MSU LIBRARIES
3 2109 00094 8019
P9-CDV-813

Anatole Jakovsky

Peintres naïfs

A Dictionary of Primitive Painters

Anatole Jakovsky

Peintres naïfs

A Dictionary of
Primitive Painters

Universe Books Inc.
New York, N.Y.

First Printing
published in the United States of America by
Universe Books Inc.
381 Park Avenue South
New York, N.Y. 10016

Library of Congress Catalog Card Number: 67–15570

Printed in Switzerland
by Basler Druck- und Verlagsanstalt

L'histoire de nos loisirs sera un jour
la portion de notre vie
qui nous fera le plus d'honneur.

DIDEROT

Contents
Inhaltsverzeichnis
Sommaire

Foreword

During the last ten years there has been a steadily growing interest in the primitive painters. Everywhere exhibitions are devoted to their work, articles and even whole books are written about them, and the number of serious collectors of their paintings becomes greater year by year. A reliable reference book of "naive" artists has therefore become a necessity. And surely no-one is more qualified to compile such a book than Anatole Jakovsky, the great friend and promoter of these artists, who has spent over twenty years studying them.

Right from the start it was clear to both author and publisher that the preparation of such a reference book would be fraught with difficulties. The first problems lay in the selection of artists. It was not simply a case of separating the wheat from the chaff but rather of sorting out the truly "naive" painters from those who were so no longer and those who consciously tried to be so. But where should the line be drawn?

Further, since these self-taught artists generally work in secret, in the privacy of their room, we must presume that there are many whose names belong in this book but who are still flowering in seclusion. For this reason the present book lays no kind of claim to completeness. We hope, however, that the publication will serve to draw attention to those primitive artists who up to now have been but little known, and we would request all readers to forward to the publishers (Universe Books, Inc., 381 Park Avenue South, New York, N.Y. 10016) details about any authentic self-taught artists, "naive" in the true sense of the word such as Anatole Jakovsky defines it in his introduction. What we should like are: biographical information, a picture of the artist and a photograph of one of his paintings. In this way we hope to be able to publish in a few years' time either an enlarged edition or a supplement.

Occasionally in this volume certain details are missing, or a picture of the artist himself or of his work could not be found; but this is no reflection on the reliability or goodwill of the compiler. He has written thousands of letters trying to obtain material, often in vain, because certain official or semi-official sources did not see the point of giving up some of their valuable time to such a useless matter as "naive" art. However, we should like to take this opportunity of expressing our sincere thanks to all those who assisted Anatole Jakovsky in his work of preparation.

WILLY JÄGGI

Vorwort

In den letzten Jahren ist das Interesse an den Sonntagsmalern ständig gewachsen. Allenthalben werden ihnen Ausstellungen gewidmet, es werden Artikel und ganze Bücher über sie geschrieben, und die Zahl ihrer ernsthaften Sammler wird von Jahr zu Jahr größer. Ein verläßliches Nachschlagewerk über die naiven Maler und ihre Werke ist daher zu einem dringenden Bedürfnis geworden. Wer wäre berufener, ein solches Lexikon zusammenzustellen, als Anatole Jakovsky, der große Freund und Förderer der peintres naïfs, er, der bereits über zwanzig Jahre ihrem Studium aufgeopfert hat.

Autor und Verlag war es von Anfang an klar, daß die Herausgabe eines derartigen Nachschlagewerkes großen Schwierigkeiten begegnen werde. Die Probleme begannen bei der Auswahl. Es galt nicht nur die Spreu vom Weizen zu trennen, sondern vor allem auch die echten Naiven von denen, die es schon nicht mehr waren, und von jenen, die es nur sein wollten, zu scheiden. Aber wo liegen die Grenzen?

Zudem muß bei der Laienmalerei, die in aller Heimlichkeit, im stillen Kämmerlein entsteht, vermutet werden, daß manches Talent, das in dieses Buch gehören würde, noch im Verborgenen blüht. Aus diesem Grunde kann das vorliegende Werk niemals Anspruch auf Vollständigkeit erheben. Wir hoffen aber, daß wir auf Grund dieses Buches auf bisher unbekannte Maler aufmerksam gemacht werden. Wir bitten daher alle Leser, dem Verlag (Basilius-Presse, Dornacherstraße 11, 4002 Basel, Schweiz) Unterlagen über echte Laienmaler, Maler des reinen Herzens, wahrhaft Naive, wie Anatole Jakovsky sie in seiner Einleitung definiert, einzusenden. Erwünscht sind biographische Daten, eine Porträtaufnahme und die Photographie eines Gemäldes. Wir vermuten, daß dadurch in einigen Jahren entweder eine erweiterte Neuauflage oder ein Ergänzungsband notwendig werden dürfte.

Wenn auch hier und dort im vorliegenden Band einzelne Angaben nicht ermittelt und von etlichen Malern entweder keine Porträtaufnahme oder keine Kostprobe ihres Schaffens aufgetrieben werden konnte, hängt das weder an der Zuverlässigkeit noch am guten Willen des Autors. In Tausenden von Briefen hat er sich um das Material bemüht, oft vergeblich, weil gewisse amtliche und halbamtliche Stellen es nicht der Mühe wert fanden, ihre kostbare Zeit für eine derart nutzlose Sache wie die Laienmalerei zu opfern. Wir möchten aber darüber nicht vergessen, all jenen unseren herzlichen Dank auszusprechen, die Anatole Jakovsky bei seiner großen Arbeit unterstützt haben.

WILLY JÄGGI

Préface

L'intérêt pour les peintres du dimanche n'a fait qu'augmenter au cours de cette dernière décennie. Des expositions sont organisées un peu partout, des articles, voire des livres entiers leur sont consacrés et le nombre des collectionneurs avertis augmente d'année en année. Aussi le besoin se fait-il sentir de publier un lexique des peintres naïfs et de leurs œuvres. Qui aurait su entreprendre un tel travail mieux qu'Anatole Jakovsky, le grand ami et mécène des peintres naïfs, qui a passé plus de vingt ans à étudier leur art.

L'auteur et l éditeur savaient dès l'abord que la publication d'un tel ouvrage se heurterait à de grandes difficultés. Un choix judicieux s'imposait. Il ne s'agissait pas seulement de séparer le bon grain de l'ivraie, il fallait aussi faire le tri entre les authentiques naïfs et ceux qui ne l'étaient plus ou ceux qui croyaient l'être. Mais où sont les limites? Puisque les peintres amateurs travaillent d'habitude dans le secret, en se cachant du monde, il ne fait pas de doute que bien des talents, qui devraient avoir leur place dans cet ouvrage, n'ont pas encore été découverts. C'est pour cette raison que ce lexique ne peut se targuer d'être absolument complet. Mais nous espérons par le truchement de cet ouvrage attirer l attention sur ces peintres inconnus. Aussi prions-nous tous les lecteurs de signaler à l'éditeur Basilius Presse S.A., Dornacherstrasse 11, CH-4002 Bâle/Suisse, les authentiques peintres amateurs de leur connaissance, peintres de l'âme pure, peintres naïfs tels que les définit Anatole Jakovsky dans son introduction. Nous désirons des données biographiques, une photographie du peintre et de l'une de ses œuvres. Nous espérons, grâce à ce moyen, être en mesure de publier, dans quelques années, une édition augmentée ou un volume complémentaire.

Si certaines indications manquent dans cet ouvrage, si l'on n a pu fournir le portrait ou un échantillon de l'art de l'un ou l'autre peintre, on ne saurait incriminer ni la compétence ni la bonne volonté de l'auteur. Il a écrit des milliers de lettres afin d'obtenir sa documentation, mais souvent en vain car certaines sources officielles ou semi-officielles ne voyaient pas la nécessité de perdre leur temps précieux pour une affaire aussi insignifiante que la peinture d'amateurs. Que tous ceux, par contre, qui ont contribué à l'enrichissement de la documentation et facilité la tâche d'Anatole Jakovsky soient vivement remerciés.

WILLY JÄGGI

HENRI ROUSSEAU

The Primitive Painting

An Introduction

The first international exhibition of "naive" painting ever to be held in Europe finally took place in 1958, within the framework of the World Exhibition in Brussels. Without running the risk of being mistaken or of leading anyone astray, we may state that the last six or seven years since then have done more, much more to promote a knowledge of "naive" painting than the whole period, about fifty years, which preceded them.

For there were exhibitions organised soon after this impetus, all of them important ones. The one in Baden-Baden was first, and it was transferred just as it was to Hanover and Frankfurt (1961); then, in the same year, there was the "Laienmaler" one in Basle. Later it was the turn of Rome, where in the splendid Barberini Palace all the best that was available on both sides of the Alps was shown. Even Austria (Residenzgalerie in Salzburg, 1964) and Morocco (Rabat Cultural Centre, 1964) attempted similar displays, although of course on a lesser scale. Only France has had to be satisfied up to now with a purely national exhibition, which collected the French "naive" artists and included foreign painters only if they were resident in France. It is but poor consolation that France was able to precede Germany and Switzerland, among others, by one year! Furthermore, the exhibition took place on private initiative, thanks to the perspicacity of the now obsolete "Maison de la Pensée Française"; it did not even have semi-official status, as was the case everywhere else. But let us not dwell on this....

Be that as it may, most of these exhibitions not only brought to the public eye a large number of completely new artists worthy of interest but also (and most important) helped to bring about a complete change in our perspective and attitude towards this rather neglected, even ignored branch of painting. Truly it had been a poor relation.

It is a fact that all other artists without exception are discussed, criticized, referred to (whether admired or condemned is beside the point); but as soon as "naive" artists are mentioned one is immediately faced with prejudice, definite and cutting, as if in an attempt to avert some undefined but real danger. Sometimes they are simply laughed at, sometimes they are shrugged curtly aside. They are the only ones not taken seriously. This becomes still more obvious at retrospective and anthological exhibitions, which by their very nature collect together the various tendencies (sometimes contradictory) of so-called "modern art"—each time the only painter who still provokes lighthearted mockery and condescending smiles, or even conspiratorial sarcasm, is always the "Douanier" Rousseau. Every single time. This same artist, however, has for a long time held an assured place in art galleries all over the world and in all books dealing with art in general.

Where does all this misunderstanding, all this ignorance, all this dislike originate?

It is exactly on this point that the general public, who were so ill-informed, were due for a great surprise. They expected to find something to laugh at—faults of perspective, brash colours, tottering drawing and banal anecdotes which, for want of anything better, replace purely plastic qualities... in short, all that they had heard tell about this subject. And, instead, they found the work of artists: artists equally honest, equally gifted, equally worthy of admiration as any other artists, whether figurative or abstract, reflective or spontaneous, awkward or talented. As for the other public, the larger and unbiased group, they were immediately enchanted by the inventiveness and the unquestionable poetry of the "naive" artists; they were surprised by their originality, charmed by their forthrightness and their love of a beautiful piece of work. Thus the first step towards the recognition of "naive" painting as a quite distinct type was taken quite independently, without help from any quarter, simply thanks to the direct contacts between the "naive" artists and their two kinds of public (which incidentally were soon to become one). And the contacts steadily grew as the above-mentioned exhibitions travelled from town to town, from country to country.

It was only Rousseau and several other "great ones" like Vivin, Séraphine, Bauchant and Bombois whose names became widely known. But the public soon realized that there was not only a single Rousseau, a single Vivin, etc., but rather there were dozens and dozens of artists who, although completely unknown, were nevertheless worthy to be called their equals. Hierarchies crumbled, horizons enlarged, and "naive" painting gradually ceased to be the property of a single man or a single country. It spread all over the world.

Latin America and Haiti appeared on the scene, as did also what has recently been called the "Yugoslav miracle", which is capable of satisfying even those who are most difficult to please. Poland discovered the famous Nikifor, son of a prostitute and an unknown father, a poor deaf-mute who could neither read nor write, who casually, with one eye on the police, sold real little masterpieces in front of the church of his native town of Krynica. The United States brought to light Morris Hirschfield and the well-known Grandma Moses who started to paint at the age of eighty. Spain had Rivera Bagur, whom Miró discovered; Israel had Chalom de Safed; Czechoslovakia, Karel Chaba, Anna Lickova and Juraj Lauko; Germany, Paps; Morocco, Louardiri; Belgium, Micheline Boyadjian and Van den Driessche; the Netherlands, Alexandrine; and Brazil, Iracema. Finally Italy, suddenly remembering that she had been the cradle and undoubted homeland of the primitives, rounded up in next to no time five or six important names.

Even the Soviet Union, where "naive" art had been virtually forbidden because of Jdanov's Stalinist doctrine, rehabilitated her great "naive" Georgian painter Niko Pirosmanachvili, recently awarding him a posthumous exhibition in the Moscow Pushkin gallery—a supreme honour normally reserved for recognized geniuses. Furthermore, a large volume was published on the Ukrainian peasant artist Katherina Bialacour whose flower arrangements strangely resemble those of Séraphine.

All this surely proves that, far from being an accident, a happy chance or an isolated success, "naive" painting is really and truly a natural organic phenomenon, obviously obeying some historic necessity.

What other explanation is there for this incomparable, practically simultaneous flowering of a whole constellation of artists? Artists who, only in rare cases knowing each other and therefore generally unaware of each other's existence, suddenly strike up the same song in all four corners of the earth!

Naturally, some "false naive" artists have slipped in among them, and sometimes folklore is confused with the typically individual art of the "naive" painter; but these are only growing pains, which can easily be avoided or even cured, provided, however, someone gives this branch of painting careful study. For at the moment there is virtually nothing and no-one qualified to make a decision on any of the thorny questions concerning this matter. Few books have appeared, no fundamental articles and even fewer really academic works. Despite the ever-increasing interest which primitive painting has awakened, despite the success and encouragement which it visibly enjoys, everything continues exactly as before, as if "naive" art were of absolutely no importance and as if it were pointless to concern oneself with it.

In the meantime, those who do write about "naive" artists are content to pay lip-service and to quote references which are thirty or forty years old. You would think they were robots working from punched cards prepared long ago! Here we have Apollinaire, there we have Wilhelm Uhde; and then there is also the inevitable Alfred Jarry to give the whole thing a bit of spice. But Jarry saw in Rousseau only a kind of King Ubu of the palette, just the right artist to shock bourgeois minds; and Apollinaire appreciated him very belatedly and after much hesitation, even though he had known since childhood the wonderful votive pictures of Laghet[1].

As for Uhde, we must not forget that he was an art dealer and, as such, only defended his own wares. Therefore the four or five names which we know are those whose work succeeded in becoming goods for sale—much sought-after goods, of course. And it is on this that the majority of critics based their judgments, and even still continue to do so. What a farce! What a hindrance! What a disaster!

Why do these critics not remember occasionally the following words, which after all were written by their own dear Apollinaire in his "Méditations Esthétiques": "*You cannot carry the body of your father around with you. You have to leave him in the company of the dead. You remember him, you miss him, you speak of him with admiration. And, if you become a father yourself, you must not expect one of your children to drag your dead body around all his life!*"

Nevertheless, it is a fact that the ratification, or rather the logical conclusion, of this state of affairs was the most recent (and unfortunately probably the largest) international exhibition of "naive" painting. This exhibition, with its luxurious catalogue temptingly called "The World of the Naive", and with the more than sufficient means placed at the disposal of the organizers, could have—indeed, *should* have been the finest and most complete of its kind. But it was neither. I refer to the exhibition which took place in 1964 at the Boymans-van Beuningen Museum in Rotterdam.

Actually, it was like entering a huge necropolis. No surprises, no revelations at all! Except perhaps for the numerous gaps, which in the normal way would be inexplicable, and for the confusion (which, it must be admitted, was fairly widespread) that consisted in trying at all costs to pass off various transpirations of folklore, whether Yugoslav or South American, as "naive" art. The remaining pictures were already catalogued and known, known by heart, by virtue of having been hung again and again on the walls of museums, art galleries and private collectors and permanently exhibited. Therefore the whole exhibition gave off the perfidious, insidious odour of old books and old pictures, the mustiness of a corpse. One had the distinct impression that the earth had ceased to rotate a long, long time ago....

Deceived and disillusioned, many unsatisfied visitors who had been gradually getting used to other pleasures and other enchantments started to try to discover the reason for this ill-fated venture, which some had no hesitation in calling a scandal.

Was it simply a blunder, an error of judgment, as can happen from time to time to incompetent people when they concern themselves with something they know nothing about? Or, rather, did this exhibition inadvertently play its part in a more machiavellian plan, a more subtle conspiracy, aimed for instance at snatching from France her present artistic domination? For the living French "naive" artists—more numerous, richer and more varied than anywhere else in the world—were represented only by three old men, whereas the dead painters were represented simply by a Belgian, Aloys Sauter, born in Stabroek near Antwerp.

There were two possibilities: either the organizers were honestly afraid that some of the artists not represented would have eclipsed the majority of the rather minor canvases exhibited and would have caused irreparable damage to them by inevitable comparisons; or else they were purposely passed over for another reason, in order to be able to say: "As you can see, France certainly did have a few good primitive artists, but now that's finished with, really and truly; now we must look to Yugoslavia and elsewhere...".

Was it, in fact, an art dealers' conspiracy?

Even now, the facts are not known. The protests and polemics in the press have not succeeded in giving us the true picture. So we still wonder in vain, vacillating between intrigue and stupidity as the explanation. For, to crown it all, even the best Dutch and Flemish artists were overlooked!

There is another question which arises immediately, one which is much more serious: how was it possible that a French art gallery worthy of the name could, in its turn, fall into such a clumsy trap? A man's house is his castle, after all. For it was finally Paris—yes, the Musée d'Art Moderne in Paris—which took over the obviously Balkan rather than Dutch machination.

It could be claimed that it served them right, since no other French art gallery had previously thought of it or had had the means to realize something similar. But what can you expect? Our museum curators are made the way they are, and why should they differ so much from their predecessors who,

---

[1] "The awe-inspired and painstaking awkwardness of primitive art which is dominant here touches even unbelievers. There are pictures of all kinds—portraits alone cannot be found. All the pictures submitted are exhibited permanently; it is sufficient that a picture commemorates a miracle brought about by the intervention of Our Lady of Laghet.

"All possible accidents, fatal illnesses, severe pain, all kinds of human misery are here depicted—with naiveté, pious devotion and ingenuousness...

"A furious sea tosses a poor, mastless shell of a boat, on which kneels a man larger than the vessel itself. All seems lost, but the Virgin of Laghet watches over him from a halo of light in the corner of the picture. The believer was saved. An Italian inscription affirms it. This was in 1811...

"A carriage drawn by bolting horses is being carried over a precipice. The travellers will perish, dashed to pieces on the rocks. Mary, in her luminous cloud, watches from a corner of the picture. She places undergrowth on the sides of the precipice and the travellers cling to it. Later, in gratitude, they hang this picture in the cloisters at Laghet. That happened in 1830...

"Again and again—in 1850, in 1860, every year, every month, almost every day, the blind saw, the dumb spoke, the consumptives were cured, thanks to Our Lady of Laghet, haloed in yellow and smiling sweetly from a corner of every picture..."

H. Rousseau

scarcely fifty years ago, refused to hang Cézanne and Van Gogh pictures in their galleries? "Naive" art is not for them. At least not yet. It is much too revolutionary, much too novel. And yet, when all is said and done, the French "naive" artists did not and do not deserve such treatment! Far from it.

Therefore, we feel it is salutary and urgently necessary to draw up a sort of objective list of "naive" painting throughout the world, giving *all* the artists their rightful place but no more than their place. Time will duly sort out the wheat from the chaff. At any rate, whatever happens, the bibliographic information and the exact references which we give here cannot but be useful for future research.

Nevertheless, it has taken half a century since the death of poor Rousseau for his myth to become demythologized, especially to rid it of all the cheapness which has clung both to him and to his painting, so that now his life and work can be examined with the seriousness and thoroughness which they deserve. Paul Valéry spoke the truth when he said: "In the beginning was legend".

As for the history itself of "naive" art, obviously we can only sketch it briefly because of lack of space. A detailed statement, fortunately, still remains to be written.

The "naive" artists as a social phenomenon appear for the first time at that particular point in history when the pre-industrial, still rather feudal society was on the point of making a decisive jump forward and confronting the "modern age". It was the meeting of a simple needle with a sewing machine, to paraphrase the gloomy Isidore Ducasse, called the Count of Lautréamont; or, to keep in the realm of metaphors, it was the violent intrusion of a factory chimney into the rustic peace of a Virgilian eclogue. The example of Yugoslavia is more than conclusive; Yugoslavia, a country as patriarchal and mediaeval as it is possible to imagine, where, on the eve of the last war, just before it too was swept into the era of socialism and the machine, there were only painters on glass and one or two other representatives of essentially rural, folklore art far removed from the type of painting with which we are concerned, and yet a country which, soon afterwards, so to speak before our very eyes, suddenly gave birth to a respectable number of authentic "naive" artists.

In France itself it coincides with the Revolution of 1789 and the abolition of the guilds.

Up to that time, in fact, all those who showed some facility for cutting, moulding or drawing entered one of these guilds at a very early age. There they learned the basic principles of a craft and were sent out to practise that trade all their lives.

Without exception, they had a certain feeling for beauty, necessarily accompanied by a great love of work well done. They could satisfy these desires to their heart's content since, as said before, their whole lives were devoted to the execution of a multitude of these absolutely perfect objects half-way between a work of art and a purely utilitarian article.

When a church was being built, the stone-masons furnished it with stone saints and the woodcarvers decorated it with wooden saints; if an inn was being opened, the village painter would produce the inn-sign—the same painter who generally, at the request of someone miraculously healed, promptly executed one of those innumerable votive pictures narrating either a cure effected in extremis or a fatal accident averted just in time. Just think of all those pictures at Laghet....

Some of these became simply artists, occasionally great artists, like J. B. Chardin, the son of a carpenter from the Rue de Seine. As for the others, well, they were craftsmen, neither more nor less, only perhaps a little further developed, a little more defined. Which does not prevent their still having been on a level with those last executors of popular art in Latin America, who still sell their work on the market squares, quite naturally, as they did a hundred years ago. They were not creative workers. Not entirely. Not by themselves. "Naive" art appears on the scene when folklore is silent.

The situation changed completely with the introduction of the machine. For the machine quickly eliminated the last vestiges of manual work. There is therefore nothing surprising in the fact that the first "naive" artists were those who, even yesterday, had been glass-painters, potters, smiths, cabinet makers, playing-card painters, and so on, all those who by force of circumstance were obliged to ply a trade quite unconnected with art.

Uprooted, confused, frustrated, embittered, repressed and wounded in their feeling and love for beauty, they seized the slightest opportunity of resuming contact with what lay nearest to their heart, in order to sing of their Paradise Lost. The man who previously had spent most of his time painting or carving little angels for churches, and who then worked in a coal mine, transformed himself into a Fallen Angel. All he could do was to tell of his fall. Others, even if they had not worked directly or indirectly at some semi-artistic trade, also deplored the hardness of life; they regretted the good old days which the tornado of economic transformation had swept away for ever, and sighed for some other lost happiness. Like Marcel Proust, who searched so obstinately and carefully his whole life for that "time" which he had in fact lived so little, the "naive" artists threw themselves into the search for a certain Sunday of life, a Sunday which—unfortunately and yet justly—lasts no longer than a Sunday dream! Hence the name "Sunday painter".

Forced to work hard, very hard, for six days at a stretch, without fresh air and behind dreary, dirty panes of glass, they suppressed within themselves all kinds of forbidden visions: skies as blue as blue can be, flowers in all colours of the rainbow, trees in springtime, rivers full of fish. The vision of the "Douanier" Rousseau was the tropical forest, which of course he had never seen but at which he had often gazed blissfully, sitting on a bench in the Jardin des Plantes, with the eyes of the soul.

"The concept of happiness is new in Europe", said Saint-Just, situated as he was on the borders of these two eras, between the 18th century and the fascinating modern age which could only be glimpsed occasionally like a mirage on a cloudless horizon. And the "naive" world, in fact the word itself, was also new then, perhaps (who knows?) for the same reason.

After all, this individual happiness, to which each human being has in recent times had a right, is what the "naive" artist is looking for in his *own* painting, and it is of course for everyone. Painting can, if not must, be done by everyone. But at what a price!

For it was no longer a matter of calmly copying from one

◄ HENRI ROUSSEAU

generation to the next, as their ancestors had done before them, but instead it was a matter of struggling, of constantly improvising, of giving shape to something which had not existed before—in other words, of creating. Further, they had at the same time to invent both subject and technique, drawing and perspective, shading and volume, absolutely everything, even to the mixing of the colours.

As it happened, the less they knew about it the more value it had. The enchantment and the surprise were all the greater. He who tries to be "naive" is not—I have to repeat this truism—and to be really, definitely "naive" in the full sense of the word a man must be consumed with a burning desire to express himself; otherwise he would not have persisted in this statement of his individuality, in the face of all kinds of opposition, nor pursued what was always threatening to escape him. And all this, simply in order to leave a trace, be it ever so faint, of his existence on earth...

They knew, in fact, that they were tenanted by a force which was beyond them; they became literally possessed. That is why the majority of their work seems to us to be like a gift, or, rather, filled with a kind of grace.

Their landscapes are naked as Adam and Eve were before the Fall. Without shame. They did not even know the difference between good and evil; they had not yet eaten of the fruit of the tree of knowledge held out to them by the Devil, and therefore they did not know, even theoretically, the plastic sin taught in the academies. They knew only that painting helped them to live, that it represented their sole and eternal Eden, i.e. happiness, ecstasy, call it what you will.

The "Douanier" Rousseau freely admitted it one day: "It is not I who paints. It is something at the end of my hand."

Be that as it may, this desire for a primitive freshness, the great burning thirst for virginal purity, in short everything which could be called "naive" for want of a better word (a word which at that time had no pejorative sense and nothing of what it later became) was already haunting everyone, great and small, educated and uneducated alike[2].

Diderot said: "All that is true is not 'naive', but all that is 'naive' is true, having an appealing, original and rare naiveté". And, a little later, Stendhal noted in his "Diary" on 16th Messidor of the year XII, i.e. 5th July 1804: "Naiveté is in my opinion the highest point of ordinary life". And it is obviously not by chance that this same Stendhal was interested in old Italian chronicles, searched for novels of ordinary life and became very enthusiastic about the famous "blue library" which peddlers sold from village to village, as well as about popular tunes which were still sung in the market-places; for his intellectual standpoint was only one step removed from that of Baudelaire or Rimbaud, to mention only two. To Baudelaire's statement: "I have come back to seek refuge in spotless naiveté", the remark of Rimbaud: "I loved absurd paintings, 'dessus de portes', charlatan stage-scenery, inn-signs, popular picture-sheets" is the perfect counterpart.

When the world changes hands, when past and present confront each other in a merciless struggle while waiting for the future, suddenly people all over the world feel a great need to bathe at the Fountain of Youth, to possess an art primitive and direct as in the first ages of man, where rules, conventions and sophistication do not take precedence over spontaneity and sincerity—in short, over truth.

Whether it was the Scotsman MacPherson, a witness to the birth of British industrialisation and author of the "Songs of Ossian", those poems which were resoundingly successful before the deceit was discovered (for this pseudo-bard from the 3rd century had never existed); whether it was the Russian composers Moussorgsky and Rimsky-Korsakoff, among others, who included in their works fairy tales and well-known tunes, sometimes even downright popular melodies, at the same time as the first blast furnaces were lit; or whether it was the Chinese Liaou Tao-Chouen who, even in the Dynasty of Songs, had said: "Look for talent in clumsiness"—they all had the same aims, the same desires: to start again, to remake the world, having the eyes and the heart of a child.

In this conjunction of forces which determined the appearance of the "naive" phenomenon, the creation of the Gothic novel, the "roman noir", with its spectres, its ghosts, rattling of chains, clanking of armour, bleeding nuns and subterranean hiding-places full of bones, can be considered as an aggressive demand, a final sign of life of the Middle Ages, cautery and exorcism at the same time—frighten me, please, it makes me feel safe! Just as, in the same way, the "avengers" were a hundred years later: Rocambole, Chéri-Bibi, Arsène Lupin, Fantomas, Judex, and so on. The "naive" artists, on the contrary, despite their unquestionable links with the old régime, should rather be considered as resigned victims of a new order; they were the swindled, the robbed, the scoffed-at, those who had put their faith in promises and fair words and especially in Progress with a capital P.

It is at any rate very clear that the Gothic novel on the one hand and "rosewater books" on the other both show equal naiveté. The only difference was that the former applied an essentially romantic technique, full of sound and fury, sweepingly and hazily drawn, directly descended from the technique of Walter Scott and Ann Radcliffe, to which even someone like Stendhal paid tribute, whereas the latter used the lens of the fingerprint expert, and later the methods of the postcard and of the photographer Adget, an incomparable poet of drawing-pen and plumbline, a sort of Rousseau of photography.

With these people is not everything clear, exact, meticulous, without fault? Never has the invisible been defined so closely. Reality, however, is elsewhere. It is called Courbet and Zola. Paradoxically, those who are known as the "realists" are not those who left behind the last touching pictures, the final sensitive witnesses of what was disappearing without hope of return; the task was left to those visionary weekend dreamers.... Our disinherited, our pariahs, our untouchables.

Thus the era of the regular Sunday escapes began.

But it was mainly from 1850, 1860 onwards, when nature was shrivelling up more and more under the hot breath of the blast furnaces (another Baudelaire image!), that weavers, cobblers, miners, postmen, market-porters, minor employees, small stockholders, even caretakers, threw themselves wholeheartedly into painting; they painted, painted, painted, sacrificing their brief minutes of freedom in their haste. Leisure time, sleep, hours of rest, mealtimes, all disappeared into their paintbrushes. Before and after the wail of the factory siren—between the evening and morning calls of that Angelus bell of the steam

[2] The word "naive", incidentally, comes from the Latin "nativus", meaning "that which is born".

LOUIS VIVIN

age. But now it is no longer Millet who copies them but the pre-expressionists Munch and Hodler.

Why did they paint? Because they could do no other.

Not very long ago I studied, in my book "Eros du Dimanche"[3], the hidden mechanism of "naive" creation, as well as this flagrant affective-frustrated side of their production, and I think I examined the question as thoroughly as possible. Therefore there is no necessity for me to return to the subject here.

For whom did they paint? First of all for themselves. For their own pleasure, then for their family and friends. The idea that their pictures could one day be sold did not even occur to them. After all, one does not give one's love letters away. Surely it would be sacrilege?

Where did they exhibit their work? Nowhere.

What became of their paintings? For the most part they disappeared, either purposely destroyed by those who had inherited them and were ashamed of them, or slowly but surely ruined by being dragged from one flea market to another. No-one noticed them except, perhaps, some other tormented soul, some kindred spirit similar in all points to that of the artist and also in quest of a touch of colour for a humble home.

It was not until the founding of the Salon des Indépendants that these Sunday painters were able to find, if not a public, at least a place to hang their work. The more so as, even here, visitors did not stay long and did not appreciate in the least all this "buffoonery", so sharply differentiated from all other kinds of artists, whether art-school graduates or not.

Even Georges Courteline, who after all was the first to have the idea and the desire to collect "naive" pictures, had to make fun of them at first. Whenever he hunted out one of these paintings in a Montmartre junkshop, he promptly gave it a humourous title, such as "The Half-Cooked Virgin", "Oysters when there is no R in the Month", "The Mausoleum Regattas", etc., etc.

What is less well known, however, is that this collection, which was originally called "The Museum of Horrors", included among its many unknown pictures two paintings by Rousseau; one of them was the "Portrait of Pierre Loti", which was given that name by Courteline himself (every single picture received a name) probably because of the tarboosh and the cat[4], even though the picture was actually a portrait of a certain Mr. Frank who lived on Montmartre hill. This picture Courteline gave away towards the end of his life for a song, while calling the buyer a fool for his purchase!

It was also as a joke that the exhibitions in the above-mentioned Museum, i.e. the "naive" paintings, were honoured by the Parisian press and found themselves reproduced in a newspaper. For that reason the issue No. 39 of the satirical newspaper "Cocorico", dated 15th August 1900, entirely devoted to this famous collection, undoubtedly constitutes not only the first document of its kind but also the very first witness, at least of any importance, of "naive" art in existence. A document indeed. A date to remember. Let us pause a little and reflect.

Apart from Courteline's commentaries, the most valuable aspect of this unexpected publication is the introduction—or rather the preface—from which the following abstract is taken:

"As we announced in our last issue, our friend Georges Courteline has kindly agreed to present his remarkable Museum for the first time in 'Cocorico'. The pictures here reproduced are, as the reader will see, the object of witty comments made by the fortunate owner of the collection.

In this connection we should like to quote the following lines from a long and very interesting study which Edouard Norès recently dedicated to his friend and colleague; they explain to our readers better than we could ourselves the aesthetic principles which guided Courteline in the choice of his paintings:

"There is a trait of Courteline's character which, to me, explains the acuteness of his perception of human absurdities: it is the deep tenderness which the spectacle of such absurdities awakes in him. As an acute observer of eternal stupidity he loves it with a brotherly love, accepts without bitterness contact with it, and savours its various manifestations with secret joy. And when he immortalizes it in the unforgettable pages of his 'Train de 8 heures 47', his 'Ronds de Cuir', his 'Gaîtés de l'Escadron' or his 'Boubouroche', his observation shows us, beneath the accuracy of the drawing, the very human feeling of the writer.

"It was this string which vibrated in Courteline's character when he acquired the first of these pictures which now constitute his 'collection'. He told himself that it would be a curious collection to make—not of bad painting in the precise meaning of the term, for one had only to bend down to pick up that sort of thing—but bizarre creations born of the conscientious endeavour of convinced 'naive' painters who, by a sustained, fruitless and admirable effort, exercised in painting the negative qualities of mistaken but sincere vocations.

"So the Courteline collection was founded.

"Patient research has enriched it each day, and now the collection is made up of about thirty pictures, thus adding to the history of French art a page of humour which had previously been lacking. signed: Edouard Norès"

Despite certain injustices, some of which certainly are injustices, in the appreciation of the work of the "naive" artists, this article, which we must remember is more than 66 years old, is clearly younger and more shrewd than so many lucubrations of more recent date, quite apart from some of the absurd descriptions with which the "naive" painters are labelled, as for instance "the popular masters of reality".

It is certainly true that since that time a lot of water has flowed down the Seine; Courteline agreed to a public exhibition of his collection, which took place from 21st November to 2nd December 1927 at the Bernheim-Jeune Gallery. But the titles and the commentaries of the humorist printed in the catalogue (the principal attraction of this exhibition) had already appeared 27 years earlier in the periodical "Cocorico" exactly as they were, except that "The Guinea-Fowl's Last Gasp" had been altered to "Painful Hours" and "Flooding in a Cemetery" to the above-mentioned "The Mauseleum Regattas". The situation had obviously not changed much, even though, in the meantime, Courteline had realized his mistake, as the very revealing N.B. inserted into the catalogue shows:

"Georges Courteline formally rejects the title of 'Museum of Horrors' which his collection has come to be called. He absolutely denies authorship of this phrase." (Between ourselves, that was a lie...) *"At the most, his collection could be referred to by the general term 'Museum of Ingenuous Effort'".*

[3] Published by J. J. Pauvert, Paris 1964.

[4] H. Certigny: "Le douanier Rousseau a-t-il peint le portrait de P. Loti?" L'information de l'histoire de l'Art, nº 1 – January 1965.

This change of appreciation is, of course, worthy of note; but one may well ask oneself whether it was really Courteline's conviction or whether he simply "moved with the times". For the rehabilitation of "naive" art had already started, and these 27 years which had passed between the two publications represented a decisive turning-point in the history of this kind of painting. Times had definitely changed.

Despite that, Rousseau continued to exhibit his work without success in the Salon des Indépendants, just like so many of his anonymous colleagues; he was scorned and laughed at, but he was used to that. Until, one day, he met quite by chance his "fellow-countryman" Jarry, who also came from Laval. Jarry immediately recognized what was exceptional in Rousseau's painting—we must give him his due here—and gave him his only commission for a lithograph "War", for the periodical "Ymagier" which Jarry and Rémy de Gourmont edited at that time. Incidentally, it has since been discovered that Rousseau had used as model for this composition a poor drawing which had appeared in a vaguely socialist periodical "L'Egalité". For him that was unimportant. Other drawings and engravings have been used by him in some way or other for his paintings. Decidedly, only "naive" artists are capable of carrying out this kind of metamorphosis.

But it is obvious that Jarry, who is mainly known for his sensational "Ubu Roi" and for the five-letter word to which he added a sixth, could do nothing for Rousseau. It did not "catch on". Mainly because it came from him. Was it in revenge or out of spite that he shot at his own portrait which Rousseau had painted? No-one knows. But at any rate he utterly destroyed it.

Tired of the struggle, he introduced Apollinaire to him.

All that finally remains from Jarry is the nickname "Douanier" (customs official), the beginning of a long and undying legend, for it was Jarry, poet and pataphysicist, who first burdened the simple Paris customs-house official with this title and who listed him under this name among the other personalities of his private and individual mythology.

As has been mentioned earlier, Apollinaire hesitated for a long time before stating his opinion, but suddenly he made up his mind and supported Rousseau openly and definitely. Then he became fully involved. He was all fire and flame, writing pages of eulogy in both verse and prose. Just before the outbreak of the war he even devoted a special issue of his "Soirées de Paris" to him. And, a little earlier, he had organised in his honour that unforgettable banquet in Picasso's studio on the "Bateau Lavoir", which has been described more than once. And practically instantaneously came the so long-awaited acceptance, recognition, fame almost. Apollinaire seemed to have completely forgotten the malicious article which he had written only a few years previously abusing this same Rousseau....

Bernheim arranged an exhibition in Paris and Joseph Brummer did so in New York. Ambroise Vollard bought his paintings. Not for very much, but he bought them. After all, that was a change from the fruitseller at the corner, the charcoalseller and the laundress, his normal clients in the Plaisance district. Another art-dealer, Paul Guillaume no less, followed suit and bought some pictures also. In a letter written from the front Apollinaire advised him: "Buy pictures at a bargain price—Rousseau, Picasso, Laurencin, Bonnard, Cézanne, etc.... you know which ones...". Rousseau, please note, heads the list. He was indeed launched. But he was already dead, poor man. From that time on, he became stele and symbol at the same time—a real tomb of the unknown "naive" painter!

Profiting by this passing infatuation, W. Uhde, a methodical and sharp-witted art-dealer, hastened to exploit as much as possible this thirst for innocence, this taste for the primitive, even for the barbarous, which was slowly beginning to spread like a patch of oil. After the first world war he added to Rousseau some other "naive" artists who were nicknamed "the great" or "the popular masters of reality" for the good of the cause. Great, because they were the only ones to be promoted by the dealers. Masters, because it was vital to differentiate them at all costs from any other similar artist. Anything to avoid confusion....

Unfortunately, those who slander "naive" painters are rather like antisemitics. It is well known that each of these scoundrels had his own "good" Jew, which permitted him to banish all the others to the pogroms and the gas chambers. Thus, because one had one's Vivin or one's Bauchant, one was entitled to exterminate all the others.

Confusion was obviously tempting, especially as many of the "inferior" artists were equal in talent, and sometimes even superior, to these "masters" among whom they were not allowed to appear. Further, their number increased steadily. They held exhibitions here and there, reaping occasionally a few condescending lines of press review—but that was all for the time being. At least, so it was thought in the high places. It was hoped that, by raising the barricade of an official "place of origin" it would be possible to cut short the dangerous expansion of these artistic works. In vain. For the fundamental point was overlooked: they were liked by the public and they amused them. (They still do, of course, only now the pictures are bought more and more openly, no longer in secret, no longer using the clandestine methods which previously were employed to avoid the gibes of others.) And they were bought for the same reason they were painted—for love. They were not purchased for their possible financial value nor as a kind of investment, but because they possessed something which had been truly lacking and which only they were able to supply. For the first time in the history of modern art, the purchase of paintings ceased to be a speculation. Thus the segregation of this kind of art, like all kinds of segregation, of course, miscarried in the face of reality, truth and justice.

Oh yes, they were liked... a little, a great deal, passionately. By simple lovers of pretty paintings and also by connoisseurs and expert collectors. Especially by avant-garde artists, by cubists and abstract painters. Picasso and Robert Delaunay were among the first purchasers of Rousseau canvases. In Picasso's strong-box at the Banque Nationale du Crédit et de l'Industrie there are works of Rousseau next to those of Cézanne, Matisse and Braque. It was also Picasso who bought the first canvases of Vivancos. It was only Jean Cocteau who permitted himself to write rather contemptuous lines, but perhaps simply because his two protégés Jean Marais and Edouard Dermit were tending to "turn naive" a little and here too it was necessary to separate the wheat from the chaff:

Dear Rousseau, can you hear us
We send you our greetings
Delaunay his wife Monsieur Queval and I
Let our luggage go duty-free through the doors of heaven

Bombois

Now everyone knows the fine epitaph which Guillaume Apollinaire wrote in pencil on Rousseau's tombstone and which Brancusi, assisted by Ortiz de Zarate, later engraved with a chisel, so that rain and dead leaves could never obliterate it. But few people know the declaration Kandinsky made shortly after the first world war, which could be paraphrased as follows: "I see nothing for the future except abstract art or 'naive' painting".

Kandinsky confirmed this opinion to me in person. I remember the occasion well: it was in his lovely apartment in Neuilly, almost opposite the Île de la Grande Jatte (immortalized by Seurat), where he was to live until the end of his life, after definitely settling in France. The conversation took place in 1934, and his confirmation of this view was made in duplicate, so to speak, for at the same time he showed me two small paintings by Rousseau which hung on the walls of his room, the only paintings he tolerated there beside his own.

In 1947 the tombstone left the sad suburban crampedness of the Bagneux cemetery, together with what remained of the coffin of poor Rousseau, for a new resting-place; and now from the Square de la Perrine it dominates the bridges of the Mayenne and the pale, peaceful, rather sleepy town of Laval, the town of his birth, although it did not recognize him as such during his lifetime. But the winged words of the poet encircled the world a long time ago; they have been translated into all languages, are read, recited and learned by heart, even if only to remind the last detractors of "naive" art that among the first discoverers and admirers of Rousseau there figured, as if by chance, one of the greatest abstract painters, Robert Delaunay himself. By chance? Surely not.

In alliance with him there stands Kandinsky, therefore, an honest and clearsighted man who knew quite well what he was doing and saying. He too settled the question of the legitimacy of "naive" art and openly foretold its future.

Should I also quote the lines written in 1930 by Michel Seuphor, the first serious historiographer of abstract painting? They appeared as a preface to an exhibition of the painter J. Torrès-Garcia's children, who were blessed with the lovely names of Olympia, Auguste and Iphigénie.

"One of the merits of our age—an age of scientific research, of desire for precision, of striving towards the knowledge of an order—will be that we have also grown closer to the child, that other pole of our being. The child is becoming for us of great educational value: he leads us back to nature and to our original moral sources, precisely to the point where the mechanism of modern life makes us forget the basis of our vital balance. Like everything which makes up our past, the child is in each one of us, but it is necessary that we make this a conscious presence to avoid being forced to submit to it in spite of ourselves and against our will. Let us hope that soon a true art of childhood will take up all the room which today is still occupied by the various manifestations of romanticism, that belated and diseased infantilism like expressionism and surrealism, for instance."

All right. With testimonials of this kind one would expect that the right to naiveté was well and truly won or, at least, tacitly recognized and that "naive" art would take its due place without further delay; that its rise would be easy, rapid and without obstacle. Nothing like that happened. On the contrary. Nothing was ever so painful and so disappointing. Year after year passed without the slightest change in this respect, without "naive" painting ceasing to be considered negligible. Ignorance, intrigue and unfairness maintained the status quo as far as possible. It is true that the mentality of the epoch between the wars was far from being mature enough to realize that, in essence, the "naive" phenomenon represented one end of the dialectic pendulum of history while abstract art represented exactly the other end—they were thesis and antithesis, positive and negative, day and night, head and tail of the same human drama, the same problem of the visible. The bomb and the mirror. Not the mirror of stupid figurative presentation, long since out-of-date and falling willy-nilly into disrepair after the abstracts had exploded it once and for all, but rather the other kind, the true kind, the fundamental vision, the original nucleus, the refreshing and fertile source of our Western vision. This partly explains why our "naive" artists, so near to, and yet so far from the earlier primitives, are the primitives of today, whether we like it or not.

Nobody realized, unless some people pretended not to do so, that the appearance of "naive" art coincided on another level, as a reflex, you could say, with the first battering-ram blows at academic art. For, faced by the "dynamiters", they began, unconsciously and by an automatic defence mechanism, to secrete a sort of antitoxin aimed at safeguarding as far as possible the best part of the surrounding world of the senses and, if the worst came to the worst, aimed at saving what could still be saved. Cézanne was only five years older than Rousseau.

Right from the time the free academies, which were frequented to a greater or lesser degree by Delacroix, Bonington, Courbet, Bonnard, Matisse and very many more, began to assault the dominant academic conventionalism, the "naive" artists in their turn began guerilla warfare to build up a world of their own more or less at the same time; a world and an art completely separate, private and secret, almost clandestine. To this can be traced the abundance, the high quality, the variety and antiquity, logical consequences of a normal, uninterrupted development, which made French "naive" art the oldest and richest in the world.

Was *this* perhaps the point where the shoe pinched the organisers of the Rotterdam exhibition? But the fact exists, and I can do nothing at all about it.

However, the second world war and the second wave of "naive" artists (more powerful, more diversified than the first) had to come about, so that the eyes of our doubting Thomases could be opened once and for all. So that a flood of international manifestations, including the Rotterdam one, could take place. As a matter of fact, the situation had started to change a little earlier, during the dark years of the occupation, partly because of the temporary disappearance of a large number of art-dealers and the perceptible decrease of their influence. An exhibition like the one in the Galerie "Claude" in 1944 would have been unthinkable at any other time.

Above all, what was necessary was a protracted, though masked, questioning of all plastic values, aggravated by excesses of all kinds: painting with guns, painting with flame-throwers, sculpting with the power hammer, not forgetting the motorcycles wrapped in nylon, the displaying of objects taken

◄ CAMILLE BOMBOIS

from a rubbish-bin, painting monkeys, Tinguely's painting machine, etc.—in short, everything that was forced to end sooner or later in Pop Art, which is art only in name. Of course, by that I mean the ancient conception of art as it has been defined for thousands of years. Further, the advanced point of analytic, strictly formal painting which, starting from Cézanne's apple, first reached the point of a circle meaning nothing and then ended in the disappearance, the suppression even of the circle, in a single-colour background, that famous blue of Klein, in other words in nothingness, was scarcely of any further value. Therefore, Pop Art definitely consummated this break, for its relation to Cézanne was like the relation of Cézanne's apple to fruit juice in a tin. This recently allowed its leader, Pierre Restany, to take his bearings and to discover, realist as he is, the presence and existence of "naive" artists, which so many writers of the so-called "avant garde" continue to ignore. Here is what he wrote: "The most impressive phenomenon of the Paris season, and also the most significant one, is the invasion of 'naive' painters." And, later: "But this time we are forced to recognize that we are facing an event of quite a different scope. Too many coincidences create a situation of actual fact."[5]

This situation of actual fact had, however, been vaguely foreseen by several people. To begin with, there are the incense-bearers of abstract art themselves, for whom yesterday the word "real" was not only a nightmare but also an insult, and who now are trying to save the situation and who secretly cheat. They do it subtly, sometimes camouflaging the wreckage behind the label "new figuration" (an old verbal fraud, since there has already existed in Paris for some time the salon of "Réalités Nouvelles" devoted to precisely the most obstruse abstraction), sometimes proposing an "Art Autre" or that "Nouveau Réalisme" which is the French substitute for Pop Art. It is the "lettrists" alone who frankly continued their quest for a "sign", for want of the thing signified: a sign, a song, a reflection of the times in which we live. So let us rather hope, waiting patiently for a miracle: a breath of fresh air, even a patch of not-so-grey, not-so-dirty blue above the housetops, whilst hungrily breathing in the fumes of exhausts during the rush hours....

But once again it was Picasso, that true seismograph of the last fifty years, who was most sensitive to the movement of the times. Suddenly he renounced the conscious deformation and ugliness which has since been canonized and turned into a cult by J. Dubuffet, and turned as if by magic to a simplicity and freshness which had up to that time been unknown with him, with the series "The Painter and his Model". If he made this inauguration of a new method with his customary desire to surprise and shock, he was very successful: these pleasing rustic paintings, sensitive and almost too "pretty", mark a very clear return to artist-painting and revolutionise once again the ready-made style. In the true sense of the word this is his "naive" epoch.

Meanwhile Morandi, the Italian Georges Braque, died at the age of 74 at his home in Bologna, perhaps even while glancing for the last time at a pen-and-ink drawing of a nude by Rembrandt and at the drawings of Rousseau pinned on the wall. They were his beacons. This was mentioned—rather courageously—in an obituary written by Marco Walsecchi which appeared on 19 June 1964 in the newspaper "Il Giorno"[6].

Confronted by the gulf which opened with the explosion of Hiroshima and which is widening daily, man is not so much terrorised, now in the second half of the twentieth century, by the old-fashioned ghosts of steam or the spectres of all-triumphant electric power as by his own self and his immediate future. His mortal enemy. Yes, man has become his own enemy, neither more nor less than a tiny atom which scientists destroy day by day. From there to chain-reaction atom-splitting it is only a question of time. Will a man die a natural death or will he perish in a universal cataclysm? And when? In other words, how much longer has he got to live? And if he hopes to survive, can he still live here or must he exile himself to other solar systems? Everything is implicated: his knowledge, his feelings, his loves, his customs, his home, his tastes, his crafts, his gastronomical desires, and so on. Man delves into his subconsciousness, penetrates into the most secret folds of his intimate life....

But it is no longer man himself who responds to the majority of these questions, but his proxy: electronic robots. Cybernetic machines now calculate for him what he will do, what he will be tomorrow. Peace and war, life and death depend on these machines. Man himself is helpless! The same machines unravel the mysteries of the infinitely small and the infinitely large, the microcosmos and the macrocosmos. Newton's fixed system no longer holds good—the chaos of the stars returns. A kiss is now only a chemical reaction, life itself simply a further proof of organic chemistry. Memory? A protein. Individuality, talent, genius a simple lottery of genes and chromosomes. Relativity reigns supreme, the relativity of time and space. Soon it will be possible to freeze living people and wake them up after a decade or so of sleep. Into what society, under what government, in which century? Why not in a few light years? Whether one believes in Heaven or not, everything is cracking and falling to pieces, there is nothing which remains firm, nothing to which one may cling. One only speaks of the past or the future, not of the present. Never of the present. History is accelerating. The earth has got much smaller since Cendrars and Paul Morand than it has since Marco Polo. The same type of buildings, the same clothes and the same films can be found in Alaska and in Tahiti, in India and in Switzerland. It is a levelling down to the lowest common denominator. However, the world has also increased infinitely more since the last "terra incognita" disappeared from the face of the earth. Rockets shoot to the moon. Soon they will land on Mars and Venus.

But what is above no longer corresponds to what is below. Even Pythagoras was in error. "Above" and "below"—do these words have any meaning at all when one can walk (or rather fly) in a state of weightlessness? Obviously not; up there it is no longer the "mask with white teeth" which lies in wait but flying saucers and the "Blue Peril".

It is curious to note that the science-fiction novel by Maurice Renard which bore this name appeared at the same time as the adventures of Arsène Lupin, as the first abstract paintings and the first "ready mades" of Marcel Duchamp—Pop Art be-

[5] Domus No. 423 (1965).

[6] Una casa semplice, con i mobili ottocenteschi che furono del padre, un estimato di canapa alcuni quadri antichi di buona firma alle pareti e poche stampe tra cui il nudo di schiena inciso da Rembrandt e i disegni del Doganiere Rousseau.

IVAN GENERALIČ

fore the term existed. But the worthy "avengers" of the good old days have gone. Only fear is left, not the old, skin-deep fear, but anguish, a bottomless, animal, visceral anguish, a longing for the past and terror of what tomorrow may bring. Not the present, I repeat! No security, no rest, no peace....

On the threshold of the second industrial revolution now in progress (and in proportion to it), that revolution which in less than twenty years has overwhelmed our lives and even our dreams, changing everything more profoundly than many a past century, everything must be made new and logical. The success of science fiction and of pseudo-scientific publications like the journal "Planet" cannot be explained in any other way. They are the marihuana of the council-house tenants. A drug just like detective stories or yeah-yeah records.

Frighten me please! Quickly! Again! ... Still more ... terribly!

And yet one would have thought at a given moment that the inventions of science fiction would eventually lead to a new evasion, a new refuge, a sort of Post-Surrealism. A third solution. Neither the mirror intact nor the broken mirror. But simply a mirror without backing, to be melted as required like in "Alice in Wonderland".

An escape and a new-found attraction, baited with all the charms of a man-made paradise.

Alas! When all is said and done, science fiction can only offer the same nothingness: brain-washing, stultification and the systematic disturbance of all the senses. Imagination is here used as a means of finally destroying whatever is left of the former individual—the residue of "pre-atomic" man. Our children will certainly use the term as we now say "pre-adamic".

Nevertheless, Pop Art cannot ignore this kind of writing, just as it cannot remain outside its determining forces. It is a true child of its time—its flesh and its being. Breach of sensations, explosion of images, accelerated speed of perception, inverted perspectives and standards of judgment, a mad cavalcade of objects, faces and spaces, everything without any kind of link between them and without any justification except that of dislocated consciousness, empty of ideas, empty of feelings and (what is worse) empty of emotion, "washed clean by life", to use the expression of one of its defenders—Pop Art is discovering all this and more. I use the word "discovering" purposely because, beyond the extra-pictorial confusions, Pop Art finally rediscovered one of the basic rules of painting: that it is created with a brush. No more rusty nails, no more rags, plaster and cement, no more lucky charms of unrelated parts, fetishes to conjure up the forces of a new age! Following automatisation, chance, accident and brute matter there come again conscious will and choice. Once again there exists something which can be called art, not like that "other" art which dare not say its name, but an art and a vision requiring only a minimum of apprenticeship and technical skill. In order to fight the "naive" artists (their only adversaries of any moment), Pop Art felt instinctively the necessity of possessing equal weapons. But are they really equal? Although the painting is very different from that created by father and grandfather, it is nevertheless executed by the same methods, and as before the future is approached palette in hand. A mixture of Zen and comic strips. A world become a puzzle, a world made up of unrelated parts. Man no longer paints the machine, but he is becoming a machine himself. That is why he imitates its language and its idiosyncrasies, and why he reproduces exactly even to the screen of a photographic block, just as previously classical plaster casts were copied. The machine which produces something, one does not quite know what...noise...terror. The hypnosis and the nirvana of the tinkling of an ordinary silver ball going "tilt".

And yet, two thousand years ago, another future began with only two or three perfectly comprehensible, perfectly static images: the Good Shepherd, the Fish of the Saviour, the Bread of the Eucharist. As Nietzsche fiercely remarked: "Ideas which revolutionize the world walk with dove's feet".

Today, that dove no longer flies—it is crucified on the ceiling of a room in the Louvre. By Georges Braque.

Thus two thousand years have passed, supported willy-nilly by these very humble images; and now another sacred sign, the fish, has made its ultimate sacrifice and drawn its last life's breath, to become the fish of that same Georges Braque: its negation, its dead letter, its whitewashed skeleton.

Previously, it had contained all the joys and the sorrows, all the blessings and troubles of humanity. It was one of those good old signs such as the "lettrists" understand and to which they aspire. Afterwards, it became simply an ornament, a decoration, a vain echo of the past. The abstracts blew it to bits. (If I repeat myself it cannot be helped.) They swept the past clean away. And yet the vital force of a symbol has nothing to do with the visible effects of an explosion. A contained force, held in reserve, is always more effective than that same force dispersed in smoke. Abstract deflagration is therefore an action, and from this come the "drippings", the "action paintings", and other pure gesture paintings. Gratuitous actions. Measures taken for no reason. An absolute of no-one. An absolute of nowhere. And again it is Pop Art which is looking (in vain) for the reason behind this deflagration and which is bringing order into the ruins and the debris. From this point of view Pop Art and "naive" painting are the beginning and the end, and vice versa. However strange it may seem, the "naive" artists are nearer to Pop Art than the abstracts! The machine and the anti-machine.... The new folklore of the skyscraper encounters the remains of the old folklore of the thatched cottages.

Therefore it was necessary to wake up one gloomy morning of the year zero, with a fine hangover after the party, to wake up in an ultra-modern machine, air-conditioned or even pressurized like a spaceship, to wake up and suddenly to be nauseated by a glance at a framed stain on the wall, supposed to be a painting, then at a pile of twisted metal on a pedestal, supposed to be a sculpture. Then to try to react, to try to think or at least to remember—with the sharp pain of remembrance like sometimes waking up on the operating table and looking for an amputated limb—that after all there had been something else, that it still existed, something true, reassuring, peaceful and clean, something resembling dew on an intensely green leaf, crying out with all its chlorophyl its joy at living, its joy at shining, its joy at existing, while the sun rises gradually in the distance and greets one as it greets those who come out of hospital or prison. This leaf and this sun-glistening dew resemble very closely a humble "naive" painting that one had noticed somewhere the day before: one's only chance and one's last greeting!

Oh, these first departures! Life... life continues, of course. It's as simple as that.

"Naive" art is quite simply the ante-room to this life. And we will never have another. Let us therefore profit by it, as long as we still have time. We must choose between Pop Art and "naive" art. That is the "naive" phenomenon. "Naive" art is that and nothing more. Everything else is just high-sounding talk.

I know that it is very difficult to explain why, over the course of centuries, the arts often change their country of residence, why the countries exchange their Muses, why Melpomene yields to Thalia, Thalia to Euterpe, and why some of these arts, after having shone with the incomparable splendour of novel and intense creation, fade away one after the other so that only a cold, dull, haughty, distant gleam remains—the sacred hunting grounds of the museums. Like long-dead stars, of which space still preserves some trace, some fugitive impression, they continue to give out the remaining sublime light of the eternal.

Yes, why indeed does one particular age express itself more fully by painting than by architecture or music, for instance? And why does that painting sometimes seek out Italy, sometimes France, rather than Spain or Flanders? And, finally, why are there entire countries apparently wrapped in a lethargic sleep which prevents them from experiencing the intoxication of inspiration and of creation, while other countries awaken suddenly and unexpectedly, without knowing why or how?

As far as the nineteenth century is concerned, and also the twentieth century so far, there is no doubt but that France has taken over the leadership—in painting, at any rate.

As inheritor of the spirit of the Venetians, the Bolognese, of Rubens and Goya, it is France who has questioned the visible world most thoroughly and, in doing so, has submitted the various forms of plastic expression, hitherto valid, to criticism. Like the serpent in the Bible, France has held out to the universe Cézanne's apple, the fruit of knowledge of modern painting. And it is also France which has presented to this civilization of pictures (the advantages and disadvantages of which we are still finding out) its third glass eye, unknown to any peoples of antiquity: photography and the film, both of them specifically and completely French inventions.

Since, however, this new painting is essentially revolutionary, it is inevitable that the struggle between the past and the future, between what the wind of change blows away, each day a little more, and what continues to flourish among the ruins, especially "naive" art, should be most easily read in the French countryside, the French countenance and the French object.

But what about other nations? Other countries?

Well, having no real artistic tradition which had at all costs to be discarded as soon as it became sterile, many countries moved directly from the prehistoric to the historic, i.e. from a jumble of anonymous objects and pictures, not differing much from drawings and carvings on rock, to signed works, where the presence of an individual can be felt. From "rough genius, if you like, but still genius" (according to Maurice Barrès) to personal and private stammerings, deprived at one fell swoop of centuries-old condensation but which, with a bit of luck, could become another kind of genius. In short, from tradition to the complete absence of tradition.

In contrast to the majority of countries of the Western world, where generation after generation passed before the people, thanks to the magic mirror of painting, arrived at the aeropagus of the immortals (reserved up to that time for gods, saints, kings and great courtesans), there are other countries where this happens virtually overnight, when the appearance of the machine radically changes their mode of existence. The spark flies up, and the nameless slave, a sort of beast of burden, becomes in the twinkling of an eye an adult man. By "machine", incidentally, I do not mean the machine itself but rather everything that it brings in its train. The city encroaches upon the village with its radio, its cinemas, its newspapers and its emptiness, that dreadful emptiness which must at all costs be filled. Shouting or creating, those are the only two escapes!

The quicker this transformation of the way of life is accomplished, the more brutal is the shock, provoking reactions bordering on delirium and madness. On a more elevated plane, there is the birth of expressionism (Germany, Belgium) or futurism (Italy, Russia). What a long way we are from French cubism, which calmly and methodically works out the disintegration of the picture as reflection, the mirror picture! The others overturn, set fire to, explode—all the difference in the world is there. And during that period a country like Great Britain remains deaf and blind; she had completed her industrial revolution a long time ago. She is the country with the fewest "naive" artists.

In Italy, where division, that break between two modes of life, appeared relatively late, and which is characterized by the anarchistic explosion of futurism, it is not until towards the end of the second world war that one sees the rise of its great, authentic and original "naive" artists—artists who, incidentally, are to some extent distinct from all other primitive painters. All of them are more or less possessed by an element of madness, as if this were the only way they could be rid of the heavy inheritance of all the worlds of art which had collected on Italy's soil. And even then, it is only in the more out-of-the-way places, the least developed and the poorest in works of art that they can express themselves and show what is theirs, theirs alone: Ligabue, a true man of the woods, in the Po valley; Rovesti and Mozzali the same; Luigi Pera in the Abruzzi; Ceccarelli in Spoleto; Luigi de Angelis in Ischia and Carmelina in Capri. Only Elena Lissia, Adriano Grande and Alfredo Ruggeri live and work in Rome. Is that the reason why these last-named artists differ so much from their compatriots and approach more the style of their fellow-artists in France?

Elena Lissia is, incidentally, a special case. First of all, she is the only "lady" among these working-class people, and secondly, the forces which determined her vocation were not social in origin, but moral. Having recovered from a serious illness, she took up painting as one takes up religion. However, the result is the same—like all the others she calls the tree her brother and the river her sister. With thirty years between them, her case recalls and repeats that of the American Gertrude O'Brady. Here too everything hangs together, and one can only be astounded at the crass ignorance of those scribblers who have come to "naive" art only recently and for whom "naive" art in Italy means only the everlasting Metelli.

Who was, after all, the first Italian "naive" painter?

Was it the adolescent shepherd boy Giotto who, even before Cimabue guided his hand, had tried as well as he could to capture the movement and graceful masses of his goats gambolling somewhere near Vespignano, among the green hills of Tuscany dotted with cypress trees?

Was it those first anonymous Christians, to whom one must unceasingly return, who traced by the light of an oil lamp in the catacombs of San Callisto that emerald fish, still stiff with hope and life?

Or was it, after all, the worthy shoemaker of Terni, Orneore Metelli, who, about 1922, being then over fifty years old, tired of receiving rewards and gold and silver medals for his models of shoes and unable to continue playing the trombone in the town band because of heart trouble, was seized by the demon of painting? The demon did not let him go until the day of his death, sixteen years later.

What does it matter? What counts, what is really important, is that in that country, once inhabited by gods and still overflowing with their heritage, more than one person has taken new measure of the truth, under the implacable sun of Italy, the enemy of all lies. And these new standards have been measured according to the artist's own heart, in all simplicity, in all spontaneity and in all honesty, entirely independent of anything which had been created and codified before, although the vast number of masterpieces, to be seen everywhere in Italy and constituting art-instruction under the open sky, was the greatest obstacle for the birth and development of "naive" art springing from the soil. This obstacle is so great that one can even see in the countless pictures lying around in the Porta Portese, the famous flea-market of Rome, (obviously painted by those who have never learned to paint and who should therefore be "naive") here and there some well-known ornamentation, some taught decoration (or rather subconsciously acquired), proving clearly the power of this ubiquitous pictorial "bel canto", against which one can do nothing. They are simply pictures in the manner of..., neither more nor less. Or else one is faced abruptly with popular art in the correct meaning of the term, which is never the same thing. Like Montesquieu, who wondered how anyone could possibly be Persian, one wondered for a long time how anyone could be Italian and yet "naive"....

Now it is a fact; the Fioretti bloom in Italy again like everywhere else, the great saga of the "naive" artists is unfolding before our very eyes. It is not a story for dry eyes.

Another typical and striking example of this passing the line, this generally unexpected mutation, when from what seems definitely exhausted ground of popular art there suddenly appear several obviously "naive" painters, painting by themselves and for themselves, is Latin America in general and the Antilles and Caribbean Islands in particular. I refer especially to Haiti, the Dominican Republic and Cuba.

The majority of the large countries of Latin America, like Argentina, developed gradually and harmoniously and did not experience the brutal shock of the encounter between two worlds, calling up those inevitable artist-witnesses whose moment of truth, "momento de verdad", coincided with the decisive moment of that encounter. Such artists must either abdicate, i.e. efface themselves and gradually adapt themselves to the new situation, or else they must proclaim their own right to beauty, a certain, unusual, never-experienced beauty, expressing this right with all the candour and vigour of young, new forces as yet untried. The Spanish "émigré", Casimir Domingo, is strictly speaking an exception—he is not really a true "naive" artist, yet he can be included in that visionary tendency which we will call, for want of a better term, "spiritistic", the group which includes Crépin, Scottie Wilson, Grauben de Monte Lima, Isabel Jesus and Vandersteen and which has recently found a new recruit in Anselme Boix-Vives; the tendency which is so to speak half way between "art brut", inspired embroidery, and simply "insania pingens", in other words the art of the mentally ill. Brazil, on the contrary, is a country where "naive" art has up to now remained almost the exclusive domain of women, while a country like Peru has brought forth only one Indian artist of any quality—Urteaga. Guatemala has also an Indian, Andres Curuchich, Honduras has Velasquez, and Chile has Herrera Guevara, the painter of Cosmopolis and other imaginary towns, as well as Fortunato San Martin and, I suppose, Violeta Parra, singer, carpet-worker and occasionally "naive" artist. Uruguay with its artists Horatio Espondabura, Ferrer Aruffe and Carlos Gonzales tends more to a renovated, up-to-date folklore, as does also the artist Diogenes Paredes from Equador. The means of expression are different, but it remains folklore based on the pittoresque or the popular—the name is immaterial—as was used even at the beginning of this century by the Mexican engraver, José Guadalupe Posada, similar in all respects to what was later invented by one of his compatriots, Diego de Rivera, except that the latter had more ability; it also resembles the folklore art of various Central European artists, for instance the Yugoslav Brašič, for this return to the soil and to the living forces of the people had been praised by Rivera's counterpart Krsto Hegedušič as far back as the end of the first world war. Hegedušič was by no means a "naive" artist, although many critics who are unfamiliar with the subject blithely class him as one. This situation in Latin America, however, which leaves much to be desired, undergoes a complete change as soon as one turns one's attention to the islands near the Tropic of Cancer—those islands which overwhelm us with the quantity and quality of their "naive" artists.

Even in 1947, when UNESCO presented for the first time in Paris a selection of more or less "naive" artists from Equador, Peru and Haiti, the superiority of those from Haiti was manifest.

But how difficult, if not impossible, everything becomes when we have to concern ourselves with this part of the world, quite apart from the confusion which exists between folklore and "naive" art!

For instance, accurate information is often missing. Dates and places of birth are uncertain or unknown. Photographs, either of pictures or of the artists, are not available. And the majority of letters receive no reply. Even official organisations, such as the Museum of São Paulo and many others which I will not specify, do not give themselves the trouble of furnishing the required information. Embassies, cultural centres are dumb.

That explains why, to my great regret, I am unable to give complete information about a number of painters from the Southern Hemisphere, and why they have less written about them in comparison to all the other artists from the other countries.

It is only thanks to the invaluable assistance given to me at the eleventh hour by Messrs. José Pedro Argul of Montevideo, Thiago de Melo of Santiago de Chile, and Mora, an artist from the Dominican Republic, that I have been able to collect a

◄ ÉMILE BRANCHARD

little material about the painters from that part of the world. I should like to express my very sincere gratitude to all three for their help.

The events in Haiti, between Cuba and Puerto Rico, confirm yet again (if any such confirmation were necessary) that the great awakening and flowering of "naive" art is not a fortuitous phenomenon but obeys certain laws and requires a special set of economic circumstances. A country may have been ready for a long time to take this decisive step forward, but in order to do so it needs an internal or external catalyst: the social revolution (Yugoslavia, Cuba) or the direct intervention of interested persons (U.S.A., Morocco, a few West European countries). In Haiti the catalyst is called De Witt Peters, an English teacher who arrived there in 1943.

Let us look more closely at the records.

A book which appeared in 1938 by a certain Herskowitz, entitled "Life in Haitian Valley", asserted the almost complete extinction of local popular art, which had once been rich and lively. "The absence of graphic and plastic manifestations in Haitian art.... The suppression of these essential forms of African tradition gives the impression that the people of Haiti have lost an important outlet for internal tension". What, then, has happened? And in such a short time?

All that was necessary was, quite simply, for this English teacher, in the course of his travels, to come quite by chance upon a curious inn in Mont-Rouis, a village between Saint-Marc and Port-au-Prince; the sign of the inn was "Ici la Renaissance". A prophetic title—well, almost. The inn had in fact been decorated in an equally strange manner by its owner, Hector Hyppolite, previously a house-painter and occasionally a priest of the Voodoo sect[7].

The impression which these decorations produced on the teacher, although they were not very different from the traditional manner of painting, was so great that he immediately started to look for works and decorations of a similar kind, travelling far and wide all over the country.

After he had rounded up two or three veterans, not very many (notably Philomé Obin, born 1891 in Cap Haitien, a self-taught painter who had tried practically all trades—hairdresser, clerk, coffee-seller, etc.—and who painted only occasionally) the teacher thought quite correctly that by initiating young coloured people into the art of painting he would be sure to obtain results as good, if not better.

No sooner said than done. One year later the Art Centre in Port-au-Prince opened its doors. To tell the truth, De Witt Peters obtained for these artists not only the wherewithal for painting but also the wherewithal for living, for as soon as a picture was finished it was sent abroad and sold to art lovers. Most of the buyers were American. Deprived of French "naive" pictures because of the war and really loving this kind of art, the Americans consoled themselves temporarily with these exotic "naive" paintings together with the paintings of their own Grandma Moses, who was discovered more or less at the same time.

The result was not slow in coming. It was extraordinary, stupefying. A whole constellation of young "naive" painters gradually collected together (not forgetting the sculptor Georges Liautard, a simple blacksmith and village mechanic born 1899 in Croix-de-Bouquets, who thanks to De Witt Peters became a particularly expressive and original artist), rivalling each other in ideas and talent. Even Philomé Obin, following the intelligent advice of De Witt Peters, passed almost without transition from his "Intercession", painted in the conventional manner of a votive tablet, to epic, monumental compositions, remarkably personal, in which for instance he described "The Burial of Charlemagne Piralte" and the arrival of "President Roosevelt in Cap Haitien". The most optimistic hopes, the wildest dreams of De Witt Peters were surpassed. Because of the strength of will of one person, Haiti revived the miracle of Yugoslavia.

But that is not all. When the new Episcopalian church of the capital was constructed in 1950, many of the frescos were painted by "naive" artists such as Philomé Obin, Rigaud Benoît, Louverture Poisson and Toussaint Auguste, to mention only a few. This church is certainly the one and only building of this kind in the world. Because of its frescos it is worthy to stand beside the Palace of the Postman Cheval and the house of broken plates in Chartres constructed by Raymond Isidore. Little by little, at least twenty "naive" artists of Haiti made their entrée on to the artistic scene, becoming known and even achieving a certain fame, principally in the United States.

Among these artists we must give a few of them special mention, beginning with the oldest: Rigaud Benoît, former shoemaker and taxidriver (born 1914); Louverture Poisson, creator of "Adam and Eve" and "Crime passionnel" (born 1914); Maurice Borno (born 1917); J. B. Bottex (born 1919); Abelard, mechanic (born 1922); Préfete Duffaut (born 1923); Castera Bazile, illiterate; Dieudonné Cédor (born 1925); Léon Aynaut (born 1929); Enguerrand Gourgues, who specialized in scenes of both white and black magic (born 1930); Wilson Bigaud (born 1931); etc....

It was the same in Cuba.

Before Fidel Castro came to power, there was in Cuba virtually only one single "naive" artist, Felicindo Iglesias y Acevedo, who was actually a Spaniard born 1898 in Orensa (Galicia) and had only lived on the island since 1933 as a wine and spice merchant. But here too, as in Haiti, the budding and flowering of new talents was not long in coming, and for good reason: the new head of the government was inspired by Marshal Tito, at least insofar as his cultural policy was concerned, and he gave the word to the people. Young men and women thus began to paint and to express themselves freely, with the imagination, freshness and sense of colour which is characteristic of this people. Isabel Castellanos, Alberto Anido, Irmina Gonzalez, Lourdes Fernandez, Angel Fernandez, Angel Hernandez, Armando Blanco, Benjamin and Angel Duarte, Gonzalez Puig, Alfonso Reyes, Horatio Leyva, José Ramon Comabella—it is impossible to name them all! "Macheteros" and computer-operators, peasants and typists, bus-conductors and cigar-factory workers, and particularly a truly authentic sugar-cane cutter, Luis Romero—perhaps I should also mention

[7] This is how, for instance, he explains his relations with the goddess of water:"You know that I have married my Guardian Angel, that is why I cannot marry anyone else. I was still a child when my grandfather, a famous Voodoo priest, married me to the Siren, and since then she has remained my mystical wife. But I have three mistresses, which is not many, for normally I have seven. Recently, however, I have had enough of women. All the time they create difficulties, and therefore I have decided to keep only three. They get on well with one another and are not jealous. Why should they be, in fact?".

JOSIP GENERALIČ

Samuel Feijoo, artist and writer, to whom we owe the first important document on this new painting madness[8].

Speaking of Samuel Feijoo, I must diverge a little from my tale. How can one define the true "naive" artist? How does he differ from a false one? Where does "naive" art end and method begin? Not counting the forgers who purposely "paint naive" while knowing how to paint otherwise—although we should mention that for one painter, who signed his work with an invented name and previously specialized in forged Corots and Sisleys, the career of a "false naive" turned out to be more lucrative. But what about all those who paint in all sincerity, who are similar to "naive" artists in more than one respect but yet surpass them because of their technical knowledge? To ignore them is not just, to assimilate them is not easy, and the criterion of not knowing how to paint is not always sufficient. The more so as certain "naive" artists start out purely self-taught but then gradually acquire sufficient technique to place them on the other side of the borderline. Jean Eve, Rimbert and Caillaud are three examples which are too well known to need emphasis. Are they still "naive" or not? The question is difficult to settle. The borderline is blurred and far too indefinite, too faint and delicate, since the reasons for and against are closely interwoven. Let us therefore be content to say that Samuel Feijoo belonged to the category of more or less "naive" artists which has a large number of representatives in the various countries of the Old and New World: Madeleine Luka, Caly, Gaston Chaissac, Véronique Filozof, Ozilici, Maclet, Maick, J. Milet and Fred Zeller in France; Breviglieri, Cesetti and Donghi in Italy; Stanley Spencer, Eden Box and L. S. Lowry in Great Britain; Carolus Paepen, Bockstael, Ferdinand and S. Dufoing in Belgium; Sydney Nolan in Australia, and many, many others.

In my view, and also to avoid confusions which can only be harmful to the true "naive" artists, these painters are not "naive". Even artists such as the Hungarian Csontvary and the Russian-born, naturalised Czech G. Moussatoff are on the borderline. I do not question their honesty, only that they could paint otherwise if they wanted to, while truly self-taught artists cannot paint in any other way. The others are simply intimists, sensitive artists, mannerists, fantasy-ruled, reminding me of the words written by Théophile de Viau in the 17th century:

"I should like to compose spontaneous verse,
To let my soul drift among plans unformed,
Seek out hidden places where nothing displeases,
Have leisure to meditate, time to reflect,
To watch for an hour my face in the water,
Dreaming, to hark to the splash of a stream,
To write in the woods, to pause and be silent,
To bring forth a quatrain without conscious thought."

(Poétique)

The works of these "semi-naive" artists necessarily reveal the same essentials, whether you call it taste or talent, in other words accuracy and delicacy of emotions, or that inimitable awkwardness of the hand which cannot be measured in carats but rather (like diamonds) by the purity of its water and the details of its cut. For even the true "naive" artists are not all equally of merit—there are some who have more talent than others. As for the forgers, you will find their names in other books but not in mine.

The only exception to this rule, which insists on drama and rebellion and on the necessity of self-taught artists' departing from the beaten track of style and expression, is America; in the United States, which has produced "naive" painters for as long a period as France, the development continues along a parallel path, neither identical nor entirely different.

As popular art as such did not exist in the United States—neither did an "official" art or any kind of art instruction—the art which instinctively wells up from the very varied cultural levels is right from its source (which goes back to the end of the 18th century) in essence "naive"; but those who create this art are neither black sheep nor the product of any kind of social catastrophe. On the contrary, they work peacefully, serenely, almost (but not quite) as half-professionals, as craftsmen, sometimes outstripping their French colleagues and comrades-in-arms. They obviously did not know their torments and wretchedness, nor did they encounter the hidden reefs of an existence much more dangerous than the skirmishes with the Indians of the Far West. All *they* had to do was to go on from ranch to ranch, from farm to farm, from plantation to plantation, from factory to factory, following the slow but relentless penetration of the pioneers and helping, while acting as itinerant portraitists, to tame that vast continent.

These Americans, therefore, glorified the individual and handed on to posterity new men, the future founders of the dynasties of money. The rising classes. From this point of view the artists are much nearer to Holbein, Clouet or even Ingres than the normal portraitists of the 18th century from whom they drew their inspiration, while the European painters like the Georgian Pirosman or the Greek Theophilos were still heart and soul in the age of elegant feasts, or in this case of country markets, painting only pictures out of the past, moments of a happy rural existence dressed in its Sunday best which already belonged to the past and was dying out. Instead of being cursed, the American primitive artists were very useful. They were much sought after, like plumbers and joiners.

To what end? Well, to satisfy that inborn need for beauty and truth, to quench that ancient and undying thirst for immortality. Everyone, in fact, had a turn: chubby-cheeked babies, stern judges, cold and shrivelled wives, worthy, young-looking old men. What a magnificent edition of Faulkner's novels could be published if it were illustrated by reproductions of all these pictures!

Furthermore, you do not have to look far for these pictures. They can be found by the score in American collections such as the "American Paintings of the M. and M. Karolik Collection" in the Boston City Art Gallery, in the collection "American Primitive Art" in the Houston City Art Gallery, in the "American Primitive Paintings" in the E.W. and Bernice Chrysler Garbish Collection at the National Gallery in Washington, and the incomparable "Folk Art Collection" of Abby Aldrich Rockefeller in "Colonial Williamsburg" in Virginia.

From time to time a farmer or a trapper, moved by the spectacle of nature and by the results of his own work, also tries his hand in all honesty at painting a fresh, pure picture. Did not this promised land become theirs for good? Rich, beautiful, just, free, and already so "modern"! Surely something to be proud of....

[8] Pittores y dibujantes populares de las Villas, Universidad de Las Villas, ed. Santa Clara (Cuba) 1962.

Or perhaps an old spinster, who attempts some pretty still-life. A mother who paints portraits of her little ones. A widow who revives the memory of those dear to her by pictures on their graves. And more, many more, who paint a family reunion, a harvest-time, a burial, a public park, mythological or biblical scenes, a paddle-steamer... a passing train....

Their language scarcely differs at all from the language of other self-taught artists from the Old World, at least in its form; the same love of detail, the same conscientious work and the same desire to continue, come what may, unites them. Except for the fact that some of them rid themselves of their original awkwardness and acquire some rudiments of the art of painting, which is characterized in the extraordinary, almost photographic likenesses of their pictures, thus placing themselves in the category of "non-naive" or "semi-naive" artists. We only need to re-read the poem of Théophile de Viau to realize that sentimental wandering and flirting with nature can adapt itself quite well both to the knowledge of painting technique and to the lack of it.

Blaise Cendrars, the appointed defender of avant-garde painting of the years around 1914, expressed the following wish during the last years of his life, disgusted by what painting had become: *"I wish that there were only Sunday painters left and that we would be left in peace for a hundred years without the others which clutter up the walls of museums, collectors, and art-dealers. After a hundred years' domination of that pleasing fantasy, amateur art and nature-inspired reverie, painting would perhaps enjoy a renaissance."*

But let us return to our Cuban primitives.

The production of the "naive" artists in Cuba was very different from that of the Haiti artists, for the reasons given. First of all in the choice of subject. For them imagination reigns supreme. The fantastic, or even the magical, takes the place of the real. This can of course be seen in the style, which fluctuates between Picasso and Wilfredo Lam (a native of the island) with the "non-naive" artists and between Chaissac and Dubuffet with the supporters of the "art brut". The lines become entangled, coil themselves up, become blurred, vague and nocturnal, not trying to depict what is in front of their eyes but as if trying to grasp the invisible. Even if from the strictly formal point of view these works approach the subconscious and slightly mediumistic type of painting (which we mentioned in connection with the Argentine painter Casimir Domingo) more than the normal, earthbound imagery of all other primitives, they are nevertheless worth a thousand times more than the works of "art brut". They are founded on art, whereas the pictures of "art brut" (where the word "art" is often superfluous) belong in the category of psychic cautery or plastic exorcism; at any rate they are all created for effect, and the concept of beauty is absent.

Here I am forced into another divergence from the text. Not to know how to paint does not mean to paint badly. Ignorance does not mean ugliness. On the other hand, a cry, however painful and moving it may be, does not necessarily have an aesthetic content. However interesting and revealing they may be for research-workers, doctors, psychologists and psychiatrists, the paintings of the mentally ill which, whether one admits it or not, form the basis of "art brut" according to the clique founded by Jean Dubuffet to serve as a springboard for his own artistic conceptions and activities, are generally completely lacking in creative inspiration and contain no plastic qualities. All those poor sick psyches, all those mentally delirious and all those mutilated, ravaged pictures suffer from extreme plastic poverty and seem, alas, like embryos in a test tube or like a hare with two heads preserved in a jar of alcohol, compared with the works of the Cuban artists, who really do create art. Art—and not a sophisticated branch of the Musée Dupuytren, which the illiteracy of certain newspapers and the snobbism of a certain public have presented as something which it is not. Never has such confusion reigned as in these last few years. A certain Schröder Sounenstera, who can often be found among the primitives (for instance in Rotterdam and in the Musée d'Art Moderne in Paris) is no more "naive" than Aloyse or Clovis Trouille.

In that case, where does this seed of madness in the Cuban "naive" artists originate? From the trade-winds or from a few drops of Spanish blood? Only a very shrewd person could answer that—certainly I can neither prove nor disprove it. That is not the main point here, anyway. Madness or not, this overflowing imagination of the Cuban painters displays primarily an immense, intact treasure of creative capabilities... and who knows what the future holds in store? From now on everything is possible. Even great, very great artists like Rousseau or O'Brady might appear. May they all continue painting undisturbed! It would really be a pity if a fine, as yet unconscious "naive" artist were smothered at birth for fear of letting another dauber develop. The history of primitive art is unfortunately littered with stillborn painters.

The situation in the Dominican Republic is similar.

And it is similar again in Morocco, although on a smaller scale; after a total silence of several centuries three fine "naive" painters came to light one after the other: Ahmed Louardiri or El Ouardiri, born 1920 in Salé; Mohamen Ben Allal, born 1924 in Marrakesh, and Moulay Ahmed Drissi, who was also born in 1924 near Marrakesh. All three attended the Koran school, which of course forbids pictures. All three were poor (Ben Allal was born in a nomad's tent), and for all three of them the origin of their art lies at the decisive moment when they encountered civilization. For Ben Allal, who was servant to a well-known French artist, the reaction was, understandably, more immediate and more normal. However, all three of them, at a particular point in time, said to themselves: why not I? They all saw and experienced a great many things which dazzled them, all collected visions and dreams which asked only to be put down on canvas. Happiness... always visions of happiness! Herds and green pastures. Living water in the desert....

The most specifically Arab, and also the most gifted of the three, Louardiri, sings of the past of his race; he tells story after story rather like his relation Scheherazade, until the note ri es and his voice is gradually transformed into a kind of singsong which jumbles everything together: jasmine and fountains, the moon and blackbirds, blue and pink embracing lovingly, the velvet of deep night and cool flagstone paths caressing one's feet so deliciously after the heat of an African day, then banks of flowers, and those patches of shadows and colours where, instead of the rose trees of Saadi, suddenly young girls appear with gazelle-like eyes, while the lanceolate, trefoil and horseshoe arches of the minarets and palaces of a thousand years

O'BRADY

of Moslem legend and enchantment listen attentively, likewise spellbound by the scene.

What does it matter, therefore, if the pictures sometimes become entangled or if a particularly clumsy effect is occasionally found? The flame of passion burns and consumes all imperfections of syntax and grammar. It is also immaterial if this beautiful dream has been paid for, sad to say, by a mediocre, monotonous life, perhaps (who knows?) with the bitter thorn of some present or past sorrow piercing the heart.

And then there is that Appenzeller peasant girl, Sibylle Neff, who watched with a heavy heart how all around her the last Swiss country painters were dying out, and who began to extemporize the same scenes, deal with the same subjects and recreate anew, yet *different,* the day-to-day life of her homeland.

And again, what about that modest Brazilian craftsman from the state of Pernambuco, Inocencio da Costa Nick, called Mestre Noza, who also goes beyond the old religious imagery of the "santeiros" to carve and engrave picture after picture containing all the mysticism and fanaticism of that province?[9]

And that Flemish artist, Van den Driessche, formerly a butcher, who at the age of over sixty suddenly took up painting and became a kind of unrefined James Ensor? No-one since the Brueghel brothers and Hieronymus Bosch has been able to express with such verve the very soul of Flemish life—the one consciously, the other unconsciously. ...

And those adolescents from the Cairo suburbs, grouped together by Ramses Wissa Wassef, who wove the carpets of a thousand and one nights, truly magic carpets?

And again, that bubbling in the heart of the Ruhr district, Recklinghausen, where an attempt is being made to establish peaceful co-existence between hand and machine? Hans Koehn, for instance, Karl Kazmierczak, Karl Hertmann, Peter Paul Hubert Schmitz, Werner Plümer, E. Bödecker, and also F. Gerlach who once said: "What interests me is that, in painting, I contribute a little to the development of man's destiny and the fate of this planet."

Who could add anything to that?

The more closely one studies "naive" art the more one realizes that the narrow path leading to it is everywhere and always the same.

From north to south, from east to west, from ocean to desert, from mountain to plain, from fields to factories and from thatched cottages to mushroom towns, hearts are suffering, hearts are bleeding, hearts are rebelling to such an extent that they become "sacred hearts". Mirages are born. Bottles are thrown into the sea with messages of survival. Lifebuoys float thus for a short time at the place of the shipwreck. They are painters of God, the Roman Catholic journalist Joseph Pichard said to me recently about them; he is definitely reserving for them a place of honour in the Salon de l'Art Sacré which he is organizing. They are painters of God, like the ladybird, the most "naive" drawing insect possible. ...

But he who mentions God mentions the Devil too. Here also temptations are not lacking; nor are torments, deviations, seductions, chimeras of all kinds. It is from this so naked and overwhelming struggle for the maintenance of the dignity of the human being that "naive" art is born.

A doctorate thesis in graphology submitted by Mme. A. M. Angeli (in press) proves this more than adequately. In the sixty writings of "naive" artists which she has studied there is none which does not reveal some secret wound. All without exception are the expression of tormented men, men in revolt against life. All of them contain the indelible traces of a Paradise Lost, a Paradise Regained through their art. Who therefore, in the face of this irrefutable, scientific proof, can claim the gratuitousness of their art? Who can continue to consider them as unimportant? Who dare define their art as a pastime?

I think the time has come to stop talking and circling round them and instead quite simply to let them speak for themselves. And how could I end this examination of "naive" art otherwise, since it is only the beginning of something which is changing and developing day by day?

---

[9] Via Sacra, gravada por Mestre Noza, Robert Morel ed. (1965).

CAMILLE BOMBOIS

Die Laienmalerei Eine Einführung

Die allererste internationale Ausstellung von naiven Malern, die in Europa veranstaltet wurde, fand im Rahmen der Brüsseler Weltausstellung schließlich und endlich im Jahr der Gnade 1958 statt. Ohne Gefahr, sich zu irren oder irgend jemand zu täuschen, kann man füglich behaupten, daß diese sechs oder sieben letzten Jahre mehr, viel mehr für die Kenntnis der naiven Malerei getan haben als die ganze übrige Zeit, das heißt die etwa fünfzig Jahre, die vorangingen.

Denn in Fortführung dieses ersten Anlaufs kamen kurz darauf weitere, ebenso wichtige Ausstellungen zustande. Zunächst eine in Baden-Baden, die in der Folge unverändert von Hannover und Frankfurt übernommen wurde (1961); im gleichen Jahr erfolgte die Ausstellung der Laienmaler in Basel. Dann kam die Reihe an Rom, wo im prachtvollen Palazzo Barberini das Beste geboten wurde, das es nördlich und südlich der Alpen zu sehen gab. Sogar in Österreich (Residenzgalerie Salzburg, 1964) und in Marokko (Kulturzentrum von Rabat, 1964) wurden ähnliche Ausstellungen versucht, obwohl sie natürlich in bescheidenerem Rahmen blieben. Einzig Frankreich mußte sich bisher mit einer rein nationalen Ausstellung begnügen, die nur die französischen Laienmaler umfaßte und an Ausländern ausschließlich die zuließ, die in Frankreich schafften. Daß sie den entsprechenden Ausstellungen in Deutschland und in der Schweiz zum Beispiel um ein Jahr vorausging, ist ein wahrhaft geringer Trost. Und dabei handelte es sich erst noch um eine private Initiative, die der Weitsicht der Maison de la pensée française (die inzwischen ihre Pforten schließen mußte) zu verdanken war und nicht etwa einer sozusagen offiziellen Stellungnahme, wie es sonst beinahe überall der Fall war. Schwamm drüber...

Wie dem auch sei, die meisten jener Ausstellungen haben den Augen der Öffentlichkeit nicht nur eine Anzahl ganz und gar neuer, interessanter Maler enthüllt, sondern auch und vor allem dazu beigetragen, sowohl unsere Optik wie unsere ganze Einstellung gegenüber diesem ziemlich vernachlässigten, wenn nicht gar völlig übersehenen Zweig der Malerei von Grund auf zu verändern. Bisher war die naive Malerei tatsächlich eine arme Verwandte.

Alle anderen Maler werden in der Tat ausnahmslos besprochen, kritisiert, erwähnt – im Guten oder im Bösen, darum geht es hier nicht –, während man sich, sobald man an die Sonntagsmaler rührt, entschiedenen, endgültigen, scharfen vorgefaßten Meinungen gegenübersieht, als gälte es, um jeden Preis irgendeine unbestimmte, aber wirkliche Drohung abzuwehren. Zum Teil macht man sich einfach über sie lustig, zum Teil schiebt man sie verächtlich und derb beiseite. Sie sind die einzigen, die nicht ernst genommen werden. Mehr noch: in den rückblickenden, gewissermaßen anthologischen Ausstellungen, in denen man infolgedessen die verschiedenen, mannigfachen, zuweilen widersprüchlichen Richtungen der sogenannten «modernen» Kunst vereint, ist der einzige Maler, der immer noch billige Späße, herablassendes Lächeln oder gar mitwisserischen Sarkasmus hervorruft, stets der Zöllner Rousseau. Unweigerlich. Und doch nimmt er schon seit langem in den Museen der ganzen Welt und in allen allgemeinen Werken über die Kunst einen hervorragenden Platz ein. Woher kommt dann so viel Unverständnis, so viel Unwissenheit, so viel Haß?

Gerade in diesem Punkt sollte nun aber das so schlecht unterrichtete Publikum die größte Überraschung erleben. Es erwartete, etwas zum Lachen zu finden, Fehler in der Perspektive, grelle Farben, wacklige Zeichnung und eine banale Anekdote, die in Ermangelung eines Besseren die rein plastischen Qualitäten ersetzen sollte, kurz alles, was man ihm zu diesem Thema erzählt hatte. Was es dann in Wirklichkeit zu Gesicht bekam, waren Maler: Maler, die ebenso ehrlich, ebenso begabt, ebenso «gültig» waren wie alle anderen Maler, ob sie nun figurativ oder abstrakt, besonnen oder spontan, unbeholfen oder geschickt seien. Was das andere Publikum betrifft, das größere, unbefangene, so nahmen die glücklichen Einfälle und die unbestreitbare Poesie der naiven Maler es vom ersten Blick an gefangen; ihre Originalität überraschte es, und es war bezaubert von ihrer Ehrlichkeit und ihrer Liebe zur sorgfältig ausgefeilten Arbeit. So kam der erste Schritt zur Anerkennung der naiven Malerei in ihrer Eigenschaft als vollwertige Malerei ganz von selbst zustande, ohne jegliche äußere Beihilfe, ganz einfach dank dieser unmittelbaren Kontakte zwischen den Laienmalern und jenen beiden Gruppen des Publikums, die übrigens bald verschmelzen werden, Kontakte, welche die genannten Ausstellungen unermüdlich begünstigten, indem sie von Stadt zu Stadt und von Land zu Land zogen.

Man sprach diesem Publikum ausschließlich von Rousseau und ein paar anderen «Großen», wie Vivin, Séraphine, Bauchant oder Bombois. Es merkte aber schnell, daß es nicht nur einen einzigen Rousseau, einen einzigen Vivin gab, sondern Dutzende und Aberdutzende anderer Künstler, die zwar völlig unbekannt sein mochten und es doch verdienten, mit den Berühmten in eine Reihe gestellt zu werden. Die Rangordnungen brachen zusammen, der Horizont erweiterte sich, und die naive Malerei hörte allmählich auf, die Sache eines einzigen Menschen oder eines einzigen Landes zu sein. Sie wurde weltumspannend.

Lateinamerika und Haiti betraten die Bühne, und was seit kurzem das «jugoslawische Wunder» genannt wird, war imstande, auch die Anspruchsvollsten zufriedenzustellen. Polen entdeckte den berühmten Nikifor, den Sohn einer Dirne und eines unbekannten Vaters, einen armen Taubstummen, der weder lesen noch schreiben konnte, der aber so beiläufig, beinahe verstohlen, auf dem Kirchplatz seiner Vaterstadt Krynica richtige kleine Meisterwerke verkaufte; die Vereinigten Staaten machten Morris Hirschfield und jene Grandma Moses bekannt, die im Alter von achtzig Jahren angefangen hatte zu malen; aus Spanien kam Rivera Bagur, den Miró entdeckte; aus Israel Chalom de Safed, aus der Tschechoslowakei Karel Chaba, Anna Lickova und Jurai Lauko, aus Deutschland Paps, aus Marokko Louardiri, aus Belgien Micheline Boyadjian und Van den Driessche, aus Holland Alexandrine, aus Brasilien Iracema; und Italien, das sich plötzlich erinnerte, daß es die Wiege und die unbestrittene Heimat der primitiven Malerei gewesen war, führte im Handumdrehen fünf oder sechs Namen von hoher Geltung ins Treffen.

Sogar die Sowjetunion, wo die naive Malerei kraft der stalinistischen Doktrin von Ždanov mehr oder weniger verboten war, hat ihren großen naiven Maler, den Georgier Niko Pirosmanachvili, rehabilitiert, indem sie letzthin im Puschkin-Museum in Moskau eine posthume Ausstellung veranstaltete, was einer wahren Weihe gleichkommt, die gewöhnlich unbestrittenen Größen vorbehalten bleibt. Außerdem wurde auch ein großes Werk über die ukrainische Bäuerin Katherina Bialakur herausgegeben, deren Blumensträuße eine seltsame Ähnlichkeit mit den Bildern von Séraphine aufweisen.

Das alles beweist doch vor allem, nicht wahr, daß die naive Malerei bei weitem kein Zufall, keine Glückssache, kein vereinzelter Treffer ist, sondern wirklich und wahrhaftig eine organische, natürliche Erscheinung, die ganz ohne Zweifel einer historischen Notwendigkeit gehorcht.

Wie anders könnte sich dieses unvergleichliche, sozusagen gleichzeitige Aufblühen eines ganzen Wundergartens von Künstlern erklären, die sich gegenseitig kaum kannten und daher nichts voneinander wußten und doch plötzlich über die ganze Welt verstreut das gleiche Lied anstimmen?

Natürlich haben sich ein paar unechte Naive unter die echten eingeschlichen; zuweilen verwechselte man die Folklore mit der so typisch individualisierten Kunst der Naiven, aber alles in allem handelte es sich dabei nur um Kinderkrankheiten, Übel, die man mit Leichtigkeit verhüten, wenn nicht gar heilen konnte, allerdings unter der Bedingung, daß jemand sich ernsthaft mit dem Problem der naiven Malerei abgab. Denn auch heute noch existiert sozusagen nichts und niemand, der wahrhaft befugt wäre, gegebenenfalls mit Autorität die mit diesem Problem verbundenen heiklen Fragen zu entscheiden. Wenig Bücher, keine grundlegenden Artikel und noch weniger wahrhaft wissenschaftliche Untersuchungen. Trotz der stets wachsenden Anteilnahme, die sie erregt, trotz des Erfolgs und der Förderung, die sie, wie man sieht, in immer größeren Kreisen des Publikums erfährt, geht es leider immer noch genau so zu wie früher, das heißt als hätte die naive Malerei überhaupt keine Bedeutung und als wäre es völlig überflüssig, sich damit zu befassen.

Wer inzwischen über die Naiven schreibt, begnügt sich ganz einfach mit schon Gesagtem und fährt fort, sich mit Hinweisen zu begnügen, die dreißig oder vierzig Jahre alt sind. Man könnte meinen, diese Leute seien Roboter, die mit lange im voraus vorbereiteten Lochkarten arbeiten. Apollinaire hier, Wilhelm Uhde dort, und um das Ganze etwas zu würzen, der unvermeidliche Alfred Jarry. Aber Jarry sah im Zöllner Rousseau nur eine Art König Ubu der Palette, gerade recht, um die Spießbürger zu skandalisieren; Apollinaire hat seinen Wert erst spät und, wie man offen zugeben muß, nach vielem Zögern erkannt, obwohl er seit seiner Kindheit besser als jeder andere die wunderbaren Votivtafeln von Laghet kannte[1].

Was schließlich Uhde anbelangt, so müssen wir uns daran erinnern, daß er vor allem Kunsthändler war und als solcher nur seine eigene Ware in Schutz nahm. Daher diese vier oder fünf Namen, die man kennt, da sie die einzigen waren, denen es gelang, eine Ware zu werden, natürlich eine, die hoch im Kurs stand. Darauf aber basiert sich die Mehrheit der Kritiker, gestern so gut wie heute. Welch ein Hohn! Welche Obstruktion!... Welch ein Elend!...

Warum erinnern sie sich nicht von Zeit zu Zeit an die Worte, die doch ihr lieber Apollinaire in seinen «Méditations Esthétiques» sagte: *«Man kann nicht den Leichnam seines Vaters überall mit sich herumtragen. Man läßt ihn in Gesellschaft der anderen Toten zurück. Und wenn man sich an ihn erinnert, trauert man ihm nach und spricht voll Bewunderung von ihm. Und wenn man selber Vater wird, darf man nicht erwarten, daß eines unserer Kinder sich sein Leben lang mit unserem Leichnam herumschleppt!»*

Wie dem auch sei, fest steht, daß dieser Zustand seine Bestätigung, ja mehr, eine Art logischen Abschluß gefunden hat in der neuesten großen internationalen Ausstellung der naiven Malerei (leider vielleicht auch der umfangreichsten); mit ihrem verschwenderisch ausgestatteten Katalog, der den verlockenden Titel «Die Welt der Naiven» trug, und den mehr als nur bedeutenden Mitteln, die den Organisatoren zur Verfügung standen, hätte diese Ausstellung sehr schön und sehr vollständig sein können und sein müssen. Sie war es aber keineswegs. Ich meine die Ausstellung, die 1964 im Museum Boymans-Van Beuningen in Rotterdam stattfand.

Man hatte da tatsächlich den Eindruck, eine gewaltige Nekropole zu betreten. Nicht die geringste Überraschung, nicht die geringste Entdeckung. Außer der natürlich, daß zahlreiche, unter normalen Umständen unerklärliche Lücken zu verzeichnen waren, sowie der allerdings ziemlich häufigen Konfusion, die darin besteht, um jeden Preis die verschiedenen folkloristischen Ausdünstungen, seien sie jugoslawischer oder südamerikanischer Herkunft, als naive Werke ausgeben zu wollen. Der Rest war katalogisiert, bekannt, altbekannt, so oft wird er an den Wänden der Museen, der Kunstgalerien und der Sammler aufgehängt und in Permanenz gezeigt. Aus diesem Grund verströmte diese Ausstellung einen heimtückischen, eindringlichen Geruch nach alten Bildern und alten Büchern, einen Leichengeruch. Man hatte deutlich den Eindruck, die Erde sei schon vor einer guten Weile stillgestanden...

Betrogen und enttäuscht suchten darauf zahlreiche zu kurz gekommene Besucher, die sich allmählich bereits an andere Feste und eine andere Zauberwelt gewöhnt hatten, den Grund dieses Mißlingens herauszufinden, das von manchen ohne Zögern als Skandal bezeichnet wurde.

War es ganz einfach ein Schnitzer, ein Versehen, wie sie hin und wieder unzuständigen Leuten passieren, wenn sie etwas an die Hand nehmen, von dem sie keine Ahnung haben? Oder war diese Ausstellung vielmehr zufällig Teil eines machiavellistischeren Plans, einer geheimeren Verschwörung, die zum Beispiel darauf abzielte, Frankreich seine gegenwärtige künstlerische Vorherrschaft zu entreißen? Denn der lebende Teil der französischen naiven Malerei – der zahlenmäßig stärksten,

---

[1] «Die vom Wunder geblendete und sorgsame Unbeholfenheit der primitiven Kunst, die hier herrscht, hat etwas an sich, das selbst den Ungläubigen anrührt. Es gibt hier Bilder aller Art zu sehen, einzig Porträts sind nicht zu finden. Alle Einsendungen werden ausgestellt und nie mehr entfernt. Es genügt, daß das Bild ein Wunder darstellt, das von der Lieben Frau von Laghet bewirkt wurde. Alle möglichen Unglücksfälle, die tödlichen Krankheiten, die tiefen Schmerzen, alles Elend der Menschheit wird hier naiv, fromm, vertrauensselig geschildert... Das entfesselte Meer spielt mit einer armseligen Nußschale ohne Mast, auf der ein Mann kniet, der größer ist als das ganze Schiff. Alles scheint verloren, aber in der Ecke des Bildes wacht die von einem hellen Heiligenschein umgebene Jungfrau von Laghet. Der fromme Schiffer wurde gerettet. Eine italienische Inschrift bezeugt es. Das geschah im Jahr 1811...

... Ein von scheugewordenen Pferden mitgerissener Wagen stürzt in den Abgrund. Die Reisenden werden auf den Felsen zerschellen. Maria mit ihrem strahlenden Heiligenschein wacht in einer Ecke des Bilds. Sie ließ Gestrüpp an den Hängen des Abgrunds wachsen. Die Reisenden klammerten sich daran fest und hingen später aus Dankbarkeit dieses Bild im Kreuzgang von Laghet auf. Das war im Jahr 1830...

Und stets und immer, 1850, 1860, jedes Jahr, jeden Monat, beinahe jeden Tag wurden Blinde sehend, fanden Stumme die Sprache, überlebten Schwindsüchtige dank Unserer Lieben Frau von Laghet, die, von einem sanften gelben Glorienschein umstrahlt, in den Ecken der Bilder lächelt...»

Guillaume Appolinaire, L'Hérésiarque et Cie, 1910, Stock ed. Paris

Ph. Obin
cap-Haïti
1945

reichsten und mannigfaltigsten der Welt – war alles in allem nur durch drei Greise vertreten, während der in Stabroek bei Antwerpen geborene Belgier Aloys Sauter die Toten vertrat.

Es gab nur zwei Möglichkeiten: entweder hatte man ausgesprochen Angst, ein paar dieser Abwesenden könnten die Mehrzahl der ausgestellten, nicht eben bedeutenden Bilder in den Schatten stellen und ihnen nicht wieder gutzumachenden Schaden zufügen, oder man hat sie absichtlich aus einem anderen Grund ferngehalten, und zwar um behaupten zu können: da seht ihr, Frankreich hat zweifellos ein paar gute naive Maler besessen, aber das war früher, jetzt ist Schluß damit, wirklich Schluß, jetzt muß man sie in Jugoslawien und anderswo suchen... War es, mit anderen Worten, eine abgekartete Sache der Händler?

Man weiß es heute noch nicht. Die Proteste und die Polemiken in der Presse haben es nicht fertiggebracht, die wahren Hintergründe aufzudecken. Man fragt sich also vergeblich und schwankt immer noch zwischen Betrug und Dummheit. Denn um das Ganze zu krönen, fehlten auch die besten holländischen und flämischen Maler!

Da stellt sich nun sofort eine andere, weit schwerer wiegende Frage, nämlich wie es möglich war, daß ein seines Namens würdiges französisches Museum seinerseits sich so grob hereinlegen ließ. Schließlich ist jeder Herr im eigenen Haus. Und doch hat zum Schluß Paris, jawohl, das Musée d'Art Moderne in Paris diese ausgesprochen mehr balkanesische als holländische Machenschaft geerbt.

Man könnte sagen, es geschehe ihnen ganz recht, wenn doch kein anderes französisches Museum vorher daran gedacht habe oder nicht imstande gewesen sei, etwas Derartiges selber zu verwirklichen. Aber was will man? Unsere Konservatoren sind eben, wie sie sind, und warum sollten sie sich schließlich so sehr von ihren Vorgängern unterscheiden, die vor kaum fünfzig Jahren einem Cézanne und einem Van Gogh ihre Säle verweigerten? Die naive Malerei ist nichts für sie. Noch nichts. Viel zu revolutionär, viel zu neu. Aber trotzdem... Die französischen naiven Maler haben das weder in der Vergangenheit noch jetzt verdient! Bei weitem nicht.

Darum scheint es uns heilsam und dringend, zuallererst eine Art objektives Verzeichnis der naiven Malerei auf der ganzen Welt aufzustellen, in dem *alle* naiven Maler ihren Platz finden, aber wirklich nur ihren Platz. Die Zeit wird die Auslese besorgen und die Spreu vom Weizen zu sondern wissen. Auf jeden Fall und was auch immer geschehe, die biographischen Angaben und die genauen Referenzen, die wir hier veröffentlichen, können den zukünftigen Forschern nur von Nutzen sein.

Immerhin mußte genau ein halbes Jahrhundert nach dem Tod des armen Zöllners vergehen, bis sein Mythus demystifiziert und vor allem von jener kitschigen Literatur befreit wurde, die sich sowohl seiner Person wie seines Werks bemächtigt hatte, damit seine Bilder und sein Leben mit dem Ernst und der Strenge untersucht werden können, die sie verdienen. Wie wahr ist doch das Wort von Paul Valéry: «Am Anfang war die Legende...»

Was die eigentliche Geschichte der naiven Malerei angeht, so können wir hier natürlich infolge Platzmangels nur ihre großen Linien skizzieren. Ihre Niederschrift ist Gott sei Dank noch eine Sache der Zukunft.

◄ PHILOMÉ OBIN

Die naiven Maler als soziales Phänomen treten im allgemeinen zum erstenmal in dem Augenblick der Geschichte auf, da die vorindustrielle, noch ein wenig feudale Gesellschaft sich anschickt, einen entscheidenden Sprung nach vorne zu machen und sich der modernen Zeit zu stellen. Es ist die Begegnung einer einfachen Nadel mit einer Nähmaschine, um den düsteren Isidore Ducasse, genannt Graf von Lautréamont, abzuwandeln, oder, um ein weiteres Bild zu gebrauchen, das gewaltsame Eindringen eines Fabrikschlots in den noch ländlichen Frieden einer Ekloge von Vergil. Das Beispiel Jugoslawiens ist mehr als beweiskräftig. Dieses Land, das höchst patriarchalisch und mittelalterlich war, das vor dem letzten Krieg, kurz ehe es seinerseits in das Zeitalter des Sozialismus und der Maschine eintrat, nur Glasmaler hervorbrachte, abgesehen von ein paar anderen Vertretern der im wesentlichen ländlichen, der naiven Malerei ziemlich fernstehenden Volkskunst, erweckte sogleich danach, sozusagen vor unseren Augen, ganz plötzlich eine erkleckliche Anzahl echter naiver Maler.

In Frankreich fällt die Geburt der naiven Malerei mit der Revolution von 1789 und der Aufhebung der Zünfte zusammen.

Bis dahin waren in der Tat alle, die eine gewisse Fähigkeit zum Schneiden, Formen oder Zeichnen bewiesen, in frühester Jugend in eine jener Zünfte eingetreten; dort wurden ihnen die Anfangsgründe eines Handwerks beigebracht, das sie dann ihr Leben lang ausübten.

Sie alle besaßen einen gewissen Sinn für das Schöne, notwendigerweise verbunden mit einer großen Liebe für die gut ausgeführte Arbeit; diesen Sinn konnten sie von nun an nach Herzenslust befriedigen, da ja ihre ganze Existenz, wie schon gesagt, der Herstellung einer Vielzahl jener ganz und gar vollkommenen Gegenstände geweiht war, die sich halbwegs zwischen dem Kunstwerk und dem reinen Gebrauchsartikel situieren.

Wenn eine Kirche gebaut wurde, so versahen die Steinmetzen sie mit ihren steinernen Heiligen, während die Holzschnitzer sie mit ihren hölzernen Heiligen schmückten; wurde ein Gasthof eröffnet, so malte ihr der Dorfmaler ihr Schild, derselbe Maler, der meistens im Auftrag eines durch ein Wunder Geheilten auf der Stelle eine jener unzähligen Votivtafeln ausführte, die entweder eine im letzten Augenblick erfolgte Heilung oder einen mit knapper Not vermiedenen tödlichen Unfall schildern. Wir brauchen nur an die Bilder von Laghet zu denken...

Manche unter ihnen wurden Maler schlechthin, zuweilen große Maler, wie jener J. B. Chardin, Sohn eines Schreiners aus der Rue de Seine. Was die anderen angeht, nun, so waren sie noch Handwerker, nicht mehr und nicht weniger, höchstens ein bißchen höher entwickelt, ein bißchen verfeinert. Das hindert nicht, daß sie sich immer noch auf der Ebene jener letzten Verfertiger von Volkskunst in Lateinamerika befanden, die heute noch mir nichts dir nichts ihre Erzeugnisse wie vor hundert Jahren auf den Marktplätzen verkaufen. Sie waren nicht schöpferisch tätig. Nicht ganz. Nicht von sich aus. Die naive Malerei tritt da auf, wo die Folklore verstummt.

Mit der Einführung der Maschine verändert sich die Lage von Grund auf. Denn die Maschine bringt alles, was noch schlecht und recht an manueller Arbeit übrigbleibt, schnell zum Verschwinden. Es ist darum nicht verwunderlich, daß die ersten naiven Maler sich gleich auf den ersten Anhieb unter denen finden, die gestern noch Glasmaler, Töpfer, Schmiede, Kunsttischler, Spielkartenmaler, Bilderbogenmaler und was weiß ich noch waren, unter all denen, die vom Zwang der Umstände getrieben werden, jetzt ein anderes Handwerk auszuüben, das keinerlei Beziehung zur Kunst mehr hat.

Entwurzelt, verwirrt, betrogen, verbittert, verdrängt und in ihrem Schönheitssinn und ihrer Schönheitsliebe verletzt, ergreifen sie nun die kleinste Gelegenheit, um mit dem, was ihnen am meisten am Herzen liegt, wieder anzuknüpfen, damit sie ihr verlorenes Paradies besingen können. Der Mann, der seine meiste Zeit damit verbrachte, für die Kirchen Engelchen zu malen oder zu meißeln und der von nun an in einem Kohlenbergwerk arbeitet, verwandelt sich selber in einen gefallenen Engel. Es bleibt ihm nichts anderes übrig, als von seinem Fall zu erzählen. Andere, selbst wenn sie weder von nahe noch von ferne mit irgendeiner künstlerischen Beschäftigung zu tun hatten, beklagen ebenfalls die Härte des Lebens, trauern der guten alten Zeit nach, die der Wirbelsturm der wirtschaftlichen Veränderungen unwiderruflich mit sich fortgetragen hat, und sehnen sich nach irgendeinem verlorenen Glück. Wie Marcel Proust, der sein Leben lang so hartnäckig, so sorgsam jene Zeit suchte, die er in Wirklichkeit so wenig gelebt hat, machen sich die naiven Maler ihrerseits auf die Suche nach einem gewissen Sonntag des Lebens, einem Sonntag, der leider, doch gerechterweise, nicht länger dauert als die Sonntagsträume! Daher der Name Sonntagsmaler.

Gezwungen, sechs Tage hintereinander ohne frische Luft, hinter traurigen, schmutzigen Scheiben hart, sehr hart zu arbeiten, verdrängten sie auf diese Weise alle verbotenen Visionen: einen Himmel, wie er blauer nicht sein kann, Blumen in allen Regenbogenfarben, Frühlingsbäume, fischreiche Bäche. Für den Zöllner Rousseau war es der Urwald, den er natürlich nie gesehen hat, den er aber oft, auf einer Bank im botanischen Garten sitzend, voll Glückseligkeit mit den Augen der Seele betrachtet hat.

«Der Begriff des Glücks ist neu für Europa», sagt Saint-Just, der am Wendepunkt dieser zwei Zeiten steht, zwischen dem ausgehenden 18. Jahrhundert und dieser faszinierenden modernen Zeit, von der man im Augenblick kaum nur die wolkenlosen Fata Morganen erblickte. Und das Wort naiv und die naive Welt sind, wer weiß, ebenso neu, und wäre es nur aus diesem selben Grund.

Im übrigen sieht der naive Maler dieses individuelle Glück, auf das seit kurzem jeder Mensch ein Anrecht hat, zum ersten Mal in *seiner* Malerei, und es gehört ebenfalls jedem einzelnen. Die Malerei kann, ja muß die Sache eines jeden sein. Aber um welchen Preis!

Denn es handelte sich nicht mehr darum, vom Vater auf den Sohn ruhig zu kopieren, wie es früher ihre Vorfahren taten, sondern nun mußte man kämpfen, ununterbrochen improvisieren, etwas, das vor ihnen nicht existiert hatte, wirklich Gestalt verleihen, das heißt schöpferisch tätig sein. Zudem mußten sie zugleich Thema und Technik erfinden, Zeichnung und Perspektive, Schatten und Körper, alles, tatsächlich alles, bis zum Mischen der Farben. Den Seinen gibt's der Herr im Schlafe...

Je weniger sie übrigens davon verstanden, desto besser war es. Die Zauberwirkung und die Überraschung waren dann nur um so größer. Nicht jeder, der will, ist naiv – ich muß diese Selbstverständlichkeit wiederholen –, und um es wirklich, unbestreitbar im vollen Sinne des Wortes zu sein, mußte einer wahrlich von einem brennenden Wunsch besessen sein, sonst hätte er nicht allen Widerständen zum Trotz dieser Bestätigung seines Ichs nachjagen und all das verfolgen können, was ihm zu entgehen drohte! Und dies alles, um eine wenn auch noch so schwache Spur seines Erdendaseins zu hinterlassen...

Sie fühlten sich tatsächlich von einer Kraft beseelt, die über sie hinausging; sie wurden tatsächlich Besessene. Darum erscheint uns die Mehrzahl ihrer Werke als Gabe, mehr noch, gleichsam von einer Art Gnade erfüllt.

Ihre Landschaften sind nackt, wie Adam und Eva es vor dem Sündenfall waren. Ohne jegliche Scham. Sie wissen nicht, was gut und was schlecht ist; sie haben noch nicht von der Frucht der Erkenntnis gegessen, die der Teufel hinhält, und kennen infolgedessen nicht einmal den Begriff der plastischen Sünde, die man in den Akademien lehrt. Sie wissen nur, daß die Malerei ihnen hilft, zu leben, und daß sie ihr einziges und immerwährendes Eden darstellt, das heißt das Glück, die Ekstase, das Unendliche, wie immer man es nennen mag.

Der Zöllner Rousseau bekannte es eines Tages ohne Umschweife: «Nicht ich male, sondern etwas vorne an meiner Hand.»

Wie dem auch sei, der Wunsch nach einer ursprünglichen Frische, das große, brennende Verlangen nach unbefleckter Reinheit, kurz, was man äußerstenfalls in Ermangelung eines besseren Wortes mit naiv bezeichnen könnte – das Wort hatte zu Anfang nichts Pejoratives an sich und nichts von dem, was in der Folge daraus geworden ist –, ließ bereits niemand mehr in Ruhe, die Großen so wenig wie die Kleinen, die Gebildeten so wenig wie die Ungebildeten [2].

Diderot sagte: «Alles, was wahr ist, ist nicht naiv, aber alles, was naiv ist, ist wahr, von einer reizvollen, originellen und seltenen Naivität.» Und Stendhal verzeichnete etwas später unter dem Datum des 16. Messidor des Jahres XII, das heißt am 5. Juli 1804 in seinem *Tagebuch:* «Die Naivität scheint mir das Erhabene des täglichen Lebens.» Es ist selbstverständlich auch kein Zufall, daß dieser gleiche Stendhal sich für die alten italienischen Chroniken interessierte, volkstümliche Romane aufstöberte und sich für die berühmte «Blaue Bibliothek» begeisterte, welche die Hausierer von Dorf zu Dorf feilhielten, dann auch für die Bänkelsängerlieder, die noch auf den Märkten zum Besten gegeben wurden, denn von seiner geistigen Haltung zu der eines Baudelaire oder eines Rimbaud, um nur die beiden zu nennen, war es bloß ein Schritt. Dem «ich bin zurückgekommen, um in der makellosen Naivität Zuflucht zu suchen» von Baudelaire entspricht auf vollkommene Weise das «ich liebte die idiotischen Bilder, die Sopraporten, die Bühnenbilder der Gaukler, die Aushängeschilder, die volkstümlichen Bilderbogen» von Rimbaud!

Wenn die Welt in andere Hände übergeht, wenn Vergangenheit und Gegenwart in Erwartung der Zukunft sich in einem gnadenlosen Kampf messen, empfindet man überall plötzlich das übermächtige Bedürfnis nach einem Jungbrunnen, man strebt nach einer primitiven, direkten Kunst aus den Urzeiten der Menschheit, in der die Regeln, die Konventionen und das technische Können nicht wichtiger sind als die Spontaneität, die Aufrichtigkeit, mit einem Wort: das Echte.

Es mag der Schotte MacPherson sein, Zeuge der beginnenden Industrialisierung in England, Verfasser der «Gesänge des

[2] Das Wort «naiv» kommt übrigens vom lateinischen «nativus», das «der geboren wird» bedeutet.

EMERIK FEJEŠ

Ossian», jener Gedichte, die einen so gewaltigen Erfolg hatten, ehe man die Fälschung erkannte, denn dieser angebliche Barde aus dem 3. Jahrhundert hat gar nie gelebt; es mögen die russischen Komponisten sein wie Moussorgskij und Rimskij-Korsakoff, um nur diese zu erwähnen, die in ihre Werke Märchen, bekannte Melodien, wenn nicht gar Volkslieder aufnehmen, wiederum in dem Augenblick, da die ersten Hochöfen angezündet werden; es mag der Chinese Liau Tao-Tschuen sein, der schon unter der Sung-Dynastie sagte: «Such das Talent in der Ungeschicklichkeit» – ihrer aller Wünsche stimmen überein, ihr Verlangen deckt sich: sie wollen die Welt neu schaffen, neu anfangen mit den Augen und dem Herzen eines Kindes.

In diesem Verhältnis der Kräfte, welches das Auftreten des naiven Phänomens bestimmt hat, kann die Schöpfung des «Gruselromans» mit seinen Phantomen, seinen Gespenstern, dem Rasseln der Ketten, dem Klirren der Rüstungen, den blutigen Nonnen und den unterirdischen Verließen voll Gebeinen als eine aggressive Forderung, als ein letztes Aufbäumen des Mittelalters verstanden werden, als Ätzmittel und gleichzeitige Dämonenbeschwörung – bitte mach mir Angst, das beruhigt mich! – so wie übrigens auch die um hundert Jahre jüngeren «Rächer», Rocambole, Chéri-Bibi, Arsène Lupin, Fantomas, Judex und wie sie alle heißen. Die Naiven dagegen sind trotz ihrer unbestreitbaren Bindungen an das Ancien Régime eher als die resignierten Opfer der «neuen Ordnung» anzusehen; sie sind die Betrogenen, die Bestohlenen, die Verhöhnten, die Leute, die an das Evangelium, an die Versprechungen und vor allem an den großgeschriebenen Fortschritt geglaubt haben.

Auf jeden Fall besteht kein Zweifel, daß der Gruselroman der einen und die Rosenwasserliteratur der anderen eine gleiche Naivität an den Tag legen. Der Unterschied besteht einzig darin, daß die ersteren eine hauptsächlich romantische Technik anwenden, voll von Lärm und Raserei, breitgepinselt und verschwommen, eine Technik, die in direkter Linie von Walter Scott und Ann Radcliffe herkommt, der übrigens sogar ein Stendhal seinen Tribut gezollt hat, während die letzteren sich der Linse des gerichtlichen Erkennungsdienstes bedienen, später jener der Ansichtspostkarte und des Photographen Adget, der ein unvergleichlicher Dichter der Reißfeder und des Senklots war, eine Art Zöllner Rousseau der Photographie.

Ist bei ihnen nicht alles sauber, genau, sorgsam, makellos? Noch nie hat man das Unsichtbare so eng eingekreist. Und doch befindet die Wirklichkeit sich anderswo. Sie heißt Courbet und Zola. Paradoxerweise sind es also nicht die sogenannten Maler des Wahren, welche die letzten rührenden Bilder, die letzten empfindsamen Zeugnisse dessen hinterlassen haben, was im Begriff steht, unwiederbringlich verloren zu gehen, sondern diese Visionäre, diese Träumer des Wochenendes... Unsere Enterbten, unsere Parias, unsere Ausgestoßenen.

Und es begann die Zeit der allsonntäglichen Flucht!

Während die Natur unter dem heißen Atem der Hochöfen immer mehr einschrumpft (auch das ist ein Bild von Baudelaire), das heißt vor allem von 1850, 1860 an, stürzen Weber, Schuster, Grubenarbeiter, Briefträger, Lastenträger, kleine Angestellte, kleine Rentenempfänger, Hauswarte, warum nicht, sich kopfüber ins Malen und malen, malen, malen, auch wenn sie um die Wette ihre kurzen Augenblicke der Freiheit opfern. Freizeit, Schlaf, Ruhestunden, Essenszeit, alles wird dem Pinsel zuliebe aufgegeben. Vor und nach dem Heulen der Fabriksirenen. Zwischen dem abendlichen und dem morgendlichen Ruf des neuen Angelus des Dampfzeitalters. Nur ist es nicht mehr Millet, der es abmalt, sondern die ersten Expressionisten, Munch und Hodler.

Warum malen sie? Weil sie nicht anders können.

Ich habe vor noch nicht sehr langer Zeit und, wie ich hoffe, so gründlich als möglich den verborgenen Mechanismus der naiven Schöpfung untersucht, sowie jene offenkundig zu kurz gekommene affektive Seite, und zwar in meinem Buch «Eros du Dimanche»[3]; es ist darum nicht nötig, hier darauf zurückzukommen.

Für wen malen sie? Zuallererst für sich selber. Zu ihrem eigenen Vergnügen, dann für die Familie, für die Freunde. Der Gedanke, ihre Bilder könnten eines Tages verkauft werden, streift sie nicht einmal. Man gibt ja schließlich auch seine Liebesbriefe nicht her. Wäre das nicht frevelhaft?

Wo stellen sie aus? Nirgends.

Was wird aus ihren Werken? Die meisten verschwinden; entweder werden sie von Erben, die sich ihrer schämen, willentlich zerstört, oder aber sie gehen langsam doch sicher zugrunde, während sie auf einem Flohmarkt nach dem anderen herumliegen. Niemand schenkt ihnen Beachtung, außer wahrscheinlich irgendeine andere gequälte Seele, ein Bruderherz, welches dem des Malers in allen Punkten gleicht und ebenfalls nach ein bißchen Blau für seine Hütte sucht.

Erst als der Salon des Indépendants gegründet wurde, konnten alle diese Sonntagsmaler wenn nicht ein Publikum, so doch eine Wand zum Aufhängen ihrer Bilder finden. Um so mehr, als selbst hier die Besucher nicht lange verweilten und all diesem Firlefanz, der so deutlich von allen anderen Kunstmalern, seien sie nun diplomiert oder nicht, abstach, ganz und gar keinen Geschmack abgewannen.

Sogar Georges Courteline, der doch als erster den Einfall und die Lust hatte, naive Bilder zu sammeln, konnte nicht umhin, zuerst einmal darüber zu spotten. Sobald er bei einem Trödler in Montmartre ein solches Bild aufstöberte, gab er ihm einen humoristischen Titel, in der Art «Die halbgesottene Jungfrau», «Die Austern der r-losen Monate», «Die Regatten der Mausoleen», usw.

Indessen ist weniger bekannt, daß diese Sammlung, die ursprünglich «Das Museum der Greuel» genannt wurde, unter den Bildern unbekannter Maler auch zwei Bilder des Zöllners Rousseau enthielt, wovon das eine das «Porträt von Pierre Loti» war, das, wie ausnahmslos alle andern, von Courteline selber so getauft worden war, höchstwahrscheinlich wegen der Zuavenmütze und der Katze[4], obwohl der Dargestellte niemand anders ist als ein gewisser Herr Frank, der auf der Butte wohnte. Das Bild veräußerte Courteline gegen Ende seines Lebens um einen Pappenstiel, wobei er den Käufer erst noch einen Dummkopf schimpfte!

Ebenfalls im Zeichen des Ulks wird dem genannten Museum, das heißt den Naiven, die Ehre zuteil, in der Pariser Presse erwähnt und in einer Zeitung reproduziert zu werden. Aus diesem Grund stellt diese Nummer 39 der satirischen Zeitung «Cocorico» vom 15. August 1900, die in ihrer Ganzheit dieser berühmten Sammlung gewidmet ist, unbestreitbar nicht nur das erste Do-

[3] Verlag J. J. Pauvert, Paris, 1964.

[4] H. Certigny: «Le douanier Rousseau a-t-il peint le portrait de P. Loti?» L'information de l'histoire de l'Art, Nr. 1, Januar 1965.

kument dieser Art dar, sondern auch die allererste Aussage, zumindest von dieser Bedeutung, die es auf der Welt über ein naives Ensemble gibt. Ein Dokument also. Ein Datum. Sie verdienen es, daß man sich ein bißchen länger dabei aufhält.

Das Kostbarste an dieser so ganz unerwarteten Veröffentlichung ist, von Courtelines Kommentaren abgesehen, die Einführung, um nicht zu sagen, das Vorwort, in dem wörtlich steht:

«Wie wir in unserer letzten Nummer angezeigt haben, hat unser Freund Georges Courteline sich liebenswürdigerweise bereit erklärt, sein höchst wunderliches Museum zum erstenmal in «Cocorico» vorzustellen; die abgedruckten Bilder sind, wie der Leser sehen wird, der Gegenstand würziger Kommentare von seiten des glücklichen Besitzers der Galerie.

In diesem Zusammenhang zitieren wir aus einer langen, sehr interessanten Studie, die Edouard Norès kürzlich seinem Freund und Mitarbeiter widmete, die folgenden Zeilen, die, besser als wir es vermöchten, unsere Leser über die ästhetischen Grundsätze aufklären werden, die Courteline in der Wahl seiner Bilder geleitet haben:

‹... *Es existiert bei Courteline ein Charakterzug, der in meinen Augen die Schärfe seines Blicks für das Lächerliche an den Menschen erklärt: es ist dies die tiefe Rührung, die der Anblick dieses Lächerlichen in ihm hervorruft. Als scharfsinniger Beobachter der ewigen Dummheit liebt er sie mit brüderlicher Liebe, läßt sich ohne Bitterkeit ihre Berührung gefallen, genießt ihre verschiedenen Äußerungen mit inniger Freude; und wenn er ihnen in den unvergeßlichen Seiten des Train de 8 heures 47, der Ronds de Cuir, der Gaîtés de l'Escadron oder des Boubourouche ein Denkmal setzt, so läßt seine Beobachtung unter der Präzision der Zeichnung die menschliche Gemütsbewegung des Schriftstellers durchschimmern.*

Diese Saite geriet bei Courteline in Schwingung, als er das erste der Bilder erwarb, die jetzt sein ‹Museum› bilden. Er sagte sich, da könnte man eine seltsame Sammlung aufbauen – nicht von schlechten Bildern im genauen Sinn des Wortes, da brauchte man sich nur zu bücken, um sie aufzuheben –, sondern von merkwürdigen Erzeugnissen, entstanden aus dem Fleiß der überzeugten Naiven, die in der Malerei mit einem ständigen, unfruchtbaren und bewunderungswürdigen Bemühen die negativen Qualitäten der falschen, aber aufrichtigen Berufungen zur Anwendung bringen.

Damit war das Courteline-Museum gegründet.

Geduldiges Suchen hat es seither jeden Tag bereichert, und heute umfaßt die Sammlung etwa dreißig Nummern; sie fügt der Geschichte der französischen Malerei eine humoristische Seite hinzu, die ihr bisher gefehlt hat.› gez.: Edouard Norès.»

Trotz gewissen Ungerechtigkeiten und unbestreitbaren Fehlern, die dem Autor in der Beurteilung des Werks der Naiven unterlaufen, erscheint dieser Text, der, das dürfen wir nicht vergessen, gut fünfundsechzig Jahre alt ist, jünger und einsichtiger als eine ganze Anzahl neuerer Ergüsse, ganz zu schweigen von ein paar widersinnigen Bezeichnungen, die den Naiven zuweilen angehängt werden, wie zum Beispiel «Die volkstümlichen Meister der Wirklichkeit».

Gewiß ist inzwischen viel Wasser die Seine hinuntergeflossen; Courteline erlaubte eine öffentliche Ausstellung seiner Sammlung, die vom 21. November bis am 2. Dezember 1927 in der Galerie Bernheim-Jeune auch tatsächlich stattfand. Die Titel und die Kommentare des Humoristen, die im Katalog, dem Hauptanziehungspunkt der Ausstellung, angeführt waren, hatten zwar schon unverändert 27 Jahre früher in der Zeitung «Cocorico» gestanden, selbst wenn «Das Perlhuhn beim letzten Seufzer» in «Die schweren Stunden» umgewandelt war und «Überschwemmung in einem Friedhof» zu den schon zitierten «Regatten der Mausoleen» wurde. Nichts hatte sich offenbar geändert, außer daß Courteline in der Zwischenzeit seinen Irrtum eingesehen hatte, wie das in den Katalog eingeschobene N.B. höchst aufschlußreich bezeugt:

«Georges Courteline weist den Namen ‹Museum der Greuel›, mit dem seine Sammlung zu bezeichnen man sich angewöhnt hat, in aller Form zurück. Er lehnt die Urheberschaft dafür kategorisch ab.» (Unter uns gesagt: er war es doch...) *«Es wäre höchstens möglich, diese Bilder unter der generellen Bezeichnung ‹Museum des unschuldigen Fleißes› zusammenzufassen.»*

Diese Verschiebung in der Bewertung ist natürlich bemerkenswert, obwohl man sich, und zu Recht, fragen darf, ob sie wirklich von Courteline ausging oder ob er nicht bloß sein Mäntelchen nach dem Wind hängte. Denn die Rehabilitierung der Naiven war schon auf guten Wegen, und die 27 ereignisreichen Jahre, die zwischen diesen beiden Kundgebungen verflossen, stellen einen entscheidenden Wendepunkt in der Geschichte der naiven Malerei dar. Der Wind drehte jäh.

Dessen ungeachtet, fährt Rousseau fort, wie so viele seiner namenlosen Kollegen im Salon des Indépendants auszustellen; er wird verlacht und verhöhnt, aber er ist es schon gewohnt. Bis zum Tag, da er zufällig seinem «Landsmann» Jarry begegnet, der wie er aus Laval gebürtig ist. Jarry erfaßt sofort, was Rousseaus Malerei Außergewöhnliches an sich hat – das muß man ihm lassen – und gibt ihm seine einzige Lithographie «La guerre» in Auftrag; sie ist für die Zeitschrift «Ymagier» bestimmt, die Jarry damals mit Rémy de Gourmont zusammen herausgab. Man hat übrigens in diesem Zusammenhang neulich herausgefunden, daß eine in einer sozialistisch angehauchten Zeitung, «L'Egalité», erschienene armselige Zeichnung dem Zöllner als Vorlage für die Komposition gedient hat. Darauf kam es ihm nicht an. Andere Zeichnungen und Stiche haben ihm schlecht und recht für seine Bilder gedient. Ganz entschieden sind nur die naiven Maler fähig, solche Metamorphosen zu bewirken.

Aber Jarry, der vor allem durch seinen Aufsehen erregenden Ubu Roi und das Fünf-Buchstaben-Wort bekannt ist, dem er den sechsten Buchstaben anhängt, vermag offensichtlich nichts für Rousseau. Es «schlägt» nicht ein. Besonders weil es von ihm kommt. Will er sich rächen oder schießt er aus Zorn mit seinem Revolver auf sein eigenes Porträt, das Rousseau von ihm gemalt hat? Man weiß es nicht. Auf jeden Fall zerstört er es gründlich.

Des Kämpfens überdrüssig, stellt er ihn Apollinaire vor.

Von Jarry bleibt schließlich und endlich nur der Übername «Zöllner», der Anfang einer langen, unausrottbaren Legende, denn Jarry, der Dichter und Pataphysiker, ist der erste, der dem einfachen Beamten des Pariser Zollamtes diesen Titel anhängt und ihn unter diesem Namen unter die anderen Persönlichkeiten seiner ganz privaten Mythologie einreiht.

Apollinaire, wie wir schon gesehen haben, zögerte lange, ehe er sich ausspricht, aber ganz plötzlich ergreift er offen und deutlich Partei für Rousseau. Nun setzt er sich vorbehaltlos ein. Er ist Feuer und Flamme und schreibt in Versen und in Prosa ganze Seiten des Lobs über ihn. Kurz vor dem Krieg widmet

EMERIK FEJEŠ

er ihm sogar eine Sondernummer seiner «Soirées de Paris». Etwas zuvor hatte er ihm zu Ehren in Picassos Atelier im «Bateau Lavoir» das unvergeßliche Bankett veranstaltet, das mehr als einmal beschrieben worden ist. Und beinahe augenblicklich ist die so lange erwartete Anerkennung da, der Ruhm, oder doch beinahe. Apollinaire scheint den boshaften Artikel, in dem er ein paar Jahre zuvor den gleichen Rousseau mißhandelt hat, völlig vergessen zu haben...

Bernheim macht eine Ausstellung in Paris und Joseph Brummer eine in New York. Ambroise Vollard kauft seine Bilder. Nicht teuer, aber er kauft. Das ist für Rousseau doch etwas anderes als die Obsthändlerin an der Straßenecke, der Kohlenhändler und die Wäscherin, seine gewohnten Kunden des Stadtviertels Plaisance. Ein anderer Kunsthändler, kein geringerer als Paul Guillaume, schließt sich an und kauft ebenfalls. Apollinaire rät ihm in einem an der Front geschriebenen Brief: «Kaufen Sie billige Bilder, Rousseau, Picasso, Laurencin, Bonnard, Cézanne, usw.... Sie wissen schon was...» Wie man sieht, steht Rousseau an der Spitze. Ja, der Zöllner ist lanciert. Aber er ist bereits tot, der Ärmste. Von nun an wird er zugleich Stele und Symbol – ein wahrhaftes Grab des Unbekannten Naiven!

Diese vorübergehende Begeisterung nutzend, beeilt sich der methodische, kluge Händler Wilhelm Uhde, dieses Verlangen nach Unschuld und diese Freude am Primitiven, ja Barbarischen, die sich wie ein Ölfleck auszudehnen beginnen, gründlich auszubeuten. Nach dem Ersten Weltkrieg fügt er zu Rousseau ein paar andere naive Maler, die man, um der Sache zu dienen, die «Großen» oder die «volkstümlichen Meister der Wirklichkeit» nennt. Groß waren sie, weil sie die einzigen waren, die von den Händlern unterstützt wurden. Meister, weil man sie um jeden Preis von allen anderen naiven Malern unterscheiden mußte. Nur ja keine Verwechslungen...

Mit den Verleumdern der Naiven steht es leider wie mit den Antisemiten. Bekanntlich besaß jeder dieser Schmutzfinken seinen «anständigen» Juden, was ihm erlaubte, alle anderen den Pogromen und den Gaskammern zu überlassen. Unter der Bedingung, daß man seinen Vivin oder seinen Bauchant hatte, besaß man das Recht, die übrigen alle auszurotten.

Die Verwechslung war natürlich verlockend, um so mehr, als manche unter diesen «minderwertigen» Naiven ebensoviel oder gar mehr Talent besaßen als die «Meister», zu denen sie ja nicht gezählt werden durften. Zudem nahm ihre Zahl ständig zu. Sie stellten hier und dort aus, ernteten ein paar Zeilen einer herablassenden Besprechung, aber für den Augenblick hatte es damit sein Bewenden. Zumindest glaubte man das höheren Ortes. Man hoffte, mit diesem Damm der «Herkunftsbezeichnung» der gefährlichen Ausbreitung der Naiven ein klares Halt zu gebieten. Vergeblich. Denn man vergaß das Wesentliche: sie gefielen. Sie belustigten, sie belustigen auch heute noch, das ist ganz unzweifelhaft. Aber man kaufte sie je länger desto mehr in aller Offenheit, nicht mehr im Versteckten, mehr oder weniger geheim, wie es früher der Fall gewesen war, damit man nicht die faulen Witze der Umgebung auf sich zog. Und zwar kaufte man sie aus dem gleichen Grund, aus dem diese Maler malten: aus Liebe. Man kaufte sie auch nicht als Börsenwerte oder als eine Art Geldanlage, sondern weil sie etwas brachten, das wirklich fehlte und das zu beschaffen sie allein fähig waren. Zum erstenmal in der Geschichte der modernen Malerei hörten die Bilderkäufe auf, eine Spekulation zu sein. So daß die Absonderung der Naiven, wie alle Segregationen natürlich, nicht lange vorhielt angesichts der Wirklichkeit, der Wahrheit und der Gerechtigkeit.

Ja eben, sie gefielen... Ein wenig, von Herzen, über alle Maßen. Sie gefielen den einfachen Liebhabern hübscher Bilder ebenso wie den Kennern und den gewitzten Sammlern. Insbesondere den avantgardistischen Malern. Den Kubisten und den Abstrakten. Picasso und Robert Delaunay gehören zu den allerersten Besitzern von Werken des Zöllners Rousseau. In Picassos Tresor, den er in der Banque Nationale du Crédit et de l'Industrie gemietet hat, liegen die Bilder von Rousseau neben denen von Cézanne, Matisse und Braque. Picasso hat ebenfalls die ersten Bilder von Vivancos gekauft. Nur Jean Cocteau hat sich erlaubt, eher abschätzige Zeilen über die naive Malerei zu schreiben, aber vielleicht gerade weil seine beiden Schützlinge Jean Marais und Edouard Dermit sich in einer leicht naiven Richtung «versuchten» und man auch hier ja die Spreu vom Weizen scheiden mußte.

Lieber Rousseau hörst du uns
Wir grüßen dich
Delaunay, seine Frau, Monsieur Queval und ich
Laß unser Gepäck zollfrei durch die Himmelstür.

Heutzutage kennt jedermann diese schöne Grabschrift, die Guillaume Apollinaire mit dem Bleistift direkt auf Rousseaus Grabstein schrieb und die Brancusi unter Mithilfe von Ortiz de Zarate später mit dem Meißel nachzog, damit der Regen und das vermodernde Laub sie nie verwischen können. Aber wenig Leute kennen dagegen die Erklärung, die Kandinsky kurz nach dem ersten Krieg abgab und die sich ungefähr folgendermaßen zusammenfassen läßt: «Ich sehe für die Zukunft nur die abstrakte Kunst oder die naive Malerei.»

Kandinsky hat mir diese Ansicht 1934 persönlich bestätigt; ich erinnere mich noch sehr wohl: es war in seiner schönen Wohnung in Neuilly, die beinahe gegenüber der von Seurat unsterblich gemachten Ile de la Grande Jatte lag und wo er bis an sein Lebensende wohnen sollte, nachdem er sich endgültig in Frankreich niedergelassen hatte. Und er bekräftigte seine Meinung gleichsam doppelt, denn gleichzeitig zeigte er mir seine zwei kleinen, an der Wand hängenden Rousseau, die einzigen Bilder, die er neben seinen eigenen Werken duldete.

Der Grabstein und alles, was vom Sarg des armen Zöllners übrigblieb, verließ 1947 die traurige Vororts-Enge des Friedhofs von Bagneux und überragt heute vom Square de la Perrine aus die Brücken über die Mayenne und die ganze helle, ruhige, etwas schläfrige Stadt Laval, wo er das Licht der Welt erblickte und die ihn trotzdem nicht erkannte, wenigstens nicht zu seinen Lebzeiten. Aber die beschwingten Worte des Dichters haben seither schon lange die Welt umkreist, sind in alle Sprachen übersetzt, werden gelesen, zitiert und auswendig gelernt, und wäre es nur, um den letzten Schmähern der naiven Malerei in Erinnerung zu rufen, daß sich unter den ersten Entdeckern und den ersten Bewunderern Rousseaus gleichsam zufällig einer der größten abstrakten Maler befindet: Robert Delaunay. Zufällig? Sicher nicht.

Zu ihm gesellt sich also Kandinsky, ein ehrlicher, klarblikkender Mann, der sehr wohl wußte, was er tat und was er sagte; auch er beantwortete die Frage nach der Gültigkeit der naiven Malerei eindeutig und sagte ohne Umschweife ihre Zukunft voraus.

Soll ich auch die Zeilen zitieren, die Michel Seuphor, der erste ernsthafte Historiograph der abstrakten Kunst, 1930 in Form eines Vorworts zu einer Ausstellung der Kinder des Malers J. Torrès-Garcia mit den schönen Namen Olympia, August und Iphigenie schrieb? «Eines der Verdienste unserer Epoche – einer Epoche der wissenschaftlichen Forschung, des Willens zur Präzision, des Bemühens um ein Ordnungsbewußtsein – wird darin bestehen, daß sie uns auch dem Kind, diesem zweiten Pol des Menschen, näherbrachte. Das Kind wird für uns zu einem großen erzieherischen Wert: es führt uns zur Natur zurück und zu den Ursprüngen unseres Seelenlebens, genau dorthin, wo der Mechanismus des modernen Lebens uns die Grundlage unseres lebenswichtigen Gleichgewichts vergessen läßt. Wie alles, was unsere Vergangenheit ausmacht, lebt auch das Kind in einem jeden von uns; aber es ist wichtig, daß diese Gegenwart bewußt wird, damit wir nicht gezwungen sind, sie wider Willen und als feindliche Macht zu erleiden. Wir wollen wünschen, daß in sehr naher Zukunft eine wahrhafte Kunst der Kindheit den ganzen Platz einnehmen wird, den heute noch die mannigfachen Äußerungen der Romantik innehaben, jener verspätete, krankhafte Infantilismus wie zum Beispiel der Expressionismus und der Surrealismus.»

Schön. Mit Referenzen solcher Art hätte man in der Tat annehmen können, das Recht auf Naivität sei endgültig erworben, zumindest wortlos anerkannt, und die naive Malerei werde nun ohne weiteres Zögern den Platz einnehmen, der ihr gebührt. Man durfte mutmaßen, ihr Aufstieg werde leicht, schnell und glatt vor sich gehen. Keineswegs. Im Gegenteil. Es gab nichts Mühsameres und Enttäuschenderes. Jahr um Jahr verging, ohne daß die geringste Änderung auf diesem Gebiet eintrat, ohne daß man aufhörte, die naive Malerei als belanglos zu betrachten. Unwissenheit, Intrigen und Unehrlichkeit hielten, so gut es ging, diesen Zustand aufrecht. Allerdings war die Mentalität der Zwischenkriegszeit bei weitem nicht reif genug, um einzusehen, daß das naive Phänomen im Grunde das eine Ende des dialektischen Waagebalkens der Geschichte darstellte, der mit der abstrakten Kunst am anderen Ende die These und die Antithese, das Positive und das Negative, den Tag und die Nacht, Vorder- und Kehrseite des gleichen menschlichen Dramas, des gleichen Problems des Sichtbaren bildete. Die Bombe und der Spiegel. Nicht der Spiegel der dummen figurativen Darstellung, der längst überholt ist und wohl oder übel stets weiter zerfällt, nachdem die Abstrakten ihn ein für allemal in tausend Stücke gesprengt haben, sondern der andere, der wahre, jene Vision im Rohzustand, der Urkern, die stärkende und fruchtbare Quelle unseres abendländischen Schauens. Das erklärt zum Teil, warum unsere Naiven, die den Primitiven von einst gleichzeitig so nah und so fern stehen, die Primitiven von heute sind, ob man es will oder nicht.

Man hatte auch keine Ahnung, oder tat wenigstens dergleichen, daß das Auftreten der naiven Maler auf einer anderen Ebene, man könnte sagen als Rückwirkung, mit den ersten gewaltigen Stößen zusammenfiel, die der akademischen Kunst versetzt wurden. Denn angesichts der Dynamiteros begannen sie ohne ihr Wissen, gleichsam in einem Reflex der Selbstverteidigung, eine Art Gegengift auszuscheiden, mit dem Ziel, nach Maßgabe des Möglichen den besten Teil der uns umgebenden Sinnenwelt zu bewahren und im schlimmsten Fall zu retten, was noch zu retten war. Cézanne war nur fünf Jahre älter als der Zöllner Rousseau.

Sobald die freien Akademien, die mehr oder weniger fleißig von Delacroix, Bonington, Courbet, Bonnard, Matisse und unzähligen anderen besucht wurden, gegen die herrschende akademische Salonkunst Sturm zu laufen beginnen, fangen die Naiven ihrerseits an, als Heckenschützen gleichzeitig eine Welt für sich zu errichten, eine Welt und eine Kunst, die völlig abseits stehen, eine so gut wie geheime, vertrauliche und verstohlene Welt. Daher diese Fülle, diese Qualität, diese Verschiedenheit und dieses Alter, logische Folgen einer normalen, völlig ununterbrochenen Entwicklung, die bewirkt, daß die französische naive Malerei die älteste und reichste der Welt ist.

Sollte etwa hier die Stelle sein, wo die Veranstalter der Ausstellung von Rotterdam der Schuh drückt?

Und doch ist es so, ich kann wirklich nichts dafür.

Indessen waren der Zweite Weltkrieg und die zweite, mächtigere, mannigfaltigere Welle der Naiven nötig, damit unseren ungläubigen Thomas die Augen endgültig geöffnet wurden. Damit die ganze Reihe der internationalen Kundgebungen, die von Rotterdam inbegriffen, stattfinden konnte. In Tat und Wahrheit hatte sich die Lage schon ein bißchen vorher, nämlich während der finsteren Jahre der Besetzung, grundlegend geändert, und zwar infolge des vorübergehenden Ausscheidens einer großen Anzahl von Händlern und der sehr spürbaren Verminderung ihres Einflusses. Eine Ausstellung wie die in der Galerie «Claude» (1944) wäre in anderen Zeiten völlig undenkbar gewesen.

Vor allem brauchte es eine wenn auch verhüllte Dauerkrise aller plastischen Werte, verschärft durch Ausschreitungen aller Art: Malen mit dem Gewehr, mit dem Flammenwerfer, Bildhauerei mit dem Dampfhammer, nicht zu vergessen die in Nylon verpackten Motorräder, die Zurschaustellung von aus dem Mülleimer geholten Gegenständen, die malenden Affen und die Malmaschine von Tinguely, kurz alles, was früher oder später in der Pop-Kunst münden mußte, die von Kunst nur noch den Namen hat. Ich meine natürlich damit den alten Begriff von Kunst, so wie man sie seit Jahrtausenden auffaßte. Die Vorhut der analytischen, streng formalen Malerei, die von Cézannes Apfel ausging und zuerst zu einem Kreis gelangte, der nichts mehr besagen wollte, und dann zum Verschwinden, ja zur Aufhebung dieses Kreises, zu einem einfarbigen Grund, jenem berühmten Blau von Klein, mit anderen Worten zum Nichts, war nicht viel mehr wert. Die Pop-Kunst vollzog infolgedessen diesen Bruch endgültig, denn sie verhält sich zu Cézanne wie Cézannes Apfel zu einem Fruchtsaft in einer Blechdose. Das hat ihrem Führer, Pierre Restany, neulich erlaubt, eine Standortsbestimmung vorzunehmen und als Realist die Gegenwart, die Existenz der Naiven zu entdecken, die von so vielen anderen Schriftstellern der sogenannten Avantgarde beharrlich weiter übersehen wird. «Das hervorstechendste und auch das bedeutungsvollste Merkmal der Pariser Saison», schreibt er, «ist die Invasion der Naiven.» Und etwas weiter: «Aber diesmal sind wir gezwungen, festzustellen, daß wir uns einem Ereignis von ganz anderem Umfang gegenübersehen. Die stets häufiger auftretenden Übereinstimmungen schaffen einen Tatbestand.»[5]

Dieser Tatbestand ist indessen von ein paar Leuten verschwommen vorausgeahnt worden. Zunächst einmal von den Beweihräucherern der Abstraktion, für die das bloße Wort

[5] Domus Nr. 423 (1965).

IVAN RABUZIN

«wirklich» gestern nicht nur ein Schreckgespenst, sondern eine Beleidigung war und die jetzt versuchen, den Einsatz zu retten, und im Verstohlenen mogeln, so viel sie nur können, bald indem sie die Scherben mit dem Etikett «Nouvelle Figuration» tarnen (was ein alter sprachlicher Betrug ist, denn es gibt in Paris schon seit einer geraumen Weile den Salon der «Réalités Nouvelles», der gerade die undurchdringlichste Abstraktion beherbergt), bald indem sie «Art autre» oder diesen «nouveau Réalisme» vorschlagen, den französischen Ersatz für Pop-Art. Einzig die Lettristen verfolgen ehrlich ihre Suche nach dem «Zeichen», in Ermangelung der damit bezeichneten Sache: Zeichen, Gesang und Fata Morgana der Zeit, in der wir leben. Da will man lieber hoffen, sich gedulden und auf irgendein Wunder warten: einen Hauch frischer Luft oder ein kleines Stück weniger graues, weniger schmutziges Blau über den Dächern, während man gierig die Auspuffgase der Stoßzeiten einatmet...

Aber es ist wiederum Picasso, der wahrhafte Seismograph der letzten fünfzig Jahre, der am besten gespürt hat, woher der Wind weht. Er hat plötzlich auf die gewollte Deformierung und Häßlichkeit verzichtet, die seither von J. Dubuffet seliggesprochen und zum Kult erhoben worden ist, und ist gleichsam wie mit einem Zauberschlag mit der Reihe «Der Maler und sein Modell» zu einer Einfachheit und Frische zurückgekehrt, wie sie bis dahin bei ihm unbekannt sind. Wenn er wie gewohnt wünschte, mit seiner neuen Art zu überraschen und zu schockieren, so hat er sein Ziel vollauf erreicht: diese ländlichen, gefälligen, empfindsamen und beinahe zu «hübschen» Bilder bezeichnen eine sehr deutliche Rückkehr zur Maler-Malerei und revolutionieren ein weiteres Mal die Konfektion. Sie stellen im wahren Sinn des Wortes seine «naive» Epoche dar.

Und Morandi, der italienische Georges Braque, stirbt mit 74 Jahren bei sich zu Hause in Bologna, während er, wer weiß, einen letzten Blick auf einen Stich von Rembrandt wirft, der einen Akt darstellt, und auf die an die Wand gehefteten Zeichnungen des Zöllners Rousseau. Seine Leitsterne. Ein am 19. Juni 1964 in der Zeitung «Il Giorno» veröffentlichter Nekrolog von Marco Walsecchi berichtet es mit einem gewissen Mut[6].

Angesichts des Abgrunds, der sich mit der Explosion von Hiroshima auftut, jenes Abgrunds, der von Tag zu Tag weiter klafft, sind es darum auch nicht mehr die altmodischen Phantome der Dampfkraft und auch nicht die Gespenster der siegreichen Elektrizität, die den Menschen der zweiten Hälfte des 20. Jahrhunderts terrorisieren, sondern er selber und seine nahe Zukunft. Sein Todfeind. Dieser Mensch ist sein eigener Feind geworden, nicht mehr und nicht weniger als ein winziges Atom, das die Gelehrten Tag für Tag zertrümmern. Von da bis zur Atomspaltung in Kettenreaktion ist es nur eine Frage der Zeit. Wird er eines natürlichen Todes sterben oder in einer weltumfassenden Katastrophe umkommen? In wieviel Zeit? Mit anderen Worten: wieviel Zeit bleibt ihm noch zum Leben? Und wenn er hoffen kann, davonzukommen, lebt er dann immer noch hier oder muß er in andere Sternsysteme auswandern? Alles ist in Frage gestellt: sein Wissen, seine Gefühle, seine Liebe, seine Gewohnheiten, seine Heimat, sein Geschmack, seine Künste, seine Feinschmeckerei usw. Man wühlt in seinem Unbewußten, man dringt in die geheimsten Winkel seines Seelenlebens...

Nun ist er es aber nicht mehr selber, der auf die meisten dieser Fragen Antwort gibt, sondern seine Prokuristen: die Elektronen-Roboter. Die kybernetischen Maschinen rechnen an seiner Stelle aus, was er tun wird, was morgen ist. Krieg und Frieden, Leben und Tod hängen von ihnen ab. Er, der Mensch, ist ratlos. Die Maschinen erforschen die Mysterien des unendlich Kleinen und des unendlich Großen, den Mikrokosmos und den Makrokosmos. Das starre System Newtons hält nicht mehr stand, es wird wieder zur Unordnung der Sterne. Der Kuß ist nur noch eine chemische Reaktion, das Leben ein anderes Versprechen der organischen Chemie. Das Gedächtnis? Eine Eiweißverbindung. Die Individualität, das Talent, das Genie eine bloße Lotterie der Genen und Chromosomen. Überall herrscht die Relativität. Relativität der Zeit und des Raums. Bald wird man lebende Menschen einfrieren können und sie nach ein paar Lustren wieder erwachen lassen. In was für einem Milieu, unter was für einer Herrschaft, in welchem Jahrhundert? Warum dann nicht in ein paar Lichtjahren? Ob man an den Himmel glaubt oder nicht, alles bricht zusammen, alles geht kaputt, nichts bleibt bestehen, nichts, an das man sich anklammern könnte. Man spricht nur von der Vergangenheit oder von der Zukunft, nicht von der Gegenwart. Nie von der Gegenwart. Die Geschichte beschleunigt sich. Die Erde ist seit Cendrars und Paul Morand viel mehr zusammengeschrumpft als seit Marco Polo. Man findet die gleichen Bauten, die gleichen Kleider und die gleichen Filme in Alaska und auf Tahiti, in Indien und in der Schweiz. Gleichschaltung nach unten. Nun ist aber die Welt auch unendlich viel größer geworden, seit die letzte «terra incognita» von der Erdkarte verschwunden ist. Die Raketen sausen auf den Mond zu. Und bald auf Mars und Venus.

Was oben ist, findet keine Entsprechung mehr im Unten. Aber was ist oben, was ist unten? Auch Pythagoras hat sich geirrt. Hat oben oder unten überhaupt eine Bedeutung, wenn man im Zustand der Schwerelosigkeit geht oder vielmehr fliegt? Natürlich nicht, und dort oben wartet nicht mehr die «Maske mit den weißen Zähnen» auf einen, sondern die fliegenden Untertassen und die «Blaue Gefahr».

Seltsamerweise ist der Zukunftsroman von Maurice Renard, der diesen Titel trägt, zur gleichen Zeit erschienen wie die Abenteuer des Arsène Lupin, zur gleichen Zeit wie die ersten abstrakten Bilder und die ersten «Ready-Made» von Marcel Duchamp, Pop-Art, bevor der Begriff existierte. Aber die braven Rächer aus der guten alten Zeit sind überholt. Es bleibt nur die Angst übrig, nicht die alte Angst, die hautnahe Angst, sondern eine innere Bangigkeit, eine ungeheure Bangigkeit, die in den Eingeweiden steckt, eine instinktive Beklommenheit, die Sehnsucht nach der Vergangenheit und das Grauen vor dem Morgen. Keine Gegenwart, ich sage es noch einmal! Keine Sicherheit, keine Ruhe, kein Friede...

An der Schwelle und im Maßstab der sich vollziehenden zweiten industriellen Revolution, die in weniger als 20 Jahren unser Leben, selbst auf dem Gebiet des Traums, grundlegender umgewälzt hat als vorher viele Jahrhunderte, muß Neues und Vernünftiges geschaffen werden. Der Erfolg der «Science-Fiction» und der pseudowissenschaftlichen Veröffentlichungen in der Art der Zeitschrift Planète ist nicht anders zu er-

[6] Una casa semplice, con i mobili ottocenteschi che furono del padre, un estimato di canapa, alcuni quadri antichi di buona firma alle pareti e poche stampe tra cui il nudo di schiena inciso da Rembrandt e i disegni del Doganiere Rousseau.

klären. Sie sind das Marihuana der Mieter des sozialen Wohnungsbaus. Ein Rauschgift von der gleichen Art wie Kriminalromane oder Yeah-Yeah-Platten.

Bitte mach mir Angst! Schnell! Nochmals... Noch fester... Schrecklich fest!

Und doch hätte man in einem bestimmten Augenblick meinen können, die Einfälle der Science-Fiction würden mit der Zeit zu einem neuen Ausbruch, einer neuen Zuflucht, einer Art Nach-Surrealismus führen. Eine dritte Lösung. Weder der intakte noch der zerbrochene Spiegel. Sondern ganz einfach ein Spiegel ohne Folie, der sich nach Belieben auflösen würde wie in «Alice im Wunderland».

Eine Flucht und ein neugefundenes Lockbild, versehen mit allen Reizen eines künstlichen Paradieses.

Ach! Die Science-Fiction bietet alles in allem nur das gleiche Nichts: Gehirnwäsche, Verdummung und systematische Störung aller Sinne. Denn die Phantasie dient hier nur dazu, endgültig zu zermalmen, was vom ursprünglichen Individuum noch übrigbleibt – Rückstand des prä-atomaren Menschen. Unsere Kinder werden ihn sicher so nennen, wie wir den Ausdruck prä-adamisch brauchen.

Wie dem auch sei, die Pop-Kunst konnte nicht über diese Literatur hinwegsehen, so wie sie auch nicht außerhalb der Kräfte bleiben konnte, die sie bestimmen. Sie ist völlig ein Kind ihrer Zeit, sie ist ihr Fleisch und ihr Wesen. Bruch der Empfindungen, Explosion der Bilder, beschleunigte Geschwindigkeit der Wahrnehmung, umgestürzte Perspektiven und Maßstäbe, wilde Jagd von Gegenständen, Gesichtern und Räumen, alles ohne irgendwelche Verbindung untereinander und ohne andere Rechtfertigung als dieses aus den Fugen geratene Bewußtsein, das leer ist an Ideen, leer an Gefühlen und, was schlimmer ist, leer an Gemütsleben, irgendwie «reingewaschen vom Leben», wie einer ihrer Verteidiger sagt – das alles ist die Pop-Kunst im Begriff zu entdecken. Ich brauche wirklich das Wort entdecken, denn über die außerhalb der Malerei liegenden Verirrungen hinaus entdeckt sie in der Tat endlich wieder eines der Hauptgesetze der Malerei, daß sie nämlich mit dem Pinsel hervorgebracht wird. Schluß mit den verrosteten Nägeln, Schluß mit den Lumpen, dem Gips und dem Zement, Schluß mit dem Talisman der Ersatzteile, all diesen Fetischen, welche die Kräfte einer neuen Ära heraufbeschwören sollen. Auf den Automatismus, das Ungefähr, den Zufall, die rohe Materie folgen von neuem Wille und Wahl. Darum kann man wieder von Kunst sprechen, nicht wie jene «andere» Kunst, die ihren Namen nicht zu sagen wagt, sondern eine Kunst und eine Vision, die ein Mindestmaß an Lernen und Können erfordert. Um gegen die Naiven, den einzigen großen Gegner, kämpfen zu können, hat die Pop-Kunst instinktiv die Notwendigkeit gespürt, gleiche Waffen zu besitzen. Wirklich gleiche? Obwohl ihre Malerei sehr verschieden ist von jener der Väter und der Großväter, so wird sie doch mit den gleichen Mitteln geschaffen, und wie früher wird die Zukunft wieder mit der Palette in der Hand angegangen. Eine Mischung aus Zen und comic strips. Eine Welt, die zum Puzzle geworden ist, eine Welt, die aus Einzelteilen besteht. Der Mensch malt die Maschine nicht mehr, er wird zur Maschine. Darum ahmt er ihre Sprache, ihre Eigenheiten nach, er reproduziert genau bis auf den Raster eines photographischen Klischees, so wie man früher die Gipsabgüsse der Antike kopierte. Die Maschine, die, man weiß nicht recht was, fabriziert – Lärm... Schrecken. Die Hypnose und das Nirwana des Klingelns einer gewöhnlichen Silberkugel, die «tilt» scheppert.

Und doch nahm vor 2000 Jahren eine andere Zukunft ihren Anfang mit nur zwei, drei durchaus verständlichen, durchaus statischen Bildern: der Gute Hirte – der Fisch des Retters – und das Brot des Abendmahls. Nietzsche sagt grimmig, daß die Ideen, welche die Welt revolutionieren, auf Taubenfüßen gehen...

Heute geht und fliegt die Taube nicht mehr, sie wurde an der Decke eines Saals im Louvre ans Kreuz genagelt. Von Georges Braque.

2000 Jahre haben wohl oder übel von diesen ganz bescheidenen Bildern gelebt, ehe ein anderes heiliges Zeichen, der Fisch, seine letzte Hoffnung und seinen letzten Lebenshauch dahingab und zum Fisch des gleichen Georges Braque wurde: seine Verneinung, sein toter Buchstabe, sein übertünchtes Skelett.

Vorher enthielt er alle Freuden und alle Leiden, alles Glück und alles Unglück der Menschheit. Er war eines jener Zeichen, jener guten alten Zeichen, wie unsere Lettristen sie verstehen und erstreben. Nachher war er nur noch ein Ornament, ein Schmuck, ein leeres Echo der Vergangenheit. Die Abstrakten haben ihn in die Luft gesprengt. Gleichviel, wenn ich mich wiederhole. Sie haben tabula rasa gemacht mit der Vergangenheit. Und doch hat die Lebenskraft eines Zeichens oder eines Bildes nichts zu tun mit den offenkundigen Wirkungen einer Explosion. Eine verhaltene Kraft ist immer wirksamer als diese gleiche Kraft, wenn sie in Rauch aufgegangen ist. Die abstrakte Verbrennung ist demnach eine Tat; daher die «drippings», die «action paintings» und wie diese rein gestuellen Malereien alle heißen. Unverbindliches Tun. Zwecklose Maßnahmen. Ein Niemands-Absolutum. Ein Nirgends-Absolutum. Und wiederum ist es die Pop-Kunst, die (vergeblich) den Sinn dieses Verbrennens sucht. Sie ist es, welche die Ruinen, die Trümmer organisiert. Von diesem Gesichtspunkt aus sind Pop-Art und Naive der Anfang und das Ende und umgekehrt. So seltsam es scheinen mag, die Naiven stehen der Pop-Kunst näher als den Abstrakten! Die Maschine und die Anti-Maschine... Die neue Folklore der Wolkenkratzer trifft sich mit dem, was von der alten noch vorhanden ist, mit der Folklore der Strohhütten.

So mußte man also an einem trüben Morgen des Jahres Null erwachen, mit einem schönen Kater nach dem Fest, erwachen in einer ultramodernen, mit Klimaanlage, ja wie eine Weltraumkapsel bereits mit Druckausgleich versehenen Wohnmaschine, erwachen und plötzlich Ekel verspüren beim zufälligen Blick auf einen gerahmten Flecken an der Wand, der ein Bild darstellt, auf einen Haufen verkrümmten Eisens auf einem Sockel, der eine Skulptur darstellt. Und dann mußte man versuchen, zu reagieren, versuchen, das Denken wieder zu lernen oder doch zumindest sich zu erinnern, und zwar sich um so schmerzlicher zu erinnern, als man zuweilen auch auf einem Operationstisch erwacht und im Begriff ist, ein amputiertes Glied zu suchen, probieren, sich zu erinnern, daß es trotzdem etwas anderes gab und gibt, etwas Echtes, Tröstliches, Ruhiges, Heilsames, etwas, das an Tau auf einem leuchtend grünen Blatt gemahnt, einem Blatt, das mit seinem ganzen Chlorophyll seine Lebensfreude kundgibt, seine Freude zu glänzen, seine Freude, da zu sein, während allmählich in der Ferne die Sonne aufgeht und uns begrüßt, wie sie sonst nur beim Verlassen eines Krankenhauses oder eines Gefängnisses

NIKIFOR
MATEIKO
FLRYBOW

grüßt. Dieses Blatt und dieser sonnenbestrahlte Tau gleichen zum Verwechseln einem armseligen naiven Bild, das man zufällig am Tag vorher irgendwo gesehen hat: unsere einzige Chance und unser einziges Heil!...

Ah, dieses erste Ausgehen! das Leben... Das Leben, das weitergeht. So einfach ist das.

Die naive Malerei ist nichts anderes als das Vorzimmer zu diesem Leben. Und wir werden kein anderes mehr haben. So wollen wir es denn ausnützen, solange uns noch Zeit dazu bleibt. Man muß wählen zwischen Pop-Art und naiver Malerei. Das eben ist das naive Phänomen. Die naive Malerei ist das und nichts anderes. Alles übrige sind schöne Worte.

Ich weiß, daß es sehr schwer ist, zu erklären, warum die Künste im Verlauf der Jahrhunderte oft ihre Heimat wechseln, warum die verschiedenen Länder die Musen austauschen, warum Melpomene vor Thalia zurücktritt und Thalia vor Euterpe und warum manche dieser Künste, nachdem sie mit unvergleichlichem Glanz die neuartigste und intensivste Schöpfung zum Strahlen gebracht haben, eine nach der anderen erlöschen und nur noch einen kalten, kraftlosen, hochmütigen, fernen Schein durchschimmern lassen – wohl behütetes Jagdrevier der Museen. Wie die seit langem erloschenen Gestirne, von denen der Raum indessen noch eine Spur, einen flüchtigen Abdruck bewahrt, fahren sie fort, uns den erhabenen Rückstand des Bleibenden zu spenden.

Ja, warum drückt eine Epoche sich in der Malerei besser aus als zum Beispiel in der Architektur oder in der Musik? Warum wählt die genannte Malerei manchmal Italien, manchmal Frankreich, eher als Spanien oder Flandern? Warum schließlich gibt es ganze Länder, die von einem lethargischen Schlaf befallen sind, so daß es ihnen verwehrt ist, den Rausch der Inspiration und der Schöpfung zu kosten, während ein paar andere jäh erwachen, ohne zu wissen wie und warum?

Was das 19. Jahrhundert und den bereits vergangenen Teil des 20. betrifft, so besteht kein Zweifel, daß die Rolle des Spielführers, jene berühmte Leadership, wie die Angelsachsen sagen, Frankreich zufällt. Zumindest in der Malerei.

Als Erbe der Venezier, der Bologneser, als Erbe von Rubens und Goya hat Frankreich das Sichtbare gründlich befragt und damit die verschiedenen bis dahin gültigen Formen des plastischen Ausdrucks eingehend durchleuchtet. Wie die Schlange in der Bibel hat Frankreich dem Universum Cézannes Apfel hingestreckt, die Frucht der Erkenntnis der modernen Malerei. Und der Zivilisation des Bildes, deren Wohl- und Missetaten wir ebenfalls noch nicht alle ausgeschöpft haben, hat wiederum Frankreich jenes dritte Auge aus Glas geschenkt, das kein Volk des Altertums gekannt hat; Photographie und Film sind spezifisch und hundertprozentig französische Erfindungen.

Da es sich nun aber um eine im wesentlichen revolutionäre Malerei handelt, ist es unvermeidlich, daß dieser Kampf zwischen der Vergangenheit und der Zukunft, zwischen dem, was der Wind jeden Tag ein bißchen mehr verweht, und dem, was inmitten der Trümmer weiterblüht, insbesondere die naive Malerei, an der französischen Landschaft, am französischen Antlitz und am französischen Gegenstand am deutlichsten abzulesen ist.

Und die anderen Völker? Die anderen Länder?

◄ NIKIFOR

Nun, es kommt häufig vor, daß sie in Ermangelung einer wahrhaften künstlerischen Überlieferung, von der es sich um jeden Preis zu befreien gilt, sobald sie unfruchtbar wird, unmittelbar von der Prähistorie zur Geschichte übergehen, das heißt von einer Anhäufung anonymer Dinge und Bilder, die sich nicht sehr stark von Felsenreliefs und Felsenmalereien unterscheiden, zu signierten Werken, in denen die Gegenwart des Individuums spürbar ist. Von «meinetwegen ungehobeltem Genie, aber Genie», wie Barrès sagt, zu persönlichem, privatem Gestammel, das mit einem Schlag der ganzen jahrhundertealten Verdichtung entbehrt und mit ein wenig Glück zu einer anderen Art von Genie werden kann. Mit einem Wort: von der Tradition zum vollständigen Fehlen von Tradition.

Im Gegensatz zu der Mehrzahl der Länder des Westens, wo Generationen auf Generationen folgten, ehe die Leute aus dem Volk dank dem magischen Spiegel Malerei Zugang erlangten zu jenem Areopag der Unsterblichen, der bis dahin den Göttern, den Heiligen, den Königen und den großen Kurtisanen vorbehalten war, gibt es andere Länder, in denen diese Entwicklung sich von einem Tag auf den anderen vollzieht, sobald nämlich das Auftreten der Maschine ihre Daseinsformen radikal verändert. Der Funke springt auf, und der namenlose Sklave, eine Art Lasttier, wird im Handumdrehen ein mündiger Mensch. Ich meine übrigens mit Maschine nicht die Maschine selber, sondern alles, was sie in ihrem Gefolge mit sich bringt. Die Stadt überflutet das Dorf mit ihrem Radio, ihrem Kino, ihren Zeitungen und ihrer Leere, jener gräßlichen Leere, die es um jeden Preis auszufüllen gilt. Schreien oder schöpfen, einen anderen Ausweg gibt es nicht!

Je schneller sich diese Verwandlung der Sitten vollzieht, desto brutaler ist der Zusammenprall, der an Delirium und Wahnsinn grenzende Reaktionen hervorruft. Da kommt es auf einer höheren Ebene zur Geburt des Expressionismus (Deutschland, Belgien) oder des Futurismus (Italien, Rußland). Wie weit sind wir hier vom französischen Kubismus entfernt, der ruhig und methodisch Punkt um Punkt den Zerfall des Bildes als Abbild, des Bildes als Spiegel erforscht! Die anderen stürzen um, stecken in Brand, sprengen mit Dynamit – hierin liegt der Unterschied. Und unterdessen bleibt ein Land wie Großbritannien völlig taub und blind; es hat bereits vor einer guten Weile seine erste industrielle Revolution beendet. Es ist das Land, das die kleinste Zahl von Naiven aufweist.

In Italien, wo die Trennung, jener Bruch zwischen zwei Lebensstilen relativ spät auftritt und sich eben gerade durch die anarchische Explosion des Futurismus auszeichnet, findet der Aufstieg der großen authentischen und ursprünglichen Naiven erst gegen Ende des Zweiten Weltkriegs statt. Sie unterscheiden sich übrigens ziemlich stark von allen anderen Naiven. Alle sind sie mehr oder weniger von einem Gran Wahnsinn besessen, als könnte nur er sie von der lastenden Erbschaft all dieser auf Italiens Boden aufgehäuften Kunstwerke befreien. Und selbst dann noch! Eigentlich können sie sich nur in den entferntesten, am weitesten zurückgebliebenen und an Kunstwerken ärmsten Gegenden verwirklichen und zeigen, was nur ihnen, ihnen allein gehört: Ligabue, ein wahrhafter Waldmensch, in der Po-Ebene; Rovesti und Mozzali desgleichen; Luigi Pera in den Abruzzen; Ceccarelli in Spoleto; Luigi de Angelis in Ischia und Carmelina in Capri. Nur Elena Lissia, Adriano Grande und Alfredo Ruggeri wohnen und arbeiten in Rom. Unterscheiden sich diese letzteren darum so merklich von ihren übrigen Landsleuten, so daß sie ihren französischen Kollegen näherzustehen scheinen?

Elena Lissia ist übrigens ein ganz besonderer Fall. Erstens ist sie die einzige « Dame » unter diesen Leuten aus dem Volk, und zweitens sind die Kräfte, die ihrer Berufung zugrunde liegen, nicht sozialen, sondern moralischen Ursprungs. Nach einer schweren Krankheit ist sie in die Malerei eingetreten, wie man ins Kloster eintritt. Das Ergebnis ist indessen das gleiche; wie alle anderen nennt sie den Baum Bruder und die Blume Schwester. Mit etwa dreißig Jahren Abstand erinnert ihr Fall an den gleichliegenden der Amerikanerin O'Brady. Auch hier wieder hängt alles zusammen, und man kann sich nur wundern über die krasse Unwissenheit jener Schreiberlinge, die sich erst seit kurzem mit der naiven Malerei befassen und in deren Augen sich die italienische naive Malerei auf den ewigen Metelli beschränkt.

Wer war denn eigentlich der erste italienische Naive?

War es der Hirtenjüngling Giotto, der bereits, ehe Cimabue seine Hand führte, nach besten Kräften versuchte, die Bewegung und die anmutigen Massen seiner Ziegen festzuhalten, die da in der Umgebung von Vespignano in den mit Zypressen getupften grünen Hügeln der Toskana herumhüpften?

Waren es die ersten namenlosen Christen – auf die man immer wieder zurückkommen muß –, die im Schein einer Öllampe in den Katakomben von San Callisto den smaragdgrünen, von Hoffnung und Leben noch ganz steifen Fisch zeichneten?

Oder war es am Ende der wackere Schuhmacher von Terni, Orneore Metelli? Er war über fünfzig Jahre alt, hatte es satt, für seine Schuhmodelle Auszeichnungen und Gold- und Silbermedaillen zu bekommen, konnte infolge seiner Herzkrankheit in der städtischen Blasmusik nicht weiter Posaune blasen und wurde um 1922 herum plötzlich vom Malteufel ergriffen, von dem ihn erst sein Tod sechzehn Jahre später befreite.

Was tut's! Wahrhaft wichtig ist, daß hier, auf dieser einst von den Göttern bewohnten Erde, die noch ganz gesättigt ist von ihren Spuren, mehr als ein Mensch unter der unerbittlichen, aller Lüge feindlichen Sonne das Wirkliche neu ausgemessen hat, und zwar nach seinem Herzen, in aller Einfachheit, in aller Spontaneität und Offenheit, völlig außerhalb dessen, was vor ihm geschaffen und kodifiziert worden war, obwohl dieser wegen der großen Zahl von Meisterwerken überall gegenwärtige Unterricht unter freiem Himmel das größte Hindernis sowohl für das Werden als auch für die Entdeckung der dem Heimatboden entstammenden Naiven darstellt. Das geht so weit, daß man sogar in unzähligen Bildern, die an der Porta Portese, dem berühmten römischen Flohmarkt, herumliegen und die offensichtlich von Leuten stammen, die nicht malen konnten und infolgedessen naiv sein sollten, hier und dort eine bekannte Verzierung, irgendeinen gelernten, vielmehr unwissentlich anerworbenen hübschen Schnörkel findet, was vor allem einen Beweis darstellt für die Macht dieses überall gegenwärtigen malerischen Bel Canto, gegen den nichts auszurichten ist. Es sind Werke im Stil eines..., nicht mehr und nicht weniger. Oder dann kommt man rundweg wieder zur eigentlichen Volkskunst zurück, was nie das gleiche bedeutet. Wie Montesquieu, der sich fragte, wie einer bloß Perser sein konnte, mußte man sich zu Recht lange Zeit fragen, wie einer Italiener und naiv sein konnte...

Jetzt ist der Schritt getan, die Fioretti blühen in Italien wieder wie anderswo, die große Saga der Naiven ist im Begriff, vor unseren Augen erzählt zu werden. Und sie ist nichts für nüchterne Gemüter.

Ein anderes typisches und auffallendes Beispiel dieses Passierens der Linie, dieser meistens unerwarteten Mutation, wenn auf dem Boden der volkstümlichen Kunst, der erschöpft schien, unvermutet ein paar unbestreitbar naive Maler auftauchen, die aus sich selbst und für sich selbst schaffen, bietet uns Lateinamerika im allgemeinen, die Antillen im besonderen. Ich spreche von Haiti, San Domingo und Kuba.

Die meisten großen Länder, wie zum Beispiel Argentinien, die sich langsam und harmonisch entwickeln, wurden nicht zum Schauplatz eines brutalen Zusammenstoßes zwischen zwei Welten und riefen darum auch nicht jene unvermeidlichen Maler auf den Plan, für die in ihrer Eigenschaft als Zeugen ebenfalls in diesem entscheidenden Augenblick der *momento de verdad*, die Stunde der Wahrheit schlägt. Sie müssen dann entweder abdanken, das heißt zurücktreten und sich allmählich an einen neuen Zustand der Dinge anpassen, oder im Gegenteil laut ihr eigenes Recht auf Schönheit verkünden, auf eine gewiß ungewohnte, nie gesehene Schönheit, und zwar mit der ganzen Unschuld und der ganzen Macht der jungen, neuen, bisher unverbrauchten Kräfte. Zu ihnen kann man notfalls auch den spanischen Emigranten Casimir Domingo zählen, der zwar kein echter Naiver ist, den man aber doch zu jener visionären Richtung zählen könnte, die wir in Ermangelung einer besseren Bezeichnung *spiritistisch* nennen könnten; zu ihr gehören Crépin, Scottie Wilson, Grauben de Monte Lima, Isabel Jesus und Vandersteen, und neuerdings der ausgezeichnete Anselme Boix-Vives; diese Tendenz steht gewissermaßen zwischen dem Art Brut, der inspirierten Stickerei oder ganz einfach der *insania pingens*, das heißt der Kunst der Geisteskranken. In Brasilien andererseits ist die naive Kunst bis zum heutigen Tag ein Gebiet, das fast ausschließlich den Frauen vorbehalten ist, während ein Land wie Peru nur einen einzigen Indianermaler von hohem Rang hervorgebracht hat: Urteaga. In Guatemala muß ebenfalls ein Indianer erwähnt werden: Andres Curuchich, in Honduras Velasquez, und in Chile Herrera Guevara, der Maler von Cosmopolis und anderen imaginären Städten. Ihm kann man einen Fortunato San Martin zur Seite stellen und notfalls auch Violeta Parra, eine Sängerin, Teppichwirkerin und gelegentlich naive Malerin. In Uruguay tendieren die Maler Horatio Espondabura, Hilario Ferrer Aruffe und Carlos Gonzales eher zu einer erneuerten, aktualisierten Folklore, genau wie der Ekuadorianer Diogenes Paredes. Die Ausdrucksmittel sind anders, aber es bleibt eben doch Folklore auf der Grundlage von Pittoreskheit oder Volkstümlichkeit – der Name tut nichts zur Sache –, wie sie schon zu Beginn dieses Jahrhunderts von einem mexikanischen Graveur, José Guadalupe Posada, vorausgenommen wurde, in jeder Beziehung jener ähnlich, die später von einem seiner Landsleute, Diego de Rivera, erfunden wurde, nur daß bei diesem letzteren noch das Können dazukam. Diese Folklore ist der von mehreren Malern Mitteleuropas, zum Beispiel von dem Jugoslawen Brašič, geübten sehr ähnlich, denn diese Rückkehr zur Erde und zu den lebendigen Kräften des Volkes wurde hier schon seit dem Ersten Weltkrieg von Riveras Pendant Krsto Hegedušič gepriesen, einem Maler, der keineswegs naiv ist, den aber gewisse Kritiker, die das Problem schlecht kennen, unverfroren unter die Naiven einreihen. Diese Lage in Lateinamerika, die

HORACE PIPPIN

einiges zu wünschen übrig läßt, ändert sich jedoch mit einem Schlag, sobald man sich den Inseln unter dem Wendekreis des Krebses zuwendet. Diese Inseln überfluten uns buchstäblich mit der Quantität und der Qualität ihrer Naiven.

Als die UNESCO 1947 zum erstenmal in Paris eine Auswahl mehr oder weniger naiver Maler aus Ekuador, Peru und Haiti zeigte, war die Überlegenheit dieser letzteren bereits offensichtlich.

Aber wie schwierig, wenn nicht gar unmöglich, wird alles, sobald man es mit diesem Teil der Welt zu tun hat, ganz zu schweigen von der Verwechslung zwischen Folklore und naiver Malerei!

Genaue Angaben fehlen. Die Geburtsdaten und -orte sind ungewiß oder unbekannt. Photographien, sei es von Bildern oder von ihren Malern, sind unauffindbar. Und die Briefe bleiben in der Mehrzahl der Fälle ohne Antwort. Sogar die offiziellen Stellen, so zum Beispiel das Museum von São Paulo, um keine Namen zu nennen, machen sich nicht die Mühe, die gewünschten Auskünfte zu erteilen. Die Botschaften, die Kulturabteilungen bleiben stumm.

Das erklärt, warum zu meinem großen Bedauern die Angaben über eine gewisse Anzahl Maler aus der südlichen Hemisphäre nicht vollständig sind; darum kommen sie im Vergleich mit allen anderen Malern aus allen Ländern ein bißchen zu kurz.

Das wenige an Material, das ich über diesen Kontinent zusammentragen konnte, verdanke ich übrigens nur der in letzter Minute gewährten kostbaren Hilfe der Herren José Pedro Argul, Montevideo, Thiago de Melo, Santiago de Chile, und Mora, einem Kunstmaler aus Santo Domingo. Ich drücke allen dreien meinen sehr aufrichtigen Dank dafür aus.

Was in Haiti, auf der Insel Hispaniola, zwischen Kuba und Porto Rico gelegen geschehen ist, bestätigt ein weiteres Mal, wenn eine Bestätigung noch nötig wäre, daß das Erwachen und Blühen der naiven Kunst keine zufällige Erscheinung darstellt, sondern bestimmten Gesetzen gehorcht und eine besondere wirtschaftliche Lage voraussetzt. Das betreffende Land mag lange bereit sein zu diesem entscheidenden Sprung nach vorne, er vollzieht sich erst mit Hilfe eines inneren oder äußeren Katalysators: die soziale Revolution (Jugoslawien, Kuba) oder das direkte Eingreifen interessierter Personen (USA, Marokko, ein paar westeuropäische Länder). In Haiti heißt dieser Katalysator De Witt Peters und ist ein Englischprofessor, der 1943 ins Land kommt.

Schauen wir uns die Umstände etwas näher an.

Ein gewisser Herskowitz konstatiert in dem 1938 erschienenen und «Life in Haitian Valley» betitelten Buch das beinahe völlige Aussterben der eingeborenen Volkskunst, die einst reich und lebendig gewesen war. «Das Fehlen von graphischen und plastischen Äußerungen in der haitischen Kunst... Die Verdrängung dieser wesentlichen Formen der afrikanischen Überlieferung erweckt den Eindruck, daß das haitische Volk ein wichtiges Ventil für seine inneren Spannungen verloren hat.» ... Was ist denn geschehen? In so kurzer Zeit?

Es genügte ganz einfach, daß dieser Professor völlig zufällig im Verlauf seiner Reisen in der zwischen Saint-Marc und Port-au-Prince gelegenen Ortschaft Mont-Rouis auf eine seltsame Herberge stieß, deren Schild besagte *Ici la Renaissance*. Prophetischer Name – oder doch beinahe. Ihr Besitzer, Hector Hyppolite, ehemaliger Anstreicher und gelegentlicher Voodoo-Priester [7], hatte sie in der Tat nicht weniger seltsam ausgemalt.

Der Eindruck, den der Professor von dieser Dekoration empfing, obwohl sie nicht besonders von der traditionellen volkstümlichen Art abwich, war so stark, daß er sich unverzüglich auf die Suche nach ähnlichen Werken und Dekorationen machte. Zu diesem Zweck bereiste er das Land kreuz und quer.

Nachdem er ein paar wenige Veteranen aufgespürt hatte, in erster Linie Philomé Obin, einen 1891 in Cap Haïtien geborenen Autodidakten, der so ungefähr alle Berufe ausgeübt hatte – Frisör, Angestellter, Kaffeehändler – und nur hin und wieder in seinen freien Augenblicken malte, dachte der Professor völlig zu Recht, daß er mit Sicherheit ähnliche, wenn nicht bessere Ergebnisse erreichen würde, wenn er junge Neger in die Malerei einweihte.

Gesagt, getan. Ein Jahr später öffnete das Kunstzentrum von Port-au-Prince seine Pforten. In Tat und Wahrheit beschaffte De Witt Peters diesen Schwarzen nicht nur das Nötige zum Malen, sondern auch das Nötige zum Leben, denn sobald ihre Werke beendet waren, wurden sie ins Ausland verschickt, wo Kunstliebhaber sie kauften. Die Kundschaft bestand hauptsächlich aus Amerikanern. Der Krieg machte es ihnen unmöglich, französische Naive zu kaufen, und da sie diese Bilder wahrhaft liebten, begnügten sie sich vorübergehend mit diesen exotischen Naiven und mit ihrer eigenen Grandma Moses, die ungefähr zur gleichen Zeit entdeckt wurde.

Das Ergebnis ließ nicht lange auf sich warten. Außerordentlich. Verblüffend. Es bildete sich allmählich eine ganze Gruppe von jungen naiven Malern heran (ohne den Bildhauer Georges Liautard zu vergessen, der 1899 in Croix-de-Bouquets zur Welt kam und einfacher Schmied und Dorfmechaniker war, bis er dank De Witt Peters' Bemühungen zu einem ganz besonders ausdrucksvollen und originellen Künstler wurde), die an Einfällen und Begabung miteinander wetteiferten. Sogar Philomé Obin fand dank De Witt Peters' gescheiten Ratschlägen beinahe übergangslos den Weg von seiner noch in der konventionellen Art der Votivtafeln gemalten «Intercession» zu monumentalen, epischen, auffallend persönlichen Kompositionen, in denen er zum Beispiel «Das Begräbnis von Charlemagne Piralte» oder die Ankunft von «Präsident Roosevelt in Cap Haïtien» schilderte. Die optimistischsten Hoffnungen, die wildesten Träume, die De Witt Peters gehegt haben mochte, waren übertroffen. Dank dem Willen eines einzigen Mannes erneuerte Haiti das jugoslawische Wunder.

Aber das ist noch nicht alles. Als man 1950 in der Hauptstadt eine neue Episkopalkirche baute, wurden ihre Fresken zum größten Teil von naiven Malern ausgeführt, unter anderen von Philomé Obin, Rigaud Benoît, Louverture Poisson und Toussaint Auguste. Diese Kirche ist zweifellos das einzige Bauwerk dieser Art auf der ganzen Welt! Sie kann dank ihren Fresken würdig neben dem Palast des Briefträgers Cheval und dem

[7] Seine Beziehungen zur Göttin des Wassers erklärt er zum Beispiel folgendermaßen: «Sie wissen, daß ich meinen Schutzgeist geheiratet habe, darum kann ich niemand anders heiraten. Ich war noch ein Knabe, als mein Großvater, ein berühmter Voodoo-Priester, mich mit der Sirene vermählte, und seither ist sie meine mystische Gemahlin geblieben. Aber ich habe drei Mätressen, was nicht viel ist, denn gewöhnlich habe ich deren sieben. In letzter Zeit habe ich allerdings genug von den Frauen. Sie schaffen sich die ganze Zeit Schwierigkeiten, darum habe ich beschlossen, mich auf drei zu beschränken. Sie verstehen sich gut untereinander und sind nicht eifersüchtig. Warum sollten sie es übrigens sein?»

Scherbenhaus von Raymond Isidore in Chartres bestehen. Nach und nach betraten so über zwanzig naive Maler aus Haiti die Bühne der Kunst, machten ihre Namen bekannt und erlangten eine gewisse Berühmtheit hauptsächlich in den Vereinigten Staaten...

Unter ihnen möchten wir besonders die folgenden Maler erwähnen (in der Reihenfolge ihres Alters): Rigaud Benoît, ehemaliger Schuhmacher und Taxichauffeur (geb. 1914); Louverture Poisson, Maler von «Adam und Eva» und «Affektverbrechen» (geb. 1914); Maurice Borno (geb. 1917); J. B. Bottex (geb. 1919); Abelard, Mechaniker (geb. 1922); Prefete Duffaut (geb. 1923); Castera Bazile, Analphabet; Dieudonné Cédor (geb. 1925); Léon Aynaut (geb. 1929); Enguerrand Gourgues, Spezialist für Szenen weisser und schwarzer Magie (geb. 1930); Wilson Bigaud (geb. 1931), usw. ...

Das gleiche gilt für Kuba.

Vor der Machtübernahme durch Fidel Castro gab es in Kuba sozusagen nur einen einzigen naiven Maler, Felicindo Iglesias y Acevedo, der überdies ein 1898 in Orense (Galizien) geborener Spanier war und sich erst seit 1933 als Wein- und Gewürzhändler auf der Insel niedergelassen hatte. Aber auch hier ließ das Erblühen und Wuchern neuer Talente nicht auf sich warten, und zwar nicht ohne Grund: der neue Chef der kubanischen Regierung ließ sich, zumindest in seiner Kunstpolitik, von Marschall Tito inspirieren und erteilte wirklich dem Volk das Wort. Junge Männer und Frauen fingen an zu malen und sich mit der Ungezwungenheit, der Frische und dem Farbensinn, die dieses Volk auszeichnen, frei auszudrücken. Isabel Castellanos, Alberto Anido, Irmina Gonzalez, Lourdes Fernandez, Angel Fernandez, Angel Hernandez, Armando Blanco, Benjamin und Angel Duarte, Gonzalez Puig, Alfonso Reyes, Horatio Leyva, José Ramon Comabella – es ist unmöglich, sie alle aufzuzählen! «Macheteros» und Maschinenbuchhalter, Bauern und Typistinnen, Omnibusschaffner und Arbeiterinnen in den Zigarrenfabriken und ein ganz besonders unverfälschter, wahrhafter Zuckerrohrschneider, Luis Romero. Zu ihnen allen sollte man vielleicht noch Samuel Feijoo fügen, einen Maler und Schriftsteller, dem wir das erste wichtige Dokument über diese neue Malwut verdanken [8].

Im Zusammenhang mit Samuel Feijoo muß ich einen kleinen Exkurs einflechten. Wie definiert man den echten Naiven? Worin unterscheidet er sich von dem falschen? Wo endet die Naivität und wo fängt die Technik an? Die Fälscher, die absichtlich «in naiv machen», obwohl sie anders malen können, mögen noch hingehen. Immerhin ist festzuhalten, daß sich für einen von ihnen, der mit einem erfundenen Namen signiert und früher Spezialist für gefälschte Corot und Sisley war, der Beruf eines falschen Naiven als ergiebiger erwies. Aber wie steht es mit all jenen, die voll Aufrichtigkeit malen, in mehr als einer Beziehung den Naiven nahestehen und doch infolge ihres technischen Könnens über sie hinausreichen? Sie beiseite zu lassen, ist nicht gerecht, sie ihnen gleichzustellen, ist nicht leicht, und das Kriterium des Nicht-malen-Könnens genügt nicht immer. Dies um so weniger, als gewisse Naive, die ursprünglich echte Laienmaler waren, mit der Zeit jene Technik erwerben, die sie auf die andere Seite der Schranke hinüberwechseln läßt. Die Fälle Jean Eve, Rimbert und Caillaud sind zu bekannt, als daß wir uns dabei aufhalten wollen. Sind sie noch naiv, sind sie es nicht mehr? Die Frage ist schwer zu entscheiden. Die Grenze ist unbestimmt, allzu verwischt, zu schwach und zu fein, da Für und Wider sich hier eng vermischen. So wollen wir denn sagen, daß Samuel Feijoo zu jener Gattung der mehr oder weniger Naiven gehört, die in den verschiedenen Ländern der Alten und der Neuen Welt eine ganze Anzahl Vertreter zählt: Madeleine Luka, Caly, Gaston Chaissac, Véronique Filozof, Quilici, Maclet, Maïck, J. Milet und Fred Zeller in Frankreich; Breviglieri, Cesetti und Donghi in Italien; Stanley Spencer, Eden Box und L. S. Lowry in England; Carolus Paepen, Bockstael, Ferdinand und S. Dufoing in Belgien, Sydney Nolan in Australien, und andere mehr.

In meinen Augen, und um Verwechslungen vorzubeugen, die den echten Naiven nur zum Schaden gereichen können, sind sie es nicht. Schon Maler wie der Ungar Csontvary und der Tscheche gewordene Russe G. Mussatoff bilden Grenzfälle. Ich ziehe ihre Ehrlichkeit nicht in Zweifel, nur hätten sie anders malen können, wenn sie gewollt hätten, während die echten Naiven nur können, was sie wirklich tun. Die andern sind bloß Intimisten, Empfindsame, Manieristen, Phantasten, die mich an die Worte gemahnen, die Théophile de Viau im 17. Jahrhundert schrieb:

«Ich möchte Verse schreiben ungezwungen,
Planlos schweifen lassen meinen Geist,
Verschwiegene Orte aufsuchen, wo nichts mir mißfällt,
Nach Belieben meditieren, nach Lust und Laune träumen,
Eine Stunde lang im Wasser mich spiegeln,
Wie im Traum dem Plätschern eines Baches lauschen,
Im Walde schreiben, mich unterbrechen, schweigen.
Einen Vierzeiler verfassen, absichtslos.» *(Poétique)*

Die Werke dieser Halb-Naiven hängen notwendigerweise von diesen gleichen Imponderabilien ab, ob man sie nun guten Geschmack oder Begabung nenne, das heißt Richtigkeit und Feinheit einer Gefühlsbewegung, oder von jener unnachahmlichen Unbeholfenheit der Hand, die sich nicht nach der Anzahl der Karat mißt, sondern nach der Reinheit des Wassers und der Besonderheit des Schliffs! Denn selbst unter den echten Naiven sind nicht alle gleichwertig: es gibt welche, die begabter sind als die andern. Was die Fälscher betrifft, so sind ihre Namen in anderen Werken zu finden, nicht in dem meinen.

Die einzige Ausnahme von dieser Regel, die Drama und Bruch und die Notwendigkeit verlangt, daß Stil und Ausdrucksart der Naiven die ausgetretenen Pfade verlassen, bilden die Vereinigten Staaten, ein Land, das seit ebenso langer Zeit wie Frankreich naive Maler hervorgebracht hat, dessen Entwicklung jedoch auf einem parallelen, weder ganz identischen noch völlig verschiedenen Weg verläuft.

Da es in den Vereinigten Staaten eine Volkskunst sozusagen nicht gab – so wenig wie eine offizielle Kunst oder irgendeinen Kunstunterricht –, ist die Kunst, die instinktiv aus den verschiedensten volkstümlichen Schichten hervorgeht, von ihrem Ursprung an, der auf das Ende des 18. Jahrhunderts zurückgeht, naturgegeben naiver Art, aber die Menschen, die sie ausüben, sind weder schwarze Schafe noch das Erzeugnis irgendeiner sozialen Katastrophe. Nein, sie arbeiten ruhig, heiter, beinahe als halbe Berufsmaler, als Handwerker, ohne es wirklich zu sein, und sind zuweilen ihren französischen Gefährten und Waffenbrüdern voraus. Sie haben natürlich weder deren Qua-

[8] Pittores y debujantes populares de las Villas. Universidad de Las Villas, ed. Santa Clara (Cuba), 1962.

HORACE PIPPIN

len noch ihr Elend noch die Klippen einer Existenz gekannt, die viel gefährlicher war als die Scharmützel mit den Indianern des Far-West. Sie brauchten nur von Ranch zu Ranch, von Bauernhof zu Bauernhof, von Plantage zu Plantage, von Fabrik zu Fabrik dem langsamen, doch unerbittlichen Vordringen der Pioniere zu folgen und, während sie deren wandernde Porträtisten waren, an der Dienstbarmachung dieses unermeßlichen Kontinents mitzuwirken.

Diese Amerikaner verherrlichten also das Individuum und überlieferten der Nachwelt neue Männer, die zukünftigen Gründer der Gelddynastien. Die aufsteigenden Schichten. In dieser Beziehung stehen sie einem Holbein, einem Clouet oder selbst einem Ingres viel näher als den üblichen Porträtisten des 18. Jahrhunderts, von denen sie sich inspirieren ließen, während die europäischen Maler wie der Georgier Pirosman oder der Grieche Theophilos noch völlig jener Welt der galanten Feste, im vorliegenden Fall der Bauernjahrmärkte angehörten und nur die Bilder der Vergangenheit, die Augenblicke eines glücklichen, sonntäglichen Landlebens festhielten, das indessen dem Gestern verfallen war und vor dem Aussterben stand. Anstatt verflucht zu sein, waren die amerikanischen Naiven im Gegenteil nützlich. Sie waren gesucht wie Spengler und Schreiner.

Zu welchem Zweck? Nun, um dieses angeborene Bedürfnis nach dem Schönen und Wahren zu befriedigen, um jenes alte, unlöschbare Verlangen nach Unsterblichkeit zu stillen. In der Tat kamen sie alle dran: pauspäckige Kleinkinder, strenge Richter, ausgedörrte, kalte Gemahlinnen, würdige, jugendliche Greise. Was für eine prachtvolle Ausgabe von Faulkners Romanen könnte man zustande bringen, wenn man sie mit Abbildungen all dieser Bilder illustrierte!

Man müßte sie übrigens nicht lange suchen. Diese Porträts sind massenweise in den amerikanischen Sammlungen vertreten, wie zum Beispiel in der «American Paintings of the M. and M. Karolik Collection» im Kunstmuseum von Boston, in «American Primitive Art» im Kunstmuseum von Houston, in «American Primitive Paintings» in der Sammlung E.W. und Bernice Chrysler Garbish in der Nationalgalerie von Washington und in der unvergleichlichen «Folk Art Collection» von Abby Aldrich Rockefeller im «Colonial Williamsburg» in Virginia.

Von Zeit zu Zeit macht sich auch ein Bauer oder ein Fallensteller, vom Schauspiel der Natur und dem Ergebnis seiner eigenen Arbeit aufgerührt, daran, in allen Ehren ein frisches, reines Bildchen zu malen. Wurde dieses verheißene Land doch endgültig zu dem ihren! Reich, schön, gerecht, frei, und bereits so «modern»! Grund genug, stolz zu sein...

Oder eine alte Jungfer, die sich an einem hübschen Stilleben versucht. Eine Mutter, welche die Porträts ihrer Sprößlinge malt. Eine Witwe, die auf dem Grab ihrer Lieben Andacht hält. Andere und nochmals andere, die eine Familienversammlung malen, eine Ernte, ein Begräbnis, einen öffentlichen Park, mythologische oder biblische Szenen, einen Raddampfer... einen vorüberbrausenden Zug...

Ihre Sprache unterscheidet sich kaum von der aller anderen Naiven in der Alten Welt, zumindest in der Form: eine gleiche Liebe zur Einzelheit, eine gleiche Beflissenheit, ein gleicher Wunsch, sich von keinen Schranken zurückhalten zu lassen, eint sie alle. Nur befreien sich einige schon ein wenig von der ursprünglichen Ungeschicklichkeit und erwerben gewisse Grundbegriffe des Handwerks, was sie ein bißchen in die Nähe unserer Nicht- oder Halb-Naiven rückt. Auf jeden Fall zeichnet sich ihre Technik durch eine sozusagen photographische, außergewöhnliche Ähnlichkeit aus. Man muß nur die Verse von Théophile de Viau nachlesen, um zu verstehen, daß das sentimentale Umherschweifen und der Flirt mit der Natur sich sehr wohl mit Malen-Können oder Nichtkönnen vertragen.

Blaise Cendrars, der ausgesprochene Verteidiger der avantgardistischen Malerei um 1914 herum, wünschte in seinen letzten Lebensjahren, angeekelt durch das, was sie geworden war: *«Ich möchte, es gäbe nur noch Sonntagsmaler und man ließe uns hundert Jahre lang mit den andern in Frieden, welche die Wände der Museen, der Sammler und der Händler mit Beschlag belegen. Nach hundert Jahren Herrschaft einer solchen liebenswürdigen Phantasie, Amateurkunst und Träumerei angesichts der Natur wird die Malerei vielleicht eine neue Blüte erleben.»*

Doch kehren wir zu unseren kubanischen Naiven zurück.

Die naive Malerei auf Kuba unterscheidet sich deutlich von jener in Haiti. Zunächst in der Wahl der Themen. Bei ihnen herrscht die Einbildungskraft vor. Das Phantastische, wenn nicht gar Magische ist stärker als das Wirkliche. Das drückt sich natürlich in Stil und Faktur aus, die bei den Nicht-Naiven zwischen Picasso und Wilfredo Lam (einem Eingeborenen), bei den Anhängern des Art Brut zwischen Chaissac und Dubuffet hin- und herschwanken. Die Linien verflechten sich, ringeln sich ineinander, dicht, ungenau, nächtlich, nicht um festzuhalten, was man vor Augen hat, sondern um gleichsam das Unsichtbare zu fassen. Auch wenn vom rein formalen Standpunkt aus diese Werke eher dem unbewußten und leicht mediumistischen Malen nahestehen (von dem im Zusammenhang mit dem Argentinier Casimir Domingo die Rede war) als der gewöhnlichen, erdverhafteten Bilderwelt aller anderen Naiven, so hindert das doch nicht, daß sie tausendmal mehr wert sind als der Art Brut. Sie sind Kunst, während die meisten Werke des Art Brut, wo das Wort Art oft überflüssig ist, in die Kategorie des psychischen Ätzmittels oder der plastischen Geisteraustreibung gehören; auf jeden Fall handelt es sich dabei um eine Affektentladung, in welcher der Begriff des Schönen fehlt.

Hier drängt sich eine zweite Abschweifung auf. Nicht zu malen verstehen, heißt nicht schlecht malen. Unkenntnis bedeutet nicht Häßlichkeit. Ein Schrei, so schmerzlich und ergreifend er auch sein mag, enthält jedoch nicht notwendigerweise eine ästhetische Erschütterung. So interessant und aufschlußreich sie für die Forscher, die Gelehrten, die Psychologen und die Psychiater sein mögen, die Werke der Geisteskranken, die, ob man es zugibt oder nicht, die Basis des Art Brut bilden, und zwar in der Bedeutung der von Jean Dubuffet erfundenen Clique, die seinen eigenen künstlerischen Anschauungen und Betätigungen als Sprungbrett dienen soll, entbehren im allgemeinen der schöpferischen Gemütsbewegung und weisen einen völligen Mangel an plastischen Werten auf. Alle diese armen kranken Psychen, alle diese geistigen Delirien und alle diese verstümmelten, wunden Bilder sind von einer ausgesprochenen plastischen Dürftigkeit und erscheinen leider wie Embryos in einem Reagenzröhrchen oder wie zweiköpfige Hasen in einem alkoholgefüllten Glas neben den Werken der kubanischen Künstler, die im Gegensatz dazu Kunst hervorbringen. Kunst – und nicht eine gezierte Ablage des Musée Dupuytren, welches das Analphabetentum einer gewissen Presse und der

Snobismus eines gewissen Publikums als etwas hingestellt haben, das es beim besten Willen nicht ist. Nie hat eine so große Konfusion geherrscht wie in den letzten Jahren. Ein Schröder Sonnenstern, der oft unter den Naiven zu finden ist (zum Beispiel in Rotterdam und im Musée d'Art Moderne von Paris), ist ebensowenig naiv wie eine Aloyse oder ein Clovis Trouille.

Woher stammt dann dieses Körnchen Verrücktheit bei den kubanischen Naiven? Von den Passatwinden oder ein paar Tropfen spanischen Bluts? Ein Schlaukopf, wer diese Frage zu beantworten wüßte. Auf jeden Fall könnte ich es nicht beweisen oder widerlegen. Übrigens liegt das Problem nicht hier. Verrückt oder nicht, diese überbordende Phantasie der kubanischen Maler zeugt vor allen Dingen von einem gewaltigen, intakten Schatz schöpferischer Fähigkeiten, und wer weiß, was die Zukunft uns bereithält. Von jetzt an ist alles möglich. Sogar das Auftauchen großer, sehr großer Maler, die einem Rousseau oder einer O'Brady gleichkommen. So mögen sie doch alle ruhig malen! Es wäre wahrhaftig schade, ließe man einen guten, unbewußten, naiven Maler im Keim ersticken aus Angst, einen weiteren Schmierer zur Welt zu bringen. In der Geschichte der naiven Malerei wimmelt es leider von solchen Totgeburten.

Ähnliches gilt für die Dominikanische Republik.

Und wiederum das gleiche Phänomen ist, obwohl in kleinerem Maßstab, in Marokko festzustellen, wo nach einem mehrere Jahrhunderte dauernden völligen Schweigen hintereinander drei gute naive Maler auftauchen: Ahmed Louardiri oder El Ouardiri, geboren 1920 in Salé; Mohamed Ben Allal, geboren 1924 in Marrakesch, und Moulay Ahmed Drissi, der ebenfalls 1924 in der Umgebung von Marrakesch zur Welt kam. Alle drei haben die koranische Schule besucht, die ja Bilder untersagt. Alle drei sind arm (Ben Allal ist unter einem Nomadenzelt zur Welt gekommen), und bei allen dreien liegt der Ursprung ihrer Kunst in dem entscheidenden Augenblick, da sie mit der Zivilisation in Berührung kamen. Bei Ben Allal, der bei einem bekannten französischen Maler Dienstbote war, fand die Reaktion verständlicherweise auf unmittelbare, normale Art statt. Wie dem auch sei, alle drei sagten sich zu einem bestimmten Zeitpunkt: und warum nicht ich? Alle haben sie eine Menge Dinge gesehen und erlebt, die sie geblendet haben, alle haben sie Visionen und Träume angesammelt, die nichts anderes begehrten, als auf einem Stück Leinwand festgehalten zu werden. Das Glück... Immer die Phantome des Glücks! Herden und saftige Weiden. Rieselndes Wasser in der Wüste...

Der arabischste und auch der begabteste unter den dreien, Louardiri, besingt die Vergangenheit seines Geschlechts, und er erzählt, erzählt, erzählt, ein bißchen in der Art seiner Verwandten Scheherazade, bis der Ton sich steigert und seine Stimme unmerklich in eine Art Singsang übergeht, der kunterbunt alles umfaßt, Jasmin und Springbrunnen, Mond und Nachtigall, Blau und Rosa, die sich liebend umarmen, den Samt der dunklen Nacht und die kühlen Steinplatten der Gartenwege, die nach einem schwülen nordafrikanischen Tag die nackten Füße so köstlich liebkosen, dann auch die dichten Blumenbeete, jene Zonen von Schatten und Farben, in denen anstelle der Rosenbäume von Saadi plötzlich junge Mädchen mit Gazellenaugen auftauchen, während hinter den lanzettenförmigen, dreipässigen oder hufeisenförmigen Bogen der Minarette und Paläste die tausend Jahre muselmanischer Legenden und Zauberbilder ihm aufmerksam lauschen, ebenfalls von wunderndem Staunen ergriffen.

Was tut's, wenn die Bilder sich zuweilen überschneiden oder wenn eine ganz besondere Ungeschicklichkeit hier oder dort durchbricht: die Flamme der Leidenschaft brennt und verzehrt alle Unvollkommenheiten der Syntax und der Grammatik. Es hat auch keine Bedeutung, wenn dieser schöne Traum leider mit einem mittelmäßigen, eintönigen Leben bezahlt werden muß, in dessen Herz vielleicht ein gegenwärtiges oder vergangenes Unglück steckt wie ein bitterer Stachel.

Und dann gibt es da jene Appenzeller Bäuerin Sibylle Neff, die bedrückt zusehen muß, wie rings um sie die letzten schweizerischen Bauernmaler einer nach dem anderen dahingehen, und die anfängt, die gleichen Szenen, die gleichen Themen aus dem Stegreif zu malen und das tägliche Leben ihrer Heimat neu, aber bereits *verändert* erstehen zu lassen.

Und wie steht es mit jenem bescheidenen brasilianischen Handwerker aus dem Staat Pernambuco, Inocencio da Costa Nick, genannt Mestre Noza, der ebenfalls über die alte religiöse Bilderwelt der «santeiros» hinausgeht und Platte um Platte schneidet und sticht, auf denen der ganze Mystizismus und der ganze Fanatismus dieser Provinz wieder auflebt?[9]

Und jener Flame, Van den Driessche, ein ehemaliger Metzger, der mit über sechzig Jahren plötzlich anfängt zu malen und eine Art James Ensor im Rohzustand wird? Seit den Gebrüdern Brueghel und Hieronymus Bosch hat keiner die Seele des flämischen Lebens mit so viel Schwung auszudrücken verstanden: der eine bewußt, der andere unbewußt...

Und diese Halbwüchsigen in der Bannmeile von Kairo, die Ramses Wissa Wassef vereint und die Teppiche aus Tausendundeiner Nacht weben, die reinsten fliegenden Teppiche?

Und dann dieses Brodeln im Herzen der Ruhr, in Recklinghausen, wo man versucht, ein friedliches Zusammenleben zwischen der Hand und der Maschine zu verwirklichen? Dieser Hans Koehn, dieser Karl Kazmierczak, dieser Karl Hertmann, dieser Peter Paul Hubert Schmitz, dieser Werner Plümer, dieser E. Bödecker und dieser F. Gerlach, der sagt: «Was mich interessiert, ist, daß ich mit meinem Malen ein wenig zur Entwicklung des Schicksals der Menschen und ihres Planeten beitrage.»

Wer hätte da noch etwas hinzuzufügen?

Je mehr man sich mit den Naiven beschäftigt, desto klarer wird einem bewußt, daß der schmale Weg, der zu ihrer Kunst führt, überall und immer der gleiche ist.

Von Norden bis Süden, von Ost bis West, vom Ozean zur Wüste, vom Gebirge zur Ebene, von den Feldern zu den Fabriken und von den Strohhütten zu den wie Pilze aus dem Boden geschossenen Städten – überall leiden die Herzen, bluten die Herzen, rebellieren die Herzen so stark, daß sie *heilige Herzen* werden. Fata Morganas entstehen. Man wirft Flaschen ins Meer mit einer Botschaft vom Überleben. So schwimmen Rettungsgürtel einen Augenblick lang am Ort des Schiffbruchs. Sie sind die Maler des lieben Gottes, hat mir neulich der katholische Journalist Joseph Pichard von ihnen gesagt. Er behält ihnen unfehlbar in dem Salon de l'Art Sacré, den er veranstaltet, einen Ehrenplatz vor. Die Maler des lieben Gottes, wie das Gottesschäfchen, der Käfer mit der so naiven Zeichnung...

Wer aber Gott sagt, sagt auch alsogleich Teufel. Es fehlt nicht an Versuchungen. An Qualen, Verirrungen, Verlockun-

---

[9] Via Sacra, gravada por Mestra Noza, Robert Morel ed. (1965).

gen, Chimären aller Art. Aus diesem offenen, erschütternden Kampf um die Aufrechterhaltung der Menschenwürde ist die naive Kunst entstanden.

Eine von Madame A. M. Angeli unterbreitete Doktorarbeit in Graphologie (in Druck) beweist es zur Genüge. Unter den 60 Schriften von naiven Malern, die sie untersucht hat, gibt es keine, die nicht eine geheime Verwundung aufwiese. Alle sind sie der Ausdruck umgetriebener Menschen, Menschen, die sich gegen das Leben auflehnen. Alle tragen sie die unauslöschlichen Spuren des verlorenen und des dank ihrer Kunst wiedergefundenen Paradieses. Wer also könnte nach diesem unwiderlegbaren, diesmal wissenschaftlichen Beweis behaupten, ihre Kunst sei unverbindlich? Wer könnte sie weiterhin als Nebensächlichkeit betrachten? Wer kann es wagen, ihre Kunst als Zeitvertreib zu bezeichnen?

Es wäre Zeit, glaube ich, ihnen ganz einfach das Wort zu überlassen, anstatt um sie herumzukreisen und zu reden. Und wie hätte ich diese Untersuchung über die Naiven anders beenden können, da es sich ja nur um den Anfang einer Sache handelt, die sich wandelt und sich jeden Tag unaufhörlich weiter entwickelt?

Skurjeni M. 1960.g.

La peinture naïve

Une introduction

◄ MATO SKURJENI

Depuis la toute première exposition internationale des peintres naïfs qui ait jamais eu lieu en Europe, et qui s'est tenue enfin, l'an de grâce 1958, dans le cadre de l'Exposition Universelle de Belgique, on peut affirmer, désormais, sans courir le risque de se tromper ni d'induire quiconque en erreur, que ces six ou sept dernières années ont fait plus, beaucoup plus pour la connaissance de la peinture naïve que le reste du temps, c'est-à-dire une cinquantaine d'années, environ, qui les ont précédées.

Car d'autres expositions, tout aussi importantes, furent organisées peu après sur cette lancée. Celle de Baden-Baden d'abord, transportée par la suite telle quelle à Hanovre et à Francfort (1961); celle des Laienmaler de Bâle ensuite, toujours la même année. Puis vint le tour de Rome qui, dans son splendide palais Barberini, présentait ce qu'il y avait de meilleur des deux côtés des Alpes. Même l'Autriche (Residenzgalerie, à Salzburg, 1964) et le Maroc (Centre culturel de Rabat, 1964) ont tenté des manifestations semblables, bien que de moindre envergure, bien sûr. Seule la France dut se contenter jusque-là d'une exposition purement nationale, ne réunissant que les peintres naïfs français, ainsi que les naïfs étrangers travaillant sur son sol. Qu'elle ait pu devancer d'une année l'Allemagne et la Suisse, par exemple, reste quand même une piètre consolation. Et encore! Ce fut une initiative privée, due à la perspicacité de la feue Maison de la Pensée Française et non une prise de position quasi officielle, comme c'était le cas à peu près partout ailleurs. Mais passons...

De toute façon, la plupart de ces expositions-là ont non seulement révélé aux yeux du monde une quantité d'artistes absolument neufs et dignes d'intérêt, mais elles ont contribué, également et surtout, à changer de fond en comble aussi bien l'optique que tout notre comportement vis-à-vis de cette branche plutôt délaissée, pour ne pas dire ignorée de la peinture. Sa parente pauvre.

En effet, tous les autres peintres, sans exception, on les discute, on les critique, on en parle en bien ou en mal – la question n'est pas là – tandis que, dès que l'on touche aux naïfs, on se trouve aussitôt en présence des partis pris, nets, définitifs, tranchants, comme si on voulait conjurer à tout prix quelque vague mais réelle menace. Tantôt on s'en moque purement et simplement, tantôt on les écarte d'une chiquenaude. Ce sont les seuls à ne pas être pris au sérieux. Bien mieux: lors des expositions rétrospectives, anthologiques en quelque sorte, où l'on réunit par conséquent les diverses, les multiples tendances, contradictoires parfois, de l'art dit «moderne», le seul et unique peintre qui provoque encore tant soit peu des plaisanteries faciles, sans oublier les sourires condescendants, si ce n'est les sarcasmes complices, c'est toujours le Douanier Rousseau. Immanquablement. Lui, pourtant, a déjà depuis bien longtemps une place de choix dans les musées du monde entier, ainsi que dans tous les ouvrages sur l'art en général.

D'où vient, alors, tant d'incompréhension, tant d'ignorance, tant de haine?

Or, c'est justement là que la plus grande surprise attendait le public si mal renseigné. Il s'attendait à y trouver de quoi rire, les fautes de perspectives, les couleurs criardes, le dessin bancal et l'anecdote tout court, remplaçant, faute de mieux, les qualités purement plastiques, bref tout ce qu'on lui a raconté à ce sujet, et il n'y a vu, en réalité, que des peintres; des peintres aussi probes, des peintres aussi doués, des peintres aussi valables que tous les autres peintres, qu'ils soient figuratifs ou abstraits, réfléchis ou spontanés, maladroits ou savants. Quant à l'autre public, plus vaste, non prévenu celui-là, il a été séduit d'emblée par les trouvailles et l'incontestable poésie des naïfs; il a été surpris par leur originalité, charmé par leur honnêteté et leur amour de la belle ouvrage. Ainsi le premier pas vers la reconnaissance de la peinture naïve en tant que peinture à part entière, s'est fait tout seul, sans aide de qui que ce soit. Tout simplement grâce à ces contacts directs entre les naïfs et ces deux publics, qui ne feront bientôt plus qu'un, du reste, que les dites expositions favorisaient sans relâche, allant de ville en ville et de pays en pays.

On lui parlait uniquement de Rousseau et de quelques «grands», tels que Vivin, Séraphine, Bauchant, Bombois et il s'est vite aperçu aussi qu'il n'y avait pas qu'un seul Rousseau, qu'un seul Vivin, etc... mais des dizaines et des dizaines d'autres artistes totalement inconnus, soit, tout en étant dignes, cependant, de figurer à côté d'eux. Les hiérarchies croulaient, les horizons s'élargissaient et la peinture naïve cessait peu à peu d'être le fait d'un seul homme ou d'un seul pays. Elle devenait mondiale.

L'Amérique latine et Haïti faisaient leur entrée, et ce que l'on appelle depuis peu le «miracle yougoslave», avait de quoi contenter les plus difficiles. La Pologne révélait le fameux Nikifor, fils d'une prostituée et d'un père inconnu, un pauvre sourd-muet ne sachant ni lire ni écrire, mais qui vendait comme ça, sur le parvis de son église natale de Krynica, presqu'à la sauvette, de véritables petits chefs-d'œuvre; les Etats-Unis faisaient connaître Morris Hirschfield et cette Grandma Moses, venue à la peinture à l'âge de 80 ans; l'Espagne, Rivera Bagur, découvert par Miró; l'Israël, Chalom de Safed; la Tchécoslovaquie, Karel Chaba, Anna Ličkova et Juraj Lauko; l'Allemagne, Paps; le Maroc, Louardiri; la Belgique, Micheline Boyadjian et Van den Driessche; la Hollande, Alexandrine; le Brésil, Iracema, et l'Italie, enfin, se souvenant soudain d'avoir été le berceau et la patrie incontestée des primitifs, alignait en un tourne-main cinq ou six noms de grande envergure.

Même l'Union Soviétique, où la peinture naïve était plus ou moins proscrite en vertu de la doctrine stalinienne de Jdanov, a réhabilité, elle aussi, son grand naïf géorgien Niko Pirosmanichvili en lui faisant dernièrement une exposition posthume au musée Pouchkine de Moscou – consécration suprême, réservée d'ordinaire à des gloires incontestées – tout en éditant par ailleurs un ouvrage important sur une paysanne ukraïnienne, Catherina Bilacour, dont les bouquets se rapprochent étrangement de ceux de Séraphine.

Tout cela prouve avant tout, n'est-ce pas, que loin d'être un accident, un hasard heureux, ou une réussite isolée, la peinture naïve représente bel et bien un phénomène organique, naturel, obéissant, sans aucun doute, à quelque nécessité historique.

Comment expliquer autrement cette éclosion sans pareille, simultanée, ou peu s'en faut, de toute une pléiade d'artistes qui, ne se connaissant guère entre eux, donc ignorant tout les uns des autres, entonnent subitement, des quatre coins du globe, le même chant?

Quelques faux naïfs se sont glissés naturellement parmi eux; on confondait parfois le folklore avec l'art si typiquement individualisé des naïfs, mais tout compte fait, ce n'était que des maladies de croissance, des maladies que l'on pouvait éviter facilement, sinon guérir, à condition, toutefois, que quelqu'un se soit penché sérieusement sur le problème de la peinture naïve. Parce qu'il n'existe rien pour ainsi dire, à l'heure qu'il est, ni personne de vraiment qualifié qui pourrait trancher avec autorité, le cas échéant, les questions épineuses touchant à ce problème. Peu de livres, pas d'articles de fond et encore moins de travaux vraiment scientifiques. Malgré la curiosité sans cesse croissante qu'elle suscite, malgré le succès et l'encouragement qu'elle obtient, comme on le voit, auprès des couches de plus en plus larges du public, tout se passe, hélas, exactement comme par le passé, c'est-à-dire comme si la peinture naïve n'avait aucune espèce d'importance et qu'il est inutile de s'en occuper.

En attendant, ceux qui écrivent sur les naïfs se contentent tout bonnement des ouï-dire et continuent à exhiber des références, si on peut appeler cela des références, vieilles de trente ou de quarante ans. On dirait des robots qui travaillent sur des fiches perforées; établies, préparées longtemps à l'avance. Apollinaire par-ci, Wilhelm Uhde par là et l'inévitable Alfred Jarry pour corser le bouquet. Mais Jarry ne voyait en Rousseau qu'une sorte de Père Ubu de la palette, tout juste bon pour scandaliser les bourgeois; Apollinaire n'y est venu que sur le tard, après pas mal d'hésitations, il faut l'avouer, bien qu'il connût mieux que quiconque, depuis son enfance, les merveilleux Ex-voto de Laghet[1], quant à Uhde, il fut marchand avant tout, ne l'oublions pas et, en tant que marchand, ne défendait que sa propre marchandise. D'où ces quatre ou cinq noms que l'on connaît, les seuls parvenus à devenir une marchandise, une marchandise cotée, cela s'entend. Voilà donc sur quoi se base et continue à se baser la majorité de la critique. Quelle dérision! Quelle obstruction... Quelle misère!...

Que ne se souviennent-ils pas de temps à autre de ce que disait pourtant leur cher Apollinaire dans ses «Méditations Esthétiques»: *On ne peut pas transporter partout avec soi le cadavre de son père. On l'abandonne en compagnie des autres morts. Et, l'on s'en souvient, on le regrette, on en parle avec admiration. Et, si l'on devient père, il ne faut pas s'attendre à ce qu'un de nos enfants veuille se doubler pour la vie de notre cadavre!*

Toujours est-il que cet état de choses a trouvé sa consécration, que dis-je, une sorte de conclusion logique dans la dernière en date de ces grandes manifestations internationales de la peinture naïve (peut-être la plus vaste, malheureusement), celle qui avec son catalogue luxueux, au titre alléchant: «le Monde des Naïfs» et les moyens plus qu'importants mis à la disposition de ses organisateurs, aurait pu, aurait dû être fort belle et fort complète et qui ne l'était nullement. Je veux parler de l'exposition qui a eu lieu, en 1964, au musée Boymans-van Beuningen de Rotterdam.

On y entrait, en effet, comme dans une énorme nécropole. Aucune surprise, aucune révélation. Sauf, sans doute, pour les nombreuses lacunes, inexplicables normalement, de même que pour la confusion assez fréquente, il est vrai, consistant à vouloir faire passer à tout prix pour des œuvres naïves les différents relents folkloriques, qu'ils soient yougoslaves ou sud-américains. Le reste était catalogué, connu, archi-connu, à force d'être vu et revu en permanence sur les cimaises des musées, des collectionneurs et des galeries, et exhalait de ce fait une de ces perfides et insinuantes odeurs de vieux tableaux et de vieux livres, celle qui se confond, précisément, avec l'odeur du cadavre. On avait une impression très nette que la terre a cessé de tourner il y a belle lurette...

Trompés, déçus, restés sur leur faim, de nombreux visiteurs, habitués déjà petit à petit d'autres fêtes et à d'autres féeries, cherchaient alors le pourquoi de cette mésaventure, que d'aucuns n'hésitaient pas à qualifier de scandale.

Etait-ce tout simplement une bévue, une maldonne, comme il en arrive de temps en temps à des gens incompétents lorsqu'ils s'occupent de ce qu'ils ignorent complètement, ou, au contraire, cette exposition ne faisait-elle pas partie, par hasard, d'un plan plus machiavélique, d'une conspiration plus occulte, visant, par exemple, à ravir à la France sa prépondérance artistique actuelle, d'autant plus que la partie vivante de la peinture naïve française – la plus nombreuse, la plus riche, la plus variée du monde – n'y était représentée que par trois vieillards en tout et pour tout, tandis qu'un belge, Aloys Sauter, né à Stabroek, près d'Anvers, représentait ses morts?

De deux choses l'une: ou on avait franchement peur que quelques-uns parmi ces absents n'éclipsent et ne portent un irréparable préjudice à la plupart des toiles, plutôt mineures, exposées là-bas, ou bien, on les a écartés exprès pour une autre raison, ceci pour pouvoir affirmer: vous voyez, la France a, certes, eu quelques bons peintres naïfs dans le temps, mais maintenant c'est fini, fini, c'est en Yougoslavie et ailleurs qu'il faut les chercher, désormais...

Etait-ce, enfin, une «combine» des marchands?

Aujourd'hui encore, on ne sait. Les protestations et les polémiques dans la presse n'ont pas permis de savoir le fin mot de l'histoire. On s'interroge donc en vain. On hésite toujours entre l'imposture et la bêtise. C'est que, pour comble, même les meilleurs peintres hollandais et flamands n'y étaient pas!

Une autre question se pose aussitôt, autrement plus grave celle-là: comment se fait-il qu'un musée français digne de ce nom fût tombé, à son tour, dans un piège aussi grossier? Le charbonnier est maître chez lui, pourtant. Car, en fin de compte, c'est Paris, oui, le Musée d'Art Moderne de Paris qui a hérité de cette machination nettement plus balkanique que néerlandaise.

Certains diraient que c'est bien fait, puisque aucun autre musée français n'y avait songé auparavant, ou n'était pas en

---

[1] La gaucherie, émerveillée et minutieuse, de l'art primitif qui règne ici a de quoi toucher ceux même qui n'ont pas la foi. Il y a là des tableaux de tous genres, le portrait seul n'y a point de place. Tous les envois sont exposés à perpétuité. Il suffit que la peinture commémore un miracle dû à l'intervention de Notre-Dame de Laghet.

Tous les accidents possibles, les maladies fatales, les douleurs profondes, toutes les misères humaines y sont dépeintes naïvement, dévotement, ingénument...

La mer déchaînée ballotte une pauvre coque dématée sur laquelle est agenouillé un homme plus grand que le vaisseau. Tout semble perdu, mais la Vierge de Laghet veille dans un nimbe de clarté, au coin du tableau. Le dévot fut sauvé. Une inscription italienne l'atteste. C'était en 1811...

...Une voiture emportée par des chevaux indociles roule dans le précipice. Les voyageurs périront, fracassés, sur les rochers. Marie veille au coin du tableau dans le nimbe lumineux. Elle mit des broussailles aux flancs du précipice. Les voyageurs s'y accrochèrent et, par la suite, suspendirent ce tableau dans le cloître de Laghet, en reconnaissance. C'était en 1830...

Et toujours: en 1850, en 1860, chaque année, chaque mois, presque chaque jour des aveugles virent, des muets parlèrent, des phtisiques survécurent grâce à la Dame de Laghet qui sourit doucement nimbée de jaune au coin des tableaux...

Guillaume Apollinaire, L'Hérésiarque et Cie, 1910, Stock éd., Paris

ORNEORE METELLI

mesure de réaliser quelque chose de semblable par lui-même. Que voulez-vous, nos conservateurs sont ce qu'ils sont et pourquoi voulez-vous qu'ils soient tellement différents de leurs prédécesseurs qui, il y a cinquante ans à peine, refusaient leurs salles et à Cézanne et à Van Gogh? La peinture naïve n'est pas pour eux. Pas encore. Beaucoup trop révolutionnaire, beaucoup trop neuve. Mais quand même... Les peintres naïfs français n'ont pas mérité et ne méritent pas cela! Loin de là!

C'est pourquoi, il nous a paru salutaire et urgent de dresser pour commencer, une sorte de répertoire objectif de la création naïve de par le monde, afin que *tous* les naïfs y aient leur place, mais rien que leur place. Le temps fera son tri et saura éliminer l'ivraie du bon grain. De toute façon et quoi qu'il arrive, les renseignements biographiques et les références exactes que nous donnons ici ne pourront que servir utilement les chercheurs de l'avenir.

Il a fallu, néanmoins, un demi-siècle tout juste après la mort du pauvre Douanier – on s'en rend de plus en plus compte –, pour que son mythe soit enfin démystifié, débarrassé surtout de toute cette mauvaise littérature qui s'est agglutinée aussi bien autour de sa personne qu'à son œuvre, et pour que celle-ci, ainsi que ses faits et gestes, soient examinés avec le sérieux et la rigueur qu'ils méritent. Il est vrai que, comme disait Paul Valéry: «Au commencement était la légende...»

Quant à l'histoire à proprement parler de la peinture naïve, nous ne pourrons, évidemment, faute de place, qu'esquisser ses grandes lignes. Elle reste encore à faire, Dieu merci.

Les peintres naïfs, en tant que phénomène social, apparaissent donc, généralement, pour la première fois, à ce moment précis de l'Histoire où la société pré-industrielle, un tantinet féodale, est sur le point de faire un bond décisif en avant et d'affronter les Temps modernes. C'est la rencontre d'une simple aiguille avec une machine à coudre, pour paraphraser ainsi le ténébreux Isidore Ducasse, dit le comte de Lautréamont, ou bien, pour rester toujours dans les images, la violente intrusion d'une cheminée d'usine dans la paix encore champêtre d'une églogue de Virgile. L'exemple de la Yougoslavie, pays tout ce qu'il y a de patriarcal et de moyenâgeux, pays où à la veille de la dernière guerre, juste avant qu'il ne bascule à son tour dans l'ère du socialisme et de la machine, il n'existait que des imagiers sur verre, sans compter quelques autres représentants du folklore essentiellement rural, passablement éloigné de la peinture naïve, et qui, aussitôt après, pour ainsi dire sous nos yeux, donne brusquement naissance à un nombre respectable d'authentiques peintres naïfs, est plus que probant.

La naissance de la peinture naïve en France coïncide, elle, avec la Révolution de 89 et l'abolition des Corporations.

Jusque-là, en effet, tous ceux qui montraient quelque aptitude pour la taille, le modelage ou le dessin, entraient dès leur plus jeune âge dans une de ces corporations qui leur inculquaient les rudiments d'un métier, quitte à l'exercer toute leur vie.

Tous, ils avaient un certain sens du beau, accompagné nécessairement d'un grand amour pour les choses bien faites, qu'ils pouvaient satisfaire dorénavant à loisir, puisque toute leur existence, je le répète, était vouée à l'exécution d'une multitude de ces objets absolument parfaits, à mi-chemin entre une œuvre d'art et un objet purement utilitaire.

Si on bâtissait une église, les tailleurs de pierre lui fournissaient ses saints en pierre, tandis que les tailleurs sur bois la garnissaient de leurs saints en bois; si on ouvrait une auberge, le peintre du village lui brossait son enseigne, le même qui, le plus souvent, à la demande d'un miraculé, lui exécutait aussi sur le champ l'un de ces innombrables ex-voto, narrant soit une guérison in extremis, soit un accident mortel évité de justesse. Souvenez-vous de ceux de Laghet...

Certains d'entre eux devenaient des peintres tout court, des grands peintres parfois, tel ce J. B. Chardin, fils d'un menuisier de la rue de Seine. Quant aux autres, eh bien, c'étaient encore des artisans ni plus ni moins, un peu plus évolués, un peu plus fins, voilà tout. N'empêche qu'ils se trouvaient toujours au stade de ces derniers faiseurs de l'art populaire de l'Amérique latine qui vendent encore, comme si de rien n'était, comme il y a cent ans, leur production sur les places des marchés. Ils ne créaient pas. Pas tout à fait. Pas d'eux-mêmes. La peinture naïve apparaît là où le folklore se tait.

Cette situation change du tout au tout avec l'introduction de la machine. Car la machine fait vite éliminer ce qui subsiste encore, tant bien que mal, du travail manuel. Il n'y a rien d'étonnant, alors, à ce que les premiers peintres naïfs se recrutent d'emblée parmi ceux qui, hier encore, étaient verriers, potiers, forgerons, ébénistes, cartiers, imagiers, et j'en passe, tous ceux qui par la force des choses sont obligés d'exercer un autre métier à présent, n'ayant plus aucun rapport avec l'art.

Déracinés, désorientés, frustrés, aigris, refoulés et blessés dans leurs sens et l'amour du beau, ils saisissent maintenant la moindre occasion pour renouer avec ce qui leur tient le plus à cœur, afin de pouvoir chanter leur Paradis Perdu. Celui qui peignait ou sculptait le plus clair de son temps des angelots pour les églises, et qui travaille désormais dans une mine de charbon, se transforma lui-même en un Ange Déchu. Il ne lui reste plus qu'à raconter sa chute. D'autres, même sans avoir travaillé ni de loin ni de près à une branche semi-artistique quelconque déplorent, eux aussi, la dureté de la vie, regrettent le bon vieux temps que la tornade de la transformation économique vient d'emporter à jamais et soupirent après quelque autre bonheur perdu. A l'instar de Marcel Proust, qui rechercha si obstinément, si méticuleusement sa vie durant ce Temps qu'il a si peu vécu, en vérité, les peintres naïfs se lancent de leur côté à la recherche d'un certain Dimanche de la vie, celui qui ne dure, malheureusement, que ce que durent les rêves du dimanche, comme de juste! D'où le surnom.

Obligés de travailler dur, très dur les six jours d'affilée, ceci sans air, sous les verrières tristes et sales, ils refoulaient de la sorte toutes les visions interdites: un ciel on ne peut plus bleu, des fleurs de toutes les couleurs de l'arc-en-ciel, des arbres au printemps, des rivières poissonneuses. Pour le Douanier Rousseau, ce fut la forêt tropicale qu'il n'a, bien entendu, jamais connue, mais qu'il contempla souvent, béatement, assis sur un banc du Jardin des Plantes, avec les yeux de l'âme.

L'idée du bonheur est neuve en Europe, disait Saint-Just, placé à la frontière de ces deux vies, entre le XVIIIe siècle finissant et ces fascinants Temps modernes, dont on n'entrevoyait pour l'instant que les mirages sans nuages, et le mot et le monde naïf le sont tout autant, qui sait, ne fût-ce que pour cette même raison.

Au demeurant, ce bonheur individuel, auquel tout être humain a droit depuis peu, le peintre naïf le cherche pour la première fois dans *sa* peinture et il est, également, à tout un chacun. La peinture peut, sinon doit être faite par tous. Mais à quel prix!

Parce qu'il ne s'agissait plus de copier tranquillement, de père en fils, comme le faisaient naguère leurs ancêtres, mais de lutter sans cesse, d'improviser sans arrêt, de donner réellement corps à ce qui n'existait pas avant eux, c'est-à-dire créer. De plus, il fallait inventer à la fois le sujet et la technique, le dessin et la perspective, les ombres et les volumes, tout, absolument tout, jusqu'au mélange des couleurs. Aux innocents les mains pleines...

D'ailleurs, moins ils en savaient, mieux cela valait. La féerie et la surprise étaient d'autant plus grandes. N'est pas naïf qui veut, force m'est de répéter cette lapalissade, et pour l'être vraiment, indiscutablement, dans toute l'acception de ce terme, de quels désirs brûlants fallait-il être la proie pour pouvoir continuer comme cela, envers et contre tous, cette affirmation de leur moi et poursuivre ce qui leur échappe! Tout cela afin de laisser une trace, aussi minime qu'elle soit, de leur passage sur la terre...

C'est qu'ils se sentaient vraiment habités par une force qui les dépasse; c'est qu'ils devenaient vraiment des possédés. C'est pourquoi la plupart de leurs œuvres nous apparaissent sous la forme d'un don, bien mieux, touchées par une sorte de grâce.

Leurs paysages sont nus comme l'étaient Adam et Eve avant la chute. Sans aucune honte. Ils ne savent même pas ce qui est bon et ce qui est mauvais; ils n'ont pas encore goûté à la pomme de la connaissance tendue par le diable et ignorent, par conséquent, jusqu'à la notion même du péché plastique que l'on enseigne dans les académies. Ils savent seulement que la peinture les aide à vivre, et qu'elle est leur seul et perpétuel Eden, c'est-à-dire le bonheur, l'extase, l'infini, ou appelez cela comme vous voulez.

Le Douanier Rousseau l'avoua un jour sans ambages: «Ce n'est pas moi qui peins. C'est quelque chose au bout de ma main.»

Quoi qu'il en soit, le désir d'une fraîcheur première, la grande et ardente soif d'une pureté immaculée, bref ce que l'on pourrait qualifier à la rigueur, faute de mieux de *naïf* – mot qui n'avait rien de péjoratif au départ et rien de ce qu'il est devenu par la suite – hantait déjà tout le monde, les grands et les petits, les lettrés et les illettrés[2].

Aussi Diderot disait: «Tout ce qui est vrai n'est pas naïf, mais tout ce qui est naïf est vrai, d'une naïveté piquante, originale et rare.» Tandis que, un peu plus tard, Stendhal notait dans son *Journal*, à la date du 16 Messidor, l'an XII, c'est-à-dire le 5 juillet 1804: «La naïveté me semble le sublime de la vie ordinaire.» Ce n'est évidemment pas par hasard, non plus, que ce dernier s'intéressait aux vieilles chroniques italiennes, recherchait les romans populaires et se passionnait à la fameuse «Bibliothèque Bleue», que les colporteurs vendaient de village en village, puis aux complaintes populaires que l'on chantait encore sur les places des marchés, puisque, de son état d'esprit, à celui d'un Baudelaire ou d'un Rimbaud, entre autres, il n'y avait qu'un pas. A «je suis revenu chercher asile dans l'impeccable naïveté» de Baudelaire, répondait parfaitement: «j'aimais les peintures idiotes, dessus de portes, décors de saltimbanques, enseignes, enluminures populaires» de Rimbaud!

Partout, lorsque le monde change de mains, lorsque le passé et le présent, en attendant le futur, s'affrontent dans une lutte sans merci, on éprouve soudain l'impérieux besoin d'un bain de Jouvence, on aspire à un art primitif et direct des premiers âges de l'homme, sans que les règles, les conventions et le savoir-faire ne prennent le pas sur la spontanéité, la sincérité, en un mot, sur le vrai.

Que ce soit cet Ecossais MacPherson, témoin de l'industrialisation anglaise naissante, auteur de surcroît des «Chants d'Ossian», ces chants qui ont connu un très grand succès, avant que l'on ne s'aperçoive de la supercherie, car ce prétendu barde du IIIe siècle n'a jamais existé, ou bien les compositeurs russes, Moussorgsky et Rimsky-Korsakoff, pour ne nommer que ceux-là, faisant entrer dans leurs œuvres des contes de fées, des mélodies, si ce n'est carrément des chants populaires, toujours au même moment où s'allument les premiers haut-fourneaux, ou encore ce Chinois, Liaou Tao-Chouen, qui disait déjà sous la dynastie des Songs: «Recherche le talent dans l'inhabilité», leurs vœux sont identiques, leurs désirs se confondent: refaire, recommencer le monde selon les yeux et le cœur d'un enfant.

Dans cette conjoncture des forces qui a déterminé l'apparition du phénomène naïf, si la création du «Roman noir», ou «gothique», si vous préférez, avec ses spectres, ses revenants, le grincement de ses chaînes, le cliquetis des armures, les nonnes sanglantes et ses cachots souterrains, pleins d'ossements, peut être considérée comme une revendication agressive, comme un dernier sursaut du Moyen Age, cautère et acte d'exorcisme en même temps – fais-moi peur, veux-tu, cela me rassure! – tout comme les «vengeurs», d'ailleurs, de cent ans plus tard, les Rocambole, les Chéri-Bibi, les Arsène Lupin, les Fantomas et autres Judex, les naïfs, par contre, malgré leurs attaches incontestables à l'ancien régime, se présentent plutôt comme des victimes résignées du nouvel ordre: ce sont les trompés, les volés, les bafoués, ceux qui ont cru à la bonne parole, aux promesses et surtout au Progrès, avec un grand P.

De toute évidence, aussi bien le Roman Noir des uns, que la Bibliothèque Rose des autres, tous deux peuvent être taxés d'égale naïveté. Avec cette différence seulement que les premiers appliquent une technique essentiellement romantique, pleine de bruit et fureur, de touches larges et de flous, dérivée en ligne directe de Walter Scott et d'Ann Radcliffe, à laquelle même un Stendhal a payé son tribut, tandis que les seconds se servent de l'objectif de l'identité judiciaire, puis de celui de la carte postale et d'Adget, poète incomparable du tire-ligne et du fil à plomb, une sorte de Douanier Rousseau de la photographie.

Chez eux, tout n'est-il pas net, exact, minutieux, sans bavure? Jamais on n'a cerné l'invisible d'aussi près. La réalité est pourtant ailleurs. Elle se nomme Courbet et Zola. Paradoxalement, ce ne sont donc pas ceux que l'on appelle les «vrais» peintres qui auront laissé les dernières images touchantes, les derniers témoignages sensibles de ce qui est en train de s'en aller sans espoir de retour, mais ces visionnaires, ces rêveurs des fins de semaine... Nos deshérités, nos parias, nos intouchables.

Et l'ère des évasions dominicales commença!

---

[2] Le mot «naïf» provient, d'ailleurs, du mot latin «nativus», ce qui veut dire: *qui naît.*

ANDRÉ BAUCHANT

Mais c'est surtout à partir de 1850, 1860, pendant que la nature se recroqueville de plus en plus sous l'haleine chaude des fourneaux – c'est encore une image de Baudelaire! – que des tisserands, des cordonniers, des mineurs, des facteurs, des forts des Halles, des petits employés, des petits rentiers, des concierges, pourquoi pas, se jettent à corps perdu dans la peinture, et peignent, peignent, peignent, en sacrifiant ainsi à qui mieux leurs courts instants de liberté. Les loisirs, le sommeil, les heures du repos et de repas, s'en vont aussi au fil de leurs pinceaux. Avant et après le hurlement de la sirène d'usine. Entre ces deux appels du nouvel Angélus de la vapeur. Or, ce n'est plus Millet qui les fixe, mais les expressionnistes avant la lettre: Munch et Hodler.

Pourquoi peignent-ils? Parce qu'ils ne peuvent pas faire autrement.

J'ai étudié, il n'y a pas si longtemps, et autant que j'ai pu, à fond, j'espère, le mécanisme caché de la création naïve, de même que ce côté affectif-frustré flagrant de leur production dans mon «Eros du Dimanche»[3]; il est inutile donc que je revienne là-dessus.

Pour qui peignent-ils? D'abord pour eux-mêmes. Pour leur propre plaisir. Pour la famille ensuite, pour des amis. L'idée ne leur viendrait même pas que leurs tableaux pourront être vendus un jour. Enfin, est-ce qu'on peut se défaire de ses lettres d'amour? Ce serait sacrilège, pas vrai?

Où exposent-ils? Nulle part.

Que deviennent-elles, leurs œuvres? Elles disparaissent, pour la plupart, détruites volontairement par des héritiers qui en ont honte, ou s'abîment lentement mais sûrement à force de traîner d'un Marché aux Puces à l'autre. Personne ne fait attention à elles, excepté, sans doute, quelqu'autre âme en peine, une âme sœur quelconque, à tout point semblable à celle de leurs auteurs, en quête, elle aussi, d'un peu d'azur pour son gourbi.

Ce n'est qu'avec la fondation du Salon des Indépendants que tous ces velléitaires de la peinture ont pu trouver, à défaut d'un public, une cimaise. D'autant plus que, même là, les visiteurs ne s'attardent pas et n'apprécient pas le moins du monde toutes ces «drôleries», tranchant tellement à côté de tous les autres artistes-peintres, diplômés ou non.

Même G. Courteline, qui eut le premier, cependant, l'idée et l'envie de collectionner les tableaux naïfs, ne put s'empêcher d'en rire pour commencer. Dès qu'il dénichait l'un de ces tableaux chez les brocanteurs de Montmartre, il lui donnait aussitôt des titres humoristiques dans le genre de: «La vierge à moitié cuite», «Les huîtres des mois sans R», «Les régates des mausolées», et caetera, et caetera.

Or, ce que l'on sait moins, c'est que cette collection, appelée primitivement *le Musée des Horreurs,* contenait aussi, parmi les tableaux d'inconnus, deux tableaux du Douanier Rousseau, dont le «Portrait de Pierre Loti», baptisé ainsi, comme tous les autres, sans exception, par Courteline lui-même, à cause fort probablement de la chéchia et du chat[4], bien que le personnage en question ne soit autre qu'un dénommé M. Frank, habitant de la Butte. Tableau que Courteline céda vers la fin de sa vie pour une bouchée de pain, tout en traitant son acheteur d'imbécile par-dessus le marché!

Et c'est encore sous le signe de la plaisanterie que ledit musée, voire les naïfs, ont les honneurs de la presse parisienne et se voient reproduits sur les pages d'un journal. De ce fait, ce numéro 39 du journal satirique Cocorico, datant du 15 août 1900 et consacré entièrement à cette fameuse collection, constitue indiscutablement non pas uniquement le premier document de ce genre, mais aussi le tout premier témoignage, du moins de cette importance, qui existe dans le monde sur un ensemble naïf. Un document, donc. Une date. Ils méritent qu'on s'y arrête un peu.

Néanmoins, ce qu'il y a de plus précieux dans cette publication tout à fait inattendue, les commentaires de Courteline mis à part, c'est cette introduction, pour ne pas dire préface, où il est dit textuellement:

«Ainsi que nous l'avons annoncé dans notre précédent numéro, notre ami Georges Courteline a bien voulu réserver au Cocorico la primeur de son très curieux musée; les reproductions de ces tableaux font, ainsi qu'on va le voir, l'objet de pittoresques commentaires dus à l'heureux propriétaire de la galerie.

A ce propos, nous détachons d'une longue et très intéressante étude que M. Edouard Norès consacrait dernièrement à son ami et collaborateur, les lignes suivantes, qui, mieux que nous ne pourrions le faire, mettront nos lecteurs au courant de l'esthétique qui a guidé Courteline dans le choix de ses tableaux:

... Il est chez Courteline, dit-il, un trait de caractère qui à mon sens expliquerait l'acuité de sa vision des ridicules humains; c'est le profond attendrissement que lui procure le spectacle de ces ridicules. Observateur sagace de l'éternelle sottise, il l'aime d'un fraternel amour, il se complaît sans amertume à son contact, il en savoure dans une intime joie les manifestations diverses; et, quand il les traduit dans les inoubliables pages du «Train de 8 heures 47», des «Ronds de Cuir», des «Gaîtés de l'Escadron» ou de «Boubouroche», son observation laisse percer, sous la précision du trait, l'émotion humaine de l'écrivain.

Ce fut cette fibre attendrie qui vibra chez Courteline lorsqu'il fit l'acquisition du premier des tableaux qui constituent actuellement son «musée». Il se dit qu'il y aurait une curieuse collection à réunir – non pas de mauvaise peinture au sens précis du mot, il n'y aurait qu'à se baisser pour en prendre – mais des productions bizarres nées de l'application des naïfs convaincus, exerçant dans la peinture, d'un effort soutenu, stérile et admirable, les qualités négatives des fausses mais sincères vocations.

Le musée Courteline était fondé.

De patientes recherches l'ont depuis enrichi chaque jour, et une trentaine de numéros constituent aujourd'hui cette collection qui ajoute à l'histoire de la peinture française une page humoristique qui y manquait. signé: Edouard Norès»

Malgré certaines injustices et injustices certaines dans l'appréciation de l'œuvre des naïfs, ce texte, qui va avoir bientôt plus de 65 ans, il ne faut pas l'oublier, se révèle quand même plus jeune et plus perspicace que tant d'élucubrations plus récentes, sans compter quelques dénominations absurdes dont on affuble parfois les naïfs; «Les Maîtres populaires de la Réalité» parmi tant d'autres.

Certes, beaucoup d'eau a passé depuis sous les ponts de Paris et d'ailleurs; G. Courteline consentit à une exposition

[3] J. J. Pauvert, éditeur, Paris, 1964.

[4] H. Certigny, «Le douanier Rousseau a-t-il peint le portrait de P. Loti?» L'information de l'histoire de l'Art n° 1 – janvier 1965.

publique de sa collection, qui eut lieu effectivement du 21 novembre au 2 décembre 1927, à la galerie Bernheim-Jeune, et si on s'est aperçu que les titres et les commentaires de l'humoriste figurant dans le catalogue, principal attrait de cette exposition, paraissaient déjà tels quels, vingt-sept ans plus tôt dans le journal Cocorico, même si «La pintade à son dernier soupir» se transformait en «Les heures pénibles» et que «L'inondation dans un cimetière» devenait «Les régates des mausolées», citées tout à l'heure, rien, semble-t-il, ne changeait à la chose, si toutefois, entre temps, Courteline ne s'était rendu compte de son erreur, comme l'atteste ce N.B. inséré dans le catalogue, ce qui est autrement significatif:

Georges Courteline repousse formellement le titre du «Musée des Horreurs» dont on a pris l'habitude d'appeler sa collection. Il en décline absolument la paternité (ce qui est faux, entre nous soit dit...) *Tout au plus conviendrait-il de réunir ces tableaux sous la dénomination générique du Musée du Labeur Ingénu.*

Ce changement d'appréciation est à noter, naturellement, bien que l'on puisse se demander et à juste titre, s'il venait vraiment de Courteline, ou si Courteline ne se mettait pas tout simplement «dans le vent», comme on le dirait aujourd'hui.

C'est que la réhabilitation des naïfs était déjà en marche, et ces vingt-sept ans, riches en événements, qui se sont écoulés entre ces deux témoignages, représentent un tournant décisif dans l'histoire de la peinture naïve. Le vent a tourné brusquement.

Au demeurant, Rousseau continue à exposer sans succès tout comme tant d'autres de ses anonymes confrères, au Salon des Indépendants, moqué et méprisé, il en a l'habitude, ceci jusqu'au jour où il rencontre par hasard son «pays» Alfred Jarry, originaire également de Laval, lequel Jarry comprend immédiatement ce qu'il y a d'exceptionnel dans sa peinture – il faut lui rendre cette justice – et lui commande sa seule et unique lithographie «La guerre» pour la revue Ymagier qu'il dirigeait alors avec Rémy de Gourmont. A ce propos, on a découvert dernièrement que c'est un pauvre dessin, paru dans un journal vaguement socialisant, L'Egalité, qui lui a servi de canevas pour cette composition. Il n'était pas à cela près, du reste. D'autres dessins et d'autres gravures lui ont servi tant bien que mal pour ses tableaux. Décidément, il n'y a que les peintres naïfs pour être capables d'opérer de pareilles métamorphoses.

Mais Jarry, connu surtout pour son fracassant Ubu Roi et le mot en cinq lettres auxquelles il a ajouté la sixième, ne peut vraisemblablement rien pour Rousseau. Cela ne prend pas. Surtout venant de sa part. Est-ce par vengeance, est-ce par dépit qu'il fait feu alors, à coup de revolver, dans son propre portrait «tiré» par Rousseau, l'anéantissant corps et biens?

On ne sait. De guerre lasse, il le présente à Apollinaire.

De Jarry, il ne restera finalement que ce sobriquet du Douanier, le commencement de sa longue et indéracinable légende, puisque c'est le poète et le pataphysicien qui affuble le premier de la sorte ce simple gabelou de l'octroi de Paris et le fait figurer sous ce titre parmi tous les autres personnages de sa mythologie personnelle, dont voici quelques-uns:

Carrière	celui qui vaporise.
Pierre Louys	celui qui Aphrodite.
Vallette	celui qui Mercure.
Renard	celui qui écorche vif.
Rachilde	celle qui hors nature.
Déroulède	celui qui patrouille quand-même.
Sarah	celle qui Mède.
Saint-Pol-Roux	celui qui magnifique.
Tristan Bernard	celui qui berne, nickelle les pieds et chasse les chevelures.
Huysmans	celui qui digère par la trappe.
Claude Debussy ...	celui qui Pelle (et as et Mélisande)
Odilon Redon	celui qui mystère.
Toulouse-Lautrec ..	celui qui affiche.
Détaille	celui qui uniforme.
Anatole France	celui qui rôtit chez la reine.
et Rousseau	*celui qui douanait!*

Apollinaire hésite, je viens de le dire, longtemps à son sujet avant de se prononcer; mais voilà que, tout d'un coup, il prend parti, franchement, ouvertement, pour Rousseau. Il s'engage maintenant à fond. Il est tout feu et flamme. Il écrit sur lui des pages élogieuses en vers et en prose. A la veille de la guerre, il lui consacre même un numéro spécial de ses «Soirées de Paris». Un peu plus tôt, il a organisé en son honneur, dans l'atelier de Picasso, au «Bateau Lavoir», l'inoubliable banquet décrit plus d'une fois, et c'est quasi instantanément la renommée tant attendue, la gloire ou presque. Apollinaire semble avoir complètement oublié un méchant article où, quelques années plus tôt, il a malmené ce même Rousseau...

Bernheim l'expose à Paris et Joseph Brummer à New York. Ambroise Vollard lui achète ses tableaux. Pour pas grand chose, mais il achète. Cela le change de la fruitière du coin, du charbonnier et de la blanchisseuse, ses clients ordinaires du quartier de Plaisance. Un autre marchand, et non des moindres, Paul Guillaume prend la suite et les achète aussi. Apollinaire lui conseille dans une lettre écrite du front: «achetez des tableaux bon marché, Rousseau, Picasso, Laurencin, Bonnard, Cézanne, etc... Vous savez quoi...» Rousseau est en tête, comme on le voit. Oui, le Douanier est lancé. Mais il est déjà mort, le pauvre. Dès lors, il devient à la fois la stèle et le symbole – un véritable tombeau du naïf inconnu!

Profitant de cet engouement passager, W. Uhde, marchand méthodique et avisé, s'empresse d'exploiter à fond cette soif d'innocence et ce goût du primitif, pour ne pas dire du barbare, qui commence à faire tache d'huile. Après la première guerre mondiale, il adjoint à Rousseau quelques autres peintres naïfs que l'on surnommera pour le besoin de la cause: «les Grands», ou «Maîtres populaires de la Réalité». Grands, parce qu'ils étaient les seuls à être soutenus par les marchands. Maîtres, parce qu'il fallait les séparer à tout prix de tous les autres peintres naïfs. Des fois qu'on les confondrait...

Il en est ainsi, hélas, des détracteurs de naïfs comme des antisémites. On se souvient que chacun de ces salauds avait son «bon» juif, ce qui lui permettait de vouer tous les autres aux pogromes et aux chambres à gaz. Alors, à condition d'avoir son Vivin ou son Bauchant, on avait le droit d'exterminer tous les autres.

Evidemment, la confusion était tentante, d'autant plus que certains parmi ces naïfs «inférieurs» égalaient et parfois avaient même plus de talent que ces «maîtres» auxquels ils ne devaient pas être mêlés. De plus, leur nombre grossissait sans cesse. Ils exposaient par-ci, par-là, récoltaient quelques lignes

ADOLF DIETRICH

d'un compte rendu condescendant, mais tout s'arrêtait là pour l'instant. Du moins on le pensait dans les hauts lieux. On espérait qu'en dressant le barrage de l'appellation contrôlée, on arrêterait net la dangereuse expansion des naïfs. En vain. Car on oubliait l'essentiel: ils plaisaient. Ils amusaient, ils amusaient encore et toujours, c'est un fait, sauf qu'on les achetait de plus en plus ouvertement, plus en cachette, d'une façon plus ou moins clandestine, comme c'était le cas auparavant, afin de ne pas attirer les quolibets de leur entourage, et cela pour la même raison pour laquelle ces peintres peignaient: par amour. On ne les achetait pas non plus comme des valeurs boursières, ou comme une sorte de placement, mais parce qu'ils apportaient quelque chose qui manquait réellement et qu'eux seuls étaient capables de satisfaire. Pour la première fois dans l'histoire de la peinture moderne, les achats de tableaux cessaient d'être une spéculation. De sorte que la ségrégation naïve, comme toutes les ségrégations, bien sûr, faisait long feu devant la réalité, la vérité et la justice.

Eh oui, ils plaisaient... Un peu, beaucoup, passionnément. Aux simples amateurs de jolis tableaux, comme aux connaisseurs et aux collectionneurs avisés. Aux peintres d'avant-garde notamment. Aux cubistes et aux abstraits. Picasso et Robert Delaunay s'inscrivent parmi les tout premiers possesseurs des toiles du Douanier Rousseau. Dans le coffre-fort de Picasso, à la B.N.C.I., les toiles de Rousseau ne voisinent-elles pas avec celles de Cézanne, de Matisse et de Braque? Et c'est encore Picasso qui a acheté les premières toiles de Vivancos. Seul Jean Cocteau s'est permis d'écrire des lignes plutôt désobligeantes en ce qui concerne la peinture naïve, mais peut-être justement parce que ses deux protégés, Jean Marais et Edouard Dermit «faisaient» dans la tendance un tantinet naïve et que là encore, il ne fallait pas mélanger les serviettes avec les torchons.

Gentil Rousseau tu nous entends
Nous te saluons
Delaunay, sa femme, Monsieur Queval et moi
Laisse passer nos bagages en franchise à la porte du ciel

Il n'empêche que si tout le monde connaît à présent ce beau poème épitaphe, tracé au crayon par Guillaume Apollinaire à même la pierre tombale du Douanier Rousseau, celui que Brancusi, aidé par Ortiz de Zarate, gravera plus tard au ciseau, afin que la pluie et les feuilles mortes ne l'effacent jamais, peu de personnes connaissent, en revanche, cette déclaration de Kandinsky, faite peu après l'autre guerre et qui se résume à peu près à ceci: *je ne vois pour l'avenir que l'art abstrait ou la peinture naïve*.

Kandinsky me l'a confirmé lui-même, de vive voix, en 1934, je m'en souviens très bien, dans son bel appartement de Neuilly, presqu'en face de l'Ile de la Grande Jatte, immortalisée naguère par Seurat, où il devait résider jusqu'à la fin de sa vie, après s'être fixé définitivement en France; même doublement en quelque sorte, puisqu'il me montrait en même temps ses deux petits Rousseau accrochés à ses murs, les seuls tableaux qu'il tolérait à côté de ses propres œuvres.

La pierre a quitté, en 1947, ainsi que ce qui restait du cercueil du pauvre Douanier, la triste promiscuité banlieusarde du cimetière de Bagneux pour dominer, du haut du square de la Perrine, les ponts sur la Mayenne et cette ville blonde, quiète, un peu endormie de Laval, ville qui lui a donné le jour sans le reconnaître pour autant, toujours pas de son vivant, mais les paroles ailées du poète ont fait déjà depuis longtemps le tour du monde, traduites dans toutes les langues, lues, récitées et apprises par cœur, ne serait-ce que pour rappeler aux derniers détracteurs de la peinture naïve que parmi les premiers découvreurs, les premiers acheteurs et les premiers admirateurs de Rousseau figure, comme par hasard, l'un des plus grands peintres abstraits, Robert Delaunay. Par hasard? Sûrement pas.

Se joignant à lui, en homme honnête et clairvoyant, sachant fort bien, et ce qu'il faisait, et ce qu'il disait, Kandinsky tranchait donc lui aussi, la question de la légitimité de la peinture naïve et augurait sans ambages de son avenir.

Faut-il que je cite également ces lignes qu'écrivait, en 1930, Michel Seuphor, le premier historiographe sérieux de la peinture abstraite, en guise de préface à une exposition des enfants du peintre J.Torrès-Garcia, aux si beaux noms d'Olympia, Auguste et Iphigénie?

«Un des mérites de notre époque – époque de recherches scientifiques, de volonté de précision, de l'effort vers une conscience d'un ordre – sera de nous avoir rapproché aussi de l'enfant, cet autre pôle de l'être. L'enfant devient pour nous d'une grande valeur éducatrice: il nous ramène à la nature et à notre première source morale, là précisément où le mécanisme de la vie moderne nous fait oublier la base de notre équilibre vital. Comme tout ce qui compose notre passé, l'enfant est en chacun de nous; mais il importe de rendre cette présence consciente, afin de ne pas être réduit à la subir malgré nous et contre nous. Souhaitons que, dans un temps très proche, un art effectivement de l'enfance prenne la place entière qu'occupent encore aujourd'hui les multiples manifestations du romantisme, cet infantilisme tardif et maladif, tels que l'expressionisme et le surréalisme.»

Bon. Avec des références de cette qualité, on aurait pu supposer, en effet, que le droit à la naïveté était bel et bien acquis, du moins reconnu tacitement, et que la peinture naïve allait prendre, sans tarder, la place qui lui est due. Que son ascension serait facile, rapide et sans heurts. Il n'en fut rien. Au contraire. Rien n'a été aussi pénible et aussi décevant. Des années et des années passaient encore sans que le moindre changement se manifestât dans ce domaine, sans que la peinture naïve cessât d'être considérée comme une quantité négligeable. L'ignorance, la cabale et la mauvaise foi maintenaient tant bien que mal ce statu quo. Il est vrai que la mentalité de l'époque d'entre-deux-guerres était loin d'être mûre pour se rendre compte que le phénomène naïf représentait, tout compte fait, l'autre bout du balancier dialectique de l'histoire qui, avec l'art abstrait, précisément, à l'opposé, forme la thèse et l'antithèse, le positif et le négatif, le jour et la nuit, le pile et face du même drame humain, du même problème du visible. La bombe et le miroir. Non pas le miroir de la figuration imbécile, caduc depuis longtemps, ne faisant que se dégrader bon gré, mal gré – celui que les abstraits ont fait voler une fois pour toutes en éclats – mais l'autre, le vrai, cette vision à l'état brut, son noyau immémorial, si ce n'est la source tonique et féconde des yeux mêmes de notre Occident. Ce qui explique en partie pourquoi nos naïfs à nous, si proches et si lointains en même temps des primitifs d'autrefois, sont, qu'on le veuille ou non, les primitifs d'aujourd'hui.

On ne se doutait guère davantage, si on ne feignait de l'ignorer, que l'apparition des peintres naïfs coïncidait sur un autre plan, au second degré, pourrait-on ajouter, avec les premiers coups de bélier portés à l'art académique. Lorsque ceux-ci, face aux dynamiteurs, commencèrent à secréter, à leur insu, par un réflexe d'auto-défense, une sorte d'anti-toxine dans le but de sauvegarder, dans la mesure du possible, la meilleure part du monde sensible qui nous entoure, et de sauver, le cas échéant, ce qui pouvait être encore sauvé. Cézanne n'avait que cinq ans de plus que le Douanier Rousseau.

Dès le début, dès que les académies libres, fréquentées peu ou prou par Delacroix, Bonington, Courbet, Bonnard, Matisse – leur nom est légion! – montent à l'assaut du pompiérisme régnant, les naïfs, de leur côté, commencent à édifier presqu'en même temps, en francs-tireurs certes, un monde à eux, un monde et un art absolument à part, confidentiel et secret, clandestin, ou tout comme. D'où cette abondance, cette qualité, cette variété et cette ancienneté, conséquences logiques d'un développement normal, sans interruption aucune, qui font de la peinture naïve française la plus vieille et la plus riche du monde.

Ne serait-ce pas là où le bât blesse les organisateurs de l'exposition de Rotterdam?

Pourtant c'est ainsi, et je n'y puis rien.

Il a fallu, néanmoins, la seconde guerre mondiale et la seconde vague des naïfs, plus puissante, plus diversifiée que la première, pour que les yeux de nos Thomas se déssillent cette fois pour de bon. Pour que la cascade des manifestations internationales, celle de Rotterdam y inclus, ait pu avoir lieu. En vérité, cette situation change déjà du tout au tout un peu avant, pendant les noires années de l'occupation; ceci du fait de la disparition provisoire d'un bon nombre de marchands et de la diminution assez sensible de leur influence. Une exposition comme celle de la Galerie «Claude» (1944), n'était même pas pensable en d'autres temps.

Il a fallu surtout une crise permanente, bien que larvée, de toutes les valeurs plastiques, aggravée d'excès de toutes sortes, la peinture à la carabine, la peinture au lance-flammes, la sculpture au marteau-pilon, sans oublier les motocyclettes emballées dans du nylon, l'étalage d'objets tirés de la poubelle, les singes peignant et la machine à peindre de Tinguely, bref tout ce qui devait aboutir tôt ou tard au Pop'Art, qui n'a plus d'art que le nom. Je veux dire par là art ancien, tel qu'on le concevait depuis des millénaires. D'ailleurs la pointe avancée de la peinture analytique, strictement formelle, celle qui, partie de la pomme de Cézanne, aboutissait d'abord à un rond ne voulant plus rien dire, puis à la disparition, à la suppression même de ce rond, à un fond uni, à ce fameux bleu de Klein, autrement dit le néant, ne valait guère mieux. Le Pop'Art consommait par conséquent, définitivement, cette rupture, car il est à Cézanne ce que sa pomme à lui est à un jus de fruit dans un conditionnement métallique. Ce qui a permis à son leader, M. P. Restany, de faire récemment le point et de découvrir, en réaliste qu'il est, la présence, l'existence des naïfs, que tant d'autres écrivains de la soi-disant avant-garde continuent d'ignorer: «Le phénomène le plus marquant de la saison parisienne, le plus significatif aussi, c'est l'invasion des naïfs.» Et, plus loin: «Mais cette fois-ci, force est de reconnaître que nous sommes en présence d'un événement d'une toute autre ampleur. Les coïncidences qui se multiplent, provoquent une situation de fait.»[5]

Cette situation de fait a été pressentie, pourtant, confusément, par quelques-uns. A commencer par les thuriféraires de l'abstraction eux-mêmes pour qui rien que le mot de «réel» fut hier encore plus qu'un épouvantail, une injure, et qui essayent, désormais, de sauver la mise et trichent tant et plus, en douce, tantôt en camouflant ses débris sous l'étiquette de la «Nouvelle Figuration» (vieille escroquerie verbale, puisqu'il existe déjà, à Paris, depuis un bon bout de temps, le salon des «Réalités Nouvelles», voué, précisément, à l'abstraction la plus obtuse); tantôt en proposant un «Art Autre», sinon ce «Nouveau Réalisme», le succédané français du Pop'Art. Seuls les Lettristes poursuivent honnêtement leur quête du «signe» à défaut de la chose signifiée: signe, chant et mirage des temps que nous vivons. On préfère espérer, patienter et attendre quelque miracle: une bouffée d'air frais, si ce n'est un peu de bleu moins gris, moins sale au-dessus des toits, tout en respirant goulûment le benzopyrène des heures de pointe...

Mais c'est encore et toujours Picasso, le véritable sismographe de ces cinquante dernières années, qui a senti le mieux d'où vient le vent, en renonçant soudain à la déformation et à la laideur voulues, béatifiées et érigées depuis en culte par J. Dubuffet, ceci en revenant comme par enchantement à la simplicité et à la fraîcheur, inconnues jusque là chez lui, avec la série de son «Peintre et son modèle». Si c'est par son habituel désir de surprendre et de choquer qu'il a inauguré cette nouvelle manière, il ne pouvait, évidemment, faire mieux: ces tableaux agrestes et plaisants, sensibles et presque trop «jolis», marquent un retour très net à la peinture-peinture, révolutionnent une fois de plus le prêt à porter, et constituent son époque «naïve» par excellence.

Quant à Morandi, le Georges Braque italien, il meurt à 74 ans chez lui, à Bologne, en jetant, qui sait, un dernier coup d'œil sur une gravure représentant un nu de Rembrandt et les dessins du Douanier Rousseau épinglés sur son mur. Ses phares. Un article nécrologique de Marco Walsecchi, paru le 19 juin 1964 dans le journal Il Giorno, le dit non sans courage[6].

Aussi, devant le gouffre qui s'ouvre avec l'explosion d'Hiroshima, ce gouffre qui ne fait que s'approfondir de jour en jour, ce ne sont plus les vétustes fantômes de la vapeur ni les spectres de l'électricité triomphante qui terrorisent l'homme de la seconde moitié du XXe siècle, mais lui-même et son proche avenir. Son ennemi mortel. C'est son propre ennemi qu'est devenu cet homme, un minuscule atome ni plus ni moins, que les savants désintègrent à longueur de journée. De là à la désintégration en chaîne, ce n'est que question de temps. Finira-t-il de sa belle mort, ou périra-t-il dans un cataclysme universel? Dans combien de temps, autrement dit combien de temps lui reste-t-il encore à vivre? Et s'il peut espérer survivre, vivra-t-il toujours ici ou devra-t-il s'expatrier dans d'autres galaxies? Tout est remis en cause; son savoir, ses sentiments, ses amours, ses habitudes, son habitat, ses goûts, ses arts, sa gastronomie et ainsi de suite. On fouille dans son inconscient, on pénètre dans les replis les plus secrets de sa vie intime...

Or, ce n'est plus lui-même qui répond à la plupart de ces interrogatoires, mais ses fondés de pouvoir: les robots électroniques. Les machines cybernétiques calculent à présent

[5] Domus n° 423 (1965).

[6] Una casa semplice, con i mobili ottocenteschi che furono del padre, un estimato di canapa, alcuni quadri antichi di buona firma alle pareti e poche stampe tra cui il nudo di schiena inciso da Rembrandt e i disegni del Doganiere Rousseau.

MIJO KOVAČIČ

pour lui ce qu'il fera, ce qu'il sera demain. La paix et la guerre, la vie et la mort dépendent d'elles. Lui, il ne sait plus. Ce sont elles aussi qui sondent les mystères de l'infiniment petit et de l'infiniment grand, le microcosme et le macrocosme. Le rigide système de Newton ne tient plus; il redevient le désordre des étoiles. Le baiser n'est plus qu'une réaction chimique. La vie, une autre prouesse de la chimie organique. La mémoire? Une protéine. L'individualité, le talent, le génie, une simple loterie des gènes et des chromosomes. La relativité règne partout. La relativité du temps et de l'espace. Bientôt on pourra congeler les vivants et les faire réveiller après quelques lustres de sommeil. Dans quel milieu, sous quel régime, dans quel siècle? Pourquoi pas, alors, dans les années lumière? Que l'on croie ou que l'on ne croie pas au ciel, tout craque, tout casse, rien ne reste debout, rien à quoi l'on pourrait s'accrocher. On ne parle que du passé ou du futur, mais pas du présent. Jamais du présent. L'histoire s'accélère. La terre s'est rétrécie bien plus depuis Cendrars et Paul Morand que depuis Marco Polo. On trouve les mêmes constructions, les mêmes habits et les mêmes films en Alaska et à Tahiti, aux Indes et en Suisse. Le nivellement par le bas. Or le monde s'est agrandi aussi infiniment plus depuis que la dernière «terra incognita» a disparu du planisphère. Les fusées foncent sur la lune. En attendant Mars et Vénus.

Mais ce qui est en haut, n'est plus comme ce qui est en bas. Pythagore s'est trompé, lui aussi. Le haut et le bas, est-ce que cela a, du reste, une signification quelconque lorsqu'on marche, ou plutôt vole en état d'apesanteur? Non, évidemment, et là-haut, ce n'est plus le «Masque aux dents blanches» qui vous guette, mais les soucoupes volantes et le «Péril Bleu».

Chose curieuse, le roman d'anticipation de Maurice Renard qui porte ce titre, a paru, cependant, en même temps que les aventures d'Arsène Lupin, – en même temps que les premiers tableaux abstraits et les premiers «Ready-Made» de Marcel Duchamp, le Pop'Art avant la lettre. Mais les braves justiciers du bon vieux temps ont vécu. Il ne reste plus que la peur, non pas la vieille peur, la peur à fleur de peau, mais une angoisse, une immense angoisse, viscérale, animale, la nostalgie du passé et l'épouvante du demain. Pas de présent, je vous le répète! Pas de stabilité, pas de repos, pas de paix...

Au seuil et à l'échelle de la seconde révolution industrielle en marche, celle qui, en moins de vingt ans, a bouleversé notre vie plus profondément que ne l'ont fait des siècles et des siècles, même dans le domaine des songes, il faut faire du neuf et du raisonnable. Le succès de la «Science-Fiction» et des publications pseudo-scientifiques, genre revue «Planète», n'ont pas d'autre explication. C'est de la marihuana pour les locataires des H.L.M. Une intoxication du même genre que la «Série Noire», ou les disques yé-yé.

Fais-moi peur, veux-tu? Vite! Encore... Plus fort encore... Terriblement!

On aurait pu croire, néanmoins, à un moment donné, que les trouvailles de SFIC pouvaient devenir, à la longue, une nouvelle évasion, un nouveau refuge, une sorte de Post-Surréalisme. Une troisième solution. Ni le miroir intact ni le miroir brisé. Mais tout bonnement une glace sans tain, fondant à volonté, comme dans *«Alice aux pays des merveilles»*.

Une fuite et un nouveau leurre en date, doublé de tous les attraits d'un paradis artificiel.

Las! La Science-Fiction n'offre en tout et pour tout que le même néant: le lavage du cerveau, le décervellage et le dérèglement systématique de tous les sens. L'imagination ne servant qu'à broyer définitivement, ce qui subsiste encore de l'individu ancien – le résidu de l'homme pré-atomique. Nos enfants l'appelleront certainement comme cela, comme nous qui employons le terme de l'homme pré-adamique.

Quoi qu'il en soit, le Pop'Art ne pouvait ignorer cette littérature-là, comme il ne pouvait pas rester en dehors des forces qui la déterminent. Il est parfaitement de son temps; il est sa chair et son essence. Bris de sensations, explosions d'images, vitesse accélérée de la perception, perspectives et échelles renversées, chevauchées démentes d'objets, de visages et d'espaces, tout cela sans aucun lien entre eux et sans autre justification que cette conscience disloquée, vide d'idées, vide de sentiments et ce qui est plus grave, vide d'émotion, «lavée de vie» en quelque sorte, selon l'expression d'un de ses défenseurs, voilà ce qu'est en train de découvrir le Pop'Art. Je dis bien découvrir, car, effectivement, par delà des errements extra-picturaux, il redécouvre enfin l'une des lois primordiales de la peinture; c'est qu'elle se fait au pinceau. Finis les clous rouillés, finis les chiffons, le plâtre et le ciment, finis les grigris des pièces détachées, fétiches pour conjurer les forces d'une nouvelle ère. A l'automatisme, au hasard, à l'accident, à la matière brute, succèdent à nouveau la volonté et le choix. Il redevient de ce fait un art, pas comme cet art «autre», qui n'ose dire son nom, mais un art quand même; un art et une vision qui nécessitent un minimum d'apprentissage et du travail manuel. Pour lutter contre les naïfs, le seul adversaire de taille, le Pop'Art a senti, instinctivement, la nécessité de posséder des armes égales. Egales, vraiment? Bien que très différente de la peinture de papa et de grand papa, la sienne se fait quand même avec les mêmes moyens et elle aborde à nouveau le futur, exactement comme par le passé, la palette à la main. Un mélange de Zen et de la bande dessinée. Un monde devenu puzzle, un monde en pièces détachées. L'homme ne peint plus la machine, mais il devient la machine. C'est pourquoi il imite son langage, ses tics, il reproduit jusqu'à la trame des clichés photographiques, tout comme on copiait autrefois les plâtres des antiques. La machine qui fabrique on ne sait pas trop quoi – le bruit... la terreur. L'hypnose et le nirvanha provoqués par le son d'une banale bille d'argent qui fait «Tilt».

Pourtant, il y a deux mille ans, un autre futur prenait son essor avec deux ou trois images seulement, parfaitement lisibles, parfaitement statiques: le Bon Pasteur – le Poisson du Sauveur – et les pains de l'Eucharistie. «Les idées qui révolutionnent le monde, remarque le féroce F. Nietzsche, marchent au pas de colombe...»

Aujourd'hui, cette colombe-là, ne vole et ne marche plus, crucifiée sur le plafond d'une salle du musée du Louvre. Par G. Braque.

Aussi deux mille ans ont vécu bon gré mal gré sur ces images tout ce qu'il y a de plus humble, avant qu'un autre signe sacré, le poisson, ne rende son ultime espérance, ainsi que son dernier souffle de vie et ne devienne le poisson de ce même G. Braque: sa négation, sa lettre morte, son squelette blanchi à la chaux.

Avant, il contenait toutes les joies et toutes les peines, tous les heurs et tous les malheurs de l'humanité. C'était donc l'un de ces signes, de bons vieux signes comme les comprennent et auxquels aspirent nos Lettristes. Après, ce n'était plus qu'un ornement, un décor, un vain écho du passé. Les abstraits l'ont dynamité. Tant pis si je me répète. Ils ont fait table rase du passé. Pourtant la force vitale d'un signe ou d'une image, n'a rien à voir avec les effets apparents d'une déflagration. Une force contenue est toujours plus efficace que cette même force partie en fumée. La déflagration abstraite est donc un acte; d'où les «dripping», les «actions painting» et autres peintures purement gestuelles. Des actes gratuits. Des mesures pour rien. Un absolu de personne. Un absolu de nulle-part. Et c'est encore le Pop'Art qui recherche (vainement) le sens de cette déflagration. C'est lui qui organise les ruines, les débris. De ce point de vue, le Pop'Art et les naïfs, c'est le commencement et la fin, et vice-versa. Aussi étrange que cela puisse paraître, les naïfs sont plus près du Pop'Art que des abstraits! La machine et l'anti-machine... Le nouveau folklore des gratte-ciel se rencontre avec la survivance de l'ancien, celui des chaumières.

Il a fallu donc se réveiller comme ça, par une aube maussade de l'année zéro, avec un beau cafard après la fête, se réveiller dans une machine ultramoderne à habiter, climatisée, pressurisée déjà, à l'instar d'une cabine spatiale, se réveiller et avoir eu soudain la nausée, en regardant machinalement une tache encadrée sur le mur en guise de peinture, puis un tas de ferraille tordue sur un socle en guise de sculpture, pour essayer de réagir, sinon de réapprendre à penser, du moins se souvenir d'autant plus douloureusement, comme on se réveille parfois sur une table d'opération, en train de chercher un membre amputé, qu'il y avait et qu'il y a quand même autre chose, quelque chose de vrai, de rassurant, de tranquille, de salubre, quelque chose qui ressemble à de la rosée sur une feuille intensément verte, criant de toute sa chlorophylle sa joie de vivre, sa joie de briller, sa joie d'exister, tandis que le soleil se lève peu à peu au loin et vous salue comme il ne salue de la sorte qu'à la sortie d'un hôpital ou d'une prison. Cette feuille et cette rosée au soleil, se confondant à s'y méprendre avec un pauvre tableau naïf aperçu quelque part, la veille, par hasard, votre seule chance et votre dernier salut!...

Ah, ces premières sorties! La vie... La vie qui continue, quoi. Simple comme bonjour!

La peinture naïve, c'est tout bonnement l'anti-chambre de cette vie-là. Et nous n'en aurons pas d'autre. Profitons donc, tant que nous avons encore le temps. Entre le Pop'Art et la peinture naïve, il faut choisir. C'est cela le phénomène naïf. La peinture naïve, c'est bien cela et rien d'autre. Tout le reste n'est que littérature.

Je sais qu'il est fort malaisé d'expliquer pourquoi, au cours des siècles, les arts changent souvent de pays, les pays de muses, pourquoi Melpomène passe la main à Thalie, Thalie à Euterpe, et pourquoi quelques-uns de ces arts, après avoir brillé avec un éclat incomparable de la création la plus neuve et la plus intense, s'éteignent les uns après les autres, ne laissant filtrer qu'une lueur froide, pâle, hautaine, lointaine – chasse gardée des musées. Tels les astres morts dans le temps, mais dont l'espace garde encore quelque trace, quelque fugace empreinte, ils continuent à nous dispenser ce résidu sublime de ce qui reste, de ce qui demeure.

Oui, pourquoi une époque s'exprime-t-elle plus pleinement par la peinture que par l'architecture ou la musique, par exemple; pourquoi ladite peinture élit-elle tantôt l'Italie, tantôt la France, plutôt que l'Espagne ou la Flandre? Pourquoi existe-t-il enfin des pays entiers frappés d'un sommeil léthargique, les empêchant de goûter à l'ivresse de l'inspiration et de la création, tandis que quelques autres s'éveillent brusquement, sans savoir ni pourquoi, ni comment?

En ce qui concerne le XIXe siècle, sinon ce que nous avons déjà vécu du XXe, il est hors de doute que c'est à la France qu'a été dévolu le rôle de meneur de jeu, ce fameux leadership, comme disent les anglo-saxons. Dans la peinture du moins.

Héritière des Vénitiens, des Bolonais, de Rubens et de Goya, c'est elle qui a interrogé le mieux le visible et, ce faisant, a soumis à la question les différentes formes d'expression plastique en usage jusque-là. Tel le serpent de la Bible, c'est elle qui a tendu à l'univers la pomme de Cézanne, le fruit du bien et du mal de la peinture moderne. A la civilisation de l'image dont nous n'avons pas fini, non plus, de goûter tous les bienfaits et tous les méfaits, c'est encore elle qui lui a fait présent de ce troisième œil de verre qu'aucun peuple de l'antiquité n'a connu: la photographie et le cinéma, inventions spécifiquement et cent pour cent françaises.

Or, comme c'est d'une peinture essentiellement révolutionnaire qu'il s'agit, c'est donc inévitablement à travers le paysage français, le visage français et l'objet français que se lit le plus distinctement cette lutte entre le passé et l'avenir, entre ce que le vent emporte chaque jour davantage et ce qui continue à fleurir parmi les ruines, la peinture naïve notamment.

Mais les autres peuples? Les autres pays?

Eh bien, fréquemment, à défaut d'une véritable tradition artistique dont il fallait s'affranchir coûte que coûte, du moment qu'elle devenait stérile, ils passent parfois directement de la pré-histoire à l'histoire tout court, c'est-à-dire d'un amoncellement d'objets et d'images anonymes, qui ne diffèrent pas tant que cela des sculptures et des peintures rupestres, à des œuvres signées, où l'on sent la présence de l'individu. *Du génie grossier, si l'on veut, mais du génie,* selon Maurice Barrès, à des balbutiements personnels, privés, dépourvus d'un seul coup de toute la condensation séculaire; à ce qui, avec un peu de chance, peut devenir une autre sorte de génie. De la tradition, à l'absence totale de la tradition en un mot.

Contrairement à la majorité des pays du monde occidental, qui ont vu se succéder des générations et des générations avant que les gens du peuple accèdent, grâce à ce miroir magique qu'est la peinture, à cet aréopage d'immortels, réservé jusqu'alors aux dieux, aux saints, aux rois et aux grandes courtisanes, il est d'autres pays où cela se fait du jour au lendemain, lorsque l'apparition de la machine transforme radicalement leur mode d'existence. L'étincelle jaillit et l'esclave sans nom, une sorte de bête de somme, devient, en un tournemain, un homme majeur. J'entends d'ailleurs, par la machine, non pas la machine elle-même, mais tout ce qu'elle amène dans son sillage. La ville envahit le village avec sa radio, son cinéma, ses journaux et son vide, l'affreux vide qu'il faut combler coûte que coûte. Crier ou créer, il n'y a pas à sortir de là!

Plus la vitesse à laquelle cette transformation des mœurs s'accomplit est grande, plus le choc est brutal, provoquant des réactions touchant au délire et à la folie. On assiste alors, sur un plan plus élevé, à la naissance de l'expressionnisme (Allemagne, Belgique) ou du futurisme (Italie, Russie). Que nous sommes loin ici du cubisme français si mesuré, exploitant tranquillement, méthodiquement, point par point, la désintégration

JEAN GOURGUE

du tableau-reflet, du tableau-miroir. Les autres bouleversent, incendient, dynamitent, toute la différence est là. Et pendant ce temps-là, la Grande-Bretagne demeure absolument sourde et aveugle: elle a fini sa première révolution industrielle il y a belle lurette. C'est le pays qui compte le plus petit nombre de naïfs.

En Italie, où le divorce, cette rupture entre deux modes de vie survient relativement tard, caractérisés, précisément, par l'explosion anarchique du futurisme, ce n'est que vers la fin de cette guerre-ci que l'on assiste à la montée de ses grands naïfs, authentiques et originaux, assez différents d'ailleurs de tous les autres naïfs. Tous, ils sont plus ou moins touchés par un grain, par un brin de folie, comme s'il n'y avait qu'elle qui pouvait les affranchir du lourd héritage de toutes ces œuvres d'art qui s'accumulent sur son sol. Et encore! C'est justement dans les endroits les plus éloignés, les moins évolués et les plus pauvres en œuvres d'art qu'ils peuvent se réaliser et donner à voir ce qui n'est qu'à eux, à eux seuls: Ligabue, le véritable homme des bois, dans la vallée du Pô; Rovesti et Mozzali, idem; Luigi Pera dans les Abruzzes; Ceccarelli à Spoleto; Luigi de Angelis à Ischia et Carmelina à Capri. Seuls Elena Lissia, Adriano Grande et Alfredo Ruggeri habitent et travaillent à Rome. Est-ce pour cela que ces derniers se différencient sensiblement du reste de leurs compatriotes et se rapprochent plutôt de leurs confrères français?

Le cas d'Elena Lissia est, d'ailleurs, tout à fait particulier. D'abord c'est la seule «Dame» parmi ces gens du peuple, puis les forces qui ont déterminé sa vocation ne sont pas d'origine sociale, mais morale. Au sortir d'une grave maladie, elle est entrée dans la peinture comme on entre en religion. Le résultat est pourtant le même. Comme tous les autres, elle appelle l'arbre mon frère, et la rivière ma sœur. A une trentaine d'années de distance, son cas rappelle et répète le cas de l'Américaine O'Brady. Là encore, tout se tient, et on ne peut que s'étonner de l'ignorance crasse de ces scribouillards venus à la peinture naïve sur le tard, pour qui la peinture naïve italienne se limite toujours au sempiternel Metelli!

Au fait, qui fut le premier naïf Italien?

Est-ce ce berger adolescent de Giotto qui, avant que Cimabue ne guide sa main, s'essayait déjà, de son mieux, à saisir le mouvement et la grâce des volumes de ses chèvres gambadant quelque part, aux environs de Vespignano, parmi les collines verdoyantes de la Toscane, ponctuées de cyprès?

Est-ce ces premiers chrétiens anonymes, auxquels il faut revenir sans arrêt, qui traçaient à la lueur d'une lampe à huile, dans les catacombes de San Callisto, ce poisson émeraude, tout raide encore d'espérance et de vie?

Est-ce enfin ce brave cordonnier de Terni, Orneore Metelli, qui vers 1922, la cinquantaine passée, las de recevoir des récompenses et des médailles d'or et d'argent pour les modèles de ses chaussures et ne pouvant plus jouer du trombone dans l'orphéon municipal, à cause de sa maladie de cœur, s'est senti possédé par le démon de la peinture dont il ne se délivrera que seize ans plus tard, le jour de sa mort?

Qu'importe! Ce qui compte et ce qui est autrement important, c'est qu'ici, sur cette terre habitée autrefois par les dieux, gorgée, toute saturée encore de leurs empreintes, plus d'un homme a pris sous un soleil implacable, ennemi du mensonge, des nouvelles mesures du réel, ceci selon son cœur, en toute simplicité, en toute spontanéité et en toute franchise, absolument en dehors de ce qui a été fait et codifié avant lui, bien que cet enseignement à ciel ouvert, présent partout, en raison même de la prolifération des chefs-d'œuvre, constitue justement le plus grand obstacle, et à la venue, et à la découverte des naïfs du terroir. De sorte que même dans maint et maint tableau qui traîne à La Porta Portese – les fameuses «Puces» romaines – fait visiblement par quelqu'un qui ne savait pas peindre et qui aurait dû être, par conséquent, naïf, on retrouve quand même çà et là quelques fioritures connues, quelque joliesse apprise, acquise plutôt comme ça, sans le savoir, ce qui dénote avant tout la puissance de ce Bel Canto pictural infus contre lequel on ne peut rien. Ce sont des œuvres à la manière de, ni plus ni moins... Ou, alors, on retombe carrément, dans l'art populaire à proprement parler, ce qui n'est jamais la même chose. Longtemps, à l'exemple de Montesquieu qui se demandait comment peut-on être persan, on pouvait se demander, avec raison, comment pouvait-on être italien et naïf...

Maintenant, c'est fait, les Fioretti refleurissent en Italie, comme partout ailleurs, la grande Saga des naïfs est en train de se conter sous nos yeux. Mais elle n'est pas faite pour les yeux secs.

Un autre exemple typique et frappant de ce passage de la ligne, de cette mutation le plus souvent inattendue, lorsque, sur un terreau épuisé définitivement, semble-t-il, de l'art populaire, surgissent sans crier gare quelques peintres indiscutablement naïfs, créant par eux-mêmes et pour eux-mêmes, nous est fourni par l'Amérique latine en général et les Antilles et les Caraïbes en particulier; j'ai nommé Haïti, la République Dominicaine et Cuba.

En effet, si la plupart des grands pays, tels que l'Argentine, évoluant lentement, harmonieusement, n'ont pas été le théâtre d'un choc brutal entre les deux mondes et n'ont pas suscité par là l'apparition de ces inévitables peintres-témoins, pour qui, également, sonne à ce moment crucial *el momento de verdad,* l'heure de la vérité, consistant soit à abdiquer, c'est-à-dire à s'effacer, tout en s'adaptant progressivement à un nouvel état des choses, soit à clamer, au contraire, leur propre droit à la beauté, à une beauté insolite, certes, jamais vue, avec toute la candeur et toute la vigueur des forces jeunes et neuves, inemployées jusque là, à l'exception, au pis aller, de cet émigré espagnol, Casimir Domingo, pas tout a fait un vrai naïf, mais que l'on pourrait rattacher à la rigueur à cette branche ou tendance visionnaire que nous appellerions, faute de mieux, *spirite,* bref celle des Crépin, des Scottie Wilson, des Grauben de Monte Lima, des Isabel Jesus, et des Vandersteen, et qui a trouvé récemment une nouvelle recrue de marque en la personne d'Anselme Boix-Vives, à mi-chemin en quelque sorte entre l'art brut, la broderie inspirée, ou tout simplement l'*Insania Pingens,* ou l'art des malades mentaux; si d'autre part, l'art naïf du Brésil demeure jusqu'à l'heure qu'il est le domaine presqu'exclusivement réservé aux femmes, tandis qu'un pays comme le Pérou n'a donné naissance qu'à un Indien de grande classe, Urteaga, le Guatemala à un autre Indien, Andres Curuchich, le Honduras à Vélasquez, et le Chili à Herrera Guevara, auteur de Cosmopolis et autres villes imaginaires, à qui ont peut adjoindre un Fortunato San Martin, et au besoin Violeta Parra, chanteuse, tapissière et peintre naïf à ses heures; si, enfin, l'Uruguay, avec Horatio Espondabura, Hilario Ferrer Aruffe et Carlos Gonzalès, de même que l'Equateur, avec Diogenes Paredes, versent plutôt dans un folklore rénové, actualisé, exprimé par d'autres moyens, soit, mais folklore quand même, à base du pittoresque ou du populisme – le nom importe peu! – préfiguré dès le début de ce siècle par un graveur mexicain, José Guadalupe Posada, à tous les points semblable à celui qui va être inventé plus tard, le savoir faire en plus, par l'un de ses compatriotes, Diego de Rivera, semblable aussi à celui que pratiquent plusieurs peintres de l'Europe Centrale, le Yougoslave Brašič entre autres, puisque ce retour à la terre et aux forces vives du peuple a été déjà prôné là-bas à partir de la première après-guerre par l'homologue de Rivera, Krsto Hegedušič, peintre nullement naïf mais que d'aucuns, connaissant mal la question, rangent sans vergogne parmi les naïfs, cette situation, donc, laissant franchement à désirer, évolue considérablement et change complètement dès que l'on se tourne vers les îles du tropic du Cancer, ces îles qui nous submergent littéralement par la quantité et la qualité de leurs naïfs.

Déjà, quand en 1947, l'UNESCO a présenté pour la première fois à Paris une sélection des peintres plus ou moins naïfs de l'Equateur, du Pérou et d'Haïti, ces derniers dominaient très nettement.

Mais que tout devient difficile, pour ne pas dire impossible, dès que l'on aborde cette partie du globe, la confusion entre le foklore et la peinture des naïfs mise à part!

Les indications précises manquent. Les dates et les lieux de naissance sont incertains ou inconnus. Les photographies, que ce soit des tableaux, ou de leurs auteurs, demeurent introuvables. Quant aux lettres, elles restent dans la plupart des cas sans réponse. Même les organismes officiels, le Musée de São-Paulo entre autres, pour ne pas le nommer, ne se donnent pas la peine de fournir les renseignements désirés. Les ambassades, les services culturels sont muets. Ce qui explique, à mon grand regret, l'absence de fiches signalétiques complètes pour un certain nombre de peintres de l'hémisphère Sud, ce qui les fait un peu jurer à cause de cela, à côté de tous les autres peintres de tous les autres pays.

D'ailleurs, ce n'est que grâce à l'aide précieuse, apportée in extremis par MM. José Pedro Argul de Montévidéo, Thiago de Melo de Santiago de Chili et Mora, artiste peintre dominicain, que j'ai pu réunir le peu de documentation sur ce continent. Je leur exprime, à tous les trois, ma très sincère gratitude.

Or, ce qui s'est passé à Haïti, entre Cuba et Porto Rico, confirme une fois de plus, si besoin était, que l'éclosion, puis la floraison de l'art naïf n'est pas un phénomène fortuit, mais qu'il obéit à certaines lois et exige une conjoncture économique spéciale. Le pays en question a beau être prêt, afin d'accomplir ce saut décisif en avant, il ne se produit pourtant qu'à l'aide d'un catalyseur intérieur ou extérieur: la révolution sociale (Yougoslavie, Cuba), ou bien la mainmise de personnes intéressées (USA, le Maroc, et quelques pays de l'Europe Occidentale). A Haïti, ce catalyseur s'appelle De Witt Peters, arrivé là-bas, en tant que professeur d'anglais, en 1943.

Voyons quand même de plus près les pièces du dossier.

En 1938, un livre écrit par un nommé Herskowitz, dont le titre exact est: «Life in Haithien Valley», constate l'extinction quasi-totale de l'art populaire indigène, quoique riche et vivace dans le temps. «L'absence de manifestations graphiques et plastiques dans l'art haïtien... le refoulement de ces formes essentielles de la tradition africaine, donne l'impression que le peuple haïtien a perdu un important débouché pour ses tensions intérieures» ... Que s'est-il alors passé? En si peu de temps?

Il a suffi, ni plus ni moins, que ce professeur tombât tout à fait par hasard, au cours de ses déplacements, sur une curieuse auberge à Mont-Rouis, située entre Saint-Marc et Port-au-Prince, qui portait comme enseigne: *Ici la Renaissance*. Titre prophétique, ou peu s'en faut. Son propriétaire, Hector Hyppolite, ancien peintre en bâtiment et prêtre d'un rite Vaudou à l'occasion[7] l'avait décorée, en effet, d'une façon non moins étrange. Le choc que ces décorations ont produit sur le professeur, bien qu'elles ne sortissent pas tellement de la veine traditionnelle populaire, fut tel que, sans perdre un instant, il se mit à la recherche des œuvres et des décorations similaires, en parcourant dès lors en long et en large le pays.

Après avoir repêché deux ou trois vétérans, pas si nombreux que cela, à commencer par Philomé Obin, né en 1891 à Cap Haïtien, autodidacte ayant fait à peu près tous les métiers, coiffeur, employé, marchand de café et ne peignant que par intermittence, à ses moments perdus, le professeur pensa donc, à juste raison, qu'en initiant des jeunes noirs à la peinture, il obtiendrait à coup sûr des résultats semblables, sinon des plus intéressants.

Ce qui fut fait. Un an plus tard, le Centre d'Art de Port-au-Prince ouvrait ses portes. A dire la vérité, De Witt Peters ne procurait pas uniquement à ces noirs de quoi peindre, il leur donnait aussi de quoi vivre, car leurs œuvres, une fois terminées prenaient le chemin de l'étranger, où elles étaient revendues aux amateurs. A la clientèle américaine de préférence. Privée de naïfs français du fait de la guerre, et les aimant vraiment d'amour, elle se contentait provisoirement de ces naïfs exotiques, ainsi que de sa grandma Moses, découverte à peu près en même temps.

Le résultat ne se fit pas attendre. Extraordinaire. Vraiment stupéfiant. Toute une pléiade de jeunes peintres naïfs (sans oublier le sculpteur Georges Liautard, qui, de simple forgeron et mécanicien de village, né en 1899 à Croix-de-Bouquets, devenait, toujours grâce à De Witt Peters un artiste particulièrement expressif et original), se formait ainsi peu à peu, rivalisant de trouvailles et de talents. Même Philomé Obin, conseillé intelligemment par lui, passait presque sans transition de son «Intercession», peinte encore dans le genre conventionnel d'ex-voto, à des compositions épiques monumentales, remarquablement personnelles, narrant tantôt «Les funérailles de Charlemagne Piralte», tantôt «L'arrivée du Président Roosevelt au Cap Haïtien». Les espérances les plus optimistes, les rêves les plus fous de De Witt Peters étaient dépassés, Haïti, par la volonté d'un seul homme, renouvelait le miracle yougoslave.

Mais il y a mieux. Lorsqu'on a construit, en 1950, la nouvelle église épiscopale de la capitale, ses fresques ont été exécutées en majorité par des peintres naïfs: Philomé Obin, Rigaud Benoît, Louverture Poisson et Toussaint Auguste, pour ne citer que ceux-là, y ont pris part. C'est certainement le seul et unique

[7] Voici comment il explique, par exemple, ses rapports avec la Déesse de l'Eau: «Vous savez que j'ai épousé mon Esprit Gardien, c'est pourquoi je ne puis me marier à personne d'autre. J'étais encore enfant lorsque mon grand-père, un célèbre prêtre Voudou, me maria à la Sirène et, depuis lors, elle est restée mon épouse mystique. Mais j'ai trois maîtresses, ce qui n'est pas beaucoup, car habituellement j'en ai sept. Ces derniers temps, j'en ai toutefois assez des femmes. Elles se créent tout le temps des difficultés et j'ai donc décidé de m'en tenir à trois. Elles s'entendent bien et elles ne sont pas jalouses. Pourquoi le seraient-elles d'ailleurs?»

MARIO URTEAGA

monument de ce genre qui existe de par le monde! Il peut figurer dignement, à cause de ces fresques, et à côté du palais du facteur Cheval, et à côté de la maison en assiettes cassées de Raymond Isidore à Chartres. Petit à petit, une bonne vingtaine de noms de peintres naïfs haïtiens faisait ainsi son entrée sur la scène artistique, se faisait connaître et accédait à la notoriété, principalement aux Etats-Unis...

Parmi eux, il faut mentionner de préférence, en commençant par les plus âgés: Rigaud Benoît, ex-cordonnier et chauffeur de taxi (né en 1914); Louverture Poisson, auteur d'«Adam et Eve» et du «Crime passionnel» (né en 1914); Maurice Borno (né en 1917); J. B. Bottex (né en 1919); Abelard, mécanicien (né en 1922); Préfete Duffaut (né en 1923); Castera Bazile, illettré; Dieudonné Cédor (né en 1925); Léon Aynant (né en 1929); Enguerrand Gourgues, spécialisé dans les scènes de magie blanche et noire (né en 1930); Wilson Bigaud (né en 1931); etc...

La même chose pour Cuba.

Là encore, si à la veille de l'avènement de Fidel Castro il n'y avait pour ainsi dire qu'un seul et unique peintre naïf, Félicindo Iglesias y Acevedo, un espagnol de surcroît, né en 1898 à Orense (Galicie), établi seulement depuis 1933 dans l'île comme négociant en vins et épices, l'éclosion et la prolifération de nouveaux talents ne s'y fit pas attendre non plus, et pour cause: s'inspirant du Maréchal Tito, du moins en ce qui concerne sa politique des Beaux-Arts, le nouveau chef du gouvernement cubain a réellement donné la parole au peuple. Des jeunes femmes et des jeunes gens se mirent alors à peindre et à s'exprimer librement, avec toute la fantaisie, la fraîcheur et le sens de la couleur qui caractérisent ce peuple. Isabel Castellanos, Alberto Anido, Irmina Gonzalez, Lourdes Fernandez, Angel Fernandez, Angel Hernandez, Armando Blanco, Benjamin et Angel Duarte, Gonzalez Puig, Alfonso Reyes, Horatio Leyva, José Ramón Comabella – jamais je ne pourrai les nommer toutes et tous! Des «macheteros» et des mécanographes, des paysans et des dactylos, des receveurs d'autobus et des confectionneuses de cigares, parmi lesquels se détache tout particulièrement Luis Romero, un coupeur de canne à sucre authentique, et auxquels il faudrait ajouter, peut-être, Samuel Feijoo, peintre et écrivain, à qui on doit le premier document important sur cette nouvelle rage de peindre[8].

Ici, à propos de Samuel Feijoo, il faut que j'ouvre une parenthèse. Comment définit-on le vrai naïf? En quoi se distingue-t-il des faux naïfs? Où finit la naïveté et où commence le procédé? Passe encore pour les faussaires qui «font du naïf» intentionnellement, tout en sachant peindre autrement. Toujours est-il que pour l'un d'eux, qui signe d'un nom imaginaire, spécialisé auparavant dans les faux Corot et les faux Sisley, le métier du faux naïf se révéla plus rentable. Mais tous ceux qui peignent avec sincérité, se rapprochant par plus d'un côté des naïfs, tout en les dépassant par leur science? Les écarter n'est pas juste, les assimiler n'est pas facile, et le critère de ne pas savoir peindre ne suffit pas toujours. D'autant plus que certains naïfs, de vrais naïfs au départ, acquièrent peu à peu ces connaissances qui les font basculer de l'autre côté. Le cas de Jean Eve, de Rimbert et de Caillaud sont trop connus pour y insister. Sont-ils encore naïfs, ou ne le sont-ils plus? Cette question est difficile à trancher. La frontière est floue, par trop imprécise. Trop menue et trop délicate, puisque les pour et les contre s'y mêlent étroitement. Disons donc que Samuel Feijoo appartient à cette catégorie des plus ou moins naïfs, qui compte pas mal de représentants dans les différents pays du vieux et du nouveau monde: Madeleine Luka, Caly, Gaston Chaissac, Véronique Filozof, Quilici, Maclet, Maïck, R. Tattin, J. Jokvin, J. Milet et Fred Zeller en France; Breviglieri, A. Incerti, Cesetti et Donghi en Italie; Stanley Spencer et L. S. Lowry en Angleterre; Carolus Paepen, Bockstael et S. Dufoing en Belgique, Sidney Nolan en Australie, Euridyce au Brésil et j'en passe.

Pour moi, et pour éviter les confusions, qui ne peuvent être que préjudiciables aux vrais naïfs, ils ne le sont pas. Déjà les peintres tels que le Hongrois Csontvary et le Russe, naturalisé tchèque, G. Moussatoff se situent vraiment à la limite. Je ne mets pas leur bonne foi en doute, seulement ils auraient pu peindre autrement s'ils le voulaient, tandis que les vrais naïfs ne peuvent faire que ce qu'ils font. Les autres ne sont que des intimistes, des tendres, des maniéristes, des fantaisistes qui me font penser à ce qu'écrivait au XVIIe siècle Théophile de Viau:

Je veux faire des vers qui ne soient pas contraints
Promener mon esprit par des petits desseins
Chercher des lieux secrets où rien ne me déplaise
Méditer à loisir, rêver tout à mon aise
Employer tout une heure à me mirer dans l'eau
Ouir, comme en songeant, la course d'un ruisseau
Ecrire dans les bois, m'interrompre, me taire
Composer un quatrain sans songer à le faire. *(Poétique)*

Les œuvres de ces semi-naïfs relèvent nécessairement de ces mêmes impondérables, qu'on les appelle le goût ou le talent, c'est-à-dire la justesse et la finesse d'une émotion, ou bien de cette gaucherie inimitable de la main qui ne se mesure pas au nombre des carats, mais à la pureté de l'eau d'une pierre précieuse, sinon à la particularité de son clivage. Car même parmi les vrais naïfs, tous ne sont pas égaux: il y a ceux qui ont plus de talent que les autres. Quant aux faussaires, vous trouverez leurs noms dans d'autres ouvrages, pas dans le mien.

La seule exception à cette règle qui veut qu'il y ait drame et rupture, et que le style et la façon de s'exprimer des naïfs sortent des sentiers battus, nous est donné par les Etats-Unis, pays tout aussi vieux que la France en tant que générateur des peintres naïfs, mais dont l'évolution suit une route parallèle, sans être ni identique, ni tout à fait différente pour cela.

Comme l'art populaire n'y existait pour ainsi dire pas – pas plus que l'art officiel ou un enseignement quelconque – l'art qui sourd instinctivement des couches populaires les plus variées est, dès son origine, qui remonte à la fin du XVIIIe siècle, d'essence naturellement naïve, maix ceux qui le pratiquent ne sont ni en rupture de ban, ni le produit d'un cataclysme social quelconque; non, ils l'exercent tranquillement, sereinement, presqu'en semi-professionnels, en artisans sans en être. En devançant parfois leurs compagnons et leurs frères d'armes de France. Ils n'ont pas connu évidemment ni leurs tourments, ni la misère, ni les écueils d'une existence bien plus dangereuse que les escarmouches avec les Indiens du Far-West. Ils n'avaient qu'à suivre de ranch en ranch, de ferme en ferme, de plantation en plantation, de manufacture en manufacture, la lente mais implacable pénétration des pionniers, et tout en étant leurs portraitistes ambulants, coopérer à la domestication de cet immense continent.

Ces Américains glorifiaient donc l'individu et faisaient passer

[8] Pittores y dibujantes populares de la Villas, Universidad de Las Villas, ed. Santa Clara (Cuba) 1962.

à la postérité des hommes neufs, les futurs fondateurs des dynasties d'argent: les couches montantes. De ce point de vue, ils sont beaucoup plus près de Holbein, de Clouet, ou même d'Ingres, que des portraitistes courants du XVIIIe siècle, dont ils s'inspiraient, tandis que les peintres européens, tels que le Georgien Pirosman ou le Grec Théophilos, sont encore en plein dans ce siècle des fêtes galantes, kermesses paysannes en l'occurrence, ne fixant que les images du passé, des moments d'une vie rurale, heureuse et endimanchée, mais révolue et prête à s'éteindre. Au lieu d'être maudits, au contraire, les naïfs américains étaient utiles. On les recherchait, comme on recherchait les plombiers et les menuisiers.

Dans quel but? Mais pour satisfaire ce besoin inné du beau et du vrai; répondre à cette vieille et inextinguible quête de l'immortalité. Toutes et tous y passaient, en effet: des bébés joufflus, des juges sévères, des épouses desséchées et frigides, des vieillards dignes et verts. Quelle édition magnifique pourrait-on faire des romans de Faulkner, en les accompagnant, en guise d'illustration, des reproductions de tous ces tableaux!

Ils ne manquent pas; d'ailleurs. Ces portraits fourmillent dans les collections américaines telles que «American Paintings» de la M. et M. Karolik Collection au musée des Beaux-Arts de Boston; «American Primitive Art», au musée des Beaux-Arts de Houston; «American Primitive Paintings» de la collection de E.W. et Bernice Chrysler Garbish à la Galerie Nationale de Washington, et l'imcomparable «Folk Art Collection» de Abby Aldrich Rockefeller au «Colonial Williamsburg» de Virginie.

Puis, de temps à autre, c'est un fermier ou un trappeur, ému par le spectacle de la nature, aussi bien que par le résultat de son propre labeur, qui se risque, en tout bien tout honneur, à brosser quelque tableautin frais et pur. Cette terre promise ne devenait-elle pas la leur pour de bon? Riche, belle, juste, libre, et déjà si «moderne»! Il y avait de quoi être fiers...

Une vieille demoiselle aussi, qui s'essaye à quelque jolie nature morte. Une mère, qui fixe les portraits de ses bambins. Une veuve, qui se recueille sur l'image des tombes de ceux et de celles qui lui sont chers. D'autres et d'autres encore, qui peignent une réunion de famille, des moissons, des enterrements, des parcs publics, des scènes mythologiques, ou inspirées par la Bible; un bateau à roues... un train qui passe...

Leur langage ne diffère guère du langage de tous les autres naïfs de l'ancien continent, pour la forme, du moins: un même amour du détail, une même application et un même désir d'aller jusqu'au bout les unit. Sauf que certains s'affranchissent déjà peu à peu de la maladresse native et acquièrent quelques rudiments du métier, se caractérisant par une extraordinaire ressemblance quasi-photographique, qui les apparentent un peu à nos non ou semi-naïfs. On n'a qu'à relire les vers de Théophile de Viau pour comprendre que le vagabondage sentimental et le flirt avec la nature s'accommodent fort bien avec le savoir ou le non savoir à peindre.

Blaise Cendrars, le défenseur attitré de la peinture d'avant-garde des années quatorze, ne souhaita-t-il pas, dans les dernières années de sa vie, écœuré par ce qu'elle est devenue: *Je voudrais qu'il n'y ait que les peintres du dimanche et que durant cent ans on nous fiche la paix avec les autres qui encombrent les cimaises des musées, des collectionneurs et des marchands. Après cent ans de ce régime d'aimable fantaisie, d'amateurisme et de rêverie devant la nature, la peinture connaîtra peut-être un renouveau.*

Mais revenons à nos naïfs cubains.

Aussi, la production naïve cubaine diffère-t-elle sensiblement de celle d'Haïti. D'abord par le choix des sujets. Chez eux, c'est l'imagination qui domine. Le fantastique, pour ne pas dire le magique, prend le pas sur le réel. Le style et l'écriture s'en ressentent, bien sûr, oscillant entre Picasso et Wilfredo Lam (natif de l'île) du côté des non-naïfs, et entre Chaissac et Dubuffet du côté de l'art brut. Des lignes s'enchevêtrent, se lovent, touffues, imprécises et nocturnes, non pas pour fixer ce qui est devant leurs yeux, mais comme pour saisir l'invisible. Il n'empêche que, si du point de vue strictement formel ces œuvres se rapprocheraient plutôt de l'écriture automatique et tant soit peu médiumnique, dont il était question à propos de l'Argentin Casimir Domingo, que de l'imagerie ordinaire, plus terre à terre de tous les autres naïfs quels qu'ils soient, elles valent quand même mille fois mieux que l'art brut. Elles relèvent de l'art, tandis que la plupart des œuvres de l'art brut, où le mot art est souvent de trop, relèvent du cautère psychique ou de l'exorcisme plastique. De l'auto-défoulement, dans tous les cas, où la notion même du beau est absente.

Une seconde parenthèse s'impose de toute évidence. Ne pas savoir peindre, ne veut pas dire mal peindre. L'ignorance ne signifie pas laideur. Un cri, aussi douloureux et aussi émouvant qu'il soit, ne contient pas nécessairement une émotion esthétique. Pour aussi intéressantes et aussi révélatrices qu'elles soient pour les chercheurs, les savants, les psychologues et les psychiatres, les œuvres des malades mentaux qui constituent que l'on veuille ou non la base même de l'art brut, ceci en tant que chapelle inventée par Jean Dubuffet, afin de servir de tremplin à ses propres conceptions et activités artistiques, sont dépourvues, généralement, de l'émotion créatrice et manquent totalement de qualités plastiques. Toutes ces pauvres Psyché malades, tous ces délires mentaux et toutes ces images mutilées et meurtries, d'une rare indigence plastique, paraissent, hélas, comme des embryons dans une éprouvette, ou un lièvre à deux têtes dans un bocal rempli d'alcool, à côté des œuvres des artistes cubains qui, eux, font de l'art. De l'art et non une succursale sophistiquée du Musée Dupuytren que l'analphabétisme d'une certaine presse et le snobisme d'un certain public ont fait passer pour ce qu'il n'est pas. Jamais la confusion n'a autant régné que ces dernières années! Un Schröder Sonnenstern, qui figure souvent parmi les naïfs (à Rotterdam, notamment, et au Musée d'Art Moderne de Paris) n'est pas plus naïf qu'une Aloyse, ou un Clovis Trouille.

Alors, ce brin de folie des naïfs cubains, viendrait-il des alizés ou de quelques gouttes de sang espagnol? Bien malin qui saurait y répondre; qui le prouverait ou le contredirait d'une façon précise; pas moi. La question n'est pas là, d'ailleurs. Folie ou pas, cette imagination débordante des peintres cubains témoigne avant tout d'un immense, intact trésor de facultés créatrices, et qui sait ce que l'avenir nous réserve. Tout est désormais possible. Même la venue de grands, de très grands peintres à l'égal de Rousseau et d'O'Brady. Qu'ils peignent donc tous et toutes tranquillement! Il serait vraiment dommage qu'en craignant de voir naître un barbouilleur de plus, on laisse assassiner dans l'œuf quelque beau peintre naïf qui s'ignore. L'histoire de la peinture naïve est jonchée malheureusement de ces morts-nés.

La même chose pour la République Dominicaine.

La même chose se répète encore, bien que sur une moindre

CAILLAUD

échelle, au Maroc, où, après un silence total de plusieurs siècles, trois bons peintres naïfs surgissent coup sur coup: Ahmed Louardiri ou El Ouardiri, né en 1920 à Salé; Mohamed Ben Allal, né en 1924 à Marrakech et Mouly Ahmed Drissi né, lui aussi, en 1924, dans les environs de cette dernière ville. Tous les trois ont passé par l'école coranique qui interdit, cependant, les images. Tous les trois sont pauvres (Ben Allal est né sous la tente des nomades), et pour tous les trois la genèse de leur art se situe à ce moment décisif où ils rencontrent la civilisation. Pour Ben Allal, domestique chez un peintre français connu, la réaction était, cela se comprend, plus immédiate, plus normale. Quoi qu'il en soit, tous les trois se sont dit à un moment donné: et pourquoi pas moi? Tous, ils ont vu et connu des tas de choses qui les ont éblouis, tous ils avaient accumulé des visions et des rêves qui ne demandaient qu'à être fixés sur un bout de toile. Le bonheur... Toujours les fantômes du bonheur! Des troupeaux et des verts pâturages. De l'eau vive dans le désert...

Le plus spécifiquement arabe et le plus doué aussi des trois, Louardiri, chante tout un passé de sa race, et il conte, conte, conte, un peu à la façon de sa consœur Schéhérazade, jusqu'à ce que le ton monte et sa voix se mue insensiblement en une sorte de mélopée qui embrasse pêle-mêle le jasmin et les jets d'eau, la lune et le rossignol, le bleu et le rose qui font l'amour, le velours de la nuit profonde et les dalles fraîches des allées, caressant si délicieusement les pieds nus après une journée chaude nord-africaine, puis ces massifs de fleurs, ces plages d'ombres et de couleurs, où, à la place des rosiers de Saadi, surgissent des jouvencelles aux yeux de gazelle, tandis que par les arcs lancéolés, trilobes ou outrepassés des minarets et des palais (je m'excuse, mais ce sont les termes architecturaux exacts), les mille ans de légendes et de féérie musulmanes l'écoutent attentivement, émerveillés à leur tour.

Qu'importe donc si les images empiètent parfois les unes sur les autres et si une insigne maladresse perce par endroits: la flamme de la passion brûle et emporte toutes les imperfections de la syntaxe et de la grammaire. Qu'importe aussi, tant pis, si ce beau rêve a été payé au prix d'une vie médiocre, monotone, sans oublier quelque malheur présent ou passé, planté comme une écharde dans son cœur, qui sait?

Et cette paysanne d'Appenzell, Sibylle Neff qui, le cœur serré, voyant s'éteindre autour d'elle les uns après les autres, les derniers peintres paysans suisses, se met à improviser les mêmes scènes, refaire les mêmes sujets et faire revivre, mais déjà *autrement*, le décor quotidien de la vie de son pays?

Et ce modeste artisan brésilien de l'état de Pernambouc, Inocencio da Costa Nick, dit Mestre Noza, qui, lui aussi, transgresse la vieille imagerie religieuse des «santeiros», sculpte et grave des planches et des planches où revit tout le mysticisme et tout le fanatisme de cette province-là? [9]

Et ce Flamand, ancien boucher de son état, Van den Driessche qui, la soixantaine passée, s'adonne tout d'un coup à la peinture et devient une sorte de James Ensor à l'état brut? Personne depuis les Brueghel et Jérôme Bosch, n'a su exprimer avec autant de verve le fond même de la vie flamande: l'un savamment, l'autre sans le savoir...

Et ces adolescents de la banlieue du Caire, réunis par Ramses Wissa Wassef, qui tissent des tapisseries des mille et une nuits, des vrais tapis volants?

Et ce bouillonnement, enfin, en plein cœur de la Ruhr, à Recklinghausen, où l'on essaye d'établir une coexistence pacifigure de la main et de la machine? Ce Hans Koehn, ce Karl Kazmierczak, ce Karl Hertmann, ce Peter Paul Hubert Schmitz, ce Werner Plümer, ce E. Bödecker et ce F. Gerlach qui dit: «Ce qui m'intéresse, c'est que, en peignant, je contribue ainsi quelque peu au développement du destin des hommes et de leur planète»?

Qui dit mieux?

Plus on se penche sur les naïfs, plus on se rend compte que cette voie étroite qui mène à leur art est partout et toujours la même.

Du Nord au Sud, de l'Est à l'Ouest, de l'océan au désert, de la montagne à la plaine, des champs aux usines et des chaumières aux villes-champignons, des cœurs souffrent, des cœurs saignent, des cœurs se rebellent au point de devenir des *cœurs sacrés*. Des mirages naissent. On jette des bouteilles à la mer avec des messages de survie. Des bouées de sauvetage flottent ainsi un moment sur les lieux mêmes du naufrage. Ce sont les peintres du Bon Dieu, m'a dit récemment, en parlant d'eux, le journaliste catholique Joseph Pichard. Il leur réserve immanquablement une place de choix dans le Salon de l'Art Sacré, dont il est l'animateur. Les peintres du Bon Dieu, comme les coccinelles, l'insecte au dessin on ne peut plus naïf...

Mais qui dit Dieu, dit aussitôt diable. Les tentations ne manquent pas, non plus. Les tourments, les égarements, les séductions, les chimères de toutes sortes. C'est de cette lutte, si franche, si bouleversante, pour le maintien de la dignité de la personne humaine qu'est né l'art naïf.

Une thèse de doctorat ès graphologie, soutenue par Mme A. M. Angeli (sous presse), le prouve amplement. Sur les soixante écritures de peintres naïfs qu'elle a étudiées, il n'y en a pas une qui ne porte quelque secrète blessure. Toutes, elles sont l'expression d'hommes tourmentés, des femmes en révolte contre la vie. Toutes elles portent les traces indélébiles des Paradis Perdus, des Paradis Retrouvés grâce à leur art. Qui donc, après cette preuve irréfutable, scientifique cette fois, pourra prétendre à la gratuité de leur art? Qui pourra continuer à les prendre pour des quantités négligeables? Qui pourra oser qualifier leur art de passe-temps?

Il serait temps, je crois, qu'au lieu de parler et de tourner ainsi autour d'eux, de leur laisser tout simplement la parole. Et comment aurais-je pu terminer autrement, en effet, cette étude sur les naïfs, puisque ce n'est que le commencement de quelque chose qui évolue et se développe sans cesse tous les jours?

[9] Via Sacra, gravada por Mestre Noza, Robert Morel, éd. (1965).

EMIL WHITE

Lexicon

Lexikon

Lexique

Van den Abeele, Albijn

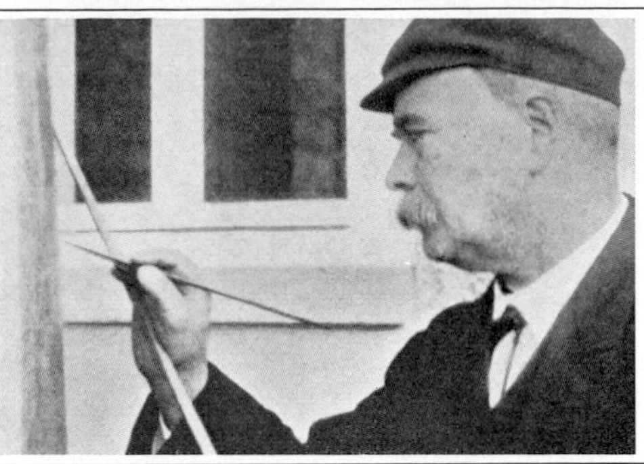

Born August 27, 1835 in Laethem Saint-Martin (Belgium).
Died December 22, 1918 in Laethem Saint-Martin (Belgium).

Geboren am 27. August 1835 in Laethem Saint-Martin (Belgien).
Gestorben am 22. Dezember 1918 in Laethem Saint-Martin (Belgien).

Né le 27 août 1835 à Laethem Saint-Martin (Belgique).
Mort le 22 décembre 1918 à Laethem Saint-Martin (Belgique).

Born in this Flemish area on the river Lys a few miles from Ghent, he could not help befriending the two generations of artists and writers who made this village famous. At one time he was burgomaster, later he became communal secretary. Up to the age of forty he was known only as a local historian and as the author of rather idyllic novels. It was only about 1875 that he too was seized by the urge to paint. His works, some of which can be seen in the art galleries of Deynze and Ghent, are imbued with their own bucolic poetry—touching, honest, meticulous. In short, he is a self-taught artist who had seen and recognized true painting.

Es war nicht anders möglich, als daß ein Sohn dieses flämischen Barbizon, das ein paar Kilometer von Gent entfernt an der Lys liegt, mit zwei Generationen von Malern und Schriftstellern befreundet war, die den Namen seines Dorfs berühmt gemacht haben. Er hatte zuerst das Amt des Bürgermeisters inne, dann das des Gemeindesekretärs. Bis zum Alter von 40 Jahren ist er nur als Lokalhistoriker und Verfasser ziemlich idyllischer Romane bekannt. Erst gegen das Jahr 1875 ergriff der Malteufel auch von ihm Besitz. Seine Bilder, von denen sich einige in den Museen von Deynze und Gent befinden, tragen alle den Stempel einer aufrichtigen, sorgfältigen, rührend bukolischen Poesie. Alles in allem handelt es sich hier um einen Autodidakten, der echte Malerei gesehen und gekannt hat.

Enfant de ce Barbizon flamand, situé sur la Lys, à quelques kilomètres de Gand, il ne put être qu'ami de deux générations de peintres et d'écrivains qui ont rendu célèbre le nom de son village. Il y remplit d'abord les fonctions de bourgmestre, puis de secrétaire communal. Jusqu'à l'âge de 40 ans, il n'est connu que comme historien local et auteur de romans plutôt idylliques. Ce n'est donc que vers 1875 qu'il fut saisi à son tour par le démon de la peinture. Ses œuvres, dont certaines figurent aux musées de Deynze et de Gand, sont empreintes d'une même poésie bucolique, touchante, probe et méticuleuse. Somme toute, c'est un autodidacte qui a vu et qui a connu la vraie peinture.

EXPOSITIONS:
«Les Peintres Naïfs», Knokke-le-Zoute 1958.
«Peintres Naïfs Belges», Théâtre National de Bruxelles 1965; Musée Royal des Beaux-Arts, Verviers 1965; Musée royal des Beaux-Arts, Hasselt 1966.

BIBLIOGRAPHIE:
A. de Ridder: «Lathem Saint-Martin», Editions Lumière, Bruxelles 1945.
«Hugo van den Abeele», Latemse Kunstenaars, Gand 1958.
Anatole Jakovsky: «Eros du Dimanche», Editions J.J. Pauvert, Paris 1964.

Abelard, Gessner

Born 1922 in Haiti.

Geboren 1922 in Haiti.

Né en 1922 à Haïti.

A mechanic. Learned to draw and paint in the Technical School of Port-au-Prince; then, in 1948, he started to attend the famous 'Art Centre' which had been founded in 1944 by De Witt Peters. This marked a turning point not only in his career but in his whole life. He became an artist. A full-time artist. Most of all he paints traditional rural scenes and decorative composition, which are very much in the early manner of Hector Hyppolite.

Mechaniker. Lernt in einem Technikum in Port-au-Prince zeichnen und malen. 1948 tritt er in das berühmte «Kunstzentrum» ein, das 1944 von De Witt Peters gegründet wurde. Dieser Schritt bestimmt sowohl seine Laufbahn als auch sein Leben im allgemeinen. Er wird Maler. Ausschließlich Maler. Er malt hauptsächlich folkloristische Szenen und dekorative Kompositionen, die von den allerersten Bildern von Hector Hyppolite beeinflußt sind.

Mécanicien. Apprend à dessiner et à peindre dans une Ecole Technique de Port-au-Prince, puis, en 1948, entre dans le fameux «Centre d'Art», fondé en 1944 par De Witt Peters, ce qui décide aussi bien de sa carrière que de sa vie en général. Il devient peintre. Peintre uniquement. Il peint surtout des scènes folkloriques et des compositions décoratives qui dérivent des tout premiers Hector Hyppolite.

EXPOSITIONS:
«La Peinture Naïve», Knokke-le-Zoute 1958.
«19 Peintres d'Haïti», Palais des Beaux-Arts, Bruxelles 1963.

BIBLIOGRAPHIE:
Selden Rodman: «Renaissance in Haiti», Pellegrini & Cudahy, New York (sans date).
Oto Bihalji-Merin: «Das naïve Bild der Welt», Köln 1959.
Oto Bihalji-Merin: «Die naïve Malerei», Köln 1959.
Oto Bihalji-Merin: «Les Peintres Naïfs», Paris (sans date).

Acevedo, Felicindo y

Born 1898 in Orense (Spain).

Geboren 1898 in Orense (Spanien).

Né en 1898 à Orense (Espagne).

Spent his childhood in France and was educated in a Roman Catholic school. About 1930 he immigrated to Cuba, where he became an importer and wholesaler of wine and groceries. Is a citizen of Cuba – in fact Cuba's first 'naive' artist; he took up painting in 1939. He is also a musician, playing and singing in a church in Havana, where he now lives. Frequently he finds inspiration for his work in historical and religious subjects. He has taken part in many collective exhibitions: in New York, São Paulo, Moscow, and elsewhere.

Er verbringt seine Kindheit in Frankreich und empfängt in einer katholischen Schule eine religiöse Erziehung. Um 1930 gelangt er nach Kuba, wo er ein Einfuhr- und Großhandelsgeschäft in Wein und Kolonialwaren gründet. Kubanischer Staatsangehöriger und erster naiver Maler Kubas, denn er beginnt schon 1939 zu malen. Er ist auch Musiker und singt und spielt in einer Kirche von Havanna, wo er von nun an lebt. Er gestaltet oft historische und religiöse Themen. Hat an zahlreichen Gruppenausstellungen in New York, São Paulo, Moskau usw. teilgenommen.

Il passe son enfance en France et reçoit une éducation religieuse dans une école catholique. Arrive vers 1930 à Cuba où il devient importateur et grossiste en vin et épicerie. Citoyen cubain et premier peintre cubain naïf, car il commence à peindre en 1939. Il est aussi musicien, joue et chante dans une église à la Havane qu'il habite désormais. Son art s'inspire souvent de sujets historiques et religieux. A participé à de nombreuses expositions collectives à New York, São Paulo, Moscou, etc.

EXPOSITIONS:
«La Peinture Naïve», Knokke-le-Zoute 1958.

BIBLIOGRAPHIE:
Oto Bihalji-Merin: «Das naive Bild der Welt», Köln 1959.
Oto Bihalji-Merin: «Die naive Malerei», Köln 1959.
Oto Bihalji-Merin: «Les Peintres Naïfs», Paris (sans date).

Adamoff, Hélène

Born March 21, 1906 in Moscow (Russia).

Geboren am 21. März 1906 in Moskau (Rußland).

Née le 21 mars 1906 à Moscou (Russie).

Arrived in Paris in 1921 and first of all lived the normal unobtrusive life of so many Russian emigrants. It was not until 1954, when her son was just completing his studies, that she began to realize that all she had seen and experienced was worthy of being preserved, and so she tried to express herself in painting. Her first pictures are full of the charm and color of Russian popular art. However, this decorative and diligent aspect quickly disappeared from her painting and then she created real works of art—rich, sonorous, filled with color. Her snow scenes, whether Russian or not, are quite remarkable.

Kommt 1921 nach Paris und führt zuerst das zurückgezogene Leben so vieler russischer Emigranten. Erst 1954, als ihr Sohn dabei ist, seine Studien abzuschließen, wird sie sich allmählich bewußt, daß alles, was sie gesehen und erlebt hat, wert ist, festgehalten zu werden. Nun versucht sie sich in der Malerei auszudrücken. Man findet übrigens in ihren ersten Bildern den ganzen Zauber und alle Farben der russischen Volkskunst. Aber dieser dekorative, beflissene Aspekt verschwindet rasch, und es entstehen Bilder, wahre Bilder, reich, wohlklingend, farbenfroh. Ihre Schneelandschaften sind, ob russisch oder nicht, sehr bedeutend.

Arrive à Paris en 1921 et mène d'abord la vie effacée de tant d'émigrés russes. Ce n'est que vers 1954, lorsque son fils était en train de finir ses études, qu'elle se rend peu à peu compte que tout ce qu'elle a vu et vécu mérite d'être fixé, et tente donc de se réaliser par la peinture. On retrouve d'ailleurs dans ses premiers tableaux tout le charme et tous les coloris de l'art populaire russe. Mais ce côté décoratif et appliqué disparaît rapidement, et ce sont des tableaux, de vrais tableaux, riches, sonores, hauts en couleur. Ses paysages de neige, russes ou pas, sont absolument remarquables.

EXPOSITIONS:
Galerie du Haut Pavé, Paris 1956.
Galerie Romi, Paris 1959. (Préface Romi.)
«Les Primitifs d'Aujourd'hui»,
Galerie Charpentier, Paris 1964.

Albertine

(real name: Albertine Bernadette Grouëc)
Born April 13, 1896 in Cayennes-de-Saurais, Deux-Sèvres (France).

(mit ihrem richtigen Namen Albertine Bernadette Grouëc)
Geboren am 13. April 1896 in Cayennes-de-Saurais, Deux-Sèvres (Frankreich).

(de son vrai nom: Albertine Bernadette Grouëc)
Née le 13 avril 1896 aux Cayennes-de-Saurais Deux-Sèvres (France).

Housekeeper for the artist and illustrator Edy-Legrand. Began to paint quite by chance, using the scraps of paint left over from her employer's palette. Great sensitivity for color. Definitely a poetic imagination. Some of her compositions, especially the large flower groups, remind one of a sort of unrefined Chagall.

Putzfrau oder vielmehr Haushälterin bei dem Maler und Illustrator Edy-Legrand. Beginnt ganz zufällig zu malen, wobei sie die Reste von der Palette ihres Brotherrn benützt. Sehr empfindsamer Farbensinn. Eine unbestreitbar poetische Phantasie. Manche ihrer Kompositionen, insbesondere die großen Blumensträuße, gemahnen an eine Art Chagall im Rohzustand.

Femme de ménage, ou plutôt gouvernante chez le peintre et illustrateur Edy-Legrand. Commence à peindre tout à fait par hasard en utilisant les déchets de la palette de ce dernier. Grande sensibilité de la couleur. Une imagination poétique incontestable. Certaines de ses compositions, les grands bouquets notamment, font penser à une espèce de Chagall à l'état brut.

BIBLIOGRAPHIE:

Anatole Jakovsky: «Eros du Dimanche», Paris 1964.

Alexandrine

(Alexandrine Kelder, née Gortmans)
Born July 31, 1903 in Djakarta (Java).

(Alexandrine Kelder, geborene Gortmans)
Geboren am 31. Juli 1903 in Djakarta (Java).

(Alexandrine Kelder, née Gortmans)
Née le 31 juillet 1903 à Djocjakarta (Java).

Born in the heart of a tropical, luxuriant environment and forced to leave it behind in early adolescence, this natural painter has always retained, subconsciously, nostalgic memories of the landscape of Java as if it were a thorn pricking her heart. But life is stronger than dreams, especially at The Hague where she lived—she raised her children and married them off before she began painting. But when she did start, her work was a revelation immediately, both for others and for herself. She is the greatest—by far!—Dutch 'naive' artist.

Diese geborene Malerin, die im Schoß einer üppigen tropischen Natur zur Welt kommt und gezwungen ist, diese Umgebung schon in der Jugend zu verlassen, bewahrt unbewußt stets eine lebendige Erinnerung daran, gleichsam einen Stachel im Herzen. Aber das Leben ist stärker als die Träume, vor allem in Den Haag, wo sie wohnt. So zieht sie denn zuerst ihre Kinder auf, verheiratet sie und beginnt erst dann zu malen. Es ist sogleich eine Offenbarung, sowohl für die andern wie für sie selber. Sie ist bei weitem der größte naive Maler Hollands.

Née au sein d'une nature tropicale, exubérante, et obligée de la quitter dès son adolescence, ce peintre-né, à son insu, en gardera toujours un souvenir ému, telle une écharde plantée à l'endroit de son cœur. Mais la vie est plus forte que les rêves, surtout à La Haye où elle habite; elle élève donc d'abord ses enfants, puis les marie avant de commencer à peindre. Et c'est une révélation aussitôt, aussi bien pour les autres que pour elle-même. C'est le plus grand – et de loin! – peintre naïf hollandais.

EXPOSITIONS:
Galerie M. Bénézit, Paris 1964
(Cat., Préface Anatole Jakovsky).
« Primitifs d'Aujourd'hui », Galerie Charpentier, Paris 1964.
Galerie M. Bénézit, Paris 1966.

BIBLIOGRAPHIE:
Anatole Jakovsky: « Eros du Dimanche », 1964.
« Alexandrine ». Petit Crapooillot, Paris, Novembre 1964.
Jardin des Arts, N° 130, Sept. 1965, Editions J.Tallandier, Paris 1965.

INTERVIEW:
à la Télévision Française, Octobre 1954.

Allegretti, Ferdinando

Born March 11, 1908 in Pesaro, Marches (Italy).

Geboren am 11. März 1908 in Pesaro, Marches (Italien).

Né le 11 mars 1908 à Pesaro, Marches (Italie).

At the age of 7 moved to Terni, the Metelli country, where his father gained employment at the blast-furnaces. He too began work early—at the age of 14 he started at the steelworks. In 1942 was deported to Germany and was not repatriated until the end of the war, by the International Red Cross. Began to paint after he had retired. His work is still a little set and awkward, but is not without charm. Entirely authentic.

Kommt im Alter von 7 Jahren nach Terni, Metellis Heimatstadt, denn sein Vater findet hier Arbeit in den Hochöfen. Er selber beginnt mit 14 Jahren in den Stahlwerken zu arbeiten. 1942 wird er nach Deutschland deportiert und erst nach Kriegsende vom Internationalen Roten Kreuz heimgeschafft. Fängt nach seiner Pensionierung zu malen an. Noch etwas steife, ungeschickte Malerei, doch nicht ohne Reiz. Echt.

Arrive à Terni, patrie de Metelli, car son père venait de s'y embaucher dans les hauts-fourneaux, à l'âge de 7 ans. A son tour, dès l'âge de 14 ans, commence à travailler dans les aciéries. En 1942, déporté en Allemagne et rapatrié seulement à la fin de la guerre par la Croix Rouge Internationale. Se met à peindre après avoir pris sa retraite. Peinture encore un peu figée, malhabile, mais non sans charme. Authentique.

EXPOSITIONS:
Bottega d'Arte Bazzi, Terni 1964.
«I Pittori Naifs», Rome 1964.
«I Pittori Naifs», Centro Internazionale di Arte Figurative, Biella 1964.

BIBLIOGRAPHIE:
«Art Naïf», Editions Marocaines et internationales, Rabat 1964.

De Angelis, Luigi

Born August 5, 1883 in Rome (Italy).
Died October 21, 1965 in Ischia (Italy).

Geboren am 5. August 1883 in Rom (Italien).
Gestorben am 21. Oktober 1965 in Ischia (Italien).

Né le 5 août 1883 à Rome (Italie).
Mort le 21 octobre 1965 à Ischia (Italie).

This artist, nicknamed 'Il barbiere d'Ischia' because he had a man's hairdressing salon there, and called 'Gigi' by his close friends, may be considered as one of the first Italian 'naive' artists, since the beginning of his painting dates back to 1920—he tells of this in a touching autobiographical story. His artistic career and the rapidity with which he became successful did not lead him to give up his profession, and he reigned in his salon, surrounded by his children and grandchildren, until only a few days before his death. His pictures are delicately colored, full of subtle shading, almost as if burned by the island's violent sun; they have appeared in exhibitions all over the world. And it was artists and writers who made him famous.

Dieser Maler, der «Il barbiere d'Ischia» genannt wird, weil er dort einen Friseurladen innehatte, «Gigi», wie ihn die Freunde nannten, kann als einer der ersten naiven Maler Italiens betrachtet werden, denn seine Anfänge gehen ins Jahr 1920 zurück, wie er selber in einer rührenden autobiographischen Erzählung berichtet. Seine Laufbahn als Maler und der sehr rasche Erfolg, mit dem sie gekrönt wurde, haben ihn nicht dazu veranlaßt, seinen eigentlichen Beruf aufzugeben. Von seinen Kindern und Kindeskindern umgeben, thronte er noch bis in seine letzten Lebenstage in seinem Salon. Seine Bilder mit den verhaltenen, nuancenreichen Farben, gleichsam verbrannt von der Heftigkeit der Sonne seiner Insel, sind auf der ganzen Welt ausgestellt worden. Maler und Schriftsteller haben ihn bekannt gemacht.

Ce peintre, surnommé «Il barbiere d'Ischia», parce qu'il y tenait un salon de coiffeur, et «Gigi» tout court pour les intimes, peut être considéré comme l'un des premiers peintres naïfs italiens, puisque ses débuts remontent vers 1920, comme il le raconte lui-même dans un touchant récit auto-biographique. Sa carrière de peintre et le succès très rapide dont elle a été couronnée, ne lui ont pas fait, pourtant, abandonner son vrai métier, où il trônait encore jusqu'à ses derniers jours, entouré de ses enfants et de ses petits-enfants. Ses peintures aux tons discrets, tout en nuances, comme brûlées par la violence du soleil de son île, ont été exposées dans le monde entier. Et ce sont les peintres et les écrivains qui l'on fait connaître.

EXPOSITIONS:
Galeria Bragaglia, Rome 1926.
Galerie Pierre, Paris 1926.
Galerie Foster et Newpart, Paris 1928.
«Montra di Pittura Popolare»,
Palazzo delle Esposizioni, Rome 1955.
Galeria d'arte Cairola, Milan 1955
(Cat., Préface Vasco Pratolini).
«Ente provinciale per il turismo», Terni 1962.
(Cat., Préface Aurelio de Felici et Ilario Ciaurro.)
«I Pittori Naifs», Rome 1964.

BIBLIOGRAPHIE:
Paolo Ricci: «Luigi de Angelis», Unità, Rome 26 octobre 1965.
Catalogo Bolaffi d'Arte Moderna 1965/66, Turin 1966.

Arcambot, Jean Pierre Albert Marius

Born May 27, 1914 in Braux, Basses-Alpes (France).

Geboren am 27. Mai 1914 in Braux, Basses-Alpes (Frankreich).

Né le 27 mai 1914 à Braux, Basses-Alpes (France).

Son of a farmer who died for his country. Works on the Paris métro. In fact, it was in one of the métro company's annual exhibitions (in 1948) that his works were noticed. His paintings themselves, which he creates with great care and which aim at reflecting reality as closely as possible, tend more and more towards what in 1925 was called 'die neue Sachlichkeit' or the New Objectivity. He generally participates in collective exhibitions.

Mündel der Nation. Sohn eines für Frankreich gefallenen Bauern. Ist Angestellter der Pariser Untergrundbahn. In einer der jährlichen von diesem Betrieb veranstalteten Ausstellungen wurden seine Werke übrigens zum ersten Mal beachtet (1948). Seine Bilder, die mit viel Sorgfalt gemalt sind und auf eine möglichst getreue Darstellung der Wirklichkeit abzielen, nähern sich mehr und mehr dem, was man um 1925 «die neue Sachlichkeit» nannte. Nimmt vor allem an Gruppenausstellungen teil.

Pupille de la Nation. Fils d'un cultivateur mort pour la France. Travaille dans le Métro parisien. C'est d'ailleurs dans un des salons annuels de cette Régie que ses œuvres ont été remarquées (1948). Quant à ses tableaux, exécutés avec beaucoup de soin et qui visent à la transcription la plus fidèle de la réalité, ils se rapprochent de plus en plus de ce qu'on appelait, vers 1925, «Die neue Sachlichkeit». Participe surtout à des expositions collectives.

EXPOSITIONS:
«Les Primitifs d'Aujourd'hui», Galerie Charpentier, Paris 1964.

BIBLIOGRAPHIE:
«Dix Ans d'Art Actuel», Editions Comparaisons, Paris 1964.

Astarita, Ugo

Born September 1, 1904 in Capri (Italy).
Died December 1964 in Capri (Italy).

Geboren am 1. September 1904 in Capri (Italien).
Gestorben im Dezember 1964 in Capri (Italien).

Né le 1 septembre 1904 à Capri (Italie).
Mort en décembre 1964 à Capri (Italie).

A baker first of all, then a general handyman in a snack shop. Began to paint in 1931 and had some success, since the Bragaglia gallery in Rome exhibited his work. But in 1935 he was overcome by a wave of mysticism; the Virgin Mary appeared before him, in full daylight.
So he stopped painting entirely. He did not begin again until 1960, and only then perhaps because of the ever-increasing success of Carmelina, who also came from Capri although was not known to him. His second group of paintings stands out, to some extent, in contrast to all the other 'naive' pictures by an inner radiance and a visionary quality.

Bäcker. Dann «Mädchen für alles» bei einem Händler von Gebratenem. Fängt 1931 an zu malen. Hat Erfolg, da die Galerie Bragaglia ihn in Rom ausstellt. Aber 1935 wird er von einer mystischen Krise heimgesucht; die Jungfrau Maria erscheint ihm am heiterhellen Tag. Da hört er völlig auf zu malen. Erst 1960 fängt er wieder an, vielleicht angespornt durch den ständig wachsenden Erfolg seiner Landsmännin Carmelina, die er übrigens nicht kennt. Seine neuen Bilder unterscheiden sich ein wenig von allen anderen Naiven durch ihr inneres Licht und jene «visionäre» Seite, die nicht trügt.

Boulanger. Puis homme à tout faire chez un marchand de frites. Commence à peindre en 1931. Obtient du succès, puisque la galerie Bragaglia l'expose à Rome. Mais une crise mystique le terrasse à partir de 1935; la Vierge lui apparaît en plein jour. Alors il cesse complètement de peindre. Il ne recommence qu'en 1960, peut-être à cause de la réussite sans cesse grandissante de sa «payse» Carmelina qu'il ne connaît d'ailleurs pas. Ses nouveaux tableaux tranchent un peu sur tous les autres naïfs par leur lumière intérieure et ce côté «visionnaire» qui ne trompe pas.

Bagur, Miguel Rivera

Born January 30, 1919 in Alcudia, Majorca, Balearic Islands (Spain).

Geboren am 30. Januar 1919 in Alcudia, Mallorca, Balearen (Spanien).

Né le 30 janvier 1919 à Alcudia, Mallorca, Baléares (Espagne).

At one time a policeman. Was discovered as an artist by the painter Miró, who was immediately enchanted by the unusual poetic feeling shown in his pictures. Whether the pictures are of landscapes or scenes with people, they are all pervaded by a gentle, warming radiance. A fine talent which is not yet exhausted.

Ehemaliger Gendarm. Er wurde durch den Maler Miró entdeckt, den der außergewöhnliche poetische Sinn seiner Bilder gefangen nahm. Ob Landschaften oder figürliche Szenen, alle seine Werke sind von einem milden, warmen Licht umspielt. Sehr schöne Begabung, von der man noch viel erwarten darf.

Ancien gendarme. Il a été découvert par le peintre Miró, séduit d'emblée par le sens poétique rare que dégagent ses tableaux. Que ce soient des paysages, ou des scènes avec des personnages, toutes ses œuvres sont auréolées par une douce et chaude lumière. Très beau talent qui n'a pas dit son dernier mot.

EXPOSITIONS:
Galerie Danus, Palma de Mallorca 1954.
Galerie Danus, Palma de Mallorca 1955.
Galerie Gralla, Palma de Mallorca 1959.
Circulo de Belles Artes, Palma de Mallorca 1960.
Club de los Poetas, Formentor 1960.
Galerie Schütze, Bad Godesberg 1962 (Cat., Préface Camilo José Cela).
Club de los Poetas, Formentor 1962 (Cat., Préface Camilo José Cela).

BIBLIOGRAPHIE:
Gabriel Cortes: «Miguel Bagur», Diario de Mallorca 29 octobre 1959.
Gafim: «Miguel Bagur», Baléares, 6 novembre 1959.
A. Cirici-Pellicer: «Miguel Bagur», Serra d'or, 1 juillet 1960.

Bauchant, André

Born April 24, 1873 in Châteaurenault, Indre et Loire (France).
Died August 12, 1958 in Montoire, Loir-et-Cher (France).

Geboren am 24. April 1873 in Châteaurenault, Indre-et-Loire (Frankreich).
Gestorben am 12. August 1958 in Montoire, Loir-et-Cher (Frankreich).

Né le 24 avril 1873 à Châteaurenault, Indre-et-Loire (France).
Mort le 12 août 1958 à Montoire, Loir-et-Cher (France).

A nursery gardener by profession. It was chance which made him, fairly late in life, take up painting. During the first world war he was engaged in telemetric drawings. An officer, impressed by the accuracy of his strokes, advised him to take up drawing—and this advice did not fall on deaf ears. Ever since his youth he had been attracted to art through his reading (books on history and mythology, for which he later drew illustrations), and he became passionately interested in painting. His first exhibition was in 1921 at the Salon d'Automne, where Le Corbusier and Ozenfant—at that time running the magazine 'L'Esprit Nouveau'—noticed his work and became the first to buy his pictures. He was launched. His works began to sell, and continued selling up to his death. A shrewd, wily and very miserly peasant, he even did series of paintings, which sold the best. Thus, following his monumental works and his fine, slightly medieval landscapes of the Touraine district, there came only very small pictures—good or bad according to his inspiration or skill. He is one of the two 'naive' artists who have been decorated with the Legion of Honour. His work is therefore, although inconsistent, very voluminous. He is probably the most prolific 'naive' painter.

Baumzüchter. Ein Zufall entscheidet über seine ziemlich späte Berufung. Während des Ersten Weltkriegs ist er mit telemetrischen Geländeaufnahmen beauftragt, und ein Offizier, dem die Genauigkeit und Richtigkeit seines Strichs auffallen, rät ihm, das Zeichnen nicht aufzugeben. Dieses Wort fällt auf fruchtbaren Boden. In seiner Jugend hatte er gern gelesen (Bücher über Geschichte und Mythologie, deren Illustrationen er später auf seine Weise interpretieren sollte) und nun begeistert er sich für die Malerei. Im Salon d'Automne 1921 stellt er zum ersten Mal aus, wo Le Corbusier und Ozenfant, die damals die Zeitschrift L'Esprit Nouveau herausgaben, ihn bemerken und sogleich seine Bilder kaufen. Der Anstoß ist gegeben. Nun verkauft er stetig bis zu seinem Tod. Als schlauer, gerissener, sehr geiziger Bauer malt er sogar Serien, denn das verkauft sich am besten. Nach seinen monumentalen Bildern und seinen schönen, etwas mittelalterlichen Landschaften aus der Touraine malt er so nur noch ganz kleine Bildchen, gute oder schlechte, je nach seiner Inspiration oder der Laune seines Pinsels. Er ist der eine der beiden naiven Maler, die mit der Ehrenlegion ausgezeichnet wurden. Sein Werk ist ziemlich ungleichmäßig, aber sehr umfangreich. Er ist wahrscheinlich der Maler, der am meisten produziert hat.

Pépiniériste. C'est encore un hasard qui a décidé de sa vocation assez tardive. Chargé de relevés télémetriques du terrain pendant la première guerre mondiale, un officier, surpris par la justesse de son trait, lui conseille de persévérer dans le dessin. Ce qui ne tombe pas dans l'oreille d'un sourd. Déjà, attiré par la lecture, au temps de sa jeunesse (livres d'histoire et de mythologie, dont il interprétera, plus tard, les illustrations), il se passionne désormais pour la peinture. Il expose pour la première fois au Salon d'Automne en 1921 où Le Corbusier et Ozenfant, qui dirigeaient alors la revue L'Esprit Nouveau le remarquent et deviennent aussitôt ses premiers acheteurs. Il est lancé. Il vend et continuera à vendre jusqu'à sa mort. Paysan fin, roublard et très avare, il peindra même en série, ce qui se vend le mieux. Ainsi, après ses pièces monumentales et ses beaux paysages, un peu médievaux de la Touraine, il ne fera plus que de tout petits tableaux, bons ou mauvais, c'est selon son inspiration, sinon disponibilité de sa main. Il est parmi les deux peintres naïfs à avoir été décoré de la Légion d'Honneur. Son œuvre est donc assez inégale, mais très importante. Il est, probablement, celui qui a produit le plus.

EXPOSITIONS:
Galerie Jeanne Bucher, Paris 1927.
Galerie Becker, New York 1931.
« Les Maîtres Populaires de la Réalité », Paris 1937.
« Les Maîtres Populaires de la Réalité », Zürich 1937.
« Masters of Popular Painting », New York 1938.
« Masters of Popular Painting », Arthur Tooth & Sons, Londres 1938.
Galerie Reid et Lefèvre, Londres 1938.
« Moderne Primitieven », Stedelijke Museum, Amsterdam 1941 (Cat., Préface D.C.R.).
Galerie Berri-Raspail, Paris 1941 (Cat., Préface Maximilien Gauthier).
Galerie de Berri, Paris 1946.
Palais des Beaux-Arts, Bruxelles 1949 (Cat., Préface W. Georges).
« Moderne primitive Maler », Kunsthalle, Bern 1949 (Cat., Préface Arnold Rüdlinger).
Galerie Charpentier, Paris 1949 (Cat., Préface Le Corbusier et Maximilien Gauthier).
Stedelijk Museum, Amsterdam 1949 (Cat., Préface non signée).
Galerie Charpentier, Paris 1951 (Cat., Préface Maximilien Gauthier).
« Maler des einfältigen Herzens », Museum am Ostwall, Dortmund 1952.
« Les Peintres Naïfs », Knokke-le-Zoute 1958.
« Les Peintres Naïfs », Maison de la Pensée Française, Paris 1960.
Galerie Bignou, Paris 1959.
Galerie M. Bénézit, Paris 1959.
Musée des Beaux-Arts, Tours 1960 (Cat., Préface B. Lossky et extraits de presse).
« Laienmaler », Gewerbemuseum, Basel 1961.
« Das naive Bild der Welt », Baden-Baden 1961.
« Les Peintres Naïfs », Arthur Tooth & Sons, Londres 1963 (Cat., Préface non signée).
Galerie Nichido, Tokyo 1964 (Cat. important en japonais).
« I Pittori Naifs », Rome 1964.
« Die Welt der naiven Malerei », Salzburg 1964.
« Primitifs d'Aujourd'hui », Galerie Charpentier, Paris 1964.
« De Lusthof der Naieven », Rotterdam 1964.
« Le Monde des Naïfs », Paris 1964.
Galerie Percier, Paris 1965.

BIBLIOGRAPHIE:

De Fayet: « Bauchant-Jeune », L'Esprit Nouveau, Paris juin 1922.
Maximilien Gauthier: « Bauchant », Ed. du Chêne, Paris 1943.
W. Uhde: « Cinq Maîtres Primitifs », Ed. Palmes, Paris 1949.
« André Bauchant », Du, N° 2, Zürich février 1951.
« André Bauchant », Graphis N° 101.
Anatole Jakovsky: « La Peinture Naïve », Paris
Anatole Jakovsky: « Les Peintres Naïfs », Paris
Anatole Jakovsky: « Naive Malerei », Zürich 1957.
Bernard Jasmand et Otto Kallir: « Sonntagsmaler », Ed. Otto Aug. Ehlers, Berlin/Darmstadt 1956.
« André Bauchant », Graphis N° 101, mai–juin 1958.
P. Courthion: « André Bauchant », L'Œil, No. 46, octobre 1958.
« André Bauchant », Du, N° 2, février 1952.
Oto Bihalji-Merin: « Das naive Bild der Welt », Köln 1959.
Oto Bihalji-Merin: « Die naive Malerei », Köln.
Oto Bihalji-Merin: « Les Peintres Naïfs », Paris (sans date).
« André Bauchant », Jardin des Arts, numéro spécial consacré aux naïfs, Paris, juin 1961.
Anatole Jakovsky: « Eros du Dimanche », Paris.
« Art Naïf », Editions Marocaines et Internationales, Rabat 1964.
Catalogo Bolaffi d'Arte Moderna, Turin 1965/66.

DÉCORS:
Apollon Musagète, Ballets russes de S. de Diaghilev, Paris 1927.

FILMS:
« Violons d'Ingres », court métrage réalisé par J.B. Brunius et G. Labrousse, Paris 1939.

ILLUSTRATIONS:
« Les Simples », vus par Violette; Ed. Jeanne Bucher, Paris 1937.
12 planches en couleurs. Tirage de 1100 exemplaires num.

Baya

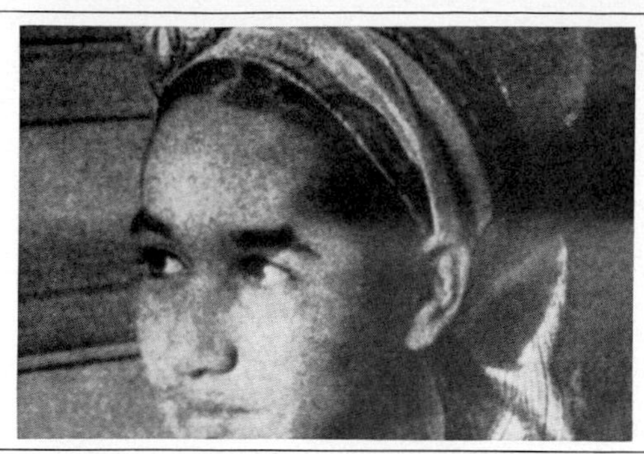

Born December 1931 near Algiers (Algeria).

Geboren Dezember 1931 in der Umgebung von Algier (Algerien).

Née en décembre 1931 dans les environs d'Alger (Algérie).

Has Arabic and Kabyle blood. She was orphaned at the age of 5 and was looked after by a certain 'Marguerite' who took her to live in her own home in Algiers, and also taught her to paint and model in clay without influencing her at all. Nor did her exhibition in Paris affect her. After attempting to do pottery work in Vallauris, at Picasso's recommendation, she returned home and married into a family bound by tradition. Then there was silence—a silence that lasted fourteen years! It is only in the course of the last year that Baya has taken up painting again.

Arabisches und kabylisches Blut. Mit fünf Jahren wird sie Waise und findet Aufnahme bei einer gewissen «Marguerite», die sie mit sich nach Algier nimmt und ihr dort Malen und Modellieren beibringt, ohne sie indessen irgendwie zu beeinflussen. Auch ihre Ausstellung in Paris hat keinen Einfluß auf sie. Nachdem sie auf Picassos Rat versucht hat, sich in Vallauris als Töpferin zu betätigen, kehrt sie in ihre Heimat zurück und heiratet in eine traditionsgebundene Familie ein. Und nun herrscht Schweigen. Vierzehn Jahre lang Schweigen! Erst im Verlauf des letzten Jahres hat Baya wieder angefangen zu malen.

Sang arabe et kabyle. Orpheline à 5 ans, elle est recueuillie par une certaine «Marguerite» qui l'emmène vivre, chez elle, à Alger, où elle lui apprend à peindre et à modeler. Sans l'influencer, toutefois, d'aucune sorte. Son exposition à Paris ne l'influence pas, non plus. Après avoir essayé à faire de la poterie à Vallauris, sur recommandation de Picasso, elle rentre chez elle et se marie dans une famille traditionnelle. Et c'est le silence. Un silence de 14 ans! Ce n'est qu'au cours de la dernière année que Baya s'est remise à peindre.

EXPOSITIONS:
Galerie Maeght, Paris 1947 (Cat., Préface André Breton et Emile Dermenghem).
Musée des Beaux-Arts, Alger 1963.

BIBLIOGRAPHIE:
«Art Naïf», Editions Marocaines et Internationales, Rabat 1964.

Bazile, Castera

Born November 26, 1928 in Jacmel (Haiti).

Geboren am 26. November 1928 in Jacmel (Haiti).

Né le 26 novembre 1928 à Jacmel (Haïti).

His first pictures were executed around 1945. He, like Abelard, attended the recently founded Art Centre in Port-au-Prince. Was awarded the first prize at Alcoa in 1955, at the general Painting Competition of the Caribbean, and later won the $ 1,000 prize offered by the American magazine 'Holiday'. Has a fresco in Port-au-Prince cathedral.

Erste Bilder um 1945. Besucht ebenfalls das Kunstzentrum von Port-au-Prince, das eben gegründet worden war. 1955 erster Preis von Alcoa im allgemeinen Kunstwettbewerb der Karibischen Inseln; dann gewinnt er auch den von der amerikanischen Zeitschrift « Holiday » ausgesetzten 1000-Dollar-Preis. Freske in der Kathedrale von Port-au-Prince.

Premières peintures vers 1945. Passe, lui aussi, par Le Centre d'Art à Port-au-Prince qui venait de se fonder. Grand Prix en 1955 à Alcoa, au Concours Artistique général des Caraïbes, puis le prix de 1000 Dollars offert par le magazine américain « Holiday ». Fresque à la Cathédrale de Port-au-Prince.

EXPOSITIONS:
« Peintures de l'Equateur, de Haïti et de Pérou », l'UNESCO, Paris 1947.
« Das naive Bild der Welt », Baden-Baden 1961.
« 19 Peintres d'Haïti », Palais des Beaux Arts, Bruxelles 1963.
« 20th Century Latin American Naive Art », La Jolla (USA) 1964.

BIBLIOGRAPHIE:
Selden Rodman: « Renaissance in Haïti », Pelegrini & Cudahy, New York (sans date).

Becker do Vale, Rosina

Born April 4, 1914 in the state of Guanabara (Brazil).

Geboren am 4. April 1914 im Staat Guanabara (Brasilien).

Née le 4 avril 1914 dans l'état de Guanabara (Brésil).

She is another of the artists who at first attended the free classes on art given by the Museum of Modern Art in Rio de Janeiro. However, she freed herself fairly easily from the techniques she had been taught and moved more and more to the semi-folklore, semi-'naive' style of painting beloved of all the 'naive' artists of both sexes in Brazil. From 1957 to 1964 she took part in exhibitions in virtually all the art galleries of her native land. Her works are represented in the museums of São Paulo and Rio de Janeiro.

Noch eine Malerin, die zuerst die freie Malwerkstatt des Museums für Moderne Kunst in Rio de Janeiro besucht hat. Wie dem auch sei, sie löst sich ziemlich mühelos vom offiziellen Unterricht und entwickelt sich in der halb folkloristischen, halb naiven Richtung, in der sich die «naiven» brasilianischen Maler beiderlei Geschlechts so sehr gefallen. Von 1957 bis 1964 hat sie an ungefähr allen Salons ihres Landes teilgenommen. Ihre Werke sind in den Museen von São Paulo und Rio vertreten.

Encore une qui a fréquenté d'abord l'atelier libre de peinture du Musée d'Art Moderne à Rio de Janeiro. Quoiqu'il en soit, elle se dégage assez facilement de l'enseignement officiel pour donner dans la direction semi-folklorique, semi-naïve qu'affectionnent tant les peintres «naïfs» brésiliens des deux sexes. De 1957 à 1964, elle a participé à peu près à tous les salons de son pays. Ses œuvres sont représentées aux musées de São Paulo et de Rio.

EXPOSITIONS:
Galerie Gead, Rio de Janeiro 1963.

Beckles, Gillian

Born 1918 in England.

Geboren 1918 in England.

Né en 1918 en Angleterre.

A self-taught artist who paints only in her leisure time. Recalls in her work the traditional 'boat memories' painters, but is distinguishable from them either by her personality or by the absence of models to copy. Thus she also resembles all the other painters of ships the world over—the French ones, for instance, such as Pajot senior and junior. Has exhibited for some time now at the Women's International Art Club.

Reine Autodidaktin, die nur in ihrer Freizeit malt. Steht in der Nähe der traditionellen «Souvenir-Schiff-Maler», geht jedoch über sie hinaus entweder dank ihrer Persönlichkeit oder weil sie ohne Modell arbeitet. Aus diesem Grund nähert sie sich ebenfalls allen anderen Schiffsmalern auf der ganzen Welt, u.a. auch den Franzosen Pajot Vater und Sohn. Stellt seit langem in Women's International Art Club aus.

Autodidacte pur qui ne peint que pendant ses loisirs. Se rapproche des peintres des «Bateaux-Souvenir» traditionnels, tout en les transgressant déjà, soit par sa personnalité, soit par le manque de modèle. De ce fait, elle se rapproche, également, de tous les autres peintres de bateaux du monde entier, les français, Pajot père et fils entre autres. Expose depuis longtemps au Women's International Art Club.

EXPOSITIONS:
«Laienmaler», Gewerbemuseum, Basel 1961.

BIBLIOGRAPHIE:
A. Hernandez: «Naive Maler», Atlantis, N°11, Zurich novembre 1961.

Belle, Narcisse

Born September 9, 1900 in Saint-Sylvain-sous-Toulx, Creuse (France).

Geboren am 9. September 1900 in Saint-Sylvain-sous-Toulx, Creuse (Frankreich).

Né le 9 septembre 1900 à Saint-Sylvain-sous-Toulx, Creuse (France).

One-time market porter, later employed by the Parisian slaughterhouses. After enjoying a rapid rise to success, due to the reputation of the gallery of Jeanne Bucher who was interested in his work, he did not paint for many years, for reasons unknown. Later, he started again to paint, intermittently. He is at his best in monumental compositions, such as the 'Earthly Paradise', prehistorical scenes, and 'The Whalefishers'.

Ehemaliger Lastenträger in den Markthallen von Paris. Ehemaliger Angestellter im Schlachthaus von Paris. Hat schnell Erfolg als Maler, weil die bekannte Galerie Jeanne Bucher sich seiner annimmt; gibt dann aber die Malerei jahrelang auf. Dann kehrt er von Zeit zu Zeit zu ihr zurück. Zeichnet sich aus in Monumentalkompositionen, wie «Das Paradies auf Erden», prähistorischen Szenen und Bildern vom Walfischfang.

Ancien «Fort des Halles». Ancien employé aux abattoirs de Paris. Après un succès assez rapide, dû à la notoriété de la galerie Jeanne Bucher qui s'en est occupée, abandonne, on ne sait pas pourquoi, pendant des années, sa peinture. Puis, il y revient par intermittence. Excelle dans les compositions monumentales, telles que les «Paradis terrestre», les scènes préhistoriques, etc. et les «Pêches à la baleine».

EXPOSITIONS:
Galerie Else Clausen, Paris 1943
(Cat., Préface André Salmon).
«Moderne primitive Maler», Kunsthalle, Bern 1949 (Cat., Préface Arnold Rüdlinger).
Galerie Herbinet, Paris 1964
(Cat., Préface Anatole Jakovsky).
«I Pittori Naifs», Rome 1964.
«Les Primitifs d'Aujourd'hui»,
Galerie Charpentier, Paris 1964.

BIBLIOGRAPHIE:
«Art Naïf», Editions Marocaines et Internationales, Rabat 1964.

Benaboura, Hacène

Born 1898 in Algiers (Algeria).
Died 1961 in Algiers (Algeria).

Geboren 1898 in Algier (Algerien).
Gestorben 1961 in Algier (Algerien).

Né en 1898 à Alger (Algérie).
Mort en 1961 à Alger (Algérie).

Even at school he showed a taste for painting and drawing. And he even earned his living by this talent, as a coachwork painter. In his spare time he painted for his own pleasure, but it was only in 1944 that he was finally able to take part in an exhibition, namely the group exhibition organised by Mme Cuttoli. However, once the beginning was made he regularly participated in exhibitions in various Algerian galleries. In 1954 he won second prize in the competition for the Algerian Grand Prix Artistique, and in 1957 he was the winner. He made progress, it must be admitted, but even the pictures which developed and tended to draw away from 'naive' art more and more reveal a certain touch which cannot be learned or copied...

Schon in der Schule macht sich eine Neigung zum Malen und Zeichnen bemerkbar. Sein Leben verdient er als Karosseriemaler. Die übrige Zeit malt er für sich. Aber erst 1944 kann er endlich an einer von Mme Cuttoli organisierten Gruppenausstellung teilnehmen. Nun ist der Anstoß gegeben, und in der Folge ist er regelmäßig in den verschiedenen algerischen Salons vertreten. 1954 steht er an zweiter Stelle bei der Verteilung des großen algerischen Kunstpreises und 1957 ist er erster Preisträger. Gewiß hat er einen weiten Weg zurückgelegt, aber selbst in den Werken, die sich vielleicht am weitesten von der naiven Malerei entfernen, ist noch das unbestimmte Etwas spürbar, das sich weder erlernen noch imitieren läßt...

Dès l'école, il manifeste un goût pour la peinture et le dessin. Même sa vie, il la gagne comme peintre en carrosserie. Il peint pour lui le reste du temps. Or ce n'est qu'en 1944 qu'il peut participer enfin à une exposition de groupe organisée par Mme Cuttoli. Mais le départ est donné et, par la suite, il participera régulièrement aux différents salons algériens. En 1954, il obtient le second Grand Prix Artistique de l'Algérie et en 1957 il en est le lauréat. Certes, il a fait du chemin, mais même dans les œuvres qui s'éloignent le plus, peut-être, de la peinture naïve, il en reste ce on ne sait quoi qui ne s'apprend et qui ne s'imite pas...

EXPOSITIONS:
Galerie du Minaret, Alger 1946.

BIBLIOGRAPHIE:

J. de Maisonseul: « L'art naïf d'un fils d'Alger », Révolution Africaine, 16 mars 1963.

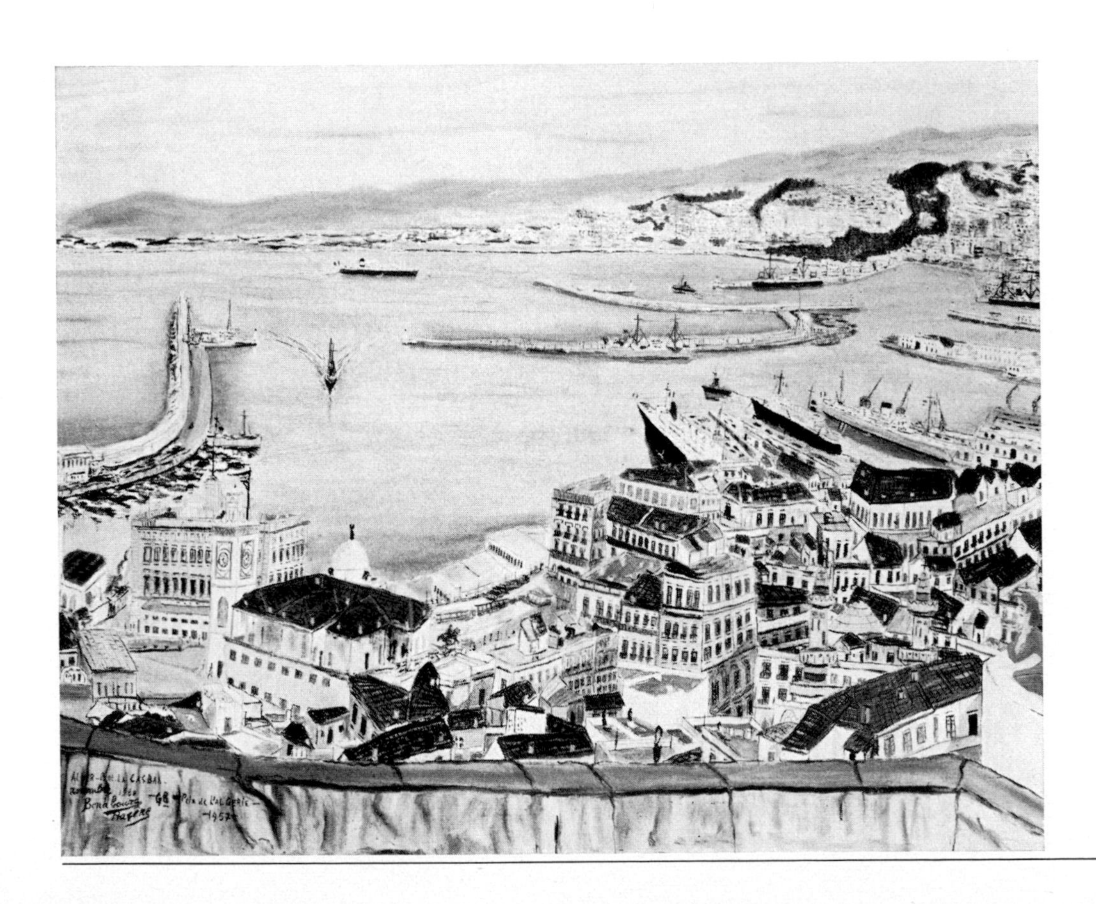

Ben Allal, Mohamed

Born 1924 in Marrakesh (Morocco).

Geboren 1924 in Marrakesch (Marokko).

Né en 1924 à Marrakech (Maroc).

Was employed as a servant by the French artist Jacques Azéma. He began to paint on the encouragement of Azéma, and soon afterwards the state of Morocco itself helped him as far as possible. At the moment he is employed by the Museum of Dar Si Said in Marrakesh. First exhibited his work in 1948, and since then has exhibited in Washington, Rabat, Tangiers, Rome and Paris, although most of these were not individual exhibitions.

Dienstbote beim französischen Maler Jacques Azéma. Dieser ermuntert ihn, sich im Malen zu versuchen, und bald unterstützt ihn der marokkanische Staat nach Maßgabe seiner Mittel. Gegenwärtig ist er Angestellter im Museum Dar Si Said in Marrakesch. Stellt seit 1948 aus. Ausstellungen in Washington, Rabat, Tanger, Rom und Paris, aber im allgemeinen immer im Rahmen einer Gruppe.

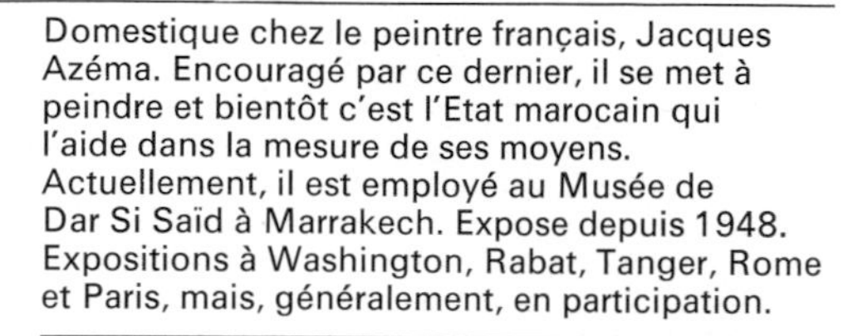

Domestique chez le peintre français, Jacques Azéma. Encouragé par ce dernier, il se met à peindre et bientôt c'est l'Etat marocain qui l'aide dans la mesure de ses moyens. Actuellement, il est employé au Musée de Dar Si Saïd à Marrakech. Expose depuis 1948. Expositions à Washington, Rabat, Tanger, Rome et Paris, mais, généralement, en participation.

EXPOSITIONS:
«2000 Ans d'Art Marocain», Galerie Charpentier, Paris 1963.
«Panorama International de la Peinture Naïve», Tanger, Rabat, Marrakech et Casablanca 1964.

BIBLIOGRAPHIE:
Jacques Azéma: «Ben Allal», Ed. des Amis de la Peinture marocaine, Rabat 1963.
«Art Naïf», Editions Marocaines et Internationales, Rabat 1964.

Benedettucci, Luigi

Born 1897 in Recanati (Italy).

Geboren 1897 in Recanati (Italien).

Né en 1897 à Recanati (Italie).

Began to work at the age of nine, as helper to a mason. Immigrated to South America and became coachbuilder and mechanic. Returned to his own country when eighteen to join the army. Afterwards he immigrated again, only to return yet again to fight in the next war. Giancarlo Vigorelli, who discovered him when visiting Recanati, found in him a 'Leopardi'[1] vein. This 'Sunday painter' is in essence a village painter, with his picturesque and rough characters, his bonfires and fireworks, etc. Even here imagination and reality are intertwined.

[1] Giacomo Leopardi, Italian poet, born June 29, 1798 in Recanati, died June 14, 1837 in Naples.

Beginnt mit 9 Jahren als Maurergehilfe zu arbeiten. Wandert nach Südamerika aus, betätigt sich als Karosseriebauer und Mechaniker. Kehrt mit 18 Jahren in die Heimat zurück, um Kriegsdienst zu leisten. Wandert wieder aus und kehrt nochmals heim, um erneut in den Krieg zu ziehen. Giancarlo Vigorelli, der ihn bei einem Besuch in Recanati entdeckt, findet, er habe eine gewisse Verwandtschaft mit Leopardi[1]. Bei diesem Sonntagsmaler ist immer Dorfsonntag, mit pittoresken, urwüchsigen Gestalten, Freudenfeuern und Feuerwerk, wobei sich bereits der Traum in die Wirklichkeit mischt.

[1] Giacomo Leopardi, italienischer Dichter, geboren am 29. Juni 1798 in Recanati, gestorben 14. Juni 1837 in Neapel.

Commence à travailler à 9 ans comme aide-maçon. Emigre en Amérique du Sud: carrossier et mécanicien. Rentre dans son pays à 18 ans pour faire la guerre. Re-émigre à nouveau pour rentrer encore une fois pour faire la guerre. Giancarlo Vigorelli qui le découvre lors d'une visite à Recanati, lui trouve une veine «Leopardi»[1]. Chez ce peintre du dimanche, c'est toujours le dimanche du village, avec ses personnages pittoresques, truculents, avec ses feux de joie et ses feux d'artifice où, déjà, le rêve se mêle à la réalité.

[1] Giacomo Leopardi, poète italien, né le 29 juin 1798 à Recanati, mort le 14 juin 1837 à Naples.

EXPOSITIONS:
«Mostra di Pittura popolare», Palazzo delle Esposizioni, Rome 1955.
Galleria l'Incontro, Rome 1958 (Cat., Préface Giancarlo Vigorelli).
Galleria di Cichi, Rome 1961 (Cat., Préface non signée).
«I Pittori Naifs», Rome 1964.

BIBLIOGRAPHIE:
Catalogo Bolaffi d'Arte Moderna 1965/66, Turin 1966.

Benoit, Jacqueline

Born January 16, 1925 in Paris (France).

Geboren am 16. Januar 1925 in Paris (Frankreich).

Née le 17 janvier 1925 à Paris (France).

Has lived in Orleans since she was a teenager. Helped her parents in their business until they retired. Her creative work, which at first produced only a few paintings, later became more regular. In the peace of that provincial town she was able to develop, little by little, a very distinguished style which is, so to speak, unique of its kind. Her mountain landscapes remind one of Brueghel, and her nudes—for she is one of the few 'naive' artists to paint nudes—bear the mark of a delicate and authentic eroticism, almost like filigree work.
One of the best modern 'naive' artists.

Wohnt seit ihrer Jugend in Orléans. Half ihren Eltern in einer Handelsfirma, bis sie sich von den Geschäften zurückzogen. Von da an malt sie mehr und regelmäßiger. In der Ruhe dieser Provinzstadt hat sie nach und nach ihr überaus beachtliches und in seiner Art sozusagen alleinstehendes Werk aufgebaut. Ihre Berglandschaften gemahnen an Brueghel, und ihre Akte, denn sie ist eine der wenigen Naiven, die Akte malen, lassen eine raffinierte und durchaus echte Erotik durchschimmern. Eine der besten naiven Malerinnen unserer Zeit.

Habite depuis son adolescence Orléans. Aidait ses parents dans une maison de commerce jusqu'à ce qu'ils se retirent des affaires. Sa production, peu importante d'abord, devient alors plus regulière. Et c'est dans le calme de cette ville de province qu'elle a élaboré peu à peu cette œuvre absolument remarquable et pour ainsi dire unique dans son genre. Ses paysages de montagne rappellent Brueghel, et ses nus, car elle est l'un des rares peintres naïfs à peindre des nus, portent l'empreinte d'un raffiné et très authentique érotisme qui se lit plutôt en filigrane. L'un des meilleurs peintres naïfs de nos jours.

EXPOSITIONS:
Galerie Herbinet, Paris 1964
(Cat., Préface Anatole Jakovsky).
«I Pittori Naifs», Rome 1964.
«Les Primitifs d'Aujourd'hui»,
Galerie Charpentier, Paris 1964.

BIBLIOGRAPHIE:
Anatole Jakovsky: «Eros du Dimanche»,
Paris 1964.

Benoît, Rigaud

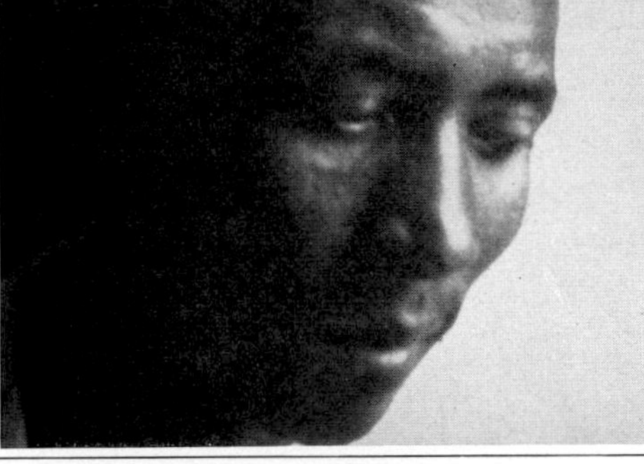

Born January 1911 in Port-au-Prince (Haiti).

Geboren Januar 1911 in Port-au-Prince (Haiti).

Né en janvier 1911 à Port-au-Prince (Haïti).

Practiced various trades: shoemaker, taxi-driver, etc. Encouraged by the extraordinary flowering of 'naive' art in Haiti, he too began to paint. Has a fresco representing the birth of Christ in Port-au-Prince cathedral.

Schuhmacher, Taxichauffeur usw. Ermuntert durch den außergewöhnlichen Aufschwung der haitischen naiven Kunst, fängt auch er an zu malen. Eine Freske, welche die Geburt Christi darstellt, befindet sich in der Kathedrale von Port-au-Prince.

Cordonnier, chauffeur de taxi, etc. Se met à peindre encouragé par l'extraordinaire essor de l'art naïf haitien. Une fresque qui représente la naissance du Christ à la Cathédrale de Port-au-Prince.

EXPOSITIONS:
«Les peintres de l'Equateur, de Haïti et de Pérou», l'UNESCO, Paris 1947.
«19 Peintres d'Haïti», Palais des Beaux-Arts, Bruxelles 1963.
«20th Century Latin American Naive Art», La Jolla, Calif. (USA) 1964.

BIBLIOGRAPHIE:
Selden Rodman: «Renaissance in Haiti», Peligrini and Cudahy, New York (sans date).
Oto Bihalji-Merin: «Das naive Bild der Welt», Köln 1959.
Oto Bihalji-Merin: «Die naive Malerei», Köln 1959.
Oto Bihalji-Merin: «Les Peintres Naïfs», Paris (sans date).

Bernhardsgrütter, Anton

Born 1925 in Hohen, canton Thurgau (Switzerland).

Geboren 1925 in Hohen, Kt. Thurgau (Schweiz).

Né en 1925 à Hohen, canton de Thurgovie (Suisse).

Schoolmaster—entirely self-taught artist. 'I began to paint at the age of 28 on impulse. I paint what I like, a landscape for instance, with Sunday strollers. Suitable details occur whilst I am painting. Some day I would like to paint scenes from the Bible', he once said. So he does have imagination in his work, which is genuine and full of charm.

Volksschullehrer. Autodidakt. « Mit 28 Jahren begann ich, einem inneren Drang folgend, Bilder zu malen. Ich male, was mich freut, z. B. eine Landschaft mit Menschen am Sonntag. Während der Malarbeit fallen mir passende Details ein. In nächster Zeit möchte ich ein biblisches Bild malen.» Er schafft also aus der Phantasie. Reizende, aufrichtige Malerei.

Instituteur. Autodidacte. « J'ai commencé à peindre à l'âge de 28 ans en suivant mes impulsions. Je peins ce qui me plaît, par exemple un paysage, avec des gens le dimanche. Je voudrais peindre à l'avenir des scènes bibliques» dit-il. Peinture d'imagination, donc. Charmante et sincère.

EXPOSITIONS:
« Laienmaler», Gewerbemuseum, Basel 1961.

Bianconi, Walter

Born February 2, 1923 in Ostiglia, Mantua (Italy).

Geboren am 2. Februar 1923 in Ostiglia, Mantua (Italien).

Né le 2 février 1923 à Ostiglia, Mantoue (Italie).

Encouraged by artists like Scitlian Guttoso and Vedova, this 'Pittore Facchino[1]', who began to paint in 1960, showed very great talent from the beginning. A kind of inborn pictorial 'Bel Canto' helped him to avoid a period of unexciting primitive painting and led him more and more to create wonderful lighting effects and chromatic orchestration. Already one can see, behind the artist, the decorator, and one may well ask oneself whether Bianconi will remain 'naive' for much longer. Whatever happens, however, a part of his work is and will remain 'naive', and this is the part which interests us most.

[1] Facchino = porter.

Von Malern wie Scitlian Guttuso und Vedova gefördert, offenbart dieser «Pittore Facchino[1]», der 1960 zu malen beginnt, schon von Anfang an außerordentliche Gaben. Eine Art angeborener bildhafter Bel Canto führt ihn sehr schnell über einen glanzlosen Primitivismus hinaus und treibt ihn immer mehr zu Lichteffekten und prunkvollen farbigen Instrumentierungen. Hinter dem Maler macht sich bereits der Dekorateur bemerkbar. So sehr, daß man sich heute schon fragen kann, ob Bianconi noch lange ein Naiver bleibt. Wie dem auch sei, ein Teil seines Werks wird immer naiv bleiben, und unser Interesse gilt natürlich diesem Teil.

[1] Facchino = Gepäckträger.

Encouragé par des peintres tels que Scitlian, Guttuso et Vedova, ce «Pittore Facchino[1]», qui commence à peindre en 1960, révèle ses dons extraordinaires dès ses débuts. Une sorte de Bel Canto pictural inné lui fait vite brûler les étapes d'un primitivisme sans éclat et le pousse de plus en plus vers les effets de lumière et les somptueuses orchestrations chromatiques. Le décorateur perce déjà sous le peintre. A tel point que l'on peut se demander dès à présent si Bianconi va rester encore longtemps naïf. Quoiqu'il en soit, une partie de son œuvre le sera toujours et c'est celle-là, bien sûr, qui nous intéresse.

[1] Facchino = porteur de bagages.

EXPOSITIONS:
Galleria d'Arte La Barcaccia, Reggio Emilia 1964 (Cat., Préface Ugo Sassi).
L'Associazione pro loco di Ostiglia, Ostiglia 1965 (Cat., Préface Anatole Jakovsky et Nevio Jori).
Centro Culturale Schivenoglia, Schivenoglia 1965 (Cat., Préface Anatole Jakovsky).

BIBLIOGRAPHIE:
Nevio Jori: «Ostiglia presenta Walter Bianconi», 1964.
Nevio Jori: «Walter Bianconi», Gazzetta di Reggio, 15 mai 1965.

Bigaud, Wilson

Born January 25, 1931 in Port-au-Prince (Haiti).

Geboren am 25. Januar 1931 in Port-au-Prince (Haiti).

Né le 25 janvier 1931 à Port-au-Prince (Haïti).

Was discovered by Hector Hyppolite, the patriarch of the 'naive' movement in Haiti, who brought him to the Art Centre in Port-au-Prince. Paints scenes from Haitian life, using rather bright colors. His fresco of the Marriage of Cana can be seen in the Port-au-Prince cathedral.

Der Patriarch der naiven haitischen Maler, Hector Hyppolite, hat ihn selber entdeckt und ins Kunstzentrum gebracht. Ziemlich farbige Szenen aus dem einheimischen Leben. Die Freske « Die Hochzeit von Kana » befindet sich in der Kathedrale von Port-au-Prince.

C'est Hector Hyppolite, le patriarche du mouvement naïf haïtien qui l'a découvert lui-même et l'a amené au Centre d'Art. Des scènes de la vie du pays assez hautes en couleur. La fresque, Les Noces de Cana, figure dans la cathédrale de Port-au-Prince.

EXPOSITIONS:
« Peintres de l'Equateur, de Haïti et de Pérou », l'UNESCO, Paris 1947.
« La Peinture Naïve », Knokke-le-Zoute 1958.
« Das naive Bild der Welt », Baden-Baden 1961.
« 19 Peintres d'Haïti », Palais des Beaux-Arts, Bruxelles 1963.
« 20th Century Latin American Naive Art », La Jolla (USA) 1964.

BIBLIOGRAPHIE:
Selden Rodman: « Renaissance in Haiti », Peligrini and Cudahy, New York (sans date).
Oto Bihalji-Merin: « Das naive Bild der Welt », Köln 1959.
Oto Bihalji-Merin: « Die naive Malerei », Köln 1959.
Oto Bihalji-Merin: « Les Peintres Naïfs », Paris (sans date).

Bilacour, Kathérina

Born December 7, 1900 in Bogdanovka, near Poltava (Russia).

Geboren am 7. Dezember 1900 in Bogdanovka, Distrikt Poltava (Rußland).

Née le 7 décembre 1900 à Bogdanovka, district de Poltava (Russie).

Daughter of a poor peasant family—therefore she had no chance to go to school. So she learned her ABCs by heart, all by herself. Her first picture dates from 1934, approximately.
She was discovered as an artist on the eve of war, during the organizing of a large exhibition of popular Ukrainian art. From 1956 onwards she has been honored officially several times.

Tochter armer Bauern, ging infolgedessen nicht zur Schule. Ihr ABC lernt sie ganz allein auswendig. Ihr erstes Werk stammt ungefähr aus dem Jahr 1934. Sie wird kurz vor dem Krieg entdeckt, als man eine große Ausstellung ukrainischer Volkskunst veranstaltete. Von 1956 an offizielle Ehrungen.

Fille de paysans pauvres; n'a donc pas fait d'études. Alors elle apprend toute seule son abécédaire par cœur. Sa première œuvre date de 1934, environ. On la découvre juste à la veille de la guerre, lorsqu'on organisait une grande exposition de l'art populaire ukrainien. A partir de 1956, les honneurs officiels.

EXPOSITIONS:
Première exposition personnelle, Poltava 1941.

BIBLIOGRAPHIE:
N. Nogaï: «Kathérina Bilacour», Editions d'Etat, Kieff 1959.

Blair, Streeter

Born July 16, 1888 in Cadmus, Kansas (USA).

Geboren am 16. Juli 1888 in Cadmus, Kansas (USA).

Né le 16 juillet 1888 à Cadmus, Kansas (USA).

Has lived since his youth in Los Angeles, where he worked first in a café and then as drummer in a band (this was to pay for his studies). In 1911 he married, and since that time he led a varied life full of unexpected changes and happenings; finally he came to painting—by chance, of course. He had tried his hand at being a secondhand dealer, after going bankrupt at the end of ten years in his clothing firm, and it was at the request of one of his customers that he dashed off a picture of an old house. Having received payment for this picture, he continued painting and has never stopped. His work is rather harsh and very realistic, despite his preference for conjuring up the past and for depicting imaginary scenes which he invents himself.

Lebt seit seiner Jugend in Los Angeles, wo er zuerst als Kellner, dann als Schlagzeuger in einem Orchester arbeitete, um seine Studien zu bezahlen. 1911 heiratet er und von nun an führt er ein bewegtes Leben, reich an Unvorhergesehenem, das ihn schließlich zur Malerei führt. Natürlich ganz zufällig. Er betätigt sich unvorbereitet als Antiquar, nachdem ein Kleidergeschäft, das er zehn Jahre lang betrieben hat, Konkurs macht. Im Auftrag eines Kunden malt er das Bild eines alten Hauses. Als dieses Bild bezahlt ist, macht er sich wieder ans Malen und hört nicht mehr auf. Etwas harte, sehr realistische Malerei, trotz der Anläufe, die Vergangenheit heraufzubeschwören oder imaginäre, von ihm erfundene Szenen darzustellen.

Vit depuis sa jeunesse à Los Angeles où il travaille d'abord comme garçon de café, puis comme tambour dans un orchestre; ceci pour pouvoir payer ses études. Il se marie en 1911 et, à partir de là, c'est une vie mouvementée, pleine d'imprévu qui le conduit, à la fin, vers la peinture. Par hasard, comme de bien entendu. Il s'improvise antiquaire, après avoir fait faillite, au bout de dix ans, d'un commerce de vêtements, aussi c'est sur la demande d'un de ses clients qu'il brosse un tableau d'une vieille maison. Le tableau payé, il recommence pour ne plus s'arrêter. Peinture un peu dure, très réaliste, malgré ses velléités d'évoquer le passé ou de peindre des scènes imaginaires, inventées par lui.

EXPOSITIONS:
«A Group of Natural Painters»,
Galerie St-Etienne, New York 1952.
Galerie St-Etienne, New York 1953.
«Amerikanische Primitive», Museum am Ostwall, Dortmund 1954–55.
«Amerikanische Malerei», Kunstmuseum, Luzern 1956.
«American Primitive Paintings»,
The Smithsonian Institution, Washington 1958.

BIBLIOGRAPHIE:
B. Jasmand et Otto Kallir: «Sonntagsmaler», Otto Aug. Ehlers, Berlin/Darmstadt 1956.
Oto Bihalji-Merin: «Das naive Bild der Welt», Köln 1959.
Oto Bihalji-Merin: «Die naive Malerei», Köln 1959.
Oto Bihalji-Merin: «Les Peintres Naïfs», Paris (sans date).

Blondel, Emile

Born August 6, 1893 in Le Havre (France).

Geboren am 6. August 1893 in Le Havre (Frankreich).

Né le 6 août 1893 au Havre (France).

Became a farmer, a sailor and finally a bus-driver. He himself summed up the various stages of his existence in a picture entitled 'My Life'. Virtually all his painting was done after he retired. All his pictures are endowed with an angelic charm. He is a fine painter of the Eternal Sunday of life.

Nacheinander Bauer, Matrose und schließlich Omnibusschaffner. Er hat die verschiedenen Etappen seines Lebens übrigens selber in einem Bild zusammengefaßt, das sich «Mein Leben» betitelt. Malt eigentlich erst, nachdem er in den Ruhestand getreten ist. Von all seinen Bildern geht ein engelhafter Zauber aus. Ein ausgezeichneter Maler des ewigen Lebenssonntages.

Tour à tour cultivateur, marin et finalement conducteur d'autobus. Il a résumé d'ailleurs lui-même les différentes étapes de son existence dans un tableau intitulé: «Ma vie». Ne peint, somme toute, qu'après avoir pris sa retraite. Un charme angélique se dégage de tous ses tableaux. Un beau peintre de l'Eternel dimanche de la vie.

EXPOSITIONS:

Galerie Cambacères, Paris 1950 (Cat., Préface Maximilien Gauthier).
Galerie J.J. Rousseau, Le Havre 1950 (Cat., Préface Maximilien Gauthier).
Hall of Art, New York 1950.
Galerie de Conti, Paris 1953 (Cat., Préface Anatole Jakovsky).
Galerie Cambacères, Paris 1955 (Cat., Préface Anatole Jakovsky).
«Les Peintres Naïfs», Knokke-le-Zoute 1958.
«Les Peintres Naïfs», Maison de la Pensée Française, Paris 1960.
Musée de l'Athénée, Genève 1962 (Cat. avec un poème de Blondel).
«I Pittori Naifs», Rome 1964.
«Les Primitifs d'Aujourd'hui», Galerie Charpentier, Paris 1964.
Galerie Cambacères, Paris 1964 (Cat., Préface Anatole Jakovsky).

BIBLIOGRAPHIE:

Anatole Jakovsky: «Les Peintres Naïfs», Paris 1956.
Anatole Jakovsky: «Naive Malerei in Frankreich», Zürich 1957.
Anatole Jakovsky: «Emile Blondel», Editions «Temps Mêlés», Verviers 1959.
Oto Bihalji-Merin: «Das naive Bild der Welt», Köln 1959.
Oto Bihalji-Merin: «Die naive Malerei», Köln 1959.
Oto Bihalji-Merin: «Les Peintres Naïfs», Paris (sans date).

Boix-Vives, Anselme

Born January 3, 1899 in Morella Herbeset, in the province of Castille (Spain).

Geboren am 3. Januar 1899 in Morella Herbeset, Provinz Kastilien (Spanien).

Né le 3 janvier 1899 à Morella Herbeset, province de Castellon (Espagne).

Arrived in France on 6 June 1917 and worked ever since then as a fishmonger. On his retirement he began to paint with gouache on large sheets of cardboard, immediately showing in his painting great strength of personality. It is curious to note that his work is more similar to the South American trend than to that of any other European 'naive' artist. He starts out with reality, as far as he sees it, but completely transforms it by giving it a primitive, savage aspect. A very fine talent, just beginning to show itself.

Kommt am 6. Juni 1917 nach Frankreich, wo er den Beruf eines Fischhändlers ausübt. Nachdem er das Geschäft aufgegeben hat, beginnt er auf großen Pappen mit Gouache zu malen und offenbart sofort eine sehr starke Persönlichkeit. Seltsamerweise stehen seine Werke der südamerikanischen Art näher als der Malerei der übrigen europäischen Naiven. Er geht vom Wirklichen aus, oder zumindest von dem, was er als Wirklichkeit ansieht, und verwandelt es vollständig in etwas Primitives, Barbarisches. Sehr große Begabung, die erst an ihren Anfängen steht.

Arrive en France le 6 juin 1917, où il exerce la profession de poissonnier, et qu'il ne quittera plus. Arrivé à l'âge de la retraite, il commence à peindre à la gouache sur de grands cartons qui révèlent aussitôt une très forte personnalité. Chose curieuse, ses œuvres se rattachent davantage à la veine sud-américaine qu'à la production des autres naïfs européens. Partant du réel, ou du moins tel qu'il le voit, il le transfigure complètement sous une apparence primitive et barbare. Très beau talent qui n'est qu'à ses débuts.

EXPOSITIONS:
Galerie Breteau, Paris 1964.
Kunsthalle, Bern 1964.
«Les Primitifs d'Aujourd'hui», Galerie Charpentier, Paris 1964.
Galerie Breteau, Paris 1965.

BIBLIOGRAPHIE:
«Art Naïf», Editions Marocaines et Internationales. Rabat 1964.

Bonnin, Maurice

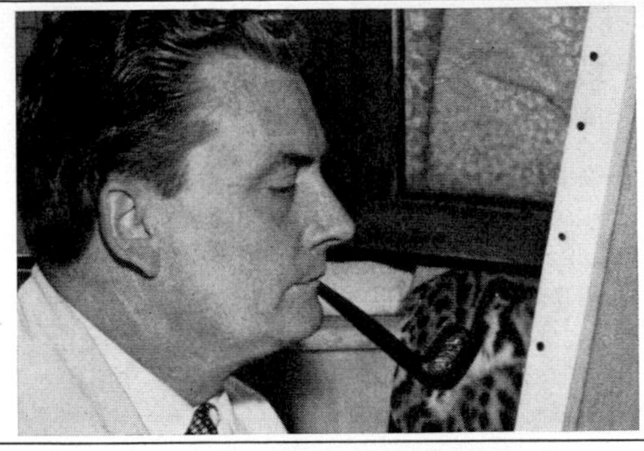

Born August 12, 1911 in Naples (Italy).

Geboren am 12. August 1911 in Neapel (Italien).

Né le 12 août 1911 à Naples (Italie).

His father was French, his mother English. Had a secondary-school education. From 1926 to 1947 he worked as a furrier with the firm of Révillon. Later he set up on his own. Had always loved to paint. After 1958 he painted more often, but without giving up his regular profession. He is an artist who is at the same time sensitive and thoughtful. Beautiful work.

Vater Franzose, Mutter Engländerin. Mittelschulbildung. Arbeitet von 1928 bis 1947 als Kürschner bei Révillon. Etabliert sich nachher auf eigene Rechnung. Liebt die Malerei seit jeher. Malt von 1958 an mehr, ohne indessen seinen wahren Beruf aufzugeben. Eine gleichzeitig empfindsame und durchdachte Malerei. Gute Bilder.

Père français et mère anglaise. Etudes sécondaires. Travaille de 1928 à 1947 comme fourreur chez Révillon. S'établit ensuite à son propre compte. A toujours aimé peindre. Peint davantage à partir de 1958, sans pour autant abandonner son vrai métier. Peinture à la fois sensible et réfléchie. Beau travail.

EXPOSITIONS:
Galerie Romi, Paris 1960 (Cat., Préface Romi).
Galerie Romi, Paris 1961 (Cat., Préface Romi).
Galerie Ror Volmar, Paris 1963
(Cat., Préface Maximilien Gauthier).
« Les Primitifs d'Aujourd'hui »,
Galerie Charpentier, Paris 1964.

BIBLIOGRAPHIE:
Robert Giraud: « L'Aventure de Maurice Bonnin », l'Information Artistique N° 65, Paris (sans date).
Maurice Cottaz: « Un Amourend de Paris, Maurice Bonnin », l'Information Artistique, N° 72, Paris (sans date).

Bombois, Camille

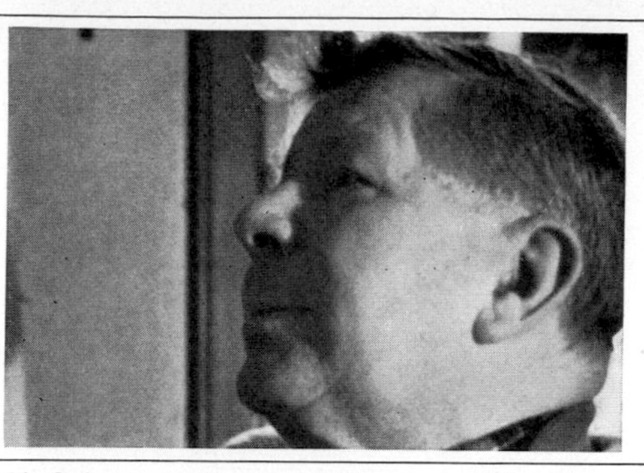

Born 1883 in Venarey-les-Laumes, Côte d'Or (France).

Geboren 1883 in Venarey-les-Laumes, Côte d'Or (Frankreich).

Né en 1883 à Venarey-les-Laumes, Côte d'Or (France).

A boatman's son, he spent his early childhood on a barge. After attending the municipal school in Laroche, he started to earn his living helping the shepherds and doing general farm work. But Paris attracted him and in order to get there, he became an itinerant wrestler. This is the source of his many pictures of circus life. The urge to paint was always present, since he started to draw at the age of 16. Once in Paris, he worked first of all as a laborer in the building of the métro, then in a printer's—at night, of course, in order to be able to paint during the day. He exhibited for the first time in 1922, at the Montmartre amateurs sidewalk exhibition. It was there that the poet and journalist Noël Bureau discovered him one day; he was soon followed by the dealers Mathot and W. Uhde. His rise to fame was abrupt, and since 1925 he has been able to live from his painting. He is one of the few 'naive' artists whose work is truly erotic. Insofar as he is the last living 'great' one, he is also at the moment the most 'expensive'. For a long time now he has painted only very small canvases.

Als Sohn eines Binnenschiffers verbrachte er seine erste Kindheit an Bord eines Schleppkahns. Er besucht die Volksschule in Laroche und lernt den Ernst des Lebens zuerst als Hirtenbube und Knecht kennen. Aber Paris lockt ihn, und um in seine Nähe zu gelangen, wird er Ringer auf den Jahrmärkten. Daher seine zahlreichen Bilder über den Zirkus. Die Malerei zieht ihn an, denn er zeichnet schon seit seinem sechzehnten Jahr. In Paris arbeitet er zuerst als Erdarbeiter beim Bau der Untergrundbahn, dann als Typograph. Mit Nachtschicht natürlich, damit er tagsüber malen kann. 1922 stellt er zum ersten Mal in Montmartre auf dem «Bildermarkt» aus, der auf dem Gehsteig abgehalten wird. Hier entdeckt ihn eines Tages der Dichter und Journalist Noël Bureau; auf ihn folgen bald die Kunsthändler Mathot und Wilhelm Uhde. Sein Aufstieg geht schnell vor sich. Schon von 1925 an kann er von seiner Malerei leben. Er ist einer der wenigen naiven Maler, die wahrhaft erotische Akte malen. Als letzter lebender «Großer» ist er gegenwärtig der «teuerste» Maler. Seit langer Zeit malt er nur noch ganz kleinformatige Bilder.

Fils d'un batelier, il passa sa prime jeunesse à bord d'une péniche. Après l'école communale de Laroche, il s'initie à la vie comme aide berger et valet de ferme. Mais Paris l'attire et, pour s'en rapprocher, il devient lutteur forain. D'où ses nombreux tableaux sur le cirque. La peinture le tourmente aussi, puisqu'il dessine dès l'âge de 16 ans. A Paris, il travaille d'abord à la construction du Métro comme terrassier, puis comme typographe. Typographe de nuit, bien sûr, pour pouvoir peindre le jour. Il expose pour la première fois en 1922 à la «Foire aux croûtes» de Montmartre, à même le trottoir. C'est là que le poète et journaliste Noël Bureau le découvre un jour, suivi bientôt par les marchands Mathot et W. Uhde. Son ascension est rapide. Dès 1925, il peut vivre, désormais, de sa peinture. Il est un des rares peintres naïfs à peindre des nus réellement érotiques. En tant que le dernier «Grand» vivant, c'est le peintre le plus «cher» à l'heure actuelle. Ne peint plus, depuis longtemps, que de tout petits formats.

EXPOSITIONS:

«Les Maîtres Populaires de la Réalité», Paris 1937.
«Les Maîtres Populaires de la Réalité», Zürich 1937.
«Masters of Popular Painting», New York 1938.
«Masters of Popular Painting», Tooth & Sons, Londres 1938.
«Moderne Primitieven», Stedelijge Museum, Amsterdam 1941 (Cat., Préface D.C.R.).
Galerie Pétridès, Paris 1944 (Cat., Préface Maximilien Gauthier).
Perls Galleries, New York 1948 (Cat., Préface non signée).
Galerie de Berri, Paris 1948.
«Moderne primitive Maler», Kunsthalle, Bern 1949 (Cat., Préface Arnold Rüdlinger).
Galerie Bing, Paris 1951.
«Maler des einfältigen Herzens», Museum am Ostwall, Dortmund 1952.
Galerie Pétridès, Paris 1953.
«Bauchant, Bombois, Séraphine, Vivin», Kunsthalle, Basel 1956.
«Les Peintres Naïfs», Knokke-le-Zoute 1958.
«Les Peintres Naïfs», Maison de la Pensée Française, Paris 1960.
«Laienmaler», Gewerbemuseum, Basel 1961.
«Das naive Bild der Welt», Baden-Baden 1961.
«Contemporary French Primitives», Marlborough Galleries, Londres 1962.
«Les Peintres Naïfs», Tooth & Sons, Londres 1963.
«Die Welt der naiven Malerei», Salzburg 1964
«I Pittori Naifs», Rome 1964.
«De Lusthof der Naieven», Rotterdam 1964.
«Le Monde des Naïfs», Paris 1964.
David B. Findlay Gallery, New York 1964 (Cat., Préface Waldemar George).

BIBLIOGRAPHIE:

Nino Franck: «Bombois peintre», L'Art Vivant, Paris, 1 avril 1929.
J. Delteil: «Bombois peintre en peinture», Formes, février 1930.
W. Uhde: «Cinq Maîtres Primitifs», Ed. Palmes, Paris 1949.
Anatole Jakovsky: «La Peinture Naïve», Paris 1949.
H. Bodmer-Bing: «Camille Bombois», Ed. de la Galerie Bing, 1951.
«Camille Bombois», in Du, N° 2, février 1952.
«Camille Bombois», in Graphis, N° 101, mai–juin 1956.
Bernard Jasmand et Otto Kallir: «Sonntagsmaler», Ed. Otto Aug. Ehlers, Berlin/Darmstadt 1956.
Anatole Jakovsky: «Les Peintres Naïfs», Paris 1956.
Anatole Jakovsky: «Naive Malerei», Zürich 1957.
Oto Bihalji-Merin: «Das naive Bild der Welt», Köln 1959.
Oto Bihalji-Merin: «Die naive Malerei», Köln 1959.
Oto Bihalji-Merin: «Les Peintres Naïfs», Paris (sans date).
«C. Bombois», in Der Spiegel, Hamburg, 20 décembre 1961.
«C. Bombois», in Düsseldorfer Hefte, N° 11, juin 1963.
Anatole Jakovsky: «Eros du Dimanche», Paris 1964.
«Art Naïf», Editions Marocaines et Internationales, Rabat 1964.
Catalogo Bolaffi d'Arte Moderna, Turin 1965/66.

Bouquet, André

Born September 19, 1897 in La Varenne-Saint-Hilaire, Seine (France).

Geboren am 19. September 1897 in La Varenne-Saint-Hilaire, Seine (Frankreich).

Né le 19 septembre 1897 à la Varenne-Saint-Hilaire, Seine (France).

A butcher by trade, who had his stall in open-air markets. In order to have more time to paint, however, he became a factory cook and later a foreman in the same factory. Is now retired. Lives only for his painting, which since he stopped work he has done every day of the week including Sundays. He is a sensitive and delicate artist, especially when depicting Parisian suburbs, of which he has caught the atmosphere remarkably. Has also painted numerous snow landscapes.

Fleischer. Verkaufte seine Ware unter freiem Himmel auf dem Markt. Um mehr Zeit zum Malen zu haben, wird er Koch in einer Fabrik, dann Vorarbeiter am gleichen Ort. Ist jetzt pensioniert. Lebt nur für seine Malerei, der er sich nun sonntags und werktags hingibt. Ein empfindsamer, zartsinniger Maler, besonders wenn er die Pariser Vororte malt, die er wunderbar erfühlt. Hat zahlreiche Schneelandschaften gemalt.

Boucher-charcutier. Vendait en plein air sur les marchés. Pour avoir plus de temps libre pour peindre, devient cuisinier dans une usine, puis contremaître dans cette même usine. A la retraite maintenant. Ne vit que pour sa peinture, qu'il fait désormais tous les jours de la semaine, dimanche y compris. Un peintre sensible et délicat, surtout lorsqu'il peint la banlieue de Paris qu'il sent admirablement. A peint de nombreux paysages de neige.

EXPOSITIONS:
Galerie de l'Institut, Paris 1958 (Cat., Préface Anatole Jakovsky).
Galerie de l'Institut, Paris 1960 (Cat., Préface, Anatole Jakovsky).
« Les Peintres Naïfs », Knokke-le-Zoute 1958.
« Les Peintres Naïfs », Maison de la Pensée Française, Paris 1960.
Galerie G. Paffrath, Düsseldorf 1961.
Galerie de l'Institut, Paris 1962 (Cat., Préface Anatole Jakovsky).
Galerie Michel Columb, Nantes 1962 (Cat., Préface Anatole Jakovsky).
« I Pittori Naifs », Rome 1964.
« Les Primitifs d'Aujourd'hui », Galerie Charpentier, Paris 1964.

BIBLIOGRAPHIE:
Anatole Jakovsky: « Les Peintres Naïfs », Paris 1956.
Anatole Jakovsky: « Naive Malerei in Frankreich », Zürich 1957.
Anatole Jakovsky: « Eros du Dimanche », Paris 1964.
« André Bouquet », Vogue, Paris décembre 1956/janvier 1957.
Oto Bihalji-Merin: « Das naive Bild der Welt », Köln 1959.
Oto Bihalji-Merin: « Die naive Malerei », Köln 1959.
Oto Bihalji-Merin: « Les Peintres Naïfs », Paris (sans date).
Anatole Jakovsky: « Les loisirs sacrés et autres », La Vie médicale, Paris mai 1963.
« Dix ans d'Art Actuel », Editions Comparaisons, Paris 1964.

FILM:
«Voyage à Paris», d'après un texte de Marcel Aymé, réalisé par Pierre Mathieu, Paris. 1959.

Box, Eden

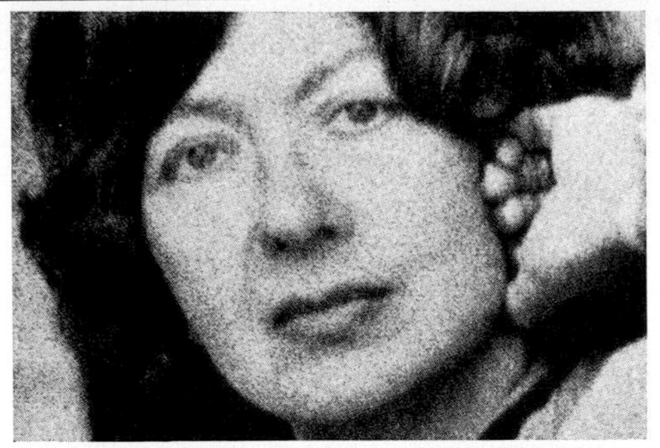

If this English artist had not exhibited her work at the Paris Musée d'Art Moderne during the 'reign' of J. Cassou (although this is not a foolproof recommendation, by the way), she would certainly not have been included in this volume. The reason for this is that there is an irritating air of cleverly maintained fraud surrounding her. The catalogue of the above-mentioned gallery does not even give her date of birth! One of her sponsors, a Yugoslav, claims her real name is Mrs. Marston Fleming. We must take the sponsor's word for this (although the book where this information is contained abounds with inaccuracies) since the art gallery where the artist has several times exhibited her work does not reply to letters. It is true that when the English decide not to reply, to be discreet, they can even beat the South Americans at the game. At any rate, whoever she is, her art is 'deliciously sophisticated' (to keep in the same key).

Wenn diese englische Malerin nicht im Musée d'Art Moderne von Paris ausgestellt hätte, als noch J. Cassou dessen Geschicke leitete, was, unter uns gesagt, keine unbedingte Empfehlung darstellt, hätten wir sie ganz sicher nicht in dieses Lexikon aufgenommen, und zwar mit gutem Grund: sie umgibt sich mit einem gewissen unerfreulichen, bewußt gepflegten Geheimnis. Der Katalog des genannten Museums gibt nicht einmal ihr Geburtsdatum an! Ein anderer ihrer Paten, zur Abwechslung ein Jugoslawe, behauptet, sie heiße in Wirklichkeit Mrs. Marston Fleming. Wir wollen es ihm aufs Wort glauben (obwohl sein Buch von Ungenauigkeiten strotzt), denn die Galerie, in der die Dame mehrmals ausgestellt hat, läßt alle Briefe unbeantwortet. Wenn die Engländer anfangen, nicht zu antworten, «diskret» zu sein, stehen sie in der Tat den Südamerikanern in nichts nach. Wie dem auch sei, ob echt oder falsch, ihre Kunst ist «himmlisch sophistisch», um in der gleichen Tonart zu bleiben

Si cette artiste anglaise n'avait pas exposé au Musée d'Art Moderne de Paris, M.J. Cassou régnant encore, ce qui n'est pas une référence à toute épreuve, entre nous soit dit, nous ne l'aurions, certes, pas incluse dans ce dictionnaire, et pour cause: un certain mystère de mauvais aloi savamment entretenu plane sur elle. Le catalogue du dit musée ne donne même pas sa date de naissance! Un autre de ses parrains, yougoslave cette fois, prétend qu'elle s'appelle en réalité Mme Marston Fleming. Croyons-le sur parole (bien que son livre soit bourré d'erreurs), puisque la galerie où la dite dame a exposé plusieurs fois, ne répond pas aux lettres. Il est vrai que lorsque les Anglais se mettent à ne pas répondre, à être discrets, ils ne le cèdent en rien aux Sud-Américains. Quoiqu'il en soit, vrai ou faux, son art est «délicieusement sophistiqué», pour rester dans la note.

EXPOSITIONS:
Hannover Gallery, Londres 1951.
Betty Parsons Gallery, New York 1953.
Institute of Contemporary Arts, London 1954.
Guildhall, Kings Lynn, USA, 1956.
Galleria dell'Obelisco, Rome 1956.
«De Lusthof der Naieven», Rotterdam 1964.
«Le Monde des Naïfs», Paris 1964.

BIBLIOGRAPHIE:
Oto Bihalji-Merin: «Das naive Bild der Welt», Köln 1959.
Oto Bihalji-Merin: «Die naive Malerei», Köln 1959.
Oto Bihalji-Merin: «Les Peintres Naïfs», Paris (sans date).
«Art Naïf», Editions Marocaines et Internationales, Rabat 1964.

Boyadjian, Micheline

(Née Erard).
Born April 27, 1923 in Bruges (Belgium).

(Geborene Erard).
Geboren am 27. April 1923 in Brügge (Belgien).

(Née Erard).
Née le 27 avril 1923 à Bruges (Belgique).

Was a secretary and shorthand-typist before her marriage. After she met her future husband, a well-known cardiologist, she signed for evening classes in drawing in order to get out of the house—later she was much blamed for this. However, nothing came of these classes. Having learned nothing, either there or elsewhere, she remains one of the purest self-taught artists. She is also specifically Belgian. Her gentle tones in their half-shades, her meticulousness, admirably wedded to an individual and unwavering sense of poetry, make her at present the best Belgian naive artist. Awarded the 'Young Belgian Painters' Prize. Various pictures purchased by the State.

Vor ihrer Heirat Sekretärin und Stenotypistin. Als sie ihren zukünftigen Mann, einen bekannten Kardiologen, kennen lernt, schreibt sie sich, um abends ausgehen zu können, in eine Abendschule für Zeichenunterricht ein, was man ihr später zum Vorwurf gemacht hat. Diese Einwände sind unbegründet. Sie hat weder in dieser Schule noch sonstwo das Geringste gelernt, sondern bleibt eine völlig reine Autodidaktin. Gleichzeitig ist sie auch typisch belgisch. Ihre weichen Farben, ihre Halbtöne, die sorgfältige Ausführung, die sich wunderbar mit einem sehr eigenen und sehr sicheren poetischen Sinn vermählt, machen sie zum besten zeitgenössischen naiven Maler in Belgien. Preis der Jungen Belgischen Malerei. Der Staat hat mehrere Bilder von ihr erworben.

Secrétaire et sténo-dactylo avant son mariage. Lorsqu'elle fait la connaissance de son futur mari, le cardiologue connu, elle s'inscrit dans une école de dessin du soir, afin de pouvoir sortir de chez elle, ce qui lui sera reproché plus tard. Or, il n'en est rien. N'ayant rien appris, ni là, ni ailleurs, elle reste l'une des plus pures autodidactes. Spécifiquement belge aussi. Ses tons doux, en demi-teintes, son exécution minutieuse, qui se marie admirablement avec un sens poétique très particulier et très sûr, font d'elle le meilleur peintre naïf belge actuel. Prix de la Jeune Peinture Belge. Plusieurs tableaux achetés par l'état.

EXPOSITIONS:
«Les Peintres Naïfs», Knokke-le-Zoute 1958.
Galerie Breughel, Bruxelles 1960
(Cat., Préface Anatole Jakovsky).
«La Peinture Naïve», Maison de la Pensée Française, Paris 1960.
Galerie de l'Institut, Paris 1960
(Cat., Préface Anatole Jakovsky).
«Das naive Bild der Welt», Baden-Baden 1960.
Galerie Albert Ier, Bruxelles 1963.

BIBLIOGRAPHIE:

Oto Bihalji-Merin: «Das naive Bild der Welt», Köln 1959.
Oto Bihalji-Merin: «Die naive Malerei», Köln 1959.
Oto Bihalji-Merin: «Les Peintres Naïfs», Paris (sans date).
«Micheline Boyadjian», «Das naive Bild der Welt», Heft 3, Frankfurt 1961.
Anatole Jakovsky: «Belle-Ile-en-Mer», La Bibliothèque des Arts, Paris 1962.
Anatole Jakovsky: «Eros du Dimanche», Editions J.J. Pauvert, Paris 1964.
André Blavier: «Micheline Boyadjian», Savoir et Beauté, La Louvière 1965.

Branchard, Emile

Born 1881 in Greenwich Village, New York, N.Y. (USA).
Died February 1938 in Greenwich Village, New York, N.Y. (USA).

Geboren 1881 in Greenwich Village, New York, N.Y. (USA).
Gestorben Februar 1938 in Greenwich Village, New York, N.Y. (USA).

Né en 1881 à Greenwich Village, New York, N.Y. (USA).
Mort en février 1938 à Greenwich Village, New York, N.Y. (USA).

Like the majority of living American 'naive' artists, or those who started to paint at the turn of the century, Branchard is of foreign origin although he was born in the United States. His father, who was French, was a pupil of Meissonier. His mother had a large house on Washington Square South, where he spent all his childhood. He took all kinds of jobs, including that of stevedore. He began to paint in 1912, for his own amusement. Despite the impression of being painted from life, each of his pictures comes from his imagination or his memory.

Wie die meisten naiven Maler Amerikas, die heute noch leben oder die zu Beginn des Jahrhunderts angefangen haben zu malen, ist auch er ausländischer Herkunft, obwohl er bereits in den Vereinigten Staaten zur Welt kam. Sein Vater, ein Franzose, war ein Schüler von Meissonier. Seine Mutter besaß ein geräumiges Haus an Washington Square South, wo er seine ganze Jugend verbrachte. Dann übte er alle möglichen Berufe aus, sogar den eines Ausladers. 1912 begann er zu seinem Vergnügen zu malen. Und das, was er gemalt hat, hat er trotz der Illusion der Wirklichkeit aus der Phantasie, aus dem Gedächtnis geschaffen.

Comme la plupart des peintres naïfs américains vivants ou ceux qui ont commencé à peindre avec le siècle, celui-ci est d'origine étrangère, bien que déjà né aux USA. Son père, français, fut un élève de Meissonier. Sa mère avait une maison spacieuse au Washington Square South où il a passé toute sa jeunesse. Puis, il a fait toutes sortes de métiers, jusqu'à celui de débardeur. Il a commencé à peindre vers 1912 pour son propre plaisir. Et tout ce qu'il a peint, malgré l'illusion du réel, a été peint d'imagination, de mémoire.

EXPOSITIONS:
Stephan Bourgeois Gallery, New York from 1919 to 1932.
«The Masters of Popular Painting», New York 1938.
« Das naive Bild der Welt», Baden-Baden 1961.

BIBLIOGRAPHIE:
Sidney Janis: «They Taught Themselves», Dial Press, New York 1942.

Braren, Oluf

Born 1787 on the island of Föhr (Germany).
Died 1839 in Toftum on Föhr (Germany).

Geboren 1787 auf der Insel Föhr (Deutschland).
Gestorben 1839 in Toftum auf Föhr (Deutschland).

Né en 1787 dans l'île de Föhr (Allemagne).
Mort en 1839 à Toftum sur Föhr (Allemagne).

Was a teacher in Braderup, Midlum and Uetersum. Not many of the pictures of this father of German 'naive' art are known, but they are generally genre paintings or portraits stamped by the 'Gemütlichkeit' so well-beloved of the Biedermeier period.

Volksschullehrer in Braderup, Midlum und Uetersum. Man kennt nicht viele Bilder von diesem Urahn der naiven Malerei in Deutschland. Es sind im allgemeinen Genrebilder und Porträts, welche die dem Biedermeier eigene Gemütlichkeit ausstrahlen.

Instituteur à Braderup, Midlum et Uetersum. On ne connaît pas beaucoup de tableaux de cet ancêtre de la peinture naïve en Allemagne. Ce sont, généralement, des scènes de genre et des portraits empreints de cette «Gemütlichkeit», chère à l'époque du Biedermeier.

EXPOSITIONS:
«Maler des einfältigen Herzens», Museum am Ostwall, Dortmund 1952.

BIBLIOGRAPHIE:
Bernard Jasmand et Otto Kallir: «Sonntagsmaler», Ed. Otto Aug.Ehlers, Berlin/Dortmund 1956.
«Schönheit», Recklinghausen 1958 (Cat., Préface Stephan Hirzel).
Oto Bihalji-Merin: «Das naive Bild der Welt», Köln 1959.
Oto Bihalji-Merin: «Die naive Malerei», Köln 1959.
Oto Bihalji-Merin: «Les Peintres Naïfs», Paris (sans date).

Brašič, Janko

Born December 27, 1905 (or January 9, 1906, because of the shifting of the date with the Gregorian calendar) in Opariče (Yugoslavia).

Geboren am 27. Dezember 1905 (oder am 9. Januar 1906 infolge der Verschiebung des gregorianischen Kalenders) in Opariče (Jugoslawien).

Né le 27 décembre 1905 (ou le 9 janvier 1906, à cause du décalage avec le calendrier grégorien) à Opariče (Yougoslavie).

Belongs to the third group of Yugoslav 'naive' artists, the one centered in his home town Opariče. This group is the smallest and least important of the three, for even Brašič, who is indubitably the best of them, leaves a lot to be desired as a painter. His work comes very close to being 'popular art'. He began to paint in 1933, whilst helping to decorate the orthodox church in his village. Before then, he was a shepherd. His first exhibition was in the village school in 1937.

Gehört zur dritten Gruppe der naiven Maler Jugoslawiens, jener von Opariče, wo er zur Welt kam. Es ist übrigens die kleinste und unbedeutendste Gruppe, denn selbst Brašič, der unbestreitbar beste ihrer Maler, läßt zu wünschen übrig. Seine Malerei kommt der Volkskunst sehr nahe. Er beginnt 1933 zu malen, als er in seinem Dorf beim Ausschmücken einer orthodoxen Kirche hilft. Vorher hütete er Schafe. Er stellt 1937 zum ersten Mal im Schulhaus seines Dorfes aus.

Appartient au troisième groupe des peintres naïfs yougoslaves, celui d'Opariče où il est né. C'est d'ailleurs le moins nombreux et le moins important, car même le peintre en question, qui est incontestablement le meilleur, laisse à désirer. Son art frise l'art populaire de très près. Il commence à peindre en 1933, lorsqu'il aide à décorer une église orthodoxe de son village. Avant, il gardait les moutons. Il expose pour la première fois dans l'école de son village en 1937.

EXPOSITIONS:
«Naivni umetnici jugoslavjie», Belgrade 1957.
«Das naive Bild der Welt», Baden-Baden 1961.
The Arthur Jeffress Gallery, Londres 1961 (Cat., Préface M. Gelen).
«Yougoslav Modern Primitives», Edinburgh 1962.
«Peintres Naïfs Yougoslaves», Moscou 1962.
«Première Quadriennale des Peintres Naïfs Yougoslaves», Čačac 1962.
«Naive Kunst in Jugoslawien», Kunstakademie, Wien 1963.
«Peintres Naïfs Populaires Yougoslaves», Leningrad 1963.
«Sonntagsmaler aus Jugoslawien», Museum am Ostwall, Dortmund 1964.
«De Lusthof der Naieven», Rotterdam 1964.
«Le Monde des Naïfs», Paris 1964.

BILBIOGRAPHIE:
«Yougoslavija» Numéro spécial (17) consacré à l'art des naïfs, Belgrade 1959.
Oto Bihalji-Merin: «Das naive Bild der Welt», Köln 1959.
Oto Bihalji-Merin: «Die naive Malerei», Köln 1959.
Oto Bihalji-Merin: «Les Peintres Naïfs», Paris (sans date).
Oto Bihalji-Merin: «Umetnost Naivnich u Jugoslavjii», Belgrade 1963.

Bray, Ernest

Born October 8, 1883 in Blois (France).

Geboren am 8. Oktober 1883 in Blois (Frankreich).

Né le 8 octobre 1883 à Blois (France).

Son of a cooper who became a shoemaker. Was a sculptor before he turned to painting. In fact, he did not start to paint until quite late in life. Is a laborious, over-meticulous worker; apart from the manual work there is virtually no sensitivity in his pictures.

Sohn eines Küfers, der Schuhfabrikant wird. Betätigt sich als Bildhauer, ehe er zur Malerei übergeht, was erst ziemlich spät geschieht. Mühsame, zu beflissene Malerei, der es zwar nicht an Fertigkeit, wohl aber an Empfindsamkeit mangelt.

Fils d'un tonnelier qui devient fabricant de chaussures. Sculpte avant de peindre. Il s'y met assez tard, du reste. Peinture laborieuse, trop appliquée, où, en déhors du travail manuel, la sensibilité est pour ainsi dire absente.

EXPOSITIONS:
Gal. R. Duncan, Paris 1955 (Cat., Préf. D. Pipard).
Galerie Notre-Dame, Paris 1959 (Cat., Préface Guy Dornand).
« Les Primitifs d'Aujourd'hui »,
Galerie Charpentier, Paris 1964.

Buktenica, Eugen

Born November 28, 1914 in Grohota on the island of Šolta, near Split (Yugoslavia).

Geboren am 28. November 1914 in Grohota auf der Insel Šolta bei Split (Jugoslawien).

Né le 28 novembre 1914 à Grohota, dans l'île de Šolta, près de Splite (Yougoslavie).

A Croatian. Both a fisherman and a farmer. Was interned by the Nazis from 1941 to 1944, and while in the concentration camp he wrote a remarkable poem entitled 'The Fight of the People of Šolta'. In 1946 he started to paint—he is the only Yugoslav 'naive' artist to paint seascapes.

Kroate. Fischer und Bauer. Von 1941 bis 1944 von den Nazis interniert. Im Lager schreibt er ein bedeutendes Gedicht: Der Kampf der Leute von Šolta. Beginnt 1946 zu malen. Er ist der einzige unter den naiven Malern Jugoslawiens, der Seestücke malt.

Donc Croate. Pêcheur et paysan. Interné par les nazis entre 1941 et 1944. Dans le camp, il écrit un remarquable poème: Le Combat du Peuple de Šolta. Se met à peindre en 1946 et c'est le seul parmi les peintres naïfs yougoslaves à peindre des marines.

EXPOSITIONS:
Musée de Dubrovnik (à l'occasion du Congrès de l'AICA) 1956.
Galerie d'Art Primitif, Zagreb 1957 (Cat., Préface M. Gvozdanovič).
« Naivni umetnici jugoslavije », Belgrade 1957.
« La Peinture Naïve », Knokke-le-Zoute 1958.
« Première Quadriennale des Peintres Naïfs Yougoslaves », Čačac 1962.
«Yugoslav Modern Primitives», Edinburgh 1962.
« Peintres Naïfs Yougoslaves », Moscou 1962.
« Naive Kunst in Jugoslawien », Kunstakademie, Wien 1963.
The Galerie St-Etienne, New York 1963 (Cat., Préface non signée).
« Peintres Naïfs Populaires Yougoslaves », Leningrade 1963.
« Sonntagsmaler aus Jugoslawien », Museum am Ostwall, Dortmund 1964.
« De Lusthof der Naieven », Rotterdam 1964.
« Le Monde des Naïfs », Paris 1964.

BIBLIOGRAPHIE:
«Yougoslavia», numéro spécial (17) consacré à l'art des naïfs, Belgrade 1959.
Oto Bihalji-Merin: « Das naive Bild der Welt », Köln 1959.
Oto Bihalji-Merin: « Die naive Malerei », Köln 1959.
Oto Bihalji-Merin: « Les Peintres Naïfs », Paris (sans date).
Oto Bihalji-Merin: « Umetnost Naivnich u Jugoslavjii », Belgrade 1963.

Caillaud, Aristide

Born January 28, 1902 in Moulins, Deux Sèvres (France).

Geboren am 28. Januar 1902 in Moulins, Deux-Sèvres (Frankreich).

Né le 28 janvier 1902 à Moulins, Deux Sèvres (France).

There was apparently nothing to predispose this little shepherd, who gradually rose in the social scale, to take up painting, especially as the pork-butcher's shop which he bought in a Paris suburb took up all his time. Nothing—except fate, except the war. He was taken prisoner, and met painters, writers and musicians. One of the painters taught him to use a brush. The effect was instantaneous—he thought of nothing else from then on! But owing to working hard at his painting, to taking part in exhibitions and moving in intellectual circles, his inborn 'naiveté' soon gave way to a kind of old-fashioned surrealism, authoritative, not far removed from fairy stories. He is a very gifted artist in the fullest sense of the term.

Nichts schien diesen Hirtenjungen für die Malerei zu bestimmen, und dies um so weniger, seit er, auf der sozialen Stufenleiter immer höher steigend, in einem Vorort von Paris eine Schweinemetzgerei gekauft hatte, die seine ganze Zeit beanspruchte. Nichts – außer dem Schicksal, außer dem Krieg. Im Gefangenenlager lernt Caillaud Maler, Schriftsteller, Musiker kennen. Einer dieser Maler lehrt ihn, wie man sich eines Pinsels bedient. Liebe auf den ersten Blick! Er denkt nur noch ans Malen. Aber das viele Arbeiten, Ausstellen und der Verkehr mit Intellektuellen hat zur Folge, daß seine ursprüngliche Naivität von einer Art archaisierendem Surrealismus verdrängt wird, eng verwandt mit Märchen. Ein im vollen Sinn des Worts sehr begabter Künstler.

Rien ne prédisposait, semble-t-il, ce petit pâtre, s'élevant de plus en plus dans l'échelle sociale, à faire de la peinture; d'autant plus que la charcuterie qu'il a achetée dans la banlieue de Paris, lui prenait tout son temps. Rien, sauf la fatalité, sauf la guerre. Fait prisonnier, Caillaud voit des peintres, des écrivains, des musiciens. L'un de ces peintres lui apprend à se servir du pinceau. Et c'est un coup de foudre! Il ne pensera plus qu'à cela. Mais à force de travailler, d'exposer et de fréquenter des intellectuels, sa naiveté native fait bientôt place à une sorte de surréalisme archaïsant, coulant de bonne source, tout près des contes de fées. Artiste très doué, dans toute l'acception de ce terme.

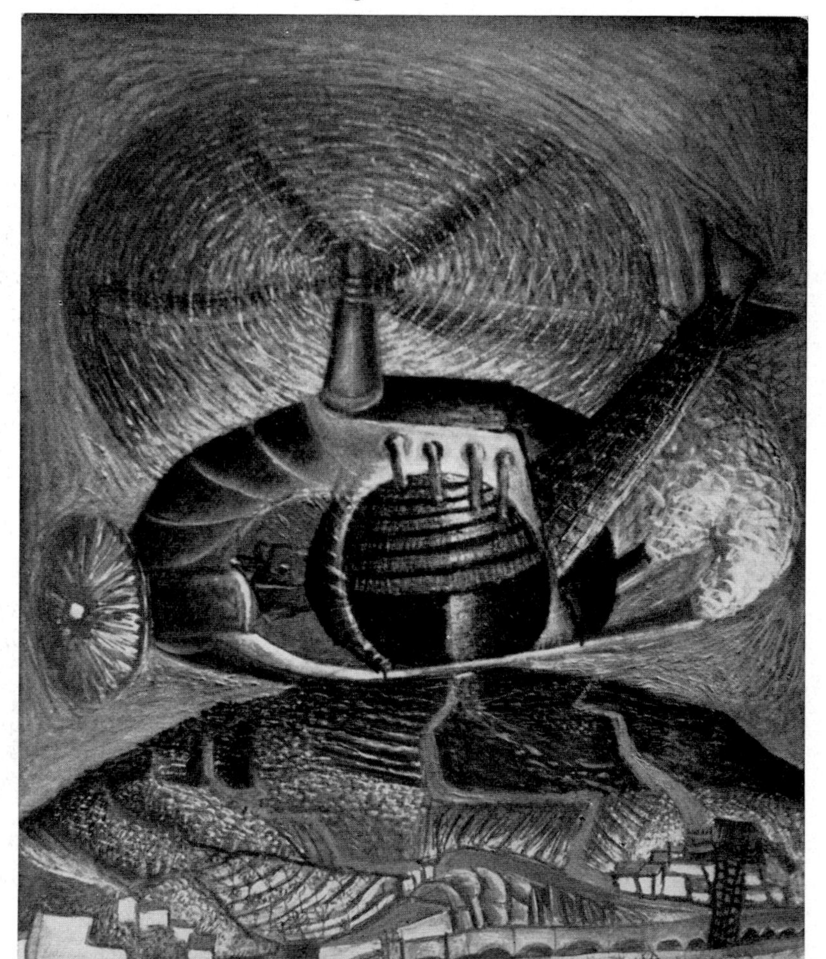

EXPOSITIONS:
Galerie Stiebel, Paris 1949.
Pavillon de Marsan, Paris 1953 (avec les tissus de Paule Marot).
Galerie Craven, Paris 1954 (Cat., Préface J. Debrix).
Galerie Bénézit, Paris 1957.
Galerie André Droulez, Reims 1959.
« Das naive Bild der Welt », Baden-Baden 1961.
Galerie Daniel Cordier, Paris 1962 (Cat., Préface Frank Elgar).
« Les Primitifs d'Aujourd'hui », Galerie Charpentier, Paris 1964.

BIBLIOGRAPHIE:
« Aristide Caillaud », Art d'Aujourd'hui, N° 7, Paris, juillet 1951.
Anatole Jakovsky: « Les Peintres Naïfs », Paris 1956.
Anatole Jakovsky: « Naive Malerei », Zürich 1957.
« Aristide Caillaud », in Documents, Ed. Pierre Cailler, Genève 1957.
Oto Bihalji-Merin: « Das naive Bild der Welt », Köln 1959.
Oto Bihalji-Merin: « Die naive Malerei », Köln 1959.
Oto Bihalji-Merin: « Les Peintres Naïfs », Paris (sans date).
« Art Naïf », Editions Marocaines et Internationales, Rabat 1964.
Anatole Jakovsky: « Eros du Dimanche », Paris 1964.

Calenda, Lucy

Born November 19, 1929 in Rio de Janeiro (Brazil).

Geboren am 19. November 1929 in Rio de Janeiro (Brasilien).

Née le 19 novembre 1929 à Rio de Janeiro (Brésil).

Rather sketchy painting of traditional folklore subjects. But has a delicate eye and a feeling for nuances, which rescue her pictures from being monotonous or even repetitive. Has lived for years in Europe.

Etwas summarische Malerei mit überlieferten folkloristischen Themen. Aber ihr sehr feines Auge und ihr Sinn für Nuancen retten ihre Bilder vor einer gewissen Monotonie, um nicht zu sagen Dürftigkeit. Lebt schon seit Jahren in Europa.

Peinture un peu sommaire, à des sujets folkloriques traditionnels. Mais son œil très fin et son sens des nuances sauvent ses tableaux d'une certaine monotonie, pour ne pas dire indigence. Vit depuis des années en Europe.

EXPOSITIONS:
Galeria Oxumare, Bahia 1956
(Cat., Préface José Pedreira).
Club des Arts, São Paulo 1957
(Cat., Préface Sergio Milliet).
Galerie Montmartre, Rio de Janeiro 1958
(Cat., Préface A.F. Schmidt).
Galeria Rose-Marie, Buenos Aires 1958.
Galerie Marcel Bernheim, Paris 1962
(Cat., Préface Anatole Jakovsky).
Galerie El Arbol, Madrid 1962
(Cat., Préface João Cabral de Melo Neto).
Galleria Giraldi, Livorno 1963
(Cat., Préface Anatole Jakovsky et Melo Neto).
Galleria La Feluca, Rome 1963
(Cat., Préface Anatole Jakovsky).
«Pittori Naifs», Centro Internazionale di Arte Figurative, Biella 1964.
Galleria La Feluca, Rome 1964.

Canal, Edmond Léon

Born December 19, 1892 in Montgaillard, Ariège (France).

Geboren am 19. Dezember 1892 in Montgaillard, Ariège (Frankreich).

Né le 19 décembre 1892 à Montgaillard, Ariège (France).

Was a maker of funeral wreaths, then a funeral director. Even in the making of these wreaths of many-colored beads (which are really works of art in that region of France, like the flower arrangements of Séraphine de Senlis) he showed a good deal of ingenuous ability—he himself designed the wreaths. But he did not actually start painting until 1954, when he felt himself to be at a loose end after a serious operation. And it was mainly after 1962 that he devoted much of his time to painting. His work depicts the customs and the legendary history of his country.

Fabrikant von Grabkränzen, dann Leichenbestatter. Schon für diese Kränze aus farbigen Glasperlen, die in dieser Gegend Frankreichs wahre Meisterwerke an gutem Geschmack darstellen und an Blumensträuße von Séraphine gemahnen, hat er viel Erfindungsgabe aufgebracht, denn er schuf die Zeichnungen für die Anordnung selber. Aber er malt noch nicht. Dazu kommt er erst 1954, als er nach einer schweren Operation nicht weiß, was anfangen. Von 1962 an widmet er sich wahrhaft seiner Malerei. Seine Bilder schildern Sitten und Gebräuche und die folkloristische Vergangenheit seiner Heimat.

Fabricant de couronnes mortuaires, puis entrepreneur des pompes funèbres. Déjà, pour ces couronnes en perles multicolores, qui sont de véritables chefs d'œuvre de goût dans cette partie de la France, pareilles à des bouquets de Séraphine de Senlis, il a depensé pas mal d'ingénuosité, car c'est lui-même qui créait les modèles de ces couronnes. Mais il ne peint pas encore. Cela n'arrive qu'en 1954, lorsqu'il se sent desœuvré après une grave opération. Et c'est surtout à partir de 1962 qu'il se consacre à sa peinture, où il évoque les mœurs et le passé folklorique de son pays.

Capel, Miguel

Born December 27, 1932 in Gochar, Almeria (Spain).

Geboren am 27. Dezember 1932 in Gochar, Almeria (Spanien).

Né le 27 décembre 1932 à Gochar, Almeria (Espagne).

A typically Spanish painter—strident colors and a strong, almost cruel design. Sometimes rather erotic. Erratic production, but as the artist is still young there is hope for development.

Eine typisch spanische Malerei; grelle Farben und schwarze, beinahe grausame Konturen. Zuweilen ziemlich erotisch. Ungleichmäßig im Wert, aber in Anbetracht des Alters des Künstlers sind Hoffnungen erlaubt.

Une peinture typiquement espagnole; couleurs stridentes et un cerne noir, presque cruel, du dessin. Parfois assez érotique. Production inégale, mais, vu l'âge de l'artiste, permet d'espérer.

EXPOSITIONS:
Galeria René Metras, Barcelone 1965 (Cat., Préface Rafael Santos Torroella).

Carlsson, Carl Johan

Born 1867 in Brandalssund (Sweden).
Died in 1953 in Gävle (Sweden).

Geboren 1867 in Brandalssund (Schweden).
Gestorben 1953 in Gävle (Schweden).

Né en 1867 à Brandalssund (Suède).
Mort en 1953 à Gävle (Suède).

Was a blacksmith by trade, but had several other jobs too. A genuine self-taught artist, who, in fact, did not take up painting until quite late. His work is rather awkward and shows signs of a definitely infantile technique. He called himself 'court painter' because, having once sent a portrait to King Gustav V, he received from him a letter of thanks.

Schmied, daneben ein paar andere Gelegenheitsberufe. Reiner Autodidakt. Er begann übrigens erst in vorgerücktem Alter zu malen. Ziemlich unbeholfen, mit offensichtlichen Zeichen von Infantilismus. Er nannte sich «Hofmaler», weil er von König Gustav V. ein Dankesschreiben erhielt für ein Porträt, das er ihm geschickt hatte.

Forgeron, sans compter quelques autres métiers occasionnels. Autodidacte pur. Il se mit, d'ailleurs, à peindre sur le tard. Assez malhabile, avec des signes d'infantilisme évident. Il se prénommait «Peintre de la Cour», car, à la suite d'un envoi d'un portrait du roi Gustave V, il a reçu de lui une lettre de remerciements.

EXPOSITIONS:
«Laienmaler», Gewerbemuseum, Basel 1961.

Carmelina

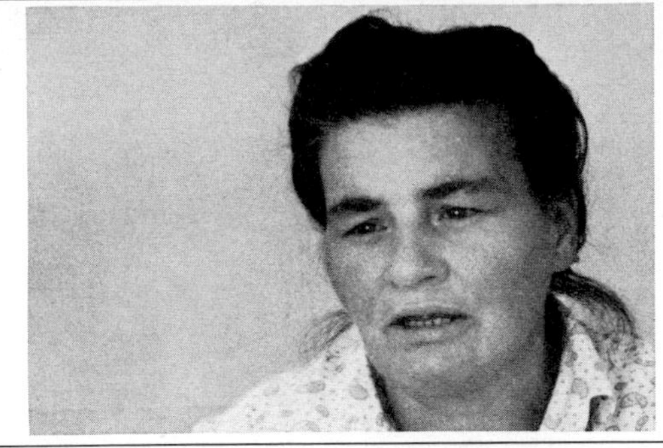

(Carmelina Alberino).
Born June 23, 1920 in Capri (Italy).

Geboren am 23. Juni 1920 in Capri (Italien).

Née le 23 juin 1920 à Capri (Italie).

Daughter of a humble family of fishermen. Married the gardener of the island's small graveyard and had two children. She has an enthusiastic and very pious nature, and she threw herself into painting with the same keenness with which she undertook the building of hcr beautiful house (this latter, however, seemed to be beyond her strength). Her pictures, which show various views of Capri, have the same attitude of challenge. Time no longer exists, distances become confused. The artist, as if gifted with ubiquity, seems to be everywhere at once. A feeling of enchantment pervades all her work.

Tochter bescheidener Fischer. Heiratet den Gärtner des kleinen Friedhofs der Insel, bringt zwei Kinder zur Welt. Sie stürzt sich voll Begeisterung und Gottvertrauen aufs Malen, mit der gleichen Spontaneität und dem gleichen Schwung, die sie zum Bau ihres sehr schönen Hauses getrieben haben, obwohl es über ihre Kräfte zu gehen schien. Ihre Bilder, die verschiedene Ansichten von Capri darstellen, zeugen vom gleichen Wagemut. Die Zeit ist aufgehoben, die Entfernungen verschwimmen; Carmelina, mit wahrer Allgegenwart begabt, ist überall gleichzeitig. Zauber herrscht in allen ihren Bildern.

Fille de modestes pêcheurs. Epouse le jardinier du petit cimetière de l'île qui lui donne deux enfants. Enthousiaste, pleine de foi, elle se jette à corps perdu dans la peinture, avec la même spontanéité et le même élan qui l'a poussée à entreprendre la construction de sa fort belle maison qui semblait être, pourtant, au-dessus de ses forces. Ses tableaux, qui représentent les différents aspects de Capri, relèvent de la même gageure. Le temps n'existe plus, les distances se brouillent; douée d'un véritable don d'ubiquité, Carmelina est partout à la fois. La féerie règne d'un bout à l'autre de ses tableaux.

EXPOSITIONS:
Galleria La Feluca, Rome 1961
(Cat., Préface Lorenza Trucchi).
Galleria La Feluca, Rome 1963
(Cat., Préface Lorenza Trucchi).
«I Pittori Naifs», Rome 1964.
Galerie M. Bénézit, Paris 1964
(Préface Anatole Jakovsky).
«I Pittori Naifs», Centro Internazionale di Arte Figurative, Biella 1964.

BIBLIOGRAPHIE:
Salvatore Maffei: «Carmelina», Oggi, 26 novembre 1961.
Lorenza Trucchi: «Carmelina», Editions All'Insegna del Pesce d'Oro, Milan 1964.
«Art Naïf», Editions Marocaines et Internationales, Rabat 1964.
Catalogo Bolaffi d'Arte Moderna 1965/66, Turin 1966.
Anatole Jakovsky: «Saluto ai naifs italiani», L'Europa Letteraria, N° 29, Rome (sans date).

Carter, Bernard

Born 1920 in London (England).

Geboren 1920 in London (England).

Né en 1920 à Londres (Angleterre).

A traditional schoolteacher who has been enthusiastic about painting ever since the age of four. Spent the war in Egypt with the R.A.F.; after the war he married and now lives in South London with his wife and child. His style is extremely delicate, using fresh light colors. He is especially fond of painting stretches of water such as pools and rivers, and he is very knowledgeable about the flora and fauna of such districts. Everything is clearly and accurately presented—its very naturalness gives it a supernatural air.

Ein Schulmeister von altem Schrot und Korn, der sich schon als Vierjähriger für das Malen begeistert. Kämpft während des Kriegs in der RAF in Ägypten. Nach dem Krieg heiratet er und läßt sich mit Frau und Kind im Süden von London nieder. Seine Kunst ist äußerst zart, mit frischen, hellen Farben. Er liebt es ganz besonders, Wasserflächen darzustellen, Teiche und Flüsse, deren Fauna und Flora er ausgezeichnet kennt. Alles ist genau, präzis und vor lauter Wirklichkeit etwas überwirklich.

Un bon vieux maître d'école qui se passionne pour la peinture dès l'age de 4 ans. Fait la guerre dans la R.A.F. en Egypte et, à la fin de la guerre, se marie et se fixe avec son enfant dans le Sud de Londres. Son art est extrêmement délicat, avec des coloris frais et clairs. Il affectionne surtout les étendues d'eau; les étangs et les rivières dont il connait admirablement la faune et la flore. Tout est net, exact et presque surréel à force d'être si réel.

EXPOSITIONS:
Portal Gallery, Londres 1963
(Cat., Préface non signé).
Portal Gallery, Londres 1965
(Cat., Préface non signé).

Ceccarelli, Marino

Born July 15, 1909 in Spoleto, Umbria (Italy).

Geboren am 15. Juli 1909 in Spoleto, Umbrien (Italien).

Né le 15 juillet 1909 à Spoleto, Umbria (Italie).

This artist, who signs his work simply 'Marino' apparently because of another painter called Ceccarelli, was born and still lives in one of Italy's loveliest towns, in the heart of Umbria—a town which has festivals but no motor traffic. Before he took up painting (in 1954) he held a number of jobs, including that of a policeman. Now his painting is done in a studio at the top of the town which resembles at once a picture-seller's booth and the cell of a Franciscan monk. His work is filled with tranquillity, peace and humility—he approaches his landscapes as St. Francis used to speak to animals and birds.

Der Mann, der bloß Marino signiert, weil es, wie es scheint, bereits einen anderen Maler namens Ceccarelli gibt, lebt seit seiner Geburt in einer der schönsten Städte Italiens, im Herzen Umbriens, einer Stadt, wo es Festspiele, aber keine Autos gibt. Ehe er 1954 zu malen anfängt, übt er verschiedene Berufe aus, so auch den eines Polizisten. Jetzt arbeitet er ganz oben in der Stadt, in einem Raum, der zugleich die Butike eines Bildchenmalers und die Zelle eines Franziskanermönchs sein könnte. Denn in Ceccarellis Werk ist alles Friede, Sanftheit und Demut; er spricht zu seiner Landschaft, wie einst der hl. Franz zu den Tieren und Vögeln sprach.

Celui qui signe Marino tout court, à cause, paraît-il d'un autre peintre portant déjà le nom de Ceccarelli, est né et vit dans une des plus belles villes d'Italie, au cœur de l'Ombrie, ville où il y a des festivals, mais pas de voitures. Avant de commencer à peindre, en 1954, il a changé souvent de métier, jusqu'à celui d'agent de police. Maintenant, il travaille tout en haut de la ville, dans une pièce qui pourrait être à la fois l'échoppe d'un marchand d'images et la cellule d'un moine franciscain. Car tout est paix, douceur et humilité dans l'œuvre de Ceccarelli: il s'adresse à son paysage comme autrefois saint François parlait aux bêtes et aux oiseaux.

EXPOSITIONS:
«Mostra di Pittura Popolare», Palazzo delle Espossizioni, Rome 1955.
«I Pittori Naifs», Rome 1964.
«I Pittori Naifs», Centro Internazionale di Arte Figurative, Biella 1964.
Galerie Herbinet, Paris 1965
(Cat., Préface Anatole Jakovsky).

BIBLIOGRAPHIE:
Nevio Jori: «Marino Ceccarelli», Gazzetta di Reggio, 29 juin 1964 et 8 juin 1965.
Anatole Jakovsky et Nevio Jori: «Marino Ceccarelli», Spoleto 1965.
«Le Petit Crapouillot», Paris 1965.
L. Bo: «Marino Ceccarelli», Corriere della Sera, 10 mars 1965.
Catalogo Bolaffi d'Arte Moderna 1965/66, Turin 1966.

Cervantez, Pedro

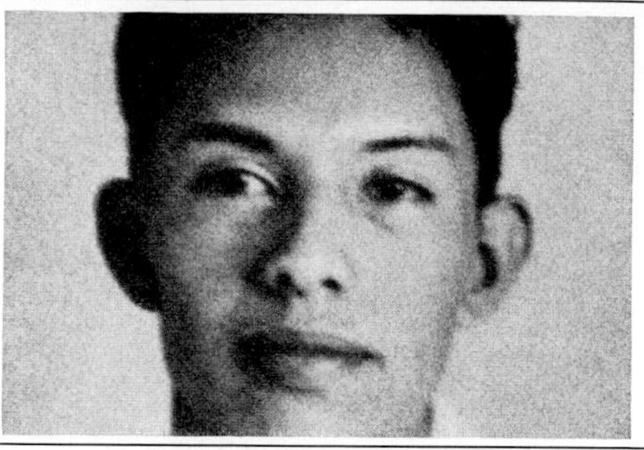

Born 1915 in Arizona (USA).

Geboren 1915 im Staate Arizona (USA).

Né en 1915 dans l'Arizona (USA).

His maternal grandparents ran a pottery works in Mexico, but during the revolution it was burned down and so the whole family immigrated to the United States. Cervantez, whose last position was with the WPA, Federal Art Project in New Mexico, works unhurriedly and conscientiously; his work jars rather by the almost mathematical precision of his design and his execution.

Seine Großeltern mütterlicherseits betrieben in Mexico eine Töpferei. Diese ging während der Revolution in Flammen auf, und darum wanderte die ganze Familie in die Vereinigten Staaten aus. Der Maler, der zuletzt bei WPA, Federal Art Project in New Mexico, beschäftigt war, arbeitet langsam, gewissenhaft, und seine Kunst steht etwas abseits infolge der beinahe mathematischen Strenge sowohl in der Komposition wie in der Ausführung.

Ses grands-parents maternels exploitaient une poterie au Mexique. Cette poterie a brûlé pendant la révolution, et c'est pourquoi toute la famille a émigré aux Etats-Unis. Le peintre, dont le dernier emploi était au WPA, Federal Art Project in New Mexico, travaille lentement, conscienscieusement, et son art détonne un peu par la rigueur presque mathématique aussi bien de la composition que de l'exécution.

EXPOSITIONS:
« Masters of Popular Painting », New York 1938.

BIBLIOGRAPHIE:

Oto Bihalji-Merin: « Das naive Bild der Welt », Köln 1959.
Oto Bihalji-Merin: « Die naive Malerei », Köln 1959.
Oto Bihalji-Merin: « Les Peintres Naïfs », Paris (sans date).

Chaba, Karel

Born August 3, 1925 in Sedletz (Czechoslovakia).

Geboren am 3. August 1925 in Sedlec (Tschechoslowakei).

Né le 3 août 1925 à Sedlec (Tchécoslovaquie).

An unskilled workman, he has had any number of jobs, although he has been attracted to painting from early childhood. He was a self-taught artist so he could not think about exhibiting. But it was only with the de-Stalinization of the country that he was able to show his paintings. Sometimes his art goes beyond true 'naive' painting; he introduces a certain stylization indicating a knowledge, however small, of modern art. His colors are beautiful and delicate and his landscapes are more poetical than anything else. A very talented artist and a very individual one, at any rate.

Ungelernter Arbeiter, der alle möglichen Berufe ausübt, obwohl ihn die Malerei von früher Jugend an anzieht. Als Autodidakt konnte er nicht daran denken, auszustellen. Erst nach der Entstalinisierung konnte er seine Bilder endlich zeigen. Aber seine Kunst geht zuweilen über die eigentlich naive Malerei hinaus. Er unternimmt eine gewisse Stilisierung, die darauf hinweist, daß er die moderne Kunst ein wenig kennt. Seine Farben sind zart und schön, und seine Landschaften vor allen Dingen poetisch. Ein begabter, auf jeden Fall sehr persönlicher Künstler.

Ouvrier non spécialisé qui pratique toutes sortes de métiers, bien qu'attiré depuis son plus jeune âge par la peinture. Autodidacte, il ne pouvait tout de même pas songer à exposer. Ce n'est qu'avec la destalinisation qu'il a pu enfin montrer ses tableaux. Mais son art dépasse parfois la peinture naïve à proprement parler. Il y introduit une certaine stylisation qui dénote un tant soit peu la connaissance de l'art moderne. Ses couleurs sont fines et belles, et ses paysages sont plutôt poétiques qu'autre chose. Un artiste de talent et très personnel dans tous les cas.

EXPOSITIONS:
Divadlo E.F. Buriana, Prague 1960 (Cat., Préface Josef Raban).
Divadlo na Zabradli, 1961.
Galeria Fronta, Prague 1962 (Cat., Préface Alexej Kusak).
Nove Mesto nad Metuji, 1962 (Cat., Préface J. Buzek).
Vinarna Viola, Prague 1963.
Usti nad Orlici, 1963 (Cat., Préface Jaromir Pecirka).
Dum Osvety, Ceska Lipa 1960.
«De Lusthof der Naieven», Rotterdam 1964.
«Le Monde des Naïfs», Paris 1964.

BIBLIOGRAPHIE:
Josef Raban: «Karel Chaba», Vitvarne Umeni Nº 6, 1963.
Karel Trinkewiz: «Karel Chaba», Im Herzen Europas, Mai 1963.

Chabauty, Malvina

(Née Gaborieau).
Born January 28, 1911 in La Ferrière, Vendée (France).

(Geborene Gaborieau)
Geboren am 28. Januar 1911 in La Ferrière Vendée (Frankreich).

(Née Gaborieau).
Née le 28 janvier 1911 à La Ferrière, Vendée (France).

A true peasant. Raises Angora rabbits. Has always painted, moved by a kind of religiosity which leads her to relate stories making life more beautiful. But she never considered her work of any importance and destroyed the majority of her paintings, until an artist who lived nearby encouraged her to take them more seriously. She is very sensitive and imaginative, despite the inadequacies of her drawing.

Eine echte Bäuerin. Züchtet Angora-Kaninchen. Hat von früh auf gemalt, getrieben von einer Frömmigkeit, die ihr erlaubt, das Leben verschönernde Geschichten zu erzählen. Aber sie maß ihren Bildern keinerlei Bedeutung bei, zerstörte die meisten, bis ein Maler in der Umgebung sie ermunterte, ernstlich weiterzumachen. Eine große Empfindsamkeit und eine nicht weniger große Phantasie trotz der Unzulänglichkeit der Zeichnung.

Une authentique paysanne. Elève des lapins Angora. A toujours peint, mue par une sorte de réligiosité qui lui permet de raconter des histoires qui embellissent la vie. Mais elle n'attachait aucune importance à ce qu'elle faisait, détruisant la plupart de ses œuvres, ceci jusqu'au jour où un peintre des environs l'encourage à persévérer très sérieusement. Une grande sensibilité et une non moins grande imagination malgré les insuffisances du dessin.

EXPOSITIONS:
Galerie du Verseau, Paris 1965
(Cat., Préface Anatole Jakovsky et E. Grekoff).

Chalgalo

(real name: Charles Albert Gaston Lombard)
Born August 18, 1882 in Chalons-sur-Marne (France).

(mit seinem richtigen Namen Charles Albert Gaston Lombard)
Geboren am 18. August 1882 in Chalons-sur-Marne (Frankreich).

(De son vrai nom: Charles, Albert, Gaston Lombard)
Né le 18 août 1882 à Chalons-sur-Marne. (France).

At one time a casino croupier. Distrustful and touchy in character. Began to paint when he lost the great love of his life. The memory of this woman obsesses him, and he is doomed to spend the rest of his life lonely, misogynous and unsociable. He prefers to give his paintings away to friends instead of selling them, and to hand them over to the official sales-rooms rather than to have directly to do with art dealers. After his death no doubt many fine works will come to light.

Ehemaliger Croupier. Eigensinniger, mißtrauischer Charakter. Fängt an zu malen, nachdem er die große Liebe seines Lebens verloren hat. Die Erinnerung an diese Frau verfolgt ihn, und er verbringt den Rest seines Lebens in Einsamkeit, Menschenscheu, Ungeselligkeit. Er verschenkt seine Bilder lieber seinen wenigen Freunden, als daß er sie verkauft, und läßt sie lieber versteigern, als in die Hände von Händlern geraten. Nach seinem Tod wird man ein schönes Werk entdecken.

Ancien croupier des Casinos. Caractère entier et ombrageux. Se met à peindre après avoir perdu l'amour de sa vie. Le souvenir de cette femme l'obsède et il passera le reste de sa vie solitaire, mysogine, insociable. Il préfère donner ses tableaux aux amis plutôt que de les vendre, et les passer à l'Hôtel des Ventes au lieu d'avoir affaire à des marchands. Il restera une belle œuvre à découvrir après sa mort.

BIBLIOGRAPHIE:
Anatole Jakovsky: «La Peinture Naïve», Paris 1949.
Anatole Jakovsky: «Les Peintres Naïfs», Paris 1956.
Anatole Jakovsky: «Naive Malerei in Frankreich», Zürich 1957.

Chambers, Thomas

Born ca. 1800 in the United States.
Died ca. 1855 in the United States.

Geboren ca. 1800 in den Vereinigten Staaten.
Gestorben ca. 1855 in den Vereinigten Staaten.

Né vers 1800 aux Etats-Unis.
Mort vers 1855 aux Etats-Unis.

Nothing definite is known about this very gifted artist, except that he worked from 1835 until his death in the State of New York. Most of his paintings show the banks of the Hudson River in a vaguely romantic style. He also painted Niagara Falls. He left between 40 and 50 signed paintings, which are considered among the finest in 19th-century American 'naive' art. Two of his pictures are in the famous collection of E.W. and Bernice Chrysler Garbish (National Gallery of Art, Washington).

Man weiß nichts Genaues über diesen wertvollen Künstler, außer daß er von 1835 bis zu seinem Tod im Staat New York gearbeitet hat. Er hat vor allem mit einem leicht romantischen Gefühl die Ufer des Hudson gemalt. Auch die Niagara-Fälle hat er dargestellt. Er hinterließ etwa 40 bis 50 signierte Bilder, die zu den schönsten Werken der naiven amerikanischen Malerei des 19. Jahrhunderts gehören. Zwei seiner Bilder befinden sich in der berühmten Sammlung E.W. und Bernice Chrysler Garbish (National Gallery of Art, Washington).

On ne sait rien de précis sur cet artiste de grande qualité, sinon qu'il a travaillé à partir de 1835 jusqu'à sa mort dans l'Etat de New York. Il a peint surtout les rives de l'Hudson dans un sentiment vaguement romantique. Il a peint également les chutes du Niagara. Il a laissé entre 40 et 50 tableaux signés qui comptent parmi les belles œuvres de la peinture naïve américaine du XIXe siècle. Deux de ses œuvres figurent dans la célèbre collection E.W. and Bernice Chrysler Garbish (National Gallery of Art, Washington).

EXPOSITIONS:
«Amerikanische Primitive», Museum am Ostwall, Dortmund 1954–55.
Pavillon Américain à l'Exposition Universelle, Bruxelles 1958.

BIBLIOGRAPHIE:
«Thomas Chambers», Antiques Magazine, New York, mars–avril 1948.
Jean Lipman et Alice Winchester: «Primitive Painters in America», Dodd Mead & Co, New York 1950.
B. Jasmand und Otto Kallir: «Sonntagsmaler», Otto Aug. Ehlers, Berlin/Darmstadt 1956.
Oto Bihalji-Merin: «Das naive Bild der Welt», Köln 1959.
Oto Bihalji-Merin: «Die naive Malerei», Köln 1959.
Oto Bihalji-Merin: «Les Peintres Naïfs», Paris (sans date).

Chesher, William A.

Born 1897 in Wooton, near Bedford (England).

Geboren 1897 in Wooton, bei Bedford (England).

Né en 1897 à Wooton, près de Bedford (Angleterre).

A 'specialist in agricultural machinery', as they are called in his country. He knows these machines intimately, and no detail is omitted in his paintings. His pictures are very colorful, bordering sometimes on the picturesque art (or rather the chromolithography) of the last century, and sometimes reminding one of certain pictures by Blondel—he too was at one time a bus-driver. The paintings are not without charm and genuine feeling. Unfortunately, traces of 'splendid isolation' still persist, even in the field of 'naive' art, and detailed information about this artist is not available. (This is the case with the majority of English 'naive' painters.)

«Spezialist für landwirtschaftliche Maschinen» wird er in seiner Heimat genannt. Er kennt ihre Mechanik aufs gründlichste, und so fehlt in seinen Bildern auch nicht die geringste Einzelheit. Sehr farbige Malerei, die ein wenig an die Bilderbogenmalerei oder vielmehr an die Chromolithographie des letzten Jahrhunderts gemahnt und zuweilen an gewisse Bilder von Blondel erinnert, der zufällig auch ehemaliger Omnibuschauffeur war. Es fehlt seiner Malerei weder an Charme noch an Echtheit. Leider ist die «splendid isolation» selbst auf dem Gebiet der naiven Malerei noch nicht spurlos verschwunden, so daß genaue Auskünfte über diesen Maler (wie über die meisten englischen Naiven) nicht erhältlich sind.

«Spécialiste», comme on l'appelle chez lui, des «machines agricoles». Il connaît à fond leur mécanique, donc pas un détail ne manque dans ses tableaux. Peinture très colorée, frisant un tantinet l'imagerie, ou plutôt la chromolithographie du siècle passé, et rappelant parfois certains tableaux de Blondel, lui aussi, comme par hasard, un ancien conducteur d'autobus. Ne manque pas de charme et d'authenticité. Malheureusement, les traces du «Splendide Isolement» persistent encore, même dans le domaine naïf, et les renseignements détaillés nous manquent en ce qui le concerne. (Comme pour la plupart des naïfs anglais.)

EXPOSITIONS:
Portal Gallery, London 1962
Portal Gallery, London 1965
(carte d'invitation illustrée).
«Les Peintres Naïfs», Galerie J.Verrière, Cannes 1966.

BIBLIOGRAPHIE:
Barrie Sturt-Penrose: «Primitives in Private», Observer, 13 février 1966.

Chiappini, J.

Born 1922 in Haiti.

Geboren 1922 in Haiti.

Né en 1922 à Haïti.

Very little is known about this very individual artist who affects a rather old-fashioned, flattened style taken from the old votive pictures of his country. His work reminds one of Dieudonné Cédor, for instance, who also painted Toussaint Louverture, a legendary hero of Haiti.

Man weiß sehr wenig von diesem eigenartigen Künstler, der eine ziemlich altmodische, farblich unabgestufte, den alten Votivtafeln des Landes entlehnte Faktur bevorzugt. Seine Malweise ist übrigens verwandt mit jener von Dieudonné Cédor zum Beispiel, der ebenfalls einen Toussaint Louverture, den sagenhaften Helden der Insel, gemalt hat.

On sait très peu de chose sur cet artiste assez particulier qui affectionne une écriture passablement surrannée, aux applats, empruntée aux anciens Ex Voto du pays. Elle s'apparente, du reste, à celle de Dieudonné Cédor, par exemple, qui a peint, lui aussi, un Toussaint Louverture, héros légendaire de cette île.

EXPOSITIONS:
«Das naive Bild der Welt», Baden-Baden 1961.
«Naive Painters of Latin America», Duke University, Durham (N.C.) 1963.
«De Lusthof der Naieven», Rotterdam 1964.
«Le Monde des Naïfs», Paris 1964.

BIBLIOGRAPHIE:
«Art Naïf», Editions Marocaines et Internationales, Rabat 1964.

Christiaens, Désiré

Born December 21, 1859 in Zele (Belgium).
Died August 4, 1941 in Kallo.

Geboren am 21. Dezember 1859 in Zele (Belgien).
Gestorben am 4. August 1941 in Kallo.

Né le 21 décembre 1859 à Zele (Belgique).
Mort le 4 août 1941 à Kallo.

Was the first tailor's cutter of the store 'Nine Provinces'. It was not until he was almost 35 that he married and settled down in Termonde, as a master tailor. His house was destroyed during the first world war, and so he returned to Zele and later went to St. Nicolas. Became interested in highly improbable inventions and lost all his money. As a consolation he played the violin, the piano, and the cornet; he also took up photography and ... painting. Fairly soon. Naturally. The majority of his works recall the time at Termonde. He often signed his pictures with the pseudonym 'Ed. Snea'.

Erster Zuschneider im Warenhaus «Neuf Provinces». Er war beinahe 35 Jahre alt, als er sich verheiratete und sich als Schneidermeister in Termonde niederließ. Während des Ersten Weltkriegs wird sein Haus zerstört; da kehrt er nach Zele zurück und zieht später nach St. Nicolas. Beschäftigt sich mit ziemlich schrulligen Erfindungen und verliert sein ganzes Geld. Um sich zu trösten, spielt er Geige, Klavier, Klapphorn, betätigt sich als Photograph und – als Maler. Schon ziemlich früh. Natürlich. Die meisten seiner Werke gemahnen an die Schule von Termonde. Oft signierte er seine Bilder mit dem Pseudonym Ed. Snea.

Premier coupeur aux «Neuf Provinces», il avait près de 35 ans quand il se maria et se fixa à Termonde en qualité de maître-tailleur. Sa maison est ravagée pendant la première guerre mondiale, il retourne, alors, à Zele et, plus tard, à St-Nicolas. S'occupe d'inventions assez fantasques et perd tout son argent. Pour se consoler, il joue du violon, du piano, du piston, fait de la photographie et ... de la peinture. D'assez bonne heure. Naturellement. La plupart de ses œuvres font songer à l'école de Termonde. Souvent, il signait ses tableaux d'un pseudonyme: Ed. Snea.

EXPOSITIONS:
«Les Peintres Naïfs Belges», Le Théâtre National, Bruxelles 1965.
«Les Peintres Naïfs Belges», Musée Royal des Beaux-Arts, Verviers 1965.
«Les Peintres Naïfs Belges», Musée Royal des Beaux-Arts, Hasselt 1966.

Clerc, Joseph

Born April 14, 1878 in Saint-Trivier de Courtes, La Haute Bresse (France).

Geboren am 14. April 1878 in Saint-Trivier de Courtes, Haute Bresse (Frankreich).

Né le 14 avril 1878 à Saint-Trivier de Courtes, La Haute Bresse (France).

Previously employed by the post office. Played around with painting in his spare time. After his retirement he worked more regularly at his art. Most of his pictures are of woodland scenery. His deep forests, which are drawn with extreme accuracy and affection, make him a sort of 'naive' Courbet.

Ehemaliger Postbeamter. Pinselt ein bißchen in seinen Mußestunden, arbeitet aber regelmäßiger, seit er in den Ruhestand getreten ist. Malt hauptsächlich Waldlandschaften. Seine tiefen Wälder, die mit ebenso viel Genauigkeit wie Liebe gesehen sind, machen eine Art naiven Courbet aus ihm.

Ancien employé des postes. Taquine le pinceau à ses heures perdues. Travaille plus regulièrement après avoir pris sa retraite. Fait surtout des paysages sylvestres. Ses forêts profondes, conçues avec autant d'exactitude que d'amour, font de lui une espèce de Courbet naïf.

EXPOSITIONS:
Ancien Hôtel de Ville, Lyon 1955.

Cloes, Nicolas

Born March 24, 1889 in Othee, Liege province (Belgium).

Geboren am 24. März 1889 in Othee, Provinz Lüttich (Belgien).

Né le 24 mars 1889 à Othee, province de Liège (Belgique).

Organist. Began by painting on Sundays then did so on other days of the week also, especially after he retired. After delicate landscapes with slightly old-fashioned people there came flower groups and still-life paintings, which constitute his best work.

Organist. Malt zuerst nur am Sonntag, dann auch an den Wochentagen, vor allem nachdem er in den Ruhestand getreten ist. Auf die zarten Landschaften mit den ein bißchen altmodischen Figuren folgen bald Blumensträuße und Stillleben, die als seine besten Werke anzusehen sind.

Organiste. Se met à peindre d'abord le dimanche puis les autres jours de la semaine. Surtout après avoir pris sa retraite. Aux paysages tendres, avec des personnages un tantinet surannés, succèdent bientôt des bouquets et des natures-mortes qui constituent le meilleur de son œuvre.

EXPOSITIONS:
Librairie Gason, Verviers 1956.
Salle de la Société Royale des Beaux-Arts, Verviers 1957 (Cat., Préface Anatole Jakovsky, P. Gason et A. Blavier).
« Les Peintres Naïfs », Knokke-le-Zoute 1958.
Galerie La Proue, Bruxelles 1960.
Galerie Contacts, Liège 1960.
Mairie de Montzen 1962 (Cat., Préface G. Schmits).
Galerie Apollinaire, Stavelot 1962.
Cercle Artistique de Spa, 1963.
Galerie Rose des Vents, Bruxelles 1963/64.
Galerie du Marbre, Liège 1964.
Galerie du Marbre, Liège 1965.
« Peintres Naïfs Belges », Le Théâtre National, Bruxelles 1965.
« Peintres Naïfs Belges », Musée Royal des Beaux-Arts, Verviers 1965.
« Peintres Naïfs Belges », Musée Royal des Beaux-Arts, Hasselt 1966.

BIBLIOGRAPHIE:
G. Schmits: « Nicolas Cloes », 1966. Savoir et Beauté: Numéro spécial, paraissant à La Louvrière, et consacré entièrement aux peintres naïfs, décembre 1965.

Collier, Adolphus

Born December 14, 1880 in Baasrode, Antwerp Province (Belgium).
Died April 2, 1962 in Antwerp (Belgium).

Geboren am 14. Dezember 1880 in Baasrode, Provinz Antwerpen (Belgien).
Gestorben am 2. April 1962 in Antwerpen (Belgien).

Né le 14 décembre 1880 à Baasrode, Province d'Anvers (Belgique).
Mort le 2 avril 1962 à Anvers (Belgique).

Ferryman, taxi-driver, repairer of sails, beer merchant, café proprietor. Most of his pictures show views of Burcht, where he had the café 'De Wachtzaal' (the waiting-room), but he also liked to tell animal stories, a little in the manner of La Fontaine's fables. His style is hard, and sharp, much less dreamlike in quality than that of the other sea artists. Many of his paintings have been lost.

Binnenschiffer, Taxichauffeur, Segelflicker, Bierhändler, Wirt. Seine Bilder stellen in der Mehrzahl Ansichten von Burcht dar, wo er das Café « De Wachtzaal » (Wartesaal) führte, aber er liebte es auch, Tiergeschichten zu erzählen, ein bißchen in der Art von La Fontaines Fabeln. Sein Stil ist hart, zugespitzt, viel weniger träumerisch als die Malweise der anderen malenden Schiffer. Viele seiner Bilder sind verlorengegangen.

Batelier, chauffeur de taxi, réparateur de voiles, marchand de bière, patron de café. Ses tableaux représentent le plus souvent les vues de Burcht, où il tenait le café « De Wachtzaal » (Salle d'attente), mais il aimait à raconter aussi des histoires d'animaux, un peu à la manière des fables de La Fontaine.
Beaucoup de ses tableaux sont perdus. Son style est dur, incisif, beaucoup moins rêveur que celui des autres peintres-mariniers.

EXPOSITIONS:
« Peintres Naïfs Belges », Théâtre National de Belgique, Bruxelles 1965.
« Peintres Naïfs Belges », Musée Royal des Beaux-Arts, Verviers 1965.
« Peintres Naïfs Belges », Musée Royal des Beaux-Arts, Hasselt 1966.

Colombo, Mario

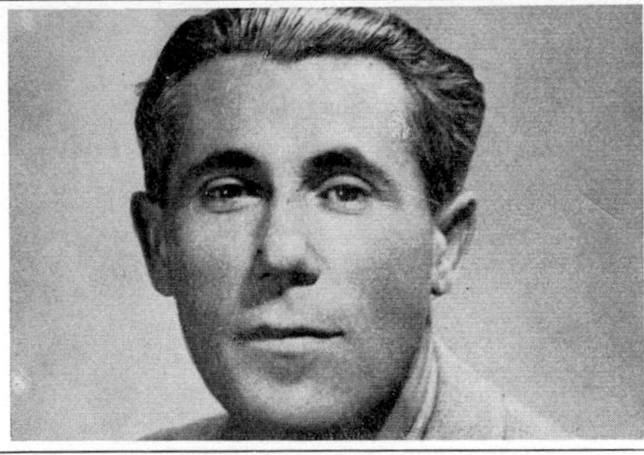

Born January 17, 1907 in Mantua (Italy).

Geboren am 17. Januar 1907 in Mantua (Italien).

Né le 17 janvier 1907 à Mantoue (Italie).

Now lives in Guastalla, one of those districts (of which there are several in the world) where quite a number of 'naive' artists seem to reside. Such a place obviously influences many people; each is attracted by it and thinks: 'Well, why not I?' Guastalla was one of these towns. Colombo's first attempts, painted in gouache, are very promising. At the moment his work is simply anecdotal but it may develop.

Lebt in Guastalla. Orte, wo naive Begabungen in großer Dichte vorhanden sind, wie es deren ein paar auf der Welt gibt, üben unvermeidlich eine viel größere Anziehungskraft aus. Zu diesen Orten gehört Guastalla. Jeder scheint sich hier zu fragen: warum nicht ich? Aber schon Colombos Anfänge in Gouache waren vielversprechend. Eine im Augenblick noch anekdotische Malerei, die sich aber weiterentwickeln kann.

Habite Guastalla. Or, des endroits à forte densité de talents naïfs, comme il en existe quelques-uns de par le monde, exercent nécessairement une attraction beaucoup plus grande que partout ailleurs. Et Guastalla en est un! Chacun semble s'y demander: et pourquoi pas moi? Mais ses débuts, à la gouache, étaient déjà prometteurs. Une peinture anecdotique pour l'instant, mais qui peut évoluer.

BIBLIOGRAPHIE:
Nevio Jori: «Colombo Mario», Gazzetta di Regio, 8 mai 1965.

Crépin, François-Joseph

Born February 8, 1875 in Henin-Liétard, Pas de Calais (France).
Died November 10, 1948 in Montigny-en-Gohelle, Pas de Calais (France).

Geboren am 8. Februar 1875 in Henin-Liétard, Pas de Calais (Frankreich).
Gestorben am 10. November 1948 in Montigny-en-Gohelle, Pas de Calais (Frankreich).

Né le 8 février 1875 à Henin-Liétard, Pas de Calais (France).
Mort le 10 novembre 1948 à Montigny-en-Gohelle, Pas de Calais (France).

Worked in the Pas de Calais mines until the day his hand began to draw all by itself on a sheet of paper. He understood immediately that this was a message from beyond and that he must obey, whatever happened. Later he heard voices. These voices foretold the exact number of 'wonderful' pictures which he would complete in his lifetime, and that the last one would be done on the day of his death. This turned out to be quite accurate, in fact. He worked at night, hiding even from his daughter. He was also a 'healer'. It is curious to note that the architecture and landscapes depicted in his work, probably Egyptian or Aztec, resemble those of another miner-healer, Lessage, whom he had obviously not known.

Arbeitete in den Gruben des Pas de Calais bis zum Tag, da seine Hand sich ganz von allein über ein Blatt Papier zu bewegen begann.
Er begreift sofort, daß es sich dabei um eine Botschaft aus dem Jenseits handelt und daß er sie unverändert wiedergeben muß. Später vernimmt er dann Stimmen. Diese Stimmen sagen ihm die Gesamtzahl der «wunderbaren» Bilder voraus, die er in seinem Leben malen wird, und daß das letzte an seinem Todestag entstehen werde. Was sich als richtig herausstellte.
Er arbeitete nachts und versteckte sein Tun selbst vor seiner Tochter. Er war andererseits auch Heilpraktikant. Seltsamerweise erinnern seine Bauten und Landschaften, die ägyptisch oder aztekisch sein könnten, an die von Lessage, der ebenfalls Medium und Grubenarbeiter war, den Crépin aber natürlich nicht gekannt hat.

Travaillait dans les mines du Pas de Calais jusqu'au jour où sa main a commencé à courir toute seule sur une feuille de papier. Il comprend aussitôt qu'il s'agit là d'un message de l'au-delà et qu'il faut qu'il l'exécute tel quel. Plus tard, il entendra des voix. Ces voix lui ont prédit le nombre total de tableaux «merveilleux» qu'il fera dans sa vie, car le dernier sera fait le jour de sa mort. Ce qui se révéla, d'ailleurs, exact. Il travaillait la nuit, se cachait même de sa fille. Il était guérisseur par ailleurs. Chose curieuse, ses architectures et ses paysages, qui pourraient être égyptiens ou aztèques, rappellent ceux d'un autre peintre-médium, Lessage, qu'il n'a, évidemment, pas connu.

EXPOSITIONS:
Galerie Lefranc, Paris 1946.
Galerie Lefranc, Paris 1948.
Galerie Lefranc, Paris 1950.
Galerie Voyelles, Paris 1954.
Galerie à l'Etoile Scelée, Paris 1955
(Cat., Préface André Breton et Ch. Estienne).

BIBLIOGRAPHIE:
André Breton: «François-Joseph Crépin», Combat, Paris 14 juin 1954.
«Collection d'André Breton», in l'Œil, N°.10, Paris octobre 1955.
Anatole Jakovsky: «Les Peintres Naïfs», Paris 1956.
Anatole Jakovsky: «Naive Malerei», Zürich 1957.
André Breton: «Le Surréalisme et la Peinture», Ed. Gallimard, Paris 1965.
«F.J. Crépin», L'Art Brut, No. 6, Paris 1965.

Crociani, Emile

Born June 25, 1902 in Santa Sofia, near Florence (Italy).

Geboren am 25. Juni 1902 in Santa Sofia bei Florenz (Italien).

Né le 25 juin 1902 à Santa Sofia, près de Florence (Italie).

Worked on the land until he was twenty. Then he immigrated to France, where for three years he was employed as a miner in the Meuse district and then, for 32 years 3 months, he worked as a stoker in a gasworks in Nice. However, before he left Florence he had visited its famous art galleries—the Pitti Palace, the Uffizi. But that was all. He waited until he retired before taking up painting himself; in other words, he did not start till 1954. His pictures flow from his brush as visions which have been confined for many years; they give free rein to a truly plastic poetry reminding one irresistibly of the earliest paintings of our Western world, such as the famous ex-votos of Our Lady of Laghet and of St. John of Garguier.

Bis zum Alter von 20 Jahren Bauer. Dann wandert er nach Frankreich aus, wo er zuerst 3 Jahre lang im Departement Meuse im Bergwerk und darauf 32 Jahre und 3 Monate als Heizer im Gaswerk von Nizza arbeitet. Bevor er Italien verläßt, besucht er als Zwanzigjähriger immerhin die beiden berühmtesten Museen seiner Stadt: Pitti und die Uffizien. Aber das ist alles. Er wartet, bis er den Ruhestand erreicht, ehe er selber zu malen anfängt. 1954 ist es endlich so weit. Und nun brechen die lange verhaltenen Bilder nur so aus ihm hervor, eine echte plastische Poesie entfaltet sich frei in seinen Gemälden und verbindet sie so, ob man es will oder nicht, mit den primitivsten Werken unseres Abendlands, den berühmten Votivtafeln von Laghet und von Saint-Jean de Garguier zum Beispiel.

Paysan jusqu'à 20 ans. Emigre en France où il est d'abord, pendant trois ans, mineur dans la Meuse, puis, pendant 32 ans et 3 mois ouvrier – chauffeur de four à l'usine à gaz de Nice. Avant d'émigrer, il visite quand-même, à l'âge de 20 ans, les deux plus fameuses galeries de sa ville: Pitti et les Offices. Mais c'est tout. Il attendra l'âge de la retraite avant de peindre lui-même, ce qui arrive, enfin, en 1954. Et c'est un déferlement d'images longtemps contenu, et c'est une vraie poésie plastique qui se donne libre cours dans ses toiles, l'apparentant ainsi, que l'on veuille ou non, aux œuvres les plus primitives de notre Occident; les fameux Ex Voto de Notre Dame de Laghet et de Saint-Jean de Garguier, par exemple.

EXPOSITIONS:
Galerie Longchamp, Nice 1960.
Hôtel le Provençal, Juan-les-Pins 1961.
Galerie Le Portal, Coaraze 1963 et 1964.
Galerie Jacques Verrières, Cannes 1966.

BIBLIOGRAPHIE:

Jacques Lepage: «Emile Crociani», Aujourd'hui Art et Architecture N° 45, avril 1964.

Csontvary

real name: Kosztka, Mihaly Tivador.
Born July 5, 1853 in Kisszeben (Hungary).
Died June 20, 1919 in Budapest (Hungary).

mit seinem richtigen Namen: Kosztka, Mihaly Tivador.
Geboren am 5. Juli 1853 in Kisszeben (Ungarn).
Gestorben am 20. Juni 1919 in Budapest (Ungarn).

de son vrai nom: Kosztka, Mihaly, Tivador.
Né le 5 juillet 1853 à Kisszeben (Hongrie).
Mort le 20 juin 1919 à Budapest (Hongrie).

Son of a country doctor and pharmacist. He too started as assistant in a pharmacy. One day, on the back of a prescription, he drew a peasant cart to which were yoked two magnificent oxen similar to those in his picture called 'Storm on the Hortobagy'. His chief, thunderstruck, said, 'You are a born painter!' Soon afterwards, he heard a voice which convinced him that he would be the greatest painter in the world. Even greater than Raphael! Spellbound by this prophecy, a little bit megalomaniac, he thought of nothing after that time but painting. He saved as hard as he could to be able to study, but it was not until he was 41 that he finally went to Munich, Karlsruhe and Paris, where he studied at the Julian Academy. From 1894 to 1908 he travelled far and wide, painting—Italy, Greece, Lebanon, Palestine. His first personal exhibitions with catalogue were in Paris in 1907 and in Budapest in 1908.
He has been called the Hungarian Douanier Rousseau, but this is not quite accurate. He is not entirely naive, because he set out to learn all that he could. Nevertheless a certain manual awkwardness, which he could not, or did not know how to overcome, brings him near the naive painters. His art swings between expressionism and a touching romantic naïveté.

Sohn eines Landarztes und -apothekers. Beginnt seine Laufbahn seinerseits als Apothekergehilfe. Und in der Offizin zeichnet er eines Tages auf die Rückseite eines Rezepts einen mit zwei prachtvollen Ochsen bespannten Bauernwagen, wie sie auf seinem «Unwetter über der Hortobagy» betitelten Bild zu sehen sind. Zutiefst beeindruckt sagt ihm sein Prinzipal: Sie sind ein geborener Maler. Kurz darauf vernimmt er eine Stimme, die ihm versichert, er werde der größte Maler der Welt werden. Größer selbst als Raffael! Von dieser etwas größenwahnsinnigen Prophezeiung entscheidend beeinflußt, denkt er von diesem Augenblick an nur noch ans Malen.
So spart er nun eisern, um studieren zu können. Aber erst im Alter von 41 Jahren kann er endlich nach München, Karlsruhe und Paris fahren, wo er sich in der Akademie Julian einschreibt. Von 1894 bis 1908 bereist er malend die Welt: Italien, Griechenland, Libanon und Palästina. Erste individuelle Ausstellungen mit Katalog: Paris 1907 und Budapest 1908.
Man hat ihn den ungarischen Zöllner Rousseau genannt. Diese Bezeichnung trifft nicht zu. Er ist kein rein naiver Maler, denn er hat das Malen gelernt, so gut es in seiner Kraft stand. Indessen rückt eine gewisse manuelle Unbeholfenheit, eben gerade der Zug, den er nicht überwinden wollte oder konnte, ihn trotzdem in die Nähe der Naiven. Seine Kunst schwingt demnach zwischen Expressionismus und einer rührenden romantischen Naivität hin und her.

Fils d'un médecin et pharmacien de campagne. Débute, lui aussi, comme préparateur en pharmacie. Et c'est là qu'il dessine un jour, au dos d'une ordonnance, une charrette paysanne, attelée de deux bœufs magnifiques, comme on peut en voir sur son tableau intitulé: «Tempête sur l'Hortobagy». Son patron sidéré lui dit: vous êtez un peintre né. Peu après, il entend une voix qui le persuade qu'il sera le plus grand peintre du monde. Plus grand que Raphaël! Traumatisé par cette prophétie, un tantinet mégalomane, il ne songe, désormais, qu'à la peinture. Ainsi, il économisera sou par sou afin de pouvoir étudier. Mais ce n'est qu'à l'âge de 41 ans qu'il se rend enfin à Munich, Karlsruhe et Paris, où il étudie à l'Académie Julian. De 1894 à 1908, il parcourt le monde en peignant: l'Italie, la Grèce, le Liban et la Palestine. Premières expositions personnelles, avec catalogue: à Paris en 1907, et à Budapest en 1908.
On l'a surnommé le Douanier Rousseau hongrois. Ce n'est pas exact. Il n'est pas tout à fait naïf, puisqu'il se mit à apprendre la peinture tant qu'il a pu. Or, une certaine maladresse manuelle, celle-là, précisément, qu'il n'a pas pu, ou n'a pas su vaincre, le rapproche quand-même des naïfs. Son art oscille donc entre un expressionnisme et une touchante naïveté romantique.

EXPOSITIONS:
Musée Ernst, Budapest 1930.
«Palais des Beaux-Arts», Bruxelles 1962 (Cat., Préface Eva Bodnar, Pages autobiographiques).

BIBLIOGRAPHIE:
Ervin Ybl: «Csontvary», Corvina, Budapest 1959.
Marcel Brion: «Csontvary, le rêveur éveillé», Jardin des Arts, N° 113, Paris avril 1964.
Lajos Nemeth: «Csontvary», Corvina, Budapest 1964.

Curuchich, Andres

Born in 1892 in Comalapa near Guatemala City (Guatemala).

Geboren 1892 in Comalapa bei Guatemala City (Guatemala).

Né en 1892 à Comalapa, près de Guatemala City (Guatemala).

A Central American Indian of the Cachiquel (Maya) tribe. He has never left his native village where, like all his fellow-countrymen, he cultivates his fields and attends to the housework. Has never learned to paint. Began with tiny landscapes but, gradually, he enlarged his scope out of pure love of his native land and even attempted to portray the life of the country.
He is a 'naive' artist (or 'primitive', as Americans say) in the truest sense of the word. So he depicts work and daily life, such as marriage ceremonies, baptisms, woodcutters at work, women at the spring, New Year's processions, burials, etc. And all have a typically Indian quality.

Indianer vom Stamm der Cachiquel (Maya), der sein Dorf nie verlassen hat, wo er wie alle seine Stammesgenossen seine Felder bestellt und die Hausarbeiten versieht. Hat nie malen gelernt. Er hat mit ganz kleinen Landschaften angefangen, jedoch aus Liebe zu seiner Heimat sein Register erweitert und sich an die verschiedenen Aspekte des Lebens dieses Landes gewagt. Er ist ein Naiver, oder wie die Amerikaner sagen, Primitiver im wahren Sinn des Wortes.
Er malt die Arbeit und das tägliche Geschehen, das heißt Hochzeiten, Tauffeste, die Holzfäller bei der Arbeit, die Frauen am Brunnen, die Prozessionen des Neujahrstages und die Begräbnisse. Das alles mit typisch indianischen Reminiszenzen.

Indien de la tribu Cachiquel (Maya) qui n'est jamais sorti de son village, où, comme tous ses autres compatriotes, il cultive ses champs et vaque aux travaux de la maison. N'a jamais appris à peindre. Il a commencé par de tout petits paysages, mais, peu à peu, par amour de son pays, il a étendu son registre, en s'attaquant aux différents aspects de la vie même de ce pays. Il est un naïf, ou «primitif», comme disent les Américains, dans le vrai sens de ce mot. Il peint donc les travaux et les jours, c'est-à-dire les céremonies du mariage, celles du baptême, les bûcherons au travail, les femmes à la fontaine, les processions du 1er Janvier et les enterrements. Tout cela avec des reminiscences typiquement indiennes.

EXPOSITIONS:
Galerie St-Etienne, New York 1958 (Cat., Préface Dr. Walter Heil).

Dapra, Regine

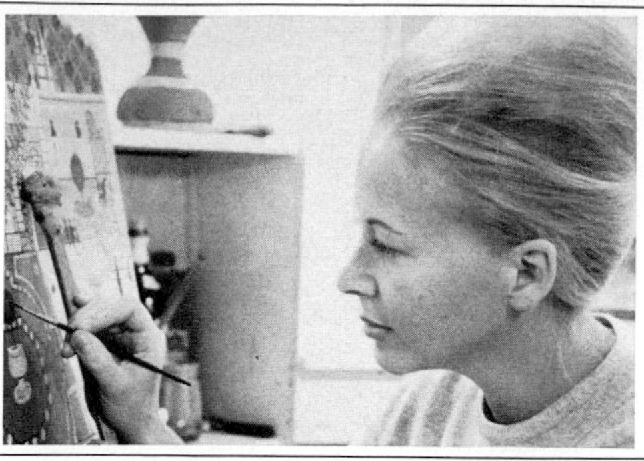

Born February 2, 1929 in Bad Hofgastein (Austria).

Geboren am 2. Februar 1929 in Bad Hofgastein (Österreich).

Née le 2 février 1929 à Bad Hofgastein (Autriche).

From 1945 to 1953 she studied music in Salzburg and Vienna, and then toured abroad as a pianist until 1959. After her return to Salzburg in 1960 she suddenly took up painting, encouraged by her photographer husband. As a general rule she paints landscapes of the countryside around Salzburg, as well as views of Salzburg itself—shimmering, sincere pictures, not without a kind of elegance.

Studiert von 1945 bis 1953 Musik in Salzburg und Wien. Pianistin im Ausland von 1954 bis 1959. Nach ihrer 1960 erfolgten Rückkehr nach Salzburg fängt sie plötzlich an zu malen, ermuntert von ihrem Mann, der Photograph ist. Malt hauptsächlich die Landschaften in der Umgebung von Salzburg und Ansichten der Stadt, schillernde, aufrichtige Bilder, denen es nicht an einer gewissen Eleganz fehlt.

De 1945 à 1953 étudie la musique à Salzburg et à Vienne. Pianiste à l'étranger de 1954 à 1959. Puis, dès son retour à Salzburg, en 1960, se met soudain à peindre, encouragée par son mari qui est photographe. Peint surtout les paysages des environs de Salzburg ainsi que les vues de Salzburg, chatoyantes, sincères et non exemptes d'une certaine élégance.

EXPOSITIONS:
« Die Welt der naiven Malerei », Residenzgalerie, Salzburg 1964.
Galerie ABC, Winterthur 1964.
Salzburger Kunstvereinigung, Mirabell-Casino 1965 (Cat., Préface Herbert Eisenreich).
« Les Primitifs d'Aujourd'hui », Galerie Charpentier, Paris 1964.
Galerie Autodidakt, Vienne 1965 (Cat., Préface Herbert Eisenreich).
Galerie Schöninger, München 1966 (Cat., Préface Herbert Eisenreich).

BIBLIOGRAPHIE:
Hans Kutschera: « Regine Dapra », Salzburger Volksblatt, 5 septembre 1964.
Calendrier mural pour l'année 1966 avec 12 reproductions en couleurs de Regine Dapra.

Dechelette, Louis-Auguste

Born January 11, 1894 in Cours, near Lyons (France).
Died November 19, 1964 in Paris (France).

Geboren am 11. Januar 1894 in Cours bei Lyon (Frankreich).
Gestorben 19. November 1964 in Paris (Frankreich).

Né le 11 janvier 1894 à Cours, près de Lyon (France).
Mort le 19 novembre 1964 à Paris (France).

Was brought up by his grandfather, an inventor and social republican in the tradition of skilled workers, who had taken part in the 1848 revolution. Did his own 'tour de France' as a painter of buildings and a plasterer. He, too, started to invent things at a very early age. Painted during his leisure time. He was 'discovered' during the Second World War and finally he gave up his trade, not without regret, to devote himself entirely to painting. His work stands out clearly from the other primitive artists by its humanitarian aspect. He protested against war, injustice, etc. Towards the end of his life he was forgotten to a certain extent, but he has pride of place in the second 'naive' wave which broke after the Second World War.

Aufgezogen von einem Großvater, der ein Erfinder war, 1848 mitgekämpft hatte und die Traditionen der fahrenden Handwerksgesellen und der Republik hochhielt. Er selber durchwandert Frankreich als Anstreicher und Gipser. Er macht auch schon in seiner frühesten Jugend Erfindungen. Malt während seiner Freizeit. Während des Zweiten Weltkrieges wird er entdeckt und verzichtet schließlich nicht ohne Bedauern auf seinen eigentlichen Beruf, um sich nur noch der Malerei zu widmen. Seine Malerei sticht durch ihre humanitäre Seite von der aller anderen naiven Maler ab. Er protestiert gegen den Krieg, gegen die Ungerechtigkeit usw. Gegen Ende seines Lebens geriet er ein wenig in Vergessenheit, doch nimmt er in der zweiten Welle der Naiven, die sich nach dem Zweiten Weltkrieg ausbreitet, einen ehrenvollen Platz ein.

Elevé par son grand-père, inventeur et quarante-huitard dans les traditions compagnoniques et républicaines. Fait lui-même le «Tour de France» en tant que peintre en bâtiment, plâtrier. Il invente aussi dès son plus jeune âge. Peint pendant ses loisirs. Découvert pendant la deuxième guerre mondiale, il renonce finalement, non sans regret, à son véritable métier pour se consacrer uniquement à la peinture. Sa peinture tranche sur tous les autres naïfs par son côté humanitaire. Il proteste contre la guerre, l'injustice, etc. Un peu oublié vers la fin de ses jours. Dechelette a une place de choix dans la seconde vague des naïfs qui a deferlé après la seconde guerre mondiale.

EXPOSITIONS:
Galerie Jeanne Bucher, Paris 1942 (Cat., Préface Robert Rey).
Galerie Jeanne Bucher, Paris 1944 (Cat., Préface Robert Rey).
«De l'Ethiopie à une Paix Stable», exposition au Mouvement de la Libération Nationale, Paris 1945.
«Les Peintres Naïfs», Knokke-le-Zoute 1958.
«Les Peintres Naïfs», Maison de la Pensée Française, Paris 1960.
«I Pittori Naifs», Rome 1964.
«Les Primitifs d'Aujourd'hui», Galerie Charpentier, Paris 1964.

BIBLIOGRAPHIE:
Anatole Jakovsky: «La Peinture Naïve», Paris 1949.
Anatole Jakovsky: «Les Peintres Naïfs», Paris 1956.
Anatole Jakovsky: «Naive Malerei», Zürich 1957.
Anatole Jakovsky: «Dechelette», Editions Temps Mêlés, Verviers 1962.
Anatole Jakovsky: «Eros du Dimanche», Paris 1964.
Oto Bihalji-Merin: «Das naive Bild der Welt», Köln 1959.
Oto Bihalji-Merin: «Die naive Malerei», Köln 1959.
Oto Bihalji-Merin: «Les Peintres Naïfs», Paris (sans date).
«Louis-Auguste Dechelette», L'Illustrazione Italiana N° 11, novembre 1960.
«Art Naïf», Editions Marocaines et Internationales, Rabat 1964.

FILM:
«Le voyage à Paris», d'après un texte de Marcel Aymé, réalisé par Pierre Mathieu, Paris 1959.

ILLUSTRATION:
Marcel Aymé: «Uranus», Editions Gallimard, Paris 1959.

Delacroix, Emilienne

Born September 11, 1893 in Chalette, Loiret (France).

Geboren am 11. September 1893 in Chalette, Loiret (Frankreich).

Née le 11 septembre 1893 à Chalette, Loiret (France).

She lives in Saint-Paul de Vence, which perhaps explains her success, although she was definitely encouraged by Verdet and Prévert. In fact, she has illustrated the text and cover of these two authors' books. She paints with a full brush, almost in relief; her drawing is childish and her inspiration does not go beyond the subjects used for calendar color-prints. Her work is more amusing than pretty, more pretty than true.

Lebt in Saint-Paul de Vence, was zweifellos ihren Erfolg erklärt. Immerhin fördern Verdet und Prévert sie wirklich. Sie hat übrigens Illustrationen und Einbände geschaffen für ihre Bücher. Ihre Farbe ist dick aufgetragen, beinahe als Relief, die Zeichnung infantil, und ihre Inspiration geht nicht über Kalenderbildchen hinaus. Ihre Bilder sind mehr lustig als hübsch, mehr hübsch als echt.

Vit à Saint-Paul de Vence, ce qui explique, sans doute, son succès. Il n'empêche que Verdet et Prévert l'encouragent réellement. Elle a, d'ailleurs, fait des illustrations et des couvertures pour les livres de ces derniers. Sa pâte est épaisse, presqu'en relief, son dessin infantile et son inspiration ne dépassent pas les sujets des chromos pour les calendriers. C'est plus amusant que joli; plus joli que vrai.

EXPOSITIONS:
« Les Primitifs d'Aujourd'hui »,
Galerie Charpentier, Paris 1964.

BIBLIOGRAPHIE:
Anatole Jakovsky: « Les Peintres Naïfs », Paris 1956.
Anatole Jakovsky: « Naive Malerei », Zürich 1957.

Delaporte, Roger

Born August 10, 1907 in Méru, Oise (France).

Geboren am 10. August 1907 in Méru, Oise (Frankreich).

Né le 10 août 1907 à Méru, Oise (France).

Wrought-iron worker by trade. However, a long illness early prevented him from continuing this fine work. Other disasters overtook him: he lost his son in Algeria, his daughter died of leukemia. In order to escape from his grief he turned to painting. Although hesitant at first, he tended more and more towards an art of simplicity—truth and honesty are his aims. His craftsman's gifts are transposed to another plane. Up to now has only exhibited his work in general exhibitions.

Kunstschmied. Aber bald macht es ihm eine lange Krankheit unmöglich, diesen schönen Beruf weiter auszuüben. Anderes Unglück trifft ihn. Er verliert seinen Sohn in Algerien, und seine Tochter stirbt an Leukämie. Um seinen Schmerz zu betäuben, fängt er an zu malen. Zuerst zögernd, dann nähert er sich immer mehr einer einfachen, wahren, ehrlichen Kunst. Seine handwerklichen Fähigkeiten übertragen sich auf ein anderes Gebiet. Er hat bisher erst in Gruppenausstellungen ausgestellt.

Ferronnier d'art. Mais bientôt une longue maladie l'empêche de continuer ce beau métier. D'autres malheurs s'abattent sur lui. Il perd son fils en Algérie, et sa fille meurt de léucemie. Alors, pour échapper aux tourments, il se met à peindre. Hésitant au début, il se dirige de plus en plus vers un art simple; de vérité et de probité. Ses vertus artisanales se sont transportées sur un autre terrain. N'a exposé jusqu à présent que dans des groupes.

BIBLIOGRAPHIE:
L. Lelong: «Roger Delaporte», Signatures, Paris.

Delattre, Louis

Born January 8, 1815 in Ghent (Belgium).
Died December 19, 1897 in Ghent (Belgium).

Geboren am 8. Januar 1815 in Gent (Belgien).
Gestorben am 19. Dezember 1897 in Gent (Belgien).

Né le 8 janvier 1815 à Gand (Belgique).
Mort le 19 décembre 1897 à Gand (Belgique).

This painter, considered for a long time as being not only the chief, but also the only primitive Belgian artist, spent a varied life: fitter, mechanic, house painter, contractor (of a business which went bankrupt), photographer and, curiously enough, inventor of a flying machine, like Sauter! But his machine did not fly either. It was about 1865 that he risked his first flights, which were a drastic failure but which brought him the nickname of 'the flying man'. Further, for a very long time, despite the investigations carried out by Fritz van den Berghe and P.G. Van Hecke, only one single painting of his could be found, namely the 'Ascension of Prince Baudoin' (collection of Franz Hellens). The reason for this is that his pictures, sold in bulk by his family after his death, had been bought by local artists to be used as canvases.

Dieser Maler, den man lange Zeit nicht nur für den ersten, sondern auch für den einzigen naiven Maler Belgiens hielt, hatte ein ziemlich bewegtes Leben: er war Schlosser, Mechaniker, Anstreicher, Unternehmer (der Konkurs machte), Photograph und seltsamerweise Erfinder einer Flugmaschine! Wie Sauter. Die seine ist übrigens so wenig geflogen wie die von Sauter. Im Jahr 1865 unternimmt er Flugversuche, die kläglich scheitern, die ihm aber den Necknamen «Der fliegende Mann» eintragen. Während sehr langer Zeit kannte man auch trotz den von Fritz van den Berghe und P.G. Van Hecke unternommenen Nachforschungen nur ein einziges Bild von ihm, betitelt «Ascension du Prince Baudoin» (Sammlung Franz Hellens). Das erklärt sich durch die Tatsache, daß seine Angehörigen nach seinem Tod seine Bilder wahllos an Maler der Umgebung verkauften, welche die Leinwand benützen wollten.

Ce peintre, considéré longtemps non seulement comme le premier mais comme l'unique peintre naïf belge, a eu une vie mouvementée: ajusteur, mécanicien, peintre en bâtiment, entrepreneur (qui a fait faillite), photographe et, chose curieuse, inventeur d'une machine à voler! Comme Sauter. D'ailleurs, comme celle de Sauter, la sienne n'a pas volé davantage. C'est vers 1865 qu'il se risque à des essais de vol qui échouèrent lamentablement, mais qui lui valurent le sobriquet de «L'Homme volant». Pendant très longtemps aussi, malgré les recherches faites par Fritz van den Berghe et P.G. Van Hecke, on ne lui connaissait que le seul et unique tableau, «Ascension du Prince Baudoin» (Coll. Franz Hellens). Ceci s'explique par le fait que ses tableaux, vendus en vrac après son decès par la famille, ont été achetés par des peintres locaux désirant se servir des toiles.

EXPOSITIONS:
«La Peinture Naïve du Douanier Rousseau à nos Jours», Knokke-le-Zoute 1958.
«De Lusthof der Naïeven», Rotterdam 1964.
«Le Monde des Naïfs», Paris 1964.
«Peintres Naïfs Belges», Théâtre National de Belgique, Bruxelles 1965.
«Peintres Naïfs Belges», Musée des Beaux-Arts, Verviers 1965.
«Peintres Naïfs Belges», Musée des Beaux-Arts, Hasselt 1966.

BIBLIOGRAPHIE:
Oto Bihalji-Merin: «Das naive Bild der Welt», Köln 1959.
Oto Bihalji-Merin: «Die naive Malerei», Köln 1959.
Oto Bihalji-Merin: «Les Peintres Naïfs», Paris (sans date).

Delplace, Rupert

Born 1896 in Herchies, Hainaut (Belgium).
Died 1951 in Brussels (Belgium).

Geboren 1896 in Herchies, Hennegau (Belgien).
Gestorben 1951 in Brüssel (Belgien).

Né en 1896 à Herchies, Hainaut (Belgique).
Mort en 1951 à Bruxelles (Belgique).

Specialized in geometry. Was badly wounded in the 1914–18 war and had to have both legs amputated. Started to paint on the advice of friends. The artist Luis Van Lint, among others, encouraged him during the last war. Had a tormented vision, rather like Ensor, which makes him in some respects similar to another Belgian 'naive' painter, the Flemish Van den Driessche. Masks, symbolical subjects, village fairs. Gave up painting in 1949.

Geometer. Kriegsverstümmelter aus dem Ersten Weltkrieg (beide Beine amputiert). Beginnt auf den Rat von Freunden hin zu malen. Unter anderen gehört während des letzten Kriegs auch Luis Van Lint zu seinen Förderern. Gequälte Schau, in der Art eines Ensor, die ihn ein wenig in Nähe eines anderen belgischen Naiven rückt, des Flamen Van den Driessche. Masken, symbolische Themen, Jahrmärkte. Hört 1949 auf zu malen.

Géomètre. Grand mutilé de la guerre 1914–18 (deux jambes amputées). Se met à peindre sur les conseils des amis. Le peintre Luis Van Lint, entre autres, l'encourage pendant la dernière guerre. Vision tourmentée, à la Ensor, qui le rapproche un tant soit peu d'un autre peintre naïf belge, flamand celui-là, Van den Driessche. Masques, sujets symboliques, kermesses. Cesse de peindre en 1949.

EXPOSITIONS:
Palais des Beaux-Arts, Bruxelles 1943.
Palais des Beaux-Arts, Bruxelles 1945.
Palais des Beaux-Arts, Bruxelles 1946.
Galerie Les Contemporains, Bruxelles 1962 (Retrospective).

BIBLIOGRAPHIE:
Thomas Owen: «Rupert Delplace», Savoir et Beauté, La Louvière, décembre 1965.

Demonchy, André

Born September 14, 1914 in Paris (France).

Geboren am 14. September 1914 in Paris (Frankreich).

Né le 14 septembre 1914 à Paris (France).

Was orphaned by the 1914–18 war. Spent his childhood and adolescence on various farms in the Yonne district, placed there by the Welfare authorities. Then, after army service, he worked on the railways. But he had suffered too much and had never known affection. He was haunted by leaden, snowladen skies. He started to paint about 1946. Fate smiled on him as an artist fairly quickly, but not to the extent of his being able to give up his work on the railway. Curious paradox of 'naive' painting!

Kriegswaise des 1. Weltkriegs. Verbringt Kindheit und Jugend in verschiedenen Bauernhöfen des Departements Yonne, wo ihn die öffentliche Armenpflege unterbringt. Nach dem Militärdienst geht er zur Eisenbahn. Aber er hat zuviel gelitten, nie Liebe erfahren, und eine gewisse Art von bleischwerem, schneeträchtigem Himmel verfolgt ihn bis in seine Träume. Gegen 1946 beginnt er zu malen. Das Glück lächelt ihm ziemlich bald. Aber doch nicht in dem Maße, daß er seinen Broterwerb aufgeben könnte. Seltsames Paradox der naiven Malerei!

Orphelin du fait de la guerre 1914–18. Passe son enfance et son adolescence dans les fermes de l'Yonne, placé par l'Assistance Publique. Puis il entre dans les Chemins de Fer, après le régiment. Mais il a trop souffert, il n'a pas connu de tendresse, et certains ciels plombés, lourds de neige, le hantent. Il commence à peindre vers 1946. La chance lui sourit assez vite. Mais pas au point de pouvoir abandonner son gagne-pain. Etrange paradoxe de la peinture naïve!

EXPOSITIONS:
Galerie de Berri, Paris 1949 (Cat., Préface André Breton).
Galerie de Berri, Paris 1952.
Knoedler Gallery, New York 1948.
Knoedler Gallery, New York 1949.
«Les Peintres Naïfs», Knokke-le-Zoute 1958.
Galerie Michel Columb, Nantes 1958 (Cat., Préface Anatole Jakovsky).
La Goujonnette, Poissy 1959.
Galerie Chassaing, Lyon 1959 (Cat., Préface M.-F. Braive et Anatole Jakovsky).
«Les Peintres Naïfs», Maison de la Pensée Française, Paris 1960.
Galerie Wolfensberger, Zürich 1960.
«Laien-Maler», Gewerbemuseum, Basel 1961.
Galerie Chappe, Toulouse 1961 (Cat., Préface Anatole Jakovsky et Max-Pol Fouchet).
«L'Ecole Buissonnière», Paris 1962 (Cat., Préface Max-Pol Fouchet).
«I Pittori Naifs», Rome 1964.
«Les Primitifs d'Aujourd'hui», Galerie Charpentier, Paris 1964.
«Le Panorama International de la Peinture Naïve», Mission Culturelle, Rabat 1964.

BIBLIOGRAPHIE:
Anatole Jakovsky: «Les Peintres Naïfs», Paris 1956.
Anatole Jakovsky: «Naive Malerei», Zürich 1957.
Anatole Jakovsky: «André Demonchy», Editions Temps Mêlés, Verviers 1962.
Anatole Jakovsky: «Eros du Dimanche», Paris 1964.
Oto Bihalji-Merin: «Das naive Bild der Welt», Köln 1959.
Oto Bihalji-Merin: «Die naive Malerei», Köln 1959.
Oto Bihalji-Merin: «Les Peintres Naïfs», Paris (sans date).
Anatole Jakovsky: «Les loisirs sacrés et autres», La Vie médicale, Paris, mai 1963.
«Art Naïf», Editions Marocaines et Internationales, Rabat 1964.
André Breton: «Le Surréalisme et la peinture», Editions Gallimard, Paris 1965.

FILM:
«Le Voyage à Paris», d'après un texte de Marcel Aymé, réalisé par Pierre Mathieu, Paris 1959.

ILLUSTRATION:
Marcel Aymé: «Le Bœuf clandestin», Editions Gallimard, Paris 1959.

PUBLICITÉ:
Pochette pour le disque de «L'Ecole Buissonnière» de J.L. Lafforgue, Paris 1962.
Affiche, éditée par l'Office Français du Tourisme (Le château de Foix) 1962.

Desnos, Ferdinand

Born July 29, 1901 in Pont-Levoy, Loir-et-Cher (France).
Died November 16, 1958 in Paris (France).

Geboren am 29. Juli 1901 in Pont-Levoy, Loir-et-Cher (Frankreich).
Gestorben am 16. November 1958 in Paris (Frankreich).

Né le 29 juillet 1901 à Pont-Levoy, Loir-et-Cher (France).
Mort le 16 novembre 1958 à Paris (France).

Son of a baker. He painted his first picture in 1923. In 1927 he moved to Paris, where he held several posts, until he was stricken by tuberculosis and had to return to the country. After the war he returned to Paris and eventually became caretaker of a block of apartments. His work is very irregular and extremely erratic. When he painted from nature or from memory, he produced sensitive pictures which were bathed in a delicate, pure light. But when he tried large compositions, they turned out barren and declamatory. He was an 'intimiste' lost in dreams of greatness.

Er war der Sohn eines Bäckers und malte sein erstes Bild 1923. 1927 läßt er sich in Paris nieder, wo er mehrere Berufe ausübt, bis ihn die Tuberkulose zwingt, aufs Land zurückzukehren. Kommt nach dem Krieg wieder nach Paris, wo er seine Tage als Hauswart beschließt. Sehr ungleichmäßiges Werk eines ausgesprochenen Dilettanten. Wenn er nach Natur oder nach Erinnerungen malt, schafft er empfindsame, in zartes, wirkliches Licht getauchte Bilder. Aber wenn er große Kompositionen ins Auge faßt, werden sie trocken und hochtrabend. Ein Intimist, den die Träume von Größe verdorben haben.

Fils d'un boulanger, il peignit son premier tableau en 1923. Il s'établit en 1927 à Paris, où il exerce plusieurs métiers, jusqu'à ce que la tuberculose l'oblige à retourner à la campagne. Revient à nouveau, après la guerre, à Paris, où il finira comme concierge d'un immeuble. Production très inégale d'un vélleitaire par excellence. Lorsqu'il peint d'après nature, sinon d'après les souvenirs, il produit des œuvres sensibles, baignées dans une lumière fine et réelle. Mais lorsqu'il envisage des grandes compositions, elles deviennent sèches et déclamatoires. Un intimiste perdu par les rêves de grandeur.

EXPOSITIONS:
Galerie La Boétie, Paris 1943 (Cat., Préface Vanderpyl).
Musée des Beaux-Arts, Tours 1943 (Cat., Extraits de presse).
Noyer de France, Blois 1943 (Cat., Extraits de presse).
Galerie Romi, Paris 1953 (Cat., Préface Romi).
Galerie Lucie Weil, Paris 1962.
Musée des Beaux-Arts, Tours 1963.
Retrospective (Cat., Préface Boris Lossky).
«De Lusthof der Naieven», Rotterdam 1964.
«Le Monde des Naïfs», Paris 1964.
«Le Panorama International de la Peinture Naïve», Mission Culturelle, Rabat 1964.

BIBLIOGRAPHIE:
Marius Richard: «Ferdinand Desnos», Point de Vue, N° 411, Paris 28 avril 1956.
«Art Naïf», Editions Marocaines et Internationales, Rabat 1964.
Anatole Jakovsky: «Eros du Dimanche», Paris 1964.

Devalck, Jan

Born May 25, 1885 in Marchienne-au-Pont, Charleroi (Belgium).
Died December 3, 1960 in Antwerp (Belgium).

Geboren am 25. Mai 1885 in Marchienne-au-Pont, Charleroi (Belgien).
Gestorben am 3. Dezember 1960 in Antwerpen (Belgien).

Né le 25 mai 1885 à Marchienne-au-Pont, Charleroi (Belgique).
Mort le 3 décembre 1960 à Anvers (Belgique).

A boatman, and son of a boatman. Began to work at the age of twelve. For forty years he traversed the canals of Belgium and France, actually on a boat already decorated with pictures including a portrait of his daughter. Finally he settled down in Antwerp where he was employed by the municipality as captain of the boat 'Het Mestschip', used to take away the household refuse. It is during this period that he painted the majority of his pictures. However, only about fifteen are known; the remainder are lost or destroyed. He died a pauper.

Flußschiffer, Sohn von Flußschiffern. Beginnt schon im Alter von 12 Jahren zu arbeiten. 40 Jahre lang durchfährt er kreuz und quer die Kanäle Belgiens und Frankreichs, und zwar auf einem Schiff, das er bereits mit Malereien schmückt, darunter mit einem Porträt seiner Tochter. Zum Schluß läßt er sich in Antwerpen nieder, wo er in den Dienst der Stadt tritt, und zwar als Kapitän von «Het Mestschip», das heißt des Schiffes, das den Kehricht abführt. Hier malt er die Mehrzahl seiner Bilder. Man kennt übrigens nur etwa 15. Die andern sind verschollen oder zerstört. Er ist als armer Mann gestorben.

Batelier, fils de bateliers. Commence à travailler dès l'âge de 12 ans. Pendant 40 ans, il sillonne les canaux de Belgique et de France, ceci sur un bateau qui était déjà orné de peintures, dont un portrait de sa fille. A la fin, il s'installe à Anvers, où il entre au service de la ville en tant que capitaine de «Het Mestschip», c'est-à-dire le bateau qui évacue les ordures ménagères. C'est là où il a peint la plupart de ses tableaux. On n'en connaît, du reste, qu'une quinzaine. Les autres sont perdus ou détruits. Il est mort pauvre.

EXPOSITIONS:
«Peintres Naïfs Belges», Théâtre National, Bruxelles 1965.
«Peintres Naïfs Belges», Musée Royal des Beaux-Arts, Verviers 1965.
«Peintres Naïfs Belges», Musée Royal des Beaux-Arts, Hasselt 1966.
(Cat., Préface Anatole Jakovsky, Alain Germoz et Paul Snoek.)

Dixon, James

Born 1889 in Tory Island (Republic of Ireland).

Geboren 1889 in Tory Island (Irland).

Né en 1889 à Tory Island (Irlande).

Up to now the only known Irish 'naive' artist. A fisherman. His pictures, which depict the life of his village, swept by the Atlantic Ocean, are of high quality, broad in scope, and truly inspired, as is generally the case with paintings of seagoing people. Full of truly pictorial qualities.

Bisher der einzige bekannte naive Maler Irlands. Fischer. Seine Malerei, die vom Leben in seinem vom Atlantik umwogten Dorf erzählt, ist schön, inspiriert, großzügig, wie die Bilder der Seeleute meistens sind. Voll von wirklich malerischen Qualitäten.

Le seul connu jusqu'à présent parmi les peintres naïfs irlandais. Pêcheur. Sa peinture qui raconte la vie de son village, balayé par l'Atlantique, est belle, inspirée, large, comme le sont généralement les peintures des gens de la mer. Pleine de qualités vraiment picturales.

EXPOSITIONS:
«Les Peintres Naïfs», Galerie J.Verrière, Cannes 1966.

BIBLIOGRAPHIE:
Barrie Sturt-Penrose: «Primitives in Private», Observer, 13 février 1966.

Dietrich, Adolf

Born November 9, 1877 in Berlingen (Switzerland).
Died June 4, 1957 in Berlingen (Switzerland).

Geboren am 9. November 1877 in Berlingen (Schweiz).
Gestorben am 4. Juni 1957 in Berlingen (Schweiz).

Né le 9 novembre 1877 à Berlingen (Suisse).
Mort le 4 juin 1957 à Berlingen (Suisse).

The most important and, above all, the best known of the Swiss 'naive' artists. He is the only foreigner to have benefited by the first success of the French 'naive' painters who later became known as the 'Popular Masters of Reality'. The son of a humble peasant, his only schooling was at the local elementary school, but even there the schoolmaster noticed his gift for drawing. And, indeed, his first sketchbook dates from 1896. Unfortunately, however, he had to earn his living—he worked in a knitting factory, then as a knitter at home, as a woodcutter, and even as a laborer. It was not until his father died that he followed in his footsteps and became a farmer. His first picture is dated 1905. He was noticed quite soon by other artists in the district and was able to devote more time to painting, without, however, giving up his means of livelihood. His work, is distinctive for both its remarkable honesty and for the faultless execution which hampers neither the artist's sensitivity nor his deep feeling for nature.

Der bedeutendste und vor allem der bekannteste naive Maler der Schweiz. Er ist der einzige Ausländer, der von der ersten Erfolgswelle der seither unter dem Namen «Maîtres Populaires de la Réalité» bekanntgewordenen naiven Maler Frankreichs profitierte. Als Sohn eines bescheidenen Bauern besucht er nur die Dorfschule, wo dem Lehrer bereits seine Zeichenbegabung auffällt. Sein erstes Skizzenbuch stammt in der Tat aus dem Jahre 1896. Aber leider muß er sein Brot verdienen, zuerst als Arbeiter in einer Strickwarenfabrik, dann als Heimstricker, als Holzfäller und sogar als Tagelöhner. Erst beim Tod seines Vaters wird er seinerseits Bauer. Sein erstes Bild stammt aus dem Jahr 1905. Die Maler der Gegend werden ziemlich früh auf ihn aufmerksam und bald kann er der Malerei mehr Zeit widmen, ohne indessen darum seinen wahren Beruf aufzugeben. Seine Kunst ist von erstaunlicher Ehrlichkeit und stellt einen beinahe alleinstehenden Fall dar, wo eine tadellose Technik weder der Empfindsamkeit noch dem tiefen Natursinn im geringsten Abbruch tut.

Le plus important et surtout le plus connu parmi les peintres naïfs suisses. Il est le seul étranger à avoir bénéficié de la première promotion des peintres naïfs français, connus depuis sous le nom de «Maîtres Populaires de la Réalité». Fils d'un modeste paysan, il ne fréquente que l'école communale où l'instituteur remarque déjà son aptitude pour le dessin. Son premier cahier de croquis date, en effet, de 1896. Mais il doit, hélas, gagner sa vie, entre temps, en tant qu'ouvrier dans une usine de tricots, puis comme tricoteur à domicile, comme bûcheron et même comme journalier. Ce n'est qu'à la mort de son père qu'il devient, à son tour, cultivateur. Sa première peinture date de 1905. Remarqué assez tôt par les peintres de la région, il pourra se consacrer bientôt davantage à la peinture, sans abandonner pour cela son véritable métier. Son art, d'une remarquable probité, présente un cas presqu'unique où le travail impeccable ne gêne en rien sa sensibilité ni son sens profond de la nature.

EXPOSITIONS:
Wassenberghaus, Konstanz 1913.
Galerie Goltz, München 1917.
Kunsthaus, Mannheim 1922 und 1925.
Kunstmuseum, Winterthur 1926.
« Maîtres Populaires de la Réalité », Paris 1937.
« Maîtres Populaires de la Réalité », Zürich 1937.
« Masters of Popular Painting », New York 1938.
« Masters of Popular Painting », Tooth & Sons, Londres 1938.
Galerie Bettie Thommen, Basel 1939.
« Moderne Primitieven », Stedelijk Museum, Amsterdam 1941 (Cat., Préface D.C.R.).
Kunsthaus Zürich 1942.
Salon Wolfsberg, Zürich 1947.
« Moderne primitive Maler », Kunsthalle Bern 1949 (Cat., Préface Arnold Rüdlinger).
Museum zu Allerheiligen, Schaffhausen 1952.
Kunstmuseum, Winterthur 1953 (Cat., Préface H. K.).
Kunsthaus, Zürich 1957 (Cat., Préface R.Wehrli).
« Schönheit », Recklinghausen 1958 (Important catalogue, signé Stephan Hirzel).
« Laienmaler », Basel 1961.
« Das naive Bild der Welt », Baden-Baden 1961.
« Die Welt der naiven Malerei », Salzburg 1964.
« De Lusthof der Naieven », Rotterdam 1964.
« Le Monde des Naïfs », Paris 1964.

BIBLIOGRAPHIE:
Margot Riess: « Adolf Dietrich », Berlin 1927 (Neuauflage Zürich und Leipzig 1937).
Karel Hoenn: « Adolf Dietrich », Huber, Zürich 1942.
Erwin Brüllman: « Begegnung mit Adolf Dietrich », Bodensee Verlag 1947.
Anatole Jakovsky: « Les Peintres Naïfs », Paris 1956.
Anatole Jakovsky: « Naive Malerei », Zürich 1957.
Oto Bihalji-Merin: « Das naive Bild der Welt », Köln 1959.
Oto Bihalji-Merin: « Die naive Malerei », Köln 1959.
Oto Bihalji-Merin: « Les Peintres Naïfs », Paris (sans date).

Djanira (Da Motta e Silva)

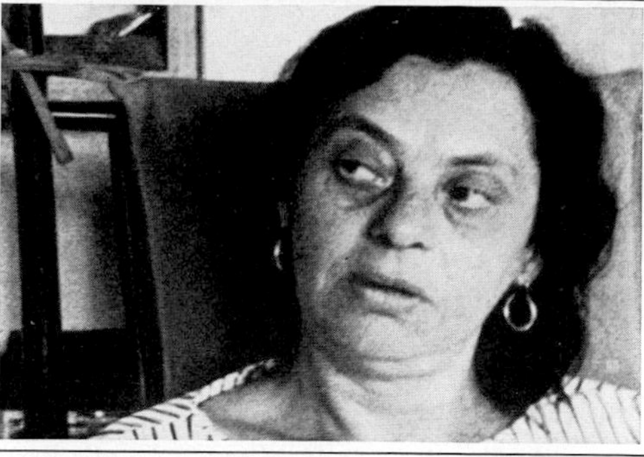

Born 1914 in São Paulo (Brazil).

Geboren 1914 in São Paulo (Brasilien).

Née en 1914 à São Paulo (Brésil).

Studied art in Brazil and the United States, and so one cannot call her work really one-hundred-percent 'naive'. However, her love for her country and her sense of color carry her beyond the knowledge she has acquired. Her painting is truculent—based on folklore, of course, but nevertheless art, 'naive' art. Has displayed her work in various collective (mainly state) exhibitions in Brazil and other countries, such as Great Britain, France, Switzerland, Argentina, Chile, Peru, Uruguay, etc. But very few individual exhibitions.

Studiert Malerei in Brasilien und den Vereinigten Staaten. Auch hier kann man nicht von einer hundertprozentig reinen naiven Malerei sprechen. Aber ihre Heimatliebe und ihr Farbensinn sind stärker als ihr gelerntes Können. Zweifellos urwüchsige, folkloristische Malerei, aber eben doch Malerei. Sogar naive Malerei! Hat an zahlreichen, meist offiziellen Gruppenausstellungen in Brasilien und im Ausland teilgenommen: England, Frankreich, Schweiz, Argentinien, Chile, Peru, Uruguay usw. Aber sehr wenig Einzelausstellungen.

Etudie la peinture au Brésil et aux Etats-Unis. Là encore on ne peut pas parler d'une veine vraiment cent pour cent naïve. Mais son amour du pays et son sens de la couleur l'emportent sur son savoir faire. Peinture truculente, folklorique, sans aucun doute, mais de la peinture quand-même. Même naïve! A participé à de nombreuses expositions collectives dans son pays et à l'étranger, officielles dans la plupart des cas: Angleterre, France, Suisse, Argentine, Chili, Pérou, Uruguay, etc. Mais très peu d'expositions individuelles.

EXPOSITIONS:
Musée d'Art Moderne, Rio de Janeiro 1958.
«Artistes brésiliens», Musée d'Art Moderne de la Ville de Paris 1959.

Domingo, Casimiro

Born March 4, 1882 in Pinilla de Jadraque, Guadalajara (Spain).

Geboren am 4. März 1882 in Pinilla de Jadraque, Guadalajara (Spanien).

Né le 4 mars 1882 à Pinilla de Jadraque, Guadalajara (Espagne).

Began to work at the age of ten as an apprentice shoemaker, which trade he continued to practice all his working life. In 1910 he visited Cuba but returned promptly to Madrid, where he worked twelve years. In 1923 he left for South America, and in Buenos Aires in 1935 he began to paint. Strange as it may seem, his art is of the kind which several Cuban artists practiced much later, after the revolution there. When studying Domingo's pictures one is in the presence of an art which is most definitely inspired, having no connection with reality.

Beginnt im Alter von 10 Jahren eine Lehrzeit als Schuhmacher; diesen Beruf übt er sein ganzes Leben lang aus. 1910 macht er eine kurze Reise nach Kuba, kehrt jedoch gleich nach Madrid zurück, wo er 12 Jahre lang arbeitet. 1923 fährt er nach Südamerika, wo er 1935 in Buenos Aires zu malen anfängt. So seltsam es scheinen mag: er hat viel Gemeinsames mit ein paar kubanischen Künstlern, die erst viel später, das heißt nach der Revolution, zu malen anfingen. Wir befinden uns in Gegenwart einer unbestreitbar inspirierten Kunst, die keinerlei Verbindung mit dem Wirklichen besitzt.

Commence à travailler à 10 ans comme apprenti cordonnier, métier qu'il exercera toute sa vie. En 1910, il effectue un court voyage à Cuba pour retourner aussitôt à Madrid où il va travailler pendant 12 ans. En 1923, il part pour l'Amérique du Sud, où il commence à peindre, à Buenos Aires, en 1935. Aussi étrange que cela paraisse, son art s'apparente à celui que vont pratiquer beaucoup plus tard, après la Révolution, quelques-uns des artistes cubains. Nous sommes en présence d'un art incontestablement inspiré, n'ayant aucune attache avec le réel.

EXPOSITIONS:
Au sous-sol du Consejo Deliberante, Buenos Aires 1938.
Galerie Guttierez, Buenos Aires 1938.
A la Banque Municipale, Buenos Aires 1943.
Galerie Comte, Buenos Aires 1945 (Cat., Préface non signée).
A la Banque Municipale, Buenos Aires 1952.
«La Peinture Naïve», Knokke-le-Zoute 1958.

BIBLIOGRAPHIE:
Anatole Jakovsky: «Eros du Dimanche», Paris 1964.

Donati, Valentina

Born December 20, 1897 in Nikolaieff (Russia).

Geboren am 20. Dezember 1897 in Nikolajew (Rußland).

Née le 20 décembre 1897 à Nikolaieff (Russie).

Italian by nationality, she was born in Russia where her father was Consul. In Florence she met the Russian painter Portkoff, whom she married and to whom she gave three sons.
For the first years of her marriage she was fully occupied in looking after the children and helping in her husband's business (an antique shop and restorer's workshop). Lived in Paris.
It was not until 1955, after a trip to Brittany, that she was able to achieve a lifetime's ambition and to start painting. Has won the 'médaille de la ville de Paris' and the 'médaille de la ville de Rimini'.

Italienerin, geboren in Rußland, wo ihr Vater Konsul war. Lernt in Florenz den russischen Maler Portkoff kennen, dem sie drei Söhne schenkt. Kümmert sich zunächst um die Kinder und den Laden ihres Mannes, der ein Antiquitäten- und Restaurierungsgeschäft betreibt. Lebt in Paris. Erst nach einer 1955 unternommenen Reise in die Bretagne verwirklicht sie den Traum ihres Lebens und malt. Medaille der Stadt Paris, Medaille der Stadt Rimini.

Italienne, née en Russie où son père était consul. A Florence, rencontre le peintre russe Portkoff à qui elle donnera trois fils. S'occupe donc d'abord des enfants et de l'affaire de son mari qui tient un magasin de restauration et d'antiquités. Vit à Paris. Ce n'est qu'en 1955, après un voyage en Bretagne, qu'elle réalise le rêve de sa vie qui est de peindre. Médaille de la Ville de Paris, médaille de la Ville de Rimini.

EXPOSITIONS:
Galerie Cambacerès, Paris 1963.
Chambre de Commerce Italienne, Paris 1964 (Cat., Préface Pierre Mornand, André Neba et Pierre Imburg).

Doriani, William

Born January 27, 1893 in the Ukraine (Russia).

Geboren am 27. Januar 1893 in der Ukraine (Rußland).

Né le 27 janvier 1893 en Ukraine (Russie).

American citizen. Although he went to America as a very young man, he visited Europe several times, especially Russia and Italy, in his profession as a singer. It was at the age of forty that he began to paint. Much of his work is inspired by the theatre, of course, and he also paints crowd scenes from various angles. His art is gay and rather childlike.

Amerikanischer Staatsbürger. Er kommt ganz jung in die Staaten, doch kehrt er in seiner Eigenschaft als Sänger mehrmals nach Europa zurück, insbesondere nach Rußland und nach Italien. An seinem 40. Geburtstag beginnt er zu malen. Er läßt sich natürlich in hohem Maß vom Theater inspirieren, malt aber auch Menschenmengen in verschiedenen Perspektiven. Seine Kunst ist fröhlich, etwas kindlich.

Citoyen américain. Arrivé tout jeune ici, il retourne néanmoins plusieurs fois en Europe, en Russie et en Italie notamment, en tant que chanteur. Il commence à peindre le jour de sa quarantième année. Il s'inspire beaucoup du théâtre, bien sûr, et il peint aussi des foules sous des différentes perspectives. Son art est gai, un peu enfantin.

EXPOSITIONS:
«La Peinture Naïve», Knokke-le-Zoute 1958.

BIBLIOGRAPHIE:
Sidney Janis: «They taught themselves», The Dial Press, New York 1942.

Van den Driessche, Ernest

Born December 25, 1894 in Eine, Audenarde (Belgium).

Geboren am 25. Dezember 1894 in Eine, Audenarde (Belgien).

Né le 25 décembre 1894 à Eine, Audenarde (Belgique).

Started to work extremely early in life. Assistant to a carpenter, then to a house painter, then a cabinetmaker, then an apprentice at the slaughter house. Eventually became the owner of a large butcher's shop in Brussels. Nevertheless, after the last war he returned to his native town and threw himself into the antique-dealer's business. For him, painting is describing one's dreams. That is why most of his pictures are inspired by folklore; he paints Christmas processions, popular legends, giants, village fairs, etc. A truly Flemish painter, a kind of unrefined James Ensor.

Beginnt in früher Jugend zu arbeiten. Zimmermannsgehilfe, Malergehilfe, Tischler, Lehrling im Schlachthaus. Erwirbt schließlich eine große Metzgerei in Brüssel. Kehrt indessen nach dem letzten Krieg in seine Vaterstadt zurück, wo er einen Handel mit Antiquitäten anfängt. Für ihn bedeutet malen seine Träume erzählen. Darum sind die meisten seiner Themen der Folklore entliehen: die Weihnachtsprozession, die volkstümlichen Legenden, die «Riesen», die Jahrmärkte usw. Er ist ein zutiefst flämischer Maler, eine Art James Ensor im Rohzustand.

Commence à travailler de fort bonne heure. Aide charpentier, aide peintre en bâtiment, ébéniste, apprenti aux abattoirs. Finit par devenir propriétaire d'une importante boucherie à Bruxelles. Il revient toutefois, après la dernière guerre, dans sa ville natale où il se lance dans le commerce des antiquités. Peindre, pour lui, c'est raconter ses rêves. C'est pourquoi la plupart de ses sujets sont inspirés par le folklore: la procession de Noël, les légendes populaires, les «Géants», les kermesses, etc. C'est un peintre essentiellement flamand. C'est une espèce de James Ensor à l'état brut.

EXPOSITIONS:
Musée Historique, Gand 1964.
Galerie Margarethe de Boeve, Assenede 1965 (Cat., Préface Paul Snoek).
Galerie M. Bénézit, Paris 1965 (Cat., Préface Paul Snoek et Anatole Jakovsky).
«Peintres Naïfs Belges», Théâtre National, Bruxelles 1965.
Musée Royal des Beaux-Arts, Verviers 1965.
Musée Royal des Beaux-Arts, Hasselt 1966.
Galerie Pierre Vanderborght, Bruxelles 1966.

BIBLIOGRAPHIE:
Paul Snoek: «Van den Driessche», Monographie en préparation, avec une Introduction par Anatole Jakovsky.

Drissi, Moulay Ahmed

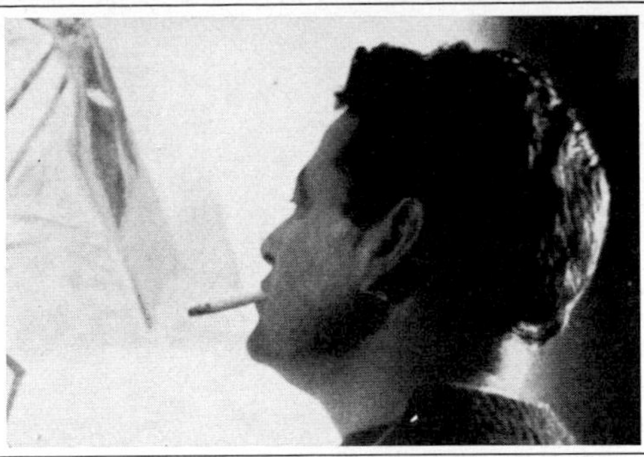

Born 1924 near Marrakesh (Morocco).

Geboren 1924 in der Umgebung von Marrakesch (Marokko).

Né en 1924 aux environs de Marrakech (Maroc).

Purely self-taught artist. It was a chance meeting with two Swiss painters which prompted him to make a career of painting. Between 1948 and 1960 he travelled widely outside Morocco, exhibiting and selling his work—Italy, Switzerland, France, Sweden, Germany, Spain. His art is more primitive than that of Ben Allal, and his tonality is darker. But nevertheless these two are perfect expressions of certain aspects of the traditional life of their country.

Reiner Autodidakt. Eine zufällige Begegnung mit einem Schweizer Malerehepaar bestimmt seine Malerlaufbahn. Von 1948 bis 1960 reist er viel im Ausland, stellt seine Werke aus und verkauft sie: Italien, Schweiz, Frankreich, Schweden, Deutschland, Spanien. Seine Kunst ist primitiver als die von Ben Allal und seine Farbtöne sind dunkler. Aber beide drücken auf vollkommene Weise gewisse Seiten des volkstümlichen Lebens ihres Landes aus.

Autodidacte pur. Une rencontre fortuite avec un couple de peintres suisses décide de sa carrière de peintre. Dès 1948 et jusqu'en 1960, il voyage beaucoup à l'étranger en exposant et en vendant ses œuvres: Italie, Suisse, France, Suède, Allemagne, Espagne. Son art est plus primitif que celui de Ben Allal et ses tonalités sont plus sombres. Il n'empêche que tous les deux expriment parfaitement certains côtés de la vie populaire de leur pays.

EXPOSITIONS:
« Panorama International de la Peinture Naïve»; Tanger, Rabat, Marrakech et Casablanca 1964.

BIBLIOGRAPHIE:
Mohamed Tanjaoui: « Drissi», Ed. de la Mission Universitaire Française, Rabat (sans date).
«Art Naïf», Editions Marocaines et Internationales, Rabat 1964.

Duffaut, Prefete

Born January 1, 1923 in Jacmel (Haiti).

Geboren 1. Januar 1923 in Jacmel (Haiti).

Né le 1 janvier 1923 à Jacmel (Haïti).

Boat-builder. Also a poet and a mystic, with a bent for the supernatural. Generally he paints his dreams—his real dreams, not, like so many other painters, embroidered by the imagination. That is why his pictures undeniably have a strange kind of life of their own, saturated with belief in magic, which is not yet dead in that country. Has a fresco in Port-au-Prince cathedral.

Schiffsbauer. Dichter und Mystiker, dem das Übernatürliche am Herzen liegt. Gewöhnlich malt er seine Träume, richtige Träume, nicht das, was so viele andere mit Hilfe ihrer Phantasie heraufbeschwören. Darum besitzen seine Kompositionen ein unbestreitbares, seltsames Leben, das ganz von dem noch nicht völlig ausgestorbenen magischen Glauben des Landes erfüllt ist. Eine Freske in der Kathedrale von Port-au-Prince.

Constructeur de bateaux. Poète et mystique. Porté sur le surnaturel. Il peint généralement ses rêves, de vrais rêves et non ce que tant d'autres élaborent grâce à leur imagination. C'est pourquoi ses compositions ont une vie indéniable et étrange, toute imprégnée des croyances magiques, pas tout à fait mortes du pays. Une fresque à la Cathédrale de Port-au Prince.

EXPOSITIONS:

«Das naive Bild der Welt», Baden-Baden 1961.
«Naive Painters of Latin America», Duke University, Durham, N.C. 1963.
«19 Peintres d'Haïti», Palais des Beaux-Arts, Bruxelles 1963.
«20th Century Latin American Naive Art», La Jolla (USA) 1964.

BIBLIOGRAPHIE:

Selden Rodman: «Renaissance in Haiti», Pelegrini & Cudahy New York (sans date).
Oto Bihalji-Merin: «Das naive Bild der Welt», Köln 1959.
Oto Bihalji-Merin: «Die naive Malerei», Köln 1959.
Oto Bihalji-Merin: «Les Peintres Naïfs», Paris (sans date).

Elmer, Edwin Romanzo

Born 1850 in Ashfield, Mass. (USA).
Died 1923 in Ashfield, Mass. (USA).

Geboren 1850 in Ashfield, Mass. (USA).
Gestorben 1923 in Ashfield, Mass. (USA).

Né en 1850 à Ashfield, Mass. (USA).
Mort en 1923 à Ashfield, Mass. (USA).

Childhood and adolescence were spent on a farm. Attended the local village school. Later, he invented agricultural machines, when he was not busy painting portraits of his fellow-countrymen from photographs. In order to improve his abilities on that score he left for New York in 1895 and took a course of training at the National Academy of Design. One year later he returned to his native village and continued to paint until his death. His most famous picture shows his daughter Effie (who died at an early age) in front of their house at Shelburne Falls. The parents are seated in the background. This picture is almost like a hallucination, perhaps because of the extraordinarily lifelike presence of these three people.

Verbringt Kindheit und Jugend auf einem Bauernhof. Besucht die Dorfschule. Später erfindet er landwirtschaftliche Maschinen, wenn er nicht nach Photographien die Porträts seiner Mitbürger malt. Um sich in dieser Kunst zu vervollkommnen, begibt er sich 1895 nach New York, wo er die Kurse der National Academy of Design besucht. Ein Jahr später kehrt er in sein Heimatdorf zurück, wo er bis zu seinem Tod weitermalt. Sein berühmtestes Bild stellt seine Tochter Effie dar, ein frühverstorbenes Kind, das er vor seinem Haus in Shelburne Falls abbildet. Die Eltern sitzen im Hintergrund. Dieses Bild hat etwas Halluzinierendes, denn die drei Personen scheinen tatsächlich gegenwärtig zu sein.

Enfance et adolescence dans une ferme. Fréquente l'école rurale. Plus tard, il invente des machines agricoles, quand il ne peint pas les portraits de ses concitoyens d'après les photographies. Pour se perfectionner dans cet art, il se rend, en 1895, à New York où il suit les cours de la National Academy of Design.
Un an après, il rentre dans son village natal où il continuera à peindre jusqu'à sa mort. Son tableau le plus célèbre représente sa fille Effie, enfant morte prématurément, devant leur maison à Shelburne Falls. Les parents sont assis derrière. Ce tableau a quelque chose d'hallucinant, ne serait-ce que par la présence quasi réelle de ces trois personnages.

EXPOSITIONS:
Smith College Museum of Art, Northampton Mass. 1952.
«American Primitive Art», The Museum of Fine Arts, Houston 1956 (Cat., Préface Edith Gregor Halpert).
«American Art», Bruxelles 1958 (Cat. de la section U.S.A. à l'Exposition Universelle de Belgique).
«De Lusthof der Naieven», Rotterdam 1964.
«Le Monde des Naïfs», Paris 1964.

BIBLIOGRAPHIE:
Oto Bihalji-Merin: «Das naive Bild der Welt», 1959.
Oto Bihalji-Merin: «Die naive Malerei», Köln 1959.
Oto Bihalji-Merin: «Les Peintres Naïfs», Paris (sans date).

Escudier, Jean

Born September 28, 1896 in Toulouse, Haute Garonne (France).

Geboren am 28. September 1896 in Toulouse, Haute Garonne (Frankreich).

Né le 28 septembre 1896 à Toulouse, Haute Garonne (France).

Attendant at the Musée des Augustins in Toulouse. Began to paint at the age of 47. His fine pictures were immediately noticed, both by the curator of the Museum and by passing artists. Now lives in the neighborhood of Toulouse in a pretty, tastefully furnished house. Now he can paint as much as he likes...

Kustos im Musée des Augustins in Toulouse. Beginnt im Alter von 47 Jahren zu malen. Seine Bilder sind gut und werden sofort sowohl vom Konservator des Museums als auch von durchreisenden Künstlern beachtet. Er lebt jetzt in der Umgebung von Toulouse in einem geschmackvoll eingerichteten hübschen Haus. Jetzt kann er nach Herzenslust malen...

Gardien au Musée des Augustins de Toulouse. Commence à peindre à l'âge de 47 ans. Ses peintures de belle qualité sont remarquées aussitôt, aussi bien par le conservateur du Musée que par les artistes de passage. Vit maintenant aux environs de Toulouse, dans une jolie maison arrangée avec goût. Maintenant, il peut peindre tant qu'il voudra...

EXPOSITIONS:
Galerie Chappe-Lautier, Toulouse 1950.
Galerie Vendôme, Paris 1957.
Galerie du Taur, Toulouse 1959.

Eve, Jean

Born in 1900 in Somain, near Douai, Nord (France).

Geboren 1900 in Somain bei Douai, Nord (Frankreich).

Né en 1900 à Somain, près de Douai, Nord (France).

Comes from a family of miners; however, he wanted to escape from this landscape of slag-heaps, and left home. He became a surveyor, draughtsman, customs-house officer—but, most important of all, he was an artist. He was lucky enough to participate as a very young man. in the first exhibition to promote the primitives. Since then he has lived for his art. Works regularly, especially in Normandy, near Giverny (Claude Monet country). His technique developed steadily, except for the short diversion of his 'Venice', to the extent that one sometimes wonders whether he may still be called 'naive'. But he certainly is a naive painter, in fact a very, very fine one—for him, the craft of painting is used, fundamentally, to express his sensitivity to, and love for nature.

Familie von Bergarbeitern. Er jedoch will dieser Landschaft von Schlackenhalden entrinnen. Vermesser, technischer Zeichner, Zöllner – aber vor allem wichtig ist die Malerei. Das Glück ist ihm übrigens hold, denn er nimmt als Jüngster an der ersten «Welle» der Naiven teil. Seither lebt er nur von seiner Malerei. Arbeitet regelmäßig, besonders in der Normandie, in der Nähe von Giverny, der Domäne von Claude Monet. Mit Ausnahme einer kurzen Verirrung in seiner Bilderserie über Venedig reift seine Kunst so sehr, daß man sich zuweilen fragen muß, ob er noch ein Naiver ist. Natürlich ist er einer, ein sehr guter Naiver, dessen großes Können im Grunde nur im Dienst seines Natursinnes und seiner Naturliebe steht.

Famille de mineurs. Mais lui, il veut échapper à ce paysage de crassiers et de terrils. Métreur, dessinateur industriel, gabelou, mais ce qui compte avant tout, c'est la peinture. Il est d'ailleurs favorisé par la chance, car il participe, en tant que benjamin, à la première promotion des naïfs. Depuis, il vit de sa peinture. Travaille régulièrement, surtout en Normandie, près de Giverny, fief de Claude Monet. Son art mûrit aussi, à l'exception d'un court égarement de ses «Venise», à tel point que l'on peut se demander parfois s'il est encore naïf. Il l'est, certes, même un très, très beau naïf chez qui un grand métier ne fait que servir, somme toute, son sens et son amour de la nature.

EXPOSITIONS:
Galerie Alice-Manteau, Paris 1930.
Galerie Santi, Douai 1931.
Galerie Moderne, Lille 1932.
«Les Maîtres Populaires de la Réalité», Paris 1937.
«Les Maîtres Populaires de la Réalité», Zürich 1937.
«Masters of Popular Painting», New York 1938.
Perls Galleries, New York 1938.
Galerie Berri-Raspail, Paris 1943
(Cat., Préface Maximilien Gauthier).
Perls Galleries, New York 1951.
Galerie Romanet, Paris 1956
(Cat., Préface Maximilien Gauthier).
«La Peinture Naïve», Knokke-le-Zoute 1958.
«La Peinture Naïve», Maison de la Pensée Française, Paris 1960.
«I Pittori Naifs», Rome 1964.
«Les Primitifs d'Aujourd'hui», Galerie Charpentier, Paris 1964.
«Le Panorama International de la Peinture Naïve», Mission Culturelle, Rabat 1964.

BIBLIOGRAPHIE:
«Jean Eve», Beaux-Arts, Paris, 20 mai 1943.
«Jean Eve» in Femina-Noël, Paris, janvier 1948.
Maximilien Gauthier: «Jean Eve», Editions Les Gemeaux, Paris 1950.
Anatole Jakovsky: «La Peinture Naïve», Paris 1949.
Anatole Jakovsky: «Les Peintres Naïfs», Paris 1956.
Anatole Jakovsky: «Naive Malerei», Zürich 1957.
Oto Bihalij-Merin: «Das naive Bild der Welt», Köln 1959.
Oto Bihalji-Merin: «Die naive Malerei», Köln 1959.
Oto Bihalji-Merin: «Les Peintres Naïfs», Paris.
«Art Naïf», Editions Marocaines et Internationales, Rabat 1964.

ILLUSTRATIONS:
Calendrier mural, avec 4 Saisons du peintre, Verlag Conzett und Huber, Zürich 1964.

Favier, Cécile

(Née Mattys).
Born March 29, 1906 in Orcyne, Puy-de-Dôme (France).

(Geborene Mattys).
Geboren am 29. März 1906 in Orcyne, Puy-de-Dôme (Frankreich).

(Née Mattys).
Née le 29 mars 1906 à Orcyne, Puy-de-Dôme (France).

Has liked to paint ever since her childhood in South America, and especially to depict landscapes of the Argentine countryside spread out around her parents' house. She returned to France in 1918 and became first a milliner, then a florist, later a maker of funeral wreaths—the orderly arrangement of flowers was a kind of inspiration for her. In 1956 her painting changed decisively to become what it is now.

Malt zu ihrem Vergnügen seit ihrer in Südamerika verbrachten Kindheit, vor allem die argentinische Landschaft, die sich vor dem Haus ihrer Eltern erstreckt. 1918 kehrt sie nach Frankreich zurück, wird Putzmacherin, dann Blumenbinderin; insbesondere fertigt sie Kränze an, deren artig angeordnete Blumen ihr zu einer Quelle der Inspiration werden. Das Jahr 1956 bringt eine entscheidende Wendung in ihrer Malerei, die zu dem wird, was sie heute ist.

S'amuse à peindre depuis son enfance en Amérique du Sud. Surtout les paysages de la campagne argentine qui s'etendent devant la maison de ses parents. Revenue en France, en 1918, elle exerce successivement les métiers de modiste, puis de fleuriste, confectionneuse de couronnes mortuaires en l'occurrence, dont les fleurs sagement ordonnées lui seront une source d'inspiration. L'année 1956 marque un tournant décisif dans sa peinture qui deviendra ce qu'elle est maintenant.

EXPOSITIONS:
Galerie « Montparnasse 89 », Paris 1959 (Cat., Préface Anatole Jakovsky).
« Les Peintres Naïfs », Maison de la Pensée Française, Paris 1960.
Galerie Berri-Lardi, Paris 1963 (Cat., Préface Anatole Jakovsky).
« I Pittori Naifs », Rome 1964.
« Les Primitifs d'Aujourd'hui », Galerie Charpentier, Paris 1964.
« Le Panorama International de la peinture Naïve », Mission Culturelle, Rabat 1964.

BIBLIOGRAPHIE:
Maurice Colinon: « Peintres du Dimanche », Femmes d'Aujourd'hui, No 900 Bruxelles Août 1962.
« Art Naïf », Editions Marocaines et Internationales, Rabat 1964.

Favre, Marcel

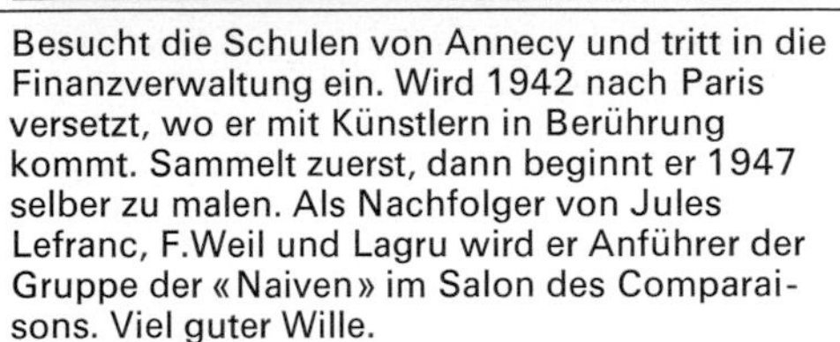

Born December 16, 1907 in Dingy-Saint-Clair, near Annecy, Haute Savoie (France).

Geboren am 16. Dezember 1907 in Dingy-Saint-Clair bei Annecy, Haute Savoie (Frankreich).

Né le 16 décembre 1907 à Dingy-Saint-Clair, près d'Annecy, Haute Savoie (France).

Studied in Annecy and entered the state Financial Department. In 1942 was transferred to Paris, where he came into contact with artists. First he collected pictures, then began to paint himself, in 1947. Became the leader of the 'naive' group in the 'Salon des Comparaison', succeeding Jules Lefranc, F.Weil and Lagru. Is full of good intentions.

Besucht die Schulen von Annecy und tritt in die Finanzverwaltung ein. Wird 1942 nach Paris versetzt, wo er mit Künstlern in Berührung kommt. Sammelt zuerst, dann beginnt er 1947 selber zu malen. Als Nachfolger von Jules Lefranc, F.Weil und Lagru wird er Anführer der Gruppe der «Naiven» im Salon des Comparaisons. Viel guter Wille.

Fait ses études à Annecy et entre dans l'Administration des Finances. En 1942 est nommé à Paris, où il prend contact avec le milieu des arts. Collectionne d'abord, puis commence à peindre lui-même. En 1947, succédant à Jules Lefranc, F.Weil et Lagru, devient le chef de groupe des «Naïfs» au Salon des Comparaisons. Beaucoup de bonne volonté.

EXPOSITIONS:
«Les Primitifs d'Aujourd'hui», Galerie Charpentier, Paris 1964.

BIBLIOGRAPHIE:
«Dix Ans d'Art Actuel», Editions Comparaisons, Paris 1964.

Feješ, Emeric

Born 1904 in Osijek (Yugoslavia).

Geboren 1904 in Osijek (Jugoslawien).

Né en 1904 à Osijek (Yougoslavie).

Came of a poor family. Was the seventh of fourteen children. Worked with his hands as a comb-maker and a button-cutter. In 1945 he tried his hand as a secondhand dealer in Novi-Sad. It was in 1949 that he began to paint, depicting towns which he had never seen but which he made look attractive and lifelike by his exceptional gift for the use of color and by the touch of poetry which he gave each picture. He is sometimes compared to Vivin, who also painted from photographs or other pictures; but Vivin's precise vision and impeccable, pure craftsmanship unfortunately cannot be found in Feješ. Nevertheless, he is one of the best Yugoslav artists at the present time.

Stammt aus ärmlichen Verhältnissen. Er ist das siebte von vierzehn Kindern. Manuelle Berufe: Kammacher und Knopfschneider. 1945 betätigt er sich ausnahmsweise aus dem Stegreif als Antiquitätenhändler in Novi-Sad. Beginnt 1949 jene Stadtlandschaften zu malen, die er nie besucht hat, die er aber dank seiner unbestreitbaren Farbbegabung und dank des sie beseelenden poetischen Atems anziehend und lebendig gestaltet. Man vergleicht ihn zuweilen mit Vivin, der ebenfalls nach Photographien oder anderen Dokumenten malte, aber die Strenge der Schau und das tadellose, glatte Können eines Vivin gehen Feješ leider ab. Wie dem auch sei, er ist einer der besten jugoslawischen Maler der Gegenwart.

Famille pauvre. Lui, il est le septième des quatorze enfants. Métiers manuels: tourneur de peignes et tailleur de boutons. En 1945, il s'improvise, exceptionnellement, marchand d'antiquités à Novi-Sad. Commence à peindre en 1949 ces paysages de villes qu'il n'a jamais visitées, mais qu'il rend attrayants et vivants grâce à son don incontestable de coloriste, ainsi que grâce au souffle poétique qui les anime. On le rapproche parfois de Vivin qui, lui aussi, peignait d'après les documents photographiques ou autres, mais la rigueur de la vision, jointe à un métier racé, impeccable, de Vivin manque, hélas à Feješ. Quoiqu'il en soit, il reste l'un des meilleurs peintres yougoslaves actuels.

EXPOSITIONS:
Musée de Dubrovnik 1956.
« Naivni umetnici jugoslavije », Belgrade 1957.
« La Peinture Naïve », Knokke-le-Zoute 1958.
« Das naive Bild der Welt », Baden-Baden 1961.
The Arthur Jeffress Gallery, London 1961 (Cat., Préface M. Gelen).
«Yugoslav Modern Primitives», Edinburgh 1962.
« Peintres Naïfs Yougoslaves », Moscou 1962.
« Première Quadriennale des Peintres Naïfs Yougoslaves », Čačac 1962.
Galleria La Feluca, Rome 1963.
« Naive Kunst in Jugoslawien », Kunstakademie, Wien 1963.
Centro per la Cooperazione Mediterranea, Palerme 1963 (Import. Cat., Préface Vittore Querel).
Galerie St-Etienne, New York 1963.
« Peintres Naïfs Populaires Yougoslaves », Leningrad 1963.
«Sonntagsmaler aus Jugoslawien», Museum am Ostwall, Dortmund 1964.
« Die Welt der naiven Malerei », Salzburg 1964.
« De Lusthof der Naieven », Rotterdam 1964.
« Le Monde des Naïfs », Paris 1964.

BIBLIOGRAPHIE:
«Yougoslavia» Numéro spécial (17) consacré à l'art naïf. Belgrade 1959.
Oto Bihalji-Merin: « Das naive Bild der Welt », Köln 1959.
Oto Bihalji-Merin: « Die naive Malerei », Köln 1959.
Oto Bihalji-Merin: « Les Peintres Naïfs », Paris (sans date).
Oto Bihalji-Merin: « Umetnost Naivnich u Jugoslavjii », Belgrade 1963.
« Art Naïf », Editions Marocaines et Internationales, Rabat 1964.

Fereoli, Enrico

Born December 1, 1901 in Sala Baganza, Parma (Italy).

Geboren am 1. Dezember 1901 in Sala Baganza, Parma (Italien).

Né le 1er décembre 1901 à Sala Baganza, Parme (Italie).

Has always lived in Parma. Was a cabinet-maker by profession, but a serious accident in 1958 injured him permanently and prevented him from working any more. So, in order to keep idleness at bay, and above all in order to continue creating things of beauty, he took up painting; this was about 1960. His attitude is humble – he approaches reality with awe. Not even the slightest detail is omitted, for he respects even the smallest things. The epitome of a 'peintre intimiste'

Wohnt seit jeher in Parma. Tischler. Aber 1958 hat er einen schweren Unfall, der ihn auf lebenslänglich verstümmelt und ihm das Arbeiten unmöglich macht. Um dem Müßiggang zu entgehen und vor allem um weiterhin etwas Schönes zu schaffen, fängt er 1960 an zu malen. Schüchtern. Er geht mit viel Ehrfurcht an die Wirklichkeit heran und läßt nicht die geringste Einzelheit aus, respektiert auch winzige Dinge. Seine Malerei ist im wahren Sinne des Wortes intimistisch.

Réside depuis toujours à Parme. Ebéniste. Mais un grave accident survenu en 1958 le rend mutilé jusqu'à la fin de ses jours et l'empêche désormais de travailler. Alors, pour fuir l'oisiveté ét surtout pour continuer à faire de belles choses, il commence à faire de la peinture. Vers 1960. Timidement, il approche le réel avec beaucoup de respect. Il n'omet aucun détail, il respecte de toutes petites choses. C'est une peinture intimiste par excellence.

EXPOSITIONS:
Centro Sociale, Parme 1962.
«I Pittori Naifs», Rome 1964.
«I Pittori Naifs», Centro Internazionale di Arte Figurative, Biella 1964.
Galleria Camattini, Parme 1965
(Cat., Préface Tiziano Marcheselli).

Ferrara, Daniel

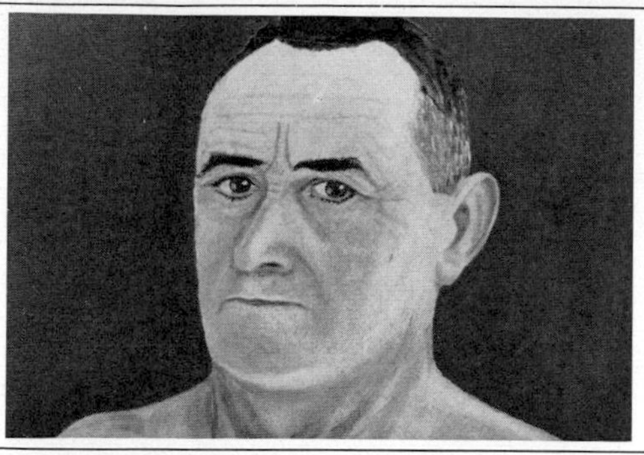

Born July 8, 1906 in Mers-El-Kebir (Algeria).

Geboren am 8. Juli 1906 in Mers-El-Kebir (Algerien).

Né le 8 juillet 1906 à Mers-El-Kebir (Algérie).

Came from a sailor's family of Italian origin. He himself became a docker in Marseilles. Is only able to paint during the short leisure hours which his job left him. Has a special liking for Biblical scenes and large landscapes of Marseilles and its environs; in such pictures it is easy to see his predilection for the Italian style. He is the most Italianate of all the French 'naive' artists.

Familie von Seeleuten italienischer Herkunft. Er selbst ist Hafenarbeiter in Marseille. Er kann also nur in der knappen Freizeit malen, die ihm sein Beruf läßt. Hat eine Vorliebe für biblische Szenen und die großen Landschaften von Marseille und seiner Umgebung. In seinen Bildern wird seine Liebe zur italienischen Malerei deutlich sichtbar. Er ist der italienischste aller französischen Naiven.

Famille de marins, d'origine italienne. Lui-même, est docker à Marseille. Il ne peut peindre donc que pendant les rares loisirs que lui laisse son métier. Affectionne les scènes bibliques et les grands paysages de Marseille et des environs de Marseille, où l'on distingue très nettement son goût pour la peinture italienne. C'est le plus italianisant de tous les naïfs français.

EXPOSITIONS:
Galerie Herbinet, Paris 1960.
Galerie Herbinet, Paris 1963.
Galerie Herbinet, Paris 1965
(Cat., Préface Anatole Jakovsky).
«I Pittori Naifs», Rome 1964.
«Les Primitifs d'Aujourd'hui»,
Galerie Charpentier, Paris 1964.

BIBLIOGRAPHIE:
Anatole Jakovsky: «Eros du Dimanche», Paris 1964.

Ferrer, Hilario Aruffe

Born September 30, 1881 in Malbajar, in the province of Durazno (Uruguay).
Died August 19, 1950 in Montevideo (Uruguay).

Geboren am 30. September 1881 in Malbajar, Provinz Durazno (Uruguay).
Gestorben am 19. August 1950 in Montevideo (Uruguay).

Né le 30 septembre 1881 à Malbajar, province de Durazno (Uruguay).
Mort le 19 août 1950 à Montévideo (Uruguay).

'Uruguayan artist, rural and primitive'; thus Ferrer has been described by his compatriot, the critic José Pedro Argul—and it is an accurate assessment. Long visits to the countryside where he spent his youth made it natural for him to choose rural subjects for his painting, while his marriage to the daughter of one of the most famous political leaders of the civil war at the beginning of the century led him to political commitment in his choice of subjects. He has often exhibited his work in his own country, making no distinction between amateur and professional exhibitions. He even won first prize in the 1927 'Salon', an honor accorded him by public vote. He came from the people, was one of them, and thus his work appealed to them. He translated into pictures their national feeling. Ferrer himself called his work 'nativism'. And it is true that something was born there....

«Ländlicher und primitivistischer uruguyanischer Maler», sagt sein Landsmann, der Kritiker José Pedro Argul, zu Recht von ihm. In der Tat haben lange Aufenthalte auf dem Land, wo er seine Jugend verbrachte, ihn für ländliche Themen empfänglich gemacht, während seine Ehe mit der Tochter eines sehr bekannten politischen Führers aus der Zeit der Bürgerkriege zu Beginn des Jahrhunderts ihm «engagierte» Themen nahelegte. Er hat in seiner Heimat viel ausgestellt, wobei er sich unterschiedslos sowohl zu den Dilettanten wie zu den Berufsmalern zählte. Er erhielt sogar im Salon von 1927 vom Publikum den ersten Preis zugesprochen. Als Sohn des Volks gefiel er dem Volk. Er drückte sein Nationalgefühl aus. Er selber nannte seine Kunst «Nativismus». Und in der Tat kam da etwas zur Welt...

«Peintre ruraliste et primitiviste uruguayen», dit de lui, avec justesse, son compatriote, le critique José Pedro Argul. En effet, de longs séjours à la campagne, où il a passé sa jeunesse, l'ont prédisposé aux sujets ruraux, tandis que son mariage avec la fille d'un leader politique des plus renommés des guerres civiles du commencement du siècle l'ont incliné vers les sujets disons «engagés». Il a beaucoup exposé dans son pays, se mêlant sans distinction aussi bien aux amateurs qu'aux professionnels.
Il a même eu le premier prix du Salon de 1927, accordé par le suffrage du public. Issu du peuple il plaît donc au peuple. Il traduit son sentiment national. Lui-même, il appelait son art «Le Nativisme». Il est vrai qu'il y a là quelque chose qui naît...

Field, Erastus Salisbury

Born 1805 in Leverett, Mass. (USA).
Died 1900 in Sunderland, Mass. (USA).

Geboren 1805 in Leverett, Mass. (USA).
Gestorben 1900 in Sunderland, Mass. (USA).

Né en 1805 à Leverett, Mass. (USA).
Mort en 1900 à Sunderland, Mass. (USA).

Is one of the few American 'naive' artists of last century (the 'anonymous' or 'unknown' ones are legion) to have a biography. He started by being a pupil of S.F.B. Morse, the portraitist and painter of New York scenes, who also later became known for his invention of the telegraphic alphabet. Later, to earn his living, he was forced to follow in the footsteps of so many of his colleagues and to become an itinerant portrait-painter, going from ranch to ranch, from farm to farm, from village to village, immortalizing in his painting those who were (unconsciously) founding the new dynasties of money. However, perhaps for his own pleasure, he also painted biblical scenes as well as mythological and historical-allegorical pictures, which are executed with great delicacy.

Einer der wenigen alten naiven Maler Amerikas – in der Mehrzahl sind sie «anonym» oder «unbekannt» –, der eine Biographie besitzt. Er beginnt als Schüler von S.F.B. Morse, der Porträtist und Maler von New Yorker Landschaften war, jedoch bekannter als Erfinder des nach ihm benannten Alphabets. Dann mußte er, um sein Brot zu verdienen, den Weg so vieler seiner Kollegen beschreiten und als fahrender Porträtist von Ranch zu Ranch, von Hof zu Hof, von Städtchen zu Städtchen ziehen, um die Männer und Frauen zu verewigen, die ohne ihr Wissen die neuen Gelddynastien begründeten. Aber wohl zu seinem Vergnügen malte er auch biblische oder mythologische und historisch-allegorische Szenen, die er mit großer Zartheit widergab.

L'un des rares, parmi les peintres naïfs américains anciens, «anonymes» ou «inconnus» – leur nom est légion! – à avoir une biographie. Il débute comme élève de S.F.B. Morse, portraitiste et peintre de paysages new-yorkais, connu davantage par son invention de l'alphabet télégraphique. Ensuite, pour gagner sa vie, il a dû prendre la filière de tant d'autres de ses collègues en tant que portraitiste ambulant, allant de ranch en ranch, de ferme en ferme, de bourgade en bourgade, afin d'immortaliser celles et ceux qui, à leur insu, fondaient les nouvelles dynasties d'argent. Mais, pour son propre plaisir, qui sait, il peignait aussi des scènes bibliques, si ce n'est mythologiques et historico-allégoriques peintes avec une grande finesse.

EXPOSITIONS:
«Amerikanische Primitive»,
Museum am Ostwall, Dortmund 1954–55.
Pavillon américain à l'Exposition Universelle, Bruxelles 1958.
Abby Aldrich Rockefeller Folk Art Collection, Williamsburg 1963.
«De Lusthof der Naieven», Rotterdam 1964.
«Le Monde des Naïfs», Paris 1964.

BIBLIOGRAPHIE:
Bulletin of the Society for the Preservation of New England Antiquities, octobre 1942.
Jean Lipman et Alice Winchester: «Primitive Painters in America», Dodd Mead & Co, New York 1950.

Filipovič, Franjo

Born October 2, 1930 in Hlebine (Yugoslavia).

Geboren am 2. Oktober 1930 in Hlebine (Jugoslawien).

Né le 2 octobre 1930 à Hlebine (Yougoslavie).

Belongs to what has since been named the 'Hlebine school', the cradle of 'naive' art in Yugoslavia. Was born of peasant stock and has remained a peasant, painting only during his free time. Took up painting in 1945, having been encouraged by his group leader, Ivan Generalič. A year later he exhibited his work with those of all the other village artists of Koprivniča. His art is strong, healthy, with a tendency to folklore.

Gehört zur «Schule von Hlebine», der Wiege der naiven Kunst in Jugoslawien. War und ist Bauer, denn er malt nur während seiner Freizeit. Beginnt 1945, ermuntert durch Ivan Generalič, den Führer der Gruppe. Ein Jahr später stellt er mit allen anderen Malern des Dorfes in Koprivniča aus. Eine saftige, gesunde Kunst mit folkloristischen Tendenzen.

Appartient à ce que l'on appelle désormais «L'Ecole de Hlebine», berceau de l'art naïf yougoslave. Paysan, resté paysan, car il ne peint que pendant ses loisirs. Commence à peindre en 1945, encouragé par le chef de file, Ivan Generalič. Un an après, il expose avec tous les autres peintres du village à Koprivniča. Un art dru, sain, avec des tendances folkloriques.

EXPOSITIONS:
«Naivni umetnici jugoslavije», Belgrade 1957.
Narodni Muzej Zemun, 1959.
The Arthur Jeffress Gallery, Londres 1961 (Cat., Préface M. Gelen).
«Yugoslav Modern Primitives», Edinburgh 1962.
«Peintres Naïfs Yougoslaves», Moscou 1962.
«Première Quadriennale des Peintres Naïfs Yougoslaves», Čačac 1962.
«Naive Kunst in Jugoslawien», Académie des Beaux-Arts, Vienne 1963.
Galerie St-Etienne, New York 1963.
«Peintres Naïfs Populaires Yougoslaves», Leningrad 1963.
«Sonntagsmaler aus Jugoslawien», Museum am Ostwall, Dortmund 1964.

BIBLIOGRAPHIE:
Oto Bihalji-Merin: «Das naive Bild der Welt», Köln 1959.
Oto Bihalji-Merin: «Die naive Malerei», Köln 1959.
Oto Bihalji-Merin: «Les Peintres Naïfs», Paris (sans date).
Oto Bihalji-Merin: «Umetnost Naivnich u Jugoslavjii», Belgrade 1963.

Fiorio, Serge

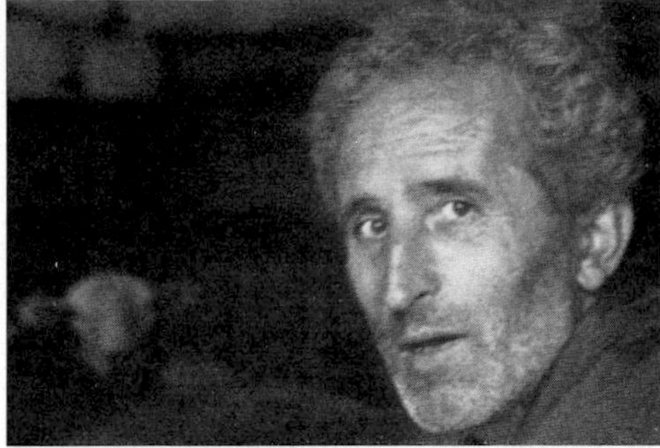

Born October 10, 1911 in Vallorbe (Switzerland).

Geboren am 10. Oktober 1911 in Vallorbe (Schweiz).

Né le 10 octobre 1911 à Vallorbe (Suisse).

Has lived for many years in Haute Provence, where he leads the life of a gentleman-farmer. Painting is his hobby. Is he 'naive'? Is he no longer 'naive'? Futile questions... He is purely self-taught and will never be able to rid himself of a certain 'naïveté'. However, his sense of grandeur seems to rank him rather among the primitives. At any rate, his painting is beautiful, elegant and rather subtle.

Lebt seit langer Zeit in der Haute Provence, wo er das Dasein eines Gentleman-Farmers führt. Die Malerei ist sein Steckenpferd. Ist er ein Naiver? Ist er es nicht mehr? Müßige Fragen... Als reiner Autodidakt wird er sich nie von einer gewissen Naivität befreien können. Aber sein Sinn für Größe rückt ihn eher in die Nähe der Primitiven. Wie dem auch sei, seine Bilder sind schön, elegant und ein klein wenig raffiniert.

Habite depuis longtemps la Haute Provence, où il mène une vie de gentleman-farmer. La peinture est son violon d'Ingres. Est-il naïf? N'est-il plus naïf? Questions oiseuses... Autodidacte pur, il ne pourra jamais se débarrasser d'une certaine naïveté. Mais son sens de la grandeur l'apparente davantage aux primitifs. Quoiqu'il en soit, c'est une peinture belle, élégante et un tantinet raffinée.

EXPOSITIONS:
Galerie du Cabaret de l'Ecluse, Paris 1956.
Galerie des Mages, Vence 1957.
Galerie du Haut Pavé, Paris 1959 (Cat., Préface Jean Cocteau).
Galerie du Haut Pavé, Paris 1961.
Musée Filke, Worpswede 1961
Galerie Dieter Brusberg, Hannover 1961.
Galerie Insel, Hamburg 1961.
Palais des Arts, Berlin-Charlottenburg 1962.
Institut Français, Stuttgart 1962
Galerie Cheval de Verre, Bruxelles 1966.

BIBLIOGRAPHIE:
«Serge Fiorio», Pâtre, No 61 Paris, février 1959.
Anatole Jakovsky: «La Peinture Naïve», Paris 1956.
Anatole Jakovsky: «Naive Malerei», Zürich 1957.
Dépliant avec textes de J. Cocteau, J. Giono etc., Grenoble (sans date)

Fortin, Edmond

Born in August 1881 in Argy, near Châteauroux, Indre (France).
Died April 24, 1955 in Le Bourget, Seine et Oise (France).

Geboren im August 1881 in Argy bei Châteauroux, Indre (Frankreich).
Gestorben am 24. April 1955 in Le Bourget, Seine et Oise (Frankreich).

Né au mois d'août 1881 à Argy, près Châteauroux, Indre (France).
Mort le 24 avril 1955 au Bourget, Seine et Oise (France).

Fortin is another of those who painted entirely for personal pleasure, or rather from an inner compulsion, not caring at all about fame or about selling pictures. Rather the contrary. He was a grocer with a shop near the airport Le Bourget, and he refused to sell his paintings, which he used to hang on the walls of his shop. Only after his death did his latest 'partner in life' sell them to a group of art-lovers. He had a tortured imagination, impeccable technique, and unusual gifts.

Noch einer, der einzig zu seinem eigenen Vergnügen und aus innerer Notwendigkeit gemalt hat, ohne sich um Ruhm oder den Verkauf seiner Bilder zu kümmern. Im Gegenteil. Er besaß ein Lebensmittelgeschäft in der Nähe des Flughafens von Le Bourget und hing seine Bilder im Laden auf, weigerte sich jedoch, sie zu verkaufen. Erst nach seinem Tod hat seine letzte Lebensgefährtin sie an eine Gruppe von Liebhabern verkauft. Gequälte Inspiration, tadellose Ausführung, außergewöhnliche Begabung.

Encore un qui a peint uniquement pour son propre plaisir, sinon par nécessité intérieure, sans se soucier ni de la gloire ni de la vente de ses tableaux. Au contraire. Etabli épicier, près de l'Aéroport du Bourget, il réfusait de vendre ses tableaux accrochés, pourtant, dans sa boutique. Ce n'est qu'après sa mort que la dernière compagne de sa vie les a vendus à un groupe d'amateurs. Inspiration tourmentée, exécution impeccable, dons hors commun.

EXPOSITIONS:
Galerie Herbinet, Paris 1965
(Cat., Préface Anatole Jakovsky).

BIBLIOGRAPHIE:
Fernand Woutaz: «Edmond Fortin», Journal des Médecins du Nord et de l'Est, N° 6, Paris, juin 1965.

Fous, Jean

Born April 9, 1901 in Paris (France).

Geboren am 9. April 1901 in Paris (Frankreich).

Né le 9 avril 1901 à Paris (France).

Son of a picture-framer living in the rue du Dragon in Saint-Germain-des-Prés. Instead of following in his father's footsteps, however, as was the custom, he chose adventure; he travelled to the south of France and finally set up a stall in an open-air market in the shade of St. Sernin Cathedral in Toulouse. Later he returned to Paris and continued to sell in the flea-market of the Porte de Vanves. This is therefore the second 'naive' artist who was a seller in a second-hand market, for Paul Lefebvre was another (c.f. the article 'A century of naive painting' by P. Lissandre, which appeared in French in 'Le Monde Illustré', October 28, 1933, at the time of the exhibition of E.Wolters's collection.) Fous's art is very personal, full of pictorial qualities. He is almost the only artist to have painted the Paris flea-markets.

Sohn eines Einrahmers aus der Rue du Dragon in Saint-Germain-des-Prés. Aber anstatt den Beruf des Vaters zu ergreifen, wie es bei den Handwerkern üblich war, wählt der junge Fous das Abenteuer. Er bereist Südfrankreich und etabliert sich schließlich als «Flohmarkttrödler» im Schatten der Kathedrale Saint-Sernin in Toulouse. Nach seiner Rückkehr nach Paris fährt er fort, auf dem Flohmarkt an der Porte de Vanves zu verkaufen. Er ist der zweite Maler, der sein Leben auf dem Flohmarkt verdient, denn es gab da schon einen gewissen Paul Lefebvre. (Siehe dazu: Un Siècle de peinture naïve, von P. Lissandre, erschienen in Le Monde Illustré vom 28. Oktober 1933, anläßlich der Ausstellung der Sammlung E. Wolters.) Fous' Kunst ist sehr persönlich, voll von bildhaften Eigenschaften. Er ist ungefähr der einzige Maler, der die Pariser Flohmärkte geschildert hat.

Fils d'encadreur de la rue du Dragon à Saint-Germain-des-Prés. Mais au lieu de continuer le métier de son père, comme il était de coutume chez les artisans, le jeune Fous choisit l'aventure; il voyage dans le Midi de la France et s'établit enfin, comme «Pucier», à l'ombre de Saint-Sernin à Toulouse. Revenu à Paris, il continue à vendre aux «Puces» de la porte de Vanves. C'est le second peintre pucier, puisqu'il y a eu déjà un certain Paul Lefebvre. (Voir à ce sujet: Un Siècle de peinture naïve, par P. Lissandre, paru dans Le Monde Illustré du 28 octobre 1933 à l'occasion de l'exposition de la collection E. Wolters.) L'art de Fous est très personnel, plein de qualités picturales. Il est à peu près le seul peintre à avoir peint les marchés aux Puces parisiens.

EXPOSITIONS:
Galerie Le Dragon, Paris 1944 (Cat., Préface Anatole Jakovsky).
Galerie de Médicis, Paris 1945 (Cat., Préface Anatole Jakovsky).
Galerie Roux-Hentschel, Paris 1948 (Cat., Préface Anatole Jakovsky).
Galerie d'Art du Faubourg, Paris 1954 (Cat., Préface Anatole Jakovsky).
Galerie Robert Prouté, Paris 1958.
«La Peinture Naïve», Knokke-le-Zoute 1958.
Galerie de Chaudun, Paris 1960 (Cat., Préface Maurice Fombeure).
«La Peinture Naïve», Maison de la Pensée Française, Paris 1960.
Galerie O'Hanna, Londres 1962.
«Les Primitifs d'Aujourd'hui», Galerie Charpentier, Paris 1964.
«I Pittori Naifs», Rome 1964.
«Aux Rois d'Aragon», Perpignan 1965.
Syndicat d'Initiative de la ville de Céret, 1966.

BIBLIOGRAPHIE:
Anatole Jakovsky: «La Peinture Naïve», Paris 1949.
Anatole Jakovsky: «Peintres Naïfs», Paris 1956.
Anatole Jakovsky: «Paris-mes-Puces», Editions les Quatre Jeudis, Paris 1956.
Anatole Jakovsky: «Die naive Malerei», Zürich 1957.
Oto Bihalij-Merin: «Das naive Bild der Welt», Köln 1959.
Oto Bihalij-Merin: «Die naive Malerei», Köln 1959.
Oto Bihalij-Merin: «Les Peintres Naïfs», Paris (sans date).
«Jean Fous», L'Illustrazione Italiana, novembre 1960.

Frost, John O. J.

Born 1852 in Marblehead, Mass. (USA).
Died 1929 in Marblehead, Mass. (USA).

Geboren 1852 in Marblehead, Mass. (USA).
Gestorben 1929 in Marblehead, Mass. (USA).

Né en 1852 à Marblehead, Mass. (USA).
Mort en 1929 à Marblehead, Mass. (USA).

His father was a fisherman; he himself became a sailor. Began to paint rather late in life, after having retired from work. Always painted from memory—reminiscences of his adventures and travels. He also depicted his little native town in paintings full of nostalgia, showing what he called 'the good old days'. Incidentally, he also wrote several stories which were characterized by the same feeling.

Sein Vater war Fischer, er selber Matrose. Beginnt in ziemlich vorgerücktem Alter zu malen, als er sich zur Ruhe setzt. Er malt aus dem Gedächtnis Erinnerungen an seine Abenteuer und seine Reisen. Er hat auch mit viel Sehnsucht seine kleine Heimatstadt verewigt, die für ihn «die gute alte Zeit» darstellt. Er hat auch ein paar Erzählungen geschrieben, die der gleichen Geistesverfassung entspringen.

Père pêcheur; lui, marin. Commence à peindre assez âgé, après avoir pris sa retraite. Il peint de mémoire. Ce sont les souvenirs de ses aventures et de ses voyages. Il a immortalisé aussi, avec beaucoup de nostalgie, sa petite ville natale. Ce qu'il appelle, du reste, «Le bon vieux temps». Il a écrit par ailleurs quelques récits qui correspondent au même état d'esprit.

EXPOSITIONS:
«Amerikanische Primitive», Museum am Ostwall, Dortmund 1954–55.
«American Primitive Paintings», The Smithsonian Institution, Washington 1958.

BILBIOGRAPHIE:
B. Jasmand und Otto Kallir: «Sonntagsmaler», Otto Aug. Ehlers, Berlin/Darmstadt 1956.

Funken, Armand

Born in 1870 in Verviers (Belgium).
Died April 28, 1940 in Verviers (Belgium).

Geboren 1870 in Verviers (Belgien).
Gestorben am 28. April 1940 in Verviers (Belgien).

Né en 1870 à Verviers (Belgique).
Mort le 28 avril 1940 à Verviers (Belgique).

Nothing much is known yet about this typically Walloon artist; he was discovered by the young poet and writer Georges Schmits, who prepared a brochure on him. But his paintings speak for themselves. They are imbued with an irresistible enthusiasm. They always depict crowds composed of extremely typical characters, and are drawn with great subtlety.

Man weiß nicht viel über diesen typisch wallonischen Maler, der von dem jungen Dichter und Schriftsteller Georges Schmits entdeckt wurde. Aber seine Bilder sprechen für sich selber. Eine unwiderstehliche Vitalität beseelt sie. Sie stellen immer Menschenmengen dar, die aus erstaunlich treffend charakterisierten und geschickt gemalten Personen bestehen.

On ne connaît pas encore grand' chose sur ce peintre typiquement wallon, découvert par le jeune poète et écrivain Georges Schmits, qui prépare une plaquette sur lui. Mais ses tableaux parlent d'eux-mêmes. Une verve irrésistible les anime. Ce sont toujours les foules composées de personnages remarquablement typés et exécutés avec finesse.

BIBLIOGRAPHIE:
G. Schmits: «Armand Funken», «Savoir et Beauté», La Louvière, numéro spécial consacré aux naïfs, décembre 1965.

Gabriel, Jean-Hubert

Born October 8, 1919 in Ligneuville (Belgium).

Geboren am 8. Oktober 1919 in Ligneuville (Belgien).

Né le 8 octobre 1919 à Ligneuville (Belgique).

A self-taught artist. Mason by trade. Depicts the landscapes of his country, of which Apollinaire once wrote. During the course of years, however, his knowledge of plastic technique gradually increased through hard work and this sometimes lifts him out of the realms of the true 'naive' artists.

Autodidakt. Maurer. Malt die Landschaften seiner einst von Apollinaire besungenen Heimat. Er arbeitet so viel, daß er sich nach und nach die plastischen Kenntnisse erwirbt, die ihn zuweilen der Ursprünglichkeit der echten Naiven berauben.

Autodidacte. Maçon. Peint les paysages de son pays, chanté jadis par Apollinaire. A force de travail, il acquiert peu à peu les connaissances plastiques qui lui enlèvent parfois le primesaut des vrais naïfs.

EXPOSITIONS:
Institut St-Remacle, Stavelot 1961.
Galerie Apollinaire, Stavelot 1962.

BIBLIOGRAPHIE:
G. Schmits: «Jean-Hubert Gabriel», «Savoir et Beauté», numéro spécial, Edité à la Louvière et consacré aux naïfs, décembre 1965.

Galeotti, Francesco

Born May 25, 1920 in S. Adriano di Marradi, Florence (Italy).

Geboren 25. Mai 1920 in S. Adriano di Marradi, Florenz (Italien).

Né le 25 mai 1920 à S. Adriano di Marradi, Florence (Italie).

Peasant. Quite definitely one of the purest Italian 'naive' artists. Began by painting traditional scenes of Italian everyday life: grape-gathering, fairs, markets, work in the fields—always with a background of Tuscan landscape and Tuscan architecture, dotted with cypress trees. But quite soon he moved away from merely depicting definite scenes to a more fantastic art, in which the shapes and objects he painted acquire an almost independent existence. His sunflowers, for instance, and his birds exist only in the realm of poetic fantasy. In this way he reminds one of Rabuzin or Alexandrine—whom he obviously did not know.

Bauer. Unbestreitbar einer der reinsten unter den italienischen Naiven. Auf dem Hintergrund der toskanischen Landschaft und der durch Zypressen unterstrichenen toskanischen Architektur malt er zuerst traditionelle Szenen aus dem Leben seiner Heimat: Weinlese, Jahrmarkt, Markt und Feldarbeit. Aber er befreit sich schnell von der anekdotischen Seite des Dargestellten, so daß die Formen und Dinge, die seine Bilder bevölkern, ein beinahe unabhängiges Leben gewinnen. So z. B. seine Sonnenblumen oder seine Vögel, die von der Maßlosigkeit der Poesie erfüllt sind. In dieser Beziehung steht er einem Rabuzin oder einer Alexandrine, die er natürlich nicht kennt, sehr nahe.

Paysan. Incontestablement l'un des plus purs parmi les naïfs italiens. Commence par peindre des scènes traditionnelles de la vie de son pays, vendanges, foires, marchés et travaux de la terre, tout cela sur un fond de paysage toscan et de l'architecture toscane ponctuée de cyprès, mais il se débarrasse bien vite du côté anecdotique de la chose représentée, à tel point que les formes et les objets qui peuplent ses tableaux acquièrent une vie presqu'indépendante. Tels sont, par exemple, ses tournesols et ses oiseaux que seule la démesure de la poésie habite. Il se rapproche, de ce fait, d'un Rabuzin ou d'une Alexandrine qu'il ne connaît, évidemment, pas.

EXPOSITIONS:
Galleria d'Arte Spinetti, Florence 1962 (Cat., Préface Antony de Witt).
«Pittori Naifs», Centro Internationale di Arti Figurative, Biella 1964.
Galleria d'Arte Spinetti, Florence 1965 (Cat., Préface Antony de Witt et Italo Spinetti).

BIBLIOGRAPHIE:
Renzo Battiglia: «Galeotti», Oggi, No. 23, Rome juin 1966.

Gaži, Dragan

Born August 5, 1930 in Hlebine (Yugoslavia).

Geboren am 5. August 1930 in Hlebine (Jugoslawien).

Né le 5 août 1930 à Hlebine (Yougoslavie).

Of peasant stock. Has been drawing ever since childhood. Generalič taught him to paint on glass. His pictures are typical country scenes; he paints only in his free time. Belongs to the 'Hlebine school'.

Bauer. Zeichnet seit seiner Kindheit. Generalič bringt ihm das Glasmalen bei. Typische Szenen aus seiner Heimat, die er ausschließlich während seiner Freizeit malt. Gehört zur «Schule von Hlebine».

Paysan. Dessine depuis son enfance. Generalič lui enseigne la peinture sur verre. Scènes typiques du pays qu'il peint uniquement pendant ses loisirs. Fait partie de l'«Ecole de Hlebine».

EXPOSITIONS:
«Naivni umetnici jugoslavije», Belgrade 1957.
The Arthur Jeffress Gallery, Londres 1961 (Cat., Préface M. Gelen).
«Yugoslav Modern Primitives», Edinburgh 1962.
«Première Quadriennale des Peintres Naïfs Yougoslaves», Čačac 1962.
«Peintres Naïfs Yougoslaves», Moscou 1962.
«Naive Kunst in Jugoslawien», Kunstakademie, Wien 1963.
«Peintres naïfs Populaires Yougoslaves», Leningrad 1963.
«Sonntagsmaler aus Jugoslawien», Museum am Ostwall, Dortmund 1964.

BIBLIOGRAPHIE:
«Yougoslavija», Numéro spécial (17) consacré à l'art des naïfs, Belgrade 1959.
Oto Bihalji-Merin: «Das naive Bild der Welt», Köln 1959.
Oto Bihalji-Merin: «Die naive Malerei», Köln 1959.
Oto Bihalji-Merin: «Les Peintres Naïfs», Paris (sans date).
Oto Bihalji-Merin: «Umetnost Naivnich u Jugoslavjii, Belgrade 1963.

Generalič, Ivan

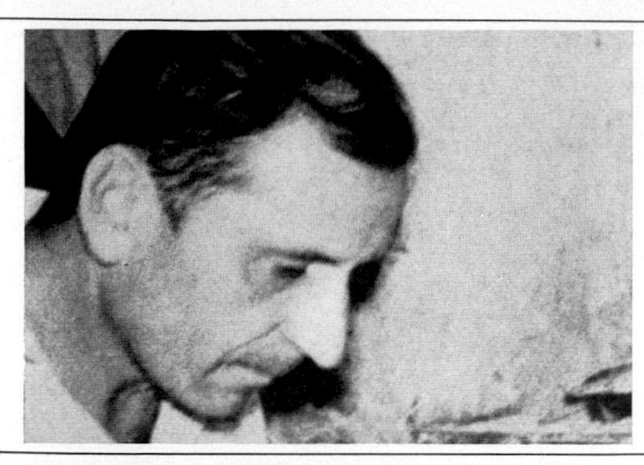

Born December 21, 1914 in Hlebine (Yugoslavia).

Geboren am 21. Dezember 1914 in Hlebine (Jugoslawien).

Né le 21 décembre 1914 à Hlebine (Yougoslavie).

Even while he was employed as a shepherd (like Giotto) he used to draw. In 1931 Generalič exhibited his first pictures in Zagreb. Since that time Generalič's path was clear—and in 1936 the 'Hlebine school' came into being. Most of his work is on glass. He is the best known of the 'naive' artists in Yugoslavia.

Wie Giotto zeichnet er schon als junger Schäfer. Generalič stellt zum ersten Mal 1931 in Zagreb aus. Von da an ist sein Weg vorgezeichnet, und bereits 1936 wird der Name «Schule von Hlebine» gebraucht. Gewöhnlich malt er auf Glas. Er ist der bekannteste naive Maler Jugoslawiens.

Déjà jeune berger, tel Giotto, il dessine. Il expose pour la première fois, en 1931 à Zagreb. Désormais son chemin est tracé, et dès 1936, l'appellation «Ecole de Hlebine» fait son apparition. Il peint généralement sur verre. C'est le plus connu parmi les peintres naïfs yougoslaves.

EXPOSITIONS:
Agence du Tourisme Yougoslave, Paris 1953.
Participation à la troisième Biennale, São Paulo 1955.
«Les Primitifs Yougoslaves», Musée, Dubrovnik 1956.
Galerie de l'Etat, Belgrade 1955.
«Les Peintres Primitifs Yougoslaves», Dubrovnik 1956.
«Naivni umetnici jugoslavije», Belgrade 1957.
«50 Ans d'Art Moderne», Exposition Universelle, Bruxelles 1958.
«La Peinture Naïve», Knokke-le-Zoute 1958.
Palais des Beaux-Arts, Bruxelles 1959 (Cat., Préface O. Bihalji-Merin).
Galerie d'Art Primitif, Zagreb 1960 (Cat., Préface par lui-même).
«Laienmaler», Gewerbemuseum, Basel 1961.
«Das naive Bild der Welt», Baden-Baden 1961.
The Arthur Jeffress Gallery, Londres 1961 (Cat., Préface M. Gelen).
«Yugoslav Modern Primitives», Edinburgh 1961.
Salon Moderne Galerie, Zagreb (puis à Sarajevo et Belgrade) 1962.
Galerie d'Art Primitif, Zagreb 1962 (Cat., Préface Mica Basicevic).
Première Quadriennale des Peintres Naïfs Yougoslaves, Čačac. 1962.
«L'Art des Peintres Naïfs Yougoslaves», Moscou 1962.
«L'Art des Peintres Naïfs Yougoslaves», Leningrad 1963.
Galerie d'Art Primitif, Zagreb 1963.
«Sonntagsmaler aus Jugoslawien», Museum am Ostwall, Dortmund 1964.
«Die Welt der naiven Malerei», Salzburg 1964.
«De Lusthof der Naieven», Rotterdam 1964.
«Le Monde des Naïfs», Paris 1964.
Galerie Friedrich und Dahlem, München 1965 (Cat., Préface Erika Billeter).
Mercury Gallery, London 1964 (Cat., Préface Earl of Harewood).
Galerie Bischofberger, Zürich 1965 (Cat., Préface Françoise Essellier).

BIBLIOGRAPHIE:

«Yougoslavija», Numéro Spécial (17) consacré à l'art des naïfs, Belgrade 1959.
Oto Bihalji-Merin: «Das naive Bild der Welt», Köln 1959.
Oto Bihalji-Merin: «Die naive Malerei», Köln 1959.
Oto Bihalji-Merin: «Les Peintres Naïfs», Paris (sans date).
Oto Bihalji-Merin: «I.G. jugoslawische Pastorale, Woldemar Klein, Baden-Baden 1960.
Oto Bihalji-Merin: «Umetnost Naivnich u Jugoslavjii», Belgrade 1963.
Dimitrije Basicevic: «Generalič», Ed. Drustro Historicara Umjetnosti, N.R.H. Zagreb 1962.
«Art Naïf», Editions Marocaines et Internationales, Rabat 1964.
Anatole Jakovsky: «Eros du Dimanche», Paris 1964.

ILLUSTRATIONS:
Album de 8 sérigraphies de Generalič, introduction par Ivan Mandelo, Ed. Znanje, Zagreb 1960. Tirage à 200 ex. numérotés et signés par l'artiste.

I. Gen. 1964

Generalič, Josip

Born 1936 in Hlebine (Yugoslavia).

Geboren 1936 in Hlebine (Jugoslawien).

Né en 1936 à Hlebine (Yougoslavie).

Called: Generalič the younger. The son of Ivan Generalič, he became a teacher and drawing-master, also a teacher of physical culture. He exhibits his painting with the Hlebine group of artists both in Yugoslavia and abroad. His first individual exhibition was in 1961 in Zagreb. The influence of his father is clearly visible but, despite this, his pictures are original and the standard of craftsmanship is high. His future seems bright.

Genannt: Generalič der Jüngere. Sohn von Ivan Generalič. Volksschullehrer, Zeichenlehrer, Turnlehrer. Stellt mit der Gruppe von Hlebine im In- und Ausland aus. Seine erste Einzelausstellung fand 1961 in Zagreb statt. Der Einfluß seines Vaters ist deutlich spürbar, aber seine Bilder sind trotzdem schön und sehr sorgfältig gemalt. Er hat eine verheißungsvolle Zukunft vor sich.

Dit: Generalič le jeune. Fils de Ivan Generalič. Instituteur et professeur de dessin. Professeur de culture physique. Expose avec le groupe de Hlebine dans son pays et à l'étranger. Sa première exposition individuelle est de 1961 à Zagreb. On sent très nettement l'influence de son père, mais malgré cela, ses peintures sont belles et remarquablement exécutées. Un bel avenir est devant lui.

EXPOSITIONS:
Galerie Bischofberger, Zürich 1964
(Cat., Préface Françoise Essellier).
Galerie Friedrich und Dahlem, München 1965
(Cat., Préface Erika Billeter).
Mercury Gallery London 1965
(Préface, Earl of Harewood).
Galerie Bischofberger, Zürich 1966.

Gerlach, Friedrich

Born 1903 in Herten (Germany).

Geboren 1903 in Herten (Deutschland).

Né en 1903 à Herten (Allemagne).

First a miner, then a skilled worker in a metallurgical concern in Herne, in the Ruhr district. Now he is retired. He is perhaps the second 'personality', at least as far as originality of his creative work is concerned, among all the many artists who have sprung up in the last ten years or so in the Ruhr basin. A visionary. His colors seem to shine with an inner radiance and remove the landscapes from their usual setting, reminding one of Millet's famous rainbow, which is also striking from this point of view.

Bergmann, dann Facharbeiter in einer Eisenhütte in Herne im Ruhrgebiet. Jetzt ist er pensioniert. Er ist zweifellos die zweitstärkste Persönlichkeit, zumindest was die Originalität betrifft, unter all den Begabungen, die in den letzten zehn Jahren im Ruhrgebiet aufgetaucht sind. Visionär. Seine gleichsam von einem inneren Neonlicht erleuchteten Farben verfremden die Landschaft und gemahnen an jenen Regenbogen von Millet, der von diesem Gesichtspunkt aus ebenfalls ein ungewöhnliches Bild schuf.

Mineur, puis ouvrier spécialisé dans un complexe sidérurgique de Herne, dans la Ruhr. Maintenant pensionné. Il est, sans doute, la seconde personnalité, en tant qu'originalité du moins, parmi tous ces talents qui ont surgi depuis une dizaine d'années à peine dans le bassin de la Ruhr. Visionnaire. Ses couleurs, comme illuminées par quelque néon intérieur, dépaysent le paysage et font penser à cet arc-en-ciel de Millet qui est, également, un tableau insolite de ce point de vue.

EXPOSITIONS:
«Schönheit», Recklinghausen 1958 (Important cat., Préface Stephan Hirzel).
«Laienkunst im Ruhrgebiet», Recklinghausen 1963 (Cat., Préface Bernhard Tacke).

BIBLIOGRAPHIE:
«Art Naïf». Editions Marocaines et Internationales, Rabat 1964.

Gerson, Alves de Souza

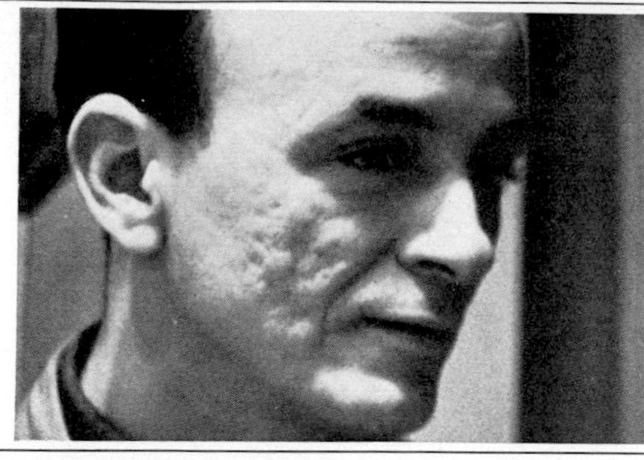

Born June 19, 1926 in Recife, Pernambuco (Brazil).

Geboren 19. Juni 1926 in Recife, Pernambuco (Brasilien).

Né le 19 juin 1926 à Recife, Pernambuco (Brésil).

Although born in the north of Brazil, Gerson has lived since 1951 in Rio de Janeiro. Since 1955 he has been employed by the post office; he likes his work and has no desire to give it up despite his recent successes. He is married and has one daughter, 15 years old. His canvases, which are mainly dark and where chestnut, blue and sepia are the dominating colors, are based on several preliminary sketches and are inspired by beliefs current in his native land, endowed with an element of magic: for example, the rather disconcerting toads' faces.

Dieser Nordbrasilianer ist seit 1955 Postbeamter und wohnt seit 1951 in Rio de Janeiro. Er ist verheiratet, Vater einer fünfzehnjährigen Tochter und liebt seinen Beruf, den er trotz seines Erfolges nicht aufgeben will. Seine meist dunklen Bilder, in denen Kastanienbraun, Blau und Sepia vorherrschen, ergeben sich aus mehreren Skizzen und sind immer von den Glaubensansichten seines Landes inspiriert, die von einer gewissen Magie geprägt sind. Daher diese Krötengesichter, die uns ein wenig befremden.

Cet originaire du Nord du Brésil est postier depuis 1955 et habite Rio de Janeiro depuis 1951. Marié, père d'une fille de 15 ans, il aime son métier qu'il ne veut pas abandonner malgré ses récents succès. Ses toiles, généralement sombres, où le marron, le bleu et le sépia dominent, sont les résultantes de plusieurs croquis et s'inspirent toujours des croyances de son pays natal, empreintes d'une certaine magie. D'où ces faces de crapauds qui nous déconcertent un tant soit peu.

EXPOSITIONS:
Xico Art Galeria, Recife 1964.
Galeria Goeldi, Rio de Janeiro 1965.
«Arte Latino-Americano», Yale University 1965.

La Giraudière, Mady

(née Couquet)
Born April 3, 1922 in Toulouse (France).

(geborene Couquet)
Geboren 3. April 1922 in Toulouse (Frankreich).

(née Couquet)
Née le 3 avril 1922 à Toulouse (France).

Has lived all her life in Lavelanet, in Ariège. She has never lost touch with this countryside and her background there, and so she can convey better than anyone else the quite individual charm of this district. In her paintings, bathed in the southern sun, can be found everything typical: customs, traditions, legends. She is susceptible to the changing seasons, and has painted the same landscape at four different times of the year. A fine touch, with enchanting stories to relate. Her 'Way of the Cross', with 13 pictures, enjoyed an enormous success at the 'Salon d'Art Sacré' in Paris in 1965.

Lebt seit jeher in Lavelanet im Departement Ariège. Da sie daher den Kontakt mit der Erde ihrer Vorfahren nie verloren hat, versteht sie es besser als jeder andere, den so besonderen Reiz dieser Gegend wiederzugeben. Gebräuche, Traditionen, Legenden, alles hat Platz in ihren Bildern, die von der Sonne des Südens bestrahlt sind. Sie besitzt ein feines Gefühl für die Jahreszeiten und hat die gleiche Landschaft unter ihren vier verschiedenen Aspekten gemalt. Eine geschickte Hand, die hübsche Geschichten zu erzählen versteht. Ihr Kreuzweg in 13 Bildern hat 1965 im Pariser Salon d'Art Sacré einen sehr großen Erfolg errungen.

Habite depuis toujours Lavelanet, en Ariège. N'ayant donc jamais rompu le contact avec la terre de ses ancêtres, elle sait mieux que quiconque rendre le charme si particulier de ce pays. Les mœurs, les traditions, les légendes, tout trouve place dans ses tableaux. Le soleil du Midi les baigne. Elle est sensible aux saisons, et elle a peint le même paysage sous les quatre aspects différents. Une belle main qui sait de jolies histoires à raconter. Son « Chemin de Croix », a eu un très grand succès au Salon d'Art Sacré de Paris en 1965.

EXPOSITIONS:
Galerie du Faubourg, Paris 1958 (Cat., Préface Anatole Jakovsky).
Galerie M. Œillet, Toulouse 1959 (Cat., Préface Anatole Jakovsky).
Galerie H. Bénézit, Paris 1961 (Cat., Préface Anatole Jakovsky).
Galerie H. Bénézit, Paris 1963 (Cat., Préface Anatole Jakovsky).
« Les Peintres Naïfs », Maison de la Pensée Française, Paris 1960.
« Laienmaler », Kunstgewerbemuseum, Basel 1961.
« I Pittori Naifs », Rome 1964.

BIBLIOGRAPHIE:
« Les Très Riches Heures de Lavelanet », Introduction par Anatole Jakovsky, Editions Temps Mêlés, Verviers 1960.
M. Colinon: « Les Peintres du Dimanche », Femmes d'Aujourd'hui N° 900, Bruxelles 2 Août 1962.
Anatole Jakovsky: « Eros du Dimanche », Paris 1964.

Di Girolamo, Giovanni

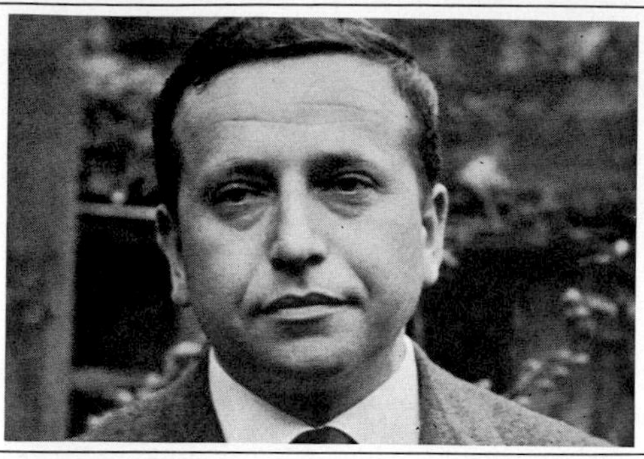

Born May 1, 1932 in Spoleto (Italy).

Geboren am 1. Mai 1932 in Spoleto (Italien).

Né le 1 mai 1932 à Spoleto (Italie).

A policeman. Took up painting only a few years ago, but is already making appreciable progress. His landscapes are mostly imaginary, but give the impression of being real; somehow they are the quintessence of his native Umbria. Has not yet held an individual exhibition.

Stadtpolizist. Malt erst seit ein paar Jahren, aber in seinen Bildern sind bereits sehr bedeutende Fortschritte festzustellen. Seine Landschaften sind in der Mehrzahl erfunden, vermitteln dabei aber den Eindruck der Wirklichkeit. Gewissermaßen eine Quintessenz seiner Heimat Umbrien. Noch keine Einzelausstellung.

Agent de police municipale. Peint seulement depuis quelques années, mais déjà, on décèle dans ses tableaux des progrès très sensibles. Ses paysages sont imaginaires pour la plupart, tout en donnant une impression du réel. Une quintessence, en quelque sorte, de son Ombrie natale. N'a pas encore eu d'exposition individuelle.

BIBLIOGRAPHIE:

Nevio Jori: «Giovanni Di Girolamo, chiaro Pittore umbro», Gazzetta dell'Emilia 10 décembre 1965.

Gourgue, Enguerrand

Born 1930 in Port-au-Prince (Haiti).

Geboren 1930 in Port-au-Prince (Haiti).

Né en 1930 à Port-au-Prince (Haïti).

Began to draw and paint at a very early age. Like Prefete Duffaut, he found his inspiration in the old traditional customs of his country, and especially in black and white magic. He seemed to find, as if by magic, the shapes and rhythms of Africa and of pre-Christian days, like those current in the Voodoo cult, for instance. One of the rare Haitian artists to look for the sad side of life.

Hat schon als ganz jung zu malen und zu zeichnen angefangen. Wie Prefete Duffaut läßt er sich von den alten folkloristischen Gebräuchen und vor allem von der schwarzen und weißen Magie inspirieren. Er findet gleichsam wie mit einem Zauberschlag zu den afrikanischen, vorchristlichen Formen und Rhythmen zurück, wie sie sich zum Beispiel im Voodookult äußern. Einer der seltenen haitischen Maler, der zur tragischen Seite der Dinge vorstößt.

A commencé à peindre et à dessiner tout jeune. Comme Prefete Duffaut, il s'inspire des anciennes coutumes folkloriques et surtout de la magie noire et blanche. Il retrouve comme par enchantement les formes et les rythmes africains, pré-chrétiens, ceux que lui fournit le culte de Vaudou, par exemple. L'un des rares peintres haïtiens à atteindre au côté tragique des choses.

EXPOSITIONS:
«La Peinture Naïve», Knokke-le-Zoute 1958.
«Das naive Bild der Welt», Baden-Baden 1961.
«Naive Painters of Latin America», Duke University, Durham, N. C. 1963.
«19 Peintres d'Haïti», Palais des Beaux-Arts, Bruxelles 1963.
«20th Century Latin American Naive Art», La Jolla, Cal. (USA) 1964.
«De Lusthof der Naieven», Rotterdam 1964.
«Le Monde des Naïfs», Paris 1964.

BIBLIOGRAPHIE:
Selden Rodman: «Renaissance in Haiti», Pelegrini & Cudahy New York (sans date).
Oto Bihalji-Merin: «Das naive Bild der Welt», Köln 1959.
Oto Bihalji-Merin: «Die naive Malerei», Köln 1959.
Oto Bihalji-Merin: «Les Peintres Naïfs», Paris (sans date).

Grande, Adriano

Born 1897 in Genoa (Italy).

Geboren 1897 in Genua (Italien).

Né en 1897 à Gênes (Italie).

A poet and writer. Began painting about 1955, like a Benedictine monk decorating his manuscripts. His style is medieval, entirely unassuming and honest. Some people call him another Donghi—who, of course is no 'naive' painter. How absurd! Grande is another of those artists whose freshness of approach has nothing to do with his cultural pursuits.

Dichter, Literat. Beginnt 1955 zu malen, und zwar auf die Art eines Benediktiners, der seine Schriften illustriert. Sein Stil ist mittelalterlich, voll Demut und von großer Gewissenhaftigkeit. Manche rücken ihn in die Nähe eines Donghi, der kein Naiver ist. Das ist absurd. Noch ein Fall, wo die Frische der Hand nichts zu tun hat mit dem Grad der Bildung.

Poète, homme de lettres. Commence à peindre vers 1955, et cela à la façon d'un bénedictin qui enluminerait ses écrits. Son style est moyenâgeux, plein d'humilité et de grande probité. Certains le rapprochent d'un Donghi qui, lui, n'est pas un naïf. C'est absurde! Encore un cas où la fraîcheur de la main n'a rien à voir avec le degré de culture.

EXPOSITIONS:
Galleria Russo, Rome 1958
(Cat., Préface Carlo Belli).
Galleria dell'Azienda di Soggiorno di Albisola Mare, 1963 (Cat., Préface Angelo Barile).
Galleria Anthea, Rome 1963
(Cat., avec des extraits de presse).
«I Pittori Naifs», Rome 1964.
«I Pittori Naifs», Centro Internazionale di Arte Figurative, Biella 1964.

BIBLIOGRAPHIE:
Catalogo Bolaffi d'Arte Moderna 1965/66, Turin 1966.

Grauben (do Monte Lima)

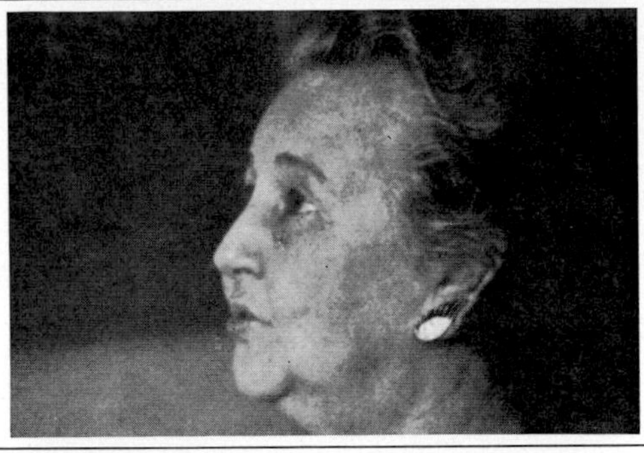

Born 1889 in Crato, Ceara (Brazil).

Geboren 1889 in Crato, Ceara (Brasilien).

Née en 1889 à Crato, Ceara (Brésil).

At a very early age she moved to Rio de Janeiro and worked as a civil servant. Her life was uneventful until, in 1960, after a long illness which confined her to bed for three years, she began to paint. And it was really a revelation, both for herself and for others. She depicts a world of enchantment, curiously recalling the work of Van der Steen which must have influenced her subconsciously, a world which seems to create itself and flow out of her pictures. A fairyland such as one finds with inspired artists spiritist or not.

Als junges Mädchen läßt sie sich in Rio de Janeiro nieder, wo sie als Staatsbeamtin arbeitet. Ein ereignisloses Leben also, bis sie 1960 nach einer Krankheit, die sie drei Jahre lang ans Bett gefesselt hat, zu malen anfängt. Eine wahre Offenbarung, sowohl für sie selber wie für die andern. Eine verzauberte Welt, die seltsam an die eines Van der Steen gemahnt und die wohl ohne ihr Wissen in ihrem Unterbewußtsein gelebt hatte, beginnt frei emporzuquellen und sich alle Tage weiter zu entfalten. Eine Zauberwelt, die sich nur innerhalb des Kreises des Inspirierten findet, seien sie nun Spiritisten oder nicht.

Très jeune, elle est venue s'installer à Rio de Janeiro où elle travaille comme fonctionnaire. Une vie sans histoire donc, jusqu'à ce que, en 1960, après une longue maladie, qui l'a clouée au lit pendant trois ans, elle commence à peindre. Et c'est une véritable révélation, aussi bien pour elle-même que pour les autres. Un monde enchanté, rappelant étrangement celui de Van der Steen, celui qui devait hanter son subconscient à son insu, commence à jaillir librement et à s'épanouir tous les jours. Une féerie que l'on rencontre rarement en dehors de ces inspirés, spirites ou non.

EXPOSITIONS:
Galeria Relevo, Rio de Janeiro 1962, 1963,et 1964.
«Peintres Naïfs Brésiliens», Galerie Jacques Massol, Paris 1965.

Greffe, Léon

Born February 13, 1881 in Charleroi (Belgium).
Died March 8, 1949 in Paris (France).

Geboren am 13. Februar 1881 in Charleroi (Belgien).
Gestorben am 8. März 1949 in Paris (Frankreich).

Né le 13 février 1881 à Charleroi (Belgique).
Mort le 8 mars 1949 à Paris (France).

First a miner in his native country. Later went to Paris where he worked in the market, and finally he became caretaker to a block of apartments on the Quai de la Mégisserie, opposite the Palais de Justice. Did his painting in an attic room. This is why he so often depicted the Palais de Justice and the quais seen from above. During the whole course of the war he was exploited by dishonest collectors, and so he did not become known until the time of his one and only Paris exhibition. Following this exhibition, an important Right-Bank dealer forced him to sign a contract obliging him to work more than he could. So he began to drink to gain inspiration, and died soon afterwards, literally killed by the money he had acquired and did not know what to do with.

Zuerst Grubenarbeiter in seiner Heimat. Begibt sich dann nach Paris, wo er in den Markthallen arbeitet und schließlich den Posten eines Hauswarts in einem Mietshaus am Quai de la Mégisserie, gegenüber dem Justizpalast, bekommt. Malt seine Bilder in einer Dachkammer. Darum hat er so oft den Justizpalast und die Quais von oben gemalt. Während des ganzen Krieges wird er von unredlichen Sammlern ausgebeutet und kennt erst einen bescheidenen Erfolg anläßlich seiner einzigen Ausstellung in Paris. Anschließend an diese Ausstellung läßt ihn ein bedeutender Händler des rechten Seineufers einen Vertrag unterschreiben, der ihn verpflichtet, mehr zu arbeiten, als in seinen Kräften steht. Da fängt er an zu trinken, um seine Inspiration zu beflügeln, und stirbt bald darauf, buchstäblich von dem Geld umgebracht, mit dem er nichts anzufangen wußte.

D'abord mineur dans son pays natal. Se rend ensuite à Paris où il travaille aux Halles et finit par avoir une loge de concierge dans un immeuble du quai de la Mégisserie, face au Palais de Justice. Fait ses peintures dans une chambre de bonne. C'est pourquoi il a peint si souvent, et ledit Palais de Justice, et les quais vus d'en haut. Exploité pendant toute la durée de la guerre par des collectionneurs de mauvais aloi, il ne connaît le succès, et encore, que lors de sa seule et unique exposition parisienne. A la suite de cette exposition, un marchand important de la rive droite lui fait signer un contrat, l'obligeant ainsi à travailler plus qu'il ne peut. Il s'adonne alors à la boisson, pour activer son inspiration, et meurt peu après, littéralement tué par cet argent dont il ne savait plus que faire.

EXPOSITIONS:
Galerie Le Dragon, Paris 1945 (Cat., Préface Anatole Jakovsky).
«Les Peintres Naïfs», Knokke-le-Zoute 1958.
«Les Peintres Naïfs», Maison de la Pensée Française, Paris 1960.
«Peintres Naïfs Belges», Théâtre National, Bruxelles 1965.
«Peintres Naïfs Belges», Musée Royal des Beaux-Arts, Verviers 1965.
«Peintres Naïfs Belges», Musée Royal des Beaux-Arts, Hasselt 1966.

BIBLIOGRAPHIE:

Anatole Jakovsky: «La Peinture Naïve», Paris 1949.
«Léon Greffe», Art d'Aujourd'hui, Nº 4, Paris, mars 1951.
«Léon Greffe», Art d'Aujourd'hui: Nº 7, Paris, juillet 1951.
Anatole Jakovsky: «Les Peintres Naïfs», Paris 1956.
Anatole Jakovsky: «Die naive Malerei in Frankreich», Zürich 1957.
Oto Bihalji-Merin: «Das naive Bild der Welt», Köln 1959.
Oto Bihalji-Merin: «Die naive Malerei», Köln 1959.
Oto Bihalji-Merin: «Les Peintres Naïfs», Editions Delpire, Paris (sans date).
«Léon Greffe», Savoir et Beauté, La Louvière, décembre 1965.

Grim

Grimaldi, Maurice
Born July 23, 1890 in Raon-l'Etape, Vosges (France).

Geboren 23. Juli 1890 in Raon-l'Etape, Vosges (Frankreich).

Né le 23 juillet 1890 à Raon-l'Etape, Vosges (France).

Has always been good at drawing and penmanship. At the age of 11 he won a handwriting competition organized by the Poulain chocolate firm. When he was 19 he took a job with the Nancy postal authorities. Then he was drafted, and finished the war as secretary to Mme Lyautey. Later he re-entered the Post Office and became a traveling postman on the Paris-Strasbourg line, with Vivin as inspector. Started to paint by chance, as a joke, using his son's paint-box. It was not until 1957 that he devoted his time entirely to painting.

Hat schon als Kind gut gezeichnet und schön geschrieben. Mit 11 Jahren gewinnt er einen von der Schokoladefabrik Poulain gestifteten Preis für Schönschreiben. Mit 19 Jahren ist er Postangestellter in Nancy, dann wird er zum Kriegsdienst aufgeboten und beendet den Krieg als Sekretär von Mme Lyautey. Er kehrt in den Postdienst zurück, arbeitet als Bahnpostbeamter auf der Linie Paris–Straßburg, wo Vivin sein Insepktor ist. Beginnt aus Zufall, zum Spaß zu malen, mit der Malschachtel seines Sohnes, und erst von 1957 an widmet er sich völlig der Malerei.

A toujours bien dessiné et bien écrit. A l'âge de 11 ans, il gagne un Prix d'Ecriture offert par le Chocolat Poulain. A 19 ans, il est employé des Postes à Nancy, puis, mobilisé, il termine la guerre comme secrétaire de Mme Lyautey. De retour dans l'administration, il est postier-ambulant sur le Paris–Strasbourg, avec Vivin comme Inspecteur. Commence à peindre par hasard, par plaisanterie, avec la boîte de couleurs de son fils, et ce n'est qu'en 1957 qu'il se consacrera entièrement à la peinture.

EXPOSITIONS:
Galerie-Café Marthe Druhle, Paris 1963.
« Les Primitifs d'Aujourd'hui »,
Galerie Charpentier, Paris 1964.
Galerie du Pont Neuf, Paris 1964.
Galerie Fetcherin, München 1965.
Galerie Mingaux, Fontainebleau 1966
(Cat., Préface Pierre Chaumeil).

BIBLIOGRAPHIE:
Alexander Watt: « Nouveaux Naïfs », Art in America, N° 2, 1963.
« Grim », Arts-PTT, No. 44, Paris 1966.

Grossin, Fernande

(called: Mémée Grossin)
Born October 28, 1886 in Bordeaux (France).

(genannt «Mémée Grossin»)
Geboren am 28. Oktober 1886 in Bordeaux (Frankreich).

(dite: «Mémée Grossin»)
Née le 28 octobre 1886 à Bordeaux (France).

The wife of a senior member of the colonial service, she lived for a long time in Martinique. After returning to Europe, to Paris as it happened, she was haunted by the remembrance of the light and colors of the tropics. So much so that, one day, she started to paint and produced her first picture, 'Flamboyant'. It was quite late in life to begin painting. She is one of the rare 'naive' artists who paint the subject directly. The others generally are satisfied with sketches. She is totally indifferent to the comments of lookers-on, since she paints the best she can and puts her whole heart into it.

Frau eines hohen Kolonialbeamten. Lebt lange Zeit auf der Insel Martinique. Nach ihrer Rückkehr nach Europa und namentlich nach Paris lassen das Licht und die Farben der Tropen sie nicht los. So daß sie eines schönen Tages ihr erstes Bild, die flammend roten Blüten einer Caesalpinia pulcherrima, malt. Übrigens erst in vorgerücktem Alter. Sie ist eine der seltenen naiven Maler, die direkt nach der Natur malen. Die anderen begnügen sich im allgemeinen mit Skizzen, die sie nachher ausarbeiten. Was die Gaffer sagen, ist ihr völlig egal, denn sie malt nach besten Kräften und mit viel Gemüt.

Femme d'un haut fonctionnaire colonial. Séjourne longtemps à la Martinique. De retour en Europe, à Paris en l'occurrence, elle est hantée par la lumière et les couleurs tropicales. Tant et si bien qu'un beau jour, elle finit par peindre un «Flamboyant», son premier tableau. Sur le tard, du reste. Elle est une des rares naïves à peindre directement sur le motif. Les autres se contentant généralement des croquis. Ce que disent les badauds l'indiffère totalement, puisqu'elle peint de son mieux et avec beaucoup de cœur.

EXPOSITIONS:
Galerie Epona, Paris 1964
(Cat., Préface Marcel Say).

BIBLIOGRAPHIE:
«Mémée Grossin», Revue Moderne, Paris, 1er juin 1965.

Guignard, Georges

Born December 1, 1861 in Paris (France).
Died May 18, 1935 in Tours (France).

Geboren am 1. Dezember 1861 in Paris (Frankreich).
Gestorben am 18. Mai 1935 in Tours (Frankreich).

Né le 1er décembre 1861 à Paris (France).
Mort le 18 mai 1935 à Tours (France).

It used to happen occasionally, before the present rather over-enthusiastic infatuation, that one could find the complete works of a 'naive' artist in a Parisian Flea Market (having drifted there no one knew how), and that one morning was sufficient for these works to be scattered to the four winds. And, as a general rule, nothing was ever heard of these pictures any more; they were never seen again. What is known now of those 99 pictures which comprised the former Wolters collection and which were exhibited in 1933 under the title 'A Century of Naive Painting' in the art gallery of the periodical 'Beaux Arts'? Nothing at all. No more than we know about those which belonged to the Courteline collection. Perhaps we know more about those remarkable personalities Guiraud de Saint-Chinan and Denimal? Unfortunately not. And with Guignard the situation is just the same, except that he had a little more luck: the person who discovered his work (which comprises several dozen paintings) found his address written on one picture, and by means of this he was able to give the artist, after much research, a legal identity. As if this varied, droll and sometime flamboyantly patriotic group of paintings needed that sort of thing!

Vor der gegenwärtigen, vielleicht etwas zu gewinnsüchtigen Begeisterung für die naive Malerei kam es vor, daß man hin und wieder auf dem Pariser Flohmarkt das ganze Werk eines naiven Malers fand, das auf unbekannte Weise hier gelandet war und das innerhalb eines Vormittags in alle vier Winde zerstreut wurde. Und gewöhnlich hörte man nie mehr etwas von diesen Bildern und sah sie auch nie wieder. Was wissen wir von den 99 Nummern, welche die ehemalige Sammlung Wolters ausmachten und die 1933 unter dem Titel «Hundert Jahre naive Malerei» in der Galerie der Zeitung «Beaux-Arts» ausgestellt wurden? Nichts. Und genau so wenig kennen wir das Schicksal der Bilder, die sich in Courtelines Sammlung befanden. Wissen wir dafür besser Bescheid über so markante Persönlichkeiten wie Guiraud de Saint-Chinan oder Denimal? Leider nicht. Und Guignard befindet sich genau im gleichen Fall, obwohl er etwas mehr Glück hatte. Der Entdecker seines Werks, das sich aus ein paar Dutzend Bildern zusammensetzt, fand auf einem Bild die Adresse des Malers, was ihm erlaubt hat, diesen nach mancherlei Nachforschungen mit einer gesetzlichen Identität zu versehen. Als ob dieses abwechslungsreiche, drollige und manchmal hurrapatriotische Werk das nötig hätte...

Il arrivait autrefois, de temps en temps, avant l'engouement actuel, peut-être un peu trop intéressé, de trouver aux «Puces» de Paris toute une œuvre d'un peintre naïf, échouée là, on ne sait pas comment, et qu'une matinée suffisait à éparpiller aux quatre vents. Et, généralement, on n'entendait plus jamais parler de ces tableaux. On ne les revoyait jamais. Que savons-nous des 99 numéros qui constituaient l'ancienne collection Wolters, exposée sous le titre: «Un Siècle de la Peinture Naïve», en 1933, à la Galerie du journal «Beaux-Arts»? Rien. Pas plus que de ceux qui constituaient la collection Courteline. Sans doute, sommes-nous renseignés davantage sur des personnalités aussi marquantes que Guiraud de Saint-Chinan ou Denimal? Malheureusement non. Le cas de cet artiste est exactement le même, bien qu'il ait eu un peu plus de chance. Le découvreur de son œuvre, se composant de plusieurs dizaines de tableaux, a trouvé sur l'un d'eux son adresse ce qui lui a permis, après bien des recherches, de le doter d'une identité légale. Comme si cette œuvre variée, cocasse et parfois cocardière avait besoin de cela...

EXPOSITIONS:
Galerie le Cadran Solaire, Paris 1966.

Guilleminot, René

Born January 15, 1900 in Bagneux, Seine (France).

Geboren am 15. Januar 1900 in Bagneux, Seine (Frankreich).

Né le 15 janvier 1900 à Bagneux, Seine (France).

A games-teacher in gymnasiums. For 30 years he taught weight lifting, table tennis, wrestling, boxing, etc., but this did not prevent him from cultivating his own 'secret blue flower' and to devote himself to being a 'Sunday painter' from the age of 26. Although he was a fine wrestler, he specialized in 'catch' and became champion of France and even of Europe. He is a wonderful example that 'naive' showing has its own 'elect'—there are no distinctions of sex, social position or fortune. An ardent, unquenchable thirst for beauty is all that is necessary. He has never exhibited his work except in local collective exhibitions.

Hilfslehrer für Sportunterricht. Lehrt während 30 Jahren Hanteln, Pingpongspielen, Ringen und Boxen, was ihn nicht hindert, eine kleine blaue Blume zu hegen und sich seit dem Alter von 26 Jahren der Sonntagsmalerei hinzugeben. Obwohl er sehr begabt ist für den Ringkampf, wirft er sich auf den «Catch» und wird französischer und sogar Europameister. Ein großartiger Beweis, nicht wahr, daß die naive Malerei ihre Erwählten aussucht, wo sie will, wo sie kann, ohne Unterschied des Geschlechts, des sozialen Rangs oder der finanziellen Lage. Ein brennender, unlöschbarer Durst nach dem Schönen genügt. Guilleminot hat erst in regionalen Gruppenausstellungen ausgestellt.

Prevôt dans les gymnases. Enseigne donc pendant 30 ans haltères, ping-pong, lutte et boxe ce qui ne l'empêche pas de cultiver une jolie fleur bleue et de s'adonner, dès l'âge de 26 ans, à la peinture du dimanche.
Très doué pour la lutte, il se lance néanmoins dans le «catch» et devient vite champion de France et même d'Europe. Une magnifique preuve, n'est-ce pas, que la peinture naïve choisit ses élus là où elle veut, là où elle peut, sans aucune distinction de sexe, de condition sociale ni de degré de fortune. Une ardente, une inextinguible soif du beau suffit. N'a encore exposé que dans les expositions collectives régionales.

Guillen, Asilia

Born 1887 in Granada (Nicaragua).
Died March 1964 in Granada (Nicaragua).

Geboren 1887 in Granada (Nicaragua).
Gestorben März 1964 in Granada (Nicaragua).

Née en 1887 à Granada (Nicaragua).
Morte en mars 1964 à Granada (Nicaragua).

Although she took music lessons as a child—which would imply a fairly high social background—she was a simple embroidress all her life. She was encouraged to take up painting by the poet Enrico Fernandez Morales. Her work reminds one a little of Velasquez, but it is more feminine; it shows the influence of embroidery (of course, this is not meant in a derogatory sense at all).

Obwohl sie in ihrer Jugend Musikstunden nahm, was auf einen anderen sozialen Stand deutet, ist sie ihr ganzes Leben lang einfache Stickerin geblieben. Der Dichter Enrico Fernandez Morales hat sie zum Malen ermuntert. Ihre Kunst gemahnt ein bißchen an José Velasquez, aber ins Weibliche übersetzt, sozusagen mit Spuren von Stickerei, was natürlich nicht in einem abschätzigen Sinn verstanden werden darf.

Bien qu'elle ait pris des leçons de musique dans sa jeunesse, ce qui dénote une autre condition sociale, elle est restée simple brodeuse toute sa vie. C'est le poète Enrico Fernandez Morales qui l'a encouragée à peindre. Son art ressemble un tant soit peu à celui de Velasquez, mais en plus féminin, avec des traces de la broderie, en quelque sorte, ce qui ne doit pas être pris dans le sens péjoratif, comme de bien entendu.

EXPOSITIONS:
«La Peinture Naïve», Knokke-le-Zoute 1958.
Union Pan-Américaine, Washington 1962 et 1963.
«Naive Painters of Latin America», Duke University, Durham N.C., 1963.
«20th Century Latin American Naive Art», La Jolla (USA) 1964.
«De Lusthof der Naieven», Rotterdam 1964.
«Le Monde des Naïfs», Paris 1964.

BIBLIOGRAPHIE:
Oto Bihalji-Merin: «Das naive Bild der Welt», Köln 1959.
Oto Bihalji-Merin: «Die naive Malerei», Köln 1959.
Oto Bihalji-Merin: «Les Peintres Naïfs», Paris (sans date).
«Art Naïf», Editions Marocaines et Internationales, Rabat 1964.

Haddelsey, Vincent

Born 1929 in Lincolnshire (England).

Geboren 1929 in Lincolnshire (England).

Né en 1929 dans le Lincolnshire (Angleterre).

A keen horseman and trainer of horses (for polo and rodeos, for horse shows and even for the Charriadas in Mexico). When he had finished studying he immigrated to Canada and lived in the wilds of British Columbia, where he had the opportunity to get to know the people and customs of the Hasla tribe of Indians. Later he went to the United States and to Mexico. It was during these long years of complete solitude that he was able to meditate on his painting and to develop, gradually and unhindered, what he had dreamed about since childhood. But it was only on his return to Europe that he was finally able to give all his time to painting.

Zuerst gehört sein ganzes Interesse den Pferden. Pferdedressur – Polo und Rodeo – Pferderennen und selbst Charriadas in Mexiko. Nach abgeschlossener Schulbildung fährt er nämlich nach Kanada, wo er im Busch von Britisch Kolumbien lebt und Gelegenheit hat, die Sitten der Hasla-Indianer aus der Nähe zu studieren. Dann begibt er sich in die Vereinigten Staaten und nach Mexiko. In diesen langen, in völliger Einsamkeit verbrachten Jahren kann er über seine Kunst nachdenken und langsam, in völliger Freiheit, reifen lassen, wovon er schon als Kind träumte. Aber erst nach seiner Rückkehr nach Europa kann er sich endlich ausschließlich der Malerei widmen.

Cavalier, homme de cheval. Entraînement de chevaux – Polo et Rodeo – concours hippiques et même les Charriadas au Mexique. Ses études terminées, il part, en effet, pour le Canada où il a vécu dans la brousse de la Colombie Britannique et où il a pu approcher et étudier les mœurs de la tribu des Indiens Hasla; repart pour les Etats-Unis et le Mexique, et c'est pendant ces longues années vécues absolument en solitaire, qu'il a pu songer à son art et mûrir, lentement, librement, ce à quoi il rêvait déjà dès son enfance. Mais ce n'est que dès son retour en Europe qu'il put se consacrer, enfin, uniquement à sa peinture.

EXPOSITIONS:
«Peintres Naïfs», Gallery Arthur Tooth and Sons, Londres 1964.
Galerie Romi, Paris 1964.
«Les Primitifs d'Aujourd'hui», Galerie Charpentier, Paris 1964.
Galaxy Gallery, Phoenix, Arizona, 1965.
Gumps Gallery, San Francisco 1965.
Gilles de Turenne Gallery, Mexico City 1965.
«Peintres Naïfs», Kunstsalon Wolfensberg, Zürich 1965.
Galerie Jacques Verrières, Cannes 1966.

Hadzimihali, Ersi

Born 1921 in Athens (Greece).

Geboren 1921 in Athen (Griechenland).

Née en 1921 à Athènes (Grèce).

After enjoying a college education she devoted herself first of all to writing. In 1962 she even obtained second prize in the Pen Club's international competition (among the jury were André Maurois, W. Barnett and S. Jameson); her work had been selected from 4500 entrants from 52 different countries. Suddenly, however, she took up painting. Entirely self-taught. Among her best works are her interior scenes, especially of churches.

Nach ihren Universitätsstudien widmet sie sich zuerst der Literatur und erhält 1962 sogar den zweiten internationalen Preis des Pen Clubs, in dessen Jury u. a. André Maurois, W. Barnett und St. Jameson saßen. Ihr Werk wurde aus den Einsendungen von 4500 Kandidaten aus 52 verschiedenen Ländern ausgelesen. Aber nun fängt sie an zu malen. Reine Autodidaktin. Zu ihren besten Bildern gehören die Interieurs, vor allem Kirchen.

Après ses études supérieures, elle se consacre d'abord à la littérature. En 1962, elle obtient même le second prix international du Pen Club, dont le jury se composait, entre autres, de M.M. André Maurois, W. Barnett et St. Jameson. Son œuvre a été remarquée parmi 4500 candidats de 52 pays différents. Mais voilà qu'elle se met à peindre. Autodidacte pure. Parmi ses meilleures choses, il faut compter les intérieurs, surtout des églises.

EXPOSITIONS:
Galerie Takis et Nikos, Athènes 1961.

Hallsten, Pehr

Born 1897 in the northern part of Sweden.

Geboren 1897 in Nordschweden.

Né en 1897 dans le Nord de la Suède.

In 1920 he immigrated to the United States and became a teacher of French and Spanish. Lived in Seattle since 1938. A purely self-taught artist, he took up painting in 1953, and it was Mark Tobey who discovered him and helped him to make his name. He creates gouaches, generally painting only small pictures recalling his memories of the far north. At the moment he lives in Basle. Has exhibited his work in New York (in 1960) and in Paris (in 1961).

Wandert 1920 in die Vereinigten Staaten aus, wo er Französisch und Spanisch unterrichtet. Wohnt von 1938 an in Seattle. Beginnt 1953 zu malen. Autodidakt. Mark Tobey entdeckt ihn und verhilft ihm zum Durchbruch. In seinen meistens kleinformatigen Gouaches malt er seine Erinnerungen an den Hohen Norden. Jetzt lebt er in Basel. Er hat 1960 in New York und 1961 in Paris ausgestellt.

Emigre en 1920 aux Etats-Unis, où il enseignait le français et l'espagnol. Habitait Seattle depuis 1938. Commence à peindre en 1953. Autodidacte C'est Mark Tobey qui le découvre et qui l'aide à percer. Dans ses gouaches, généralement de petits formats, il évoque ses souvenirs du grand Nord. Il habite maintenant à Bâle. Il a exposé en 1960 à New York et en 1961 à Paris.

EXPOSITIONS:
«Laienmaler», Gewerbemuseum, Basel 1961.

Hansen, Christian Peter

Born 1803 in Keitum auf Sylt (Germany).
Died 1879 in Keitum auf Sylt (Germany).

Geboren 1803 in Keitum auf Sylt (Deutschland).
Gestorben 1879 in Keitum auf Sylt (Deutschland).

Né en 1803 à Keitum auf Sylt (Allemagne).
Mort en 1879 à Keitum auf Sylt (Allemagne).

A friend of Oluf Braren. Was a schoolmaster by profession, and did a good deal for his native North Sea island by writing about it and doing tireless research about its vestigial past.
His art has much in common with that of some German romantic painters, especially Caspar David Friedrich, but is less skillful. He painted portraits and scenes from village life. His craft is careful, poignant, with an occasional touch of awkwardness.

Freund von Oluf Braren. Er war Volksschullehrer von Beruf und hat viel für seine kleine Nordsee-Heimat getan, indem er darüber schrieb und unermüdlich den Spuren ihrer Vergangenheit nachforschte. Seine Kunst ist verwandt mit jener der deutschen Romantik, insbesondere mit Caspar David Friedrich, nur daß ihm das Können fehlt. Er malt Porträts und Szenen aus dem Dorfleben. Gepflegtes, rührendes Malen, mit einem Schuß Unbeholfenheit hier und dort.

Ami d'Oluf Braren. Instituteur de son état, il a fait beaucoup pour sa petite patrie de la mer du Nord, ceci en écrivant sur elle et en recherchant inlassablement les vestiges de son passé. Son art s'apparente à celui des romantiques allemands, à Caspar David Friedrich notamment, métier en moins. Ce sont des portraits et des scènes de la vie villageoise. Un métier soigné, touchant, avec un brin de maladresse ça et là.

BIBLIOGRAPHIE:
Bernard Jasmand und Otto Kallir: «Sonntagsmaler», Otto Aug. Ehlers, Berlin/Darmstadt 1956.
Oto Bihalji-Merin: «Das naive Bild der Welt», Köln 1959.
Oto Bihalji-Merin: «Die naive Malerei», Köln 1959.
Oto Bihalji-Merin: «Les Peintres Naïfs», Paris (sans date).

Hefti, Anja

Born in 1911 in Padua (Italy).

Geboren 1911 in Padua (Italien).

Née en 1911 à Padoue (Italie).

Her childhood and youth were spent in Venice. Is now married to a Swiss and lives in Männedorf. A self-taught artist. She began to paint in 1956 on the encouragement of friends. Her first exhibition was held in Zürich in 1960. Her art is typically Italian—it is much closer to Rosina Viva, for instance, or even to Pasotti, than to her Swiss fellow-painters.

Kindheit und Jugend in Venedig. Mit einem Schweizer verheiratet. Wohnt seither in Männedorf. Autodidaktin. Fängt 1956, von ihren Freunden ermuntert, an zu malen. 1960 erste Ausstellung in Zürich. Ihre Kunst ist typisch italienisch und steht einer Rosina Viva zum Beispiel oder einem Pasotti viel näher als ihren schweizerischen Kollegen.

Jeunesse et adolescence à Venise. Mariée avec un Suisse. Habite depuis à Männedorf. Autodidacte. Commence à peindre en 1956, encouragée par ses amis. Première exposition en 1960 à Zurich. Son art est typiquement italien, bien plus proche d'une Rosina Viva, par exemple, ou bien d'un Pasotti que de ses collègues suisses.

EXPOSITIONS:
«Laienmaler», Gewerbemuseum, Basel 1961.
«Die Welt der naiven Malerei», Salzburg 1964.

Hel Enri

(real name Hélène Berlewi)
Born March 20, 1873 in Warsaw (at that time Russia, now Poland).

(mit ihrem richtigen Namen Hélène Berlewi)
Geboren am 20. März 1873 in Warschau (damals Rußland, heute Polen).

(de son vrai nom: Hélène Berlewi).
Née le 20 mars 1873 à Varsovie (en son temps Russie, actuellement Pologne).

Has lived since 1928 in Paris. Began to paint in 1952, at the age of 79. She is therefore (since the death of Grandma Moses) the world's 'naive' artist. Her work is very individual and does not resemble at all that of any other artist. She always paints imaginary flora, found in no part of the world, but all her pictures are sensitive and delicate, poetical and rather contemplative; they show a world of feeling and memory existing only in her imagination. She is the mother of the constructivist artist Berlewi; in fact, she began to paint, quite by chance, using the scraps of paint left on his palette.

Lebt seit 1928 in Paris. Beginnt 1952, im Alter von 79 Jahren, zu malen. Sie ist demnach seit dem Tod von Grandma Moses der älteste lebende naive Maler auf der ganzen Welt. Ihre Kunst ist etwas ganz Besonderes und läßt sich mit keiner anderen vergleichen. Sie malt immer eine nirgends existierende imaginäre Blumenwelt, empfindsam und raffiniert, poetisch und ein wenig verträumt. Sie schafft eine ganz neue Welt von Empfindungen und Erinnerungen. Sie ist die Mutter des konstruktivistischen Malers Berlewi. Übrigens hat sie mit den Resten seiner Palette ganz zufällig angefangen zu malen.

Vit depuis 1928 à Paris. Elle commence à peindre en 1952 à l'âge de 79 ans. Elle est donc, de ce fait, après la mort de Grandma Moses, la doyenne des peintres naïfs du monde entier. Son art est absolument particulier, ne ressemblant ni de près ni de loin à aucun autre. Il s'agit toujours d'une flore imaginaire, de nulle part, sensible et raffinée, poétique et un tantinet rêveuse. C'est un monde des sensations et des souvenirs entièrement recréé par elle. Elle est la mère du peintre constructiviste Berlewi. C'est d'ailleurs avec les résidus de sa palette qu'elle a commencé à peindre tout à fait par hasard.

EXPOSITIONS:
Galerie M. Bénézit, Paris 1954 (Cat., Préface Anatole Jakovsky).
Galeria Centralne Biuro-Wystaw, Varsovie 1958 (Cat., Préface Anatole Jakovsky).
Galeria Zwiazek Polskich Artystow Plastykow, Sapocie 1958 (Cat., Préface Anatole Jakovsky).
Galerie M. Bénézit, Paris 1959 (Cat., Préface G. Hugnet).
Galerie Suzanne Bollag, Zürich 1960.
Galerie d'Art Moderne, Basel 1960.
«Laienmaler», Gewerbemuseum, Basel 1961.
Galerie «Die Insel», Hamburg 1962 (Cat., Préface Hanns Theodor Flemming).
Haus am Lützowplatz, Berlin 1963 (Cat., Préface Hanns Theodor Flemming).
«Die Welt der naiven Malerei», Salzburg 1964.
«Les Primitifs d'Aujourd'hui», Galerie Charpentier, Paris 1964.

BIBLIOGRAPHIE:
Anatole Jakovsky: «Hel Enri», Monographie (sous presse).
F. Pluchard: «Pourquoi Hel Enri a-t-elle commencé à peindre à l'âge de 79 ans?» Combat, Paris, 31 janvier 1966.

Hermans, Josephine

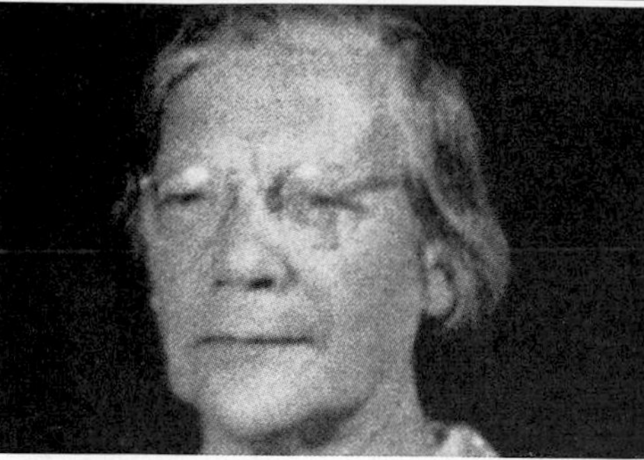

Born 1895 in Arnhem (Netherlands).

Geboren 1895 in Arnhem (Holland).

Née en 1895 à Arnhem (Hollande).

Of Flemish parents. For a long time she worked as an embroidress, then became a maid in a welfare center in Amsterdam. Suddenly, one day, she started to paint without knowing why or how. She was noticed almost straight away by W. Sandberg, the director of the Stedelijk Museum, who bought several of her paintings for his museum. Her work recalls to some extent that of E. Schipper-Schramm, who was of German origin. Now she lives with her daughter in Zürich. Here is how she describes her work: 'After the soul-destroying cleaning, life was still able to exist in the shop. I like painting skies out of my imagination and especially sunsets, which I have always loved. I cannot draw or copy anything—I only put down what I have in my head. It is not art with a capital A, nor is it nonsense'.

Die Eltern sind Flamen. Sie übte lange den Beruf einer Stickerin aus. Dann arbeitete sie als Dienstmädchen in einer Armenklinik in Amsterdam. Eines schönen Tages fing sie an zu malen, ohne zu wissen, wie und warum. W. Sandberg, Konservator des Stedelijk Museum, wird sehr schnell auf sie aufmerksam und erwirbt ein paar Bilder für sein Museum. Ihre Kunst erinnert ein wenig an die von E. Schipper-Schramm, die eine gebürtige Deutsche ist. Gegenwärtig lebt sie bei ihrer Tochter in Zürich. Sie sagt selber von ihrer Malerei: «Nach dem Putzen, das den Geist tötete, hat das Leben in der Bude trotzdem erwachen können. Ich male gern Phantasiehimmel und hauptsächlich Sonnenuntergänge, die ich immer bewundert habe. Ich bin unfähig, etwas zu zeichnen oder zu kopieren, ich gebe nur wieder, was ich im Kopf habe. Es ist keine großgeschriebene Kunst, es ist aber auch kein Kohl.»

Parents flamands. Exerça longtemps le métier de brodeuse. Elle entra ensuite comme bonne à tout faire dans un dispensaire à Amsterdam. Puis, un beau jour, se mit à peindre sans savoir ni pourquoi, ni comment. Elle a été remarquée presque aussitôt par W. Sandberg, Directeur du Stedelijk Museum qui lui achète quelques tableaux pour son musée. Son art rappelle un tant soit peu celui de E. Schipper-Schramm, d'origine allemande celle-là. Elle vit actuellement chez sa fille à Zurich. Voici ce qu'elle dit elle-même de son art: «Après les nettoyages, qui tuaient l'esprit, la vie a quand-même pu naître dans la boutique. Je peins volontiers des ciels de fantaisie et surtout les couchers de soleil que j'ai toujours admirés. Je suis incapable de dessiner ou de copier quelque chose, je ne fais que rendre ce que j'ai dans la tête. Ce n'est pas de l'art avec un grand A, ce n'est pas non plus du bidon.»

EXPOSITIONS:
«Laienmaler», Gewerbemuseum, Basel 1961.
«De Lusthof der Naieven», Rotterdam 1964.
«Le Monde des Naïfs», Paris 1964.

BIBLIOGRAPHIE:
Bernard Jasmand und Otto Kallir: «Sonntagsmaler», Otto Aug. Ehlers, Berlin/Darmstadt 1956.

Herrera Guevara, Luis

Born 1891 in Santiago (Chile).
Died 1945 in Santiago (Chile).

Geboren 1891 in Santiago de Chile.
Gestorben 1945 in Santiago de Chile.

Né en 1891 à Santiago de Chili.
Mort en 1945 à Santiago de Chili.

Formerly a barrister. After having attended the Amunatégui high school, where he was noticed for the excellence of his drawing of geography maps, he studied for his degree and obtained it in 1920. Settled in San Bernardo as a barrister,a profession he practised until 1929. In that year he visited Rome, Paris, Madrid and Lisbon, and this is most likely what decided him to take up painting as a way of life. His first pictures were exhibited in 1930 in the Free Gallery of Valparaiso. After then he devoted his entire time to art—and he enjoyed considerable success.

Ehemaliger Advokat. Nach dem Besuch des Gymnasiums Amunatégui, wo er dank der Vollkommenheit seiner Geographiekarten auffällt, besteht er sein Abitur, dann seine Lizentiatur (1920). Läßt sich als Advokat in San Bernardo nieder und übt seinen Beruf bis 1929 aus. In diesem Jahr besucht er Rom, Paris, Madrid und Lissabon, was wahrscheinlich den Anstoß gibt zu seiner Malerberufung. Stellt 1930 im Salon Libre von Valparaiso zum ersten Mal aus. Von da an widmet er sich ausschließlich der Malerei. Übrigens mit viel Erfolg.

Ancien avocat. Après ses études au lycée Amunatégui, où il se fait remarquer par la perfection de ses cartes géographiques, passe son baccalauréat, puis sa licence en 1920. S'installe à San Bernardo comme avocat, profession qu'il exerce jusqu'en 1929. Cette année-là, il visite Rome, Paris, Madrid et Lisbonne, ce qui, vraisemblablement, a décidé de sa vocation de peintre. Expose pour la première fois, en 1930, au Salon Libre de Valparaiso. Depuis, il ne fait plus que peindre. Avec beaucoup de succès, d'ailleurs.

EXPOSITIONS:
Sala del Banco de Chile, 1941 (Cat., Préface Camilo Mori, E. Campos, C. Hermostilla, Gregorio de la Fuente, Luis O. Caceres et R. d'Harnoncourt).
Sala del Ministerio de Educación, Santiago de Chili 1944
Galeria Dedalo, Santiago de Chili 1945.
Durlacher Bros. Gallery, New York 1943 (Cat., Préface Lincoln Kirstein).
Sala Nascimento, Santiago 1952.
Sala Ministerio de Educación, Santiago 1954.
Retrospective à la Librairie de l'Europe, 1957 (Cat., Préface Pablo Neruda, Gabriela Mistral, Luis Vargas Rosas, Antonio R. Romera, etc.).

BIBLIOGRAPHIE:
Antonio R. Romera: « Herrera Guevara », Ed. de Universidad de Chili, 1958.

Hertmann, Karl

Born 1918 in Recklinghausen (Germany).

Geboren 1918 in Recklinghausen (Deutschland).

Né en 1918 à Recklinghausen (Allemagne).

Was a miner, but his technical ability helped him to gain employment with the firm Ewald-Kohle AG. He can be considered a typical example of the 'Sunday painter', trying to enrich his life by creating beauty. He paints faithfully what he sees, trying to make it more solid and tangible and yet uplifting; this can be observed in his portraits as well as in his 'Morning Toilet', doubtlessly a picture of his wife.

Grubenarbeiter. Dank seiner technischen Fähigkeiten kann er nachher zu Ewald-Kohle AG übertreten. Sozusagen typisches Beispiel dieser Sonntagsmaler, die ihr Leben verschönen wollen. Er bleibt der Wirklichkeit treu, aber er will, daß sie stärker, greifbarer werde und doch erhebend bleibe. Das spürt man in seinen Porträts ebenso wie in der «Morgentoilette», die zweifellos die Frau des Künstlers darstellt.

Mineur. Passe ensuite, grâce à ses aptitudes techniques, à Ewald-Kohle AG. Exemple pour ainsi dire typique de ces peintres du dimanche qui veulent embellir leur vie. Fidèle au réel, il le veut plus solide, plus palpable, tout en restant exaltant. Cela se sent dans ses portraits aussi bien que dans la «Toilette du matin» qui représente la femme de l'artiste, sans aucun doute.

EXPOSITIONS:
«Laienkunst», Recklinghausen 1963
(Cat., Préface Bernhard Tacke).

BIBLIOGRAPHIE:
«Art Naïf», Editions Marocaines et Internationales, Rabat 1964.

Hicks, Edward

Born 1780 in Attelborough
(now called Langhorne), Bucks County,
Penn. (USA).
Died 1849 in Newton, Penn. (USA).

Geboren 1780 in Attelborough
(heute Langhorne), Bucks County, Penn. (USA).
Gestorben 1849 in Newton, Penn. (USA).

Né en 1780 à Attelborough (aujourd'hui
Langhorne), Bucks County, Penn. (USA).
Mort en 1849 à Newton, Penn. (USA).

Undisputed ancestor of 'naive' American art. This means that, among the hundreds and hundreds of paintings which are either anonymous or whose signature tells us nothing although the paintings themselves are wonderful and varied, he is the only artist to have both a body of work and a biography. From the age of 13 until he was 20 he was apprenticed to a wheelwright, but all at once he decided to earn his living as a painter of utilitarian objects such as carts, signs, signposts, and so on. A serious illness brought his mind to religious questions, and as a result of that he went off to Milford in 1801 and joined the Quakers. After that he preached. But it did not prevent him from continuing to paint his 'specialities' to earn enough to live on; and later he created real pictures mainly inspired by the 'Kingdom of Peace'.
At the end of his life he wrote his memoirs, telling of his religious experiences and activities.

Unbestrittener Vorfahre der naiven amerikanischen Malerei. Das heißt, daß er unter den Hunderten und Aberhunderten von Malern, deren Bilder entweder anonym bleiben oder deren Signatur nichts besagt, die indessen alle wunderbar und abwechslungsreich sind, ungefähr der einzige ist, der ein Werk und eine Biographie vorweisen kann. Von seinem 13. bis zu seinem 20. Jahr ist er Lehrling bei einem Wagner. Plötzlich beschließt er, sein Leben damit zu verdienen, daß er Gebrauchsgegenstände bemalt, Wagen, Schilder, Wegweiser und was weiß ich. Eine schwere Krankheit bewirkt, daß er sich der Religion zuwendet. 1801 begibt er sich nach Milford, wo er sich den Quäkern anschließt. Seither predigt er. Das hindert ihn nicht, seine «Spezialitäten» zu malen, um sein materielles Leben zu verdienen. Später malt er die eigentlichen Bilder, die vom «Reich des Friedens» inspiriert sind. Schließlich schreibt er seine Memoiren über seine religiöse Tätigkeit.

Ancêtre incontesté de la peinture naïve américaine. C'est-à-dire que parmi les centaines et les centaines d'œuvres anonymes, ou dont la signature ne dit rien qui vaille, toutes merveilleuses et variées, du reste, il est à peu près le seul à avoir, et une œuvre, et une biographie. De 13 à 20 ans en apprentissage chez un charron, il décide soudain de gagner sa vie comme peintre d'objets usuels tels que voitures, enseignes, poteaux indicateurs, et j'en passe. Une grave maladie le fait tourner vers la religion, à la suite de quoi il se rend, en 1801, à Milford où il s'affilie à la secte des Quakers. Il prêche depuis. Ce qui ne l'empêche pas de continuer à peindre ses «spécialités» pour gagner sa vie matérielle et, plus tard, les vrais tableaux inspirés surtout par le «Royaume de la Paix». A la fin de sa vie, il a écrit ses mémoires où il relate son activité religieuse.

EXPOSITIONS:
«Masters of Popular Painting», Museum of Modern Art, New York 1938.
Guild Hall, East Hampton, N.Y. 1951.
«American Primitive Art», Washington 1954.
«Amerikanische Malerei», Kunstmuseum Luzern 1954 (Cat., Préface Adolf Reinle et J. Lipman).
«L'Art Américain», Bruxelles 1958.
Abbey Aldrich Rockefeller Folk Art Collection, Williamsburg, Va. 1960.
«De Lusthof der Naieven», Rotterdam 1964.
«Le Monde des Naïfs», Paris 1964.
«Garbisch Collection»; National Gallery of Art, Washington 1959 (Cat., Préface David E. Finley et John Walker).

BIBLIOGRAPHIE:
Jean Lipman: «American Primitive Painting», Oxford University Press, London/New York/Toronto 1942.
Jean Lipman and Alice Winchester: «Primitive Painters in America», Dodd Mead & Co, New York 1950.
Oto Bihalji-Merin: «Das naive Bild der Welt», Köln 1959.
Oto Bihalji-Merin: «Die naive Malerei», Köln 1959.
Oto Bihalji-Merin: «Les Peintres Naïfs», Paris (sans date).

Hirschfield, Morris

Born 1872 in a small town in the Russian part of Poland, near the German border.
Died 1946 in New York (USA).

Geboren 1872 in einem kleinen Dorf des russischen Teils von Polen, nahe der deutschen Grenze.
Gestorben 1946 in New York (USA).

Né en 1872 dans une petite ville de la Pologne russe, près de la frontière allemande.
Mort en 1946 à New York (USA).

While still very young he created sculptures of religious subjects. In 1890 he immigrated to America, where he worked in an establishment making ladies' clothes. Only after a serious illness, which attacked him in 1936–1937, did he turn to painting—his first works were 'Beach Girl' and 'Angora Cat' copied from photographs. But his artistic temperament and his occasionally delirious imagination, which was embellished by a very definite erotic enthusiasm promptly overcame the pictures he was copying. Almost immediately Hirschfield showed himself to be one of the greatest 'naive' artists, not only in America but in the whole world. At his death he left behind about seventy pictures.

Schon als ganz jung schuf er Skulpturen über religiöse Themen. Wandert 1890 nach Amerika aus, wo er in einem Damenkonfektionsgeschäft arbeitet. Erst nach einer 1936/37 erlittenen schweren Krankheit denkt er wieder an Kunst. Da malt er nach Photographien «Beach Girl» und «Chat Angora». Aber sein Künstlertemperament und seine zuweilen überbordende Phantasie, deren sehr spezielle Erotik wahrscheinlich auf seine Beschäftigung mit weiblicher Unterwäsche zurückgeht, machen ihm das Kopieren schnell unmöglich. Beinahe alsogleich entpuppt er sich als einer der größten naiven Maler, nicht nur in Amerika, sondern auf der ganzen Welt. Bei seinem Tod hinterläßt er rund 70 Bilder.

Déjà tout jeune, il faisait des sculptures sur des sujets religieux. En 1890, émigre en Amérique, où il travaille dans une entreprise de confections pour dames. Ce n'est qu'après une grave maladie, survenue en 1936/37, qu'il repense à l'art. Il peint alors «Beach Girl» et «Chat Angora» d'après des photos. Mais son tempérament d'artiste et sa fantaisie parfois délirante, agrémentée d'un zest d'érotisme très spécial, contracté, sans doute, en maniant les sous-vêtements féminins, ont eu vite raison de la copie. Presqu'aussitôt, il se révéla comme l'un des plus grands peintres naïfs, non seulement américains, mais du monde entier. A sa mort, il a laissé quelque 70 tableaux.

EXPOSITIONS:
Museum of Modern Art, New York 1954.
Kunsthaus, Zürich 1951.
Galerie Maeght, Paris 1951 (Cat., Préface R. Queneau, Charles Estienne et H.P. Roché).
«La Peinture Naïve», Knokke-le-Zoute 1958.
L'Exposition Universelle, 50 Ans d'Art Moderne, Bruxelles 1958.
«Das Naive Bild der Welt», Baden-Baden 1961.
«De Lusthof der Naieven», Rotterdam 1964.
«Le Monde des Naïfs», Paris 1964.

BIBLIOGRAPHIE:
Sidney Janis: «They Taught Themselves», Dial Press, New York 1942.
Jean Lipman et Alice Winchester: «Primitive Painting in America», Dodd Mead, New York 1950.
Oto Bihalji-Merin: «Das naive Bild der Welt», Köln 1959.
Oto Bihalji-Merin: «Die naive Malerei», Köln 1959.
Oto Bihalji-Merin: «Les Peintres Naïfs», Paris (sans date).
Anatole Jakovsky: «Eros du Dimanche», Paris 1964.
André Breton: «Le Surréalisme et la Peinture», Editions Gallimard, Paris 1965.

Hjorth, Bror

Born 1894 in Alvkarleby (Sweden).

Geboren 1894 in Alvkarleby (Schweden).

Né en 1894 à Alvkarleby (Suède).

Sweden was certainly the first country in the West to try actively to preserve as far as possible the traces of the 'good old days' of our ancestors, i.e. an age of craftsmanship and rural life, daily endangered by the increasing importance of the machine. The first folklore museum of its kind, an open-air museum, was founded in Skanzen in 1891, thus beating the one in Arnhem (capital of the Guelder district of Holland) by more than twenty years and the one in Borkrijk (Belgium) by still more. It is therefore not suprising that several Swedish artists were attracted by popular art and drew their inspiration from it. Hjorth is one of these artists. His favorite subjects seem to be erotic and religious. He is also a sculptor. Although his art is not entirely 'naive', it follows the same general trend.

Schweden war unbestreitbar das erste Land der westlichen Welt, das so gut wie möglich die Spuren der «guten alten Zeit» unserer Vorfahren bewahren wollte, das heißt das handwerkliche und das ländliche Leben, das von der siegreichen Maschinenwelt jeden Tag neu bedroht wurde. Das erste Folklore-museum dieser Art wurde bereits 1891 in Skanzen unter freiem Himmel errichtet; es ist also mehr als zwanzig Jahre älter als das Museum in Arnhem, der Hauptstadt von Geldern (Holland), und sehr viel älter als das von Borkrijk in Belgien. Es ist darum nicht verwunderlich, daß mehrere schwedische Künstler sich von der Volkskunst anziehen ließen und ihre Inspiration darin fanden. Hjorth gehört zu diesen Malern. Er liebt ganz besonders erotische und religiöse Themen. Er ist auch Bildhauer. Seine Kunst ist zwar nicht völlig naiv, doch gehört sie zur Familie der Naiven.

La Suède fut sans conteste le premier pays du monde occidental à vouloir conserver dans la mesure du possible les traces du «bon vieux temps» de nos aïeux, c'est-à-dire de la vie artisanale et rurale, que le machinisme triomphant mettait tous les jours en péril. Le premier musée folklorique de ce genre, en plein air, fut édifié dès 1891 à Skansen, devançant ainsi de plus de vingt ans celui d'Arnhem, capitale de la Gueldre (Hollande) et encore davantage celui de Borkrijk en Belgique. Il n'est donc pas étonnant que plusieurs artistes suédois se sentirent attirés par l'art populaire y puisant leur inspiration. Hjorth est de ceux-là. Il affectionne particulièrement les motifs érotiques et réligieux. Il est également sculpteur. Son art, même s'il n'est pas tout à fait naïf, est néanmoins dans la lignée naïve.

BIBLIOGRAPHIE:
Erik Blomberg: «Bror Hjorth», Svensk Litteratur, Halmstadt 1952.

Houtman, Sipke Cornelis

Born 1871 in Dokkum (Netherlands).
Died 1945 in Amsterdam (Netherlands).

Geboren 1871 in Dokkum (Holland).
Gestorben 1945 in Amsterdam (Holland).

Né en 1871 à Dokkum (Hollande).
Mort en 1945 à Amsterdam (Hollande).

Had always wanted to be an artist, but his parents insisted on his studying and becoming a teacher. He did this for a while, but then could not stand it any longer and gave it up—he preferred to work as an assistant in a bakery. At the age of sixty he fulfilled his life's ambition, when his old age pension finally allowed him to take up painting. As he had never had any painting lessons, he liked to write on the back of his pictures: 'The Lord Jesus is my only teacher'. He died in an old people's home.

Er wollte von Anfang an Maler werden, aber seine Eltern zwangen ihn, sich als Lehrer auszubilden. Er übte den Beruf während kurzer Zeit aus, aber dann hielt er es nicht mehr aus und zog es vor, als Bäckergehilfe zu arbeiten. Sein Wunsch ging in Erfüllung, als er 60 Jahre alt war und seine Altersrente ihm endlich erlaubte, zu malen. Da er das Handwerk nie gelernt hat, pflegte er auf die Rückseite seiner Bilder zu schreiben: «Der Herr Jesus ist mein einziger Meister». Er starb im Altersasyl.

Il voulait être peintre depuis toujours, mais ses parents l'obligeaient à faire des études afin de devenir instituteur. Il le fut, du reste, pendant un court laps de temps, mais, n'y tenant plus, il préféra servir d'aide dans une boulangerie. Son rêve fut exaucé à l'âge de 60 ans, lorsque sa pension de vieillesse lui a permis enfin de peindre. Comme il n'a jamais étudié, il aimait inscrire sur le dos de ses tableaux: «Le Seigneur Jésus est mon seul maître». Il est mort à l'Hospice des Vieillards.

EXPOSITIONS:
«Moderne Primitieven», Stedelijk Museum, Amsterdam 1941 (Cat., Préface D.C.R.).
«Maler des einfältigen Herzens», Museum am Ostwall, Dortmund 1952.
«Arbeit-Freizeit-Muße», Kunsthalle, Recklinghausen 1953.
«La Peinture Naïve», Knokke-le-Zoute 1958.
«Laienmaler», Gewerbemuseum, Basel 1961.
«De Lusthof der Naieven», Rotterdam 1964.
«Le Monde des Naïfs», Paris 1964.

BIBLIOGRAPHIE:
Oto Bihalji-Merin: «Das naive Bild der Welt», Köln 1959.
Oto Bihalji-Merin: «Die naive Malerei», Köln 1959.
Oto Bihalji-Merin: «Les Peintres Naïfs», Paris (sans date).

Hoyer, Thorvald Arenst

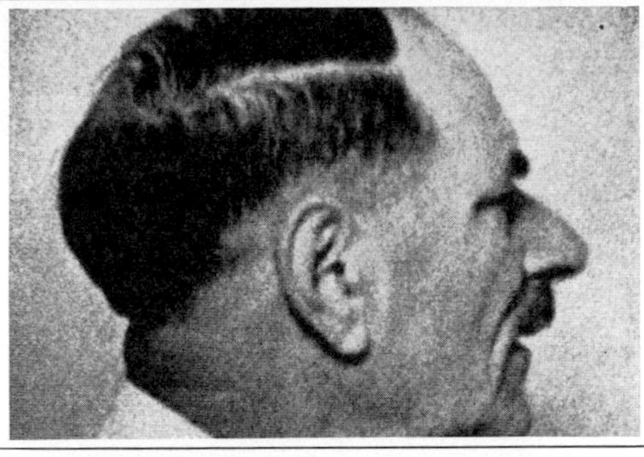

Born 1872 in Copenhagen (Denmark).

Geboren 1872 in Kopenhagen (Dänemark).

Né en 1872 à Copenhague (Danemark).

Has lived since 1902 in the United States, and is an American citizen. Since 1915 he has been in Chicago. Is an acrobat by profession, and has traveled a good deal—but his first love is painting. Is always visiting art galleries. He is full of admiration for the old masters, and in his own work he takes over their style—as well as he can, of course. He is one of the very few 'naive' artists to be interested in the effects of light.

Seit 1902 in den Vereinigten Staaten. Amerikanischer Staatsbürger. Lebt seit 1915 in Chicago. Akrobat. Reist viel, aber was ihn vor allem begeistert, ist die Malerei. Darum besucht er überall die Museen. Von der Kunst der alten Meister hingerissen, bemüht er sich, nach Maßgabe seiner Mittel natürlich, um ihren Stil. Er gehört zu den ganz seltenen naiven Malern, die sich für Lichteffekte interessieren.

En U.S.A. depuis 1902. Citoyen américain. Vit à Chicago depuis 1915. Acrobate. Voyage beaucoup, mais ce qui le passionne avant tout, c'est la peinture. C'est pourquoi il visite toujours les musées. Emerveillé par l'art des vieux maîtres, il adopte donc leur style, dans la mesure de ses moyens, évidemment. Il est parmi les très rares peintres naïfs à s'intéresser aux effets de la lumière.

EXPOSITIONS:
Findlay Galleries, Chicago 1936.
«Masters of Popular Painting», New York 1938.
«La Peinture Naïve», Knokke-le-Zoute 1958.

BIBLIOGRAPHIE:
Oto Bihalji-Merin: Das Naive Bild der Welt, Köln 1959.
Oto Bihalji-Merin: Die Naive Malerei, Köln 1959.
Oto Bihalji-Merin: Les Peintres Naïfs, Paris (sans date).

Hubaček, Zigmunt

Born March 8, 1906 in Lucenec (Czechoslovakia).

Geboren am 8. März 1906 in Lucenec (Tschechoslowakei).

Né le 8 mars 1906 à Lucenec (Tchécoslovaquie).

Bookbinder by trade. In 1957 he started to create unusual chased copperwork, halfway between painting and sculpture, which has an undeniable, slightly barbaric charm. Together with Kemko's sculptured wood, Vavercak's wrought-iron animals like old-fashioned votive pictures, and Kerac's metal wire sculptures, Hubaček extends the fascination of Czechoslovak 'naive' art. Like most of his colleagues, his work came to the attention of the public at the amateurs' exhibition held in 1962 in Prague and Martin.

Buchbinder. Beginnt 1957 jene seltsamen getriebenen Kupfer zu schaffen, die zwischen Malerei und Bildhauerei liegen und einen unbestreitbaren, etwas barbarischen Charme besitzen. Wie Kemko mit seinen Holzschnitzereien, Vavercak mit seinen schmiedeisernen Tieren, die an Votivtafeln gemahnen, und Kerac mit seinen Drahtskulpturen, läßt Hubaček den Zauber der naiven tschechischen und slowakischen Kunst weiterleben. Wie die meisten seiner Kollegen ist er dank der Ausstellung «Dilettantenkunst» bekannt geworden, die 1962 in Prag und in Martin stattfand.

Relieur. A partir de 1957, commence à créer ces cuivres repoussés étranges, se situant entre la peinture et la sculpture et qui possèdent un charme incontestable, un tantinet barbare. Avec les bois sculptés de Kemko, les animaux en fer forgé de Vavercak, pareils à des anciens Ex Voto, et les sculptures en fil de fer de Kerac, Hubaček prolonge les enchantements de l'art naïf tchèque et slovaque. Comme la plupart de ses confrères, il a été révélé par l'exposition des amateurs qui a eu lieu, en 1962, à Prague et à Martin.

EXPOSITIONS:
«Naivni Umeni», Dum mesta, Brno 1964.
«Naivni Umeni», Narodni Galerie, Prague 1964.

Van Hyfte, Camille

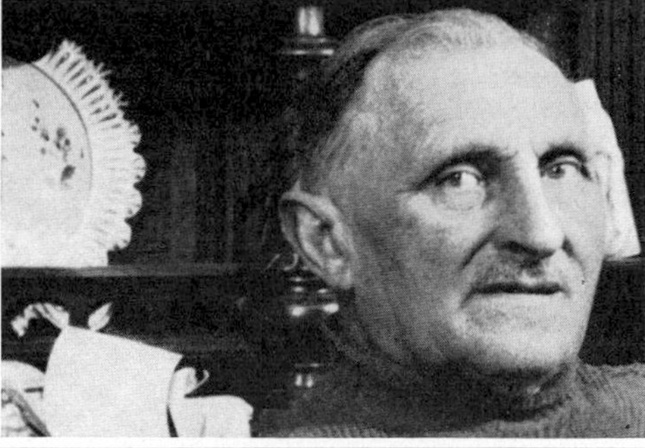

Born 1886 in Ertvelde (Belgium).
Died June 11, 1966 in Mouy, Oise (France).

Geboren 1886 in Ertvelde (Belgien).
Gestorben am 11. Juni 1966 in Mouy, Oise (Frankreich).

Né en 1886 à Ertvelde (Belgique).
Mort le 11 juin à Mouy, Oise (France).

Began as a farmer like his father. Immigrated to France where land was less expensive and easier to find. Settled down in Mouy in the district of Oise, and finally bought a horseflesh butcher's shop. He is blessed with marvellously good health and took part in bicycle races for many years despite his advanced age. When his doctor forbade him to continue, he found distraction in painting. Here too he did everything himself: made the frames, the canvases, fitted them, etc. Decorated his house with rather fine pictures. His art is at the same time fresh and yet sensitive, especially in his wonderful use of pearly grey tones.

Ist zuerst Bauer wie sein Vater. Wandert nach Frankreich aus, wo das Land billiger und leichter zu finden ist. Läßt sich in Mouy im Departement Oise nieder und erwirbt schließlich eine Pferdemetzgerei. Seine unverwüstliche Gesundheit erlaubt es ihm, noch in vorgerücktem Alter an Radrennen teilzunehmen. Als der Arzt ihm solche Strapazen verbietet, findet er eine Ablenkung in der Malerei, denn auch hier macht er alles selber: Rahmen, Blendrahmen, Leinwand. Er schmückt sein Haus mit ziemlich schönen Bildern. Seine Kunst ist zugleich frisch und empfindsam, vor allem in den perlgrauen Tönen, die er meisterhaft beherrscht.

Commence par être agriculteur comme son père. Emigre en France où les terrains sont moins chers et plus faciles à trouver. Se fixe à Mouy, dans l'Oise, et finit par avoir une boucherie hippophagique. Doué d'une santé prodigieuse, il participe encore aux courses cyclistes malgré son âge avancé. Aussi, lorsque le médecin lui défend de continuer, il trouve un dérivatif dans la peinture, car, là encore, il fait tout lui-même: les cadres, les châssis, les toiles. Il décore sa maison d'assez belles peintures. Son art est frais et sensible à la fois, surtout dans les tons gris-perle où il excelle.

EXPOSITIONS:
Galerie de l'Institut, Paris 1955 (Cat., Préface Anatole Jakovsky).
Galerie Merz, Beauvais 1958.
«Les Peintres Naïfs», Knokke-le-Zoute 1958.
«Les Peintres Naïfs», Maison de la Pensée Française, Paris 1960.
«Peintres Naïfs Belges», Théâtre National, Bruxelles 1965.
«Peintres Naïfs Belges», Musée Royal des Beaux-Arts, Verviers 1965.
«Peintres Naïfs Belges», Musée Royal des Beaux-Arts, Hasselt 1966.

BIBLIOGRAPHIE:
Anatole Jakovsky: «Les Peintres Naïfs», Paris 1956.
Anatole Jakovsky: «Die naive Malerei in Frankreich», Zürich 1957.
Paul Guth: «Un Naïf chez les Peintres Naïfs», Vogue, Paris 1956.
Oto Bihalji-Merin: «Das naive Bild der Welt», Köln 1959.
Oto Bihalji-Merin: «Die naive Malerei», Köln 1959.
Oto Bihalji-Merin: «Les Peintres Naïfs», Editions Delpire, Paris (sans date).
Anatole Jakovsky: «Le Douanier et les Contrebandiers», Jardin des Arts, No 79, Paris, juin 1961.
«Camille van Hyfte», Savoir et Beauté, La Louvière, décembre 1965.

Hyppolite, Hector

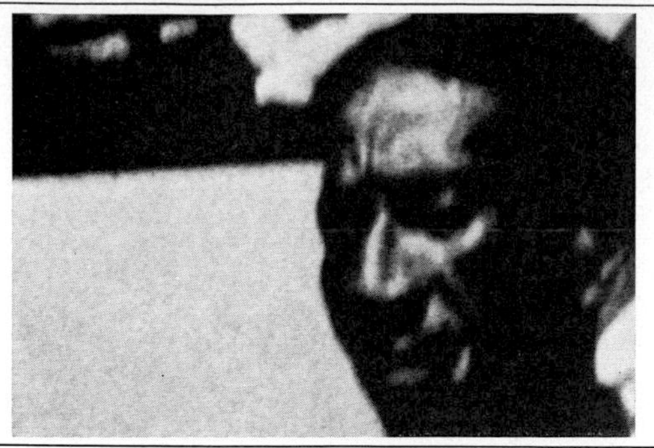

Born 1894 in Saint-Marc (Haiti).
Died 1948 in Port-au-Prince (Haiti).

Geboren 1894 in Saint-Marc (Haiti).
Gestorben 1948 in Port-au-Prince (Haiti).

Né en 1894 à Saint-Marc (Haïti).
Mort en 1948 à Port-au-Prince (Haïti).

At the age of twelve he became apprenticed to a shoemaker. During his youth he traveled to America and also to Africa. On his return to Haiti he became a house painter and decorator, and later an innkeeper. Was a priest of the strange voodoo cult which allowed prayer to St. Joseph but also to the Siren. Nevertheless, he and Philomé Obin were the island's only artists until DeWitt Peters came. He is the greatest 'naive' artist of Haiti, and of course the best known one, thanks to the surrealists who became familiar with his work before the war through the Cuban painter Wilfredo Lam. Died of a heart attack.

Erlernt mit 12 Jahren das Schuhmacherhandwerk. In seiner Jugend bereist er Amerika und Afrika. In seine Heimat zurückgekehrt, wird er Anstreicher, Dekorationsmaler und schließlich Hotelier. Priester des Voodoo-Kultes, jener seltsamen Religion, die sich gleichzeitig an den hl. Joseph und an die Sirene wendet. Auf jeden Fall waren vor DeWitt Peters' Ankunft in Haiti Philomé Obin und er die beiden einzigen Maler der Insel. Er ist der größte naive Maler Haitis und natürlich der bekannteste, vor allem dank den Surrealisten, die vor dem Krieg durch den kubanischen Maler Wilfredo Lam auf ihn aufmerksam gemacht wurden. Er ist an einem Herzschlag gestorben.

Apprenti cordonnier à 12 ans. Il voyage dans sa jeunesse en Amérique et en Afrique. Plus tard, de retour au pays natal, devient peintre en bâtiment, peintre décorateur et, finalement, hôtelier. Prêtre du culte Vaudou, ce culte plus qu'étrange qui permet d'évoquer à la fois, et saint Joseph et la Sirène. Toujours est-il qu'il n'y avait que lui et Philomé Obin qui peignaient déjà avant l'arrivée de DeWitt Peters dans l'île. Il est le plus grand peintre naïf haïtien et, évidemment, le plus connu, surtout grâce aux surréalistes qui l'ont célèbre avant la guerre par l'intermédiaire du peintre cubain, Wilfredo Lam. Il est mort d'une crise cardiaque.

EXPOSITIONS:
« Peintres de l'Equateur, de Haïti et de Pérou », l'UNESCO, Paris 1947.
« Das naive Bild der Welt », Baden-Baden 1961.
« Naive Painters of Latin America », Duke University, Durham, N. C. 1963.
« 19 Peintres d'Haïti », Palais des Beaux-Arts, Bruxelles 1963.
« 20th Century Latin American Naive Art », La Jolla, Cal. (USA) 1964.
« De Lusthof der Naieven », Rotterdam 1964.
« Le Monde des Naïfs », Paris 1964.

BIBLIOGRAPHIE:
Selden Rodman: « Renaissance in Haiti », Pelegrini and Cudahy, New York (sans date).
E. et R. Mason Pollock: « Haiti », Readers Digest, décembre 1958.
Oto Bihalji-Merin: « Das naive Bild der Welt », Köln 1959.
Oto Bihalji-Merin: « Die naive Malerei », Köln 1959.
Oto Bihalji-Merin: « Les Peintres Naïfs », Paris (sans date).
Anatole Jakovsky: « Eros du Dimanche », Paris 1964.
André Breton: « Le Surréalisme et la Peinture », Gallimard, Paris 1965.

Ilija (Bosilj)

Born 1905 near Nish, Serbia (Yugoslavia).

Geboren 1905 bei Nisch, Serbien (Jugoslawien).

Né en 1905 près de Nich, Serbie (Yougoslavie).

Began to paint in 1957 on wrapping paper and old sacking. But his very individual vision, which in no way resembles that of any other artist, soon became the object of attention. His characters are fantastic, bearing no relation to reality. Even when he paints sputniks they look more like medieval inventions of the Devil than modern technical machines. Could this be due to the icons in the Orthodox Church of his country? Possibly—one cannot be sure. But what is much more disturbing is that his very identity has been challenged, his existence called in question. Some have claimed he is the father of the curator of the Zagreb Gallery of Primitive Art, whereas others say... but that is not our concern. The pictures are truly remarkable, whoever painted them.

Beginnt 1957 auf Packpapier und alte Säcke zu malen. Aber seine ganz eigenständige Sicht, die sich mit keiner anderen vergleichen läßt, lenkt sofort die Aufmerksamkeit auf ihn. Seine Personen sind phantastisch und haben gar keine Beziehung mit der Wirklichkeit. Selbst wenn er Sputniks malt, gleichen sie eher diabolischen Erfindungen des Mittelalters als mechanischen Schöpfungen unserer Zeit.
Ist es der Einfluß der orthodoxen Ikone seiner Heimat? Man kann es nicht mit Gewißheit sagen. Noch verwirrender ist jedoch die Tatsache, daß sogar seine Identität angefochten, seine Existenz angezweifelt worden ist. Die einen haben behauptet, er sei der Vater des Konservators der Galerie für Primitive Kunst in Zagreb, während die anderen... Das geht uns nichts an. Wir stehen einem sehr bedeutenden Werk gegenüber, wer immer sein Urheber sein mag.

Commence à peindre en 1957 sur des papiers d'emballage et des vieux sacs. Mais sa vision toute particulière, ne ressemblant ni de près ni de loin à aucune autre, a attiré immédiatement l'attention sur lui. Ses personnages sont fantastiques, n'ayant aucun contact avec le réel. Même s'il peint les spoutniks, ils ressemblent davantage à des créations diaboliques du Moyen Age qu'à des engins mécaniques de notre temps. Est-ce l'influence des icônes orthodoxes de son pays? On ne saurait le dire avec certitude. Mais ce qui est plus troublant encore, c'est que même son identité a été contestée, son existence mise en doute. Les uns ont prétendu que c'était le propre père du conservateur de la Galerie d'Art Primitif de Zagreb, tandis que les autres... Cela ne nous regarde pas. Nous sommes en présence d'une œuvre absolument remarquable quel que soit son auteur.

EXPOSITIONS:
«Naïfs 63», Galerie d'Art Primitif, Zagreb 1963.
Duro Sajaj, Belgrade 1963
(Cat., Préface signée M. G.).
«Sonntagsmaler aus Jugoslawien», Museum am Ostwall, Dortmund 1964.
«De Lusthof der Naieven», Rotterdam 1964.
«Le Monde des Naïfs», Paris 1964.

BIBLIOGRAPHIE:
«Art Naïf», Editions Marocaines et Internationales, Rabat 1964.

Imbrogno, Pietro

Born January 6, 1917 in Lappano, Cosenza (Italy).

Geboren am 6. Januar 1917 in Lappano, Cosenza (Italien).

Né le 6 janvier 1917 à Lappano, Cosenza (Italie).

Lives in Rome and works as night watchman at the Corsini Palace art gallery. He took up painting simply to while away the long hours of his watch, in 1963. It was for exactly the same reason as lighthouse keepers who paint sailing boats or who put ships in bottles; in other words, to escape from loneliness and from having nothing to do.

Lebt in Rom, wo er in der Galerie des Palazzo Corsini als Nachtwächter arbeitet. Er hat 1963 angefangen zu malen, um die langen Stunden des Wachens auszufüllen. Genau wie die Leuchtturmwärter, die ebenfalls Segelschiffe malen oder Schiffe in Flaschen einbauen, um der Untätigkeit, der Einsamkeit zu entgehen.

Vit à Rome où il travaille comme gardien de nuit à la galerie du palais Corsini. Il a commencé à peindre justement pour meubler ses longues heures de veille. En 1963. Exactement comme les gardiens de phare qui peignent, eux aussi, des voiliers ou mettent des bateaux en bouteille, c'est-à-dire pour échapper au desœuvrement, à la solitude.

EXPOSITIONS:
«I Pittori Naifs», Rome 1964.
«I Pittori Naifs», Centro Internazionale di Arte Figurative, Biella 1964.

BIBLIOGRAPHIE:
«Art Naïf», Editions Marocaines et Internationales, Rabat 1964.

Ze Inacio, or José Inacio

(real name: Luiz Ruffolo)
Born August 1, 1927 in São Paulo (Brazil).

(Pseudonym von Luiz Ruffolo)
Geboren am 1. August 1927 in São Paulo (Brasilien).

(Pseudonyme de Luiz Ruffolo)
Né le 1 août 1927 à São Paulo (Brésil).

Brother of Iracema. Has led an active, even a fairly adventurous life. During a serious illness which he had, his sister tried to cure him by teaching him to paint. To start with, she even guided his hand. And gradually an inborn talent for art was revealed. His technique is to use very tiny strokes, almost dots, of color. His landscapes have a depth almost like tapestry work.

Bruder von Iracema. Bewegtes, ziemlich abenteuerliches Leben. Als er schwer erkrankt, versucht seine Schwester ihn zu heilen, indem sie ihm das Malen beibringt. Am Anfang führt sie ihm sogar die Hand. Und allmählich erwachen die angeborenen Gaben. Er malt in ganz kleinen, beinahe pointillistischen Strichen. Landschaften von einer Dichte, die an Wandteppiche gemahnt.

Frère d'Iracema. Vie mouvementée, passablement aventureuse. Tombé assez gravement malade, sa sœur essaye de le guérir en lui apprenant à peindre. Pour commencer, elle va jusqu'à guider sa main. Et les dons innés se reveillent petit à petit. Il peint par de toutes petites touches presque pointillistes. Des paysages d'une densité qui voisine avec celle des tapisseries.

EXPOSITIONS:
Galeria Vila, São Paulo 1963.
Galerie Vernon, Rio de Janeiro 1964.
Galerie Vernon, Rio de Janeiro 1966
(Cat., Préface Anatole Jakovsky).

BIBLIOGRAPHIE:
Noticios da Galeria Barcinski, Copacabana, septembre 1964.

Iracema

(Arditi, née Ruffolo)
Born February 1, 1924 in São Paulo (Brazil).

(Arditi, geborene Ruffolo)
Geboren am 1. Februar 1924 in São Paulo (Brasilien).

(Arditi, née Ruffolo)
Née le 1 février 1924 à São Paulo (Brésil).

Before turning to painting she tried her hand at practically all possible jobs: typist, journalist, air hostess, etc. An extraordinarily gifted woman of great sensitivity, she became interested in popular art and encouraged the primitive artists in the neighborhood. Finally, she too began to paint. Her pictures are of vast stretches of water and tropical forests, as in 'Rio Sobre-natural', haunted by some indefinable, unalterable loneliness. She is definitely the greatest Brazilian 'naive' painter, perhaps among the best of the whole of Latin America.

Bevor sie zur Malerei übergeht, versucht sie eine ganze Reihe Berufe: Typistin, Journalistin, Stewardess usw. Sie ist außerordentlich begabt, überaus empfindsam, interessiert sich zuerst für die Volkskunst und fördert die naiven Maler in ihrem Bekanntenkreis. Dann fängt sie selber an zu malen. Und es entstehen weite Wasserflächen und Urwälder, ihr "Rio Sobre-natural", heimgesucht von einer unnennbaren, unheilbaren Einsamkeit. Sie ist zweifellos der größte naive Maler Brasiliens und einer der besten in ganz Lateinamerika.

Avant de faire de la peinture, elle a essayé à peu près tous les métiers: dactylo, journaliste, hôtesse de l'air, etc. Remarquablement douée, d'une extraordinaire sensibilité, elle s'intéresse d'abord aux arts populaires et encourage les peintres naïfs de son entourage. Puis, elle se met à peindre à son tour. Et ce sont les vastes étendues des eaux et des forêts tropicales de son «Rio Sobre-natural», hantées par on ne sait quelle inguérissable solitude. C'est certainement le plus grand peintre naïf brésilien, et, sans doute, l'un des meilleurs de toute l'Amérique latine.

EXPOSITIONS:
Galerie Herbinet, Paris 1965
(Cat., Préface Anatole Jakovsky).
Maison de France, São Paulo 1965.
Galerie Vernon, Rio de Janeiro 1966
(Cat., Préface Anatole Jakovsky).

Passage à la télévision Française, novembre 1965.

Isabel
(Isabel de Jesus)

Born February 28, 1938 in Minas Gerais (Brazil).

Geboren am 28. Februar 1938 in Minas Gerais (Brasilien).

Née le 28 février 1938 à Minas Gerais (Brésil).

A servant in Iracema's house. Seeing her mistress paint, she tried also—imaginative compositions bringing to life a wealth of legends belonging to this new continent. Siren-birds, for instance. In this she resembles some of the artists of Haiti and Cuba, since they too treat the myths of their country in a kind of embroidered, mediumistic fashion.

Magd bei Iracema. Da sie ihre Herrin malen sieht, versucht auch sie sich an imaginären Kompositionen, in denen ein ganzer Legendenhintergrund des neuen Kontinents auflebt. Sirenen-Vögel zum Beispiel. Sie gleicht darin einigen Malern in Haiti und Kuba, wo dieser mythische Grund ebenfalls in einer Art beinahe mediumistischer Stickerei behandelt wird.

Servante chez Iracema. Voyant peindre sa maîtresse, elle s'essaye, elle aussi, à des compositions imaginaires où revit tout un fond légendaire de ce nouveau continent. Des oiseaux-sirènes, par exemple. Elle ressemble en cela à quelques peintres de Haïti et de Cuba où, également, ce fond mythique est traité dans une sorte de broderie quasi-médiumnique.

EXPOSITIONS:
Galeria J.D., São Paulo 1965.
Galerie Vernon, Rio de Janeiro 1966.

Isidore, Raymond Edouard

Born September 8, 1900 in Chartres (France).
Died September 7, 1964 in Chartres (France).

Geboren am 8. September 1900 in Chartres (Frankreich).
Gestorben am 7. September 1964 in Chartres (Frankreich).

Né le 8 septembre 1900 à Chartres (France).
Mort le 7 septembre 1964 à Chartres (France).

A really exceptional case of mediumistic architecture and decoration. However, in contrast to the postman Cheval who always restricted himself to the art of construction, Isidore decorated his house sometimes with frescos and sometimes with mosaics, using broken plates and other rubbish collected from the town's refuse pit. This work of art, which took him thirty years to complete, he claimed to have been commissioned him by spirits. He was employed by the town of Chartres as a cemetery sweeper.

Ein völlig außergewöhnlicher Fall mediumistischer Architektur und Dekoration. Aber im Gegensatz zum Briefträger Cheval, der sich immer auf die Kunst des Bauens beschränkt hat, schmückt Isidore sein Haus bald mit Fresken, bald mit Mosaiken, wozu er zerbrochene Teller und andere in der Müllabfuhr der Stadt gesammelte Scherben und Abfälle gebraucht. Dieses Werk, das ihn etwa 30 Jahre seines Lebens beschäftigt hat, wurde ihm, wie er behauptete, von Geistern aufgetragen. Von Beruf war er städtischer Straßenkehrer im Friedhof von Chartres.

Un cas absolument exceptionnel d'architecture et de décoration médiumnique. Mais, à l'encontre du facteur Cheval qui s'est toujours limité à l'art de bâtir, Isidore décore sa maison tantôt à la fresque, tantôt à la mosaïque, se servant pour cela des assiettes cassées et autres rebuts ramassés dans les décharges de sa ville. Cette œuvre qui lui a pris trente ans de sa vie, environ, a été dictée, prétendait-il, par des esprits. Il était de son état balayeur municipal du cimetière de Chartres.

BIBLIOGRAPHIE:

R. Giraud: «Raymond Edouard Isidore», Nouveau Femina, Paris, Septembre 1955.
R. Giraud: «Raymond Edouard Isidore», Bizarre, N°5, Paris, Juillet 1956.
«Raymond Edouard Isidore», Point de vue Images, Paris, 26 octobre 1956.
«Raymond Edouard Isidore», Sunday New York News, New York, July 21, 1957,
J. Capit: «Raymond Edouard Isidore», Panorama No. 25/27, 1958.
«Les Inspirés et leurs Demeures», Préface d'André Breton, Editions Le Temps, Paris 1962.
«Les Inspirés et leurs Demeures», Arts, No. 892, Paris, 28 novembre 1962.
Anatole Jakovsky: «Dämonen und Wunder», DuMont-Schauberg, Köln 1963.

Itaya, Foussa

Born October 14, 1919 in Fukuoka (Japan).

Geboren 14. Oktober 1919 in Fukuoka (Japan).

Né le 14 octobre 1919 à Fukuoka (Japon).

Came to Paris after having already studied art in his own country. Contact with the Western world helped him to rid his work of the conventionalism of the Far East, but also of his individualism in general. He does not even preserve a definite style, like Foujita, for instance. This makes his painting develop towards a genuine primitivism—a very rare occurrence among the Japanese. He has shown his work in various collective exhibitions, but has never had an individual one.

Kommt nach Paris, nachdem er in seiner Heimat Malerei studiert hat. Die Berührung mit dem Westen befreit ihn von allen Schablonen der fernöstlichen Kalligraphie sowie von der Virtuosität im allgemeinen. Es bleibt ihm nicht einmal ein gewisser Stil, wie er zum Beispiel bei Foujita festzustellen ist. Das bewirkt, daß seine Malerei sich in Richtung eines echten Primitivismus entwickelt, etwas ziemlich Seltenes bei seinen Landsleuten. Hat an zahlreichen Gruppenausstellungen teilgenommen, keine Einzelausstellung.

Vient à Paris après avoir étudié la peinture dans son pays. Le contact avec l'Occident le débarrasse de tous les poncifs de la calligraphie extrême-orientale, ainsi que de la virtuosité en général. Il n'en garde même pas un certain style, comme Foujita, par exemple. Ce qui fait que sa peinture évolue vers un primitivisme de bon aloi, chose assez rare chez ses compatriotes. A participé à de nombreuses expositions collectives, mais n'a pas eu d'exposition individuelle.

Jaeger, Paul

Born 1893 in Kaiserslautern (Germany).

Geboren 1893 in Kaiserslautern (Deutschland).

Né en 1893 à Kaiserslautern (Allemagne).

Is a practicing dentist in Munich. A dilettante, a self-taught 'Sunday painter'. His craftsmanship is of a delicate quality, especially in his snow scenes; basically this is due to his perfectionist's eye which notices everything. In this way he resembles the many other 'naive' artists who, although in other ways may be very different, are also possessed by the same meticulous respect for the smallest details, like Grandma Moses, for instance.

Gegenwärtig Zahnarzt in München. Dilettant, Autodidakt und Sonntagsmaler. Sehr zarte Malerei, besonders in den Schneelandschaften. Sein Können steht im Dienst einer sorgsam genauen Schau, die sich nichts entgehen läßt. Er steht demnach in der Nähe aller anderen Naiven, wer immer sie seien, die, wie Grandma Moses z. B., von der gleichen unerbittlichen Prüfung des Sichtbaren besessen sind.

Actuellement dentiste à Munich. Dilettante, autodidacte et peintre du dimanche. Métier très fin, surtout dans les paysages de neige. Métier qui est, au fond, au service d'une vision méticuleuse qui ne laisse rien échapper. Se rapproche donc de tous les autres naïfs, quels qu'ils soient, possédés par la même et implacable intérrogation du visible. De Grandma Moses, entre autres.

BIBLIOGRAPHIE:
Bernhard Jasmand und Otto Kallir: «Sonntagsmaler», Otto Aug. Ehlers, Berlin/Darmstadt 1956.

Jean-Ferdinand

(real name: Hannoset)
Born June 12, 1898 in Brussels (Belgium).

(mit seinem richtigen Namen Hannoset)
Geboren am 12. Juni 1898 in Brüssel (Belgien).

(de son vrai nom: Hannoset)
Né le 12 juin 1898 à Bruxelles (Belgique).

Hairdresser. Signed his paintings with his two first names to avoid confusion with his son, who is a decorator. His art is droll and mainly devoted to attempts to recapture the charm of life at the turn of the century, not without some eroticism; however, his paintings are unfortunately rather too cold and somehow forced, so that he resembles the many "naive" imitators who flourish in the rue de Seine in Paris.

Friseur. Signiert mit seinen beiden Vornamen, um eine Verwechslung mit seinem Sohn, der Dekorateur ist, zu vermeiden. Seine drollige, hauptsächlich den Reizen von «1900» gewidmete Kunst, in der eine Spur Erotik nicht fehlt, ist leider etwas zu kalt und irgendwie gewollt, so daß er ein bißchen jenen unzähligen falschen Naiven gleicht, die in der Rue de Seine in Paris ihre Blüten treiben.

Coiffeur. Signe de ses deux prénoms pour éviter la confusion avec son fils qui est décorateur. Son art cocasse, voué surtout à l'évocation des charmes de «1900», non sans une pointe d'érotisme, est malheuresement un peu trop froid et en quelque sorte voulu, ce qui le fait ressembler un tantinet à ces innombrables faux naïfs qui fleurissent rue de Seine à Paris.

EXPOSITIONS:
Galerie Vanderboght, Bruxelles 1962
(Cat. avec une Introduction autobiographique).

BIBLIOGRAPHIE:
Paul Caso: «Révélation d'un Peintre Naïf», Le Soir, Bruxelles, 6 avril 1962.
G. Schmits: «Jean Ferdinand», Savoir et Beauté, La Louvière, décembre 1965.

Jean-Jean

Born in 1877 in Matha, Charente (France).
Died in September 1948 in La Roche-sur-Yon, Vendée (France).

Geboren 1877 in Matha, Charente (Frankreich).
Gestorben September 1948 in La Roche-sur-Yon, Vendée (Frankreich).

Né en 1877 à Matha, Charente (France).
Mort en septembre 1948 à La Roche-sur-Yon, Vendée (France).

A waif, looked after by the Welfare authorities. He sailed and lived for many years in and near Indo-China. Returned to France, fever-ridden, out of work, at a loss to know what to do. In order to be able to live he began to create strange pictures, using bits of wood, cork, shells and scraps of material, which he sold to holiday-makers on the beaches of resorts. His subjects are vaguely exotic. An unusual death—he died in prison where he had been jailed for procuring. At the age of 71!

Findelkind. Öffentliche Armenpflege. Hält sich lange zur See und zu Land in Indochina auf. Als er zurückkommt, ist er arbeitslos, haltlos, fieberkrank. Um etwas Geld zu verdienen, fängt er an, ziemlich seltsame Bilder zu verfertigen, in die er Holz-, Kork-, Muschelstücke und Stoffetzen einfügt und die er den Sommerfrischlern in den Badeorten verkauft. Leicht exotische Themen. Ungewöhnlich ist sein Ende: er stirbt im Gefängnis, wo er wegen Kuppelei saß, mit 71 Jahren!

Enfant trouvé. Assistance Publique. Navigue et séjourne longtemps en Indo-Chine. Revient desœuvré, desorienté, avec des fièvres. Commence, pour subsister, à confectionner des tableaux assez étranges, auxquels il incorpore des morceaux de bois, de liège, des coquillages et des morceaux de chiffons qu'il vend aux estivants sur les plages. Sujets vaguement exotiques. Fin non banale: il meurt en prison, pour faits de proxénetisme. A 71 ans!

BIBLIOGRAPHIE:
Anatole Jakovsky: «La Peinture Naïve», Paris 1949.
Anatole Jakovsky: «Les Peintres Naïfs», Paris 1956.
Anatole Jakovsky: «Naive Malerei», Zürich 1957.

Jirlow, Lennart

Born April 24, 1936 in Stockholm (Sweden).

Geboren am 24. April 1936 in Stockholm (Schweden).

Né le 24 avril 1936 à Stockholm (Suède).

Studied in Florence from 1954 to 1957. For the greater part of the year he lives in France, on the the Côte d'Azur, a part of the world which is extremely dear to him and which he tries to reproduce as faithfully as possible in his pictures. Small villages, small people, always painted with a touch of affection. His development is similar to that of the majority of the other Swedish 'naive' artists who, although they were not 'naive' to start with, nevertheless succeeded in acquiring a so-called 'naivistic' vision, authentic and full of charm.

Studiert von 1954 bis 1957 in Florenz. Lebt einen Großteil des Jahres in Frankreich, an der Côte d'Azur, in einer Gegend, die er ganz besonders liebt und in seinen Bildern so getreu wie möglich wiederzugeben versucht. Kleine Dörfer, kleine Leute, alles mit einer gewissen Zärtlichkeit gemalt. Er befindet sich im gleichen Fall wie die meisten naiven Maler Schwedens, die zwar anfänglich nicht naiv sind, dann aber doch zu einer «naivistischen» Schau gelangen, die sehr echt ist und viel Reiz besitzt.

Etudes de 1954 à 1957 à Florence. Habite une grande partie de l'année la France, sur la Côte d'Azur, région qu'il affectionne tout particulièrement et qu'il essaye de rendre le plus fidèlement possible dans ses tableaux. Petits villages, petites gens, tout cela peint avec une certaine tendresse. Son cas est semblable à la plupart des cas des autres peintres naïfs suédois qui, tout en n'étant pas naïfs au départ, ont réussi néanmoins à élaborer une vision, disons «naïviste» pleine d'authenticité et de charme.

EXPOSITIONS:
Galerie Modern Konst i Hemmiljo, Stockholm 1964.
Galerie Aesthetica, Stockholm 1965.
Galerie des Beaux-Arts, Paris 1965.

Jonas, Martin

Born May 9, 1924 in Kovačiča (Yugoslavia).

Geboren am 9. Mai 1924 in Kovačiča (Jugoslawien).

Né le 9 mai 1924 à Kovačiča (Yougoslavie).

A typical example of the second group of Yugoslav 'naive' artists, known as the Kovačiča group. The work of this group tends to be more matter-of-fact than that of the Hlebine painters, but nevertheless their coloring is fresh, their vision impulsive, realistic and yet not sullied by tendencies towards folklore. If, sometimes, the poetic flight of fancy is lacking, we can find full compensation in the fresh, honest and direct way in which these artists depict what they see around them.

Er ist der typische Vertreter der zweiten Heimstätte der naiven Malerei in Jugoslawien, d. h. der Schule von Kovačiča. Sie scheint erdverbundener als die von Hlebine. Indessen sind ihre Farben frisch und ihre Optik ist naturwüchsig, ziemlich realistisch, doch keineswegs der Folklore verhaftet. Der zuweilen mangelnde poetische Schwung wird aufgewogen durch die aufrichtige, klare und unmittelbare Sicht der Umwelt.

C'est le représentant typique du second foyer de la peinture naïve yougoslave, dit de Kovačiča. Elle semble être plus terre à terre que celle de Hlebine. Il n'empêche qu'elle apporte des couleurs fraîches et une vision primesautière, assez réaliste, mais nullement entachée par le folklore. Si l'envol poétique manque parfois, il est compensé par une vision franche, sincère et directe de ce que les peintres voient autour d'eux.

EXPOSITIONS:
The Arthur Jeffress Gallery, Londres 1961 (Cat., Préface M. Gelen).
«Yugoslav Modern Primitives», Edinburgh 1962.
Galerie St-Etienne, New York 1963 (Cat., Préface non signée).

BIBLIOGRAPHIE:
«Yougoslavija», Numéro Spécial (17) consacré à l'art des naïfs, Belgrade 1959.
Oto Bihalji-Merin: «Umetnost Naivnich u Jugoslavjii», Belgrade 1963.

Joris, Fernand

Born August 10, 1885 in Anderlues, Hainaut (Belgium).

Geboren am 10. August 1885 in Anderlues, Hennegau (Belgien).

Né le 10 août 1885 à Anderlues, Hainaut (Belgique).

Was a miner, but later became a lamplighter, a male nurse and an explosives watchman. None of this prevented him from working on his own and of obtaining, at the age of 41, a diploma in geometry. When he was 48 he was forced to give up mining because of a stroke, so he went to the country and took up farming. Aged 65, no doubt driven by nostalgia for the mining district, he returned to his native town and began painting and modelling. Much of his inspiration is drawn from local folklore.

Grubenarbeiter. Abwechslungsweise Lampenwärter, Krankenpfleger und Sprengstoffwärter. Das hindert ihn nicht, für sich zu arbeiten und im Alter von 41 Jahren ein Geometerdiplom zu erwerben. Ein Schlaganfall zwingt ihn, im Alter von 48 Jahren die Arbeit in der Grube aufzugeben. Er läßt sich auf dem Land nieder und übernimmt einen Bauernhof. Mit 65 Jahren überwältigt ihn zweifellos das Heimweh nach den Gruben, er kehrt in seine Vaterstadt zurück und fängt an zu malen und zu modellieren. Entlehnt viel der heimatlichen Folklore.

Mineur. Tour à tour lampiste, infirmier et gardien d'explosifs. Ce qui ne l'empêche pas de travailler pour lui et de décrocher, à l'âge de 41 ans, le diplome de géomètre. A 48 ans, frappé d'une congestion, il est obligé de quitter la mine. Il s'installe alors à la campagne où il exploite une ferme. A 65 ans, repris sans doute par la nostalgie des corons, il revient dans sa ville natale où il commence à peindre et à modeler. S'inspire beaucoup du folklore local.

EXPOSITIONS:
Musée Communal, La Louvière 1958.
Musée Royal du Cinquantenaire, Bruxelles 1959.
Galerie Maya, Bruxelles 1965
(Cat., Préface Richard Noël).
«Peintres Naïfs Belges», Théâtre National, Bruxelles 1965.
«Peintres Naïfs Belges», Musée Royal des Beaux-Arts, Verviers 1965.
«Peintres Naïfs Belges», Musée Royal des Beaux-Arts, Hasselt 1966.

BIBLIOGRAPHIE:
«Fernand Joris», Paris-Match (Edition du Benelux), N° 742, 29 juin 1963.
Roger Foulon: «Fernand Joris», Savoir et Beauté, La Louvière, décembre 1965.

Jousse, Aline

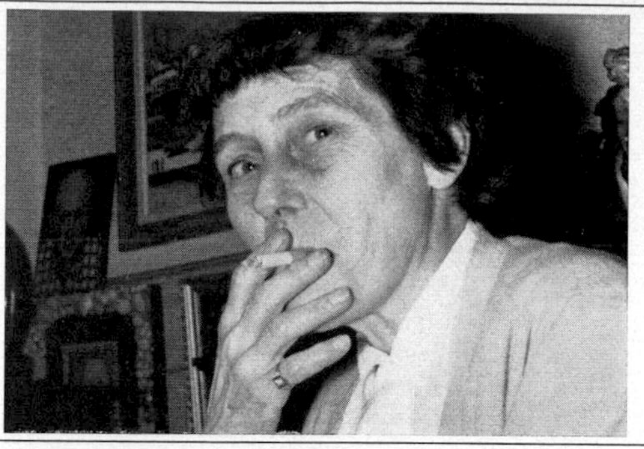

Born November 26, 1898 in Paris (France).

Geboren am 26. November 1898 in Paris (Frankreich).

Née le 26 novembre 1898 à Paris (France).

Her life was varied and on a fairly high social level. Finally she became a nurse, or rather lady-companion, on the Côte d'Azur. Painted from an inner compulsion, to express herself. Marc Chagall noticed her work and encouraged her. Her paintings have a considerable freshness.

Bewegtes und ziemlich mondänes Leben. Läßt sich schließlich als Krankenschwester und Gesellschafterin an der Côte d'Azur nieder. Malt aus innerem Zwang, um sich selber zu verwirklichen. Marc Chagall wird auf ihre Bilder aufmerksam und ermuntert die Malerin. Eine große Frische.

Vie mouvementée et passablement mondaine. Finit par s'établir comme infirmière, sinon dame de compagnie sur la Côte d'Azur. Peint par nécessité intérieure, pour se réaliser. Marc Chagall remarque ses travaux et l'encourage. Une grande fraîcheur.

EXPOSITIONS:
Galerie Mages, Vence 1954.
Galerie «La Boutique d'Art», Nice 1955.
Galerie Vidal, Paris 1958
(Cat., Préface Anatole Jakovsky).
«Les Peintres Naïfs», Maison de la Pensée Française, Paris 1960.

BIBLIOGRAPHIE:
Anatole Jakovsky: «Les Peintres Naïfs», Paris 1954.
Anatole Jakovsky: «Naive Malerei», Zürich 1957

Kane, John

Born 1860 in West Calder (Scotland).
Died 1934 in Pittsburgh, Penn. (USA).

Geboren 1860 in West Calder (Schottland).
Gestorben 1934 in Pittsburg, Penn. (USA).

Né en 1860 à West Calder (Ecosse).
Mort en 1934 à Pittsburg, Penn. (USA).

Of Irish descent, Kane worked in coal mines from the age of 9 to 19. Then he immigrated to America, where he eked out an existence by working sometimes in an ironworks and sometimes as a house painter. It was, in fact, through painting on metal that he learned to handle colors. What he valued most of all was his own painting. He tried to attend classes at the Carnegie Institute but in vain. After having been refused several times, he finally exhibited his work despite the discouragement. He was even quite successful towards the end of his life; but nevertheless, he died a pauper in the poorhouse, of tuberculosis. He is typical of the new kind of American at that time, fighting against the industrial cities, which he evoked in a somewhat similar fashion to Walt Whitman.

Irischer Abstammung. Von 9 bis 19 Jahren arbeitet er in den Kohlengruben. 1879 wandert er nach Amerika aus, wo er ein sehr hartes Leben führt, bald als Metallarbeiter, bald als Anstreicher arbeitet. Er lernt mit der Farbe umzugehen, indem er Eisen anstreicht. Was ihm jedoch am meisten am Herzen liegt, ist seine eigene Malerei. Er versucht, die Kurse am Carnegie-Institut zu besuchen. Vergeblich. Nach mehreren Abfuhren stellt er trotzdem aus. Und obwohl er in den letzten Jahren seines Lebens Erfolg hatte, ist er im Krankenhaus als armer Mann an Tuberkulose gestorben. Er ist ein gutes Beispiel für jenen neuen amerikanischen Menschen im Zwiespalt mit der Industriestadt, die er ein wenig in der Art eines Walt Whitman besingt.

D'origine irlandaise, il travaille d'abord dans les mines de charbon de 9 à 19 ans. Emigre en Amérique en 1879 où il mène une vie très dure, travaillant tantôt comme ouvrier sidérurgique, tantôt comme peintre en batiment. C'est en peignant le fer qu'il a appris à manier la couleur. Mais ce qui lui tient le plus à cœur, c'est sa propre peinture. Il a essayé de suivre les cours à l'Institut Carnegie. En vain. Après plusieurs refus, il a fini par exposer quand-même. Et bien qu'il ait connu déjà le succès, vers les dernières années de sa vie, il est mort pauvre, de tuberculose, à l'Hôpital. Il représente bien ce nouvel homme américain en conflit avec la cité industrielle qu'il chante un peu à la manière de Walt Whitman.

EXPOSITIONS:
«Masters of Popular Painting», Museum of Modern Art, New York 1938.
«Zwölf amerikanische Maler», Düsseldorf 1953 (Cat., Préface Andrew Carnduff Ritchie).
«Amerikanische Malerei», Kunstmuseum, Luzern 1954 (Cat., Préface Adolf Reinle et Lipman).
«La Peinture Naïve», Knokke-le-Zoute 1958.
«Das naive Bild der Welt», Baden-Baden 1961.
«De Lusthof der Naieven», Rotterdam 1964.
«Le Monde des Naïfs», Paris 1964.

BIBLIOGRAPHIE:
Sidney Janis: «They Taught Themselves», Dial Press, New York 1942.
Oto Bihalji-Merin: «Das naive Bild der Welt», Köln 1959.
Oto Bihalji-Merin: «Die naive Malerei», Köln 1959.
Oto Bihalji-Merin: «Les Peintres Naïfs», Paris (sans date).
«Art Naïf», Editions Marocaines et Internationales, Rabat 1964.

Kazmierczak, Karl Eduard

Born 1894 in Holbra, Mansfeldersee (Germany).

Geboren 1894 in Holbra, Mansfeldersee (Deutschland).

Né en 1894 à Holbra, Mansfeldersee (Allemagne).

A locksmith by trade, he soon gave up this craft to work in heavy industry, where one of his last responsibilities was to inspect the blast furnace pumps of the firm August Thyssen in Hamborn. The best 'naive' artist (if not the best known) of the whole constellation of painters which suddenly appeared in the Ruhr district. Has also written poetry; four of his poems are included in the catalogue 'Laienkunst im Ruhrgebiet' (1963). He is now retired and lives in Duisburg.

Schlosser. Aber er gibt dieses Handwerk auf und geht zur Schwerindustrie, wo eine seiner letzten Aufgaben darin bestand, in den August-Thyssen-Werken in Hamborn die Pumpen der Hochöfen zu überwachen. Der beste, wenn auch nicht der bekannteste naive Maler in der Gruppe, die plötzlich im Ruhrgebiet entstanden ist. Er schreibt auch Gedichte. Vier davon sind in dem Katalog zur Ausstellung «Laienkunst im Ruhrgebiet» (1963) abgedruckt. Heute ist er pensioniert und lebt in Duisburg.

Serrurier. Mais il abandonne bientôt ce métier d'artisan et passe à l'industrie lourde où l'une de ses dernières fonctions consistait à surveiller les pompes des hauts-fourneaux dans les établissements August Thyssen à Hamborn. Le meilleur peintre naïf, sinon le plus connu parmi cette pléiade qui a fleuri soudain dans la Ruhr. Il écrit aussi des poèmes. Quatre de ces poèmes figurent dans le catalogue: «Laienkunst im Ruhrgebiet» (1963). Retraité, il réside aujourd'hui à Duisburg.

EXPOSITIONS:
«Sinnvolles Laienschaffen», Recklinghausen 1954.
«Schönheit», Recklinghausen 1958 (Important cat. Stephan Hirzel).
«Arts de la Ruhr», Musée de Lille 1961.
«Laienkunst im Ruhrgebiet», Recklinghausen 1963.
«De Lusthof der Naieven», Rotterdam 1964.
«Le Monde des Naïfs», Paris 1964.

BIBLIOGRAPHIE:
Oto Bihalji-Merin: «Das naive Bild der Welt»,
Oto Bihalji-Merin: «Die naive Malerei», Köln 1959.
Oto Bihalji-Merin: «Les Peintres Naïfs», Paris (sans date).
«Art Naïf», Editions Marocaines et Internationales, Rabat 1964.

Knjazovic, Jano

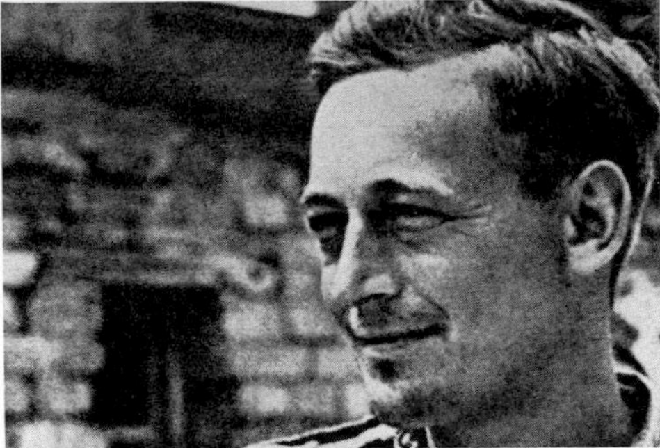

Born June 18, 1925 in Kovačiča (Yugoslavia).

Geboren am 18. Juni 1925 in Kovačiča (Jugoslawien).

Né le 18 juin 1925 à Kovačiča (Yougoslavie).

A most interesting representative of the second school of Yugoslav 'naive' painting. He took up painting in 1944. Of peasant stock, he creates pictures of village life, of farmyard animals, etc. He paints only when his work in the fields allows him a little free time. His coloring is good—resonant— even though he does not use many colors; reds and dark blues are usually all he needs.

Noch ein besonders interessanter Vertreter dieser zweiten Schule. Beginnt 1944 zu malen. Er ist Bauer und malt Szenen aus seinem Dorf, die Haustiere usw. Er malt nur, wenn die Feldarbeit ihm ein bißchen freie Zeit läßt. Seine Farben sind schön und leuchtend, obwohl er sich auf ganz wenige beschränkt. Rote und dunkelblaue Töne genügen ihm meistens.

Encore un représentant particulièrement intéressant de cette seconde école. Il commence à peindre en 1944. Paysan, il peint des scènes de son village, les animaux de basse-cour, etc. Il peint uniquement lorsque ses travaux des champs lui laissent des loisirs. Ses couleurs sont belles et sonores, bien qu'il n'en emploie pas beaucoup. Les rouges et les bleus foncés lui suffisent généralement.

EXPOSITIONS:
« Naivni umetnici jugoslavije », Belgrade 1957.
« Laienmaler », Gewerbemuseum, Basel 1961.
The Arthur Jeffress Gallery, Londres 1961 (Cat., Préface M. Gelen).
Galerie d'Art Primitif, Zagreb 1962 (Cat. Préface Miča Bašičerič, Palais de Culture, Kovain 1962.)
«Yugoslav Modern Primitives», Edinburgh 1962.
« Les Peintres Naïfs Yougoslaves », Moscou 1962.
« Première Quadriennale des Peintres Naïfs Yougoslaves », Čačac 1962.
« Naive Kunst in Jugoslawien », Kunstakademie, Wien 1963.
« Peintres Naïfs Populaires Yougoslaves », Leningrad 1963.
« Sonntagsmaler aus Jugoslawien », Museum am Ostwall, Dortmund 1964.
« De Lusthof der Naieven », Rotterdam 1964.
« Le Monde des Naïfs », Paris 1964.

BIBLIOGRAPHIE:
«Yougoslavija», numéro spécial (17) consacré à l'art des naïfs, Belgrade 1969.
Oto Bihalji-Merin: « Das naive Bild der Welt », Köln 1959.
Oto Bihalji-Merin: « Die naive Malerei », Köln 1959.
Oto Bihalji-Merin: « Les Peintres Naïfs », Paris (sans date).
Oto Bihalji-Merin: « Umetnost Naivnich u Jugoslavjii », Belgrade 1963.

Koch, Samuel

(real name Kochmeister)
Born November 13, 1887 in Warsaw (at that time Russia, now Poland).

(mit seinem richtigen Namen Kochmeister)
Geboren am 13. November 1887 in Warschau (damals Rußland, heute Polen).

(de son vrai nom: Kochmeister).
Né le 13 novembre 1887 à Varsovie (en son temps Russie, actuellement Pologne).

He was taught by his father the basics of traditional religion—the Old Testament and especially the Pentateuch. In 1901 he left home and supported himself. Went to New York in 1910 and worked in the dockyards, with Ford, with the National Biscuit Company, etc. Later he had his own shop, a cake shop. Almost at the same time as acquiring this (i.e. in 1913) he tried his hand at painting. A true 'self-made man', he was always taking up new trades—for instance, he became a hatter, and then a tobacconist. His palette was light ('despite the world's miseries', as he said); he tried his hardest to paint faithful reproductions of 'townscapes' and street scenes. His work is perhaps rather awkward but its humor cannot be denied.

Nachdem sein Vater ihm die Grundbegriffe einer religiösen Erziehung, die fünf Bücher Mosis und das Alte Testament im allgemeinen, beigebracht hat, verläßt er 1901 seine Familie und schlägt sich allein durch. 1910 kommt er nach New York, wo er im Hafen, bei Ford, bei National Biscuit usw. arbeitet. Schließlich besitzt er selber eine Konditorei. Und beinahe gleichzeitig, das heißt 1913, beginnt er zu malen. Als richtiger «Selfmademan» wechselt er noch oft den Beruf, versucht sich als Hutmacher, als Tabakverkäufer. Seine «trotz des Elends dieser Welt» helle Palette bemüht sich, so getreu wie möglich Stadtansichten und Straßenszenen wiederzugeben. Ein wenig unbeholfen vielleicht, aber mit unbestreitbarem Humor.

Après avoir reçu de son propre père des rudiments d'éducation religieuse, le Pentateuque et l'Ancien Testament en général, il quitte sa famille en 1901 pour subvenir seul à ses besoins. En 1910, il arrive à New York, où il va travailler dans les docks, chez Ford, à la National Biscuit, etc. Il finit par avoir un magasin à lui, une confiserie. Et, presqu'en même temps, c'est-à-dire en 1913, s'essaye à la peinture. En véritable «Selfmade man», il change encore souvent de métier, tantôt chapelier, tantôt buraliste. Sa palette claire, «malgré les misères de ce monde», comme il dit, s'évertue à rendre le plus fidèlement possible les paysages urbains et les scènes de la rue. Un peu maladroitement, peut-être, mais avec un incontestable humour.

EXPOSITIONS:
ACA Gallery, New York 1938.
Contemporary Art Galleries, New York 1938.
«Amerikanische Primitive»,
Museum am Ostwall, Dortmund 1954–55.
«Amerikanische Malerei», Kunstmuseum, Luzern 1956.

BIBLIOGRAPHIE:
Sidney Janis: «They taught themselves», Dial Press, New York 1942.
Oto Bihalji-Merin: «Das naive Bild der Welt», Köln 1959.
Oto Bihalji-Merin: «Die naive Malerei», Köln 1959.
Oto Bihalji-Merin: «Les Peintres Naïfs», Paris (sans date).

Koehn, Hans

Born 1897 in Treptow (Germany).

Geboren 1897 in Treptow (Deutschland).

Né en 1897 à Treptow (Allemagne).

His career is very similar to that of Kazmierczak. Trained as a locksmith, he abandoned this to work for Hoesch-Bergwerke in Dortmund.
He is now retired. For him, too, it is the peaceful, idyllic aspect of life which appeals to him as an artist; he paints old castles, amazons, etc.
In this way the blast furnaces produce their own antitoxin which enables men to enrich their lives elsewhere.

Ähnliche Laufbahn wie Kazmierczak. Zuerst Schlosser, dann arbeitet er in den Hoesch Bergwerken in Dortmund. Lebt jetzt von seiner Rente. Auch ihn fesselt die idyllische Seite des Lebens: die alten Schlösser, Amazonen, usw. So bringen die Hochöfen selber das Gegengift hervor, das den Menschen erlaubt, anderswo und ein bißchen leichter zu leben.

Carrière semblable à celle de Kazmierczak. Serrurier d'abord, il passe ensuite aux Hoesch-Bergwerke à Dortmund. Vit actuellement de sa retraite. Là encore, c'est le côté idyllique de la vie qui retient son attention: les vieux châteaux, les amazones, etc. Ainsi, les hauts-fourneaux produisent eux-mêmes l'antitoxine qui permet aux hommes de vivre un peu mieux et ailleurs.

EXPOSITIONS:
«Laienkunst», Recklinghausen 1963 (Cat., Préface Bernhard Tacke).

BIBLIOGRAPHIE:
«Art Naïf», Editions Marocaines et Internationales, Rabat 1964.

Kovačič, Mijo

Born August 5, 1935 in Gornjoi Sumi (Yugoslavia).

Geboren am 5. August 1935 in Gornjoi Sumi (Jugoslawien).

Né le 5 août 1935 à Gornjoi Sumi (Yougoslavie).

A member of the Hlebine school. Is a farmer and cattle-breeder. His age proves that even young people can be 'naive' artists of high quality. The first time he exhibited was in 1954. His first works painted on glass are in the National Museum in Koprivniča. His style is rich and elaborate, realistic and yet poetical at the same time.

Schule von Hlebine. Bauer und Viehzüchter. Sein Jahrgang beweist, daß selbst die ganz Jungen schon ausgezeichnete naive Maler werden können. Stellt 1954 zum ersten Mal aus. Seine ersten auf Glas gemalten Werke befinden sich im Nationalmuseum von Koprivniča. Seine Kunst ist reich und sorgfältig ausgearbeitet, sehr wirklich und sehr poetisch zugleich.

Ecole de Hlebine. Paysan et éleveur de bêtes. Son âge prouve que même les tous jeunes peuvent devenir encore d'excellents peintres naïfs. Il a exposé pour la première fois en 1954. Ses premières œuvres peintes sur verre se trouvent au Musée National de Koprivniča. Son art est riche et fouillé, à la fois très réel et très poètique.

EXPOSITIONS:

«Naivni umetnici jugoslavije», Belgrade 1957.
«Laienmaler», Gewerbemuseum, Basel 1961.
Galerie d'Art Primitif, Zagreb 1961.
The Arthur Jeffress Gallery, Londres 1961 (Cat., Préface M. Gelen).
Première Quadriennale des Peintres Naïfs Yougoslaves, Čačac 1962.
«Peintres Naïfs Yougoslaves», Moscou 1962.
«Yugoslav Modern Primitives», Edinburgh 1962.
«Naive Kunst in Jugoslawien», Kunstakademie, Wien 1963.
Galerie St-Etienne, New York 1963.
«Peintres Naïfs Populaires Yougoslaves», Leningrad 1963.
«Sonntagsmaler aus Jugoslawien», Museum am Ostwall, Dortmund 1964.
Mercury Gallery, London 1965 (Cat., Préface Earl of Harewood).
Galerie Bischofberger, Zürich 1965 (Cat., Préface Erika Billeter).

BIBLIOGRAPHIE:

«Yougoslavija», numéro spécial (17) consacré à l'art des naïfs. Belgrade 1959.
Oto Bihalji-Merin: «Das naive Bild der Welt», Köln 1959.
Oto Bihalji-Merin: «Die naive Malerei», Köln 1959.
Oto Bihalji-Merin: «Les Peintres Naïfs», Paris (sans date).
Oto Bihalji-Merin: «Umetnost Naivnich u Jugoslavjii», Belgrade 1963.

Kwiatkowski, Jan

Born July 21, 1894 in Halin (at that time Russia, now Poland).

Geboren am 21. Juli 1894 in Halin (damals Rußland, heute Polen).

Né le 21 juillet 1894 à Halin (en son temps Russie, actuellement Pologne).

His nationalistic schemings led him to Siberia. He escaped and immigrated to France. During the 1914–18 war he joined the army, thus acquiring French nationality. Worked later for a fashion house. Suddenly, however, he left his position (quite a good one) to devote himself entirely to painting. He bore the subsequent poverty with dignity—a poverty which lasted even until quite recently. For his art, which is extremely sensitive, full of subtleties and nuances, does not grip one immediately. But once one comes to love it, one cannot do without it.

Seine nationalistische Tätigkeit führt ihn nach Sibirien. Er flieht und wandert nach Frankreich aus. Meldet sich als Freiwilliger im Ersten Weltkrieg, was ihm die französische Staatsbürgerschaft einträgt. Nach dem Krieg arbeitet er für die Mode. Aber auf einmal gibt er seine gute Stellung auf, um sich ausschließlich der Malerei zu widmen. Er trägt mit Würde den Geldmangel, der bis in die jüngste Zeit andauert. Denn seine äußerst empfindsame Kunst, die ganz aus Zurückhaltung und Nuancen besteht, besticht nicht auf den ersten Blick. Man dringt ganz allmählich in sie ein, aber wenn man einmal drin ist, kann man sie nicht mehr entbehren.

Ses menées nationalistes le conduisent en Sibérie. S'évade et émigre en France. S'engage pendant la guerre de 1914–18, ce qui lui confère la nationalité française. Travaille pour la couture. Mais brusquement, il abandonne son assez belle situation pour se consacrer uniquement à la peinture. Supporte avec dignité le manque d'argent qui dure jusqu'à ces derniers temps. Car son art, l'un des plus sensibles qui soient, tout en discrétion et en nuance, n'accroche pas d'emblée. On y pénètre petit à petit, et une fois dedans, on ne peut plus s'en passer.

EXPOSITIONS:
Galerie du Haut Pavé, Paris 1956
(Cat., Préface Anatole Jakovsky).
Galerie 3, Quai aux Fleurs, Paris 1962
(Cat., Préface Anatole Jakovsky).
«Les Primitifs d'Aujourd'hui»,
Galerie Charpentier, Paris 1964.
Galerie M. Bénézit, Paris 1965
(Cat., Préface R. Barotte, R. Charmet, A. Jakovsky, H. Certigny).

BIBLIOGRAPHIE:
«Jan Kwiatkowski», Petit Crapouillot, N° 10, Paris, octobre 1965.
H. Certigny: «J. Kwiatkowski», avec une introduction d'Anatole Jakovsky, Plon, Paris 1966.

Laforge, Adolphe

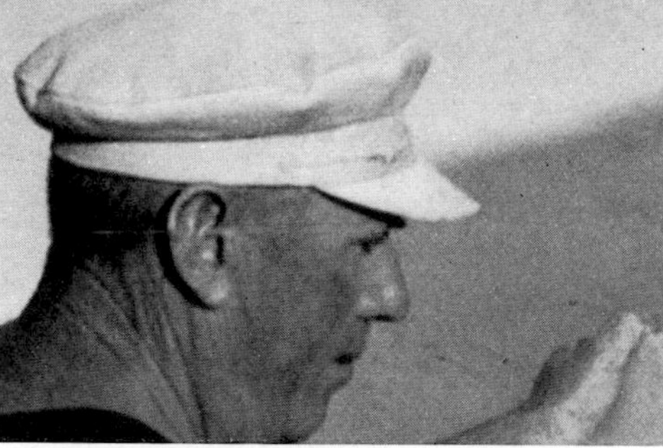

Born July 31, 1892 in Bangor, Belle-Ile-en-Mer (France).

Geboren am 31. Juli 1892 in Bangor, Belle-Ile-en-Mer (Frankreich).

Né le 31 juillet 1892 à Bangor, Belle-Ile-en-Mer (France).

Like the majority of the inhabitants of the island, he started out as a sailor; in fact, he worked on sailing boats under very hard conditions. For instance, as a ship's boy, he had to climb the main mast (with bare feet) whilst sailing near the Arctic Circle. When he had several voyages round the world to his credit, he gave up a sailor's life... and became a policeman, which he remained until he retired. Now he lives from two pensions, and when he is not fishing he paints from memories of scenes in his youth, such as the sailing boats on which he traveled. When he tries to paint pictures other than seascapes, he is less successful. For people of his generation (which is already another age) there remains only this specialized kind of art, which no longer exists.

Wie die meisten Einheimischen war er zuerst Seemann. Unter den übrigens ziemlich mühsamen Bedingungen der Segelschiffahrt. So mußte er als Schiffsjunge z. B. in der Nähe des Polarkreises barfuß den Hauptmast erklimmen. Von mehreren Reisen um die Welt erschöpft, gibt er die Marine auf und wird – Gendarm, bis er den Ruhestand erreicht. Jetzt lebt er von seinen beiden Renten, und wenn er nicht fischt, malt er seine Jugenderinnerungen, u. a. die Segelschiffe, auf denen er gedient hat. Aber wenn er versucht, etwas anderes zu malen als das Meer, hat er leider eine weniger glückliche Hand. Für die Menschen dieser Generation, die noch einer anderen Zeit angehören, zählt einzig und allein diese besondere Kunst, die nicht mehr existiert und nie mehr existieren wird.

Comme la plupart des natifs de l'île, il a commencé par naviguer. Dans des conditions assez pénibles, d'ailleurs, de la marine à voile. Ainsi, jeune mousse, il dut grimper pieds nus sur le grand mât aux abords du cercle polaire. Eprouvé par plusieurs voyages autour du monde, il renonce à la marine et... devient gendarme, ceci jusqu'à sa retraite. Il vit maintenant sur ses deux pensions, et, lorsqu'il ne pêche pas, il peint ses souvenirs de jeunesse: les voiliers sur lesquels il a navigué, entre autres. Mais, lorsqu'il essaye de peindre des paysages autres que la mer, ils deviennent, hélas, moins heureux. Pour les gens de cette génération et déjà d'un autre âge, il n'y a que cet art spécial, comme on n'en fait et n'en fera plus, qui seul compte.

BIBLIOGRAPHIE:
Anatole Jakovsky: «Couleurs du Miracle», Offrandes et Cadeaux, Paris 1948.
Anatole Jakovsky: «Belle-Ile-en-Mer», Ed. La Nef, Paris 1954.
Anatole Jakovsky: «Peintres de Bateaux-Souvenir», Arts et Traditions Populaires, No. 2, Paris 1955.
Anatole Jakovsky: «Belle-Ile-la-Bien-Nommée,» Ed. la Bibliothèque des Arts, Paris 1962.

Lagru, Dominique

Born September 30, 1873 in Perrecy-les-Forges, Saône et Loire (France).
Died February 23, 1960 in Paris (France).

Geboren am 30. September 1873 in Perrecy-les-Forges, Saône et Loire (Frankreich).
Gestorben am 23. Februar 1960 in Paris (Frankreich).

Né le 30 septembre 1873 à Perrecy-les-Forges, Saône et Loire (France).
Mort le 23 février 1960 à Paris (France).

He has been called a shepherd, a miner, and other things, but in fact he was a decorator and molder. One of the main reasons for his thundering success was his beginning to paint at the age of 76! Obviously, if he had had no talent, this would have been merely a flash in the pan—but he did have talent. A great deal, in fact. His prehistoric compositions and his visions of the future may be included among the finest 'naive' paintings of recent years.

Man hat behauptet, er sei Hirte, Grubenarbeiter, usw. gewesen. In Wirklichkeit war er Dekorateur im Baufach. Aber was ihm einen durchschlagenden Erfolg verschafft hat, war die Tatsache, daß er erst im Alter von 76 Jahren zu malen anfing! Das wäre natürlich ein Strohfeuer gewesen, hätte er kein Talent gehabt. Er hatte aber welches. Viel sogar. Sehr viel. Seine prähistorischen Kompositionen und seine Zukunftsvisionen gehören zu den schönsten naiven Bildern dieser letzten Jahre.

On l'a dit pâtre, mineur, etc. En réalité, il était staffeur, ornemaniste. Mais ce qui lui a assuré un succès foudroyant, c'est qu'il a commencé à peindre à l'âge de 76 ans! Evidemment, cela aurait été un feu de paille s'il n'avait pas de talent. Or, il en avait. Beaucoup. Enormément. Ses compositions préhistoriques et ses visions d'anticipation comptent parmi les plus beaux tableaux naïfs de ces dernières années.

EXPOSITIONS:
Galerie Romi, Paris 1951.
Galerie Romi, Paris 1952.
Galerie Vidal, Paris 1957
(Cat., Préface Anatole Jakovsky).
Galerie St-Etienne, New York 1957
(Cat., Préface Anatole Jakovsky).
«Les Peintres Naïfs», Knokke-le-Zoute 1958.
«Les Peintres Naïfs», Maison de la Pensée Française, Paris 1960.
«Laien-Maler», Kunstgewerbemuseum Basel 1961.
«Das naive Bild der Welt», Baden-Baden 1961.
Residenzgalerie, Salzburg 1964.
Galerie Bignou, Paris 1965
(Cat., Préface R. Charmet).

BIBLIOGRAPHIE:
R. Charmet: «Dominique Lagru», Paris (sans date ni nom d'Editeur).
Anatole Jakovsky: «Les Peintres Naïfs», Paris 1956.
Anatole Jakovsky: «Naive Malerei», Zürich 1957.
Oto Bihalji-Merin: «Das naive Bild der Welt», Köln 1959.
Oto Bihalji-Merin: «Die naive Malerei», Köln 1959.
Oto Bihalji-Merin: «Les Peintres Naïfs», Paris (sans date).

Lamy, Marcel

Born 1896 in Paris (France).
Died May 15, 1961 in Paris (France).

Geboren 1896 in Paris (Frankreich).
Gestorben am 15. Mai 1961 in Paris (Frankreich).

Né en 1896 à Paris (France).
Mort le 15 mai 1961 à Paris (France).

A second-hand dealer. Most of the time had a stall in the Flea Market, and also at the scrap iron fair each autumn and the 'ham market' the week before Easter each year. The rest of the time he played about with a paintbrush. His work, although erratic, has unexpected treasures, especially when he was a little more 'touched' than usual. It is curious to note that he sold some of his own pictures on his stall together with the normal Flea Market junk.

Trödler. Verkaufte hauptsächlich auf den Pariser Flohmärkten und jedes Jahr im Herbst auf der Foire à la Ferraille und eine Woche vor Ostern auf der Foire aux Jambons. Die übrige Zeit verbrachte er mit Malen. Ungleichmäßiges Werk, mit unerwarteten Einfällen, wenn das Körnchen Wahnsinn sich stärker bemerkbar macht als gewöhnlich. Das Erstaunlichste ist, daß er seine eigenen Werke neben dem gewöhnlichen Trödelkram des Flohmarkts verkaufte (nicht oft).

Brocanteur. Vendait surtout aux Marchés aux Puces et, deux fois l'an, à la foire à la Ferraille à l'automne et à la Foire aux Jambons la semaine d'avant Pâques. Le reste du temps, il taquinait le pinceau. Œuvre inégale, certes, avec des trouvailles inattendues, lorsque le grain de folie y devient plus sensible que d'habitude. Le plus curieux, c'est qu'il vendait (peu) ses propres œuvres à côté du bric à brac ordinaire des «Puces».

EXPOSITIONS:
Galerie Art Brut, Paris 1948
(Cat., Préface Michel Tapié).
Galerie Le Siècle, Paris 1949/50.

BIBLIOGRAPHIE:
Anatole Jakovsky: «Les Peintres Naïfs», Paris 1956.
Anatole Jakovsky: «Paris mes Puces», Ed. Les Quatre Jeudis, Paris 1957.
«Marcel Lamy», in l'Illustrazione Italiana, novembre 1960.

Lauga, Henri

Born February 18, 1918 in Billève, near Pau (France).

Geboren am 18. Februar 1918 in Billève bei Pau (Frankreich).

Né le 18 février 1918 à Billève, près de Pau (France).

Comes of a farming family. He too worked in the fields. Was on active service in the war and a prisoner of war for five years. Perhaps it was this enforced period of introspection which awoke a dormant vocation—its effect was belated, at any rate, for he started to paint only four years ago. At the moment he is a civil servant. His art is pure and unaffected, sometimes bordering on the fairylike, although he only paints the daily life and work of his region. Has taken part in many exhibitions in provincial galleries but has never had an individual exhibition.

Bauernsohn. Hilft mit bei den Feldarbeiten. Krieg und 5 Jahre Gefangenschaft. Vielleicht hat dieses erzwungene Insichgehen seine im Grunde späte Berufung ausgelöst, denn er malt erst seit 4 Jahren. Gegenwärtig ist er Beamter in der Präfektur. Seine Kunst ist rein und aufrichtig, grenzt manchmal ans Zauberhafte, obwohl er nur die Arbeiten und die Tage seiner Provinz darstellt. Hat in regionalen Salons oft ausgestellt, aber noch in keiner Einzelausstellung.

Fils de fermiers. Participe lui-même aux travaux des champs. La guerre et cinq ans de captivité. Et c'est peut-être ce repliement forcé sur lui-même qui a déclenché sa vocation somme toute tardive, car il ne peint que depuis quatre ans. Actuellement fonctionnaire à la Préfecture. Son art est pur et sincère, touchant parfois à la féerie, bien qu'il ne représente que les travaux et les jours de sa province. A beaucoup exposé dans des salons régionaux, mais n'a pas encore eu d'exposition individuelle.

Lauko, Yurai

Born January 28, 1894 in Szarvas (Czechoslovakia).

Geboren am 28. Januar 1894 in Szarvas (Tschechoslowakei).

Né le 28 janvier 1894 à Szarvas (Tchécoslovaquie).

A butcher by trade. Started to paint about 1928, but purely for his own pleasure and with no thought of exhibiting his works—this explains his relatively late rise to fame. For, in fact, his name did not become known until the time of the large amateur exhibition which took place in Prague and Martin in 1962. Lauko tells stories with his pictures; he narrates the customs of his country, and his art sometimes reaches the level of a real epic poem.

Schweinemetzger. Beginnt 1928 zu malen, aber wirklich nur zu seinem eigenen Vergnügen, ohne Versuch, auszustellen, was seinen ziemlich späten Erfolg erklärt. Denn man sieht seinen Namen zum ersten Mal an der großen Ausstellung der Dilettanten, die 1962 in Prag und in Martin stattfindet. Lauko erzählt Geschichten, schildert die Gebräuche seiner Heimat, und seine Kunst erhebt sich zuweilen zur Würde eines wahrhaft epischen Gesangs.

Charcutier. Commence à peindre vers 1928, mais vraiment pour son propre plaisir, sans chercher à exposer, ce qui explique son succès assez tardif. Car, en effet, on ne voit son nom pour la première fois qu'à la grande exposition des amateurs qui a eu lieu à Prague et à Martin en 1962. Lauko raconte des histoires, il narre les coutumes de son pays et son art s'élève parfois à la dignité d'un véritable chant épique.

EXPOSITIONS:
«Naivni Umeni», Dum Umeni, Brno 1963.
«Naivni Umeni v Ceskoslovensku», Prague 1964
Mestska Galeria, Bratislava 1965
(Cat., Préface Stefan Tkac).

Leal, Paulo Pedro

Born 1894 in Rio de Janeiro (Brazil).

Geboren 1894 in Rio de Janeiro (Brasilien).

Né en 1894 à Rio de Janeiro (Brésil).

Colored, nicknamed 'carioca'. His ancestors were slaves. He had several jobs—railway employee, servant to French settlers in Brazil, etc.—but in 1950 he began to paint on the pavements of Rio. A dealer discovered him and immediately exploited his find, even though Leal's painting is more concerned with telling stories than with quality, is more amusing than of intrinsic worth. Often he copies from magazine pictures of the 1914–18 war.

Neger, das heißt «carioca», der von Sklaven abstammt. Nachdem er mehrere Berufe ausgeübt hat, Eisenbahnangestellter, Dienstbote bei in Brasilien niedergelassenen Franzosen usw. usw., beginnt er 1950 in Rio auf die Gehsteige zu malen. Ein Händler entdeckt ihn und beutet seinen «Fund» alsogleich aus, obwohl Leals Malerei mehr der Anekdote als dem Wert verhaftet, mehr amüsant als wirklich gültig ist. Er kopiert vor allem Bilder aus dem ersten Weltkrieg, die er illustrierten Zeitschriften entnimmt.

Vieux noir, autrement dit «Carioca», descendant d'esclaves. Après avoir exercé plusieurs métiers, employé des chemins de fer, domestique chez des Français établis au Brésil, etc. etc., il se met à peindre sur les trottoirs de Rio. En 1950, un marchand le découvre et exploite aussitôt sa trouvaille, bien que la peinture de Leal soit plus anecdotique que de qualité, plus amusante que réellement valable. Il copie surtout, d'après les illustrés, les images de la guerre 1914–18.

EXPOSITIONS:
Petite Galerie, Rio de Janeiro 1955.
«Peintres Naïfs Brésiliens», Galerie Jacques Massol, Paris 1965.

Lebduska, Lawrence

Born 1894 in Baltimore, Maryland (USA).

Geboren 1894 in Baltimore, Maryland (USA).

Né en 1894 à Baltimore, Maryland (USA).

The son of a Czech-born mirror manufacturer. His parents returned to Europe when he was five years old, taking him with them. Schooling in Leipzig. But at the age of 18 he went back to America and has stayed there ever since. Is an American citizen. Works as an interior decorator and paints whenever he has a minute to spare. His work is solid, resonant and a little peasant in character—perhaps in memory of the fields and villages in the country of his forbears.

Sohn eines Spiegelfabrikanten tschechischer Herkunft. Seine Eltern kehren übrigens mit ihm nach Europa zurück, als er fünf Jahre alt ist. Schule in Leipzig. Aber mit 18 Jahren kehrt er endgültig nach Amerika zurück. Amerikanische Staatsbürgerschaft. Nun arbeitet er als Tapezierer und Dekorateur, malt jedoch in jeder freien Minute. Eine kräftige, volltönende, etwas bäuerliche Malerei, die sich zweifellos an die Felder und Dörfer der Heimat seiner Vorfahren erinnert.

Fils d'un miroitier d'origine tchèque. Ses parents retournent d'ailleurs en Europe, en l'emmenant à l'âge de 5 ans. Etudes à Leipzig. Mais à 18 ans, il retourne en Amérique qu'il ne quittera plus. Citoyen américain. Travaille désormais comme tapissier-décorateur, tout en peignant à chaque instant de liberté. Peinture solide, sonore, un tantinet paysanne, se souvenant, sans doute, des champs et des villages du pays de ses ancêtres.

EXPOSITIONS:
Opportunity Gallery of the Art Center, New York 1926.
Contemporary Art Galleries, New York 1936.
«Masters of Popular Painting», New York 1938.
«Amerikanische Primitive», Museum am Ostwall, Dortmund 1954–55.
«Amerikanische Malerei», Kunstmuseum Luzern 1956.

BIBLIOGRAPHIE:
Sidney Janis: «They taught themselves», Dial Press, New York 1942.
Oto Bihalji-Merin: «Das naive Bild der Welt», Köln 1959.
Oto Bihalji-Merin: «Die naive Malerei», Köln 1959.
Oto Bihalji-Merin: «Les Peintres Naïfs», Paris (sans date).
Anatole Jakovsky: «Eros du Dimanche», Paris 1964.

Leclerc

Born April 9, 1904 in d'Huison-Longueville, Seine-et-Oise (France).

Geboren am 9. April 1904 in D'Huison-Longueville, Seine-et-Oise (Frankreich).

Né le 9 avril 1904 à d'Huison-Longueville, Seine-et-Oise (France).

At the age of twelve he became a mason and has worked at this craft ever since. Became known as an artist during a brief flaring-up of interest in 'naive' art which occurred just after the second world war, when more attention was paid to the artist's trade than to his paintings; in other words, it was the era of 'shepherdesses', 'masons', 'shoemakers' and the like. His work is carefully executed, either pastiches of others or copies pure and simple.

Maurer seit seinem zwölften Jahr. Er übt seinen Beruf übrigens heute noch aus. Er wurde lanciert, als gleich nach dem Zweiten Weltkrieg während kurzer Zeit das Interesse für die naiven Maler aufflammte. Doch war damals der Beruf des Malers wichtiger als seine Malerei. Es war die Zeit der «Schäferinnen», «Maurer» und «Schuster». Mühsame Malerei, ganz einfach Nachahmung und Kopie.

Maçon depuis l'âge de 12 ans. Il exerce toujours son métier. A été lancé pendant une brève flambée de l'intérêt pour les peintres naïfs aussitôt après la seconde guerre mondiale, lorsqu'on s'attachait davantage au métier du peintre qu'à sa peinture, c'est-à-dire l'époque des «bergères», «maçons» et autres «cordonniers». Peinture laborieuse, pastiches et copies pures et simples.

EXPOSITIONS:
Galerie Cambacérès, Paris 1949 (Cat., Préface Pierre Guéguen).
Galerie Cambacérès, Paris 1949 (Cat., Préface Maximilien Gauthier).
Galerie Cambacérès, Paris 1953 (Cat., Préface Maximilien Gauthier).
«Les Primitifs d'Aujourd'hui», Galerie Charpentier, Paris 1964.

Lecossois, Victor

Born March 28, 1897 in Hal, near Brussels (Belgium).

Geboren am 28. März 1897 in Hal, bei Brüssel (Belgien).

Né le 28 mars 1897 à Hal, près de Bruxelles (Belgique).

Born in Flanders but of French ancestry; a member of Napoleon's 'Old Guard', wounded at Waterloo, had decided to stay in that part of Europe. He was a tool-maker, but in an accident at work in 1950 he lost the use of his right hand. As he only received 7% of the invalids' pension, he drew unemployment benefit, fabricated unsellable radios, constructed curtains and bedspreads, until his artistic gifts came to light. It happened quite by chance: his wife asked him to paint a still life for their dining room. It was a success. A secondhand dealer to whom he showed the picture advised him to continue painting. He became caught up in it. He did continue. His interior scenes, as well as his pictures of processions and of other local customs, are among his best works.

Flame französischer Herkunft. Ein bei Waterloo verwundeter Soldat Napoleons, der beschließt, im Land zu bleiben, ist sein Vorfahre. Er selber ist Werkzeugschlosser, doch 1950 beraubt ihn ein Arbeitsunfall des Gebrauchs seiner rechten Hand. Da er nur 7% Arbeitsunfähigkeitsrente bekommt, bezieht er Arbeitslosenunterstützung, bastelt unverkäufliche Radiogeräte, verfertigt Vorhänge und Bettüberwürfe, bis zum Tag, da er sich als Maler entpuppt. Ganz zufällig. Seine Frau bittet ihn, für das Eßzimmer ein Stilleben zu malen. Es gelingt ihm. Ein Trödler, dem er das Bild zeigt, ermuntert ihn, weiterzumalen. Lecossois findet Gefallen daran und fährt tatsächlich fort, zu malen. Seine Interieurs sowie Prozessionen und andere Volksbräuche gehören zu seinen besten Werken.

Flamand, d'origine française. Un «grognard», blessé à Waterloo, qui décide de rester dans le pays. Outilleur-ajusteur, un accident de travail le prive, en 1950, de l'usage de la main droite. N'ayant obtenu que 7% de taux d'invalidité, il émerge du Fond de chômage, fabrique des radios invendables, confectionne des rideaux et couvre-lits, ceci jusqu'au jour où il se révèle peintre. Tout à fait par hasard. Sa femme lui demande de brosser une nature-morte pour leur salle à manger. Il réussit. Un brocanteur auquel il l'a montrée, lui conseille de persévérer dans la peinture. Lecossois est pris au jeu. Il continue, en effet. Ses Intérieurs, ainsi que les Processions et autres coutumes de la vie populaire, sont parmi ses meilleures choses.

EXPOSITIONS:
Galerie La Rose des Vents, Bruxelles 1963.
Galerie l'Escalier, Bruxelles 1964.
Galerie Pan, Gand 1964.
Galerie Pan, Gand 1965.
Galerie La Rose des Vents, Bruxelles 1964.
«Peintres Naïfs Belges», Le Théâtre National, Bruxelles 1965.
«Peintres Naïfs Belges», Musée Royal des Beaux-Arts, Verviers, 1965.
«Peintres Naïfs Belges», Musée Royal des Beaux-Arts, Hasselt 1966.

BIBLIOGRAPHIE:
G. Schmits: «Victor Lecossois», Savoir et Beauté, La Louvière, décembre 1965.

Lefranc, Jules

Born May 12, 1887 in Laval, Mayenne (France).

Geboren am 12. Mai 1887 in Laval, Mayenne (Frankreich).

Né le 12 mai 1887 à Laval, Mayenne (France).

Only son of the owner of an important hardware firm. He would no doubt have taken over the business in due course, if he had not, while still a young man, quite by chance, met Claude Monet. The respect which the Master enjoyed dazzled him. He wrote to Monet, who replied casually: You must paint! So the matter was quite settled. All the same, he continued to work in his father's firm for many years before devoting all his time to painting. Besides, for him, art is a means and not an end—he has nothingt o say. He simply copies photographs, as for instance the famous 'Eiffel Tower' in the Museum of Modern Art in Paris. But despite all this the miracle happens, the miracle of the French craftsman's hand, capable of working wonders. Although his pictures have no soul, they are flawless from the point of view of form. However, his fame is unjustified.

Einziger Sohn des Besitzers einer großen Eisenwarenhandlung. Hätte zweifellos das Geschäft übernommen, hätte er nicht als Jüngling vollkommen zufällig Claude Monet kennengelernt. Das Ansehen, das der Meister genießt, blendet ihn. Er schreibt ihm, und Monet antwortet lakonisch: «Sie müssen malen!» Damit ist sein Weg vorgezeichnet. Indessen kümmert er sich noch lange Zeit um das Geschäft, ehe er sich ganz der Malerei widmet. Für ihn ist sie übrigens ein Mittel, kein Zweck. Er hat nichts auszusagen. Er kopiert sklavisch Photographien, wie jenen berühmten «Eiffelturm», der im Musée d'Art Moderne von Paris hängt. Aber das Wunder geschieht trotzdem, das Wunder der Hand jener französischen Handwerker, die Meisterwerke schaffen. Selbst ohne Seele gelingt es ihm, formal tadellose Bilder zu malen. Auf jeden Fall ist seine Berühmtheit nicht gerechtfertigt.

Fils unique du propriétaire d'une importante maison de quincaillerie. Aurait pris, sans doute, la succession des affaires, si, dans son adolescence, il n'avait pas rencontré, absolument par hasard, Claude Monet. La considération dont jouit le Maître l'éblouit. Il lui écrit, et celui-ci lui répond laconiquement: Il faut peindre! Le voilà donc fixé. Il n'empêche qu'il continuera à s'occuper encore longtemps des affaires, avant de ne faire que de la peinture. D'ailleurs, pour lui, c'est un moyen et non pas un but. Il n'a rien à dire. Il copie servilement les documents photographiques, comme c'est le cas de la fameuse «Tour Eiffel» du Musée d'Art Moderne de Paris. Mais le miracle se fait quand-même, le miracle de la main de ces artisans de France qui font des merveilles. Même sans âme, il arrive à faire une peinture impeccable du point de vue forme. Notoriété de toute façon usurpée.

EXPOSITIONS:
Galerie Carrefour, Paris 1938
(Cat., Préface Jean Cassou).
Galerie Jeanne Castel, Paris 1940.
Galerie de Berri, Paris 1941
(Cat., Préface Rob. Guérin).
Galerie Le Dragon, Paris 1945
(Cat., Préface Anatole Jakovsky).
Galerie Folklore, Lyon 1947
(Cat., Préface Aragon).
Anglo-French Center, London 1948
(Cat., Préface J. Cassou).
Galerie Arc-en-Ciel, Paris 1949
(Cat., Préface Anatole Jakovsky).
Galerie de Berri, Paris 1952/53.
Galerie Mignon-Massart, Nantes 1956
Cat., Préface Anatole Jakovsky).
«Les Peintres Naïfs», Knokke-le-Zoute 1958.
«Les Peintres Naïfs», Maison de la Pensée Française, Paris 1960.
«I Pittori Naifs», Rome 1964.
«Les Primitifs d'Aujourd'hui», Galerie Charpentier, Paris 1964.
Galerie Berri-Lardy, Paris 1964
(Cat., Préface Frédéric Mégret).
«De Lusthoof der Naieven», Rotterdam 1964.
«Le Monde des Naïfs», Paris 1964.

BIBLIOGRAPHIE:
Anatole Jakovsky: «La Peinture Naïve», Paris 1949.
Anatole Jakovsky: «Les Peintres Naïfs», Paris 1956.
Anatole Jakovsky: «Naive Malerei», Zürich 1957.
Oto Bihalji-Merin: «Das naive Bild der Welt», Köln 1959.
Oto Bihalji-Merin: «Die naive Malerei», Köln 1959
Oto Bihalji-Merin: «Les Peintres Naïfs», Paris (sans date).
«Dix Ans d'Art Actuel», Editions Comparaisons, Paris 1964.
«Art Naïf», Editions Marocaines et Internationales, Rabat 1964.
Catalogo Bolaffi d'Arte Moderna 1965/1966, Turin 1966.

Lewin, Jean

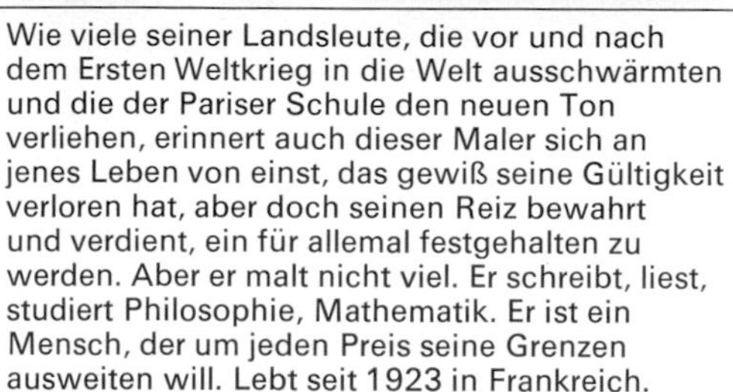

Born July 5, 1905 in Kovel (Russia).

Geboren am 5. Juli 1905 in Kowel (Rußland).

Né le 5 juillet 1905 à Kowel (Russie).

Like many of his fellow-countrymen who scattered over the world before and after the first world war, and who gave the Parisian School its new tone, this artist too recalls his previous life, out of date, no doubt, but full of charm and worthy of being set down for all time. However, he does not paint a great deal. He writes, reads, studies philosophy, also mathematics. A man who tries at all costs to widen his horizons. Has been in France since 1923.

Wie viele seiner Landsleute, die vor und nach dem Ersten Weltkrieg in die Welt ausschwärmten und die der Pariser Schule den neuen Ton verliehen, erinnert auch dieser Maler sich an jenes Leben von einst, das gewiß seine Gültigkeit verloren hat, aber doch seinen Reiz bewahrt und verdient, ein für allemal festgehalten zu werden. Aber er malt nicht viel. Er schreibt, liest, studiert Philosophie, Mathematik. Er ist ein Mensch, der um jeden Preis seine Grenzen ausweiten will. Lebt seit 1923 in Frankreich.

Comme beaucoup de ses compatriotes, qui éssemèrent dans le monde avant et après la première guerre mondiale, et qui ont donné ce ton nouveau à l'Ecole de Paris, ce peintre se souvient, lui aussi, de cette vie d'antan, périmée, certes, mais pleine de charme et qui mérite d'être fixée une fois pour toutes. Mais il ne peint pas beaucoup. Il écrit. Lit, étudie la philosophie. Les mathématiques. C'est un homme qui veut à tout prix élargir ses limites. En France depuis 1923.

Lewis, Flora

(Born Carnell)
Born January 12, 1903 in Atchison, Kansas (USA).

(geborene Carnell)
Geboren am 12. Januar 1903 in Atchison, Kansas (USA).

(née Carnell)
Née le 12 janvier 1903 à Atchison, Kansas (USA).

Has been drawing ever since she was a child and is fond of art and handwork in general: painting, music, embroidery, knitting. But she has never learned to paint. It was only in 1938, when she married a veterinary surgeon and became mistress of her own house, that she had more time to herself and was able to devote her leisure hours to painting. Her religious compositions, which show a naive and yet colorful faith, could be called the plastic equivalent of negro spirituals.

Zeichnet seit ihrer Kindheit und liebt die Künste im allgemeinen: Malerei, Musik, Sticken, Stricken. Aber sie hat nie malen gelernt. Erst als sie 1938 einen Tierarzt heiratet und ihr die Stellung als Hausfrau mehr Muße gewährt, kann sie sich ausgiebiger der Malerei widmen. Ihre religiösen Kompositionen, in denen ein naiver und farbiger Glaube spürbar ist, bilden sozusagen eine plastische Entsprechung zu den Negro Spirituals.

Dessine depuis son enfance et aime l'art en général: peinture, musique, broderie, tricotage. Mais elle n'a jamais appris à peindre. Ce n'est qu'en épousant en 1938 son mari, vétérinaire de son état et devenant donc maîtresse de maison qu'elle a pu, avec des loisirs accrus, se consacrer davantage à la peinture. Ses compositions religieuses, où l'on sent une foi naïve et colorée à la fois, représentent quelque chose comme l'équivalent plastique des Negro Spirituals.

BIBLIOGRAPHIE:

«Flora Lewis», The Art Digest; New York, novembre 1939.
Sidney Janis: «They taught themselves», Dial Press, New York 1942.

Lickova, Anna

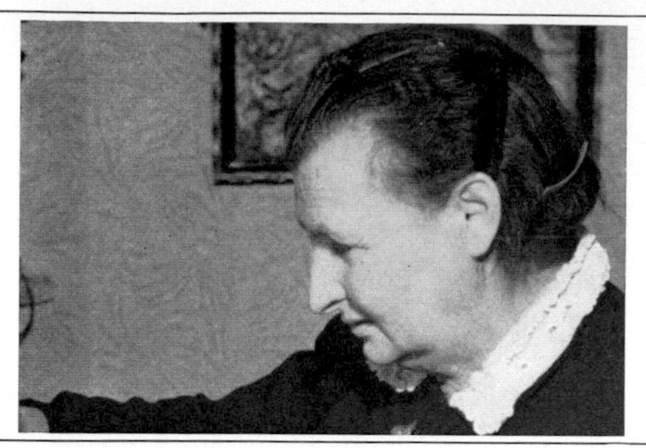

Born July 5, 1895 in Teschen (Czechoslovakia).

Geboren am 5. Juli 1895 in Teschen (Tschechoslowakei).

Née le 5 juillet 1895 à Tesin (Tchécoslovaquie).

Started to paint only about 1953. Housewife. Since 1957 she has taken part in various collective exhibitions, for instance in the 'Exhibition of Popular Artistic Activity' in Bratislava, which made her name. Her art is entirely without malice, full of grace and an innocent freshness. A typical example of a break with traditional popular art.

Beginnt um 1953 zu malen. Gute Hausfrau. Nimmt seit 1957 an zahlreichen Gruppenausstellungen teil, wie zum Beispiel der «Ausstellung des volkstümlichen künstlerischen Schaffens» in Bratislava, durch die sie bekannt wird. Ihre Kunst ist völlig arglos, voll von Anmut und ursprünglicher Frische. Ein typisches Beispiel für den Bruch mit der traditionellen Volkskunst.

Commence à peindre vers 1953. Femme d'intérieur. Dès 1957, participe à de nombreuses expositions collectives, telle, par exemple, « L'Exposition de l'activité artistique populaire» de Bratislava qui la fait connaître. Son art est absolument sans malice, tout de grâce et de fraîcheur première. Un exemple typique de rupture avec l'art populaire traditionnel.

EXPOSITIONS:

Amaterske vytvarnictvo na Slovensku, Prague 1962 (Cat., Préface Stefan Tkac).
«Naivni Umeni», Dum Umeni, Brno 1963 (Cat., Préface M.M. Micko, Stanovsky, Tkac, etc.).
«Naivni Umeni v Ceskoslovensku», Prague 1964 (Cat., Préface par les mêmes noms que le précedent).
Dom Odborov, Zilina 1965 (Cat., Préface Stefan Tkac).

BIBLIOGRAPHIE:

Stefan Tkac: «Anna Lickova», Vitvarny Zivot, N° 4, 1964.
«Anna Lickova», Umenie prostych Rúk, Stredoslovenske Vzdatelstro, 1963.

Ligabue, Antonio

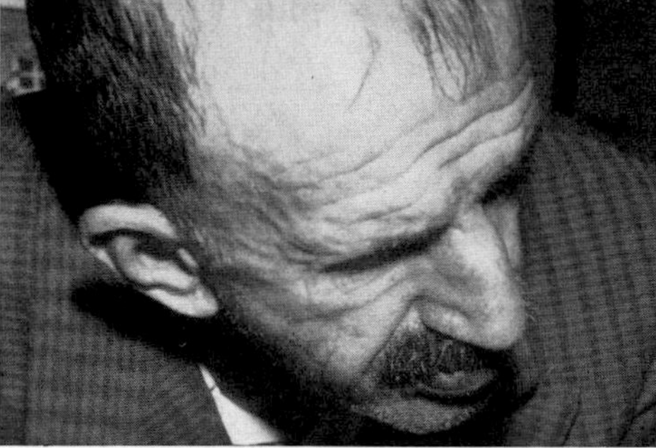

(real name: Laccabue)
Born December 18, 1899 in Zürich (Switzerland).
Died May 27, 1965 in Gualtieri, Reggio Emilia (Italy).

(mit seinem richtigen Namen Laccabue)
Geboren am 18. Dezember 1899 in Zürich (Schweiz).
Gestorben am 27. Mai 1965 in Gualtieri, Reggio Emilia (Italien).

(de son vrai nom: Laccabue)
Né le 18 décembre 1899 à Zurich (Suisse).
Mort le 27 mai 1965 à Gualtieri, Reggio Emilia (Italie).

The son of an Italian woman living abroad, he was given a name by other emigrants which was certainly not his own. He altered his name of his own free will when he returned to Italy, speaking with a slight German accent; he led a wretched and wonderful life. He is quite definitely one of the most extraordinary of the world's 'naive' artists, in other words a raw, untutored genius. He was a vagabond and a poacher, living in the Po valley, and was in and out of several psychiatric institutions until he was finally discovered by the sculptor Mazzacurati. For a little while after that he knew a kind of fame. Essentially, Ligabue has always lived 'apart', in an age and a place where animals speak. Mad rather than 'naive', clairvoyant rather than observant, a wizard rather than an artist, he will always remain living proof of the fact that art is, above all, a gift and a grace and that all the rest is artificial.

Der Fall dieses Sohnes einer italienischen Emigrantin, dem andere Emigranten einen Namen geben, der natürlich nicht der seine ist und den er übrigens später noch umändert, als er, nach Italien zurückgekehrt und mit einem leichten deutschen Akzent sprechend, ein armseliges und wunderbares Dasein führt, ist ganz ohne Zweifel einer der außerordentlichsten Fälle in der naiven Malerei der ganzen Welt. Der Fall eines Genies im Rohzustand. Als Vagabund und Wilddieb lebt er in den Nebeln der Poebene, ist dann Insasse psychiatrischer Anstalten, bis der Bildhauer Mazzacurati ihn endlich entdeckt und er zuletzt doch noch etwas Ruhm kennenlernt. Ligabue hat in Wahrheit immer anderswo gelebt, zu einer Zeit und an einem Ort, wo die Tiere noch sprechen. Mehr verrückt als naiv, mehr Seher als Beobachter, mehr Zauberer als Maler, wird er auf immer das lebende Beispiel dafür bilden, daß die Kunst zuallererst eine Gabe und eine Gnade ist und daß alles andere schöne Worte sind.

Le cas de ce fils d'une émigrante italienne à qui d'autres émigrants donnent un nom, nom qui n'est pas le sien, bien sûr, qu'il transformera d'ailleurs encore de son gré, lorsque, de retour en Italie, et parlant avec un léger accent allemand, il minera une existence misérable et merveilleuse, est, sans aucun doute, l'un des cas les plus extraordinaires de la peinture naïve mondiale. Le cas d'un génie à l'état brut. Vagabond, braconnier, vivant parmi les brouillards de la vallée du Pô, puis l'hôte des établissements psychiatriques jusqu'à ce que le sculpteur Mazzacurati le découvre enfin; puis connaissant sur le tard un semblant de gloire, Ligabue, en vérité, a toujours vécu ailleurs, dans un temps et dans un lieu où les bêtes parlent encore. Plus fou que naïf, plus voyant qu'observateur, plus magicien que peintre, il restera à jamais la preuve vivante que l'art est tout d'abord un don et une grâce et que le reste n'est que littérature.

EXPOSITIONS:
Galleria La Barcaccia, Rome 1961 (Cat., Préface Giancarlo Vigorelli).
Galleria La Perla, Modène 1963 (Cat., extraits de presse).
Galleria Viotti, Turin 1964 (Cat., Préface Gianpaolo Boetti).
E.I.D.A.C.,Milan 1964 (Cat., Préface Mario de Micheli).
«I Pittori Naifs», Rome 1964.
«I Pittori Naifs», Centro Internazionale di Arte Figurative, Biella 1964.
Instituto delle Comunità R.E. 1965 (Cat., Préface Lando Orlich, Mario de Micheli, Anatole Jakovsky et Giancarlo Vigorelli).
Galleria La Perla, Modène 1965 (Cat., Préface Giancarlo Vigorelli et Mario de Micheli).
Cita di Guastalla, R.E. 1965 (Cat., extraits de presse).

BIBLIOGRAPHIE:
«Fantasia di Ligabue», Vita, 2 mai 1961.
Liliana Gregorin: «Ligabue», Il Punto, 16 mars 1963.
Corrado Corradi: «Il Van Gogh di Reggio», ABC, 8 novembre 1964.
Serafino Prati: «Ligabue», sans lieu ni date.
Umberto Bonafini: «Pittori di casa nostra», Editions Stramese, 1964.
Ugo Sassi: «Antonio Ligabue», avec introduction par Anatole Jakovsky, Editions Barcaccia, R.E. 1964.
Catalogo Bolaffi d'Arte Moderna 1965/66, Turin 1966.

FILMS:
Quatre courts métrages sur la vie et sur l'art de Ligabue par Raffaele Andreassi.

Linderoth, Gustaf Fritz Evald

Born May 10, 1898 in Halmstad (Sweden).
Died October 6, 1962 in Antwerp (Belgium).

Geboren am 10. Mai 1898 in Halmstad (Schweden).
Gestorben am 6. Oktober 1962 in Antwerpen (Belgien).

Né le 10 mai 1898 à Halmstad (Suède).
Mort le 6 octobre 1962 à Anvers (Belgique).

A sailor. Lived at one time in Antwerp, and later in Burcht where he 'pottered'—in other words, he collected parts of abandoned boats (porthole fittings, lights, etc.) and promptly sold them to dealers. Eventually he returned to Antwerp, where he died. He was obviously a pauper, for the Consul-General of Sweden had to pay his burial expenses. His landscapes are very primitive, of high quality and painted on all kinds of surfaces: wood, advertisement posters, pieces of sheet metal.

Matrose. Wohnt zuerst in Antwerpen, dann in Burcht, wo er «bastelte», das heißt in verlassenen Schiffen Einzelteile wie Bullaugen, Laternen usw. zusammensuchte, die er dann unverzüglich den Händlern weiterverkaufte. Schließlich kehrte er an seinen Ausgangspunkt Antwerpen zurück, wo er in so großer Armut starb, daß das schwedische Generalkonsulat die Begräbniskosten übernehmen mußte. Seine Landschaften sind schön, sehr naiv und auf alles Mögliche gemalt: Holz, Pappe, Blech.

Marin. Habite d'abord Anvers, puis Burcht où il «bricolait», c'est-à-dire ramassait les pièces des bateaux abandonnés, hublots, lanternes, etc. qu'il revendait immédiatement aux marchands, pour revenir finalement à son point de départ et mourir à Anvers. Mort très pauvre, puisque c'est le consulat général de Suède qui a payé les frais de son enterrement. Ses paysages sont très naïfs, de belle qualité et peints sur n'importe quoi: bois, cartons publicitaires, morceaux de tôle.

Lissia, Elena

Born November 15, 1912 in Rome (Italy).

Geboren am 15. November 1912 in Rom (Italien).

Née le 15 novembre 1912 à Rome (Italie).

Began to paint on Good Friday 1955 when, suddenly taken seriously ill, she saw a visitor bless her. Since then she has taken to art as one takes the veil. Distinguished, restrained, with a definite sense of grandeur, she has been called 'The Roman Woman'—not without justification, even though her work resembles French 'naive' painting rather than that of the other Italian 'naive' artists. She is one of the few who dare (successfully) to tackle large compositions and large subjects.

Beginnt am Karfreitag des Jahres 1955 zu malen, als sie, die schwer krank ist, einen Priester in ihr Landhaus kommen sieht, der sie segnen will. Seither gibt sie sich der Malerei hin, wie man ins Kloster geht. Sie ist vornehm, maßvoll, mit einem unbestreitbaren Sinn für Größe begabt, und man hat sie nicht zu Unrecht «Die Römerin» genannt, obwohl ihre Malerei der französischen naiven Malerei näher steht als den andern naiven Italienern. Sie gehört zu den seltenen Naiven, die sich erfolgreich sowohl an große Kompositionen wie an große Themen getrauen.

Commence à peindre le Vendredi Saint de l'année 1955, lorsque, tombée gravement malade, elle voit arriver chez elle, dans sa maison de campagne, un prêtre venu pour la bénir. Depuis elle entre dans la peinture comme on entre en religion. Racée, mesurée, avec un incontestable sens de grandeur, on l'a appelée «La Romaine» non sans raison, du reste, bien que sa peinture se rapprocherait plutôt de la peinture naïve française que des autres naïfs italiens. Elle est parmi ces naïfs qui osent s'attaquer, avec succès, et aux grandes compositions, et aux grands sujets.

EXPOSITIONS:
Dans son atelier, Rome 1960.
Galerie de l'Institut, Paris 1962
(Cat., Préface Anatole Jakovsky).
«I Pittori Naifs», Rome 1964.
«I Pittori Naifs», Centro Internazionale di Arte Figurative, Biella 1964.
Galleria Piazza di Spagna, Rome 1965
(Cat., Préface Anatole Jakovsky).

BIBLIOGRAPHIE:
Anatole Jakovsky: «Elena Lissia», Editions Dervy-Livres, Paris 1962.
G. di San Lazzaro: «Elena Lissia», Il Tempo, 29 octobre 1962.
Alfredo Mezio: «Elena Lissia», Il Mondo, 4 août 1964.
Anatole Jakovsky: «Elena Lissia», Editions Dervy-Livres, Paris 1964.
Anatole Jakovsky: «Eros du Dimanche», Editions J.J. Pauvert, Paris 1964.
Catalogo Bolaffi d'Arte Moderna, Turin 1965.
Anatole Jakovsky: «Elena Lissia», in Saluto ai naifs italiani, L'Europa Letteraria, N° 29, Rome (sans date).

Litwak, Isreal

Born 1868 in Odessa (Russia).

Geboren 1868 in Odessa (Rußland).

Né en 1868 à Odessa (Russie).

From the age of 21 to 25 he did military service in the Czar's army. Then, in 1903, he went with his wife and his two children to the United States and became an American citizen.
A cabinet-maker by profession. When he was no longer able to work, at the age of 68, he took up painting. Lives in East Flatbush, a suburb of Brooklyn, in what he calls his 'Little Museum'. His unusual perspective and his lively imagination completely transform what he sees and give a festive atmosphere to the majority of his pictures. In this way Fifth Avenue, for instance, seems like the 'Promenade des Anglais' in Nice... Further, the people in his paintings are also not without humor.

Absolviert seinen Militärdienst vom 21. bis 25. Jahr in der zaristischen Armee. Gelangt 1903 mit seiner Frau und seinen zwei Kindern in die Vereinigten Staaten. Amerikanische Staatsbürgerschaft. Tischler. Als er im Alter von 68 Jahren nicht mehr arbeiten kann, fängt er an zu malen. Er wohnt in East Flatbush, einem Vorort von Brooklyn, in einem Haus, das er sein «kleines Museum» nennt. Seine ungewöhnliche Perspektive und seine Phantasie verwandeln alles, was er sieht, von Grund auf und verleihen den meisten seiner Bilder eine festliche Atmosphäre. So wird die Fifth Avenue z. B. eine Art Promenade des Anglais in Nizza... Auch seine Figuren entbehren nicht eines gewissen Humors.

Fait son service militaire de 21 à 25 ans dans les armées du Tsar. Arrive en 1903 avec sa femme et ses deux enfants aux Etats-Unis. Citoyen américain. Ebéniste. A 68 ans, ne pouvant plus exercer son métier, se met à peindre. Il vit à East Flatbush, banlieue de Brooklyn, dans ce qu'il appelle son « Petit Musée ». Sa perspective insolite et son imagination transforment complètement tout ce qu'il voit et donnent un air de fête à la plupart de ses tableaux. Ainsi, la cinquième Avenue devient une sorte de Promenade des Anglais à Nice... Ses personnages ne sont pas exempts, non plus, d'un certain humour.

EXPOSITIONS:
Brooklyn Museum, Brooklyn, N.Y., 1940.
«A Group of Natural Painters»,
Galerie St-Etienne, New York 1952.
«Amerikanische Primitive», Museum am Ostwall; Dortmund 1954–55.
«Amerikanische Malerei», Kunstmuseum, Luzern 1956.
«La Peinture Naïve», Knokke-le-Zoute 1958.
«American Primitive Paintings»,
Smithsonian Institution, Washington 1959.

BIBLIOGRAPHIE:
Sidney Janis: «They taught themselves»,
Dial Press, New York 1942.

Lloyd, James

Born 1906 in Skirpenbeck, Yorkshire (England).

Geboren 1906 in Skirpenbeck, Yorkshire (England).

Né en 1906 à Skirpenbeck, Yorkshire (Angleterre).

After having played an active part in the first exhibition of 'Popular Masters of Reality' England ignored 'naive' artists for a long time. It is only in the last few years that she has tried to make up this loss by actively searching out local 'naive' painters. Lloyd, who paints mainly the countryside and animals, is perhaps the most popular of this new wave of enthusiasm, this 'new look'. His work is charming, varying in quality, tending towards a more and more 'overpolished' technique which is almost photographic.

England hat an der allerersten Ausstellung der «Volkstümlichen Meister der Wirklichkeit» (1938) aktiv teilgenommen, doch sind nachher die Naiven für lange Zeit in Vergessenheit geraten. Erst seit 2 oder 3 Jahren bemüht es sich, diese Verspätung aufzuholen und sucht eifrig nach einheimischen Naiven. Lloyd malt vor allem das Landleben und Tiere. Er ist zweifellos der volkstümlichste unter den Malern dieser neuen Welle des «New Look». Seine Malerei ist gefällig, ungleichmäßig, und entwickelt sich in Richtung auf eine immer gelecktere, beinahe photographische Technik.

L'Angleterre qui, après avoir pris une part active à la toute première exposition des Maîtres Populaires de la Réalité (1938), a longtemps ignoré les naïfs. Ce n'est que depuis ces deux ou trois dernières années qu'elle essaye de rattraper ce retard en recherchant activement les naïfs du cru. Celui-ci, qui peint surtout la campagne et les bêtes, est sans doute le plus populaire de cette nouvelle vague de ce nouveau «New Look». Sa peinture est charmante, inégale, s'orientant vers une technique de plus en plus léchée, fidèle presque photographique.

EXPOSITIONS:
Portal Gallery, London 1964 (Cat. non signé).
«Les Peintres Naïfs», Galerie J.Verrière, Cannes 1966.

BIBLIOGRAPHIE:
Barrie Sturt-Penrose: «Primitives in Private», Observer, 13 février 1966.

Loirand, Maurice

Born July 24, 1922 in Montagne, Loire Atlantique (France).

Geboren am 24. Juli 1922 in Montagne, Loire Atlantique (Frankreich).

Né le 24 juillet 1922 à Montagne, Loire Atlantique (France).

Self-taught artist. Skilled workman. Took an active part in the Resistance movement. He has painted now for about twenty years. His art, clear, precise, 'modern' so to speak, could be related to that of Lefranc, but he is better than Lefranc. For he doesn't paint from photographs but from nature. He makes numerous 'live' sketches and develops and enlarges them later. His sincerity is unimpeachable. Tackles large compositions which put him among the best 'naive' artists of his generation.

Autodidakt. Facharbeiter. Nimmt aktiv an der Résistance teil. Malt seit etwa 20 Jahren. In ihrer Sauberkeit, Präzision, «Modernheit» könnte seine Kunst an Lefranc gemahnen, aber in Wirklichkeit geht sie darüber hinaus. Denn er malt nicht nach Vorlagen, sondern nach der Natur. Er macht immer eine Menge Skizzen, die er dann zu Hause in größerem Format weiterentwickelt. Seine Aufrichtigkeit steht also außer Zweifel. Wagt sich an sehr große Kompositionen, die ihn unter die besten naiven Maler seiner Generation einreihen.

Autodidacte. Ouvrier spécialisé. Prend une part active à la Résistance. Peint depuis une vingtaine d'années. Son art, par son côté net, précis, disons «moderne», s'apparenterait à celui de Lefranc, mais en vérité, il le dépasse. Car ce n'est pas d'après les documents qu'il peint mais d'après nature. Il prend toujours des quantités de croquis sur le vif, qu'il devéloppe ensuite, en grand, chez lui. Sa sincérité est donc hors de doute. S'attaque à de très grandes compositions qui le classent parmi les meilleurs peintres naïfs de sa génération.

EXPOSITIONS:
Galerie Michel Columb, Nantes 1959 (Cat., Préface Anatole Jakovsky).
«Les Peintres Naïfs», Maison de la Pensée Française, Paris 1960.
«I Pittori Naifs», Rome 1964.
«Les Primitifs d'Aujourd'hui», Galerie Charpentier, Paris 1964.

BIBLIOGRAPHIE:
Anatole Jakovsky: «Maurice Loirand», Cahiers de l'Iroise, N° 4, Brest 1957.
Anatole Jakovsky: «Eros du Dimanche», Paris 1964.
«Dix Ans d'Art Actuel», Editions Comparaisons, Paris 1964.

Louardiri, Ahmed

Born May 1928 in Salé (Morocco).

Geboren im Mai 1928 in Salé (Marokko).

Né en mai 1928 à Salé (Maroc).

After having attended the Koran school, he started work (at the age of ten) as a gardener; but from his earliest youth he had loved drawing. He was discovered about ten years ago and since 1960 has taken part in various Salons and collective exhibitions. Almost at the same time, to be precise in 1961, he became a maker of models for Salé's town-planning department, which explains his nickname 'the gardener of Salé'. He is the greatest of the Moroccan 'naive' artists. His work, which is fundamentally poetic, recalls both in its spirit and in its structure the enchanted land of a Thousand and One Nights.

Er besucht die Koranschule und lernt mit zehn Jahren den Beruf eines Gärtners, aber von früher Kindheit an zeichnet er gern. Er wurde vor rund 10 Jahren entdeckt, und nimmt seit 1960 an verschiedenen Salons und Gruppenausstellungen teil. Beinahe gleichzeitig, das heißt 1961, tritt er als Modellbauer in den Dienst der Stadtplanung. Daher sein Übername: «Der Gärtner von Salé». Er ist der größte naive Maler Marokkos. Seine vor allem poetische Kunst gemahnt sowohl im Geist wie in der Form an die Zauberwelt von Tausendundeiner Nacht.

Après être passé par l'Ecole Coranique, il apprend à dix ans le métier de jardinier, mais dès son plus jeune âge, il prend plaisir à dessiner. Découvert depuis une dizaine d'années, il participe, à partir de 1960, aux différents Salons et expositions collectives. Et presqu'en même temps, c'est-à-dire en 1961, il entre au Service de l'Urbanisme en tant que maquettiste. D'où son surnom: «Le jardinier de Salé». C'est le plus grand parmi les naïfs marocains. Son art essentiellement poétique rappelle aussi bien par l'esprit que par la forme, les féeries des Mille et Une Nuit.

EXPOSITIONS:
Galerie à Bab Rouah, 1961.
Galerie à El Jadida, 1963 (Cat., Préface Gaston Diehl).
«2000 Ans d'Art Marocain», Galerie Charpentier, Paris 1963.
Galerie M. Bénézit, Paris 1964 (Cat., Préface Anatole Jakovsky, P. Gaudibert, Fatmi M. Elfatemi, G. Diehl, Mourad Ben Embarek).
«Les Peintres Naïfs», Tanger, Rabat, Marrakech, Casablanca 1964.

BIBLIOGRAPHIE:
J. Brodskis et Mourad Ben Embarek: «Ahmed Louardiri», Ed. de la Jeune Peinture Marocaine, Rabat 1963.
«Art Naïf», Editions Marocaines et Internationales, Rabat 1964.

FILM:
«Le Jardin de Louardiri» court métrage réalisé par André Goldenberg, Rabat 1964.

Lucas, Jean

Born in 1874 in the Côtes du Nord (France).
Died in 1941 in Paris (France).

Geboren 1874 im Departement Côtes du Nord (Frankreich).
Gestorben 1941 in Paris (Frankreich).

Né en 1874 dans les Côtes du Nord (France).
Mort en 1941 à Paris (France).

First of all was a sailor. This explains his pictures of boats which are extremely similar to all the traditional 'boat memory' drawings which sailors all over the world execute during long crossings. Then he joined a circus. For many years he traveled with the small Zanfretta and Fanny circuses, during which time he gained practical experience of this kind of world. But poor Lucas was unlucky enough to fall into the hands of 'art lovers' who sought him out and stocked his paintings. That is why he has never taken part in exhibitions and why no one ever talks of him.

Zuerst Seemann. Das erklärt seine Bilder von Schiffen, die genau all den traditionellen Erinnerungs-Schiffen entsprechen, welche die Matrosen der ganzen Welt während der unendlich langen Seefahrten verfertigten. Dann wird er Zirkusgehilfe. Jahrelang zieht er mit den zwei kleinen Zirkussen Zanfretta und Fanny umher; daher stammen seine ebenfalls nicht in Büchern erworbenen Kenntnisse dieses Milieus. Aber der arme Lucas hatte das Pech, an «Liebhaber» zu geraten, die auf ihn setzten und seine Bilder einlagerten. Darum hat er nie ausgestellt, darum hat man nie von ihm gesprochen.

D'abord marin. Ce qui explique ses tableaux de bateaux qui sont absolument conformes à tous ces traditionnels «bateaux-souvenir» que les marins du monde entier confectionnaient duran les interminables traversées. Puis garçon de cirque. Il suit ainsi, pendant des années, les petits cirques Zanfretta et Fanny, d'où sa connaissance, non livresque, également, de ce milieu. Mais le pauvre Lucas a eu la malchance de tomber sur les «amateurs» qui ont misé sur lui, en stockant ses toiles. C'est pourquoi il n'a jamais exposé, c'est pourquoi on n'a jamais parlé de lui.

BIBLIOGRAPHIE:

Anatole Jakovsky: «La Peinture Naïve», Paris 1949.
Anatole Jakovsky: «Les Peintres Naïfs», Paris 1956.
Anatole Jakovsky: «Naive Malerei», Zürich 1957.

Malpas, Gilles Jean Nicolas

Born December 26, 1901 in Herstal, near Liége (Belgium).

Geboren am 26. Dezember 1901 in Herstal, Lüttich (Belgien).

Né le 26 décembre 1901 à Herstal, Liége (Belgique).

War invalid. Self-taught artist. Painted landscapes, still lifes, nudes. His style is pedantic, elaborate, virtually photographic, which sets him rather apart from the general awkwardness of primitive artists. Has taken part in exhibitions more or less all over Belgium, especially in provincial galleries.

Kriegsinvalide. Autodidakt. Landschaften, Stilleben, Akte. Sehr sorgfältiger, durchgearbeiteter, beinahe photographischer Stil, was ihn ein wenig von der gewohnten Unbeholfenheit der Naiven unterscheidet. Hat ein bißchen überall in Belgien ausgestellt, vor allem in regionalen Veranstaltungen.

Invalide à titre militaire. Autodidacte. Paysages, nature-mortes, nus. Style très minutieux, fouillé, quasi-photographique, ce qui l'éloigne un tant soit peu de la maladresse coutumière des naïfs. A exposé un peu partout en Belgique, surtout dans les salons régionaux.

EXPOSITIONS:
Hôtel du Pont, Esneux 1959.
Palace-Hôtel, Chaudfontaine 1961.
Galerie du Marbre, Liége 1961.
Dans son atelier, Hony-Esneux, 1962, 1963, et 1964.

BIBLIOGRAPHIE:
G. Schmits: «Gilles Malpas», Savoir et Beauté, La Louvière, décembre 1965.

Mandeville, Anne

Born March 11, 1915 in Fossay, Loire Atlantique (France).

Geboren am 11. März 1915 in Fossay, Loire Atlantique (Frankreich).

Née le 11 mars 1915 à Fossay, Loire Atlantique (France).

A photographer in a very small provincial town. To escape from the limitations and monotony of her life, she throws herself with zeal into painting. Her hypersensitive nature found art to be the perfect means of self-expression. She tends her pictures with loving care. A rare 'naive' painter, capable of conveying the fluid, ever-changing atmosphere of Western France.

Photographin in einer ganz kleinen Provinzstadt. Um dem engen Milieu und der Eintönigkeit des Lebens zu entgehen, wirft sie sich mit Leidenschaft auf die Malerei. Ihre überempfindsame Natur findet hier ein ideales Betätigungsfeld. Sie arbeitet ihre Bilder sorgfältig aus, poliert daran herum, liebkost sie gewissermaßen. Einer der seltenen naiven Maler, dem es gelingt, die wechselnde, flüssige Atmosphäre Westfrankreichs wiederzugeben.

Photographe d'une toute petite ville de province. Pour échapper à un milieu fermé et à la monotonie de la vie, elle se lance dans la peinture avec passion. Sa nature hypersensible y trouve un champ d'action rêvé. Ses tableaux, elle les soigne, les fignole, les caresse ou presque. Rare naïve qui arrive à rendre l'atmosphère fluide et changeante de l'Ouest de la France.

EXPOSITIONS:
«I Pittori Naifs», Rome 1964.
«Les Primitifs d'Aujourd'hui», Galerie Charpentier, Paris 1964.

BIBLIOGRAPHIE:
Anatole Jakovsky: «Anne Mandeville», Cahiers de l'Iroise, N° 4, Brest 1962.

Mary-Bisiaux, Reine

Born April 19, 1846 in Noyelles-sur-Sambre (France).
Died April 19, 1929 in Noyelles-sur-Sambre (France).

Geboren am 19. April 1846 in Noyelles-sur-Sambre (Frankreich).
Gestorben am 19. April 1929 in Noyelles-sur-Sambre (Frankreich).

Née le 19 avril 1846 à Noyelles-sur-Sambre (France).
Morte le 19 avril 1929 à Noyelles-sur-Sambre (France).

Grandmother of the artist Marcel Gromaire. She instilled in him a love for nature and taught him the basic rules of drawing. As for her—she lived on a pleasant estate in the North of France, able to spend her time happily with no need to do anything—but she chose to devote all her leisure time to painting pictures, which she executed with extreme care. Delicate and sensitive art, sometimes rather oriental in style.

Großmutter des Malers Marcel Gromaire. Sie hat ihm die Liebe zur Natur und auch die ersten Grundbegriffe des Zeichnens beigebracht. Sie selber lebte auf einem schönen Gut in Nordfrankreich, wo sie ihre Tage glücklich hätte verbringen können, ohne zu arbeiten. Indessen widmete sie ihre ganze freie Zeit der Malerei, auf die sie viel Sorgfalt verwendete. Feinsinnig, empfindsam, zuweilen an orientalische Kalligraphie erinnernd.

Grande-mère du peintre Marcel Gromaire. C'est elle qui lui a inculqué l'amour de la nature, de même que les premiers rudiments du dessin. Quant à elle, vivant dans une belle propriété du Nord de la France, où elle pouvait vivre heureuse sans rien faire, elle a consacré néanmoins tous ses loisirs à la peinture à laquelle elle apportait beaucoup de soins. Fine, sensible, frisant parfois le graphisme oriental.

BIBLIOGRAPHIE:

Marcel Gromaire: «La vie et l'œuvre de Reine Mary-Bisiaux», Editions Seheur, Paris 1931.

Maurer, Moshe

Born June 28, 1891 in Brody (Poland).

Geboren am 28. Juni 1891 in Brody (Polen).

Né le 28 juin 1891 à Brody (Pologne).

Was a manufacturer of artists' paintbrushes. Now lives in London, having acquired British nationality. Daily he handled brushes and was in contact with artists, and at the age of sixty he experienced a desire to try to paint himself. His pictures are of scenes in the life of small Jewish communities in Central Europe, still leading a pious and tradition-defined life. He is in some ways a 'naive' Chagall.

Fabrikant von Pinseln für Kunstmaler. Wohnt in London. Britische Staatsangehörigkeit. Da er ständig mit Pinseln zu tun hat und täglich mit Künstlern in Berührung kommt, erfaßt ihn im Alter von 60 Jahren der Wunsch, selber zu malen. Er schildert Szenen aus dem Leben der kleinen, noch von Glauben und Traditionen erfüllten jüdischen Gemeinschaften in Mitteleuropa. Er ist gewissermaßen ein naiver Chagall im Rohzustand.

Fabricant de pinceaux pour artistes. Habite Londres. Nationalité britannique. Or, maniant justement les pinceaux et voyant quotidiennement les artistes, le désir de peindre lui-même lui vient à l'âge de 60 ans. Et ce sont des scènes de la vie des petites communautés israëlites de l'Europe Centrale, encore pleines de foi et de traditions. Il est en quelque sorte le Chagall naïf, absolument à l'état brut.

EXPOSITIONS:
St. George Gallery, London 1955.
Ben Uri Art Gallery, London 1957 (Cat., Préface Pierre Rouve).
Genootschap d'nai B'Ritt, Anvers 1958.
Kunsthandel-Santee, Landeweer 1958.
Gallery-One, London 1960.
Galerie Vendôme, Bruxelles 1964.
Molton Gallery, London 1964 (Cat., Préface par l'artiste).
Galerie Hilt, Bâle 1965 (Cat., Préface Anatole Jakovsky).

BIBLIOGRAPHIE:
«Moshe Maurer», The Times Wednesday, 15 mai 1957.

Maynard, Bill

Born 1932 in Newbury (England).

Geboren 1932 in Newbury (England).

Né en 1932 à Newbury (Angleterre).

Was a reader in English at Cambridge University. Then, after military service, instead of continuing the academic career he had begun so brilliantly, he gave up everything and went to live quite alone in a tiny village in order to devote himself to painting. A tormented soul, searching and meditating. Although his work is very individual and original, it nevertheless has much in common with that of the 'bonesetter' in Northern France, Joseph Crépin, and also with Scottie Wilson. Has not yet held an individual exhibition of his work, although paintings of his can be found in various museums, for instance in the one in São Paulo.

Zuerst Englischlektor an der Universität Cambridge. Nach Absolvierung seines Militärdienstes kehrt er aber nicht zu seiner so glänzend begonnenen akademischen Laufbahn zurück, sondern gibt alles auf und zieht in ein winziges Dorf, wo er sich in völliger Einsamkeit der Malerei widmet. Er ist ein Sucher, ein nachdenklicher, gequälter Mensch. Seine sehr persönliche und sehr originelle Kunst weist indessen eine gewisse Verwandtschaft auf mit jener von Joseph Crépin, dem nordfranzösischen Heilpraktiker, und auch mit jener seines Landsmanns Scottie Wilson. Er hat noch keine Einzelausstellung veranstaltet, obwohl sich Werke von ihm bereits in mehreren Museen, so zum Beispiel in dem von São Paulo, befinden.

D'abord lecteur d'anglais à l'Université de Cambridge. Puis, après son service militaire, au lieu de continuer une carrière académique si brillamment commencée, il abandonne tout et va vivre, en solitaire, dans un tout petit village, afin de se consacrer à la peinture. Un chercheur. Un méditatif. Un tourmenté. Son art, très personnel et très original, s'apparente, cependant, avec celui du «rebouteux» du Nord de la France, Joseph Crépin, si ce n'est avec celui de son compatriote Scottie Wilson. N'a pas encore eu d'exposition individuelle, bien que ses œuvres se trouvent déjà dans plusieurs musées, celui de São Paulo, entre autres.

Mehkek, Martin

Born August 7, 1936 in Novacka, near Gola (Yugoslavia).

Geboren 7. August 1936 in Novacka, bei Gola (Jugoslawien).

Né le 7 août 1936 à Novacka, près de Gola (Yougoslavie).

A Croatian, who was born a peasant and has remained one all his life. A member of the Hlebine school. He depicts views of his village, perhaps rather more clumsily than the other artists; but he also paints heads—expressive, roughly hacked out, very medieval faces.

Kroate. Schule von Hlebine. Ist und bleibt Bauer. Er malt Szenen aus seinem Dorf, vielleicht ein bißchen unbeholfener als die andern, aber auch Köpfe, wie mit dem Rebmesser geschnitzte, sehr mittelalterlich anmutende Köpfe.

Croate. Ecole de Hlebine. Est et reste paysan. Il peint des scènes de son village, un peu plus maladroitement peut-être que les autres, mais aussi des têtes, des têtes expressives, taillées à coups de serpe, très mediévales.

EXPOSITIONS:
« Naivni umetnici jugoslavije », Belgrade 1957.
« Première Quadriennale des Peintres naïfs Yougoslaves », Čačac 1962.
«Yugoslav Modern Primitives», Edinburgh 1962.
« Peintres Naïfs Yougoslaves », Moscou 1962.
« Naive Kunst in Jugoslawien », Kunstakademie, Wien 1963.
« Peintres naïfs Populaires Yougoslaves », Leningrad 1963.
Galerie de la Madeleine, Bruxelles 1964 (Cat., Préface Miodrag Kolarič).
Galerie Brinken, Stockholm 1966.

BIBLIOGRAPHIE:
«Yougoslavija», numéro spécial (17) consacré à l'art des naïfs, Belgrade 1959.
Oto Bihalji-Merin: « Das naive Bild der Welt », Köln 1959.
Oto Bihalji-Merin: « Die naive Malerei », Köln 1959.
Oto Bihalji-Merin: « Les Peintres Naïfs », Paris (sans date).
Oto Bihalji-Merin: « Umetnost Naivnich u Jugoslavjii », Belgrade 1963.

Meijer, Salomon (Sal)

Born 1877 in Amsterdam (Netherlands).

Geboren 1877 in Amsterdam (Holland).

Né en 1877 à Amsterdam (Hollande).

Originally a diamond-cutter, he devoted his life to painting in 1914. He is fond of painting picturesque landscapes (which he does on visits to Belgium and Switzerland) but also paints cats and still-life pictures. At the moment he lives in Blaricum. An exhibition of his work was given at Laren to celebrate his eightieth birthday, and one year later the Amsterdam Municipal Art Gallery held a similar exhibition.

Ehemaliger Diamantenschleifer. Widmet sich von 1914 an der Malerei. Am liebsten malt er pittoreske Landschaften (wenn er zum Beispiel nach Belgien oder in die Schweiz eingeladen ist), aber auch Stilleben und Katzen. Gegenwärtig lebt er in Blaricum. In Laren wurde eine Jubiläumsausstellung veranstaltet, und ein Jahr später folgte das Städtische Museum von Amsterdam diesem Beispiel.

Ancien tailleur de diamants. Se consacre à la peinture à partir de 1914. Il peint de préférence des sites pittoresques (lorsqu'il est invité en Belgique ou en Suisse, par exemple), mais aussi des natures mortes et des chats. Il vit actuellement à Blaricum. Une exposition-jubilé a consacré son activité à Laren et, un an après, le Musée Communal d'Amsterdam suivait cet exemple.

EXPOSITIONS:
«Moderne Primitieven», Stedelijk Museum, Amsterdam 1941 (Cat., Préface D.C.R.).
«Maler des einfältigen Herzens», Museum am Ostwall, Dortmund 1952.
Hamdorf, Laren 1957.
Stedelijk Museum, Amsterdam 1958.
«La Peinture Naïve», Knokke-le-Zoute 1958.
«De Lusthof der Naieven», Rotterdam 1964.
«Le Monde des Naïfs», Paris 1964.
Galerie Meken, Amsterdam 1966.

BIBLIOGRAPHIE:
Oto Bihalji-Merin: «Das naive Bild der Welt», Köln 1959.
Oto Bihalji-Merin: «Die naive Malerei», Köln 1959.
Oto Bihalji-Merin: «Les Peintres Naïfs», Paris (sans date).
Naive Maler, par A. Hernandez, in Atlantis, Zürich No. 11, novembre 1961.

Metelli, Orneore

Born June 2, 1872 in Terni (Italy).
Died November 26, 1938 in Terni (Italy).

Geboren am 2. Juni 1872 in Terni (Italien).
Gestorben am 26. November 1938 in Terni (Italien).

Né le 2 juin 1872 à Terni (Italie).
Mort le 26 novembre 1938 à Terni (Italie).

Contrary to the general idea of this so-called 'shoemaker', he was by no means simply a humble workman but a well-known manufacturer of footwear.
He was awarded gold and silver medals in international exhibitions for his models, and was even nominated a member of the selection committee for an exhibition in Paris in 1911.
For relaxation, if it can be called that, he played the trombone. So he was very much upset when, at the age of about fifty, he was forbidden by his doctors to do that sort of thing lest he injure his heart. It was then he began to paint. His work is interesting, varied and sincere—but the main reason he is so well known in Italy and abroad is that the number of his paintings is so great. This time one can really speak of the 'complete works' of an artist.

Im Gegensatz zu dem, was man im allgemeinen von diesem «Schuster» denkt, handelt es sich hier keineswegs um einen bescheidenen Handwerker, sondern vielmehr um einen Schuhfabrikanten, der in seiner Vaterstadt und anderswo hohes Ansehen genießt. Er bekommt an internationalen Ausstellungen Gold- und Silbermedaillen für seine Schuhmodelle und wird anläßlich einer 1911 in Paris stattfindenden Ausstellung zum Ehrenmitglied der Jury ernannt. Um sich zu zerstreuen, bläst er Posaune. Groß ist daher seine Bestürzung, als ihm die Ärzte im Alter von 50 Jahren diese Anstrengungen untersagen, denn er muß sein Herz schonen. Nun erst fängt er an zu malen. Seine Malerei ist interessant, abwechslungsreich, aufrichtig, aber den beträchtlichen Widerhall in Italien und im Ausland findet sie vor allem wegen der großen Anzahl der Bilder. Hier steht man wirklich einem Werk gegenüber.

Contrairement à ce que l'on pense, généralement, de ce «Cordonnier», il ne s'agit là, nullement d'un modeste artisan, mais plutôt d'un fabricant de chaussures ayant pignon sur rue dans sa bonne ville natale. Et pas seulement à Terni. Il reçoit des médailles d'or et d'argent dans des expositions internationales, pour ses modèles, et est nommé même juré d'honneur d'une exposition en 1911 à Paris. Pour se distraire, eh bien, il jouait du trombone. Aussi quel ne fut son désarroi, lorsque, arrivant à la cinquantaine, les médecins lui interdisent ces exercices à cause de son cœur. Il s'est mis alors à faire de la peinture. Elle est intéressante, variée, honnête, mais si elle a eu un tel retentissement en Italie et à l'étranger, c'est surtout par le nombre important de toiles dont elle se compose. On se trouve vraiment en présence de ce que l'on peut appeler une œuvre. Voilà.

EXPOSITIONS:
Galleria del Secolo, Rome 1945.
Galleria di Roma, Rome 1946.
Kunsthalle Bern, Berne 1947.
Galerie d'Art moderne, Bâle 1947.
Guilde du Livre, Lausanne 1947.
Galerie Wolfensberger, Zurich 1948.
Kunstmuseum, Bâle 1949.
Galerie Palmes, Paris 1950 (Cat., Préface Aurelio de Felice, etc.).
The Hanover Gallery, London 1951.
Galerie Charpentier, Paris 1952 (Cat., Préface Maximilien Gauthier).
«Mostra di Pittura Popolare», Palazzo delle Esposizione, Rome 1955.
Galleria Galatea, Turin 1957 (Cat., Préface Ezio Metelli).
Centro Culturale Olivetti, Ivrea 1958 (Cat., Préface Ezio Metelli).
«Les Peintres Naïfs», Knokke-le-Zoute 1958.
«Das naive Bild der Welt», Baden-Baden 1961.
«Laienmaler», Gewerbemuseum, Basel 1961.
«I Pittori Naifs», Rome 1964.
«De Lusthof der Naieven», Rotterdam 1964.
«Le Monde des Naïfs», Paris 1964.
«Die Welt der naiven Malerei», Salzburg 1964.
«Galerie Bettie Thommen», Basel 1965 (Cat., Préface non signée).

BIBLIOGRAPHIE:
Luigi Bartolini: «O. Metelli», All'Insegna del Pesce d'Oro, Milan 1948.
E. Metelli, A. de Felice et L. Sinisgalli: «O. Mettelli, le cordonnier de Terni», Editions de Luca, Roma 1950.
P. Courthion: «Orneore Metelli», Editions P. Cailler, Genève 1951.
Libero Bigiaretti: «Orneore Metelli», Cercolo Culturale, Ivrea 1957.
Oto Bihalji-Merin: «Das naive Bild der Welt», Köln 1959.
Oto Bihalji-Merin: «Die naive Malerei», Köln 1959.
Oto Bihalji-Merin: «Les Peintres Naïfs», Paris (sans date).
Calendrier Publicitaire Mural, édité par la maison des machines à écrire Olivetti pour 1964.
«Art Naïf», Editions Marocaines et Internationales, Rabat 1964.
Album de 12 planches en couleurs, introduction par Libero Bigiaretti, Ivrea 1964.
Catalogo Bolaffi d'Arte Moderna 1965/66, Turin 1966.

CAVAL RIZZA UMBERTO I
O. METELLI

Mergeay, Jean-Baptiste

Born November 15, 1877 in Bertrix (Belgium).

Geboren am 15. November 1877 in Bertrix (Belgien).

Né le 15 novembre 1877 à Bertrix (Belgique).

At one time a farmer, then a joiner. Has painted since 1950. His touching pictures, which seem to tell of the 'good old days', have never been exhibited. He was discovered quite by chance by Georges Schmits.

Ehemals Bauer, dann Schreiner. Malt seit 1950. Hat seine rührenden Bilder, die an die gute alte Zeit erinnern, nie ausgestellt. Zufällig von Georges Schmits entdeckt.

Ancien cultivateur, puis menuisier. Peint depuis 1950. Il n'a jamais exposé ces tableaux touchants, comme qui dirait du «Bon, vieux temps». Découvert par hasard par M. Georges Schmits.

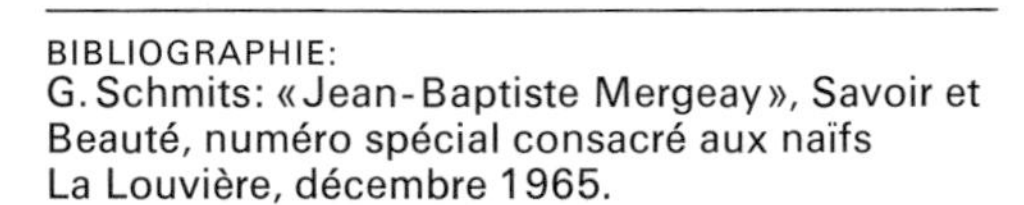

BIBLIOGRAPHIE:

G. Schmits: «Jean-Baptiste Mergeay», Savoir et Beauté, numéro spécial consacré aux naïfs La Louvière, décembre 1965.

Mozzali, Andres

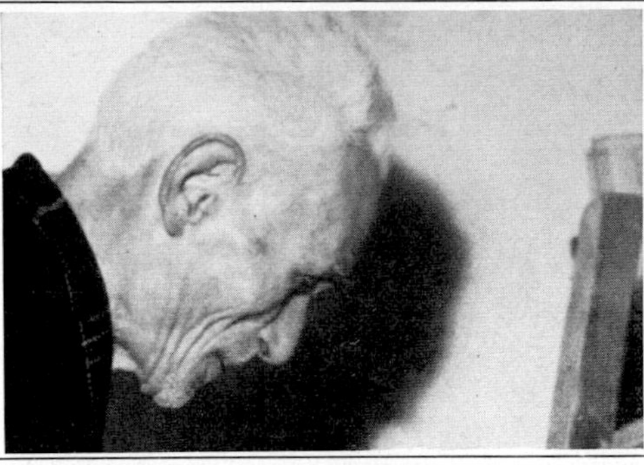

Born June 4, 1895 in Guastalla, Reggio Emilia (Italy).

Geboren am 4. Juni 1895 in Guastalla, Reggio Emilia (Italien).

Né le 4 juin 1895 à Guastalla, Reggio Emilia (Italie).

Picture restorer, repairer of old furniture, sculptor. He had artistic hands and a taste for the beautiful things he handled daily (a heritage of the medieval artisans), and began to paint about 1940, in the middle of the war. He painted to express what he thought about life and also about death. The pictures are mainly allegories, the majority of which are faintly epic in character. He has been awarded a number of prizes in local exhibitions.

Restaurator alter Möbel, Bildhauer. Er hat eine geschickte Hand und die von den Handwerkern von einst geerbte Freude an den schönen Dingen, die er täglich handhabt, und so fängt er 1940, mitten im Krieg, an zu malen. Vor allem, um zu sagen, was er vom Leben und vom Tod denkt. Seine Bilder sind in der Mehrzahl Allegorien, die eines gewissen epischen Atems nicht entbehren. Hat in regionalen Gruppenausstellungen mehrmals Preise errungen.

Restaurateur, réparateur de meubles anciens, sculpteur. Ayant une belle main et le goût des belles choses qu'il manie quotidiennement, hérité des artisans d'autrefois, il se met à la peinture vers 1940, en pleine guerre. Et c'est surtout pour dire ce qu'il pense de la vie, de la mort. Ce sont des allégories pour la plupart qui ne manquent pas d'un certain souffle épique. A obtenu plusieurs prix dans des expositions collectives régionales.

EXPOSITIONS:
Casa d'Arte, Guastalla 1962
(Cat., Préface Attillio Bertolucci, Dino Villani et Luciano Budigna).
«I Pittori Naifs», Rome 1964.
«I Pittori Naifs», Centro Internazionale di Arte Figurative, Biella 1964.

BIBLIOGRAPHIE:
Nevio Jori: «Mozzali», Gazzetta di Regio, 10 juillet 1964.
Umberto Bonafini: «Pittori di casa nostra», Edizione Stramese, Guastalla 1964.

Grandma Moses

(real name: Anna Mary Robertson)
Born September 7, 1860 in Greenwich, New York (USA).
Died December 13, 1961 in Hoosick Falls, New York (USA).

(mit ihrem richtigen Namen Anna Mary Robertson). Geboren am 7. September 1860 in Greenwich, N.Y. (USA).
Gestorben am 13. Dezember 1961 in Hoosick Falls, New York (USA).

(de son vrai nom: Anna Mary Robertson).
Née le 7 septembre 1860 à Greenwich, N.Y. (USA).
Morte le 13 décembre 1961 à Hoosick Falls, New York (USA).

What would we have had to say about this lady, who married Thomas Salmon Moses at the age of 27, became a farmer's wife when the couple bought the famous Eagle Bridge farm in 1905 (which many people erroneously think to be where she was born), who bore ten children of which only five survived, if she had not suddenly, in 1930, decided to take up painting? In fact, nothing! She had a hard life, whether happy or unhappy is not the point—it was a life without fame. Nor would we have had much to say about it if the Second World War had not suddenly brought her to the forefront of American artistic life. This was how it happened: the American people, who really love 'naive' art, felt frustrated because they were deprived of their adored French 'naive' painters, and fell back on artists of a similar style in their own country. And there was a grandmother who was still painting at the age of eighty... Imagine the publicity, the godsend this was ! Thus, in a very short time, Grandma Moses became famous, almost a national heroine. She became a Doctor honoris causa of Russell Sage College, Troy (New York) in 1949, and of the Moore Institute of Art, Philadelphia, in 1951; and her hundredth birthday was declared 'Grandma Moses' Day' by the governor of New York. So this pleasant artist, whose work is neither better nor worse than so many others who had known the United States for a large part of the nineteenth century (truly the golden age in American 'naive' painting), gradually turned into a valuable export. She died, aged over a hundred, in a Hoosick Falls, New York nursing home.

Was wäre von dieser jungen Frau zu sagen, die mit 27 Jahren Thomas Salmon Moses heiratete, Bäuerin wurde – denn das Ehepaar kaufte 1905 den berühmten Hof Eagle Bridge bei New York, der übrigens allgemein als ihr Geburtsort betrachtet wird –, die zehn Kinder zur Welt brachte, von denen nur fünf überlebten, hätte sie nicht 1930 zu malen angefangen? Nichts. Ein arbeitsames, glückliches oder unglückliches, ereignisloses Leben. Wir würden uns auch nicht besonders mit ihr befassen, hätte nicht ein bestimmter Umstand, nämlich der zweite Weltkrieg, sie plötzlich im künstlerischen Leben Amerikas auf den vordersten Platz gerückt. Die Amerikaner, welche die Naiven aufrichtig lieben, mußten nämlich unversehens auf die französischen Naiven verzichten, in die sie bisher ganz vernarrt waren, und sich mit den einheimischen Malern zufriedengeben. Dazu eine Großmutter, die noch mit achtzig Jahren malt... Welch ein Glücksfall, welch gefundenes Fressen für die Reklame! Und so wird sie in kürzester Zeit eine bedeutende Persönlichkeit, beinahe eine Nationalheldin. 1949 wird sie zum Doctor honoris causa des Russel Sage College von Troy (N.Y.) ernannt, 1951 widerfährt ihr die gleiche Ehre vom Moore Institute of Art in Philadelphia, und ihr hundertster Geburtstag wird vom Gouverneur von New York zum «Grandma Moses Day» erklärt. So wird diese hübsche Malerei, die weder schlechter noch besser ist als so manche andere, die im 19. Jahrhundert, dem wahren Goldenen Zeitalter der naiven amerikanischen Malerei, in den Vereinigten Staaten hervorgebracht wurde, allmählich ein glorreicher Ausfuhrartikel. Grandma Moses ist im Alter von über 100 Jahren in einer Privatklinik in Hoosick Falls, N.Y., gestorben.

Qu'aurions-nous à dire de cette jeune femme de 27 ans qui épouse Thomas Salmon Moses, devient fermière, puisque le couple achète, en 1905, la fameuse ferme de Eagle Bridge, près de New York, que tout le monde, du reste, lui attribue comme lieu de sa naissance, accouche de 10 enfants, dont ne survivent que cinq, si, à un moment donné, en 1930, pour être précis, elle ne s'était pas mise à peindre? Rien, n'est-ce pas? Une vie laborieuse, heureuse ou malheureuse, qu'importe –, sans histoire. Comme nous n'aurions pas épilogué sur elle outre mesure si une certaine conjoncture, qui s'appelle la guerre de 1940, ne l'avait pas placée soudain au tout premier plan de la vie artistique américaine. Eh oui, ce peuple qui aime les naïfs vraiment d'amour, s'est senti donc frustré, privé des naïfs français dont il raffolait jusque-là et dut se rabattre sur les naïfs du terroir. Puis une grand-mère qui peint encore à 80 ans... Quelle publicité, quelle aubaine! Et c'est ainsi, qu'en très peu de temps, elle devient un personnage important, presque une héroïne nationale. Elle est promue Docteur Honoris Causa de Russel Sage College de Troy (N.Y.) en 1949, celui de Moor Institute of Art de Philadelphie en 1951, et le jour de ses cent ans est proclamé Grandma Moses Day par le gouverneur de New York. Ainsi cette aimable peinture, ni plus mauvaise ni meilleure que tant d'autres, qui ont vu le jour aux Etats-Unis tout au long du XIXe siècle – véritable âge d'or de la peinture naïve américaine – devient petit à petit une gloire d'exportation. Elle est morte plus que centenaire dans la maison de santé de Hoosick Falls, N.Y.

EXPOSITIONS:
Galerie St-Etienne, New York 1940.
Ambassade des Etats-Unis, Paris 1950 (Cat., Préface Louis Bromfield et Otto Kallir).
«Amerikanische Malerei», Kunstmuseum, Luzern 1954.
«Amerikanische Primitive», Museum am Ostwall, Dortmund 1954–55.
Galerie St-Etienne, New York 1955 (Cat., Préface Thomas J.Watson.
The Mattiessen Gallery, Londres 1956 (Cat., Préface Otto Kallir).
Galerie St-Etienne, New York 1957 (Cat., Préface Hubertus von Loewenstein).
«American Primitive Paintings», The Smithsonian Institution, Washington 1958.
«La Peinture Naïve», Knokke-le-Zoute 1958.
I.B.M. Gallery of Arts and Sciences, New York 1960 (Cat., Préface par elle-même).
Musée d'Art Moderne de la Ville, Paris 1962 (Cat., Préface Otto Kallir).
Galerie St-Etienne, New York 1962 (Cat., Préface Otto Kallir).
«Die Welt der Naiven Malerei», Salzburg 1964.
«De Lusthof der Naieven», Rotterdam 1964.
«Le Monde des Naïfs», Paris 1964.
Galerie St-Etienne et Hammer Galleries, New York 1965.

BIBLIOGRAPHIE:
Sidney Janis: «They taught themselves», Dial Press, New York 1942.
Otto Kallir: «Grandma Moses», avec une introduction par Louis Bromfield, Dryden Press, New York 1946; Réédition chez Doubleday, New York 1947).
Jean Lipman et Alice Winchester: «Primitive Painters in America», Dodd Mead & Co., New York 1950.
B. Jasmand et Otto Kallir: «Sonntagsmaler», Otto Aug. Ehlers, Berlin/Darmstadt 1956.
Oto Bihalji-Merin: «Das naive Bild der Welt», Köln 1959.
Oto Bihalji-Merin: «Die naive Malerei», Köln 1959.
Oto Bihalji-Merin: «Les Peintres Naïfs», Paris (sans date).
«Grandma Moses a 100 ans», in Paris-Match N°609, 10 décembre 1960.
Anatole Jakovsky: «Grandma Moses», L'Europa Letteraria N°18 (1963).

LIVRES:
Grandma Moses: «My Life's History», Harper & Brothers, New York 1952.
Grandma Moses: «My Life's History», André Deutsch, Londres 1952.
Grandma Moses: «Meine Lebensgeschichte», Ullstein Verlag, Berlin 1957.
Grandma Moses: «Het verhaal van mijn leven», Bruna & Zoon, Utrecht 1958.

FILMS:
Documentaire en couleurs par Archibald MacLeish (sans date).

Mraz, Franjo

Born April 4, 1910 in Hlebine (Yugoslavia).

Geboren am 4. April 1910 in Hlebine (Jugoslawien).

Né le 4 avril 1910 à Hlebine (Yougoslavie).

One of the veterans of the Hlebine school of painters. In 1930 Mraz, who came of humble peasant stock, made the acquaintance of Krsto Hegedušič, who introduced him (and Generalič also) to his group 'Earth', where, in fact, he exhibited his work one year later. He paints 'pastoral' pictures and has a great gift of portraying the seasons.

Ein Veteran der Bewegung von Hlebine. Schon 1930 lernt dieser Sohn kleiner Bauern Krsto Hegedušič kennen, der ihn, wie übrigens auch Generalič, in seine Gruppe «Erde» einführt, wo er tatsächlich ein Jahr später ausstellt. Er malt Hirtenbilder und versteht es vorzüglich, die Jahreszeiten wiederzugeben.

L'un des vétérans du mouvement de Hlebine. C'est déjà en 1930 que ce fils de petits paysans fait la connaissance de Krsto Hegedušič, qui l'introduit, ainsi que Generalič, dans son groupe «Terre», où il expose effectivement un an après. Il peint des pastorales et il excelle à traduire les saisons.

EXPOSITIONS:
Participation à la troisième Biennale, São Paulo 1955.
Musée, Dubrovnik 1956.
«Naivni umetnici Jugoslavije», Belgrade 1957.
«Première Quadriennale des Peintres Naïfs Yougoslaves», Čačac 1962.
«Yugoslav Modern Primitives», Edinburgh 1962.
«Peintres Naïfs Yougoslaves», Moscou 1962.
«Naive Kunst in Jugoslawien», Kunstakademie, Wien 1963.
«Peintres Naïfs Populaires Yougoslaves», Leningrad 1963.
«Sonntagsmaler aus Jugoslawien», Museum am Ostwall, Dortmund 1964.

BIBLIOGRAPHIE:
«Yougoslavija», numéro spécial (17) consacré à l'art des naïfs, Belgrade 1959.
Oto Bihalji-Merin: «Das naive Bild der Welt», Köln 1959.
Oto Bihalji-Merin: «Die naive Malerei», Köln 1959.
Oto Bihalji-Merin: «Les Peintres Naïfs», Paris (sans date).
Oto Bihalji-Merin: «Umetnost Naivnich u Jugoslavjii», Belgrade 1963.

Musatov, (or Mussatoff), Grigorij

Born January 29, 1889 in Samra (Russia).
Died November 8, 1941 in Prague (Czechoslovakia).

Geboren am 29. Januar 1889 in Samra (Rußland).
Gestorben am 8. November 1941 in Prag (Tschechoslowakei).

Né le 29 janvier 1889 à Samra (Russie).
Mort le 8 novembre 1941 à Prague (Tchécoslovaquie).

His father was a maker of icons. He too would certainly have continued this trade, if it had not been for the Russian revolution. However, he emigrated and went first to Constantinople and then to Prague, where he settled down. Became a naturalized Czech. After holding several different posts to earn his living, he discovered painting, which promptly became his passion. First there appeared a series of pictures as primitive as one could wish for, telling of Russian life before the revolution. Little by little, however, he learned some artistic technique and aimed higher. 'Higher' is perhaps not the correct word, for his painting lost all its originality and vascillated between out-of-date impressionism and imitation Chagall fantasy.

Sein Vater ist Ikonenfabrikant. Er hätte diesen Beruf zweifellos übernommen, wäre nicht die russische Revolution ausgebrochen. Er wandert aus, zuerst nach Konstantinopel, dann nach Prag, wo er sich niederläßt. Erwirbt die tschechische Staatsbürgerschaft. Nach allen möglichen Broterwerben entdeckt er endlich die Malerei, die alsbald zu einer Leidenschaft wird. Er malt eine ganze Reihe von äußerst naiven Bildern, die das Leben in Rußland unter dem Ancien Régime schildern. Aber nach und nach erlernt er die Technik und steckt seine Ziele höher. Höher ist vielleicht nicht das richtige Wort, denn seine Malerei verliert alle Originalität und bewegt sich nun zwischen einem überholten Impressionismus und der Zauberwelt eines bereits abgegriffenen Chagall.

Son père était un fabricant d'icônes. Il aurait, du reste, certainement continué ce métier s'il n'y avait eu la révolution russe. Il émigre alors, d'abord à Constantinople, puis à Prague où il se fixe. Naturalisé tchèque. Après toutes sortes de métiers qu'il exerce pour vivre, il découvre enfin la peinture qui devient aussitôt sa passion. Une série de tableaux tout ce qu'il y a de naïfs s'ensuit alors, racontant la vie russe sous l'ancien régime. Mais, peu à peu il apprend le métier et vise plus haut. Plus haut, ce n'est peut-être pas le mot, car elle perd toute son originalité, se balançant entre un impressionnisme périmé et les féeries d'un Chagall déjà vu.

EXPOSITIONS:
Umelecka Beseda, Prague 1927, 1931, 1932, 1936.
Galerie Charpentier, Paris 1938.
Umelecka Beseda, Prague 1940.
Posova Galeria, Prague 1943 (Cat., Préface Karel Sourek).
Umelecka Beseda, Prague 1946 (Cat., Préface Ivan Smetana).
Umelecka Besada, Prague 1959 (Cat., Préface Lubos Hlavacek).

BIBLIOGRAPHIE:
Anatole Jakovsky: «Grigorij Musatov», Editions Fr. Richter, Prague 1931.
Anatole Jakovsky: «Eros du Dimanche», Editions J.J. Pauvert, Paris 1964.

Muthspiel, Agnes

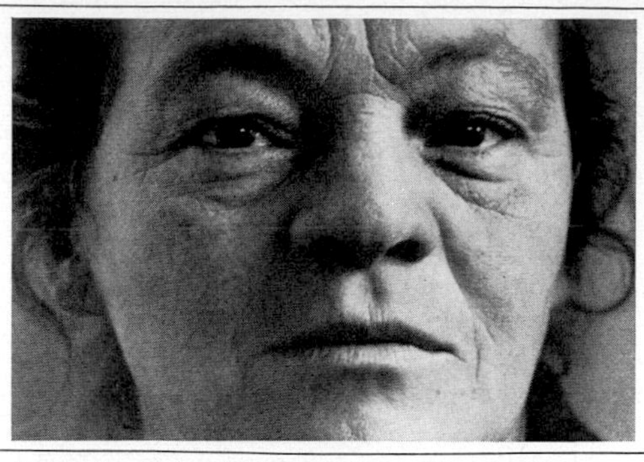

Born February 8, 1914 in Salzburg (Austria).

Geboren 8. Februar 1914 in Salzburg (Österreich).

Née le 8 février 1914 à Salzburg (Autriche).

Spent her childhood and student days in her native town. Married in 1938, but her husband was killed in the war in 1941. She turned to painting in 1946, as a means of escaping from sadness and loneliness. Her work shows a distinct religious tendency; her pictures are honest and sensitive. A completely self-taught artist.

Jugend und Ausbildung in ihrer Vaterstadt. Heiratet 1938, aber ihr Mann fällt 1941 im Krieg. Um der Traurigkeit und der Einsamkeit zu entfliehen, fängt sie 1946 an zu malen. Ausgesprochen religiöse Tendenz. Aufrichtige, empfindsame Malerei. Autodidaktin reinsten Wassers.

Jeunesse et études dans sa ville natale. Se marie en 1938, mais son mari est tué en 1941 pendant la guerre. Pour échapper à la tristesse et à la solitude, se met à peindre en 1946. Une tendance religieuse très nette. Peinture probe et sensible. Autodidacte à l'état pur.

EXPOSITIONS:
Kunstverein, Salzburg 1950.
Galleria Obelisco, Rome 1950.
« Die Welt der Naiven Malerei », Salzburg 1964.

BIBLIOGRAPHIE:
Bernard Jasmand et Otto Kallir: « Sonntagsmaler », Ed. Otto Aug. Ehlers, Berlin/Darmstadt 1956.

Naumovski, Vangel

Born March 22, 1924 in Ohrid (Yugoslavia).

Geboren am 22. März 1924 in Ohrid (Jugoslawien).

Né le 22 mars 1924 à Ohrid (Yougoslavie).

Worked at many trades: shepherd, butcher's apprentice, gardener's assistant, mason, locksmith, wheelwright and, finally, designer in a sculptor's studio in his native town. Obviously a self-taught artist. But he is distinct from all the other 'naive' painters of Yugoslavia, whichever school they belong to. His art is fundamentally lyrical, dream-like, full of legendary figures. He would be like a Pre-Raphaelite set down among ardent realists.

Schäfer, Fleischerlehrling, Gärtnergehilfe, Maurer, Schlosser, Wagner und schließlich Zeichner in einem Bildhaueratelier seiner Vaterstadt. Natürlich Autodidakt. Aber er sticht von allen anderen jugoslawischen Naiven ab. Seine Kunst ist im wesentlichen lyrisch, verträumt, sagenumwittert. Er ist gleichsam eine Art Präraffaelit, der sich unter die Realisten aller Art verirrt hätte.

Berger, apprenti-boucher, aide-jardinier, maçon, serrurier, charron et, enfin, dessinateur dans un atelier de sculpture de sa ville natale. Autodidacte, évidemment. Mais il tranche sur tous les autres naïfs yougoslaves quels qu'ils soient. Son art est essentiellement lyrique, songeur, empreint de légendes. Il serait comme une espèce de pré-raphaélite perdu parmi les réalistes de tout crin.

EXPOSITIONS:
« Première Quadriennale des Peintres Naïfs Yougoslaves », Čačac 1962.
« Galerie d'Art Primitif », Zagreb 1963 (Cat., Préface Miča Bašičevič).
« Sonntagsmaler aus Jugoslawien », Museum am Ostwall, Dortmund 1964.
Musée d'Art Contemporain, Skolije 1965 (Cat., Préface C. Grozdanov).
Salon d'Eté, Ohrid 1965 (Cat., Préface C. Grozdanov).
Studio Margutta 13, Rome 1965.

BIBLIOGRAPHIE:
«Yougoslavija», numéro spécial (17) consacré à l'art des naïfs. Belgrade 1959.
Oto Bihalji-Merin: « Das naive Bild der Welt », Köln 1959.
Oto Bihalji-Merin: « Die naive Malerei », Köln 1959.
Oto Bihalji-Merin: « Les Peintres Naïfs », Paris (sans date).
Oto Bihalji-Merin: « Umetnost Naivnich u Jugoslavjii ». Belgrade 1963.
« Art Naïf », Editions Marocaines et Internationales, Rabat 1963.
Anatole Jakovsky: « Eros du Dimanche », Paris 1964.

Neff, Sibylle

Born March 14, 1929 in Appenzell (Switzerland).

Geboren am 14. März 1929 in Appenzell (Schweiz).

Née le 14 mars 1929 à Appenzell (Suisse).

The extraordinary adventure which this young girl undertook is worth relating. When she was twenty years old, the beautiful rural painting of that region (as typified by Lämmler, J. Müller, F.A. Haim, J. Zülle and J.J. Kästli) ceased to exist; the last representative of this genre, Johann Baptist Zeller, born 20 July 1877, had given up painting. Therefore, entirely on her own initiative and inspired solely by love of her country and respect for its traditions, Sibylle Neff began to paint. The result was astonishing—not only had she revived something which had been considered dead and buried, but she gave it a new luster. Her work, which began by being pure craftsmanship, developed its own individuality and, in fact, became identified with one aspect of 'naive' painting. She continues to make progress, and we wish her further success and good luck in her endeavor.

Das Abenteuer, das außerordentliche Abenteuer dieser jungen Frau verdient es, erzählt zu werden. Als sie zwanzig war, hatte die schöne Bauernmalerei dieser Gegend, wie Lämmler, J. Müller, F.A. Haim, J. Zülle oder J.J. Kästli sie vertraten, aufgehört zu existieren. Ihr letzter Vertreter, der am 20. Juli 1877 geborene Johann Baptist Zeller, malte nicht mehr. Da fing sie an zu malen, aus eigener Initiative, einzig von Heimatliebe und Ehrfurcht vor den Traditionen getrieben. Sie malte selbstverständlich so gut sie konnte. Das Ergebnis war verblüffend. Nicht nur hat sie etwas, das als tot und abgetan galt, zu neuem Leben erweckt, sie hat ihm auch einen neuen Widerhall verschafft. Ihre Malerei entwickelte sich von einer rein handwerklichen Kunst zu einer individualisierten Kunst, kurzum: sie wurde ein Zweig der naiven Malerei. Und da Sibylle Neff nicht aufhört, Fortschritte zu machen, kann man ihr nur weiterhin gutes Gelingen und viel Glück wünschen.

L'aventure, l'extraordinaire aventure de cette jeune femme mérite d'être contée. Au moment où elle a eu ses vingt ans, la belle peinture paysanne de cette région, celle des Lämmler, des J. Müller, des F.A. Haim, des J. Zülle et autres J.J. Kästli a cessé d'exister. Son dernier représentant, Johann Baptist Zeller, né le 20 juillet 1877, ne peignait plus. Alors c'est elle, sur sa propre initiative, mue uniquement par l'amour de son pays et le respect des traditions, qui s'est mise à peindre. De son mieux, cela s'entend. Le résultat fut surprenant. Non seulement elle a ressuscité ce qui était considéré comme mort et enterré, mais elle lui a donné une nouvelle résonance. Sa peinture, d'un art purement artisanal devenait un art individualisé, bref il devenait une branche de la peinture naïve. Et comme elle ne cesse de faire des progrès, on ne peut que lui souhaiter bonne continuation et bonne chance.

EXPOSITIONS:
Kunstmuseum, St. Gallen 1965.

BIBLIOGRAPHIE:

M.: « Die Appenzeller Bauernmalerei lebt weiter », Hg. St. Galler Tageszeitung, 22 octobre 1961.
Fritz Laufer: « Sibylle Neff, die letzte Appenzeller Sennenmalerin »,
Annabelle, 12 juin 1963.

Nikifor

Born ca. 1893 in Lemkowszeryzna (Poland, previously Russia).

Geboren ca. 1893 in Lemkowszeryzna (Polen, ehemals Rußland).

Né vers 1893 à Lemkowszeryzna (Pologne, ancienne Russie).

Nothing definite is known of his background. Is a deaf-mute, the son of a beggar girl who was probably also a prostitute; he does not remember anything about his father, not even his name, and probably never knew him at all. Is frequently ill. It was while he was in the hospital once that a doctor conceived the happy idea of giving him a paintbox. Since then he has done nothing but paint. His work not only gives him a means of livelihood but also a means to make life worthwhile. He sells his pictures to residents at the spa hotel in Krynica and to tourists, rather as others sell souvenirs or postcards. He can neither read nor write, and so the letters which sometimes appear with his landscapes do not mean anything. He creates his pictures on anything he can get hold of: odd sheets of paper, cigarette packets, scraps of cardboard. His friends make tiny notices for him so that the ladies and gentlemen do not entirely forget him. Generally they are placed near his hat on the pavement. But what pictures! Pure, truly inspired art, which is undoubtedly the best in Poland, and probably among the best 'naive' work in the whole world.

Man weiß nichts Genaues über ihn. Taubstumm. Als Sohn einer Bettlerin, die wahrscheinlich auch Prostitution betrieb, hat er sogar den Namen seines Vaters vergessen. Vielleicht hat er ihn gar nie gekannt. Er ist viel krank, und während eines Aufenthalts im Krankenhaus hat ein Arzt die gute Idee, ihm eine Schachtel Wasserfarben zu schenken. Seither malt er nur noch. Seine Malerei erlaubt ihm nicht nur, sein Leben zu verdienen, sondern sich selbst zu überleben. Er verkauft seine Bilder übrigens an die Kurgäste des Thermalbades Krynica und an die Touristen, ein wenig wie man Souvenirs oder Ansichtskarten verkauft. Da er weder lesen noch schreiben kann, haben die Buchstaben, die sich zuweilen in seinen Landschaften finden, keinerlei Sinn. Er malt auf alle möglichen Materialien: Papierfetzen, Zigarettenschachteln, Pappstücke. Seine Freunde verfertigen winzige Plakätchen für ihn, damit die «Herrschaften» ihn nicht vergessen. Gewöhnlich stehen sie neben seinem Hut. Aber welch ein Maler! Rein, wahrhaft inspiriert. Zweifellos der beste Maler Polens. Einer der besten unter den naiven Malern der ganzen Welt.

On ne sait rien d'une façon précise sur lui. Sourd-muet, fils d'une mendiante doublée vraisemblablement d'une prostituée, il a oublié jusqu'au nom de son père. Peut-être, ne l'a-t-il jamais su. Toujours malade, c'est donc pendant un séjour à l'hôpital qu'un médecin a eu l'heureuse idée de lui donner une boîte de couleurs à l'aquarelle. Il ne fait que peindre depuis. Sa peinture lui permet non seulement de vivre, mais de se survivre. Il la vend, d'ailleurs, aux pensionnaires de l'établissement thermal de Krynica, de même qu'aux touristes, un peu comme on vend les objets-souvenir ou les cartes postales. Comme il ne sait ni lire ni écrire, les lettres qui accompagnent parfois ses paysages n'on aucun sens. Il les fait sur n'importe quoi: morceaux de papier, boîtes de cigarettes, bouts de carton. Ce sont ses amis qui lui confectionnent de toutes petites affichettes, afin que ces messieurs-dames ne l'oublient pas. Elles sont posées, généralement, près de son chapeau. Mais quel peintre! Pur, vraiment inspiré. Le meilleur de la Pologne, sans aucun doute. L'un des meilleurs parmi les peintres naïfs du monde entier.

EXPOSITIONS:
«La Peinture Naïve», Knokke-le-Zoute 1958.
Galerie Dina Vierny, Paris 1959.
Galerie «La Proue», Bruxelles 1959 (Cat., Préface A. Banach).
Maison franco-belge, Liège 1959 (Cat., Préface A. Banach).
«Das Naive Bild der Welt», Baden-Baden 1961.
«Laienmaler», Gewerbemuseum, Basel 1961.
«Die Welt der naiven Malerei», Salzburg 1964.
«De Lusthof der Naieven», Rotterdam 1964.
«Le Monde des Naïfs», Paris 1964.

BIBLIOGRAPHIE:

Andrzej Banach: «Nikifor», Wydawnictwo Literackie, Krakow 1957.
Aleksander Jackowski: «Nikifor», La Pologne, août 1957.
Andrzej Banach: «Pamiatka z Krynicy», Wydawnictwo Literackie, Krakow 1959.
Oto Bihalji-Merin: «Das naive Bild der Welt», Köln 1959.
Oto Bihalji-Merin: «Die naive Malerei», Köln 1959.
Oto Bihalji-Merin: «Les Peintres Naïfs», Paris (sans date).
Anatole Jakovsky: «Eros du Dimanche», Paris 1964.
«Art Naïf», Editions Marocaines et Internationales, Rabat 1964.

Obin, Philomé

Born 1892 in Cap-Haitien (Haiti).

Geboren 1892 in Cap-Haitien (Haiti).

Né en 1892 à Cap-Haïtien (Haïti).

The son of a tailor. Became a bookkeeper in his native town, then barber, coffee seller, painter and decorator in the Freemason halls. A friend of Hector Hyppolite and veteran of his first group of artists. But whereas the latter was inspired by the fables and enchantment of his country's history, Obin was filled with a kind of 'rationalism' which led him to paint vast works relating events in Haiti's history, so far as they are described in textbooks. He is now the director of an art school in his home town.

Sohn eines Schneiders. Finanzbeamter in seiner Vaterstadt, dann nacheinander Friseur, Kaffeehändler, Dekorationsmaler in Freimaurer-Tempeln. Freund von Hector Hyppolite und ältestes Mitglied der um ihn gebildeten Gruppe. Aber wenn dieser seine Wurzeln in die sagenhafte und magische Vergangenheit seiner Heimat senkt, so ist Obin im Gegenteil von einem gewissen «Rationalismus» beseelt, der ihn dazu treibt, große Kompositionen zu schaffen, die von den historischen Begebenheiten seines Landes erzählen, zumindest so wie sie in den Schulbüchern stehen. Er leitet jetzt seinerseits eine Kunstschule in seiner Vaterstadt.

Fils d'un tailleur. Commis aux finances de sa ville natale, puis tour à tour coiffeur, marchand de café, peintre-décorateur dans les temples francs-maçons. Ami et vétéran du premier groupe de Hector Hyppolite. Mais si ce dernier plonge ses racines dans le passé fabuleux et magique de son pays, celui-ci, par contre est imbu d'un certain «rationalisme» qui le conduit à peindre de vastes compositions narrant les événements historiques de son pays, du moins tels que les manuels les enseignent. Il dirige maintenant, à son tour, une école d'art de sa ville.

EXPOSITIONS:
«Peintres de l'Equateur, de Haïti et de Pérou», l'UNESCO, Paris 1947.
«La Peinture Naïve», Knokke-le-Zoute 1958.
«Das naive Bild der Welt», Baden-Baden 1961.
«Naive Painters of Latin America», Duke University, Durham, N.C., 1963.
«19 peintres d'Haïti», Palais des Beaux-Arts, Bruxelles 1963.
«20th Century Latin American Naive Art», La Jolla, Calif. (USA) 1964.
«De Lusthof der Naieven», Rotterdam 1964.
«Le Monde des Naïfs», Paris 1964.

BIBLIOGRAPHIE:

Selden Rodman: «Renaissance in Haiti», Pelegrini and Cudahy, New York (sans date).
Oto Bihalji-Merin: «Das naive Bild der Welt», Köln 1959.
Oto Bihalji-Merin: «Die naive Malerei», Köln 1959.
Oto Bihalji-Merin: «Les Peintres Naïfs», Paris (sans date).
«Art Naïf», Editions Marocaines et Internationales, Rabat 1964.

O'Brady, Gertrude

(real name: MacBrady)
Born 1904 in Chicago, Illinois (USA).

(mit ihrem richtigen Namen MacBrady)
Geboren 1904 in Chicago, Illinois (USA).

(de son vrai nom: MacBrady)
Née en 1904 à Chicago, Illinois (USA).

The life and work of this artist are themselves sufficient justification for the existence of that kind of 'possession' which mysteriously seizes certain 'naive' painters. Suddenly, after having led a completely unremarkable, dull life, she began to paint when almost forty years old and, consumed for five years with a burning passion, she produced about sixty paintings of genius. Then she sank into illness, silence and anonymity. It was in Paris, and later in the concentration camp at Vittel that she developed (probably unconsciously) her talent to the full. Since that time she has lived in Italy, after giving up painting almost twenty years ago.

Das Leben und das Werk dieser Frau allein würden genügen, um die Wirklichkeit jener Art Besessenheit darzutun, die sich, man weiß nicht wann, man weiß nicht wie, gewisser naiver Maler bemächtigt. Nachdem sie ein völlig ereignisloses, nichtssagendes Leben geführt hat, fängt sie um ihr vierzigstes Jahr herum plötzlich an zu malen, wird während 5 Jahren von einem intensiven Feuer verzehrt, schafft ungefähr 60 sozusagen geniale Werke, und versinkt dann wieder in Krankheit, Schweigen und Namenlosigkeit. In Paris und später im Konzentrationslager von Vittel hat sie, zweifellos ohne ihr Wissen, ihr Bestes gegeben. Seit bald 20 Jahren hat sie aufgehört zu malen und lebt seither in Italien.

La vie et l'œuvre de cette femme suffiraient à elles seules à justifier la réalité de cette espèce de possession qui s'empare on ne sait ni quand ni comment de certains peintres naïfs. Après avoir mené une vie absolument insipide, sans aucun intérêt, elle commence à peindre soudain, aux approches de la quarantaine, brûle d'un feu intense pendant cinq ans, produit une soixantaine d'œuvres pour ainsi dire géniales, puis sombre à nouveau dans la maladie, le silence et l'anonymat. C'est à Paris, puis au camp de concentration de Vittel qu'elle a réalisé, sans doute à son insu, le meilleur d'elle-même. Elle vit depuis en Italie, après avoir cessé de peindre, depuis bientôt vingt ans.

EXPOSITIONS:
Galerie G. Maratier, Paris 1945
(Cat., Préface Anatole Jakovsky et E. Jaguer).
Galerie du Bac, Paris 1946
(Cat., Préface Anatole Jakovsky).
Galerie Maeght, Paris 1948 (Cat., Préface Jules Supervielle et une sorte d'auto-préface).
«La Peinture Naïve», Knokke-le-Zoute 1958.
«La Peinture Naïve», Maison de la Pensée Française, Paris 1960.
«Das naive Bild der Welt», Baden-Baden 1961.
«Die Welt der naiven Malerei», Salzburg 1964.
«Les Primitifs d'Aujourd'hui», Galerie Charpentier, Paris 1964.
«De Lusthof der Naieven», Rotterdam 1964.
«Le Monde des Naïfs», Paris 1964.

BIBLIOGRAPHIE:

«O'Brady», Femina-Noël, Paris, janvier 1948.
Anatole Jakovsky: «La Peinture Naïve», Paris 1949.
Anatole Jakovsky: «Les Peintres Naïfs», Paris 1956.
Anatole Jakovsky: «Naive Malerei», Zürich 1957.
Anatole Jakovsky: «Eros du Dimanche», Paris 1964.
Oto Bihalji-Merin: «Das naive Bild der Welt», Köln 1959.
Oto Bihalji-Merin: «Die naive Malerei», Köln 1959.
Oto Bihalji-Merin: «Les Peintres Naïfs», Paris (sans date).
«Die Welt der Naiven», Der Spiegel, Hamburg, 20 décembre 1961.

Ociepka, Teofil

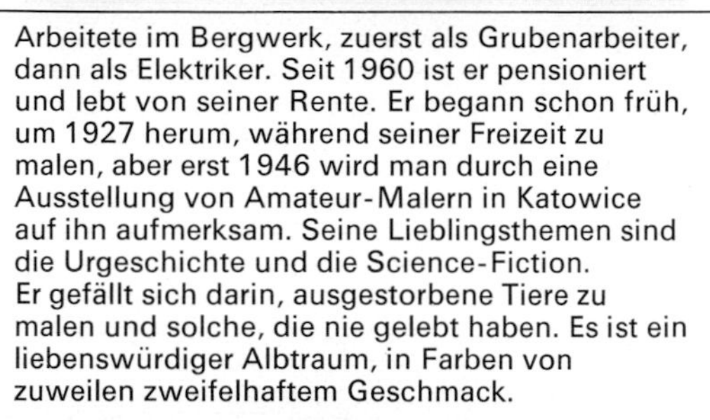

Born 1892 in Janow Slaski (Poland).

Geboren 1892 in Janow Slaski (Polen).

Né en 1892 à Janow Slaski (Pologne).

Worked in a mine as a collier and then as an electrician. Since 1960, when he retired, he has lived on his pension. Began to paint early, about 1927, during his leisure time, but it was only in 1946, at an exhibition of the work of amateur painters in Katowice, that he became known. His favorite subjects are prehistoric and science fiction scenes. He likes to depict extinct animals and also imaginary ones; a pleasant kind of nightmare. His taste in colors is sometimes questionable.

Arbeitete im Bergwerk, zuerst als Grubenarbeiter, dann als Elektriker. Seit 1960 ist er pensioniert und lebt von seiner Rente. Er begann schon früh, um 1927 herum, während seiner Freizeit zu malen, aber erst 1946 wird man durch eine Ausstellung von Amateur-Malern in Katowice auf ihn aufmerksam. Seine Lieblingsthemen sind die Urgeschichte und die Science-Fiction. Er gefällt sich darin, ausgestorbene Tiere zu malen und solche, die nie gelebt haben. Es ist ein liebenswürdiger Albtraum, in Farben von zuweilen zweifelhaftem Geschmack.

Travaillait dans la mine; comme mineur de fond d'abord, puis comme électricien. Retraité, il vit de sa pension depuis 1960. Il commença à peindre de bonne heure, vers 1927, pendant ses loisirs, mais ce n'est qu'en 1946 qu'une exposition de peintres amateurs à Katowice le fit connaître. Ses sujets de prédilection sont la préhistoire et la Science-Fiction. Il se complaît à peindre des animaux disparus, ainsi que ceux qui n'ont jamais existé. C'est un aimable cauchemar, peint avec des couleurs d'un goût parfois douteux.

EXPOSITIONS:
«La Peinture Naïve», Knokke-le-Zoute 1958.
«Laienmaler», Gewerbemuseum, Basel 1961 (Cat., Préface R.Wildhaber et A. Hernandez).
«Die Welt der naiven Malerei», Salzburg 1964.
«De Lusthof der Naieven», Rotterdam 1964.
«Le Monde des Naïfs», Paris 1964.

BIBLIOGRAPHIE:
Andrzeij Banach: «Ociepka», Wydawnictwo Literackie, Krakow 1958.
Oto Bihalji-Merin: «Das naive Bild der Welt», Köln 1959.
Oto Bihalji-Merin: «Die naive Malerei», Köln 1959.
Oto Bihalji-Merin: «Les Peintres Naïfs», Paris (sans date).
«Art Naïf», Editions Marocaines et Internationales, Rabat 1964.

Di Oliveira, Raimundo

Born 1930 in Faira di Santana-Bahia (Brazil). Died January 16, 1966 in Bahia (Brazil).

Geboren 1930 in Feira di Santana-Bahia (Brasilien).
Gestorben am 16. Januar 1966 in Bahia (Brasilien).

Né en 1930 à Feira di Santana-Bahia (Brésil). Mort le 16 janvier 1966 à Bahia (Brésil).

You would have thought this artist to be rich and happy; he became famous, even a celebrity, at the age of 23, his first individual exhibition taking place in 1951 in the Town Hall of his native town. But he was not at all happy or rich. He committed suicide in a dreary hotel room, leaving behind him a message written on the lid of a shoebox, which explained his action as being forced on him by money difficulties (his dealers took up to 80% of his income) and by solitude. So the fact that his pictures sold fairly well and his success was real was not enough to keep this artist from death. He is certainly the most vivid example of the false situation in which the majority of 'naive' artists find themselves, materially, spiritually and morally.

Man hätte meinen können, er sei reich und glücklich, dieser sehr persönliche Maler, der schon im Alter von 23 Jahren bekannt, wenn nicht gar berühmt war. Seine erste Einzelausstellung fand nämlich bereits 1951 im Rathaus seiner Vaterstadt statt. Das stimmte aber nicht. Er hat sich in einem schäbigen Hotelzimmer das Leben genommen und auf dem Deckel einer Schuhschachtel eine letzte Botschaft hinterlassen. Er erklärt seine Tat mit Geldschwierigkeiten (seine Händler beanspruchten bis zu 80% des Gewinns) und mit seiner Einsamkeit. So haben seine Bilder, die sich wirklich gut verkauften, und sein ebenfalls nicht vorgetäuschter Erfolg nicht genügt, um diesen Maler am Leben zu erhalten. Das ist zweifellos das eindrücklichste Symbol für jene schiefe Lage, in der sich die meisten unserer Naiven sowohl in materieller als auch in geistiger und moralischer Hinsicht befinden. Möge dieser Tod als Lektion dienen!

On aurait pu le croire riche et heureux, ce peintre très personnel, qui a connu la notoriété, sinon la célébrité, dès l'âge de 23 ans. Sa première exposition individuelle ayant eu lieu, en effet, en 1951, dans la Préfecture Municipale de sa ville natale. Il n'en était rien. Il s'est donné la mort, dans une sordide chambre d'hôtel, en laissant un dernier message sur le couvercle d'une boîte à chaussures. Il explique son geste par les difficultés d'argent (ses marchands lui prenaient jusqu'à 80% de bénéfices) et la solitude. Ainsi ses tableaux qui se vendaient vraiment bien et son succès non feint, non plus, n'ont pas suffi à garder en vie ce peintre. Et c'est, sans doute, le symbole le plus sanglant de cette fausse situation où se trouvent la plupart de nos naïfs, aussi bien sur le plan matériel que spirituel et moral. Que cette mort serve donc de leçon!

EXPOSITIONS:
Galeria Oxumare, Salvador, Bahia 1953.
Galerie de Arte da Folha, São Paulo 1958.
Galeria Ambiente, São Paulo 1959.
Galeria Astreia, São Paulo 1961, 1962 et 1964.
Galeria Bonino, Rio de Janeiro 1963 et 1964.
Galerie J. Massol, Paris 1965
avec d'autres naïfs brésiliens
(Cat., Préface Jacques Lassaigne).

Olson-Hagalund, Olle

Born 1904 in Hagalund (Sweden).

Geboren 1904 in Hagalund (Schweden).

Né en 1904 à Hagalund (Suède).

'Naivistic' in expression and inspiration, but nevertheless rather different both from his namesake (with a double 's') and from the genuine 'naive' Carlsson. He held his first exhibition in Stockholm in 1935. He has also done some theatre work. His art is very well thought of in his own country and his paintings are to be found in the majority of museums there.

«Naivist» in Ausdruck und Inspiration. Indessen unterscheidet sich dieser Künstler trotzdem sowohl von seinem Namensvetter mit dem Doppel-S wie von einem Carlsson, der ein echter Naiver ist. Erste Ausstellung 1935 in Stockholm. Er hat auch für die Bühne gearbeitet. Seine Kunst wird in seiner Heimat sehr geschätzt, und seine Werke finden sich in den meisten schwedischen Museen.

«Naïviste» d'expression et d'inspiration, cet artiste diffère quand-même un tant soit peu aussi bien de son homonyme avec un double s, que d'un Carlsson, un naïf authentique celui-là. Sa première exposition à Stockholm est de 1935. Il a aussi travaillé pour le théâtre. Son art est très prisé dans son pays et ses œuvres se trouvent dans la plupart des musées.

BIBLIOGRAPHIE:
Ulf Linde: «Olle Olson-Hagalund», Äthler & Akerlunds, Stockholm 1965.

Olsson, Lim-Johan

(real name Johan Erik Olsson)
Born 1865 in Mackskalen (Sweden).
Died 1944 in Kyan (Sweden).

(mit seinem richtigen Namen Johan Erik Olsson)
Geboren 1865 in Mackskalen (Schweden).
Gestorben 1944 in Kyan (Schweden).

(de son vrai nom: Johan Erik Olsson)
Né en 1865 à Mackskalen (Suède).
Mort en 1944 à Kyan (Suède).

The earliest Swedish 'naive' painter. Lived in the extreme north of Sweden and worked as a lumberman and free-lance photographer.
His work is composed of 25 known pictures, which were sold after his death in a psychiatric hospital, where he had spent the last eight years of his life.

Der älteste schwedische Naive. Lebte als Holzfäller und gelegentlicher Photograph im äußersten Norden des Landes. Sein Werk besteht, soviel man weiß, aus 25 Bildern, die nach seinem Tod verkauft wurden. Er starb in der psychiatrischen Anstalt, in der er die letzten acht Jahre seines Lebens zubrachte.

Le plus ancien parmi les naïfs suédois. A vécu dans l'extrême Nord de son pays comme bûcheron et photographe à ses heures. Son œuvre se compose de 25 tableaux connus qui ont été vendus à sa mort survenue dans un établissement psychiatrique où il a passé les huit dernières années de sa vie.

EXPOSITIONS:
Retrospective commémorative, Stockholm 1948.
« Laienmaler », Gewerbemuseum, Basel 1961.

BIBLIOGRAPHIE:
Oto Bihalji-Merin: « Das naive Bild der Welt »,
Oto Bihalji-Merin: « Die naive Malerei », Köln 1959.
Oto Bihalji-Merin: « Les Peintres Naïfs », Paris (sans date).

Pagano, Luisa

Born September 19, 1895 in Voghera, Pavia (Italy).

Geboren am 19. September 1895 in Voghera, Pavia (Italien).

Née le 19 septembre 1895 à Voghera, Pavie (Italie).

Quite a well-known singer. She is the best example of the fact that one may develop one's talents in a certain field, be successful, have training and even earn a lot of money, and still keep the poetical 'blue flower' of longing in one's heart. The more so as she began to paint before she gave up singing. Her gouache work is delicate, transparent, steeped in the Mediterranean atmosphere.

Ziemlich bekannte Sängerin. Ihr Fall beweist schlagend, daß man in einem gewissen Milieu leben, Erfolg, Bildung, ja Geld haben und doch im innersten Herzen eine kleine blaue Blume bewahren kann. Um so mehr, als die Künstlerin angefangen hat zu malen, ehe sie aufhörte zu singen. Ihre Gouaches sind zart, durchsichtig, in Mittelmeerlicht getaucht.

Chanteuse assez connue. Son cas prouve mieux qu'un autre qu'on peut évoluer dans un certain monde, avoir du succès, de l'instruction, sinon de la fortune, et garder une petite fleur bleue au fond de son cœur. D'autant plus que l'artiste a commencé à peindre avant qu'elle ne cesse de chanter. Ses gouaches sont fines, transparentes, baignées dans la Méditerranée.

EXPOSITIONS:
Galleria l'Incontro, Rome 1957
(Cat., Préface Alfredo Mezio).
«I Pittori Naifs», Rome 1964.
«I Pittori Naifs», Centro Internazionale di Arte Figurative, Biella 1964.
Galleria Al Saggittario, Milan 1965
(Cat., Préface Anatole Jakovsky).
Sala Arlecchino, Voghera 1965
(Cat., Préface A. Natoli).

Pajot, Gilbert

Born July 10, 1902 in La Chaume, Sables d'Olonne, Vendée (France).
Died May 6, 1956 in La Parée-Jésus, near Saint-Jean-des-Monts, Vendée (France).

Geboren am 10. Juli 1902 in La Chaume, Sables d'Olonne, Vendée (Frankreich).
Gestorben am 6. Mai 1956 in La Parée-Jésus bei Saint-Jean-des-Monts, Vendée (Frankreich).

Né le 10 juillet 1902 à la Chaume, Sables d'Olonne, Vendée (France).
Mort le 6 mai 1956 à La Parée-Jésus, par Saint-Jean-des-Monts, Vendée (France).

Son of Paul-Emile Pajot, born in 1873 in Talmont, died September 22, 1929 in La Chaume, formerly a sailor, who left hundreds and hundreds of large-scale water colors of ships, and who compiled the five-volume work 'The Story of my Life and my Adventures at Sea'. This book is unique—almost every page is decorated with a drawing or little gouache painting. He continued work on this until his death. The son, Gilbert Pajot, took up the same brushes that his father had used but used them slightly differently, partly because he belonged to another generation and another kind of life. He too became a sailor, but instead of sailing ships like his father he worked with fuel-driven ships, which left him much less free time. He never knew those long crossings during windless days, when gifted sailors had the leisure to learn to draw boats—these famous 'boat memories'; this tradition used to be passed on in exactly the same way as any other popular art, such as putting tiny boats into bottles (an equally widespread way of passing the time), with the result that all these boats are sadly stereotyped, those executed by French sailors, for instance, being indistinguishable from those done by American or Italian sailors. Pajot, therefore, although he had seen and was familiar with his father's work, did not learn anything directly from him; he continued where his father left off, and yet did not continue. His painting is more subjective, more touched by fantasy—in fact, it is 'naive' art.

Sohn von Paul-Emile Pajot, geboren 1873 in Talmont, gestorben 22. September 1929 in La Chaume; er war ein ehemaliger Matrose, der Hunderte und Aberhunderte von großformatigen Aquarellzeichnungen hinterlassen hat, die alle Schiffe darstellen, und vor allem jene fünfbändige «Geschichte meines Lebens und meiner Abenteuer zur See», die völlig einzig dasteht und ungefähr auf jeder Seite eine Zeichnung oder eine kleine Gouache enthält und deren Vollendung nur der Tod des Autors verhindert hat. Der Sohn ergreift den Pinsel des Vaters, doch malt er auf eine etwas verschiedene Weise, was sich durch die Tatsache erklären läßt, daß er bereits einer anderen Generation und einem anderen Milieu angehört. Auch er ist Matrose, doch nicht mehr wie sein Vater auf Segelschiffen, sondern auf Dieselfrachtern, was die Freizeit gezwungenermaßen beschränkt, denn nun ist es zu Ende mit jenen langen, windstillen Fahrten, die es den Matrosen erlaubten, zu lernen, wie man jene berühmte Souvenir-Schiffe ergänzte, eine Art Kalligraphie, die genau wie jede andere Volkskunst überliefert wurde, oder wie man winzige Schiffe in Flaschen einbaute, eine andere, ebenfalls volkstümliche Kunstform. Alle diese Schiffe waren unvermeidlich stereotypiert, und die von Franzosen angefertigten unterschieden sich nicht sehr von denen, die Amerikaner oder Italiener hergestellt hatten. Gilbert Pajot hat infolgedessen nichts gelernt, sondern nur die Werke seines Vaters gesehen und gekannt. Er tritt also in seine Fußstapfen, ohne ihn wirklich fortzusetzen. Er fügt eine unbeschwerte, persönlichere, mit einem Wort naive Note bei.

Fils de Paul-Emile Pajot, né en 1873 à Talmont, mort le 22 septembre 1929 à La Chaume, ancien marin qui a laissé des centaines et des centaines de dessins aquarellés de grand format représentant des navires et, surtout, cette «Histoire de ma vie et mes aventures en mer» en 5 volumes, absolument unique, dont à peu près chaque page est ornée d'un dessin ou d'une petite gouache et que la mort seule l'a empêché de continuer. Ce fils, donc, reprend les pinceaux de son père, mais d'une façon légèrement différente, ce qui s'explique d'abord par le fait qu'il appartient déjà à une autre génération et à un autre milieu. Marin, lui aussi, il ne navigue plus à voile, comme son père, mais au mazout, ce qui réduit forcément ses loisirs, c'est-à-dire qu'il ne connaît plus ces longues traversées par un calme plat où les marins doués pouvaient apprendre soit à dessiner les bateaux – ces fameux bateaux-souvenir – une sorte de calligraphie qui se transmettait exactement de la même façon que n'importe quel autre art populaire, soit à mettre de minuscules bateaux en bouteille, une autre forme d'art également populaire. De sorte que tous ces bateaux-là étaient fatalement stéréotypés, et ceux, faits par des Français, ne se distinguaient pas tellement des autres faits par des Américains ou Italiens. N'ayant, par conséquent, rien appris, sinon avoir vu et connu les œuvres de son père, il le continue sans le continuer en y ajoutant une note plus fantaisiste, plus personnelle, naïve en un mot.

BIBLIOGRAPHIE:
Anatole Jakovsky: «Peintres des Bateaux-Souvenir», Arts et Traditions Populaires No. 2, Paris 1955.
Anatole Jakovsky: «Les Peintres Naïfs», Paris 1956.
Anatole Jakovsky: «Naive Malerei», Zürich 1957.

Paluška, Martin

Born February 14, 1913 in Martine (Yugoslavia).

Geboren am 14. Februar 1913 in Martine (Jugoslawien).

Né le 14 février 1913 à Martine (Yougoslavie).

Was first of all a tractor-driver, then a mechanic in a flour-mill. But his leisure hours were sacred for him, entirely devoted to art. The result was that in 1938 he and his friend Sokol founded the nucleus of what was to become the Kovačiča School. His art is delicate and full of nuances, and yet at the same time it is true to life.

Arbeitet zunächst als Traktorführer, dann als Mechaniker in einer Mehlfabrik. Seine Freizeit hingegen ist heilig: sie ist der Malerei gewidmet. Schon 1938 gründet er mit seinem Freund Sokol zusammen die Urzelle dessen, was ein wenig später zur Schule von Kovačiča wird. Seine Kunst ist zart, nuancenreich und doch der Wirklichkeit treu.

Conduit d'abord le tracteur, puis travaille comme mécanicien dans une minoterie. Quant aux loisirs, ils sont sacrés; il sont consacrés à la peinture. De sorte que, dès 1938, il fonde, avec son ami Sokol, l'embryon de ce qui sera, un peu plus tard, l'Ecole de Kovačiča. Son art est fin, nuancé, tout en restant fidèle au réel.

EXPOSITIONS:
«Naivni umetnici jugoslavije», Belgrade 1957.
The Arthur Jeffress Gallery, Londres 1961 (Cat., Préface M. Gelen).
«Première Quadriennale des Peintres Naïfs Yougoslaves», Čačac 1962.
Palais de Culture, Kovačiča 1962 (Cat., Préface M. Gvozdanovič).
«Yugoslav Modern Primitives», Edinburgh 1962.
«Naive Kunst in Jugoslawien», Kunstakademie Wien 1963.
«Peintres Naïfs Yougoslaves», Moscou 1962.
«Peintres Naïfs Populaires Yougoslaves», Leningrad 1963.
«Sonntagsmaler aus Jugoslawien», Museum am Ostwall, Dortmund 1964.

BIBLIOGRAPHIE:
«Yougoslavija», numéro spécial (17) consacré à l'art des naïfs, Belgrade 1959.
Oto Bihalji-Merin: «Das naive Bild der Welt», Köln 1959.
Oto Bihalji-Merin: «Die naive Malerei», Köln 1959.
Oto Bihalji-Merin: «Les Peintres Naïfs», Paris (sans date).
Oto Bihalji-Merin: «Umetnost Naivnich u Jugoslavjii», Belgrade 1963.

Paps

(real name Waldemar Rusche) Born June 10, 1882 in Naumburg bei Kassel (Germany).
Died February 8, 1965 in Lilienthal bei Bremen (Germany).

(mit seinem richtigen Namen Waldemar Rusche) Geboren am 10. Juni 1882 in Naumburg bei Kassel (Deutschland).
Gestorben 8. Februar 1965 in Lilienthal bei Bremen (Deutschland).

(de son vrai nom: Waldemar Rusche)
Né le 10 juin 1882 à Naumburg bei Kassel (Allemagne).
Mort le 8 février 1965 à Lilienthal bei Bremen (Allemagne).

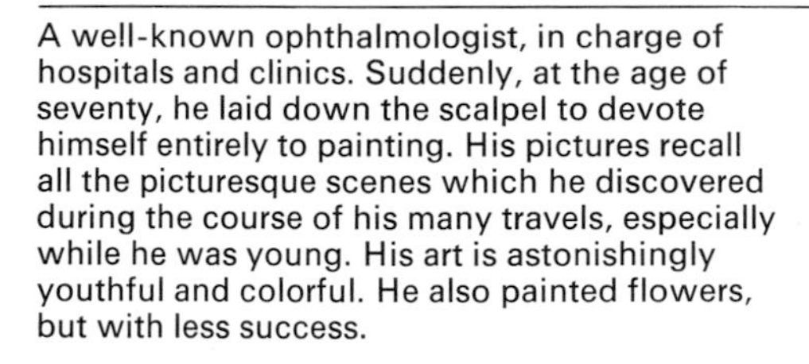

A well-known ophthalmologist, in charge of hospitals and clinics. Suddenly, at the age of seventy, he laid down the scalpel to devote himself entirely to painting. His pictures recall all the picturesque scenes which he discovered during the course of his many travels, especially while he was young. His art is astonishingly youthful and colorful. He also painted flowers, but with less success.

Sehr bekannter Ophthalmologe, der Krankenhäusern und Kliniken vorsteht. Mit 70 Jahren legt er plötzlich das Skalpell nieder, um sich ausschließlich der Malerei zu widmen. Er beschwört alle eindrücklichen Landschaften herauf, die er im Verlauf seiner zahlreichen Reisen, vor allem in seiner Jugend, gesehen hat. Eine erstaunlich junge und farbige Malerei.
Er malt auch Blumen, doch gelingen sie ihm weniger gut.

Ophtalmologiste très connu. Dirige des hôpitaux et des cliniques. Soudain, à 70 ans, il abandonne le scalpel pour se consacrer uniquement à la peinture. Il évoque alors tous les sites pittoresques qu'il a vus au cours de ses nombreux voyages, surtout pendant sa jeunesse. Une peinture étonnamment jeune et colorée. Il peint aussi des fleurs, bien qu'avec moins de bonheur.

EXPOSITIONS:
«La Peinture Naïve», Knokke-le-Zoute 1958.
Kunsthalle, Bremen 1959
(Cat., Préface non signée).
Leopold-Hoesch-Museum, Düren 1959.
Kunsthaus Schaller, Stuttgart 1960.
«Fähre», Saulgau 1960.
«Bücherschiff», Konstanz 1961.
Städtische Galerie im Lenbachhaus, München 1963 (Cat., Préface Oto Bihalji-Merin).
«Sonntagsmaler», Galerie Hella Nebelung, Düsseldorf 1963.
«Naive Malerei», Museum der Stadt Oberhausen, 1963.
«De Lusthof der Naieven», Rotterdam 1964.
«Le Monde des Naïfs», Paris 1964.
«Die Welt der naïven Malerei», Salzburg 1964.
Galerie Günther Franke, München 1965
(Cat., Préface Oto Bihalji-Merin).

BIBLIOGRAPHIE:
Oto Bihalji-Merin: «Das naive Bild der Welt», Köln 1959.
Oto Bihalji-Merin: «Die naive Malerei», Köln 1959.
Oto Bihalji-Merin: «Les Peintres Naïfs», Paris (sans date).

Parade, Marie-Pauline

(real name: Seigneurie)
Born October 5, 1904 in Paris (France).

(mit ihrem richtigen Namen Seigneurie)
Geboren am 5. Oktober 1904 in Paris (Frankreich).

(de son vrai nom: Seigneurie)
Née le 5 octobre 1904 à Paris (France).

The daughter and sister of pianists, she too became a pianist at the age of four. Her vocation as a painter, on the other hand, did not come to life until 1962. Since 1952 has been the companion of the artist Francis Pasquier, and it was purely by chance that, one rainy day in an hotel bedroom, she drew her first sketches from imagination. Art became for her more than a necessity—it became a way of escaping from everyday life. 'Each work is a poem where I live and become whole', she once said. She signs her paintings with the name of her paternal grandmother.

Tochter und Schwester der Pianisten gleichen Namens. Sie selber spielt seit dem Alter von vier Jahren Klavier. Ihre Malerberufung geht erst auf das Jahr 1962 zurück. Seit 1952 ist sie die Gefährtin des Malers Francis Pasquier und ganz zufällig kritzelt sie an einem Regentag in einem Hotelzimmer aus der Phantasie die paar ersten Zeichnungen, die bald nicht nur eine Notwendigkeit für sie werden, sondern das Bedürfnis, den Wechselfällen des Lebens zu entrinnen. «Jedes Bild ist ein Gedicht, in das ich mich einfüge und das ich erlebe», sagt sie. Sie signiert mit dem Namen ihrer Großmutter väterlicherseits.

Fille et sœur des pianistes. Pianiste elle-même dès l'âge de 4 ans. Sa vocation de peintre ne date que de 1962. Compagne, depuis 1952, du peintre Francis Pasquier, c'est tout à fait par hasard, un jour de pluie, dans une chambre d'hôtel, qu'elle griffonne d'imagination ces quelques premiers dessins qui vont devenir bientôt pour elle plus qu'une nécessité: un besoin d'évasion devant les vicissitudes de la vie. «Chaque œuvre est un poème où je m'intègre et que je vis», dit elle. Elle signe du nom de sa grand-mère paternelle.

EXPOSITIONS:
Galerie Occident, Paris 1963.
Dans son atelier, Paris 1964.
Petite Galerie, Paris 1965.
Galerie Achard de Souza, New York 1965.
Dans son atelier, Paris 1965.

Parra, Violeta

(Parra-Sandoval)
Born October 4, 1917 in the Province of Truble Chillan (Chile).

Geboren am 4. Oktober 1917 in der Provincia de Truble Chillan (Chile).

Née le 4 octobre 1917 dans la Provincia de Truble Chillan (Chili).

Is a singer, a well-known interpreter of popular songs, and also a ceramic artist and a glazer; but in her spare time this gifted woman also paints (entirely self-taught) scenes showing traditional aspects of her country. Her pictures are restrained, dark, rather magical.

Sängerin, bekannte Interpretin von Volksliedern, Keramikerin, Wandteppichweberin. Diese sehr begabte Künstlerin malt in ihren Mußestunden auch naive Bilder, die ebenfalls die verschiedenen Aspekte der Folklore ihres Landes darstellen. Schlichte, dunkle, sozusagen magische Malerei.

Chanteuse, interprète renommée de chansons populaires, céramiste, lissière, cette artiste très douée fait également, à ses moments perdu, de la peinture naïve qui représente, elle aussi, les différents aspects du folklore de son pays. Peinture sobre, sombre, pour ainsi dire magique.

EXPOSITIONS:
Foire des Arts Plastiques, Santiago 1958, 59 et 60.
Galeria Ift, Buenos Aires 1961.
«14 Chilienos», Musée d'Art Moderne, Rio de Janeiro 1961.
L'Université de Genève, 1963.
Musée des Arts Décoratifs, Paris 1964 (Cat., Préface Yvonne Brunhammer et N. Parra).

Pasotti, Bernardo

Born June 15, 1910 in Milan (Italy).

Geboren am 15. Juni 1910 in Mailand (Italien).

Né le 15 juin 1910 à Milan (Italie).

Pharmaceutical manufacturer. Self-taught artist, it is true, but one who has seen and is aware of real painting. In fact, he started to study art. This is the origin of the vague similarity (especially noticeable in his landscapes) with De Chirico's metaphysical painting, for instance. His pictures are slightly mystical in quality.

Fabrikant pharmazeutischer Produkte. Autodidakt, aber auch ein Mann, der die wahre Malerei gesehen hat und kennt. Er hat sie übrigens zuerst studiert. Daher ein schwacher Anklang (vor allem in den Landschaften) an die metaphysische Malerei eines De Chirico zum Beispiel. Leicht mystische Malerei.

Fabricant de produits pharmaceutiques. Autodidacte, certes, mais aussi quelqu'un qui a vu et qui connait la vraie peinture. Il a commencé d'ailleurs par l'étudier. D'où une vague similitude (dans les paysages, surtout) avec la peinture métaphysique de de Chirico, par exemple. Peinture légèrement mystique.

EXPOSITIONS:
Galleria Borromini, Milan 1948.
Galleria del Naviglio, Milan 1949 (Cat., Préface Raffaele Carrieri).
« Les Peintres Naïfs », Knokke-le-Zoute 1958.
Galleria del Cavalino, Venise 1953 (Cat., Préface Raffaele Carrieri).
Galleria dei Re Magi, Milan 1959 (Cat., Préface Salvatore Fiume).
Galleria del Naviglio, Milan 1964 (Cat., Préface Dino Buzzati).
Kunstsalon Wolfsberg, Zürich 1964.
« De Lusthof der Naieven », Rotterdam 1964.
« Le Monde des Naïfs », Paris 1964.
I Pittori Naifs, Rome 1964.
I Pittori Naifs, Centro Internazionale di Arte Figurative, Biella 1964.

BIBLIOGRAPHIE:
Oto Bihalji-Merin: « Das naive Bild der Welt », 1959.
Oto Bihalji-Merin: « Die naive Malerei », 1959.
Oto Bihalji-Merin: « Les Peintres Naïfs », s.d.
« 10 paesaggi di Bernardo Pasotti », Edizioni Fism, Milan (sans date).
« L'Art Naïf », Editions Marocaines et Internationales, Rabat 1964.

Pasqualini, Eo

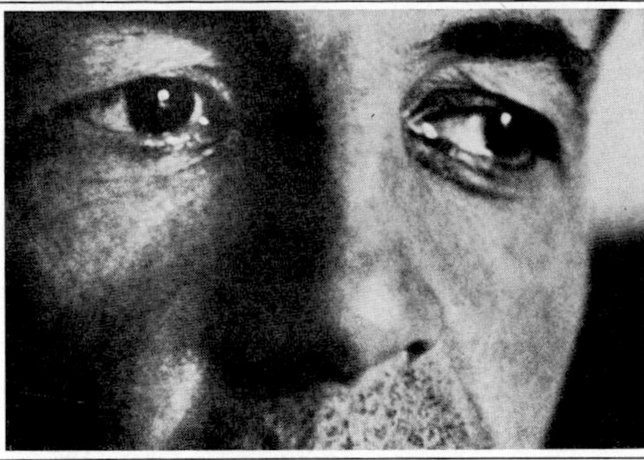

Born April 21, 1921 in Guastalla, Reggio Emilia (Italy).

Geboren am 21. April 1921 in Guastalla, Reggio Emilia (Italien).

Né le 21 avril 1921 à Guastalla, Reggio Emilia (Italie).

Was apparently not cut out to be a 'naive' artist, for he led a happy life, on the whole. However, in 1959, he was struck down by hemiplegia and lost the use of the whole right side of his body. Three years later he attempted to paint with his left hand. But his landscapes and still-lifes, rather fluid in style and somehow transparent, only faintly related to reality, did not satisfy him, it seems—for he later devoted himself to more or less surrealistic creations.

Nichts schien ihn für die naive Malerei zu bestimmen, denn er führte ein eher glückliches Leben. Aber 1959 beraubt ihn eine einseitige Lähmung der ganzen rechten Hälfte seines Körpers. Drei Jahre später versucht er, mit der linken Hand zu malen. Aber die ziemlich flüssigen, irgendwie durchsichtigen Landschaften und Stilleben, die einen schwachen Zusammenhang mit dem Wirklichen bewahren, befriedigen ihn zweifellos nicht mehr, denn von nun an wagt er sich an mehr oder weniger surrealistische Kompositionen.

Rien, semble-t-il, ne le prédisposait à la peinture naïve, car il menait plutôt une vie heureuse. Mais voilà que, en 1959, frappé d'une hémiplégie, il perd l'usage de tout le côté droit de son corps. Trois ans après, il s'essaye à la peinture, avec la main gauche. Mais les paysages, les natures-mortes, assez fluides, en quelque sorte transparents, gardant de frêles attaches avec le réel, ne le satisfont, sans doute plus, puisqu'il se lance, désormais, dans des compositions plus ou moins surréalisantes.

EXPOSITIONS:
Dominion, Guastalla 1965
(Cat., Préface Renato Massari et Nevio Jori).
Il teatro Ariosto, Reggio Emilia 1965
(Cat., Préface Paolo Uguccioni et Nevio Jori).

BIBLIOGRAPHIE:
Nevio Jori: «Eo Pasqualini», Gazzetta di Reggio, 20 février, 7 septembre et 3 novembre 1965.

Pera, Luigi

Born October 20, 1900 in Chieti (Italy).

Geboren am 20. Oktober 1900 in Chieti (Italien).

Né le 20 octobre 1900 à Chieti (Italie).

Started to paint in 1948 having never left his native village where his father built farm carts decorated in vivid colors. He too, of course, continued his father's trade until his success as an artist allowed him to give it up. As a matter of fact, monetary rewards were showered on him from all kinds of local exhibitions, and the Museum of Modern Art in Rome bought one of his pictures. His painting is fundamentally pastoral—it is fresh and sensitive, an uncritical song of praise for his native earth.

Hat 1948 angefangen zu malen, ohne seine kleine Heimatstadt, wo sein Vater bunt bemalte Bauernwagen baute, je verlassen zu haben. Er übernimmt natürlich den Beruf, bis seine Erfolge als Maler ihm erlauben, ihn aufzugeben. Er erringt in der Tat in allen regionalen Ausstellungen Preise, und das Museum für moderne Kunst in Rom erwirbt ein Bild von ihm. Seine Malerei ist im wesentlichen ländlich: frisch und empfindsam, ein ungekünstelter Gesang zum Ruhm seiner Heimaterde.

A commencé à peindre en 1948 sans avoir jamais quitté sa petite ville natale où son père était constructeur de charrettes paysannes, peintes de si vives couleurs. Lui, naturellement, continue ce métier jusqu'à ce que ses succès de peintre permettent de l'abandonner. En effet, les récompenses pleuvent dans toutes les expositions régionales et le Musée d'Art Moderne de Rome lui achète un tableau. Sa peinture est essentiellement pastorale: fraîche et sensible, c'est un chant sans malice à la gloire de son terroir.

EXPOSITIONS:
«Mostra di Pittura Populare», Palazzo delle Esposizione, Roma 1955.
«Laienmaler», Gewerbemuseum, Basel 1961 (Cat., Préface R.Wildhaber et A. Hernandez).
«I Pittori Naifs», Rome 1964.
«I Pittori Naifs», Centro Internazionale di Arte Figurative, Biella 1964.

BIBLIOGRAPHIE:
Catalogo Bolaffi d'Arte Moderna 1965/66, Turin 1966.

Perrenoud, Raoul

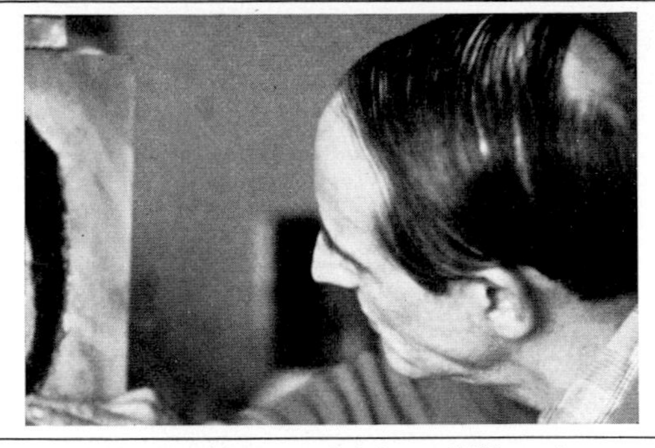

Born October 2, 1899 in Paris (France).

Geboren am 2. Oktober 1899 in Paris (Frankreich).

Né le 2 octobre 1899 à Paris (France).

Was blind until the age of eight. During that time he acquired an extreme sensitivity of touch. Later he became a masseur, and even to a small extent a 'healer by touch', and it was this gift of sensitive touch which played a dominant role. The same gift helped to make him an artist entirely on his own, since he uses neither brush nor knife but spreads the colors with his fingers. In fact, he creates sculptures—his pictures are almost all in relief. The noses protrude, the cheeks are hollowed, and you can almost run your hand through the hair of those who sat for him.

Blind bis zum Alter von 8 Jahren. Während dieser Zeit erwirbt er einen außergewöhnlich feinen Tastsinn. Als er später Masseur, Heilgymnastiker und ein bißchen Quacksalber wird, spielt gerade diese Fähigkeit eine überragende Rolle. Und der Tastsinn macht ihn auch zu einem völlig abseitsstehenden Maler, denn er malt weder mit dem Pinsel noch mit der Spachtel, sondern trägt seine Farben mit den Fingern auf. Mehr noch: er bildhauert. Seine Bilder sind beinahe alle Reliefs. Die Nase tritt vor, die Wangen fallen ein, und man kann mit der Hand durch das Haar der Leute fahren, die für seine Porträts Modell standen.

Aveugle jusqu'à l'âge de huit ans. Pendant ce temps-là, il acquiert une extrême sensibilité tactile. Plus tard, lorsqu'il deviendra masseur, kinésithérapeute et un tantinet guérisseur, c'est justement cette qualité qui jouera le rôle prépondérant. Et c'est encore ce sens tactile qui fera de lui un peintre absolument à part, car il peint sans pinceaux ni couteaux, en étalant ses couleurs avec ses doigts. Mieux encore: il sculpte. Ses tableaux sont presque tous en relief. Le nez avance, les joues se creusent et on peut passer la main dans les cheveux de ceux et de celles qui ont posé pour ses portraits.

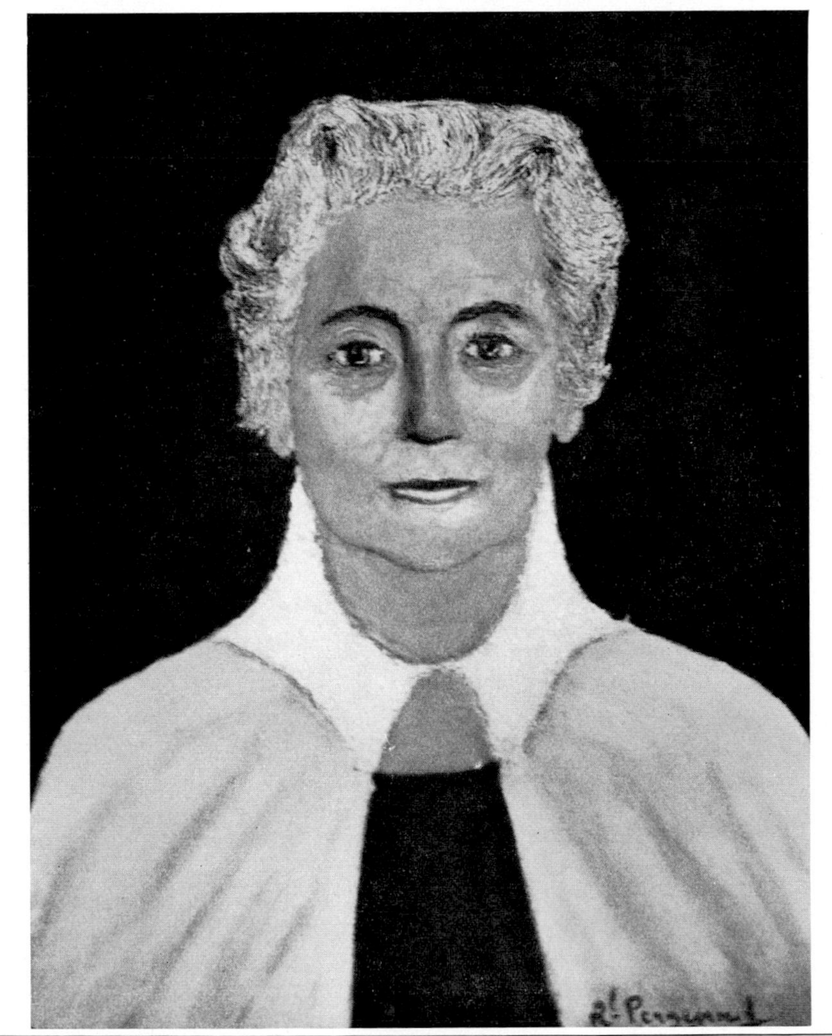

EXPOSITIONS:
Théâtre des Bouffes Parisiens, Paris 1955 (Cat., Préface Albert Willemetz).
Théâtre des Bouffes Parisiens, Paris 1957.
Galerie M. Bénézit, Paris 1961 (Cat., Préface Willemetz et Gérard Marin).
Galerie du Colisée, Paris 1962 (Cat., Préface Anatole Jakovsky).
«I Pittori Naifs», Rome 1964.
«Les Primitifs d'Aujourd'hui», Galerie Charpentier, Paris 1964.

BIBLIOGRAPHIE:

Anatole Jakovsky: «Raoul Perrenoud», La Vie Médicale, Paris mai 1963.
Anatole Jakovsky: «Raoul Perrenoud», Editions Temps Mêlés, Verviers 1964.
Anatole Jakovsky: «Eros du Dimanche», Paris 1964.

Perry, Henri

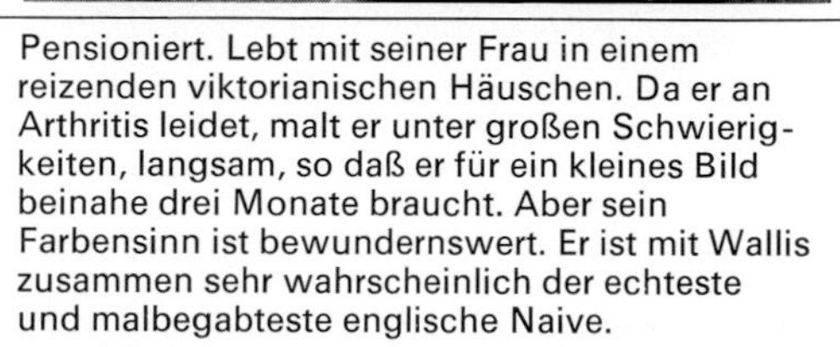

Born 1894 in Surbiton, Surrey (England).

Geboren 1894 in Surbiton, Surrey (England).

Né en 1894 à Surbiton, Surrey (Angleterre).

Is now retired. Lives with his wife in a charming little Victorian house. Suffers from arthritis and has great difficulty in painting at all—he works slowly, and can take almost three months to complete a small picture. But his sense of color is exquisite. With Wallis, he is very probably the most genuine and most artistic of all the English 'naive' painters.

Pensioniert. Lebt mit seiner Frau in einem reizenden viktorianischen Häuschen. Da er an Arthritis leidet, malt er unter großen Schwierigkeiten, langsam, so daß er für ein kleines Bild beinahe drei Monate braucht. Aber sein Farbensinn ist bewundernswert. Er ist mit Wallis zusammen sehr wahrscheinlich der echteste und malbegabteste englische Naive.

Retraité. Habite, avec sa femme, une charmante petite maison victorienne. Souffrant d'arthrite, il peint avec beaucoup de difficultés, lentement, mettant près de 3 mois pour exécuter un petit tableau. Mais son sens de la couleur est exquis. Il est, très probablement, avec Wallis, le plus authentique et le plus «peintre» parmi les naïfs anglais.

EXPOSITIONS:
«Les Peintres Naïfs», Galerie J.Verrière, Cannes 1966.

BIBLIOGRAPHIE:
Barrie Sturt-Penrose: «Primitives in Private», Observer, 13 février 1966.

Peter, Alfred Ernest

Born February 22, 1890 in Aubonne, Canton Vaud (Switzerland).

Geboren am 22. Februar 1890 in Aubonne, Kt. Waadt (Schweiz).

Né le 22 février 1890 à Aubonne, Canton de Vaud (Suisse).

The son of a banker. Before becoming a banker himself, he studied in Lausanne; he also studied music with Ansermet and was acquainted with Ramuz. Therefore he did have some contact with art and letters. Settled in Paris 1911. The 1914–18 war found him at the head of an insurance company, a position he held until 1920, the same year he married Georgina Bermyn. It was the death of his wife in 1955 which distressed him to such an extent that he sought consolation in painting. He created first of all little travel sketches but later they developed into paintings which are both 'naive' and subtle.

Sohn eines Bankiers. Ehe er selber Bankier wird, besucht er das humanistische Gymnasium in Lausanne, studiert Musik unter Ansermet und verkehrt mit Ramuz. Er beweist also eine gewisse literarische und künstlerische Veranlagung. Läßt sich bereits 1911 in Paris nieder. Bei Ausbruch des Weltkriegs leitet er die Generalagentur einer großen Versicherung; diesen Posten behält er bis 1920. In diesem Jahr verheiratet er sich mit Georgina Bermyn. Der 1955 erfolgte Tod seiner Frau erschüttert ihn so sehr, daß er von nun an in der Malerei Trost sucht. Zuerst kleine Reiseskizzen, die allmählich zu gleichzeitig naiven und raffinierten Bildern heranwachsen.

Fils d'un banquier, et avant de devenir banquier lui-même, il fait des études classiques au collège de Lausanne; étudie la musique avec Ansermet et se lie avec Ramuz. Donc une certaine prédisposition aux lettres et aux arts. Se fixe à Paris dès 1911. La guerre de 1914–18 le trouve à la tête d'un portefeuille d'assurances qu'il conservera jusqu'en 1920, l'année où il se marie avec Georgina Bermyn. Et c'est le décès de cette dernière, survenu en 1955, qui l'affecte à un tel point qu'il cherche désormais la consolation dans la peinture. De petits croquis de voyage d'abord qui deviendront peu à peu des peintures, à la fois naïves et raffinées.

EXPOSITIONS:
Galerie des Orfèvres, Paris 1964 et 1965.
« Les Primitifs d'Aujourd'hui »,
Galerie Charpentier, Paris 1964.

Petersson, Primus Mortimer

Born 1895 in Oestersund (Sweden).

Geboren 1895 in Oestersund (Schweden).

Né en 1895 à Oestersund (Suède).

Was a sailor, and traveled all over the world on American trading boats. In 1924 he had a terrible experience: two of his friends died before his eyes. So he stopped sailing and settled down in California. Then, in 1925, he went back to his home town. In the year 1929 he became a patient in a psychiatric clinic—and it was there that his gift for painting became apparent. All his paintings depict memories of his days as a sailor. Swedish art critics class him among the 'Insania pingens' but this is not accurate. There are many artists outside such institutions who paint under much greater mental stress.

Matrose. Befährt auf amerikanischen Frachtschiffen die ganze Welt. 1924 erfährt er einen furchtbaren Schock: zwei seiner Kameraden sterben vor seinen Augen. Da heuert er in Kalifornien ab. 1925 kehrt er in sein Heimatdorf zurück. 1929 wird er in einer psychiatrischen Anstalt interniert. Und hier entdeckt man sein Malertalent. Er malt immer seine Erinnerungen aus der Zeit, da er zur See fuhr. Die schwedischen Kunstkritiker reihen ihn unter die «Insania pingens» ein, was nicht ganz zutrifft. Es gibt unter den nicht als krank geltenden Malern viele, die unter bedeutend größeren geistigen Störungen leiden.

Marin. Voyages dans toutes les parties du monde sur des bateaux de commerce américains. En 1924, il reçoit un choc terrible: deux de ses camarades meurent devant lui. Il met alors pied à terre en Californie. En 1925, il retourne dans son village natal. Interné en 1929 dans un établissement psychiatrique. Et c'est là qu'on découvre ses talents de peintre. Il peint toujours ses souvenirs du temps où il naviguait. Les critiques d'art suédois le rangent parmi «Insania pingens», ce qui n'est pas tout à fait le cas. Il y a bien d'autres parmi les non malades qui peignent avec bien plus de troubles mentaux.

EXPOSITIONS:
«Laienmaler», Gewerbemuseum, Basel 1961.

Peyronnet, Dominique

Born September 23, 1872 in Talence, a suburb of Bordeaux (France).
Died March 25, 1943 in Paris (France).

Geboren am 23. September 1872 in Talence, Vorort von Bordeaux (Frankreich).
Gestorben am 25. März 1943 in Paris (Frankreich).

Né le 23 septembre 1872 à Talence, Banlieue de Bordeaux (France).
Mort le 25 mars 1943 à Paris (France).

A skilled printer, he worked in nine different towns before settling down in Paris, where he specialized in chromolithograph work. His first exhibition was held in 1932 in the Salon des Indépendants, and this exhibition made his name. Only about thirty of his canvases are known to exist, and most of them were purchased by Mme Grégory. Success went to his head to such an extent that he himself prepared a voluminous catalogue for his one and only individual exhibition. It was a masterpiece in megalomania entitled 'How I Became an Artist! Despite the defaulting of the State and a Purchasing Commission and various Selection Committees'. Then this foreword: 'In the catalogue of the "Popular Masters of Reality", an exhibition which took place from June to August 1937 and where I was only showing ten canvases, Maximilian Gauthier, the art critic, said: 'Peyronnet has created a masterpiece of which the intense dramatic power cannot be denied; he is an artist who imitates nobody, an individual artist'. He could have added (1) the only artist whose paintings one may study as closely as possible, as well as from afar; (2) the only artist who copies living things and objects from nature itself; (3) the only inimitable artist. I maintain these three definitions against and in the face of anyone, however highly placed he may be.' Truly, his genius was equaled only by his vanity.

Er war ein sehr geschickter Drucker und hat in neun verschiedenen Städten gearbeitet, bevor er sich in Paris niederließ. Hier spezialisierte er sich hauptsächlich auf Farblithographie. Stellt zum ersten Mal 1932 im Salon des Indépendants aus, wo er auffällt. Man kennt alles in allem nur etwa 30 Bilder von ihm, die in der Mehrzahl von Anne Grégory erworben wurden. Der Erfolg steigt ihm dermaßen zu Kopf, daß er einen umfangreichen Katalog für seine einzige Einzelausstellung von der ersten bis zur letzten Seite selber verfaßt. Ein Meisterwerk an Größenwahn: «Wie ich Maler wurde! Trotz des Versagens des Staates, einer Ankaufskommission und mehrerer Preisgerichte». Dann dieses Vorwort: «Im Katalog zur Ausstellung Maîtres Populaires de la Réalité, Juni bis Ende August 1937, wo ich nur 10 Bilder ausstellte, schreibt der Kunstkritiker Maximilien Gauthier: 'Peyronnet hat ein Meisterwerk geschaffen, dessen eindringliche dramatische Kraft niemand bestreiten kann'; daß ich ein Maler sei, der niemand nachahmt, und ein persönlicher Künstler. Er hätte hinzufügen können: 1) der einzige Maler, dessen Bilder man ebenso gut aus nächster Nähe wie von weitem betrachten kann; 2) der einzige Maler, der Menschen und Dinge nach der Natur abbildet; und 3) der einzige unnachahmliche Maler. Diese drei Punkte halte ich hoch, allen Widerständen zum Trotz, mögen sie von noch so hohen Stellen kommen.» In der Tat war sein Stolz so groß wie sein Talent.

Imprimeur très habile, il a travaillé dans neuf villes différentes avant de s'établir à Paris, où il s'est spécialisé surtout en chromolithographie. Expose pour la première fois en 1932 au Salon des Indépendants, qui le fait connaître. On ne connaît de lui qu'une trentaine de toiles en tout et pour tout, achetées pour la plupart par Mme Grégory. Le succès lui monte à la tête à tel point que c'est lui-même qui rédige de la première à la dernière page un important catalogue pour sa seule et unique exposition individuelle. Un chef-d'œuvre de mégalomanie: « Comment je suis devenu peintre! Malgré la carence de l'Etat et d'une Commission d'achats et de plusieurs Jurys». Puis cet avant-propos: « Dans le Catalogue des Maîtres Populaires de la Réalité, Exposition de juin à fin août 1937, où je n'avais que 10 Toiles seulement, Maximilien Gauthier, critique d'Art, dit que 'Peyronnet a fait un chef-d'œuvre dont nul ne peut contester l'intense puissance dramatique; qu'il est un peintre n'imitant personne, et un peintre personnel'; il aurait pu ajouter: a) Le seul peintre, dont on peut regarder les Toiles, d'aussi près que possible, comme de loin; 2) Le seul Peintre, imitant les êtres et les choses d'après Nature; et 3) Le seul Peintre inimitable. Je maintiens ces trois versions, envers et contre tous, aussi haut placés soient-ils». En effet son orgueil n'avait d'égal que son très grand talent.

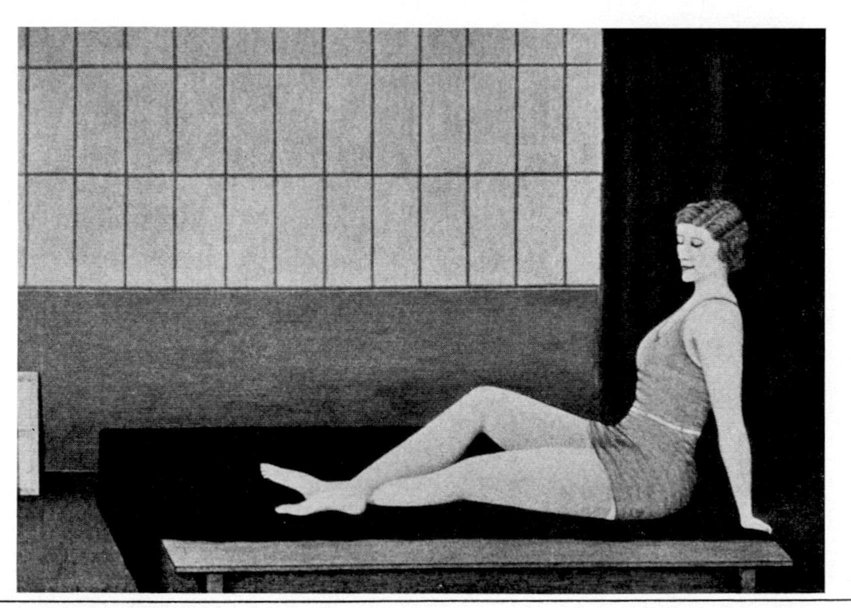

EXPOSITIONS:
«Les Maîtres Populaires de la Réalité», Paris 1937.
«Les Maîtres Populaires de la Réalité», Zürich 1937.
«Masters of Popular Painting», New York 1938.
«Masters of Popular Painting», Arthur Tooth & Sons, Londres 1938.
Studio Waroline, Paris 1939 (Cat., Préface par le peintre).
«Moderne primitive Maler», Kunsthalle, Bern 1949 (Cat., Préface Arnold Rüdlinger).
«La Peinture Naïve», Knokke-le-Zoute 1958.
«La Peinture Naïve», Maison de la Pensée Française, Paris 1960.
«Die Welt der naiven Malerei», Salzburg 1964.
«De Lusthof der Naieven», Rotterdam 1964.
«Le Monde des Naïfs», Paris 1964.

BIBLIOGRAPHIE:

A. Jakovsky: «La Peinture Naïve», Paris 1956.
Anatole Jakovsky: «Naive Malerei», Zürich 1957.
A. Jakovsky: «Eros du Dimanche», Paris 1964.
Oto Bihalji-Merin: «Das naive Bild der Welt», Köln 1959.
Oto Bihalji-Merin: «Die naive Malerei», Köln 1959.
Oto Bihalji-Merin: «Les Peintres Naïfs», Paris

Pickett, Joseph

Born 1848 in New Hope, Penn. (USA).
Died 1918 in New Hope, Penn. (USA).

Geboren 1848 in New Hope, Penn. (USA).
Gestorben 1918 in New Hope, Penn. (USA).

Né en 1848 à New Hope, Penn. (USA).
Mort en 1918 à New Hope, Penn. (USA).

He spent all his life in this small town on the edge of the Delaware River. His father owned a shipbuilding yard there. He himself, however, tormented and restless in character, preferred to wander around with a travelling circus in the neighborhood, or else to keep peacefully to his own personal shooting gallery and gaming table, which he had installed at home and for which he had painted the decorations. Perhaps his taste for painting came from that. When creating his pictures he added all sorts of substances such as sand, shells, etc. His pictures, of which all but four are lost, are considered as the finest flowering of 'naive' American painting.

Er hat demnach sein ganzes Leben in diesem Dorf am Delaware verbracht, wo sein Vater eine Schiffswerft besaß. Er war eine gequälte, unruhige Natur und zog gern unverbindlich mit einem Zirkus in der Nachbarschaft herum, wenn er nicht still in seinem eigenen Schießstand und an seinem Spieltisch blieb, die er bei sich zu Hause eingerichtet hatte und für die er die Dekoration malte. Seine Freude an der Malerei stammt vielleicht daher. Seine Bilder, denen er alle Arten von Material hinzufügt, Sand, Muscheln usw. sind uns nicht erhalten mit Ausnahme von vieren, die als die schönsten Blüten der amerikanischen naiven Malerei betrachtet werden.

Il a passé donc toute sa vie dans ce village, au bord de la rivière Delaware où son père possédait un chantier de construction navale. Lui, nature tourmentée et inquiète, il préférait plutôt les vagabondages aimables avec un cirque ambulant dans les environs, si ce n'est de rester tranquillement avec son propre tir forain et une table de jeu qu'il a amenagés chez lui et pour lesquels il a brossé les décors. Son goût de la peinture vient peut-être de là. Ses tableaux, auxquels il ajoutait toutes sortes de matières, sable, coquillages, etc. sont perdus à l'exception de quatre qui sont considérés comme les plus beaux fleurons de la peinture naïve américaine.

EXPOSITIONS:
«American Primitives», Newark Museum, Newark, N.J. 1930.
«American Folk Art», New York 1932.
«Masters of Popular Painting», Museum of Modern Art, New York 1938.
Kunstmuseum, Luzern 1954 (Cat., Préface Adolf Reinle, Jean Lipman, etc.).
«American Art», Bruxelles 1958.
«De Lusthof der Naieven», Rotterdam 1964.
«Le Monde des Naïfs», Paris 1964.

BIBLIOGRAPHIE:
Sidney Janis: «They taught themselves», Dial Press, New York 1942.
Jean Lipman: «American Primitive Painting», Oxford University Press, New York 1942.
Oto Bihalji-Merin: «Das naive Bild der Welt», Köln 1959.
Oto Bihalji-Merin: «Die naive Malerei», Köln 1959.
Oto Bihalji-Merin: «Les Peintres Naïfs», Paris (sans date).
«Art Naïf», Editions Marocaines et Internationales, Rabat 1964.

Pinçon, Charles Lucien

Born March 5, 1902 in Lamorlaye, Oise (France).

Geboren am 5. März 1902 in Lamorlaye, Oise (Frankreich).

Né le 5 mars 1902 à Lamorlaye, Oise (France).

A magistrate. Became a Justice of the Peace in Mantes-la-Jolie, then mayor of Guerville, both places in Seine-et-Oise. Came from a large family and had to start work early in life because of his father's premature death. It was his mother, née Virginie Maricourt, a cultivated and sensitive woman, who taught him to love nature in all its simplicity. He remembered her when he later began to paint, always using the same motif, in snow or in wind, and this is probably why his snowscapes, for instance, are like childhood dreams realized late in life. The honesty and sincerity of his work was soon rewarded—he received decorations and honors from several public organizations, including the silver medal of Paris.

Gerichtsbeamter. Zuerst Friedensrichter in Mantes-la-Jolie, dann Bürgermeister von Guerville, zwei Städtchen im Departement Seine-et-Oise. Stammt aus einer kinderreichen Familie und muß sehr früh verdienen, weil sein Vater vorzeitig stirbt. Seine Mutter, Virginie Maricourt, eine gebildete, empfindsame Frau, lehrt ihn, die Natur in ihrer ganzen Einfachheit zu lieben. In Erinnerung an seine Mutter fängt er später an zu malen, immer nach Natur, ob es schneit oder windet. Und daher kommen zweifellos seine Schneebilder zum Beispiel, Kinderträume, die in reifem Alter verwirklicht werden. Die Redlichkeit und Aufrichtigkeit seiner Malerei ist ziemlich bald belohnt worden. Verdienstorden des Kultus-, des Sozial- und des Landwirtschaftsministeriums, sowie Silbermedaille der Stadt Paris.

Magistrat. D'abord Juge de Paix à Mantes-la-Jolie, puis Maire de Guerville, toujours en Seine-et-Oise. Issu d'une famille nombreuse et obligé de travailler très tôt à cause du décès prématuré de son père, c'est sa mère, née Virginie Maricourt, femme cultivée et sensible qui lui a appris à aimer la nature dans toute sa simplicité. C'est donc en se souvenant d'elle qu'il commence à peindre plus tard, toujours sur le motif, qu'il neige ou qu'il vente. Et c'est de là que viennent, sans doute, ses neiges, par exemple, les rêves d'enfant réalisés à l'âge mur. Cette probité et cette sincérité de la peinture a été recompensée d'assez bonne heure. Palmes Académiques, Mérite Social et Mérite Agricole, ainsi que médaille d'argent de la Ville de Paris.

EXPOSITIONS:
Galerie Montparnasse 27, Paris 1961.
Galerie le Parnasse, Paris 1964
(Cat., Préface Anatole Jakovsky).

BIBLIOGRAPHIE:
Un dépliant par Paul Yaki, avec des extraits de presse, Paris (sans date).

Pippin, Horace

Born 1888 in West Chester, Penn. (USA).
Died 1947 in West Chester, Penn. (USA).

Geboren 1888 in West Chester, Penn. (USA).
Gestorben 1947 in West Chester, Penn. (USA).

Né en 1888 à West Chester, Penn. (USA).
Mort en 1947 à West Chester, Penn. (USA).

Began to draw with colored crayons at the age of ten. When he left school at the age of 15 he became coal-carrier, hotel porter and secondhand dealer. Spent the first world war in France, where in 1917 he was badly wounded—was an invalid for the rest of his life. The war also made a profound impression on him; when he painted his first picture (he started in 1930 and it took him three years) he called it 'The End of the War'. On his death he left behind more than 100 pictures showing war scenes, religious subjects, landscapes, still-life paintings, and scenes in the life of colored people in the United States—for he was colored himself. He said: 'One must paint from one's heart and soul; therefore it is impossible to teach art to anyone else'.

Beginnt im Alter von zehn Jahren mit farbigen Kreiden zu zeichnen. Mit fünfzehn Jahren verläßt er die Schule, wird Kohlenträger, Laufbursche in einem Hotel und Trödler. Im Ersten Weltkrieg kämpft er in Frankreich, und eine 1917 empfangene schwere Verwundung macht ihn bis zu seinem Lebensende zum Krüppel. Der Krieg hinterläßt übrigens auch sonst tiefe Spuren in ihm. Als er 1930 zu malen anfängt, betitelt er sein erstes Werk, an dem er drei Jahre arbeitet, «Das Ende des Kriegs».
Bei seinem Tod hinterläßt er mehr als 100 Bilder: Szenen aus dem Krieg, religiöse Themen, Landschaften, Stilleben und Szenen aus dem Leben der Schwarzen in den Vereinigten Staaten, denn er war selber Neger. Er sagte, man müsse mit dem Herzen und der Seele malen und darum sei es unmöglich, einem anderen Menschen Kunst beizubringen.

Commence à dessiner, avec des craies de couleur, dès l'âge de 10 ans. A 15 ans, en quittant l'école, il est porteur de charbon, commissionnaire dans un hôtel et brocanteur. Fait la guerre en France et une grave blessure, reçue en 1917, le rend invalide jusqu'à la fin de ses jours. Cette guerre l'a marqué d'ailleurs très profondément. Lorsqu'il se mettra à peindre, en 1930, son premier tableau, auquel il travaillera trois ans, s'intitulera: «La Fin de la Guerre», comme de juste. A sa mort, il a laissé plus de 100 tableaux représentant des scènes de la guerre, des sujets religieux, des paysages, des nature-mortes et les scènes de la vie des noirs aux Etats-Unis, car il était lui-même noir. Il disait qu'il fallait «peindre du cœur et de l'âme et que, à cause de cela, il était impossible d'enseigner l'art à un autre».

EXPOSITIONS:
«The Masters of Popular Painting», New York 1938.
Corcoran Gallery of Art, Washington 1943.
Downtown Gallery, New York 1944.
Institute of History and Art, Albany, N.Y. 1945.
«Amerikanische Malerei», Kunstmuseum, Luzern 1954.
«Amerikanische Primitive»,
Museum am Ostwall, Dortmund 1954–1955.
«American Primitive Paintings», The Smithsonian Institution, Washington 1958.
«Das naive Bild der Welt», Baden-Baden 1961.
«De Lusthof der Naieven», Rotterdam 1964.
«Le Monde des Naïfs», Paris 1964.

BIBLIOGRAPHIE:
Sidney Janis: «They taught themselves», Dial Press, New York 1942.
Selden Rodman: «Horace Pippin, a Negro Painter», Quadrangle Press, New York 1947.
Oto Bihalji-Merin: «Das naive Bild der Welt», Köln 1959.
Oto Bihalji-Merin: «Die naive Malerei», Köln 1959.
Oto Bihalji-Merin: «Les Peintres Naïfs», Paris (sans date).

Pirosmanichwili, Niko

(called Pirosman)
Born 1860 in Mirzaani, a village in Kakhetia, Georgia (Russia).
Died May 5, 1917 in Tiflis (Russia).

(genannt Pirosman)
Geboren 1860 in Mirzaani, einem Kharthwelierdorf in Georgien.
Gestorben am 5. Mai 1917 in Tiflis (Rußland).

(dit Pirosman)
Né en 1860 à Mirzaani, village de Kakhétie, Géorgie (Russie).
Mort le 5 mai 1917 à Tiflis (Russie).

The son of a poor apple grower. From a very early age he was attracted to painting, and in 1882 he even founded a kind of craftsman's studio with the artist Zazichvili. But the studio went bankrupt, and so to earn a livelihood he became a track inspector for the Transcaucasian railway authority. Later he took up the brush again, this time as an itinerant painter going from village to village, sometimes making signboards for 'doukhans' (taverns) and sometimes dashing off portraits of merchants and decorations for their shops. These are the works which have survived for us. Actually, it is quite possible that if he had been able to work with a real artist his technique would have developed, as happened for instance in the case of the Bulgarian Tzanco Lavrenoff, and would have become more elaborate, half-way between 'naive' painting and art pure and simple. It was the artists and poets of the 'left' (Ilja Zdanevitch, among others) who brought his work to the attention of the public in Moscow in 1913. And it was Stefan Zweig who discovered him for Western Europe in 1930. He died a pauper, in a hospital.

Sohn eines armen Bauern. Schon in seiner Kindheit hat er eine Neigung für die Malerei. Er gründet sogar 1882 mit dem Maler Zazischwili zusammen eine Art handwerkliches Atelier. Aber sie machen Pleite, und um sein Brot zu verdienen, findet er Arbeit als Bahnwärter bei der transkaukasischen Eisenbahn. Dann nimmt er den Pinsel wieder zur Hand und zieht diesmal als fahrender Maler von Dorf zu Dorf, um an Ort und Stelle bald Schilder für die Schenken, bald Porträts der Geschäftsleute oder Dekorationen für ihre Läden zu malen. Diese Werke sind uns erhalten geblieben. Es ist im übrigen nicht unmöglich, daß seine Kunst sich wie zum Beispiel die des Bulgaren Tzanco Lavrenow zu etwas entwickelt hätte, das halbwegs zwischen der naiven Malerei und Kunst schlechthin läge, wenn er weiterhin mit einem echten Maler hätte zusammenarbeiten können. « Linksstehende» Maler und Dichter, u. a. Ilja Zdanewitsch, haben ihn bereits 1913 beim Moskauer Publikum bekannt gemacht. Und im Westen hat ihn Stefan Zweig 1930 entdeckt. Er ist als armer Mann im Krankenhaus gestorben.

Fils d'un pommiculteur pauvre, il est attiré dès son plus jeune âge vers la peinture. Il fonde même avec le peintre Zazichvili une sorte d'atelier artisanal en 1882. Mais l'atelier fait faillitte et, pour vivre, il entre comme gardien des voies du chemin de fer transcaucasien. Puis il reprend à nouveau le pinceau comme peintre ambulant cette fois, allant de village en village et confectionnant sur place tantôt des enseignes des «doukhans» – cabarets –, tantôt des portraits des commerçants et des décorations pour leurs boutiques. Ce sont ces œuvres-là qui sont parvenues jusqu'à nous. Il n'est pas impossible, du reste, que, s'il avait pu continuer à travailler avec un vrai peintre, son art aurait évolué, comme celui du bulgare Tzanco Lavrenoff par exemple, vers quelque chose de plus poussé, se situant à mi-chemin entre la peinture naïve et l'art tout court. Ce sont les peintres et les poètes de «gauche», Ilja Zdanevitch, entre autres, qui l'ont fait connaître, dès 1913, au public moscovite. Et c'est Stefan Zweig qui l'a révélé en Occident en 1930. Il est mort pauvre, à l'hôpital.

EXPOSITIONS:
Première exposition d'ensemble, Tiflis 1930 (Transportée par la suite à Leningrad, Moscou, Odessa et Kiev).
Deuxième exposition d'ensemble, Tiflis 1938.
Grande rétrospective, Tiflis 1961
(Cat., Préface Amirachwili, en géorgien et en russe).
Musée Pouchkine, Moscou 1963.

BIBLIOGRAPHIE:
Première monographie de Pirosman, Tiflis 1926.
Nicolas Verjbitzky: «Rencontres avec Essenine», Tiflis 1961.
Courrier de l'UNESCO, Octobre 1962.
K. Paoustovsky: «Ma Vie», trad. franç., Gallimard, Paris 1962.
K. Paoustovsky, Interview aux «Lettres Françaises», Paris, 7 décembre 1962.
K. Paoustovsky: «Il ferroviere Pirosmanichwili» in Europa Letteraria, No. 20/21.
Kirill Zdanevitch: «Niko Pirosmanichwili», Editions d'Etat, Tbilisi 1963 (en géorgien).
Kirill Zdanevitch: «Niko Pirosmanichwili», Ed. d'Etat, Ed. Sabtchota Sakartvelo, Tbilisi 1965 (en russe).
Oto Bihalji-Merin: «Das naive Bild der Welt», Köln 1959.
Oto Bihalji-Merin: «Die naive Malerei», Köln 1959.
Oto Bihalji-Merin: «Les Peintres Naïfs», Paris (sans date).
Anatole Jakovsky: «Eros du Dimanche», Paris 1964.
Dusan Konečny: «Niko Pirosmanichwili», Editions d'Etat, Prague 1965 (en tchèque).

Plümer, Werner

Born 1909 in Essen (Germany).

Geboren 1909 in Essen (Deutschland).

Né en 1909 à Essen (Allemagne).

A woodcarver. Earns his living by working in one of the Krupp factories in Essen. He is a very sensitive artist, tending rather towards the romantic or «gemütlich» side of life. Sunday is the only day of the week he has time to paint—and it is, precisely, the Sunday of life which he depicts.

Holzschnitzer. Arbeitet in Krupps Maschinenfabrik in Essen. Große Empfindsamkeit, die hauptsächlich die romantische, «gemütliche» Seite des Lebens wahrnimmt. Er kann nur sonntags malen, und dann malt er eben den Sonntag schlechthin.

Sculpteur sur bois. Travaille chez Fried. Krupp, fabrique de machines à Essen. Grande sensibilité, orientée surtout vers le côté romantique, sinon «gemütlich» de la vie. S'il ne peut peindre que le dimanche, c'est précisément le dimanche, avec un grand D qu'il peint.

BIBLIOGRAPHIE:
«Laienkunst», Recklinghausen 1963
(Cat., Préface Bernhard Tacke).

Poisson, Louverture

Born 1914 in Haiti.

Geboren 1914 in Haiti.

Né en 1914 à Haïti.

Is always attracted by mythological subjects. His work is truly epic in inspiration, and he seems to know more than the other 'naive' painters of Haiti about traditional art, such as is taught in art schools. Unfortunately, very little is known about his life.

Hat eine Vorliebe für mythologische Themen. Er besitzt einen großen epischen Atem und ist zweifellos der Maler, der die traditionelle Malerei, jene, die man in den wahren Kunstschulen erlernt, am besten kennt. Leider weiß man nur ganz wenig über sein Leben.

Peintre attiré par des sujets mythologiques. Peintre animé par un vaste souffle épique et, sans doute, celui qui sait le mieux ce que c'est que la peinture traditionnelle, celle que l'on apprend dans les vraies écoles des Beaux-Arts. On ne sait, malheureusement, que peu de choses sur sa vie.

EXPOSITIONS:
«Peintres de l'Equateur, de Haïti et de Pérou», l'UNESCO, Paris 1947.
«Naive Painters of Latin America», Duke University, Durham, N.C. 1963.
«19 Peintres d'Haïti», Palais des Beaux-Arts, Bruxelles 1963.
«20th Century Latin American Naive Art», La Jolla, Calif. (USA) 1964.

BIBLIOGRAPHIE:
«Art Naïf», Editions Marocaines et Internationales, Rabat 1964.
Anatole Jakovsky: «Eros du Dimanche», Paris 1964.

Prazeres, Heitor dos

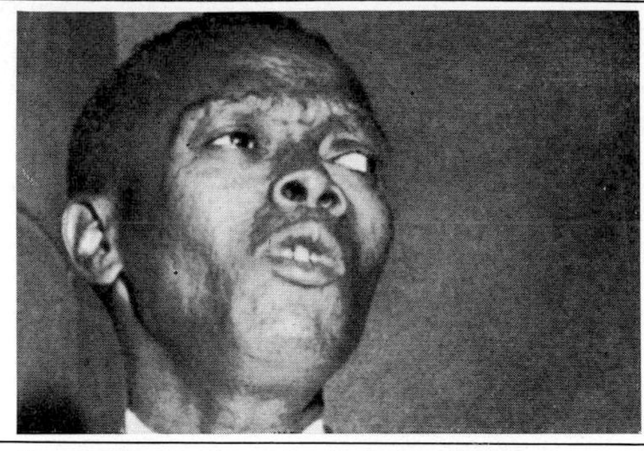

Born 1893 in Rio de Janeiro (Brazil).

Geboren 1893 in Rio de Janeiro (Brasilien).

Né en 1893 à Rio de Janeiro (Brésil).

Colored. A composer of popular folk music. Began to paint in 1937, for no particular reason and without giving up either his sambas or his guitar, which he plays surrounded by his 'pastoras' (choirs of mulatto women). Has taken part in numerous collective exhibitions both in Brazil and elsewhere. Was awarded first prize at the São Paulo Biannual Exhibition. His work is quite amusing, truly 'naive' and typically South American.

Neger. Komponist volkstümlicher Musik. Fängt 1937 an zu malen, ohne bestimmten Grund und ohne deshalb seine Sambas oder seine Gitarre aufzugeben, auf der er spielt, während seine «pastoras» (Mulattinnenchöre) dazu singen. Nimmt an zahlreichen Gruppenausstellungen im In- und Ausland teil. Wird an der ersten Biennale von São Paulo ausgezeichnet. Ziemlich amüsante, echt naive und typisch südamerikanische Malerei.

Noir. Compositeur de musique populaire. Commence à peindre en 1937, sans aucune raison précise et sans abandonner ses sambas pour cela. Ni sa guitare dont il joue entouré de ses «pastoras» (chœurs de mulâtresses). Participe à de nombreuses expositions collectives dans son pays et à l'étranger. Primé à la première Biennale de São Paulo. Peinture assez amusante, vraiment naïve et typiquement sudaméricaine.

EXPOSITIONS:
Galerie Gead, Rio de Janeiro 1959.
Musée d'Art Moderne, Rio de Janeiro 1961.
Galerie Montmartre-Jorge, Rio de Janeiro 1964.
«Peintres Naïfs Brésiliens», Galerie Jacques Massol, Paris 1965.

BIBLIOGRAPHIE:
Rubem Braga: «Tres Primitivos», Ed. par le Service de Documentation du Ministère de l'Education et de la Culture, 1953.

Prior, William Matthew

Born 1806 in Bath, Maine (USA).
Died 1873 in Boston, Mass. (USA).

Geboren 1806 in Bath, Maine (USA).
Gestorben 1873 in Boston, Mass. (USA).

Né en 1806 à Bath, Maine (USA).
Mort en 1873 à Boston, Mass. (USA).

This artist, like Mary Ann Wilson, Bradley, Eunice Pinney, H. Davis, Chambers, Erastus Salsbury, James Bard and others, was lucky enough to be able to pass on to later generations an almost complete biography (although we have no picture of the man himself). He too began as a 'Limner', in other words an itinerant portrait painter. His earliest known work carries the date "Portland, Aug. 14 (?) 1824". Rather later, he advertised in the newspapers offering his services as an artist. Incidentally, he asked fairly high prices. His rise to fame did not come until 1834, when he settled down with Nathaniel Hamblen, his brother-in-law, in Portland. In 1840 he moved again and made his home this time in Boston. He became a member of William Miller's sect, which forecast the second coming of Christ for the year 1843.

Wie so viele andere, Mary Ann Wilson, Bradley, Eunice Pinney, H. Davis, Chambers, Erastus Salsbury oder James Bard z. B., hat auch er der Nachwelt eine sozusagen vollständige Biographie hinterlassen, auch wenn wir nicht wissen, wie er ausgesehen hat. Auch er beginnt als «Limner», das heißt als fahrender Porträtist. Das älteste bekannte Bild trägt den Vermerk «Portland, Aug. 14 (?) 1824». Etwas später inseriert er in den Zeitungen, um seine Dienste anzubieten. Er läßt sich übrigens ziemlich teuer bezahlen. Seine Berühmtheit beginnt jedoch erst mit dem Jahr 1834, als er sich mit seinem Schwager Nathaniel Hamblen zusammen in Portland niederläßt. 1840 zieht er nach Boston. Er war Anhänger der Sekte von William Miller, der die Wiederkunft Christi für das Jahr 1843 voraussagte.

Lui aussi, parmi tous ces innombrables, Mary Ann Wilson, Bradley, Eunice Pinney, H. Davis, Chambers, Erastus Salsbury, James Bard et autres, a eu la chance de faire passer à la postérité, à défaut de son visage, une biographie à peu près complète. Lui aussi débute donc comme «Limner», autrement dit portraitiste ambulant. La plus ancienne œuvre connue porte: Portland, Aug. 14 (?) 1824. Un peu plus tard, il met des annonces dans les journaux afin d'offrir ses services. Il se fait payer d'ailleurs assez cher. Or, sa notoriété ne commence qu'à partir de 1834 lorsqu'il s'installe, avec Nathaniel Hamblen, son beau-frère, à Portland. En 1840, il change encore de ville et s'établit à Boston. Il a été adepte de la secte de William Miller, qui prophétisait la venue du Christ pour l'année 1843.

EXPOSITIONS:
«Amerikanische Primitive», Museum am Ostwall, Dortmund 1954–55.
«American Primitive Paintings», The Smithsonian Institution, Washington 1958.
Pavillon américain à l'Exposition Universelle, Bruxelles 1958.

BIBLIOGRAPHIE:
Oto Bihalji-Merin: «Das naive Bild der Welt», Köln 1959.
Oto Bihalji-Merin: «Die naive Malerei», Köln 1959.
Oto Bihalji-Merin: «Les Peintres Naïfs», Paris (sans date).

Rabuzin, Ivan

Born 1919 in Ključ, near Novi Masof (Yugoslavia).

Geboren 1919 in Ključ bei Novi Masof (Jugoslawien).

Né en 1919 à Ključ, près de Novi Masof (Yougoslavie).

A joiner by trade. He took up painting in 1955; although he began with a style very similar to that of the Hlebine school, he moved away from this very soon and developed into a real 'poet of space', almost cosmic in attitude. He is certainly the most truly artistic of all Yugoslav artists; his rose colors and his pale blues are unique—as is, in fact, his inventiveness, which is poetical and yet extremely plastic.

Schreiner. Fängt 1955 an zu malen; seine Anfänge entsprechen genau der Linie der Schule von Hlebine, aber er löst sich sehr rasch davon und wird zu dem, was er heute ist, nämlich ein großer Dichter des Raums, des Kosmos, oder doch beinahe. Er ist zweifellos der malbegabteste unter allen jugoslawischen Malern. Seine Rosa und seine Hellblau sind unnachahmlich. Wie übrigens auch seine zugleich poetischen und plastischen Einfälle.

Menuisier. Commence à peindre en 1955, mais si ses débuts étaient tout à fait dans la ligne de l'Ecole de Hlebine, il s'en détache très rapidement cependant pour devenir ce qu'il est maintenant, c'est-à-dire un grand poète de l'espace, cosmique ou presque. C'est certainement le plus peintre de tous les peintres yougoslaves. Ses roses et ses bleus pâles sont inimitables. Comme sont inimitables, du reste, ses trouvailles à la fois poétiques et plastiques.

EXPOSITIONS:
The Arthur Jeffress Gallery, Londres 1961.
«Laienmaler», Gewerbemuseum, Basel 1961.
«Première Quadriennale des Peintres Naïfs Yougoslaves», Čačac 1962.
«Yugoslav Modern Primitives», Edinburgh 1962.
Galerie Mona Lisa, Paris 1963 (Cat., Préface José Pierre).
«Naive Kunst in Jugoslawien», Kunstakademie, Wien 1963.
The Galerie St-Etienne, New York 1963 (Cat., Préface non signée).
«Peintres Naïfs Yougoslaves», Moscou 1962.
«Peintres Naïfs Populaires Yougoslaves», Leningrad 1963.
«Sonntagsmaler aus Jugoslawien», Museum am Ostwall, Dortmund 1964.
«De Lusthof der Naieven», Rotterdam 1964.
«Le Monde des Naïfs», Paris 1964.
Galerie Mona Lisa, Paris 1965 (Cat., Préface Anatole Jakovsky).
Galerie Renée Laporte, Antibes 1965 (Cat., Préface Nestor Somlyo).

BIBLIOGRAPHIE:
Oto Bihalji-Merin: «Umetnost Naivnich u Jugoslavjii», Belgrade 1963.
Jean-Dominique Rey: «Ivan Rabuzin», Jardin des Arts, No. 114, Paris mai 1964.
«Art Naïf», Editions Marocaines et Internationales, Rabat 1964.
Anatole Jakovsky: «Eros du Dimanche», Paris 1964.
«Ivan Rabuzin», Petit Crapouillot, No. 12, Paris décembre 1965.

Racoff, Rastislaw

Born February 5, 1904 in Petrograd (Russia).

Geboren am 5. Februar 1904 in Petrograd (Rußland).

Né le 5 février 1904 à Pétrograd (Russie).

After the Russian Revolution he lived first in Northern China and then moved to Paris, where he arrived in 1929. Studied law and worked as scene painter for the film industry. Spent the war in the French army. When he was demobilized he became a picture framer, then decided in 1946–47 to devote all his time to painting. His style is neat and accurate, sometimes recalling J. Lefranc, his patron and friend.

Nach der Revolution lebt er zunächst in Nordchina, kommt 1929 nach Paris. Studiert Jurisprudenz und arbeitet als Film-Dekorateur. Nimmt in der französischen Armee am Krieg teil. Nach seiner Entlassung aus dem Heer wird er Einrahmer und widmet sich von 1946/47 an endgültig der Malerei. Sehr präziser Stil, der zuweilen an den seines Gönners und Freundes J. Lefranc erinnert.

Après la Révolution, il vit d'abord en Chine du Nord, puis arrive à Paris en 1929. Fait des études de droit et travaille comme décorateur pour le cinéma. Fait la guerre dans l'armée française. Démobilisé, devient encadreur, pour se consacrer définitivement à la peinture à partir de 1946/47. Style très précis, rappelant parfois celui de J. Lefranc, son protecteur et ami.

EXPOSITIONS:
Galerie Vendôme, Paris 1946.
Galerie Dina Vierny, Paris 1952.
Galerie God Konst, Göteborg 1953.
«Les Primitifs d'Aujourd'hui», Galerie Charpentier, Paris 1964.

BIBLIOGRAPHIE:
«Rastislaw Racoff», Femina-Noël, Paris, janvier 1948.
Anatole Jakovsky: «La Peinture Naïve», Paris 1949.
Anatole Jakovsky: «Les Peintres Naïfs», Paris.
Anatole Jakovsky: «Naive Malerei», Zürich 1957.

Ramholz

(real name Felix Muche)
Born 1868 in Querfurt (Germany).
Died 1947 in Ramholz (Germany).

(mit seinem richtigen Namen Felix Muche)
Geboren 1868 in Querfurt (Deutschland).
Gestorben 1947 in Ramholz (Deutschland).

(de son vrai nom: Felix Muche)
Né en 1868 à Querfurt (Allemagne).
Mort en 1947 à Ramholz (Allemagne).

He took his name from the Bavarian village on the Rhön which had a castle and a large park of which he became steward in 1901. He started in 1916 by collecting works of modern painters such as Picasso, Chagall, Klee, Marc, etc., which he sometimes considered 'crazy'; then, at the age of sixty (i.e. in 1928) he began to paint himself. His work is amusing, with a German, rather grating type of humor. His son is the famous architect Georg Muche. Perhaps that is why he did not want to sign his pictures with his own name.

Er hat seinen Namen dem bayrischen Dorf am Rand der Rhön entlehnt, wo er Verwalter des Schlosses mit dem großen Park war und wo er seit 1901 lebte. Zuerst sammelt er moderne Bilder, und zwar bereits von 1916 an: Picasso, Chagall, Klee, Marc usw., die er zuweilen als «Verrückte» bezeichnet. Dann beginnt er 1928, das heißt im Alter von 60 Jahren, selber zu malen. Seine Malerei ist amüsant, geprägt von einem deutschen, etwas schwerfälligen Humor. Er ist der Vater des berühmten Architekten Georg Muche. Vielleicht wollte er deshalb seine Werke nicht mit seinem richtigen Namen zeichnen.

Il a pris son nom au village au bord du Rhœn, en Bavière, avec un château et un grand parc dont il était régisseur et où il a vécu depuis 1901. D'abord il collectionne les tableaux modernes (dès 1916), Picasso, Chagall, Klee, Marc, etc. qu'il traite parfois de «fous», puis se met à faire de la peinture lui-même, à l'âge de 60 ans, c'est-à-dire à partir de 1928. Sa peinture est amusante, empreinte d'un humour allemand, un peu grinçant. Il est père du célèbre architecte Georg Muche. C'est peut-être à cause de cela qu'il n'a pas voulu signer ses œuvres de son vrai nom.

EXPOSITIONS:
« Die Welt der naiven Malerei », Salzburg 1964.

BIBLIOGRAPHIE:
Bernard Jasmand et Otto Kallir: «Sonntagsmaler», Ed. Otto Aug. Ehlers, Berlin/Darmstadt 1956.
Oto Bihalji-Merin: « Das naive Bild der Welt», Köln 1959.
Oto Bihalji-Merin: « Die naive Malerei », Köln 1959.
Oto Bihalji-Merin: « Les Peintres Naïfs », Paris (sans date).

Rayb

(real name: Raymond Bussereau)
Born June 17, 1897 in Saint-Chiron, Seine-et-Oise (France).

(mit seinem richtigen Namen Raymond Bussereau)
Geboren am 17. Juni 1897 in Saint-Chiron, Seine-et-Oise (Frankreich).

(de son vrai nom: Raymond Bussereau)
Né le 17 juin 1897 à Saint-Chiron, Seine-et-Oise (France).

For 42 years he worked in the bank 'Le Comptoir National d'Escompte', becoming head of the service department in 1940. But this calm and ordered way of life, spent in dealing with figures, was to undergo a change—first on his retirement and second after the death of his wife. If the former left him rather at a loose end, the latter event plunged him into a state of despair which lasted for years. And it was painting which, once again, came to the rescue. His work is accurate and inventive, and it is difficult to decide whether it is the subject of the painting which pleases so much or whether it is the extreme precision of execution—each detail may be studied with a magnifying glass.

Arbeitet 42 Jahre lang auf einer Bank (Comptoir National d'Escompte), seit 1940 als Abteilungsleiter. Aber dieses geruhsame Leben, das mit dem Aneinanderreihen von Zahlen verbracht wird, sollte sich ändern. Zuerst kam die Pensionierung, dann der Tod seiner Frau. Der Ruhestand läßt ihm ein bißchen zuviel Muße, und der Verlust seiner Frau stürzt ihn in jahrelange Verzweiflung. Gerettet wird auch er durch seine Malerei.
Eine überaus sorgfältige, erfindungsreiche Malerei, bei der man nicht recht weiß, ob einen das Thema mehr besticht oder die außerordentliche Genauigkeit, die erlaubt, jede Einzelheit mit der Lupe zu betrachten.

Travaille dans une banque (Le Comptoir National d'Escompte), pendant 42 ans, ceci en tant que chef de service depuis 1940. Mais cette vie tranquille, passée à aligner les chiffres va changer; d'abord avec la retraite, puis avec la mort de sa femme. Si la retraite le laisse un tantinet désœuvré, le second événement le plonge dans un désespoir qui dure pendant des années. Et c'est sa peinture qui le sauve.
Une fois de plus. Peinture précise, inventive, où l'on ne sait pas si on est séduit davantage par le sujet ou par cette extrême minutie, où chaque détail peut être regardé à la loupe.

Rehak, Antonin

Born in 1902 in Svaty Kopecek in Moravia (Czechoslovakia).

Geboren 1902 in Svaty Kopecek in Mähren (Tschechoslowakei).

Né en 1902 à Svaty Kopecek en Moravie (Tchécoslovaquie).

Gardener and bee keeper. Began to paint when, as the eldest son, he had to look after his many brothers and sisters during the absence of his father (called up in the 1914–18 war); he kept them amused with his drawings. Later on he continued to paint. Among the most representative, if not the most interesting of his canvases is the cycle called 'Karlsbad'—he underwent treatment there in 1961. Is a very fine, truly 'naive' artist.

Gärtner, Bienenzüchter. Beginnt zu malen, weil er als der älteste Sohn einer kinderreichen Familie in Abwesenheit des im Ersten Weltkrieg mobilisierten Vaters sich um seine Geschwister kümmern muß und sie mit seinen Zeichnungen unterhält. Er hat das Malen seither nicht mehr aufgegeben. Unter seinen repräsentativsten, interessantesten Bildern befindet sich der Zyklus «Karlsbad», wo er 1961 zur Kur weilte. Sehr begabter, echt naiver Maler.

Jardinier, apiculteur. Commence à peindre lorsque, en tant que fils aîné, devant s'occuper d'une nombreuse famille en l'absence du père, mobilisé pendant la guerre de 1914–18, il amusait ses frères et sœurs avec ses dessins. Il a continué depuis. Parmi ses toiles les plus représentatives, sinon les plus intéressantes, figure le cycle «Karlsbad», là où il était soigné en 1961. Très beau peintre authentiquement naïf.

EXPOSITIONS:
«Naivni Umeni», Dum Umeni, Brno 1963.
«Naivni Umeni v Ceskoslovensku», Prague 1964.

Riec-Jestin, Raymond

Born August 11, 1905 in Landerneau, Finistère (France).

Geboren am 11. August 1905 in Landerneau, Finistère (Frankreich).

Né le 11 août 1905 à Landerneau, Finistère (France).

Son of a country blacksmith, brought up by his grandmother. Had to teach himself French, and in the same way he studied for his educational certificates (after military service) while earning his living as a bus-conductor, strong-man in fairs, bottle washer in restaurants, etc. But, like all self-respecting Bretons, he wanted to leave his native region. So he worked on a cargo boat in the Eastern Mediterranean. One day someone proposed he go and work at the excavations in Mesopotamia. He returned from there knowing as much about it as a lecturer in the 'Collège de France', where, in fact, he was welcomed as assistant teacher. But this only involved his brain. His heart also needed to develop and express itself. Painting was the answer. He started to paint in 1953 and his pictures grow more and more beautiful.

Sohn eines Schmieds auf dem Land, von seiner Großmutter aufgezogen. Kann kein Französisch, sondern lernt es später von sich aus, wie er nach dem Militärdienst auch seine Reifeprüfung besteht, während er sein Leben als Omnibusschaffner, Kraftmensch auf den Jahrmärkten, Tellerwäscher usw. verdient. Aber wie jeden Bretonen, der etwas auf sich hält, lockt ihn die Fremde. Er fährt auf einem Frachter im östlichen Mittelmeer herum. Dann wird ihm eines schönen Tages vorgeschlagen, an den Ausgrabungen in Mesopotamien teilzunehmen. Am Ende der Arbeiten weiß er so viel wie ein Professor am Collège de France, wo man ihn übrigens als Assistenten anstellt. Aber das berührt nur den Kopf. Das Herz will auch über sich hinauswachsen. Und so kommt er zur Malerei. Er beginnt 1953, und sein Werk wird immer größer und schöner.

Fils d'un forgeron de campagne, élevé par sa grand-mère. Ne sait pas le français qu'il apprend lui-même, comme il passera plus tard son baccalauréat par ses propres moyens, après le service militaire, tout en gagnant sa vie comme receveur d'autobus, casseur de chaînes dans les Foires, plongeur dans les restaurants, etc. Mais comme tout vrai Breton qui se respecte, il faut qu'il parte. Il navigue donc sur un cargo dans la Méditerranée Orientale. Puis, un beau jour, on lui propose de travailler aux fouilles en Mésopotamie. Il en sort aussi savant qu'un professeur au Collège de France, où on l'accueille, d'ailleurs, comme assistant. Mais cela ne touche que le cerveau. Il y a encore le cœur qui a besoin de se dépasser, lui aussi. Et c'est la peinture. Cette peinture, commencée en 1953, qui ne fait que croître et embellir.

EXPOSITIONS:
Galerie Norval, Paris 1960
(Cat., Préface Anatole Jakovsky).
«Les Peintres Naïfs», Maison de la Pensée Française, Paris 1960.
Galerie Michel Columb, Nantes 1962
(Cat., Préface Anatole Jakovsky).
Galerie Herbinet, Paris 1964
(Cat., Préface Anatole Jakovsky).
«I Pittori Naifs», Rome 1964.
«Les Primitifs d'Aujourd'hui»,
Galerie Charpentier, Paris 1964.
Galerie M. Bénézit, Paris 1966
(Cat., Préface Anatole Jakovsky et René Barotte).

BIBLIOGRAPHIE:
Anatole Jakovsky: «Raymond Riec-Jestin», Cahiers de l'Iroise, N°3, Brest juillet 1960.
«Art Naïfs», Editions Marocaines et Internationales, Rabat 1964.
«Dix Ans d'Art Actuel», Editions Comparaisons, Paris 1964.
Anatole Jakovsky: «Eros du Dimanche», Paris 1964.

De Rijke, Seraphin

Born in 1840 in Deurle (Belgium).
Died in 1915 in Petegem (Belgium).

Geboren 1840 in Deurle (Belgien).
Gestorben 1915 in Petegem (Belgien).

Né en 1840 à Deurle (Belgique).
Mort en 1915 à Petegem (Belgique).

This painter of buildings and, sometimes, chair-mender lived from 1892 to 1904 in Laethem. There he too became infected by the atmosphere and painted several pictures. He is a naive artist with a touching, melancholy sensitivity. His work was not without influence: it clearly affected a certain de Saedeler, which up to now has escaped the attention of the critics. Together with Albijn van den Abeele, de Rijke is one of the leading Belgian naive artists—or rather, its unknown soldier! The more so as his works, with the exception or two or three pictures, have been irretrievably lost.

Dieser Anstreicher, der gelegentlich auch als Stuhlflechter arbeitete, lebte von 1892 bis 1904 in Laethem Saint-Martin, wo er, vom Malfieber angesteckt, ebenfalls ein paar Bilder malte.
Er ist ein Naiver von rührender, schwermütiger Empfindsamkeit. Indessen hat seine Malerei ganz eindeutig einen großen Einfluß auf de Saedeler ausgeübt, was der Kritik bisher entgangen ist. Zusammen mit Albijn van den Abeele gehört er zu den allerersten naiven Malern Belgiens, man kann geradezu sagen, er sei ihr Unbekannter Soldat! Dies um so mehr, als seine Werke, mit Ausnahme von 2 oder 3 Bildern, unrettbar verloren sind.

Ce peintre en bâtiment et, à l'occasion, rempailleur de chaises, a séjourné à Laethem Saint-Martin de 1892 à 1904, où, pris par la contagion, il a peint, lui aussi, quelques tableaux. C'est un naïf d'une sensibilité touchante et mélancolique. Son œuvre n'a pas été, cependant, sans influencer très nettement un de Saedeler, ce qui a échappé jusqu'ici à la critique. Avec Albijn van den Abeele, il est l'un des premiers peintres naïfs belges, mieux: son soldat inconnu! D'autant plus que ses œuvres, à l'exception de deux ou trois tableaux, sont irrémédiablement perdues.

EXPOSITIONS:
«Peintres Naïfs Belges», Le Théâtre National, Bruxelles 1965.
«Peintres Naïfs Belges», Musée Royal de Beaux-Arts, Verviers 1965.
«Peintres Naïfs Belges», Musée Royal des Beaux-Arts, Hasselt 1956.

BIBLIOGRAPHIE:
A. de Ridder: «Laethem Saint-Martin», Editions Lumière, Bruxelles 1945.
Hugo van den Abeele: «Latemse Kunstenaars», Gand 1958.
Anatole Jakovsky: «Eros du Dimanche» Editions J.J. Pauvert, Paris 1964.

Rimbert, René

Born 1896 in Paris (France).

Geboren 1896 in Paris (Frankreich).

Né en 1896 à Paris (France).

Son of a picture framer who was also a wood-carver, such as only exist in the district Saint-Germain-des-Prés/Saint-Sulpice of Paris. He spent his entire childhood there and his paintings forever recall this district. He even belonged to the Saint-Sulpice choir school. At any rate, at the age of 17 he began to work for the Post Office, a sensible job, and remained with the same authorities until he retired—as sensible as could be. Can one ever tell? For painting, which he took up about the time he started with the Post Office, brought him great disillusionment and almost caused an open break in his life. He rose to fame in a very short time (his pictures were bought by museums the world over) but was suddenly abandoned by his art dealer, at the time of the depression. So he stopped painting. Only in 1944 did he take up a brush again, but with less success, it must be admitted. Something had broken. Nevertheless, Rimbert is still one of the greatest of modern 'naive' artists.

Sohn eines Einrahmers und Holzschnitzers, wie es sie nur in dem Viertel Saint-Germain-des-Prés und Saint-Sulpice gab; in diesem Stadtteil verbrachte er seine ganze Jugend und er hört nie auf, ihn in seinen Bildern heraufzubeschwören. Er ist sogar Mitglied des Kirchenchors von Saint-Sulpice. Schon im Alter von 17 Jahren tritt er schön brav in die Postverwaltung ein, wo er ebenso brav verbleibt, bis er den Ruhestand erreicht. Man kann ja nie wissen. Denn die Malerei, die er seit seinem Eintritt bei der Post betreibt, hat ihm schon eine große Enttäuschung beschert und hätte beinahe einen wahrhaften Bruch in seinem Leben bewirkt. Nachdem er in kurzer Zeit sehr bekannt geworden war (seine Bilder wurden von Museen auf der ganzen Welt gekauft), ließ ihn bei Einbruch der Krise sein Händler plötzlich im Stich. Da hört er auf zu malen und nimmt den Pinsel erst 1944 wieder zur Hand, allerdings mit weniger Erfolg. Irgend etwas ist zerbrochen. Das hindert nicht, daß Rimbert zu den größten naiven Malern der heutigen Zeit gehört.

Fils d'un encadreur-sculpteur sur bois, comme il n'y en avait que dans le quartier Saint-Germain-des-Prés/Saint-Sulpice, où s'écoule toute sa jeunesse et qu'il ne cessera jamais d'évoquer dans ses tableaux. Il fait même partie de la Maîtrise Saint-Sulpice. Quoiqu'il en soit, dès l'âge de 17 ans, il entre sagement à l'Administration des Postes, où il restera jusqu'à l'âge de la retraite, aussi sagement. Sait-on jamais? Car la peinture qu'il pratique depuis son entrée aux P.T.T. lui a causé déjà une grande désillusion et a failli provoquer une véritable cassure dans sa vie. Monté très haut en peu de temps (ses tableaux sont achetés par les musées du monde entier), il se voit tout d'un coup abandonné par son marchand, avec la crise. Alors il cesse de peindre. Il ne reprendra ses pinceaux qu'en 1944, avec moins de bonheur, il faut le dire. Quelque chose est cassé. Il n'empêche que Rimbert reste parmi les plus grands peintres naïfs d'aujourd'hui.

EXPOSITIONS:
Galerie Percier, Paris 1927
(Cat., Préface Max Jacob).
« Les Maîtres Populaires de la Réalité », Paris 1937.
« Les Maîtres Populaires de la Réalité », Zürich 1937.
« Masters of Popular Painting», New York 1938.
Galerie Berri-Argenson, Paris 1950.
Galerie Montmorency, Paris 1956
(Cat., Préface Maximilien Gauthier).
« La Peinture Naïve », Knokke-le-Zoute 1958.
« La Peinture Naïve », Maison de la Pensée Française, Paris 1960.
« Die Welt der naiven Malerei », Salzburg 1964.
Galerie Berri-Lardy, Paris 1964 (Cat., Préface Jean Bouret).
« Les Primitifs d'Aujourd'hui »,
Galerie Charpentier, Paris 1964.
« De Lusthof der Naieven », Rotterdam 1964.
« Le Monde des Naïfs », Paris 1964.
« Le Panorama International de la Peinture Naïve », Rabat 1964.

BIBLIOGRAPHIE:
A. Jakovsky: « La Peinture Naïve », Paris 1949.
A. Jakovsky: « Les Peintres Naïfs », Paris 1956.
Anatole Jakovsky: « Naive Malerei », Zürich 1957.
Anatole Jakovsky: « Eros du Dimanche », Paris 1964.
Oto Bihalji-Merin: « Das naive Bild der Welt », Köln 1959.
Oto Bihalji-Merin: « Die naive Malerei », Köln 1959.
Oto Bihalji-Merin: « Les Peintres Naïfs », Paris (sans date).
« Art Naïf », Editions Marocaines et Internationales, Rabat 1964.
J.N. Priou: « R. Rimbert », Arts P.T.T., No. 44, Paris 1966.

Rivas, Francisco Barbaro

Born in Venezuela.

Geboren in Venezuela.

Né à Venezuela.

Has had a number of occupations, including that of policeman. But, in spite of everything, he is truly a painter. Is mainly fond of religious subjects. Has shown his work in all his country's art museums, including the Caracas Museum of Fine Art.

Übt eine ganze Reihe von Berufen aus, darunter auch den eines Polizisten. Malt aber dennoch, allen Widerständen zum Trotz. Vorliebe für religiöse Themen. Stellt in allen Salons seines Landes aus, auch im Kunstmuseum von Caracas.

Exerce pas mal de métiers, dont celui d'agent de police. Mais peint quand-même, envers et contre tous. Sujets religieux de préférence. Expose dans tous les Salons du pays, sans excepter le Musée des Beaux-Arts de Caracas.

EXPOSITIONS:
«Naive Painters of Latin America», Duke University, Durham, N.C., 1963.

BIBLIOGRAPHIE:
«Art Naïf», Editions Marocaines et Internationales, Rabat 1964.

Roeder, John

Born 1877 in Bollendorferbruck (Luxemburg).

Geboren 1877 in Bollendorferbruck (Luxemburg).

Né en 1877 à Bollendorferbruck (Luxembourg).

One of a family of nine. He was barely two years old when his father died. As soon as he was able, he helped his mother to look after their little farm until they immigrated to the United States, where his eldest brother was waiting for them in Richmond, California. In America he worked for Standard Oil, until he was able to buy his own farm. After that he allowed himself to potter around and finally took up painting. n 19 52 he contracted a rather serious eye disease, but that did not prevent him from continuing to paint—rather the contrary. Ever since then he has proudly signed his work 'John Roeder, the blind man'. Is now an American citizen.

Stammt aus einer Familie von neun Kindern. Sein Vater stirbt, als er kaum zwei Jahre alt ist. Sobald er es vermag, hilft er der Mutter bei der Bewirtschaftung des kleinen Bauernguts, bis sie in die Vereinigten Staaten auswandern, wo sie sein ältester Bruder in Richmond (Kalifornien) erwartet. Arbeitet bei der Standard Oil, bis er einen Hof kaufen kann. Hier bastelt er nach Herzenslust und landet schließlich bei der Malerei. 1952 wird er von einer ziemlich schweren Augenkrankheit befallen, was ihn indessen nicht hindert, weiterzumalen. Im Gegenteil. Von da an signiert er voll Stolz: John Roeder the Blind Man. Er hat natürlich die amerikanische Staatsangehörigkeit erworben.

Il naît dans une famille de 9 enfants. Son père meurt lorsqu'il a à peine 2 ans. Dès qu'il peut, il aide sa mère à s'occuper de leur petite ferme, en attendant d'émigrer aux Etats-Unis, où les attend déjà son frère aîné, à Richmond, Californie. Travaille à la Standard Oil, jusqu'à ce qu'il puisse s'acheter une ferme. Là, il s'en donne à cœur joie au bricolage qui débouche finalement sur la peinture. En 1952, une maladie des yeux assez sérieuse se déclare, ce qui ne l'empêche pas de continuer à peindre. Au contraire. A partir de ce moment, il signe avec fierté: John Roeder the Blind Man. Citoyen américain, naturellement.

EXPOSITIONS:
«Das naive Bild der Welt»; Baden-Baden 1961.

Romelaert, Paul Oscar

Born January 14, 1883 in Ostend (Belgium).

Geboren am 14. Januar 1883 in Ostende (Belgien).

Né le 14 janvier 1883 à Ostende (Belgique).

Comes from a family of fishermen. Worked first all in the Ostend docks. Then, after the 1914–18 war, settled in Ghent, where he was employed by the town as a façade painter. A clever craftsman, he can make good imitations of oak and marble. In 1952 he went back to Ostend; since then he has lived in complete solitude in a fisherman's cottage. He has painted about 25 pictures, which he still owns. Sometimes he copies the great masters, which gives rise to comical compositions like, for instance, the 'Rape of the Daughters of Leucippus' which he made into 'The Rape of Mrs. Leukipose'.

Stammt aus einer Familie von Fischern. Arbeitet zuerst im Hafen von Ostende; nach dem Ersten Weltkrieg läßt er sich in Gent nieder, wo die Stadtverwaltung ihn als Fassadenmaler anstellt. Er ist sehr geschickt und versteht es bald, Eichenholz und Marmor zu imitieren. 1952 kehrt er nach Ostende zurück, wo er seither in völliger Abgeschiedenheit in seiner kleinen Fischerhütte lebt. Er hat ungefähr 25 Bilder gemalt, die sich alle noch in seinem Besitz befinden. Zuweilen kopiert er die großen Meister, was zu einigermaßen ulkigen Kompositionen führen kann; so wird zum Beispiel der «Raub der Töchter des Leukippos» bei ihm zum «Raub der Madame Leukipose».

Fils de pêcheurs. Travaille d'abord dans le port d'Ostende, puis, après la guerre de 1914–18, s'installe à Gand où il est engagé par la municipalité comme peintre de façades. Très habile, il imite vite le chêne et le marbre. En 1952, il retourne à Ostende, où il vit, désormais, dans la plus complète solitude, dans sa petite maison de pêcheurs. Il a peint 25 tableaux, environ, qu'il possède encore. Parfois, il copie les grands maîtres, ce qui donne des compositions assez cocasses comme, par exemple, ce «Rapt des filles de Leucippe» qui devient chez lui «Le rapt de Madame Leukipose».

EXPOSITIONS:
«Peintres Naïfs Belges», Le Théâtre National, Bruxelles 1965.
«Peintres Naïfs Belges», Musée Royal des Beaux-Arts, Verviers 1965.
«Peintres Naïfs Belges», Musée Royal des Beaux-Arts, Hasselt 1966.

Romero, Luis

Born at the end of last century in Cuba.

Geboren Ende des letzten Jahrhunderts, in Kuba.

Né à la fin du siècle dernier à Cuba.

An authentic 'machetero', i.e. a sugar-cane cutter. Despite this fact, his painting is more like that of the 'white' bourgeois Felicindo y Acevedo than the paintings of the Cuban 'new wave' which, although the most subtle expression of the 'art brut', nevertheless flirts with surrealism—possibly without realizing it. Romero however, paints only what he sees. There are no imaginative touches, whether the picture is an outdoor or an indoor scene. He never goes beyond the limits of the visible. He depicts the sky, the sea, and the earth which gives him so much toil. One could almost say that his dry, hard, gnarled landscapes show the effects of the work of his muscles. We should obviously be very glad to be able to give more detailed information about his life and the exhibitions of his work, but when the cultural organizations of his country and the other possible sources of information remain dumb there is nothing we can do—we are helpless.

Authentischer *machetero,* das heißt Zuckerrohrschneider. Aber seine Malerei steht derjenigen eines Felicindo y Acevedo, eines «weißen» Bürgerlichen, viel näher als der kubanischen «Neuen Welle», die zwar den raffiniertesten Ausdruck des Art Brut darstellt, jedoch trotzdem, zweifellos ohne es zu wissen, mit den muffigen Nachklängen des Surrealismus flirtet. Romero malt nur, was er sieht, nie Phantasien, seien sie nun innerer oder äußerer Art. Nie überschreitet er die Mauer des Sichtbaren. Er malt den Himmel, das Meer und die Erde, die ihn so viel Schweiß gekostet hat. Man könnte beinahe sagen, daß seine dürren, harten, knorrigen Landschaften die Anstrengung seiner Muskeln nachspüren. Natürlich möchte man Genaueres wissen über sein Leben und seine Ausstellungen, aber niemand, nicht einmal die kulturellen Organe seines Landes, nimmt sich die Mühe, Anfragen zu beantworten. Was will man da machen? Glückliche Bequemlichkeit der Länder unter dem Kreuz des Südens...

Un authentique *machetero,* c'est-à-dire coupeur de canne à sucre. Mais sa peinture se rapproche bien plus de celle du bourgeois «blanc», Felicindo y Acevedo, que de la «Nouvelle Vague» cubaine qui, tout en étant l'expression des plus raffinées de l'Art Brut, flirte néanmoins, sans doute sans le savoir, avec les relents du surréalisme. Lui, il ne peint que ce qu'il voit. Jamais les fantasmes, qu'ils soient intérieurs ou extérieurs. Il ne franchit jamais le mur du visible. Il peint le ciel, la mer et cette terre qui lui a coûté tant de sueur. On dirait même que ses paysages, secs, durs et noueux se ressentent de l'effort de ses muscles. Evidemment, on voudrait donner davantage de précisions sur sa vie, sur ses manifestations publiques, mais que faire, si personne, les organismes culturels de son pays y compris, ne se donne la peine de répondre aux demandes de renseignements? Ah, l'heureuse nonchalance des pays de l'hémisphère de la Croix du Sud...

BIBLIOGRAPHIE:
Samuel Feijo, Pittores y dibujantes populares de las Villas. Ed. Universidad de las Villas, Santa Clara (Cuba) 1962.

Rousseau, Henri

Born May 21, 1844 in Laval, Mayenne (France).
Died September 2, 1910 in Paris (France).

Geboren am 21. Mai 1844 in Laval, Mayenne (Frankreich).
Gestorben am 2. September 1910 in Paris (Frankreich).

Né le 21 mai 1844 à Laval, Mayenne (France).
Mort le 2 septembre 1910 à Paris (France).

Seemingly everything has already been said about this false 'Douanier' (customs official) and true standard-bearer of the 'naive' revolution. Everything, perhaps—but unsatisfactorily. Dozens and dozens of articles, treating the subject apparently as seriously as they can, continue now as before to mix true and false, legends and history, just right for the popular press. In other words, no one went beyond what used to be called 'sentimental life stories', until 1961 when H. Certigny's book 'The truth about the "Douanier" Rousseau' appeared. This book started a real scandal which, like all true scandals, was rapidly hushed up. Nevertheless, it had needed a full half-century before the world's most spectacular 'naive' artist was finally de-mythologized. But this does not detract at all from his genius or his greatness. So be it.

Es scheint, daß über diesen falschen «Zöllner» und echten Bannerträger des naiven Aufstands bereits alles gesagt worden ist. Dutzende und Aberdutzende von Werken, die allen Anschein von Ernsthaftigkeit an sich haben, mischten und mischen Wahres und Falsches, Legenden und Schmalzgeschichtchen. Kurz, es blieb immer bei dem, was man früher «Lebensroman» nannte. Und dies bis zum Jahre 1961, als das Buch von H. Certigny, La vérité sur le douanier Rousseau, erschien. Das rief eine Art Skandal hervor, aber wie jeder rechte Skandal wurde auch dieser rasch unterdrückt. Das hindert nicht, daß es, wie man sieht, genau ein halbes Jahrhundert brauchte, um diesen eindrucksvollsten Fall der naiven Malerei auf der ganzen Welt endlich zu entmystifizieren. Was weder Rousseaus Genie noch seiner Größe Abbruch tut. Amen.

Tout a été dit, semble-t-il, sur ce faux « Douanier » et ce vrai porte-drapeau de l'insurrection naïve. Tout, mais mal. Des dizaines et des dizaines d'ouvrages, d'aspect pourtant tout ce qu'il y a de sérieux, continuaient et continuent à mêler le vrai et le faux, les légendes et les histoires tout juste bonnes pour la presse du cœur. Bref, ce qui n'a jamais dépassé ce qu'on appelait jadis «les vies romancées». Et cela jusqu'à l'an de grâce 1961, où parut le livre de H. Certigny, « La vérité sur le douanier Rousseau ». Cela a provoqué une sorte de scandale, mais comme tout vrai scandale, celui-ci fut vite étouffé. Il n'empêche qu'il a fallu, comme on le voit, juste un demi-siècle pour que ce cas le plus spectaculaire de la peinture naïve mondiale fût enfin démythifié. Ce qui n'enlève rien, ni à son génie, ni à sa grandeur. Ainsi soit-il.

EXPOSITIONS:

Première participation au Salon des Indépendants, Paris 1886.
Rétrospective Rousseau au Salon des Indépendants, Paris 1911.
Galerie Bernheim-Jeune, Paris 1912 (Cat., Préface W. Uhde).
Galerie Paul Rosenberg, Paris 1917 (Cat., non préfacé).
« Les Maîtres Populaires de la Réalité », Paris 1937.
« Les Maîtres Populaires de la Réalité », Zürich 1937.
« Masters of Popular Painting », New York 1938.
« Masters of Popular Painting », Arthur Tooth & Sons, London 1938.
« Moderne Primitieven », Stedelijk Museum, Amsterdam 1941 (Cat., Préface D.C.R.).
Museum of Modern Art, New York 1942.
Musée d'Art Moderne, Paris 1944 (Cat., Préface Paul Eluard et Anatole Jakovsky).
Sidney Janis Gallery, New York 1951 (Cat., Préface Tristan Tzara).
« Maler des einfältigen Herzens », Museum am Ostwall, Dortmund 1952.
« La Peinture Naïve », Knokke-le-Zoute 1958.
« Les Peintres Naïfs », Maison de la Pensée Française, Paris 1960.
« Das naive Bild der Welt », Baden-Baden 1961.
Galerie Charpentier, Paris 1961 (Cat., Préface J. Bouret et R. Nacenta).
Wildenstein Gallery, New York 1963 (Cat., Préface Maximilien Gauthier).
« I Pittori Naifs », Rome 1964.
« Die Welt der naiven Malerei », Salzburg 1964.
« De Lusthof der Naieven », Rotterdam 1964.
« Le Monde des Naïfs », Paris 1964.
« Collection J. Walter-Paul Guillaume », Musée de l'Orangerie, Paris 1966.

BIBLIOGRAPHIE:

W. Uhde: « Henri Rousseau le Douanier », Editions Figuière, Paris 1911.
Soirées de Paris, numéro spécial, N° 20, Paris 15 janvier 1913.
W. Uhde: « Henri Rousseau », Verlag Flechtheim, Düsseldorf 1914.
« Dodici opere di Rousseau », Libreria de la Voce, Florence 1914.
Roch Grey: « Henri Rousseau », Editione Valori Plastici, Rome 1922.
H. Kolle: « Henri Rousseau »: Verlag Klinkhardt, Leipzig 1922.
W. Uhde: « Henri Rousseau », Verlag R. Kaemerer, 1923.
Ph. Soupault: « Henri Rousseau », Editions des Quatre Chemins, Paris 1927.
André Salmon: « Henri Rousseau », Editions Crès, Paris 1927.
A. Basler: « Henri Rousseau », Librairie de France, Paris 1927.
Ch. Zervos: « Henri Rousseau », Editions Cahiers d'Art, Paris 1927.
A. Basler: « Henri Rousseau »: Librairie Gallimard, Paris 1927.
A. Basler: « Henri Rousseau », Les Albums d'Art, Druet, Paris 1928.
J. et J. Tharaud: « Le gentil Douanier », Cahiers Libres, Paris 1929.
W. Uhde: « Henri Rousseau et les Primitifs Modernes », Alcan, Paris 1935.
Catton Rich: « Henri Rousseau », Museum of Modern Art, New York 1942.
R. Grey: « Henri Rousseau », Editions Drouin, Paris 1943.
Pierre Courthion: « Henri Rousseau », Editions Skira, Genève 1944.
Documents retrouvés, Labyrinthe, N° 21, Genève 1945.
Ch. Chassé: « D'Ubu Roi au Douanier Rousseau » Editions Nouvelle Critique, Paris 1947.
W. Uhde: « Henri Rousseau », Editions Jean Marguerat, Lausanne 1948.
Ph. Soupault: « Henri Rousseau », Editions A. Skira, Genève 1948.
W. Uhde: « Henri Rousseau », Editions Alfred Scherz, Bern 1948.
Anatole Jakovsky: « La Peinture Naïve », Paris 1949.
W. Uhde: « Cinq Maîtres Primitifs », Editions Palmes, Paris 1949.
Maximilien Gauthier: « Henri Rousseau », Editions les Gémeaux, Paris 1949.
D. Cooper: « Henri Rousseau », Editions Braun, Paris 1951.
Lo Duca: « Henri Rousseau », Les Editions du Chêne, Paris 1951.
Robert Delaunay: « Henri Rousseau », Les Lettres Françaises, Paris 1952.
M. Garçon: « Henri Rousseau Accusé naïf », Editions des Quatre Chemins, Paris 1953.
« Henri Rousseau », Introduction par R.H. Wilenski, Editions Fernand Nathan, Paris 1953.
André Salmon: « Le souvenir du Douanier », Jardin des Arts, N° 6, Paris 1955.
Maximilien Gauthier: « Henri Rousseau », Editions Flammarion, Paris 1956.
Pierre Courthion: « Henri Rousseau », Editions F. Hazan, Paris 1956.
A. Jakovsky: « Les Peintres Naïfs », Paris 1956.
Bernard Jasmand et Otto Kallir: « Sonntagsmaler », Editions Otto Aug. Ehlers, Berlin/Darmstadt 1956.
Anatole Jakovsky: « Naive Malerei », Zürich 1957.
H. Perruchot: « Henri Rousseau », Editions Universitaires, Paris 1957.
P. Courthion: « Henri Rousseau », L'Œil, N° 46, Paris octobre 1958.

Oto Bihalji-Merin: «Das naive Bild der Welt», Köln 1959.
Oto Bihalji-Merin: «Die naive Malerei», Köln 1959.
Oto Bihalji-Merin: «Les Peintres Naïfs», Paris (sans date).
H. Certigny: «La vérité sur le Douanier Rousseau», Editions Plon, Paris 1961.
«Die Welt der Naiven», Spiegel, Hamburg, 20 décembre 1961.
Jean Bouret: «Henri Rousseau», Ides et Calendes, Neuchâtel 1961.
Dora Vallier: «Henri Rousseau», Editions Flammarion, Paris 1961.
H. Certigny: «Henri Rousseau et l'Association Philotechnique», Preuves, Paris avril 1961.
A. Jakovsky: «Eros du Dimanche», Paris 1964.
Catalogo Bolaffi d'Arte Moderna, Turin 1966.
Jean Bouret: «Henri Rousseau», Edition populaires, Oldburn, London 1966.
Henri Certigny: «La vérité sur le Douanier Rousseau», Addenda N° 1, avec l'introduction de Anatole Jakovsky, Plon, Paris 1966.

FILMS:
Henri Rousseau le Douanier, réalisé par Lo Duca, Les Ecrans Modernes, Paris 1950.

TEXTES DE ROUSSEAU:
«Voyage à l'Exposition» (Extraits), Bulletin de la Vie Artistique, Paris 1922.
«La Vengeance d'une Orpheline Russe», Orbes, N° 2 et les suivants, Paris 1929.
«Une Visite à l'Exposition de 1889», avec une Préface de Tristan Tzara, Editions P. Cailler, Genève 1947.
«La Vengeance d'une Orpheline Russe», Editions P. Cailler, Genève 1947.

Rosario

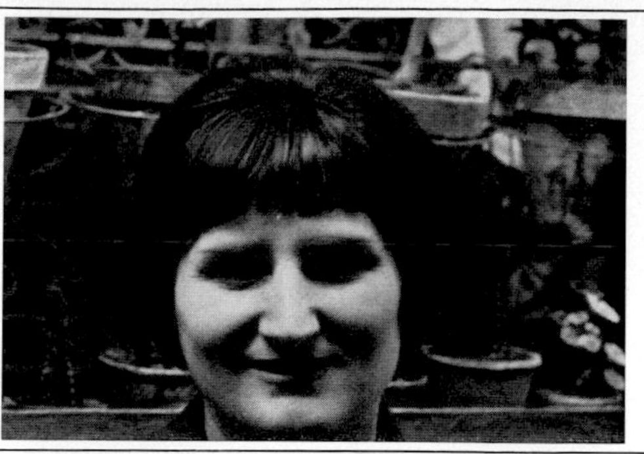

(Maria Rosario Areces-Gonzalez)
Born August 14, 1929 in Loriana-Oviedo, Asturias (Spain).

Geboren am 14. August 1929 in Loriana-Oviedo, Asturien (Spanien).

Née le 14 août 1929 à Loriana-Oviedo, Asturies (Espagne).

At the start she worked in a firm which made ceramics to a certain extent as skilled works of art. Having moved to Paris, she became a maid-of-all-work and immediately felt the frustration of the change which had deprived her both of nature and of beautiful objects. Painting brought her the relief she needed. She is a typical example of one who has transferred from the skilled craftsman to the individual artist.

Arbeitet zuerst in einem halb handwerklichen Keramik-Betrieb. Nach Paris verpflanzt, wo sie als Dienstmädchen arbeitet, verspürt sie sogleich eine Art schmerzlichen Mangel, da sie gleichzeitig der Natur und des Schönen beraubt ist. Das Malen bringt ihr eine gewisse Besänftigung. Sie ist ein typisches Beispiel für den Übergang von der handwerklichen Kunst in eine vollberechtigte individuelle Kunst.

A travaillé d'abord dans une entreprise de céramique semi-artisanale. Transplantée à Paris, où elle travaille comme bonne à tout faire, elle ressent aussitôt cette espèce de frustration qui la prive à la fois, et de la nature, et du beau. La peinture lui apporte cet apaisement. C'est un cas typique du transfert de l'art artisanal en un art individuel à part entière.

EXPOSITIONS:
Galerie Bénézit, Paris 1965 (Cat., Préface Anatole Jakovsky).
Galeria Altamira, Gijon (Asturies) 1966 (Cat., Préface Anatole Jakovsky).

Rovesti, Bruno

Born July 13, 1907 in Gualtieri, Reggio Emilia (Italy).

Geboren am 13. Juli 1907 in Gualtieri, Reggio Emilia (Italien).

Né le 13 juillet 1907 à Gualtieri, Reggio Emilia (Italie).

This artist, who signs his work 'Pittore contadino celebre' has a nature that is violent and yet tender, artful and yet 'candid' (as the Italians say). He fought in the Spanish Civil War in the international brigade, but continued later to cultivate his plot of ground and tend his vines. And his art reflects his character; one must know him (or at least have seen the excellent film which M. Andreassi made about him) in order to understand the contradictions in his work, to realize why demanding, almost expressionistic pictures are mingled with exquisite little pieces. It's just then, that he gets out a pile of medals he has won from various provincial exhibitions.... He demands high prices for his pictures, while at the same time making a present of himself to the sky and the ground of his native land. Rovesti, or the tenderness of violence!

Der Mann, der «Pittore contadino celebre» signiert, ist zugleich gewalttätig und sanft, listig und arglos. Er hat im Spanienkrieg in der internationalen Brigade gekämpft, aber er fährt fort, sein Stück Boden zu bebauen und seinen Weinberg zu jäten. Und seine Kunst ist ein Abbild seines Charakters. Man muß ihn kennen oder zumindest den ausgezeichneten Film gesehen haben, den M. Andreassi über ihn gedreht hat, um diese Widersprüche zu verstehen. Warum unter aggressiven, beinahe expressionistischen Bildern herrliche Stücke zu finden sind, auf denen der Pinsel mit der Zunge zu schnalzen scheint, als kostete er einen guten Tropfen. Und in diesem Augenblick zeigt er einen Haufen Medaillen vor, die er in den verschiedenen regionalen Ausstellungen eingeheimst hat... Er verkauft seine Bilder um teures Geld und schenkt seine Person gleichzeitig dem Himmel und der Erde seiner Heimat. Rovesti oder die Sanftmut der Gewalttätigkeit!

Celui qui signe «Pittore contadino celebre» est à la fois un violent et un tendre, un rusé et un «candide», comme disent les Italiens. Il a fait la guerre d'Espagne dans les brigades internationales, mais il continue à cultiver son lopin de terre et sarcler sa vigne. Et son art est à l'image de son caractère. Il faut le connaître ou du moins avoir vu un excellent film que M. Andreassi a fait sur lui, pour comprendre ces contradictions. Pourquoi à des toiles revendicatives, presqu'expressionnistes se mêlent des morceaux exquis, où le pinceau semble claquer la langue comme s'il goûtait une bonne bouteille. Et c'est à ce moment-là qu'il sort un tas de médailles qu'il a recoltées dans les différentes expositions régionales... Il demande très cher pour ses toiles, tout en faisant le don total de sa personne au ciel et à la terre de son pays. Rovesti, ou la tendresse de la violence!

EXPOSITIONS:
«Mostra di Pittura Popolare», Palazzo delle Esposizioni, Rome 1955.
Lido di Camaiore, Viareggio 1958.
Galleria La Perla, Modena 1963 (Cat., Extraits de presse).
«I Pittori Naifs», Rome 1964.
«I Pittori Naifs», Centro Internazionale di Arte Figurative. Biella 1964.
Personale A.N.C.R., Mantua 1965 (Cat., Préface, Carlo Segala, Orio Vergani, Giorgio Riccioli).
Ente Provinciale del Turismo, R.E. 1965.
Palazzo Principi, Città di Correggio 1966 (Cat., Extraits de presse).

BIBLIOGRAPHIE:
Nevio Jori: «Rovesti», Gazzetta di Reggio, 5 février 1965.
R. Tassi: «Rovesti», Settimo Giorno, Milan, 24 avril 1962.
«Art Naïf», Editions Marocaines et Internationales, Rabat 1964.

Roy, Louis François

Born January 11, 1891 in Niort, Creuse (France).

Geboren am 11. Januar 1891 in Niort, Creuse (Frankreich).

Né le 11 janvier 1891 à Niort, Creuse (France).

One of a large family, very poor. Attended school (irregularly) until the age of eight. Learned the cooper's trade, at which he worked until he was seventy. Set up on his own in Saint-Maixent (Ile de Ré). Now lives in La Rochelle. Began to paint in 1962, while trying to touch up an engraving soiled and worn by time. Spontaneous zest, combined with gay colors.

Kinderreiche, sehr arme Familie. Unregelmäßiger Schulbesuch bis zum Alter von 8 Jahren. Lernt den Beruf eines Küfers, den er bis zum Alter von 70 Jahren ausübt. Etabliert sich auf eigene Rechnung in Saint-Maixent (Ile de Ré). Lebt gegenwärtig in La Rochelle. Hat 1962 zu malen angefangen, als er einen beschmutzten, verblichenen Stich ersetzen wollte. Naturwüchsiger Schwung, verbunden mit einer sehr fröhlichen Farbgebung.

Famille nombreuse, très pauvre. Va à l'école, irrégulièrement, jusqu'à l'âge de 8 ans. Apprend le métier de tonnelier qu'il exercera jusqu'à l'âge de 70 ans. S'installe à son compte à Saint-Maixent (Ile de Ré). Vit actuellement à La Rochelle. A commencé à peindre en 1962, en voulant remplacer une gravure salie et abîmée par le temps. Verve primesautière, jointe à un coloris très gai.

EXPOSITIONS:
Galerie Fontenoy, La Rochelle 1965.
Galerie M. Bénézit, Paris 1966
(Cat., Préface Max Pol Fouchet et Anatole Jakovsky).

Royer, Charles

Born in 1862 in Paris (France).
Died in 1940 in Paris (France).

Geboren 1862 in Paris (Frankreich).
Gestorben 1940 in Paris (Frankreich).

Né en 1862 à Paris (France).
Mort en 1940 à Paris (France).

Typical example of a modest French craftsman. He looked after his pictures with the same loving care he devoted to the shoes in his little shoemaker's workshop, in the Gobelin district of Paris. What was important for him was not renown or money, but 'a fine piece of work'. Further, he took part in no exhibitions. The misapprehensions arose later when unscrupulous 'art lovers' seized on his work for the money it might bring them, and tried to give him a stature which is not his by rights.

Typisches Beispiel eines bescheidenen französischen Handwerkers. In seiner ärmlichen Butike im Gobelins-Viertel verwendete er ebenso viel Liebe auf seine Bilder wie auf die zu sohlenden Schuhe. Für ihn zählte vor allem die sorgfältig ausgeführte Arbeit, nicht Ehre und nicht klingende Münze. Er stellte übrigens nicht aus. Das Mißverständnis kam später, als nicht eben mit Skrupeln behaftete Liebhaber sich aus Gewinnsucht seines Werks bemächtigten und ihm einen Platz zuweisen wollten, der ihm nicht zukommt.

Un exemple typique du modeste artisan français. Il soignait ses tableaux avec le même amour avec lequel il ressemelait les chaussures, dans sa modeste échoppe du quartier des Gobelins. Ce qui comptait avant tout pour lui, c'est « La belle ouvrage »; pas les honneurs, pas l'argent. Il n'exposait, d'ailleurs, pas. Le malentendu viendra plus tard, lorsque les amateurs peu scrupuleux, s'emparant par lucre de son œuvre, ont voulu lui donner la place qui n'est pas la sienne. Voilà.

EXPOSITIONS:
Galerie Jeanne Castel, Paris 1940.
Galerie Palmes, Paris 1949
(Cat., Préface non signée).
« De Lusthof der Naieven », Rotterdam 1964.
« Le Monde des Naïfs », Paris 1964.

BIBLIOGRAPHIE:
Anatole Jakovsky: « La Peinture Naïve », Paris 1949.
Anatole Jakovsky: « Les Peintres Naïfs », Paris 1956.

Rozenberg, Hélène

Born February 1, 1908 in Belchatov (Poland).

Geboren am 1. Februar 1908 in Belchatov (Polen).

Née le 1 février 1908 à Belchatov (Pologne).

Has lived for many years in Paris. She is one of the many who have experienced and suffered much and who, not wanting all this to be in vain, sooner or later try to express themselves in some way. She herself chose painting perhaps by chance, but nevertheless she waited until she was over fifty before taking it up seriously. Her pictures are visions of paradise, imbued with an unusual and intense radiance, almost as if she wanted to show to her blind mother the wonders and magic of light. Has not yet had an individual exhibition.

Lebt seit langem in Paris. Sie gehört zu den Menschen, die viel erlebt, viel gelitten und viel gefühlt haben und die möchten, daß es nicht umsonst gewesen sei, die früher oder später auf diese oder jene Weise dieses Leiden, diese Erlebnisse, diese Gefühle zu gestalten wünschen. Hélène Rozenberg hat die Malerei gewählt, vielleicht zufällig, aber sie hat immerhin gewartet, bis sie die Fünfzig überschritten hatte, ehe sie sich ihr endgültig verschrieb. Sie malt paradiesische Visionen, die in ein ungewohntes, intensives Licht getaucht sind, genau als wollte sie ihrer Mutter, die blind war, den Zauber und die Feenwelt des Lichts zeigen. Noch keine Einzelausstellung.

Habite depuis longtemps Paris. Comme quelques-unes de ces personnes qui ont beaucoup vécu, souffert et senti, et qui voudraient que ce ne soit pas pour rien, qui voudraient donc les matérialiser tôt ou tard, d'une façon ou d'une autre, celle-ci a choisi la peinture, peut-être au hasard, mais elle a attendu quand-même la cinquantaine avant de s'y lancer définitivement. Ce sont des visions paradisiaques, baignées d'une lumière inusitée et intense, exactement comme si elle voulait faire voir à sa mère, qui était aveugle, ce que c'est que les enchantements et les féeries de la lumière. N'a pas encore eu d'exposition individuelle.

EXPOSITIONS:
« Les Primitifs Modernes », Galerie Charpentier, Paris 1964.

Ruggeri, Alfredo

Born in 1912 in San Savino, Perugia (Italy).

Geboren 1912 in San Savino, Perugia (Italien).

Né en 1912 à San Savino, Perouse (Italie).

At first a glass-blower, then attendant and restorer in the Etruscan Museum in the Valle Giulia in Rome. Has painted for about a dozen years. He is among the most distinguished and yet the most primitive of Italian 'naive' painters. The coloring of his pictures is extremely subtle, whereas the design, which is virtually superimposed on the color, is rather sketchy. Nevertheless, there is a certain greatness in his work, which could well be attributed to the influence of Rome, his present home.

Zuerst Glasbläser, dann Kustos und Restaurator im etruskischen Museum von Valle Giulia in Rom. Malt seit etwa 12 Jahren. Seine Kunst ist gleichzeitig eine der vornehmsten und der primitivsten unter den italienischen Naiven. Das äußerste Raffinement an Farbe wird sozusagen von einer ziemlich summarischen Zeichnung überdeckt. Wie dem auch sei, von seinen Bildern geht eine gewisse Größe aus, und man kann sich fragen, ob das nicht dem Einfluß von Rom zuzuschreiben ist, wo er jetzt lebt.

D'abord souffleur de verre, puis gardien et restaurateur au Musée Etrusque de Valle Giulia à Rome. Peint depuis une douzaine d'années. Son art est à la fois l'un des plus racés et des plus primitifs parmi les naïfs italiens. A l'extrême raffinement de la couleur se superpose, en quelque sorte, un dessin assez sommaire. Quoiqu'il en soit, une certaine grandeur s'en dégage, et l'on se demande si ce n'est pas l'influence de Rome où il vit à présent.

EXPOSITIONS:
Galleria La Feluca, Roma 1961
(Cat., Préface Lorenza Trucchi).
«I Pittori Naifs», Roma 1964.

Ruysbroek, Willem Cornelis

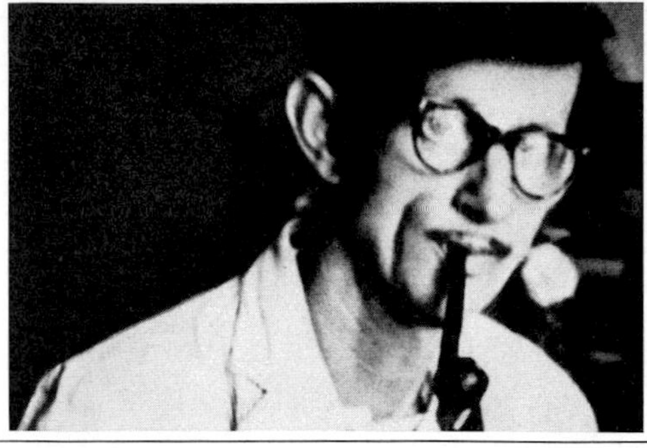

Born 1911 in Delft (Netherlands).
Died February 18, 1961 in Menton (France).

Geboren 1911 in Delft (Holland).
Gestorben am 18. Februar 1961 in Menton (Frankreich).

Né en 1911 à Delft (Hollande).
Mort le 18 février 1961 à Menton (France).

Cowherd, sailor, mattress-maker, electrician, gardener. Led a rather nomadic life before settling down in France in 1947; was in Holland, Belgium, Germany, Italy, Latin America, Asia, Japan, Indonesia, Asia Minor, Africa... only to die of consumption in a French sanatorium. He left behind the touching message of his pictures, which are like bottles thrown into the sea or like life-belts floating above the place a ship has sunk.

Kuhhirte, Matrose, Tapezierer, Elektriker, Gärtner. Führt ein eher unstetes Leben, bis er sich 1947 in Frankreich niederläßt. Holland, Belgien, Deutschland, Italien, Lateinamerika, Asien, Japan, Sundainseln, Anatolien, Afrika... und all diese Länder hat er bereist, um schließlich in einem französischen Sanatorium an Schwindsucht zu sterben. Mit seinen Bildern hat er eine ergreifende Botschaft hinterlassen; sie sind wie Flaschen, die ins Meer geworfen werden, oder Rettungsringe, die über dem Schauplatz des Schiffbruchs schwimmen.

Vacher, matelot, matelassier, électricien, jardinier. Mène une vie plutôt errante, avant de s'établir en France, où il arrive en 1947. Hollande, Belgique, Allemagne, Italie, Amérique latine, Asie, Japon, archipel de la Sonde, Anatolie, Afrique... Et c'est pour mourir de phtisie, dans un sanatorium français qu'il a fait et qu'il a parcouru tout cela. En laissant un message émouvant dans ses tableaux, qui sont autant de bouteilles jetées à la mer, ou autant de bouées de sauvetage qui flottent au-dessus du lieu de naufrage.

EXPOSITION:
«Les Peintres Naïfs», Maison de la Pensée Française, Paris 1960.

Sabine

(real name: Sabine Monory)
Born December 10, 1936 in Oran (Algeria).

(Sabine Monory)
Geboren am 10. Dezember 1936 in Oran (Algerien).

(Sabine Monory)
Née le 10 décembre 1936 à Oran (Algérie).

Is the youngest of the world's primitive artists. At any rate, her work contradicts the assertions of certain people who cannot see how 'naive' art can be executed by young painters. Meanwhile, Sabine's art is purely 'naive', unexpected, fine and delicate in quality.

Eine der jüngsten unter den naiven Malern auf der ganzen Welt. Ihr Fall beweist die Unrichtigkeit der Behauptungen jener, die vorgeben, naive Kunst sei bei Jungen nicht möglich. Sabines Kunst ist sehr wohl naiv, unerwartet, voll von Qualitäten und Feinfühligkeit.

Benjamine de la peinture naïve mondiale. Son cas, de toute façon, s'inscrit en faux contre les assertions de certains qui ne voient pas la possibilité de l'art naïf pour les jeunes. En attendant, l'art de Sabine est bel et bien naïf, inattendu, plein de qualités et de finesses.

EXPOSITIONS:
Galerie du Gouvernail, Paris 1963.
« Les Primitifs d'Aujourd'hui »,
Galerie Charpentier, Paris 1964.

BIBLIOGRAPHIE:
Anatole Jakovsky: « Sabine », Pas à Pas, N°134, mai 1963.
Anatole Jakovsky: « Eros du Dimanche », Paris 1964.

Sabo, Ladis W.

Born 1870 in Budapest (Hungary).
Died 1953 in New York, N.Y. (USA).

Geboren 1870 in Budapest (Ungarn).
Gestorben 1953 in New York, N.Y. (USA).

Né en 1870 à Budapest (Hongrie).
Mort en 1953 à New York, N.Y. (USA).

'I've always loved music, literature, and art; I even learned to play the violin', he wrote in a brief autobiography. In 1910 he immigrated to the United States, preceding his wife and five children, who joined him two years later. He worked in Greenville (North Carolina) as an assistant tailor, and in 1942 he settled in New York.
When he was not able to work any more his daughter gave him some painting equipment as a present. The result was a miracle! Sabo is definitely one of the most interesting and original 'naive' artists in America. However, unfortunately his works can be seen only rarely; the American cultural organizations are slow and ponderous, weighed down by 'Trustees' which are a group of collectors and dealers. O'Brady is another victim of this—yes, O'Brady, the best 'naive' artist in the New World (the best altogether, perhaps, after Rousseau), of an old American family, but entirely ignored by these cultural organizations. One wonders why?

«Ich liebte seit jeher Musik, Literatur, Kunst, und habe sogar Geigenspielen gelernt», sagt er in einer kurzen Autobiographie. 1910 wandert er in die Vereinigten Staaten aus, zuerst allein; zwei Jahre später folgen dann seine Frau und seine fünf Kinder nach. Er arbeitet in Greenville (North Carolina) als Schneidergehilfe. 1942 läßt er sich in New York nieder. Da er nicht mehr arbeiten kann, schenkt seine Tochter ihm eine Malausrüstung. Und alsbald entstehen Wunderwerke. Er ist unbestreitbar einer der interessantesten und der originellsten naiven Maler Amerikas. Aber leider sind seine Bilder nur sehr selten zu sehen. Die amerikanischen Kulturabteilungen sind schwerfällig und langsam, behindert durch die «Trustees», die sich aus Sammlern und Kunsthändlern zusammensetzen. Ein anderes Beispiel ist O'Brady, der beste naive Maler der Neuen Welt. Sie ist eine alteingesessene Amerikanerin, die von den genannten Stellen indessen völlig ignoriert wird, obwohl sie in der allgemeinen Wertskala zweifellos gleich auf den Zöllner Rousseau folgt. Warum?

«J'ai toujours aimé la musique, la littérature, l'art et j'ai même appris à jouer du violon», dit-il dans une courte autobiographie. Il émigre aux Etats-Unis en 1910, d'abord seul, en laissant sa femme et ses 5 enfants qui ne le rejoindront que 2 ans plus tard. Il travaille à Greenville (North Carolina) comme aide-tailleur. En 1942, il s'établit à New York. Ne pouvant plus travailler, sa fille lui fait cadeau d'un attirail de peintre. Et ce sont, aussitôt, des merveilles. Incontestablement, c'est un des plus intéressants et des plus originaux parmi les peintres naïfs américains. Mais on ne voit de ses œuvres que très rarement, hélas. Les services culturels américains sont lourds et lents, grevés par les «Trustees», c'est-à-dire les collectionneurs et les marchands mêlés. Un autre exemple: O'Brady. Oui, O'Brady, le meilleur peintre naïf du Nouveau Monde, second, sans doute, dans l'échelle des valeurs, après le Douanier Rousseau, américaine de bonne souche pourtant depuis plusieurs générations, encore que les dits services ignorent totalement. Pourquoi?

EXPOSITIONS:
«A Group of Natural Painters», Galerie St-Etienne, New York 1952.
«Amerikanische Malerei», Kunstmuseum, Luzern 1954.
«Amerikanische Primitive», Museum am Ostwall, Dortmund 1954–55.
«American Primitive Paintings», Smithsonian Institution, Washington 1958.

BIBLIOGRAPHIE:
Jasmand und Otto Kallir: «Sonntagsmaler», Otto Aug. Ehlers, Berlin/Darmstadt 1956.

Salaün, André

Born January 13, 1921 in Saint-Germain-sur Avre, Eure (France).

Geboren am 13. Januar 1921 in Saint-Germain-sur-Avre, Eure (Frankreich).

Né le 13 janvier 1921 à Saint-Germain-sur-Avre, Eure (France).

Comes of peasant stock. In 1948 started to work for the Post Office. He gradually bettered himself and, in 1955, finally was given a position which allowed him a little more leisure time for painting. Since that time his progress has been steady. Has taken part in a number of collective exhibitions but up to now has never had a private exhibition of his own work.

Kleinbauernmilieu. Tritt 1948 in die Postverwaltung ein. Dank dem Aufrücken in der administrativen Hierarchie kommt er 1955 endlich auf einen Posten, der ihm ein bißchen mehr Muße zum Malen gewährt. Seither macht er beständig Fortschritte. Hat an zahlreichen Gruppenausstellungen teilgenommen, bisher jedoch noch keine Einzelausstellung.

Milieu de petits paysans. En 1948, entre aux Postes. En avançant dans la hiérarchie administrative, obtient enfin, en 1955, un poste qui lui donne un peu plus de loisirs pour peindre. Depuis, ses progrès sont constants. A participé à de nombreuses expositions collectives, mais pas d'exposition individuelle jusqu'à présent.

BIBLIOGRAPHIE:

«Salaün», Arts P.T.T., N° 44, Paris 1966.

San Martin, Fortunato

Born 1891 in Parral, province of Linares (Chile).
Died January 1964 in Santiago (Chile).

Geboren 1891 in Parral, Provinz Linares (Chile).
Gestorben Januar 1964 in Santiago (Chile).

Né en 1891 à Parral, province de Linares (Chili).
Mort en janvier 1964 à Santiago (Chili).

As he said himself in the preface to the catalogue of the only exhibition of his work held during his lifetime, even at school he was first in drawing and since that time he never stopped drawing and painting. The only exceptions were during military service, which he spent in the 'Chorrillos' regiment, and during active service during the 1914–18 war (prolonged service for him until 1923). His art is executed with extreme care; it is full of charm and bears some resemblance to the 'naive' paintings of the 19th century. 'I am so much in love with painting that if I stopped painting one day it would mean my mission on earth were complete'—such is the last sentence of his self-written preface.

Wie er in dem Vorwort des Katalogs zur ersten und einzigen Ausstellung, die zu seinen Lebzeiten veranstaltet wurde, selber sagt, war er schon in der Schule der Beste im Zeichnen, und seither hat er nie aufgehört zu zeichnen und zu malen. Außer während seines Militärdienstes, den er in dem Regiment «Chorrillos» absolvierte, und seiner Mobilisierung während des Ersten Weltkriegs, die sich bis 1923 ausdehnte. Seine Kunst ist äußerst gepflegt, anmutig, und gemahnt irgendwie an die naiven Bilder aus dem 19. Jahrhundert. «Ich hege eine so große Liebe für die Malerei, daß es bedeuten würde, meine Mission auf Erden sei beendet, wenn ich eines Tages aufhören müßte, zu malen», so lautet der letzte Satz der von ihm verfaßten Einführung.

Comme il le dit lui-même, dans la préface au catalogue de la seule et unique exposition qu'il a eue de son vivant, déjà à l'école il était le premier en dessin, et il n'a jamais cessé de dessiner et de peindre depuis. Sauf pendant son service militaire qu'il a fait dans le régiment de «Chorrillos» et son rappel sous les drapeaux pendant la guerre de 1914–18, prolongé jusqu'en 1923. Son art est extrêmement soigné, charmant, et non sans rappeler les peintures naïves du XIXe siècle. «J'ai tellement d'amour pour la peinture que si je devais cesser de peindre un jour, cela signifierait que ma mission sur cette terre est terminée», c'est la dernière phrase de son auto-préface...

EXPOSITIONS:
Universidad de Chili, Santiago 1962
(Cat., Préface par le peintre).

Sauter, Aloys

Born April 12, 1875 in Stabroek, near Antwerp (Belgium).
Died May 14, 1952 in Chaume-en-Brie, near Argentières, Seine et Marne (France).

Geboren am 12. April 1875 in Stabroek bei Antwerpen (Belgien).
Gestorben am 14. Mai 1952 in Chaume-en-Brie bei Argentières, Seine et Marne (Frankreich).

Né le 12 avril 1875 à Stabroek, près d'Anvers (Belgique).
Mort le 14 mai 1952 à Chaume-en-Brie, près d'Argentières, Seine et Marne (France).

Son of a coachbuilder and a coachbuilder in his turn. At the age of 30 he left Belgium and his first wife, from whom he obtained a divorce in Charleroi on 30 October 1909. Together with his brother Cornelius-Alexander, Sauter worked first of all in a car factory near Paris. When they had saved enough money they set up independently of each other as secondhand dealers and restorers of furniture and pictures. The famous 'Buffet' (F. Labisse collection) is in fact a picture of these two brothers and not of Sauter alone, in two different attitudes, as has been claimed. With his second wife, who gave herself the nickname 'The Muse of Neuilly' and who wrote most of the verses for his paintings, he lived a fairly comfortable life. He was even able to devote himself to his passion for inventions—already at the age of 14 he had constructed a wooden bicycle. His inventions are a tricycle, a taxi-cycle and finally an airplane, the *Sauteral,* designed to fly with flapping wings. This airplane cost him 20.000 pre-war francs. Sauter remained Belgian and did not take French nationality, though some have claimed (and still claim) this for him. His last foreigner's identity card was renewed in 1946.

Sohn eines Wagenbauers und selber Karosseriebauer. Mit 30 Jahren verläßt er Belgien und seine erste Frau, von der er am 30. Oktober 1909 in Charleroi geschieden wird. Sauter arbeitet mit seinem Bruder Cornelius-Alexander zusammen zuerst in einer Automobilfabrik in der Umgebung von Paris. Als sie genügend Geld gespart haben, etablieren sie sich, jeder auf eigene Rechnung, als Trödler; sie bessern auch Möbel aus und restaurieren Bilder. Das berühmte «Buffet» (Sammlung F. Labisse) stellt die beiden Brüder dar und nicht Aloys allein in zwei verschiedenen Haltungen, wie das irgend jemand behauptet hat. Mit seiner zweiten Frau, die sich «Die Muse von Neuilly» nannte und die meisten der Verse zu seinen Bildern schrieb, lebte er in behaglichem Wohlstand. Er konnte sogar seiner Erfinderlust wieder frönen; schon mit 14 Jahren hatte er ein Fahrrad aus Holz gebaut. Nun erfand er ein dreirädriges Fahrrad, ein Taxi-Fahrrad und schließlich ein Flugzeug, das *Sauteral,* das beim Fliegen mit den Flügeln schlug. Dieses Flugzeug kostete ihn 20000 Vorkriegs-Francs. Sauter ist Belgier geblieben. Seine Einreihung unter die Franzosen war und bleibt ein Irrtum. Seine Identitätskarte als Ausländer wurde 1946 ein letztes Mal erneuert.

Fils d'un carrossier et carrossier à son tour. A 30 ans, quitte la Belgique et sa première femme, dont il obtient le divorce à Charleroi le 30 octobre 1909. Avec son frère Cornelius-Alexander, Sauter travaille d'abord dans une usine d'automobiles aux environs de Paris, et lorsqu'ils économisent suffisamment d'argent, ils s'installent, chacun à son compte, comme brocanteurs et réparateurs de meubles et de tableaux. Le fameux «Buffet» (Coll. F. Labisse), représente justement ces deux frères et non Sauter seul, en deux attitudes différentes, comme l'a prétendu un quidam. Avec sa seconde femme, celle qui se prénommait «La muse de Neuilly» et qui écrivit la plupart des textes en vers pour ses tableaux, ils mènent une vie assez aisée. Il peut même s'adonner à sa manie d'invention, car déjà, à l'âge de 14 ans, il avait construit une bicyclette en bois. Ce sont: une bicyclette à 3 roues, un cycle-taxi et, enfin, un avion, le *Sauteral*, volant à ailes battantes. Cet avion lui a coûté 20000 francs d'avant-guerre. Sauter est resté belge et non français, comme on le classait par erreur. Sa dernière carte d'identité d'étranger a été renouvelée en 1946.

EXPOSITIONS:
«La Peinture Naïve», Knokke-le-Zoute 1958.
«La Peinture Naïve», Maison de la Pensée Française, Paris 1960.
«De Lusthof der Naieven», Musée Boymans, Rotterdam 1964.
«Le Monde des Naïfs», Musée d'Art Moderne, Paris 1964.
«Peintres Naïfs Belges», Théâtre National, Bruxelles 1965.
«Peintres Naïfs Belges», Musée Royal des Beaux-Arts, Verviers 1965.
«Peintres Naïfs Belges», Musée Royal des Beaux-Arts, Hasselt 1966.

BIBLIOGRAPHIE:
«Aloys Sauter», Vu, N° 204, 10 février 1932.
Oto Bihalji-Merin: «Das naive Bild der Welt», Köln 1959 (Erreurs).
Oto Bihalji-Merin: «Die naive Malerei», Köln 1959 (Erreurs).
Oto Bihalji-Merin: «Les Peintres Naïfs», Paris 1960 (Erreurs).

Schal, Jacques

Born March 18, 1909 in Krautwiller, near Strasbourg (France).

Geboren am 18. März 1909 in Krautwiller bei Straßburg (Frankreich).

Né le 18 mars 1909 à Krautwiller, près de Strasbourg (France).

After having attended the local school, he became apprenticed to a shoemaker. Passed the qualifying examination in 1926. Worked as a shoemaker until 1944, the year he started to paint. In order to be able to continue painting he changed his profession and joined the French railway company, where he stayed until his retirement in 1962 on grounds of ill-health. His painting is frank, conscientious, sometimes a little too photographic in technique.

Nach dem Besuch der Dorfschule lernt er den Beruf eines Schuhmachers. Gesellendiplom 1926. Arbeitet bis 1944 als Schuhmacher, dann fängt er an zu malen. Dazu wechselt er den Beruf und geht zur französischen Eisenbahn, wo er bis 1962 bleibt. Dann wird er wegen Invalidität pensioniert. Anständige, sehr beflissene, zuweilen etwas zu photographische Malerei.

Après avoir fréquenté l'école communale, apprend le métier de cordonnier. Brevet de compagnon en 1926. Travaille donc comme cordonnier jusqu'en 1944, l'année où il commence à faire de la peinture. Pour faire de la peinture, il change de métier et entre dans les chemins de fer français où il restera jusqu'en 1962, mis à la retraite pour cause d'invalidité. Peinture honnête, très appliquée, parfois un peu trop photographique.

Schievers, Jean

Born April 22, 1876 in Louvain (Belgium).
Died October 4, 1963 in Louvain (Belgium).

Geboren am 22. April 1876 in Löwen (Belgien).
Gestorben am 4. Oktober 1963 in Löwen (Belgien).

Né le 22 avril 1876 à Louvain (Belgique).
Mort le 4 octobre 1963 à Louvain (Belgique).

Interior decorator. Did not start to paint until quite late in life. Further, his technique is very individual. Mostly he painted on ordinary canvas, or even on simple cloth or ticking. He mixed powder paint with turpentine or medicinal oil which he bought at the chemist's. In 1907 he wrote the 'Liederboek van Jean Schievers', where he described himself as 'Master Painter of Louvain'. At his death he left behind about fifty pictures, most of them small.

Tapezierer. Kommt erst ziemlich spät zur Malerei. Seine Technik ist übrigens sehr eigenartig. Er malte vor allem auf gewöhnliche Leinwand, wenn nicht gar auf bloße Laken oder Matratzenstoffe. Er mischte Farbpulver mit Terpentin und medizinischen Ölen, die er in der Apotheke kaufte. 1907 schrieb er das « Liederboek van Jean Schievers » und nannte sich selber « Maître Peintre de Louvain ». Er hinterließ etwa 50 Bilder, im allgemeinen von kleinem Format.

Tapissier. Se met à la peinture assez tard. Sa technique est d'ailleurs tout à fait particulière. Il peignait surtout sur des toiles ordinaires, si ce n'est sur de simples draps ou toiles à matelas. Il mélangeait des couleurs en poudre à de la térébenthine et à des huiles médicinales qu'il achetait chez le pharmacien. En 1907, il écrivit le « Liederboek van Jean Schievers » et se nommait lui-même « Maître peintre de Louvain ». Il laisse une cinquantaine de tableaux, généralement de petit format.

EXPOSITIONS:
« Peintres Naïfs Belges », Théâtre National, Bruxelles 1965.
« Peintres Naïfs Belges », Musée Royal des Beaux-Arts, Verviers 1965.
« Peintres Naïfs Belges », Musée Royal des Beaux-Arts, Hasselt 1966.
(Cat., Préface Anatole Jakovsky, Alain Germoz et Paul Snoek).

Schipper, Erna Maria Hermine

(née Schramm)
Born June 29, 1907 in Hamburg (Germany).

(geborene Schramm)
Geboren am 29. Juni 1907 in Hamburg (Deutschland).

(née Schramm)
Née le 29 juin 1907 à Hambourg (Allemagne).

Has lived in Holland since the age of seventeen. She is the mother of two daughters. Began to paint two years ago, just when she no longer needed to look after the children. At first the pictures were for presents—tapestries with bits of material, then later with colored crayons. Thus an enchanted world began to emerge, nearer to an Odilon Redon, for instance, than the canals and Dutch landscapes with tulips which she, in fact, tries to paint. Now one may justify the highest hopes for her.

Lebt seit ihrem siebzehnten Jahr in Holland. Mutter zweier Töchter. Hat vor 2 Jahren angefangen zu malen, als ihre Kinder sie nicht mehr brauchten. Zuerst um Geschenke zu machen. Wandteppiche aus Stoffetzen, dann mit Farbstiften gemalt. Sogleich entsteht eine zauberhafte Welt, die einem Odilon Redon zum Beispiel näher steht als den Kanälen und der holländischen Landschaft mit ihren Tulpen, die sie festzuhalten sucht. Schon heute berechtigt sie zu großen Hoffnungen.

Vit depuis ses 17 ans en Hollande. Mère de deux filles. A commencé à peindre il y a deux ans, lorsque, précisément, elle n'avait plus à s'occuper de ses enfants. D'abord pour faire des cadeaux. Des tapisseries, avec des morceaux d'étoffe, puis avec des crayons de couleur. Un monde féerique commence à se dessiner alors aussitôt, plus proche d'un Odilon Redon, par exemple, que des canaux et des vues de la campagne hollandaise, avec des tulipes, bien sûr, qu'elle essaye de saisir. Dès à présent, on peut penser que tous les espoirs sont permis.

Schmitz, Peter Paul Hubert

Born 1881 in the Ruhr district (Germany).

Geboren 1881 im Ruhrgebiet (Deutschland).

Né en 1881 dans le bassin de la Ruhr (Allemagne).

Worked for Phoenix-Rheinrohr AG in Düsseldorf, and still lives in Düsseldorf on his worker's old-age pension. He belongs to that generation of 'naive' artists for which details are more important than the picture as a whole, which is why in his work each paving-stone is counted, each tree or bush depicted minutely. It is the past which interests him more than the present, as a subject for painting.

Arbeitete bei der Phoenix-Rheinrohr AG in Düsseldorf. Wohnt immer noch in Düsseldorf und lebt von seiner Altersrente. Er gehört zu jener Generation von Naiven, für welche die Einzelheit wichtiger ist als das Ganze. Darum malt er die einzelnen Pflastersteine, zählt die Blätter. Übrigens fesselt ihn das Alte mehr als alle anderen Aspekte des Lebens.

Travaillait dans les Phoenix-Rheinrohr AG à Dusseldorf. Vit toujours à Dusseldorf de sa pension de vieux travailleur. Il appartient à cette génération des naïfs pour laquelle le détail compte plus que l'ensemble. C'est pourquoi il énumère les pavés, détaille les feuillages. C'est d'ailleurs le côté ancien qui le séduit plus que les autres aspects de la vie.

EXPOSITIONS:
«Laienkunst», Recklinghausen 1963
(Cat., Préface Bernhard Tacke).

Scholtis, Johann

Born 1897 in the Black Forest district (Germany).

Geboren 1897 im Schwarzwald (Deutschland).

Né en 1897 en Schwarzwald (Allemagne).

Half-Rumanian, half-German. At first he attended a Hungarian school; then, up to 1912, a German school. By profession a glass engraver. Became interested, one after the other, in physics, chemistry, technology, history of art and various forms of plastic expression. Took up painting in Rumania in 1934, a self-taught artist. He admits to having painted hundreds of pictures. He paints in his bedroom, by daylight. Now he lives in Dippoldiswalde, near Dresden, on a tiny pension. Art is sufficient to make him happy.

Zur Hälfte Rumäne, zur Hälfte Deutscher. Besucht zuerst eine ungarische, dann bis 1912 eine deutsche Schule. Glasgraveur. Studiert nacheinander Physik, Chemie, Technologie, Kunstgeschichte und verschiedene Formen des plastischen Ausdrucks. Beginnt 1934 in Rumänien zu malen. Wie ein Autodidakt. Er sagt, er habe Hunderte von Bildern gemalt. Er malt sie in seinem Schlafzimmer bei Tageslicht. Gegenwärtig lebt er in Dippoldiswalde bei Dresden von einer ganz kleinen Rente. Die Malerei genügt zu seinem Glück.

Moitié roumain, moitié allemand. Fréquente d'abord une école hongroise, puis, jusqu'en 1912, une école allemande. Graveur sur verre. Apprend successivement: physique, chimie, technologie, histoire de l'art et différentes formes de l'expression plastique. Commence à peindre en 1934 en Roumanie. Comme un autodidacte. Il avoue avoir peint des centaines de tableaux. Il les peint dans sa chambre à coucher, à la lumière du jour. Il vit actuellement à Dippoldiswalde, près de Dresde, d'une toute petite rente. La peinture suffit à son bonheur.

BIBLIOGRAPHIE:
Bernard Jasmand et Otto Kallir: «Sonntags-maler», Ed. Otto Aug. Ehlers, Berlin/Darmstadt 1956.

Schöttli, Emanuel

Born 1895 in Schaffhausen (Switzerland).
Died 1926 in Basel (Switzerland).

Geboren 1895 in Schaffhausen (Schweiz).
Gestorben 1926 in Basel (Schweiz).

Né en 1895 à Schaffhausen (Suisse).
Mort en 1926 à Bâle (Suisse).

Was employed as a policeman in Basel. Began to paint four years before his death—but unfortunately only in his leisure time. His very individual gift, which he managed to develop in such a short time, is astonishing. However, there are those who claim that he is simply a representative of 'ordinary' painting current at that time, and that he is by no means 'naive'. But this is a mistaken view—distressingly so. He was self-taught and therefore could only create the work of a self-taught artist. His work is very genuine. He was killed in a road accident.

Polizist in Basel. Beginnt vier Jahre vor seinem Tod zu malen. Aber leider nur in seiner Freizeit. Denn die ganz eigenartige Schau, die er in so kurzer Zeit zu schaffen verstand, ist sehr bedeutend. Es gibt indessen Leute, die der Ansicht sind, er sei ganz einfach ein Vertreter der gewöhnlichen Malerei seiner Zeit und durchaus kein Naiver gewesen. Das ist ein Irrtum. Ein betrüblicher Irrtum. Als Autodidakt konnte er nur autodidaktische Malerei hervorbringen. Sehr große Echtheit. Er kam bei einem Verkehrsunfall ums Leben.

Agent de police à Bâle. Commence à peindre quatre ans avant sa mort. Mais il n'a peint, hélas, que pendant ses loisirs. Car la vision si particulière, qu'il a su créer en si peu de temps, est absolument remarquable. D'aucuns pensent, cependant, qu'il était tout simplement un des représentants de la peinture ordinaire de son temps et nullement un naïf. Erreur. Fâcheuse erreur. Autodidacte, il n'a pu faire que de la peinture d'autodidacte. D'une grande authenticité. Il a été tué dans un accident de circulation.

EXPOSITIONS:
Kunsthalle, Basel 1927.
Kunsthalle, Basel 1947.
« Laienmaler », Gewerbemuseum, Basel 1961.
« Die Welt der naiven Malerei », Salzburg 1964.

Schubnel, Jean

Born June 24, 1894 in Château-la-Vallière, Indre et Loire (France).

Geboren am 24. Juni 1894 in Château-la-Vallière, Indre et Loire (Frankreich).

Né le 24 juin 1894 à Château-la-Vallière, Indre et Loire (France).

Descended from an Alsatian family which fled from the 1871 invasion. For many years a tobacconist in Langeais. His pictures are mainly of the historical castles of the Touraine district. He has his own individual craft, sometimes a little harsh, showing the droller aspects of his characters. Often paints from postcards and photographs. However, his sincerity is proof against everything.

Stammt aus einer elsässischen Familie, die 1871 vor der deutschen Besetzung floh. Lange Zeit war er Tabakverkäufer in Langeais. Hat hauptsächlich alle historischen Schlösser der Touraine gemalt. Eine ganz eigene, zuweilen etwas harte Technik, mit ziemlich putzigen Figuren. Malt oft nach Ansichtskarten und photographischen Dokumenten. Aber seine Aufrichtigkeit ist über jeden Zweifel erhaben.

Descendant des Alsaciens ayant fui l'invasion de 1871. Longtemps buraliste à Langeais. A peint surtout tous les châteaux historiques de la Touraine. Un métier très particulier, parfois un peu dur, avec le côté assez cocasse de ses personnages. Peint souvent d'après les cartes postales et les documents photographiques. Mais sa sincérité est à toute épreuve.

EXPOSITIONS:
Galerie Palmes, Paris 1952
(Cat., Préface M. Bedel et Anatole Jakovsky).
«Les Peintres Naïfs», Knokke-le-Zoute 1958.
«Les Peintres Naïfs», Maison de la Pensée Française, Paris 1960.
«I Pittori Naifs», Rome 1964.

BIBLIOGRAPHIE:
Anatole Jakovsky: «La Peinture Naïve», Paris 1949.
Anatole Jakovsky: «Les Peintres Naïfs», Paris 1956.
Anatole Jakovsky: «Naive Malerei», Zürich 1957.
«Jean Schubnel», Vogue, Paris, décembre 1956/janvier 1957.
Oto Bihalji-Merin: «Das naive Bild der Welt», Köln 1959.
Oto Bihalji-Merin: «Die naive Malerei», Köln 1959.
Oto Bihalji-Merin: «Les Peintres Naïfs», Paris (sans date).

FILM:
«O saisons, ô châteaux»... réalisé par Agnès Varda. Paris 1957.

PUBLICITÉ:
Une série de 8 cartes postales d'après les tableaux de Schubnel, réalisée par Cincolor, Paris 1958.

Schwartzenberg, Simon

Born September 20, 1895 in Paris (France).

Geboren am 20. September 1895 in Paris (Frankreich).

Né le 20 septembre 1895 à Paris (France).

Runs a hosiery business. Is a fine and sensitive artist, passionately fond of music. Was permanently marked by the loss of both his sons, who were assassinated by the Nazis. Thus he began to paint in 1952, whenever his business allowed him any freedom—often during the night. And every time he paints wonders which he has never seen, works of a rare poetical intensity. His paintings of a grey Paris (before the general 'cleaning' of the city's buildings) and of a light-colored Paris afterwards are among the best contemporary 'naive' works, and are likely to remain so.

Leitet ein Wirkwarenunternehmen. Dieser feinsinnige, empfindsame Künstler, der Musik über alles liebt, wird durch den Verlust seiner beiden Söhne, die von den Nazis ermordet wurden, tief gezeichnet. 1952 fängt er an zu malen, sobald seine Beschäftigungen ihm ein bißchen Muße gewähren, oft nachts. Und jedesmal entstehen nie gesehene Wunderwerke, Bilder von einer ungewöhnlichen poetischen Intensität. Seine Ansichten von Paris in Grau – vor der Häuserreinigung — und seine Ansichten von Paris in Weiß, das heißt nachher, haben und behalten ihren Platz unter den besten naiven Bildern unserer Zeit.

Dirige une entreprise de bonneterie. Artiste fin et sensible, passionné de musique, il reste marqué par la perte de ses deux fils, assassinés par les nazis. Il commence alors à peindre en 1952, chaque fois que ses occupations lui donnent quelque liberté; souvent la nuit. Et chaque fois, ce sont des merveilles jamais vues, des œuvres d'une rare intensité poétique. Ses vues de Paris gris – avant le nettoyage – et ses vues de Paris clair, c'est-à-dire après, restent et resteront parmi les meilleurs tableaux naïfs de ce temps.

EXPOSITIONS:
Galerie Bénézit, Paris 1962
(Cat., Préface Anatole Jakovsky).
« I Pittori Naifs », Rome 1964.
« Les Primitifs d'Aujourd'hui »,
Galerie Charpentier, Paris 1964.
Centre Culturel, Rabat 1964.

BIBLIOGRAPHIE:
« Simon Schwartzenberg », L'Illustrazione Italiana, Nº 11, novembre 1960.
Anatole Jakovsky: « Simon Schwartzenberg », La Vie Médicale, Paris mai 1963.
« Art Naïf », Editions Marocaines et Internationales, Rabat 1964.
Anatole Jakovsky: « Eros du Dimanche », Paris 1964.

FILM:
« Le voyage à Paris », d'après un texte de Marcel Aymé, réalisé par Pierre Mathieu, Paris 1959.

Séraphine (Séraphine Louis)

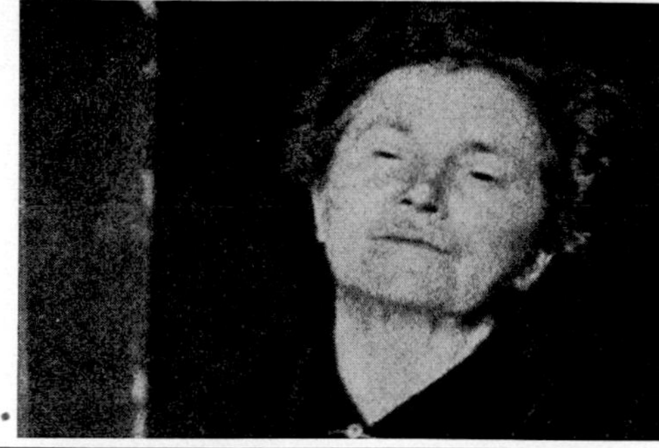

Born September 3, 1864 in Arsy, Oise (France).
Died December 11, 1942 in Clermont, Oise (France).

Geboren am 3. September 1864 in Arsy, Oise (Frankreich).
Gestorben am 11. Dezember 1942 in Clermont, Oise (Frankreich).

Née le 3 septembre 1864 à Arsy, Oise (France).
Morte le 11 décembre 1942 à Clermont, Oise (France).

Daughter of a watchmaker and a farm girl. Impecunious childhood and youth. It is not really clear why and how she started to paint. However, about 1912 she became housekeeper to W. Uhde, a picture dealer, who also bought her pictures. Since he was forced to flee France as a German subject, she did not see him again until after the first war; but then he bought all her production as if she had been under contract. This was, in fact, the time she produced her great canvases, true masterpieces. However, the general depression came and so, in 1930, Uhde stopped buying her work. Séraphine, already neurotic, thought fate was against her and that she was the subject of intrigues, and she began to behave in an eccentric manner. She was admitted to a hospital, and later to a psychiatric unit in Clermont. She did not die there in 1934 as Uhde and all the 'Master's Voices' pretended, but only eight years later. However, sick and unable to paint as she was, no one was interested in her any more... This was the end of the tragic life of one of the greatest 'naive' artists in the world and of any age.

Tochter eines Uhrmachers und einer Bauernmagd. Ärmliche Kindheit und Jugend. Im Grunde weiß man nicht, warum und wie sie zu malen angefangen hat. Auf jeden Fall wird sie gegen 1912 Putzfrau bei dem Kunsthändler Wilhelm Uhde, der auch ihre Bilder kauft.
Bei Ausbruch des Ersten Weltkriegs muß er als Deutscher Frankreich verlassen und kehrt erst nach Kriegsende zurück; nun nimmt er ihr sämtliche Bilder ab, als wäre sie vertraglich an ihn gebunden. Es ist die Zeit ihrer großen Bilder, ihrer Meisterwerke. Aber die Wirtschaftskrise naht, und 1930 stellt Uhde jäh seine Ankäufe ein. Séraphine, die bereits neurotisch ist, glaubt an eine Verhexung, an eine Intrige. Sie benimmt sich so, daß man sie zuerst ins Krankenhaus und dann in die psychiatrische Anstalt nach Clermont bringt, wo sie nicht 1934 gestorben ist, wie Uhde und nach ihm alle «Stimmen seines Herrn» behauptet haben, sondern erst acht Jahre später. Allerdings war sie geistesschwach und konnte nicht mehr malen, so daß sie niemand mehr interessierte... So endete das tragische Abenteuer einer der größten naiven Maler aller Länder und aller Zeiten.

Fille d'un horloger et d'une fille de ferme. Enfance et adolescence besogneuses. Au fond, on ne sait pas pourquoi et comment elle s'est mise à peindre. Toujours est-il que vers 1912, elle devient la femme de ménage de M.W. Uhde, marchand de tableaux, qui achète, également, les siens. Obligé de fuir la France comme sujet allemand, elle ne retrouvera celui-ci qu'après la guerre, et là, il lui prend toute sa production, comme si elle était sous contrat. C'est d'ailleurs l'époque de ses grandes toiles, des véritables chefs-d'œuvre. Mais la crise approche et, brusquement, en 1930, Uhde suspend ses achats. Déjà névrosée, Séraphine croit au mauvais sort, à la cabale. Elle se livre à des excentricités. On la conduit d'abord à l'hôpital, puis à l'établissement psychiatrique de Clermont où elle n'est pas morte en 1934 comme l'a fait croire Uhde et, à sa suite, tous les «Voix de son Maître», mais 8 ans plus tard.
Il est vrai que débile et ne pouvant plus peindre, elle n'intéressait plus personne... Ainsi finit la tragique aventure d'un des plus grands peintres naïfs du monde et de tous les temps.

EXPOSITIONS:
Galerie « Quatre-Chemins », Paris 1927.
« Primitifs Modernes », Galerie G. Bernheim, Paris 1932.
« Les Maîtres Populaires de la Réalité », Paris 1937.
« Les Maîtres Populaires de la Réalité », Zürich 1937.
« Masters of Popular Painting », New York 1938.
« Masters of Popular Painting », Tooth & Sons, Londres 1938.
« Primitifs du XXe Siècle », Galerie de Beaune, Paris 1938 (Cat., Préface G. Maratier).
« Primitifs du XXe siècle », Galerie Drouin, Paris 1942 (Cat., Préface G. Maratier).
Galerie de France, Paris 1945
(Cat., Préface Max. Gauthier et W. Uhde).
« Cinq Maîtres Primitifs », Galerie Palmes, Paris 1949 (Cat., Préface W. Uhde).
« Moderne primitive Maler », Kunsthalle, Bern 1949 (Cat., Préface Arnold Rüdlinger).
« Maler des einfältigen Herzens »,
Museum am Ostwall, Dortmund 1952.
Musée, Genève 1952.
Kunsthalle, Basel 1956.
« La Peinture Naïve », Knokke-le-Zoute 1958.
« La Peinture Naïve », Maison de la Pensée Française, Paris 1960.
Galerie P. Birtchansky, Paris 1962
(Cat., Préface Nino Frank).
« I Pittori Naifs », Rome 1964.
« Die Welt der naiven Malerei », Salzburg 1964.
« De Lusthof der Naieven », Rotterdam 1964.
« Le Monde des Naïfs », Paris 1964.

BIBLIOGRAPHIE:
W. Uhde: « Cinq Maîtres Primitifs », Paris 1949.
Anatole Jakovsky: « La Peinture Naïve », Paris 1949.
H.P. Gallot: « Séraphine », Information artistique, N° 40, mai 1957.
J.P. Weber: « Séraphine », Nouvelle Revue Française, 1er août 1958.
Bernard Jasmand et Otto Rallir: « Sonntagsmaler », Otto Aug. Ehlers Berlin/Darmstadt 1955.
Anatole Jakovsky: « Les Peintres Naïfs », Paris 1956.
Anatole Jakovsky: « Naive Malerei », Zürich 1957.
Anatole Jakovsky: « Eros du Dimanche », Paris 1964.
Oto Bihalji-Merin: « Das naive Bild der Welt », Köln 1959.
Oto Bihalji-Merin: « Die naive Malerei », Köln 1959.
Oto Bihalji-Merin: « Les Peintres Naïfs », Paris (sans date).
Catalogo Bolaffi d'Arte Moderna, Turin 1965/66.

Seron, Frédéric

Born October 3, 1876 in Brosse d'Anzy, Nièvre (France).
Died April 27, 1959 in Pressoir-Prompt, Seine-et-Oise (France).

Geboren am 3. Oktober 1876 in Brosse d'Anzy, Nièvre (Frankreich).
Gestorben am 27. April 1959 in Pressoir-Prompt, Seine-et-Oise (Frankreich).

Né le 3 octobre 1876 à Brosse d'Anzy, Nièvre (France).
Mort le 27 avril 1959 à Pressoir-Prompt, Seine-et-Oise (France).

Was a baker by profession. As soon as he retired he conceived the plan of decorating his house with concrete statues. Each statue possesses its 'secret', in other words poems of his own invention, vouchers, ration-card coupons, etc. He also painted pictures and decorated his basement with frescos. Jean Cocteau bought several of his works (he was a neighbor).

Bäcker von Beruf. Als er sich von der Arbeit zurückzieht, faßt er den Plan, sein Haus mit Zementstatuen zu schmücken. Jede Statue besitzt übrigens ihr «Geheimfach», das von ihm verfaßte Gedichte und verschiedene Belege wie Rationierungskarten usw. enthält. Er hat auch Bilder gemalt und das Kellergeschoß mit Fresken ausgeschmückt. Jean Cocteau, sein Nachbar, hat ihm ein paar Werke abgekauft.

Boulanger de son état et l'heure de la retraite sonnée, il a conçu le projet de décorer sa maison avec des statues en ciment. Chaque statue possède, du reste, son «secret», c'est-à-dire des poèmes de son cru et autres pièces justificatives, les tickets de rationnement, entre autres. Il a peint aussi des tableaux et a décoré son sous-sol à la fresque. J. Cocteau lui a acheté quelques œuvres (en voisin).

BIBLIOGRAPHIE:

Ralph Messac: «Frédéric Seron», L'Information, Paris, 7 septembre 1955.
R. Giraud: «Frédéric Seron», Paris-Presse-Intransigeant, 7 avril 1955.
«Frédéric Seron», France-Dimanche, Paris, 14 janvier 1958.
«Les Inspirés et leurs Demeures», Préface d'André Breton, Editions le Temps, Paris 1962.
Anatole Jakovsky: «Dämonen und Wunder», DuMont-Schauberg, Köln 1963.

Shalom de Safed

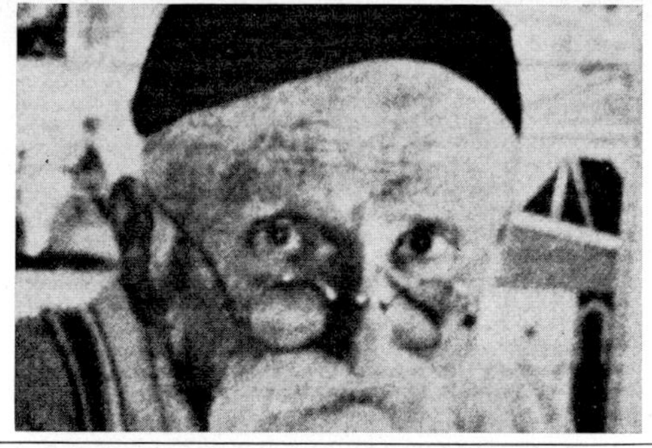

(real name Shalom Moskovitz)
Born ca. 1892 in Europe.

(mit seinem richtigen Namen Shalom Moskovitz)
Geboren ca. 1892 in Europa.

(de son vrai nom: Shalom Moskovitz)
Né vers 1892 en Europe.

Watchmaker, in humble circumstances. Began to paint towards the age of sixty, entirely by chance, like so many others. He wanted to explain the stories of the Bible in as concrete a way as possible to his grandchildren, and so he began with careful drawings, somehow 'pre-Christian' with Coptic and Ethiopian touches, which he later colored. He is an entirely self-taught artist. He lives now in a little Galilean village called Safed (hence his adopted name), once the center of cabalists and other mystical sects. His exhibitions outside Israel were an overwhelming success. But success does not affect him; he continues to work conscientiously, unhurriedly, as if nothing had happened.

Kleiner Uhrmacher. Beginnt um die Sechzig herum zu malen, ganz zufällig, wie so viele andere. Er wollte seinen Enkelkindern auf anschauliche Art die biblischen Begebenheiten erklären, und so entstanden diese sehr eigenartigen Zeichnungen, die gewissermaßen vorchristlich anmuten und koptische, ja abessinische Reminiszenzen aufweisen. Später koloriert er sie dann. Er ist reiner Autodidakt. Er lebt in einem kleinen galiläischen Dorf namens Safed – daher sein Name –, das früher eine Heimstätte für Kabbalisten und andere mystische Sekten war. Seine Ausstellungen im Ausland hatten durchschlagenden Erfolg. Aber er läßt sich dadurch keineswegs beeindrucken, sondern fährt fort, redlich zu arbeiten, ohne sich zu beeilen, als ob nichts wäre.

Petit horloger. Commence à peindre vers sa soixantième année; tout à fait par hasard, comme tant d'autres. C'est en voulant expliquer d'une façon plus concrète les événements de la Bible à ses petits enfants, qu'il trace d'abord ces dessins très particuliers, pré-chrétiens en quelque sorte, avec des réminiscences coptes, sinon éthiopiennes, et qu'il colorie par la suite. Il est pourtant un autodidacte pur. Il vit dans un petit village de Galilée nommé Safed – d'où ce surnom – foyer autrefois des cabbalistes et autres sectes mystiques. Ses expositions à l'étranger ont eu un succès foudroyant. Mais ce succès n'a aucune prise sur lui. Il continue à travailler honnêtement, sans se presser, comme si de rien n'était.

EXPOSITIONS:
Galerie Julius Carlebach, New York 1961.
Renaissance Society Gallery, Chicago 1962.
Galerie Furstenberg, Paris 1962.

BIBLIOGRAPHIE:
«Shalom», in Horizon, New York, juin-juillet 1961.

da Silva, Francesco

Born ca. 1910 in Alto Tejo, Acre (Brazil).

Geboren ca. 1910 in Alto Tejo, Bezirk Acre (Brasilien).

Né vers 1910 à Alto Tejo, territoire du Acre (Brésil).

Indian of pure stock. A Swiss artist discovered him while he (da Silva) was decorating the walls of fishermen's huts with chalk and charcoal. It is truly inspired art, despite its decorative aspect. His art is fairly similar to that of Isabel de Jesus. His work enjoyed success as a curiosity and, soon afterwards, success in the proper sense of the term. And the success is justified.

Reinrassiger Indianer. Ein Schweizer Maler entdeckt ihn, als er dabei ist, die Wände der Fischerhütten mit Kreide und Rötel zu bemalen. Wahrhaft inspirierte Kunst, trotz ihrer dekorativen Seite. Sie ist ziemlich nahe mit der Kunst von Isabel de Jesus verwandt. Snoberfolg, der sich ziemlich schnell in richtigen Erfolg verwandelt. Übrigens durchaus verdientermaßen.

Indien de pure race. Un peintre suisse le découvre lorsque celui-ci était en train de décorer à la craie et au fusain les murs des cabanes des pêcheurs. Art véritablement inspiré, malgré ses côtés décoratifs. Il s'apparente assez à celui d'Isabel de Jesus. Succès de curiosité qui se transforme assez vite en un succès tout court. Mérité, du reste.

EXPOSITIONS:
Galeria Askanasy, Rio de Janeiro 1945.
Salon Beauregard, Genève 1949.
Galerie pour l'Art, Lausanne 1950.
Palacio Foz, Lisbonne 1951.
Musée Ethnographique, Neuchâtel 1956.
Galeria Relevo, Rio de Janeiro 1963.
« Peintres Naïfs Brésiliens », Galerie Jacques Massol, Paris 1965.

BIBLIOGRAPHIE:
J. P. Chabloz: « Un Indien brézilien ré-invente la peinture », Cahiers d'Art, Paris 1952.

da Silva, José Antonio

Born 1909 in Sales de Oliveira, São Paulo (Brazil).

Geboren 1909 in Sales de Oliveira, São Paulo (Brasilien).

Né en 1909 à Sales de Oliveira, São Paulo (Brésil).

As authentic a self-taught artist as can be imagined. A kind of unspoilt Grandma Moses. Early in his life he led a nomadic existence as a rural laborer on farms and on coffee and sugar-cane plantations, as the opportunity offered, and then later he was employed as night porter in a small hotel in Rio Preto. At the age of 37 he was overwhelmed by an unconquerable urge to express himself in some way. At the same time as he wrote the story of his life (published by the Museum of Modern Art in São Paulo) he put his youthful memories down on to canvas. Has shown his paintings in collective and individual exhibitions in Rio de Janeiro and São Paulo. He even exhibited work at the Venice Biennale. Is an artist worthy of note.

Autodidakt reinsten Wassers. Eine Art Grandma Moses im Reinzustand. Als «Caboclo» führt er zuerst ein unstetes Leben als umherziehender Landarbeiter auf verschiedenen Höfen und Kaffee- oder Zuckerplantagen. Dann verdient er sein Leben als Nachtwächter in einem kleinen Hotel in Rio Preto. Im Alter von 37 Jahren ergreift ihn eine unwiderstehliche Lust, sich auszudrücken. Er schreibt den Roman seines Lebens (veröffentlicht vom Museum für Moderne Kunst in São Paulo) und hält gleichzeitig die Erinnerungen seiner jungen Jahre auf der Leinwand fest. Einzel- und Gruppenausstellungen in Rio de Janeiro und São Paulo. Er stellt sogar an der Biennale von Venedig aus! Ein Künstler, der Interesse verdient.

Autodidacte tout ce qu'il y a d'authentique. Une sorte de Grandma Moses à l'état pur. «Caboclo», il mène, pour commencer, une existence errante de travailleur rural, dans les fermes et les plantations de café et de canne à sucre en l'occurrence, puis gagne sa vie comme veilleur de nuit dans un petit hôtel de Rio Preto. A l'âge de 37 ans, il est pris par une irrésistible envie de se réaliser. En même temps qu'il écrit le roman de sa vie (publié par le Musée d'Art Moderne de São Paulo), il met sur la toile les souvenirs de ses jeunes années. Expositions individuelles et collectives à Rio de Janeiro et à São Paulo. Il expose même à la Biennale de Venise! Artiste digne d'intérêt.

BIBLIOGRAPHIE:
Rubem Braga: «Tres Primitivos», Ed. par le Service de Documentation du Ministère de l'Education et de la Culture, 1953.

da Silveira, Elisa Martins

Born 1912 in Piaui (Brazil).

Geboren 1912 in Piaui (Brasilien).

Née en 1912 à Piaui (Brésil).

Just like some of her kindred spirits, be they in Sweden or Brazil, this artist began by taking painting lessons in the normal way. Rather belatedly—for she did not begin until 1952—but nevertheless rewarded by almost immediate and resounding successes. She won prizes at the second and third São Paulo Biennale, and took part in important collective exhibitions both in Brazil and in other parts of the world. Her first individual show was in 1958. Her painting is sincere, carefully executed, sometimes with a tendency towards folklore.

Wie ein paar andere Maler und Malerinnen, sei es in Schweden oder in Brasilien, hat auch diese Künstlerin zunächst auf ganz normale Weise Malerei studiert. Ein bißchen spät allerdings, denn sie fing erst 1952 an; dafür erlebte sie großen und beinahe unmittelbaren Erfolg: Preise an der 2. und 3. Biennale von São Paulo und Teilnahme an bedeutenden Gruppenausstellungen im In- und Ausland. Ihre erste Einzelausstellung geht auf das Jahr 1958 zurück. Ihre Malerei ist ehrlich, gepflegt, zuweilen etwas folkloristisch.

Comme quelques-unes et quelques-uns de ses semblables, que ce soit en Suède ou au Brésil, cette artiste a commencé par les études absolument normales de la peinture. Un peu tardivement, puisqu'elle ne les commence qu'en 1952, mais récompensées, en revanche, par de retentissants et presqu'immédiats succès: prix à la deuxième et à la troisième Biennale de de São Paulo et participation à d'importantes expositions collectives aussi bien au Brésil qu'à l'étranger. Sa première exposition personnelle date de 1958. Sa peinture est honnête, soignée, un peu folklorique parfois.

EXPOSITIONS:
«Artistes Brésiliens», Musée d'Art Moderne de la ville, Paris 1959.

Silvia
(de Leon Chalreo)

Born April 11, 1905 in Morro de São Christovão, Rio de Janeiro (Brazil).

Geboren am 11. April 1905 in Morro de São Christovão, Rio de Janeiro (Brasilien).

Née le 11 avril 1905 à Morro de São Christovão, Rio de Janeiro (Brésil).

A well-educated woman who became in turn writer, translator, professional journalist, etc., but who finally found her vocation in painting. She is entirely self-taught as an artist, certainly, but paints nevertheless to some extent to please others. Her subjects are traditional scenes, mostly crowds. Nevertheless, she is at the extreme edge of 'naive' art, strictly speaking, as are also several other similar Brazilian artists.

Sie ist eine gebildete Frau, die nacheinander die Berufe einer Schriftstellerin, Übersetzerin, Berufsjournalistin usw. ausgeübt hat. Schließlich findet sie ihre wahre Berufung in der Malerei, die sie als Autodidaktin betreibt, doch nicht ohne den Wunsch, zu gefallen. Folkloristische Themen, Menschenmengen. Sie situiert sich trotzdem an der Grenze der reinen naiven Malerei, wie ein paar andere Brasilianerinnen, die sich im gleichen Fall befinden.

Cultivée, puisque tour à tour écrivain, traducteur, journaliste professionnel, etc. Elle ne trouve, finalement, sa vocation que dans la peinture qu'elle exerce en autodidacte, certes, mais non sans un désir de plaire. Sujets folkloriques, les foules. Elle se situe quand-même à la limite de la peinture naïve pure, comme quelques autres Brésiliennes dans son cas.

EXPOSITIONS:
Livraria Brasiliense, São Paulo 1945.
Instituto de Arquitetos de Brasil, 1946.
Galeria Velasquez, Buenos Aires 1952.
Galeria Oxumara Salvador-Bahia 1955 (Cat., Préface Carlos de Andrade).
Escola dramatica Martins Pena, Rio de Janeiro 1955 (Cat., Préface Wilson Rocha).
Galeria de Arte. São Paulo 1956 (Cat., Préface Carlos Magna).
Galeria Lemac, Recife 1958 (Cat., Préface Marcos Andre).
Galeria Municipal de Arte, Rio de Janeiro 1960.
Galeria Montmartre-Jorge, Rio de Janeiro 1961.
Galeria Macunaima, Rio de Janeiro 1961 (Cat., Préface Walmir Ayala).

Skliar, Michel

Born November 8, 1897 in Odessa (Russia).

Geboren am 8. November 1897 in Odessa (Rußland).

Né le 8 novembre 1897 à Odessa (Russie).

Came to France after the first world war and spent the second war in the French army. Became a naturalized French citizen. He was a carrier by trade, and one day he stopped in front of a box of Vlaminck's canvases. 'I could do that too, he said to himself', and set to work. But his landscapes naturally do not look at all like those of the artist who apparently inspired him. His pictures are sharply defined, often highly-colored, and represent a 'wild' tendency in Parisian 'naive' painting. Incidentally, he is among the few 'naive' artists to paint night landscapes.

Kommt nach dem Ersten Weltkrieg nach Frankreich und kämpft im Zweiten in den Reihen der französischen Armee. Erwirbt die französische Staatsbürgerschaft. Von Beruf ist er Spediteur, und so kommt ihm einmal eine Kiste mit Bildern von Vlaminck in die Hände. Das kann ich auch, sagt er sich und macht sich ans Werk. Aber seine Landschaften haben natürlich keine Ähnlichkeit mit denen, die ihm vorschweben. Stark gegliedert, oft sehr kräftig in der Farbe, stellen sie, wenn man so sagen darf, eine fauvistische Tendenz in der Pariser naiven Malerei dar. Er gehört übrigens zu den ganz wenigen naiven Malern, die Nachtlandschaften malen.

Arrive en France après la première guerre mondiale et fait celle-ci dans les rangs de l'armée française. Naturalisé français. Transporteur de son métier, il tombe en arrêt devant une caisse de toiles de Vlaminck. Je saurai le faire moi aussi, se dit-il, et il se met à l'œuvre. Mais ses paysages ne ressemblent, naturellement, pas à ceux dont il voudrait s'inspirer. Fortement maçonnés, souvent hauts en couleurs, ils représentent une tendance «fauve», si l'on peut dire, de la peinture naïve parisienne. Il est, d'ailleurs, parmi les combien rares peintres naïfs à peindre des paysages nocturnes.

EXPOSITIONS:
Galerie du Colisée, Paris 1960 (Cat., Préface Anatole Jakovsky).
«Les Peintres Naïfs», Maison de la Pensée Française, Paris 1960.
Galerie de l'Institut, Paris 1962 (Cat., Préface Anatole Jakovsky).
«I Pittori Naifs», Rome 1964.
«Les Primitifs d'Aujourd'hui», Galerie Charpentier, Paris 1964.
Residenzgalerie, Salzburg 1964.

BIBLIOGRAPHIE:
Anatole Jakovsky: «Eros du Dimanche», Paris 1964.

Skum, Nils Nilsson

Born 1872 in Lapland (Sweden).
Died 1951 in Sweden.

Geboren 1872 in Lappland (Schweden).
Gestorben 1951 in Schweden.

Né en 1872 en Laponie (Suède).
Mort en 1951 en Suède.

Was born in a nomad's tent. Taught himself to read, write and count without any help at all. Also self-taught as an artist, of course. Began quite early to make engravings and sculptures and to paint on wrapping paper—but it was mainly when he was an old man that he painted, throwing himself with delight into the task of relating stories from his early life and the life of his race. His main works, which made his name well-known, are 'Same sita' and 'Valla renar'.

Kam in einem Nomadenzelt zur Welt. Lernte ganz allein lesen, schreiben und rechnen. Selbstverständlich Autodidakt. Beginnt ziemlich früh zu gravieren, zu bildhauern und auf Packpapier zu malen, doch erzählt er vor allem in seinen alten Tagen mit Herzenslust seine Erinnerungen an das Leben von einst und an das Leben seines Volks. Seine Meisterwerke, die ihn bekannt gemacht haben, sind «Same sita» und «Valla renar».

A vu le jour sous la tente des nomades. Il a appris tout seul à lire, à écrire et à compter. Autodidacte, naturellement. Commence à graver, à sculpter et à peindre sur du papier d'emballage d'assez bonne heure, mais c'est surtout sur ses vieux jours qu'il s'en donne à cœur joie à raconter ses souvenirs de la vie d'autrefois, ainsi que de la vie de sa peuplade. Ses chefs-d'œuvre qui l'ont fait connaître sont: «Same sita» et «Valla renar».

EXPOSITIONS:
«Laienmaler», Gewerbemuseum, Basel 1961.

BIBLIOGRAPHIE:
Ernst Maurer: «Boken om Skum», Ed. Tema, Halmstad 1965.

Skurjeni, Mato

Born December 14, 1898 in Veterniča, province of Zlotar (Yugoslavia).

Geboren am 14. Dezember 1898 in Veterniča, Provinz Zlotar (Jugoslawien).

Né le 14 décembre 1898 à Veterniča, province de Zlotar (Yougoslavie).

Although he was born into a peasant family, he became a house painter and through his work came to love color. He attended evening classes in draftsmanship to improve his knowledge. As if he needed it! For the striking aspect of his paintings is precisely the elegance and the freedom from any fixed pattern. In his work everything is on the surface, is part of the melody, the whole in the mass of the picture with its so-called 'impressionistic' touches.

Stammt aus bäuerlichem Milieu, wird jedoch Anstreicher und beginnt bei dieser Arbeit die Farbe zu lieben. Abends besucht er einen Zeichenkurs, um seine Kenntnisse zu erweitern. Als hätte er das nötig! Denn was in seinen Kompositionen auffällt, ist eben gerade die Eleganz und die Freiheit, mit der er auf die Zeichnung verzichtet. Bei ihm singt die ganze Fläche, die ganze Masse des Bildes in ganz kleinen, sozusagen impressionistischen Strichen.

D'origine paysanne, il devient pourtant peintre en bâtiment, et c'est là où il commence à aimer la couleur. Le soir, il fréquente un cours de dessin afin de parfaire ses connaissances. Comme s'il en avait besoin! Car ce qui frappe, précisément, dans les compositions de Skurjeni, c'est justement l'élégance et la liberté avec lesquelles il se passe du dit dessin. Chez lui, c'est toute la surface, toute la masse du tableau qui chante en de toutes petites touches pour ainsi dire impressionnistes.

EXPOSITIONS:
«Naivni umetnici jugoslavije», Belgrade 1957.
Palais de la Culture, Belgrade 1959
(Cat.) Galerie Mona Lisa, Paris 1962
(Cat., Préface Radovan Ivsič).
The Arthur Jeffress Gallery, Londres 1961.
«Laienmaler», Gewerbemuseum, Basel 1961.
«Das naive Bild der Welt», Baden-Baden 1961.
«Yugoslav Modern Primitives», Edinburgh 1962.
«Peintres Naïfs Yougoslaves», Moscou 1962.
«La première Quadriennale des Peintres Naïfs Yougoslaves», Čačac 1962.
«Naive Kunst in Jugoslawien», Académie des Beaux-Arts, Vienne 1963.
The Galerie St-Etienne, New York 1963.
«Les Peintres Naïfs Populaires Yougoslaves», Leningrad 1963.
«Sonntagsmaler aus Jugoslawien», Museum am Ostwall, Dortmund 1964.
«Die Welt der naiven Malerei», Salzburg 1964.
«De Lusthof der Naieven», Rotterdam 1964.
«Le Monde des Naïfs», Paris 1964.

BIBLIOGRAPHIE:
«Yougoslavija», numéro spécial (17) consacré à l'art des naïfs, Belgrade 1959.
Oto Bihalji-Merin: «Das naive Bild der Welt», Köln 1959.
Oto Bihalji-Merin: «Die naive Malerei», Köln 1959.
Oto Bihalji-Merin: «Les Peintres Naïfs», Paris (sans date).
Oto Bihalji-Merin: «Umetnost Naivnich u Jugoslavjii», Belgrade 1963.
«Art Naïf», Editions Marocaines et Internationales, Rabat 1964.
Anatole Jakovsky: «Eros du Dimanche», Paris 1964.

Sokol, Jano

Born November 4, 1909 in Kovačiča (Yugoslavia).

Geboren am 4. November 1909 in Kovačiča (Jugoslawien).

Né le 4 novembre 1909 à Kovačiča (Yougoslavie).

A peasant by birth. The turning point in his life came in 1938 when he met Martin Paluska at the Municipal Library. Paluska taught him the rudiments of painting, and together they founded the famous association of peasant artists, called the Kovačiča school, in 1952. Like others of this school, Sokol painted the highlights of village life—his own village—such as weddings, burials, etc. But his style is more descriptive and has touches of folklore.

Bauer. Das entscheidende Ereignis in seinem Leben war die 1938 auf der Stadtbibliothek erfolgte Begegnung mit Martin Paluska. Dieser bringt ihm die Grundbegriffe des Malens bei, und mit ihm zusammen gründet er 1952 die berühmte Vereinigung der Bauernmaler, genannt «Schule von Kovačiča». Auch Sokol malt die wichtigen Begebenheiten des Dorflebens wie Hochzeiten, Beerdigungen usw. aber in einer mehr beschreibenden Art mit folkloristischen Reminiszenzen.

Paysan. La rencontre capitale de sa vie fut celle, à la Bibliothèque Municipale, de Martin Paluska, en 1938, qui lui enseigne les rudiments de la peinture. Toujours avec ce dernier, il fonde en 1952, la fameuse association des paysans-peintres, dite l'Ecole de Kovačiča. Lui aussi, il peint les moments capitaux de la vie de leur village, tels que mariages, enterrements, etc., mais dans un style plus descriptif, avec des réminiscences folkloriques.

EXPOSITIONS:

«Naivni umetnici Jugoslavije», Belgrade 1957.
«Laienmaler», Gewerbemuseum, Basel 1961.
The Arthur Jeffress Gallery, Londres 1961.
«Peintres Naïfs Yougoslaves», Moscou 1962.
«Yugoslav Modern Primitives», Edinburgh 1962.
«Première Quadriennale des Peintres Naïfs Yougoslaves», Čačac 1962.
Palais de Culture, Kovačiča 1962 (Cat., Préface M. Gvozdanovič).
«Peintres Naïfs Populaires Yougoslaves», Leningrad 1963.
«Naive Kunst in Jugoslawien», Kunstakademie, Wien 1963.
«Sonntagsmaler aus Jugoslawien», Museum am Ostwall, Dortmund 1964.

BIBLIOGRAPHIE:

«Yougoslavija», numéro spécial (17) consacré à l'art des naïfs, Belgrade 1959.
Oto Bihalji-Merin: «Das naive Bild der Welt», Köln 1959.
Oto Bihalji-Merin: «Die naive Malerei», Köln 1959.
Oto Bihalji-Merin: «Les Peintres Naïfs», Paris (sans date).
Oto Bihalji-Merin: «Umetnost Naivnich u Jugoslavjii», Belgrade 1963.

Speiser, Gottlieb

Born 1875 in Wintersingen, canton Basel-Land (Switzerland).

Geboren 1875 in Wintersingen, Kt. Baselland (Schweiz).

Né en 1875 à Wintersingen, canton de Bâle-Campagne (Suisse).

Country born, he was a farm hand and a cowherd. Began to paint when he was about thirty years old. A self-taught artist; but nevertheless his work shows him to be someone who not only knows nature but who has a real feeling for it, too. Now lives in Basel.

Bauer, Knecht, Kuhhirte. Beginnt um das dreißigste Lebensjahr herum zu malen. Autodidakt, mit den Eigenschaften eines Menschen, der die Natur nicht nur kennt, sondern auch erfühlt. Wohnt jetzt in Basel.

Paysan, valet, vacher. Commence à peindre vers la trentaine. Autodidacte, avec des qualités néanmoins de quelqu'un qui, non seulement connaît la nature, mais la sent. Habite à présent Bâle.

EXPOSITIONS:
«Laienmaler», Gewerbemuseum, Basel 1961.

BIBLIOGRAPHIE:
A. Hernandez: «Naive Maler», Atlantis, No. 11 Zürich, novembre 1961.

Stefula, Georgy

Born 1913 in Hamburg (Germany).

Geboren 1913 in Hamburg (Deutschland).

Né en 1913 à Hamburg (Allemagne).

His father was Hungarian, his mother French. He took up painting about 1945. His work is clearly defined, full of poetry and plastic inventiveness. He is fond of telling stories which cannot be read directly from the pictures themselves; in fact, he has much in common with the surrealists in their juxtaposition of all kinds of unexpected objects. He and his wife Dorothea (who is also an artist) live in Chiemsee.

Vater Ungar, Mutter Französin. Beginnt 1945 zu malen. Seine Kunst ist klar, poetisch, voll von plastischen Einfällen. Er liebt es auch, Geschichten zu erzählen, die nicht immer unmittelbar von seinen Bildern abzulesen sind. Man könnte ihn beinahe zu den Surrealisten zählen, denn auch er liebt es, die unvorhergesehensten Dinge nebeneinanderzustellen. Er wohnt mit seiner Frau Dorothea, die ebenfalls Malerin ist, in Chiemsee.

Père hongrois, mère française. Commence à peindre vers 1945. Son art est net, poétique, plein d'inventions plastiques. Il aime aussi à raconter des histoires qui ne sont pas toujours d'une lecture directe sur ses tableaux. Il s'apparenterait presque aux Surréalistes, avec leurs rencontres tout ce qu'il y a d'imprévues d'objets. Il habite Chiemsee avec sa femme Dorothea, qui est peintre, également.

EXPOSITIONS:
«Peintres Naïfs», Galerie Wolfsberg, Zürich 1952.
Museum am Ostwall, Dortmund 1952.
«Die Welt der naiven Malerei», Salzburg 1964.

BIBLIOGRAPHIE:
Oto Bihalji-Merin: «Das naive Bild der Welt», Köln 1959.
Oto Bihalji-Merin: «Die naive Malerei», Köln 1959.
Oto Bihalji-Merin: «Les Peintres Naïfs», Paris (sans date).

Stephane, Mucius

Born 1912 in Bainet, on the south coast of Haiti.

Geboren 1912 in Bainet, Südküste von Haiti.

Né en 1912 à Bainet, Côte sud de Haïti.

A shoemaker. Like most of the other 'naive' artists in Haiti, especially of his generation, he discovered painting through the activity of the Art Centre in Port-au-Prince. He is the most delicate, the most 'intimate' of the Haitian artists. Sometimes his works show a touch of symbolism.

Schuster. Wie beinahe allen anderen, insbesondere seinen Altersgenossen, ist ihm die Malerei durch die Tätigkeit des Kunstzentrums von Port-au-Prince offenbart worden. Der feinste, intimistischste der haitischen Maler. Er grenzt zuweilen an einen gewissen Symbolismus.

Cordonnier. Comme presque tous les autres, surtout de son âge, il a eu la révélation de la peinture par l'activité du Centre d'Art de Port-au-Prince. Le plus tendre, le plus intimiste parmi les peintres haïtiens. Il frise parfois un certain symbolisme.

EXPOSITIONS:
«Das naive Bild der Welt», Baden-Baden 1961.
«19 Peintres d'Haïti», Palais des Beaux-Arts, Bruxelles 1963.
«20th Century Latin American Naive Art», La Jolla, Calif. (USA) 1964.

Stern, Emma

Born March 13, 1878 in Saint Wendel (Saar).

Geboren am 13. März 1878 in Sankt Wendel (Saar).

Née le 13 mars 1878 à Saint-Wendel (Sarre).

Having arrived at the highest point of her life, this well-to-do woman would have no longer tried to achieve anything—if she had not kept her youthful heart. Actually, it is rare for a 'naive' artist to keep safe that first freshness which borders on the drawings of children—this comparison is by no means derogatory. One can realize this even better because we are able to meet the artist and her work in the film 'Emma's Life', prepared by Liliane de Kermadec for the publisher Delpire.

Diese wohlhabende Frau hätte sich in der Neige ihres Lebens sehr wohl dem Nichtstun hingeben können. Doch sie hat sich das Herz einer Fünfzehnjährigen bewahrt. Dünn gesät sind in der Tat die naiven Künstler, denen es gelungen ist, diese ursprüngliche Frische beizubehalten, die zuweilen an Kinderzeichnungen gemahnt, wobei dieser Vergleich nichts Abschätziges hat. Man sieht das hier um so besser, als es uns ausnahmsweise leicht gemacht wird, die Künstlerin und ihr Werk einander gegenüberzustellen, und zwar dank dem Film «Le Temps d'Emma», den Liliane de Kermadec für den Verleger Delpire gedreht hat.

Arrivée presqu'au faîte de sa vie, cette dame aisée aurait pu ne plus rien faire, si elle n'avait pas gardé son cœur de 15 ans. En effet, rares sont les artistes naïfs qui ont réussi à sauvegarder cette fraîcheur première qui voisine parfois avec les dessins d'enfants, ce qui, du reste, n'a rien de péjoratif en tant que comparaison. On s'en rend d'autant mieux compte, que, pour une fois, il nous est facile de confronter l'artiste et son œuvre grâce au film, «Le Temps d'Emma», réalisé par Liliane de Kermadec pour l'éditeur Delpire.

EXPOSITIONS:
Galerie Bruno-Bassano, Paris 1954 (Cat., Préface Loys Masson).
«Les Peintres Naïfs», Maison de la Pensée Française, Paris 1960.
«Les Primitifs d'Aujourd'hui», Galerie Charpentier, Paris 1964.
Galerie Delpire, Paris 1965.

BIBLIOGRAPHIE:
Anatole Jakovsky: «Les Peintres Naïfs», Paris 1956.
Anatole Jakovsky: «Naive Malerei», Zürich 1957.

Stolnik, Slavko

Born June 11, 1929 in Voca Donja, near Vorazdin (Yugoslavia).

Geboren 11. Juni 1929 in Voca Donja bei Vorazdin (Jugoslawien).

Né le 11 juin 1929 à Voca Donja, près de Vorazdin (Yougoslavie).

A Croatian, born of a peasant family. Even at school his gift for drawing and fashioning shapes was noticeable. He carves on juniper bark. In 1948 he worked on the construction of the Belgrade-Zagreb motorway, and then he entered the people's militia. Began to paint seriously after meeting Krsto Hegedušič. He painted on glass, somewhat in the manner of the other artists of the Hlebine school. In 1961 he immigrated to Paris, where he still lives. But that was the end of his creative work; now he only paints pictures of small importance, imitating his own work, almost as if he had outlived himself.

Kroate. Bauernsohn. Schon in der Schule äußert sich seine Begabung für das Zeichnen und Modellieren. Er schnitzt insbesondere in Wacholderrinde. 1948 arbeitet er am Bau der Autobahn Belgrad-Zagreb mit, dann tritt er in die Volksmiliz ein. Nach einer Begegnung mit Krsto Hegedušič beginnt er mit Ausdauer zu malen. Er malt auf Glas, ein wenig in der Art der anderen Maler der Schule von Hlebine. 1961 fährt er nach Paris, wo er jetzt lebt. Aber von seinem Milieu abgeschnitten, bringt er nur noch unbedeutende Werke hervor, kopiert sich selber und ist nur noch ein Abklatsch seines früheren Selbst.

Croate. Fils de paysans. A l'école déjà il manifeste ses dons pour le dessin et la taille. Il sculpte notamment dans l'écorce de genévrier. En 1948, travaille à l'autostrade Belgrade-Zagreb, puis entre dans les milices populaires. Commence à peindre d'une façon assidue à la suite de la rencontre avec Krsto Hegedušič. Il peint sur verre, un peu dans la manière de tous les autres peintres de l'Ecole de Hlebine. En 1961, il part pour Paris où il réside maintenant. Mais c'est la fin. Coupé de son milieu, il ne produit plus que des œuvres mineures, se copiant et se survivant à lui-même.

EXPOSITIONS:
«Naivni umetnici Jugoslavije», Belgrade 1957.
Galerie Suzanne de Coninck, Paris 1961 (Cat., Préface Anatole Jakovsky).
«Première Quadriennale des Peintres Naïfs Yougoslaves», Čačac 1962.

BIBLIOGRAPHIE:
«Yougoslavija», numéro spécial (17) consacré à l'art des naïfs.
Oto Bihalji-Merin: «Das naive Bild der Welt», Köln 1959.
Oto Bihalji-Merin: «Die naive Malerei», Köln 1959.
Oto Bihalji-Merin: «Les Peintres Naïfs», Paris (sans date).
Oto Bihalji-Merin: «Umetnost Naivnich u Jugoslavjii», Belgrade 1963.

Sullivan, Patrick J.

Born March 17, 1894 in Braddock, Penn. (USA).

Geboren am 17. März 1894 in Braddock, Penn. (USA).

Né le 17 mars 1894 à Braddock, Penn. (USA).

In 1916 he joined the army and became an officer. Three years later he married and settled down in West Virginia, therefore giving up army life. The war in Ethiopia gave him a guilty conscience, and he tried to express this conflict with a brush. It was about 1937 when people started to talk about his work, mainly because of the aspect of his painting which could be termed expressionistic (which sometimes even borders on caricature) and also because of his experiments in the fourth dimension. There is also always an underlying symbolism to be detected in his work.

1916 geht er zur Armee und wird Offizier. Drei Jahre später heiratet er, läßt sich in Westvirginien nieder und nimmt seinen Abschied von der Armee. Der Abessinienkrieg löst eine Gewissenskrise in ihm aus, die er mit seinem Pinsel auszudrücken versucht. Man beginnt um 1937 herum von ihm zu reden, vor allem wegen einer gewissen sozusagen expressionistischen Seite seiner Malerei (die zuweilen an Karikatur grenzt), sowie wegen seines Bemühens um die vierte Dimension. In seinen Bildern schimmert auch eine stets gegenwärtige Symbolik durch.

En 1916, il s'engage dans l'armée et devient officier. Trois ans après, il se marie, s'installe dans la Virginie Occidentale et donne sa démission de l'armée. La guerre de l'Ethiopie provoque en lui une crise de conscience qu'il essaye de traduire avec ses pinceaux. On commence à parler de lui aux environs de 1937. Surtout à cause d'un certain côté, disons expressionniste de sa peinture (qui frise parfois la caricature), ainsi que de sa recherche de la quatrième dimension. Un symbolisme sous-jacent, en filigrane, n'est pas absent, non plus, dans ses œuvres.

EXPOSITIONS:
«Masters of Popular Painting», New York 1938.
«La Peinture Naïve», Knokke-le-Zoute 1958.

BIBLIOGRAPHIE:
Sidney Janis: «They taught themselves», Dial Press, New York 1942.
Oto Bihalji-Merin: «Das naive Bild der Welt», Köln 1959.
Oto Bihalji-Merin: «Die naive Malerei», Köln 1959.
Oto Bihalji-Merin: «Les Peintres Naïfs», Paris (sans date).

Tamara, (Tamara Voltz)

Born March 23, 1898 in Berlin (Germany).

Geboren am 23. März 1898 in Berlin (Deutschland).

Née le 23 mars 1898 à Berlin (Allemagne).

Polish father, German mother. Was attracted to the arts from a very early age and finally became a film actress. Her most famous role was in Pabst's 'The joyless street' with Greta Garbo. She ended her career with the end of silent films, and retired in 1935 to a small town in the Tessin, where she married a Swiss painter. There, she too began to paint, first of all on glass and then on canvas. "In my painting I want to express all that was fine and beautiful in my life", she once said, and this describes her art much better than any commentators or critics can do.

Vater Pole, Mutter Deutsche. Hat schon sehr früh künstlerische Neigungen und wird schließlich Filmschauspielerin. Sie hat insbesondere neben Greta Garbo in « Die freudlose Gasse » von Pabst gespielt. Mit dem Aufkommen des Tonfilms nimmt ihre Filmkarriere ein Ende. 1935 zieht sie sich in ein kleines Dorf im Tessin zurück, wo sie sich mit einem Schweizer Künstler verheiratet. Hier beginnt sie zu malen. Zuerst auf Glas, dann auf Leinwand. « Alles, was in meinem Leben gut und schön war, möchte ich mit meiner Malerei ausdrücken. » Dieser Satz von ihr faßt besser als alle Kommentare und Kritiken den Sinn ihrer Malerei zusammen.

Père polonais, mère allemande. Est attirée de fort bonne heure par les arts et finit par devenir une actrice de cinéma. A joué notamment dans « La rue sans joie » de Pabst, aux côtés de Greta Garbo. Sa carrière cinématographique se termine avec le muet. Elle se retire, alors, dès 1935 dans un petit pays dans le Tessin, où elle se marie avec un artiste suisse. Là, elle commence à peindre. D'abord sur verre, puis sur de la toile. «Tout ce qui était bien et beau dans ma vie, je voudrais le dire avec ma peinture», cette phrase d'elle résume bien mieux que ne sauraient le faire les commentaires et les critiques le sens de sa peinture.

EXPOSITIONS:
Galerie Kirchgasse, Zürich 1963.
Galerie M. Bénézit, Paris 1965
(Cat., Préface Anatole Jakovsky).

BIBLIOGRAPHIE:
«Tamara Voltz», Ferien-Journal, Nr. 84/6, Ascona 21 août 1964.
«Tamara Voltz», Die Südschweiz, 15 août 1964.

Taylor, Douglas Edward

Born 1926 in Battersea, London (England).

Geboren 1926 in Battersea, London (England).

Né en 1926 à Battersea-London (Angleterre).

Married and has two children. Is an engraver by trade, specializing in religious statues, and his art reflects this in its conscious, almost carved design. Further, his liking for superimposition or juxtaposition of various graphic subjects evokes a sense of bewilderment very similar to a kind of surrealist atmosphere. But his surrealism—which lies in his form—is very different from the basic surrealism of his namesake, Jack Taylor.

Verheiratet, Vater zweier Kinder. Von Beruf ist er auf religiöse Bilder spezialisierter Graveur. In seiner Kunst drückt sich das in der deutlich sichtbaren, beinahe gestochenen Zeichnung aus. Das Übereinander oder das Nebeneinander mehrerer graphischer Themen ruft zuweilen ein Gefühl der Fremdheit hervor, das einer gewissen mehr oder weniger surrealistischen Atmosphäre sehr nahe steht. Aber sein formaler Surrealismus unterscheidet sich deutlich vom inhaltlichen Surrealismus seines Namensbruders Jack Taylor.

Marié, père de deux enfants. Graveur de son vrai métier (spécialisé dans les images religieuses), son art s'en ressent par son dessin apparent, presque gravé. Aussi la superposition, sinon le voisinage de plusieurs thèmes graphiques provoque parfois une sensation de dépaysement très proche d'une certaine atmosphère plus ou moins surréaliste. Mais son surréalisme – formel – diffère toutefois du surréalisme – de fond – de son homonyme, Jack Taylor.

EXPOSITIONS:
Portal Gallery, Londres 1964
(Cat., Préface non signé).

Taylor, Jack

Born 1931 in the East End of London (England).

Geboren 1931 in East End, London (England).

Né en 1931 à East End, London (Angleterre).

This artist and sculptor is the youngest in British 'naive' painting. But is he completely 'naive'; or is that not true any more? What is certain is that, after leading a rather varied life, he took up painting without having had any formal training, and that it gave his life a meaning. Nevertheless, his work can be distinguished from all his colleagues by a certain surrealistic note which occasionally intrudes, unexpected and with a droll effect.

Dieser Maler und Bildhauer ist der Benjamin der englischen naiven Malerei. Aber wer weiß! Ist er es wirklich? Ist er es nicht mehr? Sicher ist, daß er nach einem ziemlich bewegten Leben zur Malerei gekommen ist, ohne etwas gelernt zu haben, und daß seine Kunst für ihn ein wahrer Lebenszweck geworden ist. Sie unterscheidet sich von der all seiner Kollegen durch einen gewissen Surrealismus, der sich auf drollige Weise unvermutet bemerkbar macht.

Ce peintre et sculpteur est le benjamin de la peinture naïve anglaise. Et encore! L'est-il tout à fait? Ne l'est-il plus? Ce qui est certain, c'est que, après une vie passablement mouvementée, il y est venu sans avoir rien appris et que c'est devenu pour lui une vraie raison de vivre. Mais son art se distingue quand-même de tous les autres de ses confrères par un certain surréalisme qui y fait son intrusion cocasse et inopinée.

EXPOSITIONS:
« Les Peintres Naïfs », Galerie J.Verrière, Cannes 1966.

BIBLIOGRAPHIE:
Barrie Sturt-Penrose: « Primitives in Private », Observer 13 février 1966.

Di Terlizzi, Francesco

Born in Apulia (Italy).

Geboren in Apulien (Italien).

Né dans les Pouilles (Italie).

Where? When? No one knows. He was discovered by the writer and journalist Carlo Belli, from his work shown in a municipal exhibition in Trento during the year 1928. Two years later in Milan he displayed an astonishing series of rustic pictures which, at least to a certain extent, clash with the profession of their creator—he was a 'carabiniere'. In fact, this is the only case of a soldier turning to 'naive' painting. After this exhibition no further trace can be found of him.

Wo? Wann? Man weiß es nicht. Er wird 1928 anläßlich einer städtischen Ausstellung in Trento von Carlo Belli entdeckt. 2 Jahre später stellt er in Mailand eine ziemlich überraschende Reihe bukolischer Bilder aus, die nicht recht zum eigentlichen Beruf ihres Urhebers zu passen scheinen: er ist nämlich Carabiniere. Es handelt sich hier übrigens um den einzigen Fall, wo ein Soldat naive Bilder malt. Seither ist seine Spur wieder verloren gegangen.

Où? Quand? On n'en sait rien. Découvert par l'écrivain et journaliste Carlo Belli, dans une exposition municipale à Trento, en 1928, il expose deux ans après à Milan une assez surprenante série de tableaux bucoliques qui jurent un tant soit peu avec le véritable métier de leur auteur, qui est carabinier de son état. C'est, du reste, le seul cas d'un militaire faisant de la peinture naïve. Depuis, sa trace se perd définitivement.

EXPOSITIONS:
Galleria del Milione, Milan 1930
(Cat., Préface Carlo Belli et Tullio Garbari).
«I Pittori Naifs», Rome 1964.

Thegen, Carl-Christian

Born 1883 in Oldesloe near Lübeck (Germany).
Died 1955 in Oldesloe (Germany).

Geboren 1883 in Oldesloe bei Lübeck (Deutschland).
Gestorben 1955 in Oldesloe bei Lübeck (Deutschland).

Né en 1883 à Oldesloe, près Lübeck (Allemagne).
Mort en 1955 à Oldesloe (Allemagne).

Began by working in an abattoir, killing animals. However, perhaps nauseated by the cruelty, he underwent a complete change and worked for circuses (first the Vieux Belli circus, then the Hagenbeck one) sometimes appearing as a clown and sometimes looking after the animals. In fact, he ended up by buying his own string of horses. Called up during the first world war, he took care of the horses both on the Russian and on the French front. After the war he led a nomadic life for some years, taking on a number of jobs to earn his keep. Finally, in 1933, he took up painting and drew inspiration from his memories. A self-taught artist not without merit.

Ist zuerst Schlächter im Schlachthaus. Aber von der Grausamkeit vielleicht angeekelt, ändert er sein Leben von Grund auf und betätigt sich bald als Clown, bald als Tierwärter, zuerst im Zirkus Vieux Belli, dann bei Hagenbeck. Zum Schluß kauft er sich eine eigene Reitschule. Während des Ersten Weltkriegs betreut er Pferde an der russischen und an der französischen Front. Nach dem Krieg führt er eine Zeitlang ein unstetes Leben und übt verschiedene Berufe aus, um sein Brot zu verdienen. 1933 endlich fängt er an zu malen, wobei er hauptsächlich aus seinen Erinnerungen schöpft. Autodidakt, dem es nicht an Qualitäten fehlt.

Commence par être tueur aux abattoirs. Mais écœuré, qui sait, par ces cruautés, il change radicalement et devient tantôt clown, tantôt soigneur de bêtes; d'abord dans le cirque du Vieux Belli, puis chez Hagenbeck. Il finit, du reste, par acheter son propre manège. Mobilisé pendant la première guerre mondiale, il soigne, précisément, les chevaux aussi bien sur le front russe que français. La guerre terminée, il connaît une époque de vagabondage où il exerce plusieurs métiers pour vivre. L'année 1933 marque enfin ses débuts dans la peinture qu'il puise surtout dans ses souvenirs. Peintre autodidacte non sans qualités.

EXPOSITIONS:
«Maler des einfältigen Herzens»,
Museum am Ostwall, Dortmund 1952.
«Laienmaler», Gewerbemuseum, Basel 1961.

BIBLIOGRAPHIE:
Bernard Jasmand et Otto Kallir: «Sonntagsmaler», Ed. Otto Aug. Ehlers, Berlin/Darmstadt 1956.
Oto Bihalji-Merin: «Das naive Bild der Welt», Köln 1959.
Oto Bihalji-Merin: «Die naive Malerei», Köln 1959.
Oto Bihalji-Merin: «Les Peintres Naïfs», Paris (sans date).

Theophilos (Theophilos Hadsimichael)

Born 1866 in Lesbos (Greece).
Died 1934 in Lesbos (Greece).

Geboren 1866 auf Lesbos (Griechenland).
Gestorben 1934 auf Lesbos (Griechenland).

Né en 1866 à Lesbos (Grèce).
Mort en 1934 à Lesbos (Grèce).

The grandson of an icon maker, shepherd, coachman at the Greek consulate in Smyrna, he is first and foremost a nomad—an artist who, in return for a meal or a little money, will paint inn signs, housefronts or the portraits of Greek business men. He took an active part in the national rebellion against the Turks, in 1897. Little is known of his life; but his work—rich, varied, comprising many pictures—makes him a kind of Greek 'douanier Rousseau'. In just the same way as the immortal Zorba, he tells stories in his own way and at the same time tells of his own character. A typical example of the transformation of popular art to individual and mature art.

Enkel eines Ikonenmalers, Hirte, Kutscher beim griechischen Konsulat in Smyrna. Vor allem führt er ein unstetes Leben. Ein Maler, der um eine Mahlzeit oder ein wenig Geld Aushängeschilder malt, Fassaden anstreicht oder die Porträts der griechischen Händler pinselt. 1897 nimmt er als Soldat an der nationalen Erhebung gegen die Türken teil. Man weiß wenig über sein Leben. Aber sein reiches, vielfältiges, umfangreiches Werk macht eine Art griechischen Zöllner Rousseau aus ihm. Genau wie der unsterbliche Zorba erzählt er Geschichten auf seine Art und erzählt dabei von sich selber. Ein typisches Beispiel für die Umwandlung der Volkskunst in eine mündige, selbständige Individualkunst.

Petit fils d'un faiseur d'icônes, pâtre, cocher au consulat grec de Smyrne, il est avant tout un errant; un peintre qui pour un repas ou pour un peu d'argent brossait des enseignes, fixait les devantures ou les portraits des commerçants grecs. Guerrier, il prend part à l'insurrection nationale contre les Turcs. En 1897. On sait peu de chose sur sa vie. Mais son œuvre, riche, variée, nombreuse, fait de lui une sorte de Douanier Rousseau grec. Tout comme l'immortel Zorba, il raconte des histoires à sa façon et se raconte en même temps. C'est encore un exemple typique de la transformation de l'art populaire en un art individuel, majeur et à part entière.

EXPOSITIONS:
Kunsthalle, Bern 1960
(Cat., Préface E.Tériade, G. Seferis, etc.).
Musée des Arts Décoratifs, Paris 1961
(Cat., Préface F. Mathey, Le Corbusier, etc.).
«De Lusthof der Naieven», Rotterdam 1964.
«Le Monde des Naïfs», Paris 1964.

BIBLIOGRAPHIE:
M. Raynal: «Theophilos», Arts et Métiers Graphiques, Nº 52, Paris 1936.
Le Corbusier: «Theophilos», Le Voyage en Grèce, Nº 4, Paris 1936.

Trillhaase, Adalbert

Born 1859 in Erfurt (Germany).
Died 1936 in Königswinter (Germany).

Geboren 1859 in Erfurt (Deutschland)
Gestorben 1936 in Königswinter (Deutschland).

Né en 1859 à Erfurt (Allemagne).
Mort en 1936 à Königswinter (Allemagne).

Born of middle-class parents, who intended him to become a tradesman. But it didn't work. He was an inveterate dreamer and passionate reader, and in 1918 he began to paint. Already, six years later, he exhibited his work, in Düsseldorf. In the 'purification' of 1933, his pictures were held to belong to degenerate art and he was forbidden to paint. But the artist in him defied this ruling, and he continued to paint in secret. His daughter took all his works to Switzerland, thus rescuing them from destruction. His inspiration was often the Bible, but nevertheless his vision was fundamentally a personal one; fantasy-filled in vision and medieval in form, his work recalls to some extent the German craftsmen of the late Middle Ages. Quite definitely the best German 'naive' artist.

Gutbürgerliche Eltern, die einen Kaufmann aus ihm machen wollen. Sie vermögen nichts auszurichten. Er ist ein unverbesserlicher Träumer und leidenschaftlicher Leser. Gegen 1918 fängt er an zu malen. Sechs Jahre später stellt er bereits in Düsseldorf aus. Nach der Machtübernahme durch die Nazi werden seine Bilder der entarteten Kunst zugezählt und man verbot ihm das Malen. Der Künstler kümmerte sich nicht darum und arbeitete im Verborgenen. Seine Tochter verbrachte sein gesamtes Werk in die Schweiz und rettete es so vor der Zerstörung. Seine Themen sind der Bibel entnommen. Aber es handelt sich um eine ganz persönliche Schau, visionär in der Optik und mittelalterlich in der Form, was ihn in einem gewissen Maß in die Nähe der deutschen Maler des Spätmittelalters rückt. Unbestreitbar der beste naive Maler Deutschlands.

Parents bourgeois, qui le destinaient au commerce. Rien à faire. Rêveur invétéré et lecteur acharné, il commence à peindre vers 1918. Six ans plus tard, il expose déjà à Düsseldorf. Lors de l'épuration de 1933, ses tableaux furent considérés comme relevant de l'art dégénéré, et il lui fut même interdit de peindre. L'artiste passa outre, travaillant clandestinement. Sa fille transporta toute son œuvre en Suisse, la sauvant ainsi de la destruction. Ses sujets sont inspirés par la Bible. Mais c'est d'une vision essentiellement personnelle qu'il s'agit; hallucinée quant à l'optique et mediévale quant à la forme, ce qui l'apparente, dans une certaine mesure, aux imagiers allemands de la fin du Moyen Age. Le meilleur peintre naïf allemand, incontestablement.

EXPOSITIONS:
Galerie G. Maratier, Paris 1939.
« Moderne primitive Maler », Kunsthalle, Bern 1949 (Cat., Préface Arnold Rüdlinger).
« Maler des einfältigen Herzens », Museum am Ostwall, Dortmund 1952.
« Schönheit », Recklinghausen 1958 (Cat. important, Préface Stephan Hirzel).
« Das naive Bild der Welt », Baden-Baden 1961.
« Die Welt der naiven Malerei », Salzburg 1964.
« De Lusthof der Naieven », Rotterdam 1964.
« Le Monde des Naïfs », Paris 1964.

BIBLIOGRAPHIE:
O. Pankok: «Trillhaase», Ed. Vater und Sohn, München (sans date).
« Adalbert Trillhaase », Du No. 2, Zürich 1952.
Bernard Jasmand und Otto Kallir: « Sonntagsmaler », Otto Aug. Ehlers, Berlin/Dortmund 1956.
Oto Bihalji-Merin: « Das naive Bild der Welt », Köln 1959.
Oto Bihalji-Merin: « Die naive Malerei », Köln 1959.
Oto Bihalji-Merin: « Les Peintres Naïfs », Paris (sans date).

Trouillard, Henri

Born June 20, 1892 in Laval, Mayenne (France).

Geboren am 20. Juni 1892 in Laval, Mayenne (Frankreich).

Né le 20 juin 1892 à Laval, Mayenne (France).

Calls himself illegitimate. Led a varied and irregular life, making many totally unexpected journeys—to prison, for instance. He was imprisoned three times. Is a megalomaniac and unable to distinguish between reality and illusion; this comes out very clearly in his autobiography. From being a respectable tradesman, with a house of his own, he became simply a second-hand dealer. His art is erratic but always surprising. No individual exhibitions so far.

Behauptet, ein uneheliches Kind zu sein. Bewegtes, an allerlei unvorhergesehenen Wechselfällen reiches Leben; so saß er zum Beispiel dreimal im Gefängnis. Größenwahnsinnig, kann nicht recht zwischen der Wirklichkeit und seinen Träumen unterscheiden. Zumindest geht das ziemlich klar aus der Lektüre seines autobiographischen Buchs hervor. Aus einem angesehenen Kaufmann mit einem eigenen Haus wird ein richtiger Trödler. Ungleichmäßige, doch immer überraschende Malerei. Keine Einzelausstellungen.

Se dit fils naturel. Vie agitée, pleine de péripéties les plus imprévues, comme la prison, par exemple, où il séjourne trois fois. Mégalomane, ne discernant pas très bien la réalité de ses rêves. Du moins ce qui ressort assez clairement de la lecture de son livre autobiographique. De commerçant, ayant pignon sur rue, il est devenu tout simplement brocanteur. Peinture inégale, mais surprenante toujours. Pas d'expositions individuelles.

EXPOSITIONS:
«Les Peintres Naïfs», Maison de la Pensée Française, Paris 1960.
«Laien-Maler», Gewerbemuseum, Basel 1961.
«Les Primitifs d'Aujourd'hui», Galerie Charpentier, Paris 1964.

BIBLIOGRAPHIE:
Henri Trouillard: «Ma Vie», avec l'Introduction par Anatole Jakovsky. Editions Temps Mêlés, Verviers 1960.
Anatole Jakovsky: «Eros du Dimanche», Paris 1964.

Urteaga, Mario

Born 1875 in Cajamarca (Peru).

Geboren 1875 in Cajamarca (Peru).

Né en 1875 à Cajamarca (Pérou).

He first exhibited his work in 1934; and since that time he has been overwhelmed with all kinds of prizes and distinctions. Won first prize in the international competition in Vino del Mar (Chile); also awarded first prize by the Institute of Contemporary Art in Lima. Pictures of his can even be found in the New York Museum of Modern Art. This seems to be proof of a certain isolationist or chauvinistic tendency in the United States. It appears to me that Americans prefer mediocre paintings by artists from the New World rather than better paintings from Europe. This would account for the unprecedented success of Haitian artists and also for the lack of interest shown for the last twenty years or so in European 'naive' art.

Stellt 1934 zum erstenmal aus und seither prasseln die Auszeichnungen nur so auf ihn nieder. Erster Preis im Internationalen Wettbewerb von Vino del Mar (Chile); auch vom Institut für Zeitgenössische Kunst in Lima preisgekrönt. Seine Bilder finden sich sogar im Museum of Modern Art in New York. Das entspricht übrigens einer gewissen «isolationistischen», um nicht zu sagen chauvinistischen Tendenz der verantwortlichen Kulturträger der Vereinigten Staaten, die Werke von Künstlern des amerikanischen Kontinents, selbst wenn sie mittelmäßig sind, denjenigen aus Europa vorziehen. Daher der unvergleichliche Erfolg der haitischen Künstler und die beinahe 20 Jahre währende sozusagen vollständige Gleichgültigkeit gegenüber allen europäischen Naiven.

Expose pour la première fois en 1934, et depuis, c'est une avalanche de distinctions de toutes sortes. Premier Prix au concours international à Vino del Mar (Chili); couronné, également, par l'Institut pour l'Art Contemporain de Lima. Ses toiles se trouvent même dans le Musée d'Art Moderne de New York. Cela correspond d'ailleurs à une certaine tendance «isolationniste», sinon chauviniste des responsables culturels des USA qui leur fait préférer les œuvres médiocres des artistes du nouveau continent au détriment de ceux du continent européen. D'où le succès commercial sans précédent des artistes haïtiens et la désaffection quasi totale, pendant presque 20 ans, en ce qui concerne tous les naïfs européens.

EXPOSITIONS:
«Peintres de l'Equateur, de Haïti et de Pérou», l'UNESCO Paris 1947.
«La Peinture Naïve», Knokke-le-Zoute 1958.
«Das naive Bild der Welt», Baden-Baden 1961.

BIBLIOGRAPHIE:
Oto Bihalji-Merin: «Das naive Bild der Welt», Köln 1959.
Oto Bihalji-Merin: «Die naive Malerei», Köln 1959.
Oto Bihalji-Merin: «Les Peintres Naïfs», Paris (sans date).
«Art Naïf», Editions Marocaines et Internationales, Rabat 1964.

Valdes, Gregorio

Born 1879 in Key West, Florida (USA).
Died 1939 in Key West, Florida (USA).

Geboren 1879 in Key West, Florida (USA).
Gestorben 1939 in Key West, Florida (USA).

Né en 1879 à Key West, Florida (USA).
Mort en 1939 à Key West, Florida (USA).

A Cuban-American, who was discovered late in life by Sidney Janis. He was a sign painter—or, to be precise, a designer of letters. But he also painted pictures, mostly copying postcards. In fact, his 'discoverer' published, in his book on 'naive' artists, a view of the Boulevard Edgar Quinet in Paris (Collection Orson Welles) as well as the picture postcard which he had used as a model. And immediately we realize that all things are possible to someone capable of transforming and transmuting reality.
Did not Utrillo do just the same?

Gegen Ende seines Lebens von Sidney Janis entdeckter Kuba-Amerikaner. Er war Schildermaler oder, genauer gesagt, Schriftenmaler. Aber er malte auch Bilder, meistens nach Ansichtskarten. Janis reproduziert in seinem Buch eine Ansicht des Boulevard Edgar Quinet in Paris (Sammlung Orson Welles) und die Postkarte, die ihm als Vorbild diente. Und man wird sich augenblicklich bewußt, daß den Menschen, die das Wirkliche zu verwandeln, zu überwinden vermögen und verstehen, alles möglich ist.
Hat Utrillo denn etwas anderes getan?

Américano-cubain, découvert sur le tard par Sidney Janis. Il était peintre d'enseignes, ou, plutôt, dessinateur de lettres, pour être précis. Mais il faisait aussi de la peinture, le plus souvent d'après les cartes postales. Son découvreur reproduit justement, dans son livre, une vue du boulevard Edgar Quinet à Paris (Collection Orson Welles) et la carte postale qui a servi de modèle. Et l'on se rend compte aussitôt que tout est possible pour ceux qui peuvent et savent transformer, transgresser le réel. Utrillo a-t-il donc fait autre chose?

BIBLIOGRAPHIE:
Elisabeth Bishop: « Gregorio Valdes »,
Partisan Review, New York 1939.
Sidney Janis: «They taught themselves»,
Dial Press, New York 1942.

Vandersteen, Germain

Born July 7, 1897 in Versailles, Seine et Oise (France).

Geboren am 7. Juli 1897 in Versailles, Seine et Oise (Frankreich).

Né le 7 juillet 1897 à Versailles, Seine et Oise (France).

For some time now has signed his work 'Van-der-Steen'. Was on active service in the 1914–18 war, and was gassed. His health is delicate and he suffers from insomnia, and this has no doubt influenced his development as an artist—he paints mostly at night. After a short, so-called naturalistic period, he revealed himself as a visionary artist, not only from a personal point of view but with a very broad scope. In his work one can distinguish three periods: 1) pictures inspired by music; 2) flowers of fantasy; 3) cats. He is one of the finest modern artists. However, despite his success in France and abroad, he has not given up his chemists' shop in Paris.

Signiert seit einiger Zeit Van-der-Steen. Nimmt am Vierzehnerkrieg teil, gerät in einen Gasangriff. Er hat eine zarte Gesundheit, leidet an Schlaflosigkeit, was zweifellos nicht ohne Einfluß auf seine Malerlaufbahn geblieben ist, denn er arbeitet meistens nachts. Nach einer kurzen, sozusagen naturalistischen Periode entpuppt er sich schnell als Visionär, der nicht nur über eine sehr persönliche Schau, sondern auch über Größe verfügt. Sein Werk, in dem man drei Perioden unterscheiden kann (1. von der Musik inspirierte Gemälde, 2. imaginäre Blumen und 3. Katzen), gehört zu den schönsten unserer Zeit. Trotz seines Erfolgs sowohl in Frankreich als auch im Ausland fährt er indessen fort, seine Drogerie in Paris zu betreuen.

Signe depuis quelque temps: Van-der-Steen. Fait la guerre de 1914–18. Gazé. De santé fragile, il souffre d'insomnies, ce qui n'a pas été, sans doute, sans influencer sa carrière de peintre, car il peint, généralement la nuit. Après une courte période pour ainsi dire naturaliste, il se révèle aussitôt comme un peintre visionnaire non seulement personnel, mais de très grande envergure. Sa production, dont on distingue trois périodes, 1. tableaux inspirés par la musique, 2. fleurs imaginaires et 3. chats, est une des plus belles de notre temps. Toutefois, malgré son succès, aussi bien en France qu'à l'étranger, il continue à s'occuper de sa boutique de produits d'entretien, à Paris.

EXPOSITIONS:
Galerie Clausen, Paris 1946 (Cat., Préface F. Delanglade).
Galerie Louise, Paris 1950 (Cat., Préface Anatole Jakovsky).
Galerie Hutter, Basel 1950.
Galerie M. de Groote, Paris 1951 (Cat., Préface P. Mornand).
Galerie de la Radio, Paris 1957 (Cat., Préface Gisèle d'Assailly).
Galerie Maurice Raton, Paris 1958.
«Les Peintres Naïfs», Maison de la Pensée Française, Paris 1960.
«Laienmaler», Gewerbemuseum, Basel 1961.
Galerie Toni Brechbühl, Grenchen 1963
Galerie Lutz und Meyer, Stuttgart 1963 (Cat., Préface Anatole Jakovsky).
Galerie d'Art Primitif, Zagreb 1964 (Cat., Préface Anatole Jakovsky).
«I Pittori Naifs», Rome 1964.
«Les Primitifs d'Aujourd'hui», Galerie Charpentier, Paris 1964.
Galerie Michel Columb, Nantes 1965 (Cat., Préface Anatole Jakovsky).
Galerie Hilt, Basel 1965 (Cat. avec un texte de Vandersteen).

BIBLIOGRAPHIE:
A. Jakovsky: «La Peinture Naïve», Paris 1949.
Anatole Jakovsky: «Vandersteen», Editions Caractères, Paris 1955.
A. Jakovsky: «Les Peintres Naïfs», Paris 1956.
Anatole Jakovsky: «Naive Malerei», Zürich 1957.
Paul Guth: «Un naïf chez les peintres naïfs», Vogue, Paris 1956.
A. Hernandez: «Naive Maler», Atlantis N° II, Zürich 1961.
Anatole Jakovsky: «Le Douanier et les Contrebandiers», Jardin des Arts, N° 79, Paris 1961.
«Art Naïf», Les Editions Marocaines et Internationales, Rabat 1964.
A. Jakovsky: «Eros du Dimanche», Paris 1964.
Richard Katz et Anatole Jakovsky: «Van der Steens unheimliche Katzen», Basilius Presse, Basel 1965.

Večenaj, Ivan

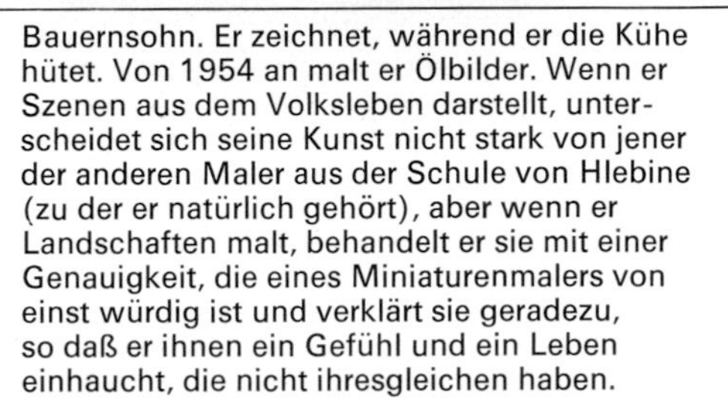

Born May 5, 1920 in Gola (Yugoslavia).

Geboren 5. Mai 1920 in Gola (Jugoslawien).

Né le 5 mai 1920 à Gola (Yougoslavie).

Comes of a peasant family. He used to draw while looking after the cows, and in 1954 he took up oil painting. When he depicts scenes of ordinary life, his style is almost indistinguishable from that of many other members of the Hlebine school (to which, of course, he belongs), but when he attempts landscapes, which he executes with the extreme attention to detail normally given to miniatures or to medieval illuminated letters, he entirely transcends their work. His landscapes have an atmosphere and a life all their own.

Bauernsohn. Er zeichnet, während er die Kühe hütet. Von 1954 an malt er Ölbilder. Wenn er Szenen aus dem Volksleben darstellt, unterscheidet sich seine Kunst nicht stark von jener der anderen Maler aus der Schule von Hlebine (zu der er natürlich gehört), aber wenn er Landschaften malt, behandelt er sie mit einer Genauigkeit, die eines Miniaturenmalers von einst würdig ist und verklärt sie geradezu, so daß er ihnen ein Gefühl und ein Leben einhaucht, die nicht ihresgleichen haben.

Fils de paysans. Il dessine en gardant les vaches. A partir de 1954, il peint à l'huile. Lorsqu'il peint les scènes de la vie populaire, son art ne diffère pas tant que cela de celui des autres peintres de l'Ecole de Hlebine (à laquelle il appartient, bien sûr), mais lorsqu'il s'attaque au paysage, le traitant avec une grande minutie, digne des miniaturistes, sinon des enlumineurs de jadis, il le transcende alors complètement, lui donnant un sentiment et une vie sans pareille.

EXPOSITIONS:
«Naivni umetnici Jugoslavije», Belgrade 1957.
Galerie d'Art Primitif, Zagreb 1959 (Cat., Préface Mica Basicevič).
«Laienmaler», Bâle 1961.
The Arthur Jeffress Gallery, Londres 1961.
«Yugoslav Modern Primitives», Edinburgh 1962.
«Peintres Naïfs Yougoslaves», Moscou 1962.
«Première Quadriennale des Peintres Naïfs Yougoslaves», Čacač 1962.
The Galerie St-Etienne, New York 1963.
«Peintres Naïfs Populaires Yougoslaves», Leningrad 1963.
«Sonntagsmaler aus Jugoslawien», Museum am Ostwall, Dortmund 1964.

BIBLIOGRAPHIE:
Oto Bihalji-Merin: «Das naive Bild der Welt», Köln 1959.
Oto Bihalji-Merin: «Die naive Malerei», Köln 1959.
Oto Bihalji-Merin: «Les Peintres Naïfs», Paris (sans date).
Oto Bihalji-Merin: «Umetnost Naivnich u Jugoslavjii», Belgrade 1963.

Velasquez, José Antonio

Born 1906 in Caridad (Honduras).

Geboren 1906 in Caridad (Honduras).

Né en 1906 à Caridad (Honduras).

Was a telegraph operator and then a hairdresser, and later became mayor of San Antonio de Oriente, the little mountain village which he has painted so often and which he still continues to paint. Although he took up water colors at an early age, his first picture in oils did not appear until 1934. His art is meticulous, almost documentary in its exactness; for instance, the variety of his greens is astonishing. Was awarded a prize for designing a Christmas card (Hallmark, Kansas City).

Telegraphenbeamter, Friseur, dann Bürgermeister in San Antonio de Oriente, jenem kleinen Bergdorf in Honduras, das er so oft gemalt hat und heute noch malt. Er hat zwar ziemlich früh zu malen begonnen, doch stammt sein erstes Ölbild erst aus dem Jahr 1934. Seine Kunst ist sorgfältig genau, beinahe dokumentarisch. Die Vielfalt seiner Grün zum Beispiel ist verblüffend. Preis für eine Weihnachts-Glückwunschkarte (Hallmark, Kansas-City).

Opérateur télégraphiste, coiffeur, puis maire de San Antonio de Oriente, ce petit village montagneux de Honduras qu'il a tant peint et qu'il continue à peindre encore à l'heure qu'il est. S'il a commencé à peindre assez tôt, son premier tableau à l'huile date seulement de 1934. Son art est minutieux, presque documentaire. La variété de ses verts, par exemple, est stupéfiante. Prix pour les cartes-vœux de Noël (Hallmark, Kansas-City).

EXPOSITIONS:
Union Pan-Américaine, Washington 1954.
«La Peinture Naïve», Knokke-le-Zoute 1958.
«Das naive Bild der Welt», Baden-Baden 1961.
«Naive Painters of Latin America», Duke University, Durham N.C., 1963.
«20th Century Latin American Naive Art», La Jolla (USA) 1964.
«De Lusthof der Naieven», Rotterdam 1964.
«Le Monde des Naïfs», Paris 1964.

BIBLIOGRAPHIE:

Oto Bihalji-Merin: «Das naive Bild der Welt», Köln 1959.
Oto Bihalji-Merin: «Die naive Malerei», Köln.
Oto Bihalji-Merin: «Les Peintres Naïfs», Paris (sans date).
«Art Naïf», Editions Marocaines et Internationales, Rabat 1964.

Venjarski, Jano

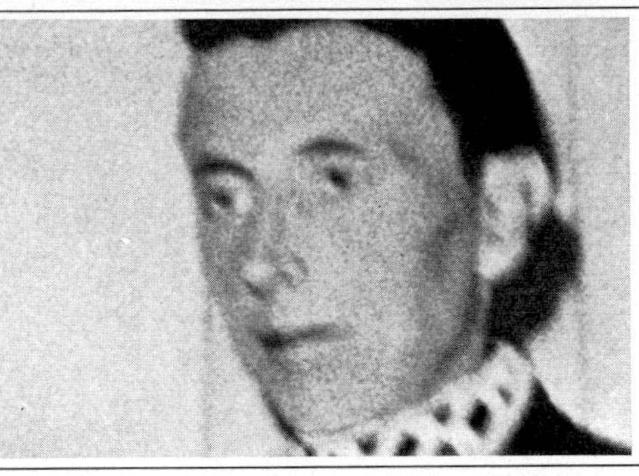

Born August 8, 1928 in Oča Andreja (Yugoslavia).

Geboren 8. August 1928 in Oča Andreja (Jugoslawien).

Né le 8 août 1928 à Oča Andreja (Yougoslavie).

He is the youngest of the Kovačiča school, a self-taught artist and also a poet. His painting, which is appreciably more 'naive' than the others of this school, is full of humor and fairly highly colored. His pictures tell stories, to the great entertainment of all who see them.

Das jüngste Mitglied der Schule von Kovačiča. Autodidakt. Maler und Dichter. Seine Malerei, die merklich naiver ist als die der andern, ist ziemlich ungestüm und voll Humor. Er erzählt Geschichten zum großen Vergnügen aller.

Le benjamin de l'Ecole de Kovačiča. Peintre autodidacte et poète. Sa peinture, sensiblement plus naïve que celle des autres, est assez truculente, pleine d'humour. Ce sont des histoires qu'il raconte toujours pour le plus grand plaisir de tous.

EXPOSITIONS:
«Laienmaler», Gewerbemuseum, Basel 1961.
The Jeffress Gallery, Londres 1961.
Palais de Culture, Kovačiča 1962.
«Peintres Naïfs Yougoslaves», Moscou 1962.
«Yugoslav Modern Primitives», Edinburgh 1962.
«Première Quadriennale des Peintres Naïfs Yougoslaves», Čačac 1962.
«Naive Kunst in Jugoslawien», Kunstakademie, Wien 1963.
The Galerie St-Etienne, New York 1963.
«Peintres Naïfs Populaires Yougoslaves», Léningrad 1963.

BIBLIOGRAPHIE:
Oto Bihalji-Merin: Umetnost Naivnich u Jugoslavjii», Belgrade 1963.

Verkouille, Emile

Born March 23, 1864 in Ostend (Belgium).
Died October 16, 1927 in Ostend (Belgium).

Geboren am 23. März 1864 in Ostende (Belgien).
Gestorben am 16. Oktober 1927 in Ostende (Belgien).

Né le 23 mars 1864 à Ostende (Belgique).
Mort le 16 octobre 1927 à Ostende (Belgique).

House painter. A deaf-mute who married, quite late in life, Octavie Quakelbeen, the widow of another deaf-mute. Worked for a brief period before the first world war with Paul Romelaert. The few pictures which are known to be his are of very high quality, combining poetical vision with careful brushwork.

Anstreicher. Taubstummer, der in schon vorgerücktem Alter Octavie Quakelbeen heiratet, die Witwe eines anderen Taubstummen. Arbeitet vor dem Ersten Weltkrieg eine Zeitlang mit Paul Romelaert zusammen. Die wenigen Bilder, die man von ihm kennt, sind sehr schön und vereinen poetischen Sinn mit gepflegter Ausführung.

Peintre en bâtiment. Sourd-muet qui, à un âge déjà avancé, épouse Octavie Quakelbeen, veuve d'un autre sourd-muet. Travaille pendant un moment, avant la première guerre mondiale, avec Paul Romelaert. Les rares tableaux que l'on connaît de lui sont d'une grande qualité, où le sens poétique se joint à une exécution soignée.

EXPOSITIONS:
« Peintres Naïfs Belges », Théâtre National, Bruxelles 1965.
« Peintres Naïfs Belges », Musée Royal des Beaux-Arts, Verviers 1965.
« Peintres Naïfs Belges », Musée Royal des Beaux Arts, Hasselt 1966
(Cat., Préface Anatole Jakovsky, Alain Germoz, Paul Snoek).

Viragova, Zuzana

Born August 15, 1885 in Kosice (Czechoslovakia).

Geboren am 15. August 1885 in Kosice (Tschechoslowakei).

Née le 15 août 1885 à Kosice (Tchécoslovaquie).

Most of the time she paints memories of the 'good old days': idyllic scenes endowed with an old-fashioned charm. Her awkwardness is made up for by her poetic vision. She became known at the famous exhibition of art by amateurs which took place in Prague and Martin.

Sie malt vor allem ihre Erinnerungen aus der guten alten Zeit, idyllische Szenen voll altmodischen Zaubers. Ihre Unbeholfenheit wird aufgewogen durch eine poetische Schau der Dinge. Wird entdeckt dank der berühmten Ausstellung der Dilettanten-Kunst in Prag und Martin.

Elle peint surtout ses souvenirs du bon vieux temps; des scènes idylliques empreintes d'un charme suranné. Sa maladresse est compensée par une vision poétique des choses. Est révélée par la fameuse exposition de l'art des amateurs à Prague et à Martin.

EXPOSITIONS:
«Naivni Umeni», Dum Umeni, Brno 1963.
«Naivni Umeni v Ceskoslovensku», Prague 1964.

Virius, Mirko

Born September 28, 1889 in Djelekovač (Yugoslavia).
Died 1943 in Zemun (Yugoslavia).

Geboren am 28. September 1889 in Djelekovač (Jugoslawien).
Gestorben 1943 in Zemun (Jugoslawien).

Né le 28 septembre 1889 à Djelekovač (Yougoslavie).
Mort en 1943 à Zemun (Yougoslavie).

A Croatian peasant, he was captured by the Russians during the first world war. In 1936 he met up with Generalič and Mraz again in Hlebine, where he painted and exhibited his work with them. He was inspired by a desire for social justice, and thus much of his work shows the difficulties and troubles of the peasant's life. The faces he draws, stamped with severity and sadness, seem to be molded from the earth of his native land. Even when he paints two people dancing together, there is no sense of joy.
He was killed by the Nazis in a concentration camp.

Kroate. Bauer. Russischer Kriegsgefangener während des ersten Weltkriegs. Schon 1936 gesellt er sich zu Generalič und Mraz und malt und stellt mit ihnen in Hlebine aus. Von einem Ideal sozialer Gerechtigkeit beseelt, malt er vor allem das Drama der Bauern, ihr schweres Leben, ihre Mühen. Seine von tiefem Ernst und Traurigkeit geprägten Gesichter sind gleichsam aus der Erde seines Landes geknetet. Selbst wenn er tanzende Paare malt, fehlt die Freude.
Er wurde von den Nazis in einem Konzentrationslager umgebracht.

Croate. Paysan. Prisonnier des Russes pendant la première guerre mondiale, il rejoint dès 1936 Generalič et Mraz à Hlebine où il peint et expose avec eux. Animé par un idéal de justice sociale, il peint surtout le drame de la paysannerie, sa vie difficile, ses peines. Ses visages, empreints d'une grande gravité et de tristesse, sont comme pétris dans la terre de son pays. Même lorsqu'il peint les couples dansant, la joie y est absente. Il a été tué par les nazis dans un camp de concentration.

EXPOSITIONS:
Participation à la troisième Biennale, São Paulo 1955.
Musée, Dubrovnik 1956.
«Naivni umetnici jugoslavije», Belgrade 1957.
«La Peinture Naïve», Knokke-le-Zoute 1958.
Narodni Musej, Zemun 1959 (Cat., Préface M. Gvozdanovič).
«Yugoslav Modern Primitives», Edinburgh 1962.
«Peintres Naïfs Yougoslaves», Moscou 1962.
«Naive Kunst in Jugoslawien», Kunstakademie, Wien 1963.
«Peintres Naïfs Populaires Yougoslaves», Leningrad 1963.
«Sonntagsmaler aus Jugoslawien», Museum am Ostwall, Dortmund 1964.
«De Lusthof der Naieven», Rotterdam 1964.
«Le Monde des Naïfs», Paris 1964.

BIBLIOGRAPHIE:
«Yougoslavija», numéro spécial (17) consacré à l'art des naïfs, Belgrade 1959.
Oto Bihalji-Merin: «Das naive Bild der Welt», Köln 1959.
Oto Bihalji-Merin: «Die naive Malerei», Köln 1959.
Oto Bihalji-Merin: «Les Peintres Naïfs», Paris (sans date).
Oto Bihalji-Merin: «Umetnost Naivnich u Jugoslavjii», Belgrade 1963.

Viva, Rosina

Born 1900 in Anacapri (Italy).

Geboren 1900 in Anacapri (Italien).

Née en 1900 à Anacapri (Italie).

Of peasant stock. Still one of those girls as described by Axel Munthe in his book about San Michele. Began to paint out of homesickness when, in 1943, she went with her husband to Switzerland. Returned to Italy, but to Naples, in 1946, and continued to paint. Her work is done entirely from memory.

Die Eltern sind Bauern. Sie ist noch ganz eines jener jungen Mädchen, wie Axel Munthe sie in seinem Buch von San Michele beschreibt. Fängt aus Heimweh an zu malen, als sie 1943 ihrem Mann in die Schweiz folgt. Kehrt 1946 nach Italien zurück, nach Neapel, wo sie fortfährt, zu malen. Sie malt ausschließlich aus dem Gedächtnis.

Parents paysans. Encore tout à fait une de ces jeunes filles décrites par Axel Munthe dans son livre de San Michele. Commence à peindre par nostalgie de son pays lorsque, en 1943, elle a suivi son mari en Suisse. Retourne en 1946 en Italie, mais à Naples où elle continue à peindre. Elle peint uniquement de mémoire.

EXPOSITIONS:
«Moderne primitive Maler», Kunsthalle, Bern 1949 (Cat., Préface Arnold Rüdlinger).
«Maler der einfältigen Herzens», Museum am Ostwall, Dortmund 1952.
«Mostra di Pittura Popolare», Palazzo delle Esposizioni, Rome 1955.
Kunsthaus Zürich 1955 (Cat., Préface Max Eichenberger).
«I Pittori Naifs», Rome 1964.

BIBLIOGRAPHIE:
Marco Valsecchi: «Rosina Viva», Edizioni del Milione, Milan 1949.
Bernard Jasmand und Otto Kallir: «Sonntagsmaler», Otto Aug. Ehlers, Berlin/Dortmund 1956.
Max Eichenberger: «Rosina Viva», Du No. 3 Zürich März 1945.
Vitali Lamberto: «Rosina Viva», Werk, Winterthur juillet 1946.
Rosina Viva: «Mein Bild, Paesaggio di Anacapri», Du, Zürich, octobre 1945.
Marco Valsecchi: «Diventa pittrice per la malinconia di Napoli», Oggi Milano 15 février 1948.
Oto Bihalji-Merin: «Das naive Bild der Welt», Köln 1959.
Oto Bihalji-Merin: «Die naive Malerei», Köln 1959.
Oto Bihalji-Merin: «Les Peintres Naïfs», Paris (sans date).

Vivin, Louis

Born July 1861 in Hadol, Vosges (France).
Died May 28, 1936 in Paris (France).

Geboren im Juli 1861 in Hadol, Vogesen (Frankreich).
Gestorben am 28. Mai 1936 in Paris (Frankreich).

Né en juillet 1861 à Hadol, Vosges (France).
Mort le 28 mai 1936 à Paris (France).

Son of a country teacher. He began to work for the post office and his monotonous life can be followed by noting his promotions. In 1880 he became supernumerary; in 1882 he got married; in 1896 became chief clerk; in 1900 supervisor; in 1910 inspector (with 5,000 francs a year); in 1910 finally promoted to inspector on the routes of East France (with 14,000 francs plus expenses—a very good salary for that time!). But he led a double life, since he was also a dedicated artist. Became an official of the Academy in 1912 and retired in 1923. Bodmer-Bing met him at the Fair of Amateur Painters, where he was exhibiting more than he was selling. Wilhelm Uhde discovered him in 1925, and since then everything was altered. People noticed him and encouraged him. He continued to work as if nothing had happened, to the best of his ability. But in 1935 he became paralyzed, and his right arm and part of his face were useless. It was the end for him as an artist. But he had the fame of which he had dreamed. Too late, as is usually the case...

Sohn eines Landschulmeisters. Um sein Brot zu verdienen, tritt er in die Postverwaltung ein. Von dem Augenblick an ist sein Leben vorgezeichnet, ereignislos, und ließe sich durch seine Beförderungen ausdrücken – Beamtenanwärter 1880, Heirat 1882, Beamter 1896, Abteilungschef 1900, Inspektor 1910, mit 5000 Francs Jahresgehalt, schließlich Inspektor auf dem Eisenbahnnetz der Ostbahn, mit 14 000 Francs Gehalt zusätzlich Spesen, was für die damalige Zeit eine ganz nette Summe darstellt –, wenn er nicht ein Doppelleben führte. Denn er ist ein in seine Kunst vernarrter Maler. Verdienstorden 1912 und Ruhestand 1923. Bodmer-Bing lernt ihn auf dem Bilder-Flohmarkt kennen, wo er mehr ausstellte als verkaufte. Wilhelm Uhde entdeckt ihn 1925, und jetzt tritt die große Wende ein. Man befaßt sich mit ihm, fördert ihn. Er fährt fort, nach besten Kräften zu arbeiten, als hätte sich nichts verändert. 1934 werden sein rechter Arm und ein Teil des Gesichts von Lähmung befallen. Das ist das Ende. Er hat den Ruhm errungen, von dem er geträumt hatte. Zu spät, wie gewohnt...

Fils d'un instituteur de campagne. Pour gagner sa vie, il entre dans l'Administration des Postes. Dès lors, sa vie est sans histoire, toute tracée, et elle se confondrait avec ses avancements – surnuméraire en 1880; se marie en 1882; commis principal en 1896; chef de brigade en 1900; Inspecteur en 1910, avec 5000 francs par an; inspecteur sur les lignes du réseau de l'Est enfin, avec 14 000 francs, plus les frais, ce qui est une jolie somme pour l'époque – si toutefois il ne menait pas une double vie, celle d'un peintre épris de son art. Officier d'Académie en 1912 et retraité en 1923. M. Bodmer-Bing fait sa connaissance à la Foire aux croûtes où il exposait plus qu'il ne vendait. Wilhelm Uhde le découvre en 1925 et tout, désormais, est changé. On s'occupe de lui, on le pousse. Lui, il continue à travailler comme si de rien n'était, de son mieux. En 1934, la paralysie le prive du bras droit et d'une partie du visage. C'est la fin. C'est la gloire aussi à laquelle il rêvait. Trop tard, comme d'habitude...

EXPOSITIONS:
«Les Maîtres Populaires de la Réalité», Paris 1937.
«Les Maîtres Populaires de la Réalité», Zürich 1937.
«Masters of Popular Painting», New York 1938.
«Masters of Popular Painting», Arthur Tooth & Sons, London 1938.
«Moderne Primitieven», Stedelijk Museum, Amsterdam 1941 (Cat., Préface D.C.R.).
Galerie Bing, Paris 1948 (Cat., Préface Jean Cassou et B. Bing).
«Moderne primitive Maler», Kunsthalle, Bern 1949.
Perrs Galleries, New York 1954.
Kunsthalle, Basel 1956; avec Bauchant, Bombois et Séraphine (Cat., Préface Arnold Rüdlinger).
«La Peinture Naïve», Knokke-le-Zoute 1958.
«La Peinture Naïve», Maison de la Pensée Française, Paris 1960.
VIII° Salon Interministériel, Musée des Beaux-Arts de la ville de Paris 1960 (Cat., Préface J.N. Priou).
«Das naive Bild der Welt», Baden-Baden 1961.
«Die Welt der naiven Malerei», Salzburg 1964.
«I Pittori Naifs», Rome 1964.
«De Lusthof der Naieven», Rotterdam 1964.
«Le Monde des Naïfs», Paris 1964.
«Le Panorama International de la Peinture Naïve», Rabat 1964.

BIBLIOGRAPHIE:
«Les grandes vacances du postier Vivin», L'Album du Figaro, Paris 1948.
W. Uhde: «Cinq Maîtres Primitifs», Librairies Palmes, Paris 1949.
Anatole Jakovsky: «La Peinture Naïve», Paris 1949.
«Vivin», Art d'Aujourd'hui, N° 4, Paris mars 1951 N° 7, juillet 1951.
Anatole Jakovsky: «Vivin», Editions J. Damase, Paris 1953.
J. Lassaigne: «Néo Primitifs du XX° Siècle», Médecine de France, N° 50, 1954
Anatole Jakovsky: «Les Peintres Naïfs», Paris 1956.
Anatole Jakovsky: «Naive Malerei», Zürich 1957.
Bernard Jasmand et Otto Kallir: «Sonntagsmaler», Editions Otto Aug. Ehlers, Berlin/Darmstadt 1956.
Oto Bihalji-Merin: «Das naive Bild der Welt», Köln 1959.
Oto Bihalji-Merin: «Die naive Malerei», Köln 1959.
Oto Bihalji-Merin: «Les Peintres Naïfs», Paris (sans date).
Francine Loriot: «L.Vivin», Style, N° 4, Lausanne 1964.
«Art Naïf», Editions Marocaines et Internationales, Rabat 1964.
J.N. Priou: «Louis Vivin», Le Jardin des Arts, No. 64, Paris, février 1960.
«Die Welt der Naiven», Spiegel, Hamburg 20 décembre 1961.
Catalogo Bolaffi d'Arte Moderna, Turin 1966.
J.N. Priou: «Vivin», Arts PTT, No. 44, Paris 1966.

L. VIVIN

Vivancos, Miguel Garcia

Born April 19, 1895 in Mazarron, Murcia (Spain).

Geboren am 19. April 1895 in Mazarron, Murcia (Spanien).

Né le 19 avril 1895 à Mazarron, Murcie (Espagne).

His poverty stricken family had to leave the country to find work. At the age of 13 he became an apprentice mechanic in the Cartagena arsenal. Then he became a docker, a house-painter, a clockmaker. When the Civil War broke out he was a taxi driver. This was the war which changed the whole course of his life. For he fought on the side of the republicans. He became a colonel and won their only definite victory, that of Teruel. But soon came defeat, exile and concentration camp in France. Naturally, he escaped and fought for the maquis. At the liberation, he was fifty years old—no job, no qualifications. He was asked to paint silk scarves, to help him earn some money, and thus his vocation was born. Picasso encouraged him, and his rise to fame is well known. At first his progress was slow, but it was always sure. Vivancos has found a meaning in life.

Stammt aus einer armen Familie, die auswandern muß, um Arbeit zu suchen. Tritt mit 13 Jahren als Mechanikerlehrling ins Zeughaus von Cartagena ein. Dann arbeitet er als Hafenarbeiter, als Anstreicher, als Uhrmacher. Bei Ausbruch des Bürgerkriegs ist er Taxichauffeur. Der Krieg bringt die große Wendung in sein Leben. Denn er kämpft auf seiten der Republikaner, steigt bald zum Oberst auf und erringt den einzigen unbestreitbaren Sieg: Teruel. Aber darauf folgt die Niederlage, das Exil und das Konzentrationslager in Frankreich. Er bricht natürlich aus und kämpft als Maquisard. Bei der Befreiung ist er fünfzigjährig, ohne Arbeit, ohne Beruf. Um ihm zu helfen, schlägt man ihm vor, er solle Halstücher bemalen... Und damit ist seine Berufung entdeckt! Picasso ermuntert ihn, er beginnt den langsamen, doch sicheren Aufstieg zu seinem heutigen Ruhm. Vivancos hat seinen Lebenszweck gefunden.

Naît dans une famille pauvre qui doit s'expatrier pour chercher du travail. A 13 ans, entre comme apprenti-mécanicien à l'arsenal de Cartagène. Puis il est docker, peintre en bâtiment, horloger. Au moment où éclate la guerre civile, il «fait du taxi». Et c'est cette guerre qui changera, radicalement, le cours de sa vie. Car il fait la guerre du côté des républicains. Il devient bientôt colonel et remporte la seule victoire incontestable, celle de Teruel. Mais bientôt c'est la défaite, l'exil et le camp de concentration en France. Il s'évade, naturellement, et se bat au maquis. A la Libération, à 50 ans, il est sans travail, sans métier. Pour l'aider, on lui propose de peindre des foulards... Sa vocation est née! Picasso l'encourage, et c'est la montée vers la notoriété que l'on sait. Lente au début, mais absolument certaine. Vivancos a trouvé sa raison de vivre.

EXPOSITIONS:
Galerie Mirador, Paris 1950
(Cat., Préface André Breton).
Royal Academy of Arts (Ecole de Paris), London 1951.
Galerie Lefèvre, London 1952.
Galerie Mirador, Paris 1956.
Galerie Lucie Weil, Paris 1957.
Galerie Norval, Paris 1958.
«La Peinture Naïve», Knokke-le-Zoute 1958.
Galerie Oeillet, Toulouse 1959.
«Les Peintres Naïfs», Maison de la Pensée Française, Paris 1960.
«Laienmaler», Gewerbemuseum, Basel 1961.
«I Pittori Naifs», Rome 1964.
«Les Primitifs d'Aujourd'hui», Galerie Charpentier, Paris 1964.
«De Lusthof der Naieven», Rotterdam 1964.
«Le Monde des Naïfs», Paris 1964.
«Le Panorama International de la Peinture Naïve», Rabat 1964.

BIBLIOGRAPHIE:
A. Jakovsky: «Les Peintres Naïfs», Paris 1956.
Anatole Jakovsky: «Naïve Malerei», Zürich 1957.
Anatole Jakovsky: «Vivancos», Editions Ch. Moulin, Paris 1961.
Anatole Jakovsky: «Les loisirs sacrés et autres», La Vie médicale, Paris mai 1963.
Oto Bihalji-Merin: «Das naive Bild der Welt», Köln 1959.
Oto Bihalji-Merin: «Die naive Malerei», Köln 1959.
Oto Bihalji-Merin: «Les Peintres Naïfs», Paris (sans date).
«Art Naïf», Editions Marocaines et Internationales, Rabat 1964.
André Breton: «Le Surréalisme et la Peinture», Editions Gallimard, Paris 1965.

FILM:
«Le Voyage à Paris», d'après un texte de Marcel Aymé, réalisé par Pierre Mathieu), 1959.

ILLUSTRATION:
Marcel Aymé: «Le Vaurien», Editions Gallimard, Paris 1959.

Wallis, Alfred

Born 1855 in Devonport (England).
Died 1942 in St. Ives, Cornwall (England).

Geboren 1855 in Devonport (England).
Gestorben 1942 in St. Ives, Cornwall (England).

Né en 1855 à Devonport (Angleterre).
Mort en 1942 à St. Ives, Cornouailles (Angleterre).

From the age of nine he traversed the seas as a ship's boy. Later, in 1890, he settled as a fisherman in St. Ives where he died a pauper. Nevertheless, it was his painting, which he had practiced since the age of seventy, which helped him to live. Was discovered in 1928 by Ben Nicholson who later also went to live in St. Ives, as did also Barbara Hepworth. Nicholson introduced him to Herbert Read, H.S. Ede, Christopher Wood, etc. Wallis said of himself: 'I never go out to paint or draw; I don't see the things I paint, for I saw them previously'.

Fährt bereits im Alter von 9 Jahren als Schiffsjunge zur See. Läßt sich 1890 als Fischer in St. Ives nieder, wo er in Armut stirbt. Der Malerei, die er von seinem 70. Jahre an treibt, verdankt er seinen Lebensunterhalt. 1928 wird er von Ben Nicholson entdeckt, der später mit Barbara Hepworth in St. Ives Wohnsitz nimmt und auch Herbert Read, H.S. Ede, Christopher Wood usw. auf ihn aufmerksam macht. Wallis sagte: «Ich gehe nie aus, um zu malen oder zu zeichnen. Ich sehe die Dinge nicht, die ich male, ich habe sie früher gesehen.»

Navigue comme mousse dès l'âge de neuf ans. Se fixe comme pêcheur à St. Ives en 1890 où il meurt pauvre. D'ailleurs, c'est sa peinture qu'il pratique à partir de sa soixante-dixième année, qui l'a aidé à vivre. Découvert en 1928 par Ben Nicholson qui s'installera, avec Barbara Hepworth, plus tard à St. Ives, il le fait connaître à Herbert Read, H.S. Ede, Christopher Wood, etc. Wallis disait: «Je ne sors jamais pour peindre ou dessiner. Je ne vois pas les choses que je peins, je les ai vues naguère».

EXPOSITIONS:
«Maler des einfältigen Herzens», Museum am Ostwall, Dortmund 1952.
Piccadilly Gallery, London 1962 (Cat., Préface H.S. Ede).
«La Peinture Naïve», Knokke-le-Zoute 1958.
«De Lusthof der Naieven», Rotterdam 1964.
«Le Monde des Naïfs», Paris 1964.

BIBLIOGRAPHIE:
Herbert Read: «Alfred Wallis», Cahiers d'Art, Paris 1938.
Bernard Jasmand et Otto Kallir: «Sonntagsmaler», Editions Otto Aug. Ehlers, Berlin/Dortmund 1956.
Oto Bihalji-Merin: «Das naive Bild der Welt», Köln 1959.
Oto Bihalji-Merin: «Die naive Malerei», Köln 1959.
Oto Bihalji-Merin: «Les Peintres Naïfs», Paris (sans date).

Van Weert, Jan

Born 1871 in Hertogenbosch (Netherlands).
Died 1955 in Düsseldorf (Germany).

Geboren 1871 in Hertogenbosch (Holland).
Gestorben 1955 in Düsseldorf (Deutschland).

Né en 1871 à Hertogenbosch (Hollande).
Mort en 1955 à Düsseldorf (Allemagne).

Began to paint after the second world war, at the age of 75. Before that he had led a checkered life, changing his job fairly often. Briefly, he left his father's transport undertaking to become a trainer of horses, and later he was a rider at horse-shows, having worked in the meantime in a hotel... In this way he visited Paris, London, Vienna, Budapest, Berlin, and many other cities, occasionally winning prizes for trick jumping horses. In Düsseldorf, he painted at the kitchen table. His reminiscences, of course!

Fängt nach dem Zweiten Weltkrieg im Alter von 75 Jahren an zu malen. Vorher führt er ein bewegtes Leben und wechselt ziemlich oft den Beruf. Er gibt das väterliche Speditionsgeschäft auf, um zuerst Pferdedresseur, dann Concoursreiter zu werden. Dazwischen war er auch in der Hotellerie tätig... Er reitet in Paris, London, Wien, Budapest, Berlin und anderswo und erringt hie und da einen Preis im Kunstspringen. In Düsseldorf malte er auf einem Küchentisch. Seine Erinnerungen natürlich!

Commence à peindre après la seconde guerre mondiale à l'âge de 75 ans. Auparavant, il mène une vie mouvementée et change assez souvent de métier. En raccourci, il abandonne l'affaire paternelle des transports pour devenir d'abord dresseur de chevaux, cavalier des concours hippiques ensuite. En passant par l'hôtellerie... Il parcourt donc Paris, Londres, Vienne, Budapest, Berlin, et j'en passe, où il décroche de temps à autre des prix pour la haute voltige. Etabli à Düsseldorf, il a peint sur une table de cuisine. Ses souvenirs, naturellement!

EXPOSITIONS:
«Maler des einfältigen Herzens», Museum am Ostwall, Dortmund 1952.
«Arbeit-Freizeit-Muße», Kunsthalle, Recklinghausen 1953.
«Laienmaler», Gewerbemuseum, Basel 1961.
«Schönheit», Kunsthalle, Recklinghausen 1958.
Galerie Hielscher, München 1955.

BIBLIOGRAPHIE:
Bernard Jasmand et Otto Kallir: «Sonntagsmaler», Ed. Otto Aug. Ehlers, Berlin/Darmstadt 1956.
Oto Bihalji-Merin: «Das naive Bild der Welt»,
Oto Bihalji-Merin: «Die naive Malerei», Köln 1959.
Oto Bihalji-Merin: «Les Peintres Naïfs», Paris (sans date).

Weil, Fernand

Born August 4, 1894 in Paris (France).
Died October 18, 1958 in Paris (France).

Geboren am 4. August 1894 in Paris (Frankreich).
Gestorben am 18. Oktober 1958 in Paris (Frankreich).

Né le 4 août 1894 à Paris (France).
Mort le 18 octobre 1958 à Paris (France).

It is very possible that this wholesale wine merchant, living in a luxury flat near the Parc Monceau, would not have known of the existence of art if it had not been for the war coming in 1939 and, one year later, the enemy occupation. Forced into hiding, and unable to remain inactive, he tried to paint. But he did not even know what it was. So he squeezed the tubes of paint out directly onto the canvas without using a brush; G. Mathieu's precedent for this method. Towards the end of his life he painted a kind of primitive 'Nympheas'—a sort of impressionism or rather of 'naive' pointillism. Rarely have colors been so sumptuous as in his paintings. He delighted in all the colors of all the famous wines which he could lay his hands on...

Man kann annehmen, dieser Weingroßhändler, der in der Nähe des Parc Monceau eine luxuriöse Wohnung besaß, hätte gar nie gewußt, daß die Malerei überhaupt existiert, wäre 1939 nicht der Krieg ausgebrochen und wäre nicht ein Jahr später die feindliche Besetzung erfolgt. Gezwungen, sich versteckt zu halten, versucht er zu malen, da er nicht untätig bleiben kann. Aber er weiß nicht einmal, was malen heißt. Da drückt er die Tuben direkt auf die Leinwand, ohne sich eines Pinsels zu bedienen; darin ist er ein Vorläufer von G. Mathieu. Gegen Ende seines Lebens malt er eine Art naive «Nymphéas»; eine Art Impressionismus, wenn nicht gar naiver Pointillismus. Als Kolorist von außergewöhnlicher Prachtliebe ergötzt er sich an allen Farben aller berühmten Weine, die durch seine Hände gingen.

On peut supposer que ce marchand de vins en gros, habitant un appartement luxueux près du Parc Monceau, n'aurait même pas su que la peinture existe, si, en 1939, il n'y avait pas eu la guerre et, un an après, l'occupation ennemie. Obligé de se cacher, et comme il ne peut pas rester inactif, il essaye de peindre. Mais il ne sait même pas ce que c'est. Alors il presse directement les tubes sur la toile, sans se servir du pinceau, en précédant en cela G. Mathieu. Vers la fin de sa vie, il peint des espèces des «Nymphéas» naïves; une sorte d'impressionnisme, sinon du pointillisme naïf. Coloriste d'une somptuosité rare, il se délecte de toutes les couleurs de tous les crus fameux qui sont passés par ses mains...

EXPOSITIONS:
Galerie du Verseau, Paris 1945 (Cat., Préface Jean Bouret).
Galerie Mac Grath, Paris 1946 (Cat., Préface Jean Bouret).
Galerie Greuse, Paris 1948.
Galerie Arc-en-Ciel, Paris 1949 (Cat., Préface Anatole Jakovsky).
Galerie J. Pascaud, Paris 1951.
Galerie Bignou, Paris 1957.
Galerie Hutton-Chambard, New York 1957.
«Les Peintres Naïfs», Maison de la Pensée Française, Paris 1960.

BIBLIOGRAPHIE:
Anatole Jakovsky: «La Peinture Naïve», Paris 1949.
Anatole Jakovsky: «Les Peintres Naïfs», Paris 1956.
Anatole Jakovsky: «Naive Malerei», Zürich 1957.
«Dix Ans d'Art Actuel», Editions Comparaisons, Paris 1964.

Westerlinck, Achilles

Born June 28, 1885 in Rupelmonde (Belgium).

Geboren 28. Juni 1885 in Rupelmonde (Belgien).

Né le 28 juin 1885 à Rupelmonde (Belgique).

Spent his youth knocking about the world as a ship's boy. Later, he traded in salt water gathered at the mouth of the Schelde and sold to a refinery in Rupelmonde, where he still lives. Did some basketwork and worked in an alcohol distilling factory, which allowed him to manufacture alcohol on his own. During the second world war he ran a café. Like all self-respecting sailors, he has constructed several ships in bottles, apart from the thirty or so pictures he has painted. He is nicknamed 'De Kat', which means 'the cat'.

Verbringt seine Jugend als Schiffsjunge auf den Weltmeeren. Später handelt er mit Salzwasser, das an der Scheldemündung geschöpft und an eine Raffinerie in Rupelmonde, wo er heute noch lebt, weiterverkauft wird. Verfertigt auch Flechtwaren und arbeitet in einer Alkoholbrennerei, was ihm erlaubt, auf eigene Rechnung Alkohol zu brennen. Betreibt während des Zweiten Weltkriegs ein Café. Außer den rund 30 Bildern, die er gemalt hat, hat er auch wie jeder Matrose, der etwas auf sich hält, ein paar Schiffe in Flaschen gebaut. Man hat ihm den Übernamen « De Kat », das heißt « Die Katze », gegeben.

Passe sa jeunesse comme mousse à bourlinguer sur tous les océans. Plus tard, fait le commerce d'eau salée recueillie à l'embouchure de l'Escaut et revendue à une raffinerie de Rupelmonde où il habite encore. Fait aussi de la vannerie et travaille à une distillerie d'alcool, ce qui lui permet de le fabriquer à son propre compte. Pendant la seconde guerre mondiale exploite un café. Comme tout bon marin qui se respecte, en plus d'une trentaine de tableaux qu'il a peints, il a mis aussi quelques bateaux en bouteille. On l'a surnommé « De Kat », autrement dit le Chat.

EXPOSITIONS:
« Peintres Naïfs Belges », Théâtre National, Bruxelles 1965.
« Peintres Naïfs Belges », Musée Royal des Beaux-Arts, Verviers 1965.
« Peintres Naïfs Belges », Musée Royal des Beaux-Arts, Hasselt 1966.

Wiacek, Joseph

Born May 28, 1910 in Oleszyce (Poland).

Geboren am 28. Mai 1910 in Oleszyce (Polen).

Né le 28 mai 1910 à Oleszyce (Pologne).

He soon immigrated to France, where he earned his living as a miner. Started to paint after his retirement. His main work is a composition of 40 pictures, making a total length of 32 meters and a total of 42 square meters of painting. It is called 'Za chlebem', which means the search for bread, and tells the story of 'the roses and the thorns', to use his own words, of the Polish immigration into France. Although the treatment is rather in the folklore style, the whole composition nevertheless represents the largest fresco which primitive painters have ever attempted. It really should go to a Polish museum which is worthy of the name.

Wandert schon früh nach Frankreich aus, wo er sein Leben als Grubenarbeiter verdient. Beginnt zu malen, als er in den Ruhestand tritt. Sein Hauptwerk besteht aus 40 Bildern, ist 32 m lang und umfaßt 42 Quadratmeter Malerei. Es heißt «Za chlebem», die Suche nach dem Brot, und erzählt «die Rosen und die Dornen», wie er selber sagt, der polnischen Einwanderer in Frankreich. Obwohl das Thema eine Spur folkloristisch behandelt ist, stellt das Werk doch das größte Fresko dar, das ein naiver Maler je versucht hat. Es gehört in ein polnisches Museum, das seinen Namen verdient.

Emigre de bonne heure en France où il gagne sa vie comme mineur. Commence à peindre avec la retraite. Son œuvre principale se compose de 40 tableaux, fait 32 mètres de long et représente 42 mètres carrés de peinture. C'est «Za chlebem», c'est-à-dire à la recherche du pain. Elle narre «les roses et les épines» selon sa propre expression, de l'émigration polonaise en France. Traitée un tantinet folkloriquement, elle représente néanmoins la plus grande fresque que les peintres naïfs aient jamais tentée. Elle doit aller dans un musée polonais qui se respecte.

EXPOSITIONS:
Galerie Y.M.C.A., Paris 1962
(Cat., Préface Anatole Jakovsky).

BIBLIOGRAPHIE:
Anatole Jakovsky: «Eros du Dimanche», Paris 1964.

De Wilde, Stefanie

Born November 8, 1913 in Antwerp (Belgium).

Geboren am 8. November 1913 in Antwerpen (Belgien).

Née le 8 novembre 1913 à Anvers (Belgique).

Her father was a sailor and afterwards a lock-keeper. She started at the age of fourteen to work as a seamstress. In 1934 she married a metallurgist and gave him a son. At the moment she lives in Antwerp and works as a housekeeper. She did not begin to paint until 1964; her work is extremely sensitive and carefully drawn. She shows a preference for painting the old buildings of Antwerp. As a general rule she makes several sketches, and a number of weeks go by before a picture is completed.

Ihr Vater war Matrose und später Schleusenwärter. Im Alter von 14 Jahren beginnt sie als Wäschenäherin zu arbeiten. 1934 heiratet sie einen Metallarbeiter, dem sie einen Sohn schenkt. Gegenwärtig lebt sie in Antwerpen und versieht den Beruf einer Hausfrau. Erst 1964 fängt sie äußerst empfindsame Bilder von gepflegter graphischer Wirkung an zu malen. Sie hat vor allem eine Vorliebe für die alten Gebäude ihrer Stadt. Gewöhnlich fertigt sie mehrere Skizzen an, und es vergehen ein paar Wochen, ehe das Bild vollendet ist.

Son père fut marin et plus tard éclusier. Dès l'âge de 14 ans, elle travaille comme lingère. En 1934, elle épouse un ouvrier métallurgiste à qui elle donne un fils. Elle vit, actuellement, à Anvers, travaille comme ménagère, et ce n'est qu'à partir de 1964 qu'elle se mit à peindre des œuvres extrêmement sensibles, d'un graphisme soigné. Elle témoigne surtout une prédilection pour les vieux bâtiments de sa ville. En général, elle fait plusieurs esquisses et plusieurs semaines se passent avant que le tableau ne soit achevé.

EXPOSITIONS:
« Peintres Naïfs Belges », Le Théâtre National, Bruxelles 1965.
« Peintres Naïfs Belges », Musée Royal des Beaux-Arts, Verviers 1965.
« Peintres Naïfs Belges », Musée Royal des Beaux-Arts, Hasselt 1966.

Wilson, Scottie

Born June 6, 1888 in Glasgow (Scotland).

Geboren am 6. Juni 1888 in Glasgow (Schottland).

Né le 6 juin 1888 à Glasgow (Ecosse).

Came of a working-class family. Never went to school. Later, other people signed his canvases for him. Did his military service in the East Indies, then traveled all over the world as a sailor. For some time he lived in Canada—is it there he received the impressions of totemism which one sees in his work? At any rate, his work, which is to a large extent stereotyped calligraphy, belongs to the group of visionary paintings. He took part in the large exhibition of 'Fantastic Art' which was held in Basel.

Sohn von Arbeitern, der nie zur Schule ging. Später sollten andere seine Bilder für ihn signieren. Militärdienst in Indien, dann Reisen um die Welt als Matrose. Läßt sich eine Zeitlang in Kanada nieder. Stammen daher gewisse totemistische Reminiszenzen? Wie dem auch sei, seine Malerei, in der schablonenhafte Kalligraphie eine große Rolle spielt, gehört zu dem Zweig der visionären Kunst. Hat an der großen Ausstellung « Die phantastische Kunst » in Basel teilgenommen.

Fils d'ouvriers. N'a jamais été à l'école. Plus tard, ce seront les autres qui signeront ses tableaux. Service militaire aux Indes, puis les voyages autour du monde en qualité de matelot. S'installe pour un temps au Canada. Est-ce de là que viennent certaines réminiscences totémiques? Quoiqu'il en soit, son art, dans lequel la calligraphie stéréotypée a une large part, appartient à la branche des visionnaires. A participé à la grande exposition de « L'Art Fantastique » à Bâle.

EXPOSITIONS:
Galerie Gimpel Fils, London 1947.
Galerie Nina Dausset, Paris 1949.
Galerie Hutter, Basel 1950.
« La Peinture Naïve », Knokke-le-Zoute 1958.
« Laienmaler », Gewerbemuseum, Basel 1961 (Cat., Préface R.Wildhaber et A. Hernandez).

BIBLIOGRAPHIE:

Oto Bihalji-Merin: « Das naive Bild der Welt », Köln 1959.
Oto Bihalji-Merin: « Die naive Malerei », Köln 1959.
Oto Bihalji-Merin: « Les Peintres Naïfs », Paris (sans date).
J. Dubuffet, Victor Musgrave et A. de Maine: « Scottie Wilson », L'Art brut No. 6, Paris 1965.

White, Emil

Born 1901 in Austria.

Geboren 1901 in Österreich.

Né en 1901 en Autriche.

American citizen. Now lives in Big Sur, the residence of Henry Miller, who acts as his patron and writes about him. His art is full of fantasy, rather decorative, and reminding one (slightly) of Vivin or rather of Feješ. He, like them, paints towns he has never seen. A pleasant style; forceful, rather magical and mysterious.

Amerikaner. Lebt jetzt in Big Sur, der Residenz von Henry Miller, der ihn fördert und über ihn schreibt. Phantastische, leicht dekorative Malerei, die von ferne an gewisse Vivin oder vielmehr Feješ erinnert. Auch er malt Städte, die er nie gesehen hat. Gefällige, urwüchsige Malerei mit einem märchenhaften, geheimnisvollen Einschlag.

Américain. Habite à présent Big Sur, résidence de Henry Miller qui le protège et qui écrit sur lui. Peinture fantastique, un peu décorative, non sans rappeler (de loin) certains Vivin, ou plutôt les Feješ. Lui aussi peint des villes qu'il n'a jamais vues. Peinture agréable, truculente, avec quelque chose de féerique et de mystérieux.

EXPOSITIONS:
« Das naive Bild der Welt », Baden-Baden 1961.

BIBLIOGRAPHIE:

Oto Bihalji-Merin: « Das naive Bild der Welt », Köln 1959.
Oto Bihalji-Merin: « Die naive Malerei », Köln 1959.
Oto Bihalji-Merin: « Les Peintres Naïfs », Paris (sans date).

Zahavit (Jacobi)

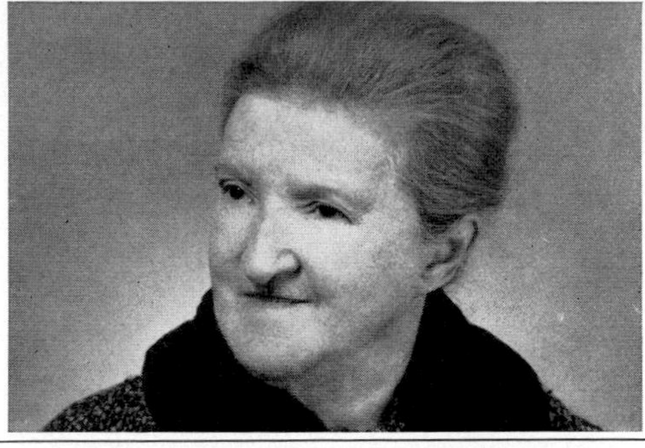

Born January 1, 1900 in Lodz (Russia, now Poland).

Geboren 1. Januar 1900 in Lodz (Rußland, jetzt Polen).

Née le 1er janvier 1900 à Lodz (Russie; actuellement Pologne).

In 1914 she left her native land and went to Israel. Was left an orphan in 1916. She had all kinds of jobs, from taking care of the sick to breaking up rocks. An unsociable, difficult woman, she left Israel again for Berlin, and later went to Montevideo, then returned to Israel only to depart again, this time for Paris, where she settled down permanently. An Israeli national. It was in Paris that she began to paint, encouraged and helped by the Baroness Alix de Rothschild. Her art is worthy of note from all points of view; it is rich, delicate and contains memories of the Near East.

1914 verläßt sie ihre Heimat und wandert nach Israel aus. 1916 verliert sie ihre Eltern. Nun übt sie alle möglichen Berufe aus, von der Krankenpflege bis zum Steinezerschlagen. Sie ist eigenbrödlerisch, hat einen schwierigen Charakter. Von Israel geht sie nach Berlin, von dort nach Montevideo, kehrt nach Israel zurück, um kurz darauf nach Paris zu fahren, wo sie sich endgültig niederläßt. Israelische Staatsbürgerin. In Paris fängt sie an zu malen, gefördert von der Baronin Alix de Rothschild. In jeder Beziehung bedeutende Malerei: reich, raffiniert, mit orientalischen Reminiszenzen.

En 1914, elle quitte son pays pour aller vivre en Israël. Orpheline en 1916, elle exerce toutes sortes de métiers, allant du soin des malades jusqu'au cassage des pierres. Insociable, de caractère difficile, elle quitte Israël pour Berlin, puis pour Montevideo; retourne en Israël pour repartir à nouveau pour Paris, où elle se fixe définitivement. Nationalité israëlienne. Et c'est à Paris qu'elle commence à peindre, protégée par la baronne Alix de Rothschild; peinture remarquable à tous points de vue: riche, raffinée, avec des réminiscences orientales.

EXPOSITIONS:
Foyer des Artistes, Paris 1962 (Cat., Préface Anatole Jakovsky).
Dans son atelier, Paris 1963/64 (Cat., Préface Waldemar George).
«Les Primitifs d'Aujourd'hui», Galerie Charpentier, Paris 1964.

Zgaib, Khalil

Born 1920 in Dbayeh (Lebanon).

Geboren 1920 in Dbayeh (Libanon).

Né en 1920 à Dbayeh (Liban).

Was a hairdresser at the Hospital of the Sacred Heart, then at the Fine Arts School in Beirut where he still works. Began to paint about 1954. Was noticed by several leading people at the American University, and presented his one and only individual exhibition at that University in 1955. One year later, he received a prize from the national education authorities. In 1962 he took part in an exhibition in Italy with other Lebanese artists.

Friseur im Krankenhaus Sacré-Cœur, dann in der Gewerbeschule in Beirut, wo er heute noch arbeitet. Fängt um 1954 zu malen an. Nachdem er ein paar Persönlichkeiten der Amerikanischen Universität aufgefallen ist, veranstaltet er seine einzige individuelle Ausstellung 1955 in dieser Universität. Ein Jahr später erhält er einen Preis des Unterrichtsministeriums. 1962 stellt er mit anderen libanesischen Malern in Italien aus.

Coiffeur à l'Hôpital du Sacré-Cœur, puis à l'Ecole des Arts et Métiers de Beyrouth, où il travaille toujours. A commencé à peindre vers 1954. Ayant été remarqué par quelques personnalités de l'Université Américaine, il fait sa seule et unique exposition individuelle, dans ses locaux, en 1955. Un an après, il obtient un prix de l'Education Nationale. En 1962, il expose en Italie, avec d'autres peintres libanais.

EXPOSITIONS:
Université Américaine, Beyrouth 1955.
«Les Primitifs d'Aujourd'hui»,
Galerie Charpentier, Paris 1964.

BIBLIOGRAPHIE:
«Art naïf», Editions Marocaines et Internationales, Rabat 1964

International Exhibitions
Internationale Ausstellungen
Expositions internationales

For all primitive painters considered in this book we only have space to list the individual exhibitions and the most important international exhibitions in which they participated. Here is a complete list of these latter, giving all useful information, catalogues, etc. When these are mentioned in the detailed information about a particular artist, as a general rule only a brief reference is given.

Bei allen naiven Malern, die in diesem Buch angeführt sind, haben wir aus Platzmangel nur die Einzelausstellungen angegeben sowie die großen internationalen Kundgebungen, an denen sie teilgenommen haben. Es folgt hier eine vollständige Liste dieser letzteren, mit allen zweckmäßigen Angaben, Katalogen usw.; in den jedem Maler gewidmeten Artikeln sind diese gleichen Veranstaltungen jedoch meistens nur abgekürzt angeführt.

Pour tous les peintres naïfs mentionnés dans ce livre, nous n'indiquons, faute de place, que leurs expositions individuelles, ainsi que les grandes manifestations internationales auxquelles ils ont participé. En ce qui concerne ces dernières, voici leur liste complète, avec tous les renseignements utiles, catalogues, etc., tandis que lorsqu'il s'agit de ces mêmes manifestations figurant dans les notices sur chaque peintre, nous n'en donnons le plus souvent que des abréviations.

LES MAITRES POPULAIRES DE LA RÉALITÉ, Salle Royale, Paris, mai 1937. Catalogue, Préface par R. Escholier et M. Gauthier.

LES MAITRES POPULAIRES DE LA RÉALITÉ, Kunsthaus Zürich, Oktober/November 1937. Katalog; Vorwort von W. Wartmann.

MASTERS OF POPULAR PAINTING, The Museum of Modern Art, New York, October 1938. Catalogue, Prefaces by Alfred H. Barr, Jr., J. Cassou, M. Gauthier and Holger Cahill.

LA PEINTURE NAIVE DU DOUANIER ROUSSEAU A NOS JOURS, Knokke-le-Zoute, juin–août 1958. Catalogue, Préfaces par A. Jakovsky et Sidney Janis.

LA PEINTURE NAIVE DU DOUANIER ROUSSEAU A NOS JOURS, Maison de la Pensée Française, juin–octobre 1960. Catalogue, Préface par A. Jakovsky.

LAIENMALER, Gewerbemuseum, Basel, Oktober–Dezember 1961. Katalog; Vorworte von R. Wildhaber und A. Hernandez.

DAS NAIVE BILD DER WELT, Staatliche Kunsthalle, Baden-Baden, Historisches Museum, Frankfurt am Main, Kunstverein Hannover, Juni–Dezember 1961. Katalog; Vorworte von D. Mahlow, Georg Schmidt, Sandberg, Anatole Jakovsky, M. F. Arntz, Miča Bašičević und R. Wildhaber.

PITTORI NAIFS, Palazzo Barberini, Rom, Mai–August 1964. Katalog; Vorworte von A. Jakovsky, G. Sangiorgio, J. Recupero, G. Vigorelli und H. Certigny.

DIE WELT DER NAIVEN MALEREI, Salzburger Residenzgalerie, Juli 1964. Katalog; Vorworte von H. Fetscherin, J. Cassou, D. Mahlow und F. Roh.

PRIMITIFS D'AUJOURD'HUI, Galerie Charpentier, Paris, octobre–décembre 1964. Catalogue, Préfaces par R. Nacenta et P. Mazars.

DE LUSTHOF DER NAIEVEN, Museum Boymans-van Beuningen, Rotterdam, Juli–September 1964. Katalog; Vorworte von J. Cassou, J. C. Ebbinge Wubben und O. Bihalji-Merin.

PANORAMA INTERNATIONAL DE LA PEINTURE NAIVE, Mission culturelle, Maroc, juillet–septembre 1964. Catalogue, Préfaces par G.-H. Rivière, M.-F. Braive, M. Gauthier, Anatole Jakovsky et G. Diehl.

Bibliography
Bibliographie
Bibliographie

The same applies to the bibliography. Here are the principal works on 'naive' painting, which are therefore those most often mentioned:

Das gleiche gilt für die Bibliographie. Die wichtigsten Werke über die naive Malerei, die am häufigsten zitierten, sind:

Le même procédé est valable pour la bibliographie. Les principaux ouvrages sur la peinture naïve, donc les plus cités, sont:

SIDNEY JANIS: THEY TAUGHT THEMSELVES, The Dial Press, New York 1942

WILHELM UHDE: CINQ MAITRES PRIMITIFS, Editions Palmes, Paris 1949

ANATOLE JAKOVSKY: LA PEINTURE NAIVE, J. Damase, Paris 1949

ANATOLE JAKOVSKY: LES PEINTRES NAIFS, La Bibliothèque des Arts, Paris 1956

ANATOLE JAKOVSKY: NAIVE MALEREI, Diogenes Verlag, Zürich 1957

ANATOLE JAKOVSKY: EROS DU DIMANCHE, J. J. Pauvert, Paris 1964

OTO BIHALJI-MERIN: DAS NAIVE BILD DER WELT, DuMont-Schauberg, Köln 1959

OTO BIHALJI-MERIN: DIE NAIVE MALEREI, DuMont-Schauberg, Köln 1959

OTO BIHALJI-MERIN: LES PEINTRES NAIFS, Editions Delpire, Paris s. d. (1960)

OTO BIHALJI-MERIN: UMETNOST NAIVNIH U JUGOSLAVJII, Jugoslavia ed., 1963

List of Pictures
Verzeichnis der Bilder
Liste des tableaux